The New
Connoisseurs' Handbook
of California Wines

Symbols used in this book to evaluate wine quality and aging characteristics are as follows:

82̶   below-average quality, a wine to avoid

85   a wine of average quality

✻   a fine example of a given type or style, an above-average wine

✻✻   a very fine wine, likely to be memorable

✻✻✻   an exceptional wine, worth a special search

---

81   a wine now past its peak

83   ready to drink now

85   drinkable now, but will improve with further aging

88   needs further aging before drinking

Examples of the wine rating system can be found in the *Wineries and Wines* chapter on p. 112.

The Producers Rated chapter uses the following symbols to provide additional information of use to consumers:

⩗   these wines are good value within their quality range

━   these wines are more ageworthy than others in their quality range

ACACIA   wines printed in boldface tend to be more consistent than others in their quality range and occasionally have earned higher ratings

~   these wines tend to be less consistent than others in their quality range and occasionally have earned lower ratings

†   these wines have been assigned preliminary ratings pending future vintage results

The New
Connoisseurs' Handbook
of California Wines

by Norman S. Roby
and Charles E. Olken

ALFRED A. KNOPF   NEW YORK

1991

THIS IS A BORZOI BOOK
PUBLISHED BY ALFRED A. KNOPF, INC.

Copyright © 1991 by Norman S. Roby and Charles E. Olken
Maps copyright © 1991 by Jean Paul Tremblay

Library of Congress Cataloging-in-Publication Data

Olken, Charles E.
The new connoisseur's handbook of California wines / Charles E.
Olken, Norman S. Roby.
p.   cm.
ISBN 0-394-56468-5
1. Wine and wine making—California. I. Title.
TP557.O55   1991
641.2'2'09794—dc20   91-52721   CIP

Manufactured in the United States of America

First Edition

Contents

Introduction

Compared to the world's other great wine-producing regions, California has a remarkably short history. Time is measured here not by centuries but by decades. Yet it is clear that today California wines can hold their own in company with the world's best, and much of this achievement is relatively recent.

It was not until the 70s that the wines of California began to attract the attention of serious wine lovers. Enjoying the role of underdog, the upstarts from California continued to challenge the old order throughout the 80s. They frequently left their mark, opening eyes and shaking old assumptions, even those of inveterate Francophiles. Now, as the pace of change slows somewhat in the 90s, it is at last possible to get a sense of what has been done—and what may be done in the future.

As will be seen from the size of this book compared to the original *Connoisseurs' Handbook* published in 1980, the sheer number of producers has increased dramatically. Nearly twice as many individuals and companies are making wine now as were a decade ago. The majority of the new names combine limited volume with great ambition. At the other extreme, an important trend of the 80s was the acquisition of California wineries and vineyards by international companies headquartered in the United Kingdom, Japan, Germany, France, Switzerland, and elsewhere.

Changes in wine geography have paralleled to some degree the changes in personalities and ownership. New wine-growing regions such as the Edna Valley and Santa Maria Valley have been developed and many of their wines are now earning accolades alongside those from the better-known valleys in Napa and Sonoma counties. In short, where once the California wine scene was relatively uncomplicated, there is now a maze of names and places capable of challenging the attention and memory of any wine buff.

The quality and character of California wines continue to reflect this dynamic background. At the beginning of the 80s the style of California wine was moving away from the heaviness that characterized many offerings of the 70s. After a brief flirtation with lighter, less ripe "food wines" that often proved to be thin and uninteresting, California's winemakers continued throughout the 80s to experiment, refining their techniques and winemaking procedures. By the end of that decade, it was obvious that overall standards had risen to a point where mediocre wines could no longer be blamed on lack of experience or error.

What we have today, therefore, is a wine scene that demands a balanced critical approach. Some producers have clearly emerged as quality leaders while others are just as clearly mired in inconsistency, or worse. The consumer deserves to know which is which. This book is intended to help him or her to do just that, and to make sense out of the entire business of California and West Coast wines, from grapes to growing areas to production techniques to the finished wines themselves.

We begin with the technology of winemaking, an area in which winemakers from California and the Northwest are rightly regarded as world leaders. The first chapter, BASICS OF WINEMAKING, covers such topics as fermentation, aging, and bottling in a comprehensive way. By detailing the options and choices open to winemakers throughout the entire process, it offers wine drinkers the opportunity to understand some of the behind-the-scenes activities and provides insights into the language of winemaking.

The next chapter, GRAPES AND WINE TYPES, contains essential information about every grape variety planted, ranging from the long-established Cabernet Sauvignon and Zinfandel to such less familiar names as Viognier and Nebbiolo, increasingly grown in West Coast vineyards. Also included are full explanations of all the wine types and wine names seen on labels.

The third chapter, WINE GEOGRAPHY, examines the increasing importance of California's grape-growing locations, with particular attention given to officially designated Viticultural Areas, the emerging appellations of the West Coast. It is a sign of California's coming of age that so many regions have been carved out and planted to those varieties best suited to the growing conditions. After a period of random plantings in the 70s that led to hit-or-miss results, new vineyard developments have kept quality grape-growing practices in mind. Unfortunately, the White Zinfandel boom and the as-yet-unchecked demand for Chardonnay and Cabernet Sauvignon sometimes led to the planting of these varieties in inappropriate locations. This chapter is a guide to all areas in which grapes are grown, and wherever possible spells out the characteristics and relative merits of the wines from each place name.

The fourth chapter, VINTAGE COMMENTARY, deals with the effects of weather on the vintages. Each year presents growers with a new set of conditions, and the differences in grape quality from one year to the next add up to qualitative differences in the wine produced. Such differences particularly include the aging characteristics of given wines, so our vintage discussion touches on the relative ageworthiness of those wines likely to benefit from aging—Chardonnay, Cabernet Sauvignon, Merlot, Pinot Noir, and Zinfandel.

Producers and their wines represent the central focus of this book. In the chapter WINERIES AND WINES, each winery receives its own entry and its wines are reviewed in detail. The chapter has two sections. The first, *California*, is a statewide comprehensive listing of producers, special trademarks, and labels. Each entry provides a profile of the winery— its history, its special interests, its goals, and its quality performance— followed by a review of those wines with some sort of track record. The second section, *The Northwest*, presents the same information for that up-and-coming region. Though the annual output of Oregon, Washington, and Idaho together pales in comparison to that of California, each of these states has a nucleus of pioneering and committed wineries.

The sixth chapter, THE PRODUCERS RATED, extends the critiques of individual wines reviewed in the previous chapter. Here will be found comparative ratings of virtually all experienced producers in seven major categories of varietals and sparkling wines. Producers are ranked according to the quality of their Chardonnay, Sauvignon Blanc, Cabernet Sauvignon, Pinot Noir, Merlot, Zinfandel, and sparkling wine output. Best Buys are indicated. This section serves as a quick review and easy reference guide.

Our final chapter deals with wine terms. WINE LANGUAGE presents definitions for all the words and phrases likely to be found on labels, and also covers all of the sensory terms used regularly to describe the appearance, smell, taste, feel, and aftertaste of wine, especially those employed in the hundreds of critical evaluations in this book.

Our intention in *The New Connoisseurs' Handbook* is to provide useful information in a comprehensive yet easily accessible form. Each section approaches the California or Northwest wine scene from a specific angle; yet together they comprise a complete guide to the wines of the West. We hope this book leads to a greater understanding of California wines and the wines of the Northwest. Even more, we hope it leads to the greater enjoyment of them.

The wine ratings and descriptions in this book are based substantially on evaluations that appear in *Connoisseurs' Guide to California Wine*, a monthly newsletter edited and published by Charles Olken and Earl Singer and distributed only by subscription. A one-year subscription is $40. Each year the *Guide* reviews up to 2,000 wines, mostly vintage-dated varietals. Readers of this *Handbook* interested in learning more about the *Guide* may receive a free copy of the latest issue by writing to *Connoisseurs' Guide to California Wine*, P.O. Box V, Alameda, California 94501.

The New

Connoisseurs' Handbook

of California Wines

Basics of
Winemaking

How a wine is made, especially a fine, priceworthy wine, does influence the way it tastes. However, winemaking techniques are not regarded in the same light in Europe as they are in the United States. In general, the technical side of winemaking takes on far greater importance in the United States among both winemakers and consumers.

In Europe, where most fine wines are identified by the name of the growing region, the internal regulations and traditions of the region often predetermine how the wine must be made. Little latitude is allowed for variation and experimentation. As a result, there is some reasonable expectation that every distinctive Vouvray, Pouilly-Fumé, or Puligny-Montrachet should have a particular taste. Champagne is an extreme case, in which every producer must follow the same specified procedures. Thus the region and the growing conditions during a given year take top billing as the most important variables in European wines.

California winemakers, on the other hand, are not bound by tradition. By using different techniques, producers can radically change the style of wine from one vintage to the next, or else experiment in subtle ways or explore various combinations in hopes of finding something different or better. Sometimes they test what consumers prefer by offering a single varietal made using several different techniques. It is becoming common, for example, for a winery to make a barrel-fermented Chardonnay and a stainless-steel-fermented Chardonnay from the same vintage. Similarly, a growing number of winemakers are making both a Reserve-style Cabernet Sauvignon that is blended with Merlot and Cabernet Franc and aged in one type of small oak barrel, and an additional Cabernet Sauvignon that is 100% varietal in composition, aged in a different type of barrel. Therefore, the names Napa Valley Cabernet Sauvignon or Central Coast Chardonnay are attached to wines that conform to no regional norm; you cannot tell what to expect in terms of taste and style by those geographical names alone.

One key indicator of how a given wine will taste is knowledge of how it was made. Who made it, the producer's name, remains the most important information provided on the label, especially if that producer is well established and has been consistent. Otherwise, details of production methods may provide clues. Winemakers in the United States seem to be quite chatty when they talk about their wines, either in person or in print. Labels often describe the residual sugar or what type of fermentation was employed. Back labels often go on at length about the blending procedures, the yeast strain, and the aging regime.

To help you wend your way through this fascinating aspect of California wines, the following section divides winemaking into its five primary functions, discussing all the related concepts and defining the terminology involved. The sequence is that of winemaking itself: crushing and pressing; fermentation; clarification; aging and blending; and, finally, stabilizing and bottling.

Crushing

After grapes have been harvested, the first stage in winemaking is extracting their juice. The most common method for obtaining juice from grapes is known as crushing. Pressing is a second method, while the third is the old-fashioned way still practiced in remote parts of the wine world, treading or stomping grapes. When ripe, grapes are plump and their skins so soft that they can be broken easily. Both grapes and juice are vulnerable to deterioration. During crushing, therefore, which is far less brutal than the term suggests, winemakers are careful to avoid any delays. The juice, moreover, must be extracted without breaking the bitter seeds, or "pips," which most wine grapes contain. The stems that hold each grape to the spinelike clusters must normally be detached and discarded because they too may contribute bitterness to wines. With improvements made in modern crushing machinery, the process has become both standardized and continuous as the equipment separates the grapes from the stems, breaks the grape skins without damaging the seeds, and ejects the stems.

In California, the juice for still (nonsparkling) wines is usually obtained through a crushing and pressing combination. A typical large winery prefers high-capacity crushers for the sake of speed, and generally employs at least two sets of crushers for making red and white wines. This avoids color problems in the white wines. The crushing stations usually consist of a receiving hopper with the actual crushing device concealed below. Because grapes are normally delivered in trucks, crush equipment is often located outdoors, near the fermentation areas and connected to the winery through large pipes known as "must lines." The actual crushers consist of paddles and/or nylon rollers through which grapes are pushed, breaking the skins. Inside the crusher, surrounding the paddles is a stainless-steel or nylon-perforated drum, which immediately receives the juice, skins, seeds, and any leaves. The drum rotates so that the juice, seeds, and skins easily fall through the holes to a basin beneath, while the stems and leaves, which are too large to slip through, stay inside. In most crushers, the stems are immediately expelled from the machine and trucked away. The majority of winemakers favor this system, in which the grapes are crushed and de-stemmed in a continuous process.

Visitors to most wineries won't see the actual crushing, which takes place within a covered cylinder. What is visible is the receiving hopper into which the grape clusters are dumped. Inside the hopper, a large rotating auger collects the grapes and feeds them steadily to the crusher. Once the grapes are dumped into the hopper, the process becomes a continuous one. An average-sized winery crusher is capable of receiving and crushing about 40 tons per hour. Large-volume wineries can set up larger units and process as many as 150 tons an hour. A ton of grapes yields somewhere between 60 to 70 cases of wine.

While the majority of all wines made in California begin with crushing, noteworthy exceptions exist. Occasionally, a winemaker decides that crushing is not the best method of extracting the juice for a particular wine. In the process of crushing, juice inevitably spends some time in contact with the grape skins. This can contribute both color and possibly some degree of bitter flavor, depending upon the length of exposure and the temperature of the grapes. (Most winemakers prefer handling grapes that are relatively cool, so they harvest in the early morning to avoid the transfer of excessive color from the skins to the juice.) The main reason to avoid crushing, therefore, is to minimize color and bitter components in the juice; these can show up in the finished wine.

Pressing

Because treading is illegal in the United States, the most likely alternative to crushing is pressing. The basic mechanics of pressing involve forcing the just-harvested grapes against an immovable object to extract juice through pressure. The pressure applied can be regulated so that the amount of juice extracted is also controllable. To put it simply, the more pressure applied, the more juice extracted. But the juice quality may decline.

Sometimes grapes are so fat and juicy that little external effort is required to start the juice flowing. When grapes are piled high, the weight of the grapes alone may be sufficient to break the skins. In winemaking circles, this juice that flows easily with little or no external pressure is known as free-run juice. As the amount of pressure used in a winepress increases, so does the likelihood that the juice will contain unwanted flavor compounds. Under extreme pressure, grape skins can be so severely pressed that they shred and release harsh, bitter flavors; but with light or only medium pressure, unwanted compounds can be wholly or at least partly avoided. In winemaking, the juice from heavy pressure may be used as some percentage of the blend or not at all. Pressing brings a great range of options to winemakers.

The modern winepress has evolved from the often-depicted wooden slotted basket press, with its ratchet handle, into a highly sophisticated and versatile technological tool. Historically, the press was used to extract as much juice from the grapes as possible. In the early days of winemaking, most white wine grapes went directly into a winepress prior to fermentation. The basket press would exert downward pressure and juice would escape through the slots. The pressure was first limited to human muscle, and later increased by mechanical means. Since all of the activities can be easily visible and therefore monitored, a basket press remains perfectly suited for small-batch efforts and, in fact, is used by some small wineries. It is also well known to many home winemakers for its reliability. Large-capacity basket presses are still used in the French region of Champagne by many famous, well-financed producers who believe that for them the best-quality juice is obtained by means of pressing.

Large-volume producers intent on capturing every possible ounce of juice from the grape, regardless of quality, inspired the development of an efficient winepress known as the continuous screw press. Though widely used for many years, this press is not really suited for high-quality wines. In the screw press, grapes are placed in one end of a cylinder and pushed under pressure to be compressed at the other end. As the grape skins become compacted, potentially good wine is often pushed through potentially harmful skins, seeds, and other solids. As a result, quality is highly variable. The early design of the screw press did not allow for tight control over the degree of pressure, and all wine varieties ended up by being treated the same way. Some fared better than others. Even today the screw-type press works well enough with varieties intended for jug-wine quality.

In the late 60s and early 70s many winemakers working for small-volume wineries adopted a relatively new press, the bladder press, in which an inflatable bladder pushes the grapes against a perforated outer drum. Recovered juice slides through the holes and into a pan beneath. This kind of winepress applies pressure evenly, and is programmable, meaning it can be adjusted to suit each grape variety. One major drawback is that it must be carefully cleaned after each batch. Another drawback is that the same perforations which allow juice to escape also allow air to enter, which can possibly oxidize the juice. Nevertheless, bladder presses remain widely used today throughout the West Coast for both red and white varieties.

By the early 80s, another kind of winepress called a tank press was being installed in California wineries. Early versions were designed in Germany by the Wilmes Company. A Swiss firm, Bucher, soon developed a following for its tank presses. This type of press eliminates the problems of the bladder press because it is a single unit that becomes airtight once the only access door is shut. Instead of a bladder, this press uses a membrane that applies very gentle pressure (30 psi maximum) to the grapes. The tank press can handle batches of different sizes and does not need to be full to operate. According to winemakers, juice coming out of a tank press is freer from solids than is juice from the same varieties coming from other types of press. (To winemakers, "grape solids" means all constituents other than juice, such as skins, seeds, and pulp; juice with many solids often ferments rapidly, but not cleanly.)

To those who look to the bottom line, the best feature is that the tank press is capable of extracting a high percentage of wine or juice at much lower pressure levels. As a result, the quality level of the juice is higher overall. With the use of tank presses, the yield per ton is increased, and the quantity is especially higher for white varieties. This obviously makes tank presses even more appealing to winery owners. At first the tank press appealed for use with small batches, but success soon encouraged the installation of large-scale, 45-ton-capacity versions. Smaller tank presses, however, can be portable, and some winemakers enjoy being able to bring the press to the grapes rather than moving the grapes to the press. All of the screw and most of the bladder-type presses are too heavy to move.

Regardless of their type, all winepresses are capable of performing a variety of functions, and winemakers use them at different stages of the winemaking process. In actual practice, it is important to emphasize that pressing is most often used in conjunction with, not in place of, crushing. However, as noted, the major reason for sometimes preferring pressing over crushing is that it allows greater control over the quality of the juice when bitterness and astringency are to be avoided. With white grapes, pressing the whole fruit allows for quick removal of the juice and thus avoids any skin contact or maceration effect. At warm temperatures this can contribute unwanted components to some of the more delicate and fragile wines, such as Chardonnay, Johannisberg Riesling, and especially sparkling wine made from Pinot Noir and Pinot Blanc grapes.

There are other winemaking situations in which pressing plays a vital role. Besides the initial extraction of juice from grapes, pressing also comes into play when winemakers want to recover finished red wine trapped in solids following fermentation, or to remove red wine from the solids during fermentation. The solids consist of skins, seeds, yeasts, and sometimes stems, and are commonly known as pomace. They contribute color, flavor, and aroma components, along with less desirable bitter notes.

In making red wines, pressing is typically employed when fermentation is completed or nearly so. After the free run has been removed by siphoning it above the sediment level, some remaining wine is trapped within the mass of grape skins. The volume trapped, as much as 15% of the total yield, can represent a significant value to the winery. To separate the usable wine from the skins, the entire remaining mass (pomace) is pumped or shoveled from the fermenters into a press. The wine recovered from the skins is known as press wine. In earlier presses, press wine was coarser and heavier than free-run wine, as well as darker and more tannic. Since the winepresses available today can be both efficient and gentle, the quality of press red wine may be almost indistinguishable from that of free run.

The color of red wines, pink wines, and Blanc de Noirs (blush types) may be readily controlled with the aid of a winepress. The red skins used to make these wines need to be removed immediately after the desired color has been obtained; normally this occurs a few hours after fermentation has begun. Typically, the free-run juice is drained and the rest of the fermenting wine is pumped to a press which separates more—and darker-colored—wine from the skins. Then, with the two lots blended, the properly pink or tinted wine continues to ferment for as long as the winemaker wants it to, or until all of the naturally fermentable sugar is used up.

In the production of sparkling wine, pressing is one of the keys to fine quality. The tiny bubbles of carbon dioxide trapped in Champagne bottles act like amplifiers, broadcasting every little defect in the wine. Therefore, right from the beginning, Champagne makers rely on pressing to give them juice with as little color and the lowest percentage of bitter flavors and grape solids possible. Those adhering to the traditional *méthode champenoise* process harvest grapes from very cool growing regions, when they are physiologically "ripe" but low in sugar, tiny, and thick-skinned. Traditionally, the grapes are harvested in the cool early morning, and then they are not crushed, but rather pressed whole. With most winepresses, Champagne makers can separate the free-run, light-press, medium-press, and heavy-press batches, and use only the desirable components. The portions of juice removed in segments from a press are known in wine talk as fractions. Overall, through selection of the fractions, the initial juice chosen for sparkling wine production is said to be cleaner, meaning freer from bitter and astringent components. Additionally, Champagne makers insist on pressing to avoid excess coloration of the juice. As greater and greater amounts of red varieties such as Pinot Noir become used in sparkling wine production, the winepress is becoming even more valuable for its ability to extract juice while not taking too much color from the skins.

Fermentation

Wine is the result of fermentation, a natural process in which the sweet juice of grapes is converted into alcohol, carbon dioxide, and another entirely different liquid through the action of yeast and other microflora. Fermentation is a natural biochemical reaction that brings us many delightful edibles, such as bread and cheese, and many potables, including beer and wine. The enzymes in yeast are the crucial ingredients; but when the fermentation is intended to produce alcohol, the other essential is sugar, helped along by inorganic and organic nutrients. Grapes used for wine contain both yeast and sugar, so it is no surprise that wine has been around for a long time. In simplest terms, fermentation occurs when the yeast metabolizes the sugar and in the process converts it into carbon dioxide and ethanol, an alcohol. As soon as all available sugar has been consumed, the yeasts stop working. With a little luck, the liquid that was once grape juice has been converted into flavorful wine.

What we normally refer to as fermentation is known to winemakers technically as the primary fermentation. Actually, this "primary" fermentation is a complex biological and biochemical process, consisting of numerous intermediate reactions. About 55 to 60% of the sugar in grapes, a combination of fructose and dextrose, is converted into alcohol by the yeasts, with the remaining 40 to 45% becoming carbon dioxide that escapes into the air. In addition, many side reactions during the fermentation create aroma compounds known as esters, and flavor compounds known as congeners. At its most active stage, fermentation generates considerable heat.

A typical fermentation starts slowly, as the yeast cells begin to work, and builds to an active tumultuous stage, only to slow down as the amount of available sugar and nutrients diminishes. Before winemakers were able to manipulate temperature and ferment wines cold, a typical fermentation would last from five to seven days from beginning to end. Cold fermentations proceed more slowly and last longer than warm ones, sometimes extending for two to three weeks or more. However, the yeasts don't always cooperate by starting things smoothly and continuing without a hitch. They often refuse to work at temperatures in the mid-90s or higher, and they sometimes stop when the alcohol level created is over 14%. The temperature range best suited to yeast populations is 48° to 65° F. for best growth on a commercial scale. A smooth fermentation is encouraged by a few nonsugar nutrients such as nitrogen and phosphorus, both usually supplied from the uptake of nutrients by the grapevines. Sometimes, however, the yeast will stop working for no apparent reason. Most winemakers speculate that the yeast stops because of either a shortage or an excess of amino acids.

Winemakers pay full attention to both the rate and the temperature of the primary fermentation. In general, the cooler the temperature, the longer the fermentation time. Red wines normally ferment at the warmer ranges (70° to 85° F.), but the trend is to ferment the more complex reds such as Cabernet Sauvignon and Zinfandels in the 80° to 90° range, with an occasional batch of Pinot Noir deliberately fermented at temperatures in the high 80s or low 90s. Winemakers generally prefer longer fermentations (two to three weeks) for white wines, and tend to ferment them in the cool range of 45° to 60° F. White wines destined to be made in a slightly sweet or sweeter style are usually fermented longer at even cooler levels. Cool fermentations are known to retain the grape's fruity characteristics, the esters, which are desirable today. Extreme warmth (above 80° F.) tends to cause the fruitiness to become volatile and escape into the air, leaving more subtle characteristics often desired in red wines. When the juice is extremely high in sugar content, as in late harvest–style wines, the primary fermentation is often a slow, difficult process. In every fermentation, as the grape juice ferments, the carbon dioxide created rises to the surface, tending to protect the wine from excessive air and from premature oxidation. Also, it has been established that the fermentation process creates a small amount of sulfur dioxide, a natural protective by-product that retards oxidation. The two biggest potential problems during the primary fermentation are the development of vinegar and the premature halt of the yeast action before all the sugar has been consumed.

A "stuck fermentation" is the technical description of the latter event. It is always unplanned and usually represents a big problem. The yeast cells simply stop metabolizing the sugar and become inactive, leaving the winemaker with unwanted sugar in the partially fermented wine. Usually, knowing how difficult it is to reactivate the fermentation, winemakers will combine the stuck batch with an actively fermenting batch of the same wine. If that's not possible, they will add vitamins and yeast nutrients in hopes of reactivating the yeast. Fermentation involving extremely sweet juice for a late harvest wine stops or sticks, and the point at which this occurs determines the amount of natural residual sugar in the wine.

CARBONIC MACERATION

Carbonic maceration is a variation in the primary fermentation that is frequently used to make fruity-style red wines such as French Beaujolais. Nouveau Beaujolais may be the best-known wine made by this fermentation procedure, but it can be used to produce any red table wine. The purpose of making wines by carbonic maceration is to obtain a deep, dark red wine that avoids harsh tannins or bitterness while accentuating youthful fruitiness. The general procedure involves macerating the whole berries in a carbon dioxide atmosphere for several days.

In carbonic maceration, winemakers will dump the just-picked grapes—without crushing or pressing—cluster by cluster into a tank which when full is sealed tight. The weight of the grapes as they pile up automatically crushes those at the tank's bottom, and this in turn leads to a fermentation. The carbon dioxide from this fermentation is trapped within the tank and the remaining grapes are bathed in it. These special conditions result in an intracellular fermentation—in effect, a fermentation within each individual berry. After a few days, the result is deep color, an aroma similar to fresh berries, cherries, and grapes, and low levels of tannin. The objection to wines produced 100% by carbonic maceration is that they are simple, one-dimensional, and fragile. In the mid-70s, a minor trend emerged when over a dozen California producers worked with this type of fermentation to offer Nouveau-style wines. The trend fizzled within a few years, mainly because consumers didn't understand what a Nouveau wine was all about. In the 80s only two or three California wineries offered wine made entirely by this technique. However, over the last few years several Oregon winemakers have been making Nouveau-style Pinot Noir by carbonic maceration in hopes that the reception will be more favorable.

WHOLE BERRY FERMENTATION

This is a variation on the carbonic maceration approach, and is now rather widely practiced by winemakers. The purpose is to add lively, berryish character to otherwise heavy-bodied and usually tannic red wines. In this procedure, the winemaker follows the conventional fermentation practice but at certain times he will add clusters of whole, uncrushed berries to the fermentation container. This tends to prolong the fermentation as well as to add desirable components. The chemical reaction involved in whole berry fermentation is such that the uncrushed berries undergo an enzyme breakdown that stretches out the fermentation process without adding alcoholic strength. The resulting wines tend to be intensified in color, fruitiness, and aroma, without being overburdened by tannins and alcohol.

Just about every red wine varietal has been produced at some time by some winemaker with an assist from whole berry fermentation. The wines that winemakers currently believe are definitely improved by it are Pinot Noir and those reds prone to excessive alcohol levels, such as Zinfandel, Petite Sirah, and Syrah. Every so often we hear of winemakers adding whole berries to fermenting Cabernet Sauvignon and Merlot.

MALOLACTIC FERMENTATION

What winemakers call the "secondary" fermentation is a biochemical reaction differing from the primary one in several ways. Also known technically as malolactic fermentation, it is induced by bacteria and does not create alcohol at all. Instead, malolactic fermentation involves a conversion of the acidity in the wine: through bacterial action one kind of acid, called malic acid (which, along with tartaric acid, is a principal acid in grapes), is converted into another kind of acid, lactic acid. Since lactic acid is much softer and smoother than malic, the malolactic fermentation is desirable in some wines under certain circumstances. Winemakers can choose either to allow it to occur or to prevent it from happening.

The bacterium itself is prevalent on the grape skins in all winemaking countries, although it wasn't identified until the 30s. It is known to belong to the large *Lactobacillus* genus. In wineries the bacterium is encouraged by warm conditions, and discouraged and inhibited by cold. Most of the time the bacterium can also be inhibited by sulfur dioxide. One of the more widely used chemicals in winemaking, sulfur dioxide protects wine from damage from air and from bacteria, and at reasonably low levels is regarded as a handy preservative.

The malolactic bacterium, which is generally found in wineries on their walls and storage containers, as well as in all vineyards, cannot be totally eradicated. However, it can be kept in check in the vineyards through application of sulfur dust, which inhibits its activity, and in wineries through filtration, which can remove it from wine. Malolactic fermentation is something that wine is predisposed to undergo, though the process remains capricious and unpredictable. The bacterium itself has been isolated and cultured, and is now available commercially. Rather than waiting around for each batch of wine to decide whether it wants to undergo this secondary fermentation, winemakers can now introduce a malolactic culture to induce it. This is usually done shortly after the primary fermentation is finished, and winemakers working with high-acid wines consider it a natural way to lower the total acidity. One of the beneficial side effects is the creation of a natural compound called diacetyl, akin to butter in aroma and in texture. So, malolactic fermentation contributes a softness through the increase of lactic acid, a buttery-smooth texture through the development of diacetyl, and an aroma that by combining both lactic and diacetyl components at the expense of simple fruitiness is regarded as more complex.

There are, however, drawbacks. One is that malolactic fermentation in process can give off unpleasant aromas along the lines of skunk cabbage and garlic. Also, it is difficult for winemakers to know for certain when a malolactic fermentation is completed. Should it continue after a batch of wine has been bottled, the results are gassy, turbid, and sometimes downright stinky wines. Another problem is that, while it adds a different character, malolactic fermentation can reduce or flatten out a wine's simple fruitiness. Thus, winemakers will choose whether or not to encourage the malolactic fermentation depending on the wine's acidic characteristic after fermentation and on the style of finished wine they believe is best suited to the market. In many instances, winemakers divide a vintage into batches, allowing one portion to experience malolactic fermentation while the remainder does not. The batches are later combined. The point to be emphasized is that for the majority of California wines, the decision to put a wine completely through malolactic fermentation, partially through it, or not at all depends on the style and characteristics the winemaker wants to achieve.

In the Western United States, malolactic fermentation is encouraged in nearly all red wines, and is a frequent option where white wines are concerned. It is particularly common (and often necessary) in dry-style white varietals (Chardonnay and Pinot Gris) from Oregon and Idaho, because the cold climatic conditions there result in extremely high acidity. The same holds true for white wines originating in cool Region I California locations. However, for most California white wines, inducing malolactic fermentation is a matter of personal choice; some winemakers have no real need to lower acidity, but simply like the flavor that results. Chardonnay is the wine most often associated with malolactic fermentation. In the 70s, an increasing number of California Chardonnays were put through the process because the resulting bold flavor dimensions were fashionable. With greater knowledge and experience came a degree of restraint. Winemakers now seem to agree that the desired buttery character will begin to manifest itself when at least 25% of the wine has undergone malolactic fermentation. Today, winemakers in California favoring 100% malolactic fermentation for Chardonnay are in the minority. In actual practice, most winemakers will encourage a certain percentage of Chardonnay to undergo such fermentation to add flavor nuances, while preventing it in the rest in order to retain essential fruity characteristics.

NATIVE YEAST FERMENTATION

Occasionally we will encounter a wine said to have been fermented by means of a native or natural yeast fermentation rather than by a cultivated variety. In the 80s, more winemakers were trying native yeasts for some wines. Winemakers refer to this wild yeast fermentation as a "bronco" fermentation. A few believe that wild yeasts should be used exclusively, though the reasons cited for their position vary widely. Those favoring such an approach tend to be found among winemakers devoted to harnessing Pinot Noir. Then there are other winemakers dedicated to the natural, nothing-added way. To date, winemakers advocating using native yeasts believe they encounter fewer stuck fermentations and fewer hydrogen sulfide problems. Also, they believe the native yeasts produce lower alcohol in wines.

BARREL FERMENTATION

Wines that undergo the conventional fermentation in a small barrel instead of a vat or tank are said to be barrel-fermented. Today, white wines such as Chardonnay and Sauvignon Blanc are most likely to be made this way. Occasionally, Chenin Blanc, Semillon, Pinot Blanc, or late harvest Sauternes-style white wine will be barrel-fermented. Just about all such fermentations take place in oak barrels of 55- to 60-gallon size, though a few wineries use larger oak containers called puncheons, holding about 150 gallons. Winemakers favoring this type of fermentation claim it contributes more subtle oak character, a richer, creamier body, and greater longevity to the wine. Barrel fermentations are expensive because more labor is required to monitor the fermentation and to clean each barrel before and after use.

Barrel fermentations became more common throughout California in the 70s, but they really represent the traditional and classic form of white wine fermentation employed in France for several centuries, primarily in Burgundy and Bordeaux. Not only are they costly, but they also bring greater risks. The temperature can only be regulated externally, so winemakers have less control over the progress of the fermentation. Specially designed barrel-fermentation "cold rooms" are one way now used to protect the wine.

Contrary to a widespread assumption, barrel-fermented wines do not have more oak aroma and flavor than wines that are only oak-aged. But the now-numerous proponents maintain that barrel-fermented wine offers a smoother integration of oak and wine. They also believe that as wines ferment in barrels, they go through a natural kind of filtration which removes overt oak tannins and bitterness along with unwanted sediment.

"Partial" barrel fermentation means that a percentage of the wine is fermented in barrels, and the remainder in another type of container. Before being bottled, the batches are combined. Many skilled winemakers prefer having an option, or several, when it comes down to combining barrel-fermented and stainless-steel-fermented lots into the final blend.

BOTTLE FERMENTATION

Champagne and all other sparkling wines produced by the traditional *méthode champenoise* are fermented the second time only in a bottle. Sparkling wine made by the modern transfer process also undergoes the second fermentation in the bottle. In both production methods, the bubbles result from bottle fermentation. In either approach, once the base wine blend or cuvée is selected, it is put into each bottle along with a carefully measured amount of sugar and yeast, which activates the second fermentation.

Many yeasts are available, but the preferred ones are known to have an ability to ferment in an alcohol solution, to add a strong yeasty aroma, and to flock and granulate together for easy collection afterwards. Each bottle in this sparkling wine fermentation is closed with a crown cap, fitting tightly over the lip. Typically, producers place the bottles in a cool location, and ideally the fermentation takes place around 55° F. and lasts between 45 to 60 days on average. When it proceeds as desired, the resulting wine acquires numerous tiny bubbles that create a persistent bead and a creamy texture. The pressure that builds up is usually around 90 psi in a standard-style sparkling wine. This second fermentation continues until all sugar has been metabolized. The spent yeasts will later be removed after a specified aging period.

FERMENTATION CONTAINERS

For centuries most wines were fermented in oak containers, either small barrels or large vats. In the early days, California wine was usually fermented in vats made of redwood, the durable wood that was widely available, then and now. With modernization in the 20th century, wineries were designed for large volume and efficiency, and new types of fermentation containers were introduced. For a time the most popular type was a glass-lined concrete tank and, to a lesser degree, concrete tanks coated with a special epoxy seal. These tanks varied in size, and could be tailored to fit into a winery. In general wine talk, a vat is an open-top container and a tank is a sealed container. In the 50s, wineries began experimenting with tanks made of stainless steel, and soon thereafter a variety of designs and sizes of stainless-steel tanks appeared in both old and new winemaking facilities.

Stainless steel has become the most common fermenting container for several reasons. Stainless-steel containers are easy to clean and to keep free of spoilage organisms. They can be sealed airtight, and once in place last much longer than any wooden container, perhaps indefinitely. Winemakers find that stainless-steel tanks are relatively easy to combine with refrigeration systems, and this ability to control temperature during fermentation sets stainless steel apart from the competition. Being easy to clean, a stainless-steel fermenting tank can also be used as a storage container after fermentation is completed. Furthermore, stainless steel is neutral in flavor to begin with, and, unlike wood, will not develop leaks with age.

Wooden containers are still used to ferment some wines. Small oak barrels are used for white wine fermentations. Redwood was once widely used at a time when most red wine fermentations took place in large open-top vats. However, by 1970 all but a few winemakers had converted to stainless steel. Some of the holdouts were stubborn old-timers, but a few—notably Beaulieu and Caymus, among others—continue to prefer open-top vats for Cabernet Sauvignon fermentations. They are joined by a few underfinanced winemakers who have acquired some of the old redwood vats and sealed them off, and use them as fermentation tanks.

Concrete fermenting tanks have all but disappeared. Only the giant factorylike wineries continue using them just to save money. Every now and then a batch of Pinot Noir from a curious hands-on type of winemaker will have been fermented in concrete tanks as an experiment. Bouchaine Winery is one Pinot Noir producer still fermenting some of its wine in its old rectangular concrete vats.

FERMENTATION YEASTS

Grapes contain yeasts on their surface, and these yeasts are capable of bringing about a fermentation. However, the natural yeasts can't always be relied upon to ferment all of the sugar and to work quickly, cleanly, and smoothly. After World War II California winemakers heeded the advice of university professors at the Davis Campus who advocated selected yeast strains. These selected yeasts were naturally occurring, and the most promising ones were isolated, cultured, and propagated for commercial use. Just about all winemakers now use cultured yeasts, and it is standard practice to inoculate the must (that is, to add pure-culture yeasts to the juice) to start fermentation. A standard practice at most wineries used to be to sprinkle a sulfur dioxide compound on the newly crushed grapes in order to stun or inhibit the wild yeast activity before the cultured yeast could be introduced. In the late 80s many winemakers gave up doing this, instead adding the sulfur dioxide compound later, at the juice stage, or even after fermentation.

Winemakers select each yeast for certain properties. A major way in which yeasts vary is in the amount of foam produced during the fermentation, which is an important consideration for anyone who is barrel-fermenting. Further, yeasts vary in their tolerance of such conditions as cold, warmth, degree of alcohol, viscosity, sugar, and acidity. Yeasts are also capable of contributing a range of aromas and flavors (sometimes distinctly undesirable aromas and flavors). Moreover, they work at different speeds, some being extremely slow and a few others very fast fermenters. In addition, the pure-culture strains are grown specifically for their ability to inhibit the growth of natural but less desirable yeasts. All of these properties must be taken into consideration when yeasts are selected.

Most wineries today simply purchase yeasts from supply houses rather than cultivate their own strains. The commercial yeasts are available in liquid as well as a freeze-dried form, which is now preferred. Winemakers with large-volume brands normally use one strain of yeasts for all red wines and another for all of the whites. We know of some using a single yeast for all wines—red, white, rosé, and sparkling. However, winemakers striving to produce individualized wines believe that the selection of a cultured yeast should be on a grape-variety-by-variety basis. Each vintage provides another chance to try out a different combination. After the 1980 vintage in California produced some wines thought to be flawed by the yeasts used, vintners began to speed up their efforts in the field of yeast selection. What follows is some general assessments of the yeasts most frequently used today.

MONTRACHET yeast has been the most popular among winemakers for many years, and is used for both red and white wines. It is frequently used for Chardonnay in both barrel and stainless-steel fermentations. Montrachet is popular because it tolerates sulfur dioxide better than most other yeasts. However, it is said to be slow and sluggish in its performance, and it does not work well with high-sugar (greater than 23.5%) grapes. Overall, with grapes within normal sugar levels, Montrachet produces some complex whites, especially Chardonnays. In the late 70s (and sometimes even today) this strain was blamed for stuck fermentations and wines with excessive levels of hydrogen sulfide, but it has since been at least partially cleared of these charges by researchers.

CHAMPAGNE yeast is probably the second most popular. It was isolated in the region of Champagne and is technically a mixed-population culture, not a pure single strain. It is favored for sparkling wines because it ferments rapidly and is tolerant of both low temperatures and high alcohol levels—both conditions commonly met with when making sparkling wines.

PASTEUR WHITE, also known by some as French White, is used for a range of white wines. It pairs well with white wines because it works slowly and tolerates cold conditions. Some winemakers like its ability to impart yeasty aromas, and a few believe it helps retain high acidity. Its liability is that it foams considerably, so it is used in stainless-steel fermentations but seldom in barrel fermentations.

STEINBERG is a strain developed in Germany's famous wine school at Geisenheim, and is generally favored for white wines that winemakers prefer to ferment long (two, three weeks or more) and cold. It is said to be the most tolerant of cold of all strains, which makes it a natural for Johannisberg Riesling, Gewurztraminer, Chenin Blanc, and Muscat varieties. This yeast contributes an aroma described as tropical-fruit in nature, which is either a plus or a minus, depending on the winemaker. It is best suited to stainless-steel fermentations.

PASTEUR RED, or French Red, is a mixed-population strain developed from yeasts prevalent in the Bordeaux region of France. Its positive attributes are a tolerance to heat and to sulfur dioxide. It also has a history of working smoothly and of rarely, if ever, being involved in a stuck fermentation. Used for red wines generally, it has recently been matched with Cabernet Sauvignon, Merlot, and Zinfandel.

ASSMANNSHAUSEN is a strain from Germany, where research on yeast strains has been going full-tilt for decades. Advocates for this strain have proclaimed it a wonder yeast for red wines because it seems to intensify the color and impart a strong spicy fragrance. At first it was used for Zinfandel and Pinot Noir exclusively; more recent vintages have witnessed its increased employment with Cabernet Sauvignon. The strain, however, is definitely not well suited for musts with high solid content, such as are characteristically found with several white grape varieties, and so should not be used with these varieties.

PRISE DE MOUSSE is a specific type of Champagne yeast which is best known for being strong-acting and very low-foaming. Both attributes make it a likely partner in barrel fermentations. Winemakers also classify it as a yeast with a strong inclination to ferment to dryness without a hitch. Those who prefer it claim that it intensifies the fruitiness of certain varietals. The only liability, at least to some, may be its strong yeasty aroma. This one attribute, however, makes it highly desirable for the second fermentation in sparkling wine among sparkling-wine producers.

EPERNAY is another specific strain isolated in Champagne that has found some advocates in the U.S. It is frequently used for bottle-fermented sparkling wine because it is an extremely slow fermenter that tolerates cold temperatures. It is also viewed as a moderate-foaming yeast. Winemakers use it for a range of white varietal wines, as well as for the primary fermentation for sparkling-wine stock.

PASTEUR CHAMPAGNE yeast is another that is often employed by winemakers. It is a very active strain, and is a popular choice for sparkling wines because it is unusually tolerant to carbon dioxide. Among those making sparkling wine by the Charmat process this is usually the yeast of choice.

All of the above-mentioned yeast cultures are widely used in California as well as by winemakers in all other states. The Robert Mondavi Winery is the only producer we are aware of that prepares its own strains of yeasts and has isolated and propagated one or two special strains. At Woodbridge, Mondavi found and later propagated a low-foaming yeast suited for barrel fermentation; it named the yeast Woodbridge. Several of the sparkling-wine producers such as Chandon and Piper Sonoma acquire their yeast strains directly from their respective headquarters in Champagne. Most cultured yeasts are sold by a variety of companies located in and around the major U.S. wine regions.

Fermentation Techniques

Winemakers can manipulate the wine during fermentation in many ways in order to achieve a certain predetermined style. The winemaker exerts as much influence on the style of a wine as do the climate and the soil conditions. Choices of containers, yeasts, and types of fermentation bear directly on specific wine styles ultimately achieved. During fermentation, winemakers have numerous other technical options before them. Though it is not our intent to chronicle every minute technical possibility, we do want to highlight the major technical areas, which are quite frequently referenced on back labels or in winery-disseminated information.

SKIN-CONTACT TIME involves the juice of white wines between crushing and the beginning of fermentation. White wines generally ferment without the grape skins, but winemakers have learned that these skins contain many aromatic and flavor-contributing compounds that can enhance their wine. To leach out these compounds hidden within the layers of the skins, they allow the white wine juice to remain in contact with the skins in a closed tank for a period of time ranging from a few hours up to a day or two. One risk involved is that the juice may pick up darker-than-desired color from the skins, and another danger is the possibility of added bitterness. Both can be avoided by frequent monitoring of the temperature during the skin-contact process. This procedure of giving white wines time in contact with the skins has certainly helped to improve the overall quality of Gewurztraminer and Chardonnay, and perhaps others.

WHOLE CLUSTER PRESSING emerged in the late 8os as a reaction among some winemakers to giving white wine skin-contact time. This approach, specifically used with Chardonnay, involves pressing the entire clusters in a gentle membrane press to minimize the time the juice spends with the skins. It involves no crushing or maceration. Whole cluster pressing is slow, and lends itself to small-batch winemaking. Used almost entirely in Burgundy, where most wines are made in small volume, whole cluster pressing appears to be best suited to grapes grown in cool climates. In relatively warm climates grapes mature sooner, and therefore their flavors are still lodged within the skins. Whole cluster pressing is advocated by those winemakers in the United States who either work with cool-climate grapes whose flavors are in the pulp, or who are fearful of the bitter flavors and browning tendency associated with maceration and skin contact.

TEMPERATURE MANAGEMENT While it is true that slow, cool fermentations in stainless-steel tanks are the rule and that most whites ferment at colder levels (45° to 60° F.) and reds somewhat warmer (65° to 75° F.), a number of winemakers employ still warmer fermentations for a few types of wine, mostly reds. Many Cabernets, Merlots, and full-bodied Zinfandels have been fermented in the 80° to 90° F. range, on the assumption that complexity is gained and simple fruitiness avoided. Warmer fermentations are also used by some to diminish the unwanted vegetative notes in reds such as Cabernet Sauvignon and Merlot. Producers of heavyweight Pinot Noirs are the strongest advocates of warm fermentations. A few winemakers allow Pinot Noir fermentations to reach the low 90s to extract more from the skins and to increase the tannin level. Barrel-fermented white wines are not subject to precise temperature controls, but winemakers usually want to maintain relatively cool (55° to 68° F.) conditions. So, most winemakers place their barrels in specially designed, temperature-controlled rooms, isolated from the rest of the winery. Another precautionary step taken by meticulous winemakers is to pre-chill the juice before running it into the barrels for fermentation.

CAP MANAGEMENT The "cap" is the solid mass, consisting mostly of grape skins and seeds, that rises to the surface during red wine fermentations. This mass of skins needs to be repeatedly pushed down into the fermenting wine because it contributes color and flavors. Left on the surface, it becomes dry and might develop ugly bacterial problems to ruin the wine. In order to manage the cap, the traditional winemaking procedure is to punch it down once or twice a day, submerging it with a long paddle. Among the traditionalists, punching down is performed several times a day throughout the active fermentation. Another way to manage the cap is to "pump over," which means that wine from the bottom of the tank is pumped over to the top, where it moistens the cap and forces it to sink beneath the surface. The modern, labor-free way is to use specially designed tanks. One popular design has a screen fixed inside the tank at around the halfway level that prevents the cap from rising to the surface. This tank requires careful cleaning after use. Another special design, first used by both the Robert Mondavi Winery and Beringer Vineyards, is a roto-tank.

This horizontal tank, now used by dozens of producers, is programmed to rotate at intervals and so mix the cap and the fermenting wines enough to keep the cap from staying at the surface for any length of time.

STEM RETENTION This first became a winemaking strategy in California in the mid-70s after many heated discussions about Pinot Noir. By the late 70s the grape stems, removed by the crusher-stemmer, were being returned to the fermenting Pinot Noir on an experimental basis. Stems—usually only a portion of the total—can augment the wine's viscosity, and add richness and aroma. With Pinot Noir, the stems are thought also to help fight off bacterial problems. According to experiments conducted by the Robert Mondavi Winery, wines such as Pinot Noir are said to benefit when the proportion of stems retained is 30% or higher. However, some winemakers claim differences are noted at 20%, and a few others say the desirable changes require more than 40% stem retention. Just about all agree that the risk involved in stem retention is excessive bitterness. Many winemakers have made wines by stem retention, and most maintain that the stems must be dried somewhat before being included, or else the bitterness can really become a major problem.

EXTENDED MACERATION involves red wines only, which are allowed to remain in contact with the skins, seeds, stems, and yeasts after fermentation is complete. The wine rests in sealed containers, usually stainless-steel tanks, for a period of time. The goals in mind are to increase color intensity, to enhance aroma, and to rid the wine of harsh, bitter tannins while retaining only soft tannins. The technical explanation is that during this maceration period the small tannin molecules combine to form larger molecules. In addition, many of these large (polymeric) molecules are less soluble and therefore will precipitate out of solution. According to winemakers, these larger tannin molecules are softer and less bitter than the smaller ones. They are also more complex tannins that provide greater stability, which allows wine from this procedure to age long.

Extended maceration is widely used in Bordeaux, and Californians began using it for Cabernet and Merlot in the late 70s. French vintners have a special name, *cuvaison,* for the combined time of fermentation and maceration. Advocates claim the beneficial effects occur only after 10 days of maceration, but the time devoted ranges considerably. Quite a few winemakers feel 21 days of maceration is the norm, while others allow the period to extend from 30 on up to 45 days. After maceration the fermented wines are pressed to remove them from the grape skins, racked three or four times, and most likely placed in oak barrels. The one definite liability of maceration is that it ties up fermentation tanks, which at many wineries are needed for other wines during the ongoing harvest.

CHAPTALIZATION is the official French term for adding sugar to wine during the fermentation period. Though illegal in California, it is permitted in several states under special circumstances. In extremely cool climates, grapes sometimes fail to develop sufficient sugar to yield balanced wines. Before they are spoiled by harsh late-season weather, the grapes are picked unripe, crushed, and then sugar is introduced into the fermentation tanks. In Oregon, where it is sometimes necessary, vintners prefer to chaptalize toward the middle or the end of fermentation in order to stretch out the fermentation time. Chaptalizing increases the wine's body because it increases the alcohol. Different states limit the amount of alcohol that can be gained through this technique. Oregon law, for instance, allows "when necessary" the addition of as much as 2% sugar to augment fermentation. This is fairly consistent with the policy in most European wine regions.

ARRESTING FERMENTATION has emerged as the primary way to preserve residual sugar in wine. Of the many methods to stop a fermentation, winemakers prefer chilling the wine when it reaches the desired sugar level. Chilling wine to or slightly below 32° F. will force the yeasts to stop working. At that point the wine has retained the residual sugar and is eventually siphoned or racked away from the yeasts. Sending wine that is still fermenting through a centrifuge to remove the yeasts is another way to leave the desired degree of sugar in a wine. The old technique for stopping the fermentation in order to make a wine with some level of sweetness was to add a large dose of sulfur dioxide when the wine had fermented to the desired stage. The only drawback was that the wines then became so sulfurous they needed to be aged for a time before they were drinkable.

ACIDULATION is a fancy expression for the addition of acidity to wine. In many warm growing regions, wine grapes develop high sugars but at a loss of acidity. In California, it is legal to add acids to wine so long as the acids are those that occur naturally in grapes—tartaric, malic, or citric. Such "acid adjustments" are needed far more often for white varietals than for reds. In California the acid added is usually tartaric, purchased in a dry, powdery form which dissolves in the wine. Winemakers disagree over whether the acid adjustment should be made during or after fermentation.

Clarifying Wine

After fermentation, a range of particles, both visible and invisible, remain in wine—among the most common being spent yeast cells, protein particles, tannins, and grape skins. Clarification is the process of removing such particles from newly fermented wines so as to leave the wines bright, clear, and visually acceptable. The process, moreover, is necessary for more than cosmetic reasons—it also serves to remove many potential dangers and prepare the wine for bottling. Today, four clarification procedures are commonly practiced by winemakers throughout the world: racking, fining, filtering, and centrifuging.

RACKING

Racking is the oldest and, in a way, the only natural system of clarifying wines. Basically, racking is the transfer of wine from one container to another so carefully that only clear wine moves, and sediment along with a small amount of wine is left behind. It is natural primarily because it relies on gravity to pull unwanted particles to the bottom of a container. Just about all wines are racked at least once, most commonly out of the fermentation container. After allowing some time for settling to occur, the winemaker removes the clearer wine from the fermentation lees—mainly yeast cells, skins, and seeds. Normally, a fermentation tank has a racking valve located at about the anticipated sediment level. The clearer wine is pumped into its next home through a hose attached to the valve. Most wines are racked three or four times over a year, and by the end become quite clear and bright to the eye. Although necessary, frequent rackings are labor-intensive.

Three ways exist to move wines from one container to another. They can be pumped, which is the common way; pushed by pressure of an inert gas (carbon dioxide or nitrogen); or they can flow naturally by gravity. A few winemakers suspect that pumping agitates wine unduly, so these few go the extra yard and rack their wines, usually reds, relying only on gravity in what's known as a barrel-to-barrel racking.

FINING

Racking removes only those particles that precipitate out from the wine naturally. But not all substances settle to the bottom, and some of those that remain can cause problems later on. Therefore, winemakers must resort to other methods. One of the most widely used procedures is fining by the addition of an outside agent. Fining agents absorb or adsorb (that is, they help collect dissolved substances) particulate matter, and are later removed together with the unwanted substances by racking or filtering. Another property of many fining agents is that they make larger particles out of smaller ones, causing them to settle to the bottom of the container. Basically, fining agents enable winemakers to remove microscopic, dissolved material, and also to improve a wine's color, aroma, and flavor. When used by competent winemakers, fining agents will leave no residue or unpleasant side effects. The agents are either natural or synthetic, though the majority are natural. The most frequently used natural agents are egg whites, bentonite, gelatin, isinglass, and casein. Among the synthetic types, the best known are activated carbon, nylon, and polyvinyl poly-pyrrolidone, known as PVPP. Each agent removes a specific unwanted constituent in wine—two of the most common being proteins that cause cloudiness and bitter components known as phenolics. Fining also helps remove unwanted aromas and atypical colors.

Bentonite is a widely used agent, especially for white wines. A powdery clay found in Wyoming, South Dakota, and Germany, it works extremely well in removing protein particles. When left in wine, proteins create a hazy, cloudy appearance, especially if the wines experience warmth during shipping or cellaring. Bentonite is otherwise gentle on wine and does not strip away desirable constituents.

Egg whites—fresh, frozen, or dried—have long been used in fining red wines to reduce tannins and bitter phenolics. In all forms egg whites consist of protein, but their ability to remove excess tannin more than makes up for any trace of protein they may leave behind. Traditionally, egg whites are added to wines such as Cabernet Sauvignon and Merlot during aging in small oak barrels (frequently, they are added after blending in large containers). The number of egg whites added to the barrel is usually four to six, depending on the amount of tannin to be removed. Winemakers are willing to expend the extra labor required because, when used properly, egg whites do not strip away color and are particularly gentle on the wine.

A range of other fining agents can be used for both red and white wines. Gelatin is a protein substance derived from collagen and in fining wine is specifically used to remove tannins. It is very active, and has sometimes been used by winemakers to lower the limited but nevertheless undesirable tannic astringency in white wines before fermentation. Gelatin can remove color and even strip away fruity flavors, however. So most winemakers, given a choice, would opt for casein when the need is to remove tannic astringency from white wines. Casein, a form of milk protein, removes tannins but with few side effects. Another fining agent used occasionally for table wines is isinglass. Made from sturgeon bladder, isinglass is a protein scoring high marks from winemakers for tannin reduction and overall clarity. Unfortunately it is expensive, and seems to be used by only a handful of Chardonnay producers. However, in Champagne and in the production of many quality California sparkling wines, isinglass is often preferred for clarification.

Here we should also mention several of the unpublicized treatments used. Though few winemakers would brag about it, activated charcoal is widely used to remove just about anything from wine. With the strong demand for White Zinfandel in the 80s, many winemakers had to work with bulk wines which needed adjustments in their color. In this context, activated charcoal served as a great tool. It also helps remove unpleasant aromas, and its "deodorizing" ability is no secret among producers. One widely used synthetic fining agent is PVPP. To date, this relatively new agent has scored well. It is known to help adjust color and aroma without any negative effects. In practice it seems to be called into action frequently to remove brown tones or other unwanted colors in white wines. One of its best attributes is that it is not soluble in wine, and therefore leaves no residual amounts behind.

Usually, after fining in tanks or in barrels, winemakers allow settling to occur. Then typically wines are clarified by racking, filtering, or centrifuging.

FILTERING

Of all clarifying procedures, filtering is one of the last procedures called upon to remove particles from wine. It also is the one that is potentially dangerous in that, if carried out improperly, filtering can strip away positive constituents. The purpose of filtering wine is to remove yeast cells and other microbes that could create off-character and instability.

Filtering consists of pumping the wine through a series of screens holding pads or special membranes. The pads may be coated with a material such as diatomaceous earth or simply made of cellulose. The pads available to most wineries vary in porosity. Filters using the finest pads are able to capture the smallest suspended particle, even a single yeast cell. (In the latter case, the process is known among winemakers as a "sterile" filtration.) More recently, membrane filters are being used in conjunction with pads because the membranes are finer and tighter in their clarifying ability. They are believed to have no adverse affects on quality. Immediately before bottling, wines often receive a final polishing filtration, with a sterile membrane filter which ensures that they are free from harmful organisms.

CENTRIFUGING

A centrifuge, even a small one, is a costly piece of equipment. Though many winemakers believe strongly in the merits of centrifuges, others refuse to use them for premium-quality wines. Those swearing by the centrifuge maintain it works fast and requires little manpower. Because particles of all sizes can be removed through centrifugal force, centrifuging easily replaces several rackings in winery operations and can make clarification simpler. The centrifuge also enables winemakers to combine fining and clarifying in a single step: after the fining agent settles out, the wine can be centrifuged immediately and is then ready for bottling. As for the detractors, they maintain that the centrifuge removes too much from wine, no matter how carefully it is monitored. The detractors are usually winemakers without a centrifuge at their disposal.

In recent years the centrifuge has proven itself an indispensable tool, when used wisely, for moderate-sized (100,000 cases) and larger-sized wineries. It has also been a great boon to those frequently producing late-harvest-style wines.

Two aspects of winemaking that may be considered to belong together are aging and blending. The two often take place within the same time frame. Moreover, both are optional, since not all wines are aged significantly, nor are all wines blended. The processes are also linked in that it is through them especially that winemakers can really assert and distinguish themselves, and thereby set themselves and their wines apart from others. Aging and blending are much more than just stages preparatory to bottling. They are functions in which winemakers have an opportunity to demonstrate their artistry.

Aging

Many wines age in wooden containers, and the general public usually equates aging with cool cellars full of cobweb-draped oak barrels. The fact is that not all wines are aged substantially before bottling, nor are all aging vessels made of oak. Quite a few wines are bottled just a few weeks or a few months after the harvest. In most instances they will have been stored in stainless-steel tanks, not in oak barrels or even larger wood containers. Though airtight, stainless-steel tanks allow wines to marry and come together as they shed some of their youthful aggressive flavors and harshness. Long aging of wine is rarely performed in stainless-steel tanks, however. On the contrary, wine stored in such tanks may be deliberately held without aging by blanketing the top of each tank with carbon dioxide or an inert gas such as nitrogen. Thus covered, the wine has no contact with air and tends to retain its fruitiness. In actual practice, wines held in stainless steel change very little, and what change there is occurs very slowly.

Most wineries wishing to age wine before bottling will keep the wine in wood. Wines are wood-aged for several reasons. One traditional reason is that the process takes young green wines, rough to the point of being unpleasant, and makes them softer, smoother, and more enjoyable. Red wines are more often in need of aging than whites, because tannins and bitter flavors are more pronounced in young red wines. A few white wines, especially barrel-fermented versions, also benefit from the softening effect of additional wood aging. Wood is porous, and the slow, controlled, but inevitable air contact with the wine results in some degree of evaporation. As evaporation takes place, the wine becomes concentrated, which is another traditional reason for placing wine in wood. As wine ages in wood, the alcohol and tannins leach out flavors from the container, and these wood flavors are usually desirable additions. Many winemakers wood-age white wines naturally low in tannins to enable them to pick up tannins—which at low levels are desirable preservatives—from the wood itself.

Today, the subject of wood aging for wine has been elevated to a science, with major emphasis given to the type of wood, the size of the container, and the origin of the wood and production method of the barrel-maker. The general requirements for a wood container for wine are that it be durable, slightly porous, and pleasantly flavored. Many kinds of wood have been used by winemakers, from chestnut to pine to redwood and white oak. But it is the last two types that are today's favorites on the West Coast. Of course it helps that both white oak and redwood are readily available.

Redwood was preferred by a wide margin in California until the mid-60s. As an aging container, redwood remains as suitable as most other types of wood. However, because it is fairly neutral in flavor, redwood places a distant second to oak when it comes to selecting small barrels intended to contribute flavor to wine. Large vats and storage tanks in California have often been made from redwood. For the early stages of aging and often for the malolactic fermentation, redwood tanks are still used today. The large tanks that stand vertical, known as uprights, are usually made of redwood, which is less expensive than oak, although many wineries may spend money on oak uprights either for the extra measure of character delivered or simply for the prestige. As prices for a winery's product go up, so does the winemaker's propensity to rely exclusively on stainless steel and oak for his wine fermentation and storage vessels.

The shape and storage capacity of an aging container will be determined by its use within the winery. Generally, the smaller the container, the faster the aging process, and vice versa. Most winemakers prefer to start out using large containers for new wine and then complete the aging process with small barrels—a barrel being an oak container with a capacity of between 55 and 60 gallons. This traditional barrel is used for the primary aging period, after the wine has been clarified. Most barrel fermentations occur in this size barrel. Several wineries prefer using a larger oak container known as a puncheon for fermenting their wines. A puncheon has a capacity of 135 to 150 gallons.

In most wineries the larger tanks—oak or redwood—are usually used for the early stages of aging, in which the wines are still in need of clarification. Most fining treatments are conducted in large containers, and the same holds true for malolactic fermentations. It is simply more efficient to employ large tanks when performing these functions. Like their stainless-steel counterparts, redwood tanks range in size from a capacity of a few hundred gallons on up to many thousands. Usually, the largest storage container in a winery will be the blending tank, which is almost always stainless steel. The various batches or lots of wine are eventually combined in blending tanks in order to achieve uniformity before bottling.

In contemporary winemaking, the small oak barrel has emerged as one of the most important factors in achieving wine's ultimate aroma and flavor. The origin of the wood—that is, where the tree grew—has emerged as a primary consideration for winemakers. The most popular kind of oak used in winemaking is white oak, belonging to the species *Quercus sessilis* in Europe and *Quercus alba* in the U.S. White oak is durable, and just porous enough to make it ideal for aging wine. This kind of oak can be found in many states, Kentucky, Tennessee, Ohio, Missouri, and Wisconsin being the leaders. The same oak also thrives in France and Yugoslavia.

In general, the flavors extracted from white oak are the vanillins—flavors obtained from the toasting of the barrel which are believed to be compatible with many wines. There are other subtle oak-provided taste sensations described variously as "spicy," "roasted," "tangy," "creamy," and "lemony." Studies have shown that the flavors and characteristics imparted by white oak barrels vary according to the origin of the oak trees. Manufacturing techniques can also influence the types of characteristics given off by the barrel during the wine-aging process.

Beginning in the 60s and continuing into the 70s California winemakers, both newcomers and veterans, became compulsive students of oak aging. The first stages in the study of oak aging revolved around research into the differences between French oak barrels made from oak trees grown in several locations within France. For example, there are three important French forests supplying white oak barrels. One is the Limousin Forest in south-central France, where the climate is relatively warm and mild. Oak from Limousin develops looser grains, which in turn contribute overt oak flavors and rough, aggressive tannins. Furthermore, Limousin oak contributes a perfumed aroma and a sharp aftertaste. Limousin has been, and still is, used mostly for Cognac. The second important source, known as the Center of France, includes the Nevers and Allier forests, which are found further north, where the climate is cooler and the wood therefore tighter-grained. For wine barrels, this tighter grain creates more subtle oak phenolics, meaning less obvious oak character. The Vosges area in northeastern France is the third important source. While Limousin, the Center of France, and the Vosges supply most of the oak for French barrels, other locations make a contribution. For instance, Allier is a small forest not far from Nevers, but even within Allier is a still smaller area known as Tronçais. Its oak barrels are thought by winemakers to leave a subtle but slightly perfumed character.

The initial obsession of Americans with French oak barrels eventually gave way to a more even-tempered understanding. French winemakers had never engaged in a systematic study of oak barrels, but knew from traditional practice that the methods employed by specific coopers (barrel-makers) were important in some vital way. After added research, California winemakers learned that most subtle differences among oak barrels could actually be attributed to a particular cooper and his techniques rather than to the choice of wood or the superiority of one forest over another.

COOPERS

Quality oak barrels imported from France are hand-crafted in the sense that no two barrels are precisely the same. Furthermore, the ways in which the oak is treated and handled by French coopers differ substantially from the methods originally used in the United States to build barrels. Historically, barrel-building in the U.S. developed to serve the whiskey industry—bourbon and rye primarily—rather than the wine business. Not surprisingly, therefore, American techniques have varied considerably from those in France.

The majority of whiskeys produced in the U.S. acquire most of whatever flavors they end up with primarily from the barrels. Traditionally, the flavors American coopers emphasized in their barrels were woody, along with a strong flavor of char and charcoal. This char or burnt-wood flavor is created automatically when the straight pieces of wood—known as staves—are treated in order to be bent and then set to form a round barrel. In the process of applying high heat, the early American coopers literally charred the inside layers of the staves. The general coopering techniques adopted in the U.S. eventually all worked toward making barrels with a strong char flavor. Even today, American-made distilled spirits display a typical character from American-made barrels.

The traditional coopering techniques followed in the United States involve sawing the timber rather than hand-splitting it, and then drying it in a kiln to expose a coarse rough surface easier to char. The staves selected to be part of a barrel are bent by being steamed, which further opens the grain for the charring to follow. Barrels produced by the American coopering method tend to be more uniform and consistent, and can be produced in volume. But such efficiency comes at a cost of the finer points.

Barrelmaking in France developed along different lines. After the oak trees have been felled, they are split by hand. Then the wood is hand-sawn, and according to tradition, seasoned or weathered for about two years by being air-dried outdoors. Next, the wood is cut by hand into planks destined to become the barrel staves, which ultimately number 30 individual pieces. Only about 20% of an oak tree is suitable for use as barrel staves, by the way. In order to bend each stave, French coopers make the wood pliable by heating it directly over a fire fueled only by oak chips and shavings. Once they are warm enough to bend, the staves are shaped into a barrel. The cooper again applies heat from the fire to set the staves into their final position, where the hoops holding them together are secured in place along with the endpieces, or heads, as they are called. The direct-fire technique used to set the wood actually impregnates the inside with a toasted character. The cooper, however, is careful to avoid burning or charring the barrel by controlling both the temperature of the fire and also the distance between the staves and the fire. It is the firing, or toasting, that imparts a special flavor to French oak barrels, or to barrels made by French techniques.

The most successful French coopering companies add their own individual touches to the barrel, while using standard techniques. Oak barrels for aging wine are usually purchased directly from a builder or cooper, and many American winemakers specify how they want their barrels to be built—the origin of the oak, the thickness of the staves, the hoops used, and the degree of toast built in—in effect ordering them custom-made. Though American barrel-builders are now willing to follow the French coopering practices, several French firms still control the lion's share of the market. At one point in 1980 a single company—Demptos—was responsible for making 50% of all new oak barrels purchased by California wineries. Other companies have since made inroads into the competitive U.S. market. Following are the leading coopers producing barrels today, with a consensus view from winemakers about their respective products:

DEMPTOS is headquartered in a suburb of Bordeaux. Along with its once-thriving export market, this firm once supplied a significant percentage of barrels used in Bordeaux. The company now buys oak from throughout France, and builds to each buyer's specifications. The Demptos barrel was so much in demand in the United States that in 82 the company established a barrelmaking and -repairing facility in Napa Valley. However, by the end of the 80s the Napa Valley Demptos, greatly expanded, was purchased by local vintners headed by the Jaegers of Rutherford Hill Winery. In mid-89, the main operation in France was sold to François Frères, which now makes Demptos barrels.

FRANÇOIS FRÈRES is a cooper based in Burgundy, where the typical barrel is fat and stocky, usually finished with traditional wood hoops. This cooper is noted for barrels that are strongly flavored and heavily toasted. Many wineries age Pinot Noir in François Frères's barrels.

SÉGUIN MOREAU is a large barrelmaker based in Cognac. It buys oak from all regions of France, but specializes in a sturdy barrel known as the Bordeaux barrel or château barrel, with distinct willow hoops. Séguin Moreau supplies barrels to many of the famous châteaux of Bordeaux, and by the mid-80s this barrel was being widely used in the U.S. for Cabernet Sauvignon, Merlot, and other red wines. Many winemakers refer to Séguin Moreau as "the Cadillac of oak barrels." Its American base of operations is in the Napa Valley.

SIRUGUE is another well-known cooper from the Burgundy region, but it is a small firm. While the majority of Burgundy coopers favor strong toasty character, Sirugue is an exception. Its light oak, with subtle toastiness, is often used for both Chardonnay and Pinot Noir.

TARANSAUD is a name seen on many barrels. This firm is located in the Cognac region and owned by the conglomerate Moët-Hennessey. The oak is air-dried for three years or more, and Taransaud's barrels thus contribute more subtle effects than are usually associated with oak from Limousin. This firm's Limousin barrels are often used with West Coast Chardonnays. In the 80s many producers of Cabernet and Merlot began using Taransaud's barrels made from Center of France oak, and the same barrel is now widely used by many Bordeaux châteaux.

TONNELLERIES DE BOURGOGNE is a Burgundy cooper whose name is quite prominent in California. Actually, it represents a group of small coopers who banded together in 67 to form a co-operative venture. Made by traditional techniques, the barrels are toasted usually in a light to medium range and are said to be extremely spicy in character. In the 80s they enjoyed a slight price advantage over other French producers.

Just about all of the major French coopering houses have agents on the West Coast. Quite a few of them have established barrel companies in California, either to build new barrels or to repair used barrels. Today, some of the firms ship staves from France and then assemble the barrels in California, often under the watchful eye of the local winemaker.

Once built and in place, a well-cared-for wine barrel will last for decades. However, an oak barrel will contribute oak flavors to a wine for only five years on average; thereafter the barrel is close to neutral in flavor. Several companies specialize in breaking barrels down stave by stave, shaving away the inner layers to expose a new layer, and then recombining the parts to make the barrels functional for flavoring again. This procedure remains controversial because the staves are often not toasted at all or, when they are, the flavors are not always acceptable.

Oak-barrel aging adds substantially to the cost of producing premium-level wine. The average price of a French-made oak barrel has ranged from a low of about $225 in the 80s to a high of $550 in 90. For comparison, the price of an American oak barrel ranged from $75 to $160 in the same time period. Once put into use, oak barrels continue to add to the cost of the final wine. Maintaining wine in oak barrels is more labor-intensive than using large-capacity stainless-steel tanks or larger wood tanks. Furthermore, in an average year about 5% of the wine placed in barrels is lost through evaporation. As a result, winemakers must protect the remaining wine from oxidation by periodically refilling each barrel to the brim, a process known as "topping up." To facilitate this topping procedure, and the required number of rackings, winemakers have devised several systems for storing and stacking their oak barrels. Whatever the system, and regardless of how high they may be stacked, oak barrels take up considerable space. Finally, oak barrels, like all wooden containers, require careful cleaning between vintages or batches, first to avoid bacterial buildup, and second to remove normal tartrate deposits. In most wineries, barrels are rinsed with warm water and sometimes with an alkaline solution of soda ash to both clean and neutralize them. At some wineries the barrels are cleaned by special, expensive machines. In today's world, in sum, aging wine in the traditional oak barrels has become very costly.

BARREL-AGING PROGRAMS

Winemakers have come to employ wood containers for purposes other than the simple aging of wine. Usually, wines are clarified long before they are placed in small barrels. Yet for those white wines that are fermented in barrels, winemakers sometimes prefer to age the wine in the same barrels because the wine will remain in contact with the lees, which consist mostly of inactive yeast cells.

Sur lie is the technical name for this type of barrel aging of wine together with the expired yeast. It is common in cool climates where the high-acid wines need to undergo the malolactic fermentation and deacidification process. Remaining in contact with the yeast lees, the new wine is encouraged by the available nutrients to begin malolactic fermentation. The *sur lie* technique can bring other benefits. Aging wine with the yeast leads to the decomposition of the yeast cells, or autolysis. This reaction will over time release amino acids to enhance the body of the wine, tone down the acid finish, and even imbue the wine with a yeasty, toasty aroma. This process is now used to produce many Chardonnays and even a few Sauvignon Blancs on the West Coast. In the making of Champagne by the classic procedure, the *méthode champenoise,* the same biochemical principle is at work when the Champagne in the bottle ages in contact with the yeast after the second fermentation is completed.

"Barrel rotation" is a winemaker's term for a system in which barrels of different ages are used to age a single vintage. Brand-new barrels may cause rapid aging and hard-to-control oakiness, so winemakers move the wine through a series of barrels of different ages. The frequent pattern for barrel-aged wine like Cabernet Sauvignon is to replace 20% of the barrels with new ones each year—thus, after five years of use, the oldest barrels, which by then have imparted all of the oak character they can give, are phased out. The replenishing is systematic, as winemakers keep close track of how old each barrel is, and where it can best be used in the winemaking process.

One final note about barrel aging relates to the physical storage conditions. In most wine facilities, barrels are stored in areas that are quiet and temperature-controlled. In the early 80s, winery proprietors became intrigued by the concept of barrel-aging wines in cool underground cellars. California has no natural caves, but at the end of the last century a few wineries, notably Beringer, Schramsberg, and Buena Vista, were using caves, dug by hand into the hills by ill-paid immigrants. Today, making a cave simply to age wines in may sound rather extravagant, yet the conditions achieved are ideal—a high humidity, as well as constant temperature and natural air conditioning. A typical cave may have a humidity level around 95% at a temperature around 60° F., conditions in which wines aging in barrels experience little evaporation and age very well. Wineries that have them claim that man-made caves can recover their construction costs within five years through the savings in wine and in energy expense.

Blending

Blending is a time-honored winemaking process that some winemakers have raised to an art form. It definitely is not synonymous with stretching, though some people do add inferior wine for that purpose. Blending, however, involves much more than just merging or mixing different wines. Winemakers blend by combining wines by region, by vineyard, by vintage, and by type of aging container. Blending to us becomes a noteworthy topic when the purpose behind it is to create a wine whose total quality impression is greater than the sum of its parts.

Combining two or more grape varieties is the most typical example of the act of blending. Many of the standard combinations now produced are classic blends originating in Europe. From Bordeaux we have Cabernet Sauvignon, Cabernet Franc, and Merlot as a standard blend which may also include Malbec and Petit Verdot. The standard white Bordeaux wine blend merges Sauvignon Blanc and Semillon, with a small amount of a Muscat wine (Muscadelle de Bordelaise) as an option. From Champagne, Chardonnay has joined with Pinot Noir and Pinot Meunier to form the classic blending trio for sparkling wine. Originating in the Rhone Valley, another common blend brings together Grenache, Syrah, and Mourvedre.

Trying to follow a classic European blend in the United States is not without its problems. The first is how to label the wine itself. Some California winemakers comply with federal rules regarding varietal labeling, using no more than 25% of other wines in order to retain the varietal name. Others, to achieve a stylistic goal, blend without retaining at least 75% of one variety and forfeit the chance to identify the resulting wine as a varietal. In the 80s, a number of producers began replicating Bordeaux red wine as closely as possible. The result is known as a Bordeaux blend, meaning the wines were made from Cabernet Sauvignon, Merlot, Cabernet Franc, and, if available, Malbec and Petit Verdot. These Bordeaux-style blends become so popular that the name Meritage was coined for them and adopted by many California winemakers, who had formed a voluntary Meritage Association. Most of the Meritage blends, both red and white, are also given proprietary names.

Blending the Bordeaux grape varieties in California has become fairly widespread. But another question raised is when to assemble the blend. The French traditionally assemble the blend before barrel aging, and therefore the components are forced to harmonize early. Californians are divided. Most will hold off on the final blend until the individual components have been aged. The logic in this case is that once a blend is made, winemakers can't change it, so it is better to hold off as long as possible.

Winemakers long ago discovered numerous other ways in which to blend for a better final product. Blending by region involves combining the same type of wine from different growing regions, such as Napa Valley and Santa Barbara County, or the same varietal wine from different Viticultural Areas within one county. In Napa Valley, many varietals are composed of wine from grapes grown in the Carneros or an adjacent area and another, more northerly locale. Some of the original vineyards in California were laid out in what is known as a "field blend." In this blend, the grower has interspersed different varieties within the vineyards and made his blend in the field. This planting system makes it next to impossible for winemakers to change the blend. When two or more varieties in the same field are harvested at the same time, they are bound to become parts of a blend. In Europe, especially in southern France, some of the traditional blends bring together red and white grapes that are harvested separately and then fermented together. The technical term for this is "co-fermenting."

In a similar way, winemakers can use different cooperage to blend wines. More often than not, Chardonnays are a blend of barrel-fermented and stainless-steel-fermented wine. The same Chardonnay can then be blended further by combining wines held in barrels of different ages, barrels made by different coopers, barrels made from different types of wood, or even barrels made of the same oak but from diverse regions and countries.

One of the last ways to blend wines is a method unfairly disparaged in the U.S.: the blending of wines from different vintages. The majority of fine Champagne in the traditional Brut mode represents a blend of several grape varieties and of vintages. Using wines from different years serves as a way to strike a needed balance when winemakers work with grapes grown under extreme conditions of hot or cold weather. Blended sparkling wines often originate in cold climates; blended fortified wines in warm or even hot ones. In California, however, the overwhelming majority of table wines and a surprisingly high percentage of sparkling wines are vintaged. The best explanation for this is that wines with a vintage are easier to market than those without. Chances are that in the future more sparkling wines will be multi-vintage blends because the mixing of old wine with new plays a significant role in the best French sparkling wine.

It is important for consumers to realize that blending has its place, and that 100% of one grape variety does not necessarily always mean better wine. Nevertheless, in the present scheme of things, we can't recall any Chardonnays that have been improved by blending, nor do we believe Pinot Noir benefits by being anything but 100% varietal. Johannisberg Riesling is said to be too delicate to be blended, and many winemakers believe that neither Zinfandel nor Gewurztraminer should be anything but 100% in composition. But a good case has been made in Europe, and is currently being made in the United States, in favor of blending for several other types of wine, notably those modeled after the wines of Bordeaux, the Rhone Valley, and Champagne.

Stabilizing and Bottling

Putting the wine safely into bottles is the final step in the winemaking process. In recent years bottling facilities have shifted from semi-primitive to clean and efficient to, in some instances, ultra-modern—more sanitary and sterile than many hospital operating rooms. The purpose of these advances is to try to prevent any yeast particle or bacterium from entering the bottle. Indeed, at many modern facilities, wines are bottled in a specially designed bottling room, sealed off from the rest of the winery. Today, at nearly all wine facilities, new and old, when it comes to readying the wines for bottling and actual bottling, the accent falls on cleanliness.

In the last decade it was not uncommon for many new producers on the North Coast to install elaborate bottling lines costing from $100,000 to as much as $750,000. This kind of money brings fully automated bottling lines that can be monitored by one or two workers with push-button control. In a typical continuous process, new bottles are loaded into the conveyor belt, unscrambled and sorted, rinsed, dried, and sterilized. Then each bottle is filled with wine, corked, and dressed in the appropriate garb, which is usually a color-coordinated capsule and label. Bottling doesn't require much labor anymore. The fully automated lines only need someone to inspect the bottles for uniformity of fill level, and to spot any defects in the bottles or in the machine's performance. Actually, the most expensive lines now have sensors which can detect any low or high levels of fill, and even spot bottles with capsules and no corks, or corks and no capsules. Humans are still needed to push the appropriate buttons (start, stop) at the appropriate time.

Not all producers can afford such elaborate bottling equipment, but most reasonably well-financed wineries producing over 50,000 cases will probably have invested in their own automated bottling line. The old adage that it's better to be safe than sorry applies perfectly to bottling. In the past, more than a few fine wines were ruined at the bottling stage by careless workers or dirty conditions. In addition to sterile bottling areas, some wineries now even have equipment that blows an inert gas such as nitrogen or carbon dioxide into each bottle to remove dust and lint, and to protect the wine from oxidation. One winery we visit regularly has installed an ozone bottle sterilizer for the absolute in cleanliness; and equipment is available to extract oxygen from the bottle neck after the bottles are filled to the required level and before the cork is introduced. Most modern bottling rooms maintain positive air pressure to help keep bacteria and yeast out.

Such extreme attention to cleanliness is not always necessary. Those wines that are likely to be harmed at bottling, and therefore need special protection, are the low (below 10%) alcohol types and all sweet wines; in these, a single yeast cell in a bottle could create a refermentation. Today, when most U.S. wine production is devoted to white wines, particularly those varying in sweetness, just about all of the small and even the long-established large wineries have upgraded their bottling lines. However, a winemaker producing limited amounts of red wines only, or of red wines and barrel-aged whites, most likely can make do with the bare essentials, even hand-corking equipment, so long as the conditions are sanitary.

Speed and efficiency are also important factors behind the preference for high-tech bottling lines. A new and fully automated line equipped with 75 fillers can bottle 350 to 1,000 regular-sized bottles per minute, or over 12,000 cases in a day. That is known as a high-speed line, which it literally is. Most of the very large wineries will have several of these bottling lines running at the same time, making 50,000 cases bottled per day just "a day's work."

Prior to the actual bottling, a number of important cellar activities take place. Most wines on the market are rendered heat and cold stable by the winery. Cold stabilization refers to forcing the wine to form natural tartrate crystals in a storage vessel to prevent the harmless but unsightly crystals from showing up in your bottle later on. Wines are cold-stabilized by being chilled below 32° F. for several days. Heat stability, on the other hand, assures that a wine will not develop a protein haze should it be kept under warm storage conditions. This is common among white wines, and the remedy for such harmless haziness is to fine with bentonite prior to bottling. The mid-sized to large-scale producers as a rule prefer to stabilize their wines for both heat and cold.

Wineries of all sizes assemble what is known as the master blend, usually in a large tank just before bottling. Allowing all wines but especially the barrel-aged wines time to be combined and "marry" helps achieve uniformity of the entire bottling. The various batches and lots are combined in the blending tank, where they remain for a day or two. Paddles within the tank mix the fractions and make the entire batch homogeneous. Then the wine is moved from the blending tank to the adjacent bottling room.

BOTTLE TYPES

Winemakers may or may not go through great mental anguish over which size, shape, and color of bottle they want to use. Sometimes the cheapest available ones are the best. For table wines, producers can choose from among four distinct shapes—the newer California or universal bottle, along with three traditional bottles, the Bordeaux, Burgundy, and Hock. The Burgundy and Bordeaux bottles can be either flat-bottom or the slightly more expensive push-up style. The indentation at the bottom, common in Champagne bottles, is also known as a kick-up or a punt. Its function has aroused some debate. We are content to believe the push-up makes it difficult for any sediment formed during aging to cling to the bottom and it originally helped to strengthen the bottle so that it could withstand the pressure. We also sense that producers know the push-up bottle makes for a more handsome package, for which they can charge more money. Hock bottles came our way via Germany, and the name originates from the wine village of Hochheim. In Great Britain, German wines, particularly Rhine wines, are known as Hock. The long, cylindrical bottle shape is more traditional than functional. Winemakers select the Hock shape because the wines placed into it are Germanic in type, such as Riesling and Gewurztraminer, or Germanic in style, sweet wines such as Chenin Blanc.

A mention of Hock bottles, though, leads naturally into a discussion of color. Hock is either dark green or dark brown, better known as amber. Dark glass was first used long ago to keep harmful ultraviolet light away from low-alcohol, sweet-finished table wines. Along Germany's Mosel River, producers preferred the green color, but along the meandering Rhine River the favorite color was brown. The Bordeaux bottle is traditionally made in either of two colors, dark green and clear: dark green for red Bordeaux and clear glass for white. Such traditions are more or less followed as well in California. Cabernet Sauvignon and Merlot, the two red grapes of Bordeaux, usually appear in a Bordeaux bottle. But many Zinfandels also come in the same bottle, because at times winemakers like to think Zinfandel resembles a Cabernet Sauvignon.

The use of the clear Bordeaux bottle for Sauvignon Blanc follows the strict tradition only when the wine contains Semillon in some proportion, or else when the winemaker has assembled a proprietary blend of Sauvignon Blanc and Semillon. Similarly, a naturally sweet white wine fashioned along the lines of Sauternes, a Bordeaux region, is frequently placed in the clear Bordeaux bottle. But now, of course, many White Zinfandels, which have nothing to do with Bordeaux or its wines, appear in a Bordeaux clear bottle. Otherwise, Bordeaux-shaped bottles with a dark brown color are traditional in some parts of Italy, primarily Piedmont, but the bottle is rarely used by any California winery. Also in Italy, Chianti producers use either a brown or, more typically, a dark green Bordeaux bottle.

The Burgundy bottle bears a resemblance to a Champagne bottle and is widely used for a variety of wines, red and white, dry and sweet. The color of the popular Burgundy bottle is a dark green known as "champagne green." Pinot Noir and Chardonnay, the traditional grapes of Champagne and Burgundy, are at home in this bottle. Some of the older Burgundy bottles used for white wines, such as Montrachet, were made of a thicker glass with a special tint of green known as "dead-leaf green." Many Californians associated this shade with prestige and began adopting it for their Chardonnays. Here, as in many other instances, traditions associated with wine bottles have been distorted for the purpose of promoting and packaging the product.

The different bottle sizes, however, are often of great interest to wine lovers. Bottle size influences the rate of aging: in general, the smaller the bottle, the more quickly the wine will reach maturity, and vice versa. In practice, however, wine in a magnum bottle (twice the regular 750-ml bottle) does not age twice as slowly; nor does the imperial (the largest bottle made commercially for wine and equal to eight bottles) reduce the aging speed by anything like eight times. Any bottles larger than the imperial will have been made by hand for some special occasion such as a wine auction, and the contents may have been poured in from smaller containers a short time before the special occasion takes place. The 187 ml, the bottle known as a "split" and sold primarily on airplanes, is now making a comeback as a container for serious wine, even Champagne.

CORKS

The use of a cork to seal a bottle is surrounded with even more murky mythology than the evolution of bottles. In fact, the cork is often unnecessary and purely ornamental for wines that won't improve if aged in bottle—which covers most of the wines made. A cork became associated with quality years back when screw caps first appeared and were scoffed at. Corks offer many advantages for protecting and aging wines, but they also cause problems because of their tendency to leak, to harbor bacteria, and to dry out when not kept moist. The best features about a cork are that it is compressible and adheres well to glass. Corks are thus well suited to bottled wine, and particularly those wines one intends to keep for some time.

Cork is actually the inner layer from a type of oak tree found growing mostly in Portugal and Spain today. The variety is known as *Quercus suber,* and the tree must be at least 20 years old before it can yield its cork commercially. Stripping it does not kill the tree, and cork can subsequently be harvested at nine-year intervals. The bark is first removed and cut into strips, then corks are stamped out of the strips, washed, bleached, dried, and ranked into quality levels. In Portugal, there are six grading categories for corks, with extra superior ranking above superfine, which is right above extra first, which is above first quality in a system amusing for its silly superlatives. First quality is usually good enough for most wines.

Cork suppliers try to make sure that their product is free of defects. Typically, a cork is dusted in a special vacuum system, rendered relatively sterile, and finally coated with paraffin and/or silicone for ease of insertion. Some wineries purchase corks in quantities of 1,000, packaged in sealed bags containing a blanket of sulfur dioxide for further protection. Despite all of these efforts, an average of 3 out of every 100 corks is said to contain some defect. The primary problem associated with a "corky" or "corked" wine is caused when a mold indigenous to cork reacts to the cleaning agent used.

The three top grades of cork are offered by manufacturers in three standard sizes. For most wines with a cork as an ornament, the small 1¼-inch cork is adequate. The more common size is 1¾ inches, the next size up being a 2-inch cork. Longer corks are made, but usually are purchased through special order by the winery. Ordered in quantities of 1,000, corks range in price from a low in 90 of 8 cents each to a high of 20 cents for the 2-inch versions. For wines likely to be cellared for 10 years or more, the longest cork available is the one that we like to discover when we remove it from our corkscrew. By the way, one belief fairly well substantiated now is that part of the aged bouquet developed over time in the bottle can be traced to the interaction between the cork and the wine.

DRESSING

The next step in the bottling process is the dressing, which includes capsules and labels. Usually the capsule goes on right after the cork has been inserted. All wine is required by federal law to have something covering the closure or cork. The most common materials for capsules are plastic, lead foil, a poly-aluminum, various laminated types and, on occasion, wax. Image-conscious producers favor lead foil by a great margin, primarily because the foil can be fitted smoothly and tightly, and so helps give the bottle an upscale appearance. Plastic, because it is plastic, lacks the association with fine wine. But it serves the purpose. The lead capsule will be phased out in the 90s in response to consumer concerns. It will be replaced by a pure tin capsule which is very expensive or by a heat-shrink plastic capsule, cheaper but less pretty.

LABELING

Labeling completes the activity on the bottling line. Present laws require only a front label; though popular, side or back labels are optional. Mandatory information in the U.S. includes the type of wine, the alcohol content, the fluid contents, the brand name, the address of the brand, and the area supplying the grapes. All wine labels must be approved by the federal government prior to their use. The particular federal agency overseeing wine labels is the Bureau of Alcohol, Tobacco and Firearms, a division of the U.S. Treasury Department. The watchful eye of our federal government looks out for misleading statements or implications, and guards against nudity, obscenity, and any suggestion that wine could be the least bit healthful. The government also watches for trademark infringements and look-alike logos.

Designing labels that can catch the eye of a potential consumer is now a big part of wine marketing. The label designers in California have become numerous, and many rather prosperous, in a short time. Sometimes a colorful or artsy label is the only reason a wine will sell at all. In any event, though France's Château Mouton-Rothschild was the first to use specially designed artistic labels, hundreds of California wineries have entered the competition, with no end in sight. As a result, collecting wine labels has become something of a fad. Since a few winery owners prefer to be sure their labels will not become unglued when placed in a refrigerator or ice bucket, they use a water-resistant super-glue to affix labels. However, most labels can be removed by soaking.

BOTTLE AGING

The next step following bottling and labeling is one of the more important ones: bottle aging. Most wine will experience a reaction known as "bottle shock" immediately after being bottled. There are several reasons for this, among them the fact that a wine picks up excessive oxygen during bottling, which flattens its aroma and leaves a chemical stink. Within one to three weeks, the wine will show signs of recovering and regaining its appeal. Bottle shock also has to do with levels of sulfur dioxide in the wine and how much was added during the bottling procedure.

Bottle aging by the winery is well worth the extra time and effort. Winemakers universally agree that with a wine like Chardonnay, the bottle-aging minimum should be 3 months and the ideal is from 9 to 12 months. It takes some time for the wine to begin to reveal its full potential. Since the average barrel-aging time for most serious Chardonnay is from 6 to 9 months, consumers can begin to understand why Chardonnays from one vintage trickle into the market over a two-year period. Red wines such as Cabernet and Merlot are bottle-aged by the more quality-minded winemakers for about a full year, and some even longer. To hold back wines in order to bottle-age them indicates a general interest in quality, a most admirable trait.

Grapes
and Wine Types

There is a tendency among people who write about California wine to talk as if the vinous millennium had arrived. They, and we, are probably encouraged in this because of the extraordinary quality now being exhibited by the best wines produced from the local wineries, and because of the continuing series of tastings in Europe at which California wines have frequently been rated higher than their European counterparts by experienced and objective tasters.

Here in California, of course, wineries designate almost all of their leading wines by the grape from which the wine was made, whereas most leading European wines carry the name of the vineyard or commune where the grapes were grown. Grape names are employed here for reasons of history—or perhaps the lack of history. The French, with their centuries of experimentation, have arrived at a system of grape and wine laws under which only certain varieties may be used in the production of vineyard-designated wines. Vouvray, for example, can be made only from Chenin Blanc; Clos Vougeot, only from Pinot Noir. West Coast grape growers and winemakers have not had this opportunity to learn from centuries of experience; and even though the producers have proven capable of making world-class wine, California and the West are still in their formative years when it comes to the knowledge of exactly where best to grow specific varieties. If the truth be known, California winemakers are still experimenting with the question of *which* varieties they should be growing, let alone *where* those varieties should be grown.

In this chapter, we take a look at grapes from the standpoint of what they have meant to California winemakers up to the present, and also examine the role they may play over time.

ALICANTE BOUSCHET   Here is a grape that the French use only to add color to their thinnest, most meager red *vin ordinaire*, but which in California has enjoyed a modest success beyond its value as a tinting agent. It gained this standing with home winemakers and commercial wineries because it yields a full-bodied, deeply colored wine with a noticeable tannic edge to toughen its otherwise soft structure. Even at best, however, it has never been much of a commercial hit as a varietal wine. It is now losing its popularity with the do-it-yourself crowd, and has been gradually disappearing from California vineyards. From a peak of 30,000 acres at the end of Prohibition, it now occupies only 2,100 acres, almost all of them in the hot Central Valley. It has only occasionally been offered as a varietal within the last decade.

BARBERA   Not more than two decades ago, Barbera was probably the fourth-leading red varietal in California. But its early history as a source of fuller-bodied, tannic, fairly high-acid red wines grown in California's coastal areas is now substantially behind it—the limited offerings from Martini and Sebastiani notwithstanding. Rather, Barbera has blossomed into the darling of the Central Valley jug-wine producers, who rely on its high-acid propensities to balance their otherwise soft red plonk. Interestingly, Barbera's fall from grace in California has been paralleled in its native Italy, where it is disappearing from the famous Piedmont grape-growing area while at the same time becoming that country's most widely planted red wine grape, especially in the hotter regions.

In California there are now over 10,000 acres planted and, with the exception of some 300 acres along the coast or in the Sierra Foothills, the grape is entirely restricted to the Central Valley. Recent plantings in Texas and New Mexico parallel the California jug-wine experience. Although some two dozen wineries around the country report making Barbera (most of them in California), it is rare to find more than one or two labels in even the most handsomely stocked wine shop.

BLANC   Literally "white," the term *Blanc,* in any of its forms, is used to denote a white wine. Names like Zinfandel Blanc, Cabernet Blanc, Gamay Blanc, and others that combine "Blanc" with the names of red wine grapes mean that a white wine has been made from the identified grape. The designations of "White" Zinfandel, "White" Cabernet, and their related brethren in name calling have exactly the same meaning. A few producers label their generic whites as "Chablis Blanc," perhaps on the theory that one good white wine name deserves another.

BLANC DE BLANCS   Literally "white from whites," this term applies both to sparkling wines and to still wines made from white grapes, often but not always a blend of varieties. Many champagnes called Blanc de Blancs typically contain substantial fractions of Chardonnay in their makeup.

BLANC DE NOIRS   Literally applied, the term denotes white wine made from black-skinned (red wine) grapes and applies to either champagne or still wines. Although employed most visibly on sparkling wines, it has been seen increasingly on California table wines. In theory, the color ranges from the palest hint of pink to light onionskin. However, in actual practice, wines labeled Blanc de Noirs, especially table wines but now even including some champagnes, are often outright pink or even light red in color. So, for some wineries, the name has become a marketing gambit under which rosés have become more easily salable.

BLUSH   Another alternative name for white or pink wines made from red wine grapes, this trademarked term belongs to Mill Creek Vineyards, which collects a fee from anyone else who uses it on a wine label. The term has also gained wide recognition as the generic category under which the industry lumps its so-called "White" or "Blanc" offerings made from red wine grapes.

BURGER   Back in the days when jug wines were the rule rather than the exception in California's North Coast, this white vinifera grape was more plentiful than all major white varieties combined. Its bountiful crop (about two to three times that of Chardonnay) of neutral, pleasant stuff was just fine for the gallon-bottle crowd and there was no point in planting better-tasting but less generous grapes for which no market existed. When the American wine palate changed for the better, Burger's fortunes changed for the worse, and the total acreage devoted to it fell off from the 3,000 acres extant just after Prohibition to about 1,500 acres by the mid-80s. (For comparison, Chardonnay zoomed from less than 100 acres to over 50,000.) A minor rebound of sorts has occurred in recent years, with a few hundred acres of new vines being planted in the North Coast reportedly to go into the production of sparkling wine as an inexpensive extender, and for wine coolers, with the result that total acreage now has come back to 2,300.

BURGUNDY   This term, borrowed from the famous wine district of France in which some of the world's best and most expensive table wines are produced, in California wine parlance invariably refers to inexpensive wines of indeterminate parentage—generally red unless otherwise specified (for instance, White Burgundy or Sparkling Burgundy). A few wineries have recently dropped this generic moniker in favor of "Red Table Wine." California burgundies are usually soft, often slightly to medium sweet, and aimed at a broad market. Needless to say, they have absolutely nothing in common with French Burgundies.

CABERNET FRANC   Ignored in California until the last decade, and still treated by most wineries as an experiment, this red wine variety has enjoyed a much happier role in its native France, where it is used variously to make light, fruity red wines in the Loire Valley, to blend with Merlot in the cool-climate vineyard areas of Bordeaux, and to blend with and perhaps add a slight raspberryish or violetty perfume to Cabernet Sauvignon in the Médoc area of Bordeaux. It is this latter role, as a complexing and prettifying agent for Cabernet Sauvignon, that has brought about the recent California interest in Cabernet Franc (see also the discussion of Cabernet Sauvignon).

About two dozen California wineries have vinified Cabernet Franc on its own at this point, and only a few of those wines have enjoyed widespread critical success. Some of the early efforts were pushed too much toward overripeness, while others, possibly because of the grape's tendency to overcrop, seem to have been dilute and unfocused. Almost all have been much more coarsely astringent than their fruit character could comfortably balance.

It is too early, however, for judgments about how Cabernet Franc will ultimately fare. Of the existing 1,620 acres in California (including 640 in Napa, 460 in Sonoma), three-quarters has been planted since the mid-80s. It has also been spotted in a few East Coast vineyards—possibly on the theory that it tolerates cooler locations better than Cabernet Sauvignon. Important plantings (by county): Mendocino (100 acres), Monterey (100), Napa (600), Sonoma (500).

CABERNET SAUVIGNON   For most of the world, Cabernet Sauvignon is the undisputed king of red wine grapes. With the exception of some limited patches of Pinot Noir in France, Nebbiolo in Italy, and local favorites in lesser locations, it is Cabernet Sauvignon that is planted and admired as the quality leader in the majority of wine-growing and wine-drinking places around the globe. This is true in California, where Cabernet is planted in the most precious soils and its wines are valued more highly than any other red produced. The only grapes that exceed Cabernet in acreage, either in California or around the world, are planted for their copious production of inexpensive table wines.

Grown here for more than a century, and producing award-winning wines in international competitions for most of that time, California Cabernet Sauvignon has come into its own only in the last two decades as a widely planted, widely successful grape. Back in 1961, just before the dawn of the current era for California premium winemaking, Cabernet Sauvignon plantings totaled 606 acres, or about ½ of 1% of all wine grapes in the state. Now there are some 33,000 acres of Cabernet, and they represent 10% of all wine grapes here.

More important for devotees of premium wine, Cabernet is grown almost exclusively in the cooler coastal vineyards, where it has a chance to produce wines worthy of its regal reputation. In Napa County alone, 9,100 acres of Cabernet produce a wealth of world-class wines from makers as venerable as Beaulieu and Beringer, as 60s-ground-breaking as Robert Mondavi and Heitz, as newly matured as Stag's Leap Wine Cellars, Caymus, and Diamond Creek, as upstart as Dunn, Spottswoode, and Forman. Before 1970, there were barely two dozen Cabernet Sauvignon bottlings available. Today, that number is closing in on 600.

Not only does Napa lead the way in Cabernet acreage, it also sets the California standard for quality, and does so with deeply fruity, rich wines whose variations in style are typically focused on flavors and structure of world-class depth and beauty. In the area of the Napa Valley lying at the western edge of the valley floor, from Yountville northward through Oakville and Rutherford, extending to St. Helena, Cabernet reaches optimal ripeness and fruitiness with a black-currant richness and firm but not imposing tannins. Referred to as the West Rutherford Bench (or more simply as the Rutherford Bench), this 10-mile stretch of well-drained, slightly elevated alluvial soils is home to some of the world's most famous Cabernet Sauvignons, including Beaulieu Private Reserve, Robert Mondavi, Opus One, Heitz (both Martha's Vineyard and the Bella Oaks Vineyard are located here), as well as Inglenook, Niebaum-Coppola, Dominus, Grgich Hills, Spottswoode, Freemark Abbey's Bosché, and others of great fame and beauty.

On the opposite side of the Napa Valley is the smaller but rightfully famous Stags Leap District, whose wines, while a little less bold than those of the West Rutherford Bench, contain an equal measure of fruit and typically a rich, elusive hint of earth and truffles. Wineries of note in this area are Stag's Leap Wine Cellars, Clos du Val, Pine Ridge, Shafer, and Silverado.

The hillsides of coastal valleys, most notably those of the Napa (Diamond Creek, Dunn) and Sonoma (Carmenet, Laurel Glen) valleys, but also including some fairly prominent vineyards in the Santa Cruz Mountains (Ridge, Mount Eden) and a sprinkling of locations in Mendocino, Lake, and Monterey counties, also contribute their share of award-winning, exemplary Cabernets.

Finally, one dare not leave this subject without a mention of the many fine Cabernets that come directly from valley floor locations. Whether it is Caymus sitting beside the Napa River in Rutherford, or the Monterey Peninsula Winery employing grapes from the Salinas Valley in Monterey County, proof is available that good Cabernet is not the sole province of benchland or hillside soils.

Nevertheless, all that's Cabernet does not glitter. In a great vintage, 12% to 15% of the labels on the market (but not so high a percentage of the total Cabernet gallonage) will rise into the most praiseworthy classes. Another 25% to 30% of the labels will front very sound, highly enjoyable wines of above-average quality, often selling at more reasonable prices and providing the world with a large supply of very good, representative wines worthy of almost any table. The remainder runs the gamut from acceptably average/eminently drinkable to lousy—and "lousy" is not necessarily limited to wines of low price.

But, whether full-bodied and rich or underfilled and uninteresting, the majority of California Cabernets share the grape's tendencies toward currranty, or sometimes cherryish, fruit, fairly firm structure, and noticeable tannins and astringency. Other frequently used analogies to Cabernet's varietal character include herbs, green olives, truffles, loam, briar, tobacco leaf, raspberry, violet, mint, tea, cedar, bell pepper, tar, and black cherry. Wineries seeking to make more accessible, early-drinking bottlings employ a variety of winemaking techniques, such as reducing the amount of hard-pressed wine in the final blend, cutting back on skin-contact time during fermentation, and fining and filtration to ease the grape's propensity for producing hard wine.

Another technique for altering and, at least theoretically, improving the character of Cabernet Sauvignon wines is the blending in of other varieties. The practice has existed in France for decades, but was rarely followed in California except by those few wineries that were looking for ways to stretch their Cabernets and, in some instances, to make them less expensive to market. However, it is only since the early 70s that California has possessed the so-called "classic" blending varieties used in Bordeaux.

The most popular among them is Merlot, employed both because its herbal and cherry character fits so well with Cabernet and also because its softer, more open structure helps mitigate Cabernet's coarseness. In theory, such a Cabernet-dominated blending with Merlot will maintain its strong varietal focus, gain some added complexity, and become a little more approachable in its youth.

The second most likely grape to appear in what might be called "classic" Cabernet Sauvignon blends is its upcountry relative, Cabernet Franc. This latter grape is a minor player in French wines dominated by Cabernet Sauvignon, but has found the beginnings of a home in California, where major wineries like Robert Mondavi and Joseph Phelps employ it generously in their leading Cabernet Sauvignon–based wines. While the structure of Cabernet Franc does little to soften or round out Cabernet Sauvignon, its fragrant, herb-laced, strawberry/raspberryish fruit seems to its fans to extend and enhance the tighter, somewhat brooding nature of the best young Cabernet Sauvignons.

Whether blended or not, however, it is the aromas and flavors, the depth and ageability of Cabernet Sauvignon that are prized above all else. Winemakers fill it with hard tannins or soften it by blending and fining, grow it on hillsides or valley floors, sell it for $50 or $5. But, whatever its blend, whatever its structure, whatever its assigned place in the market, Cabernet Sauvignon reigns as the king of red wine grapes in California. Important plantings (by county): Alameda (200 acres), Lake (1,200), Mendocino (1,300), Monterey (3,800), Napa (9,100), Sacramento (1,100), San Joaquin (3,200), San Luis Obispo (2,500), Santa Barbara (900), Sonoma (6,500).

CARIGNANE This workhorse of a grape, the most widely planted red variety in France and for many years the most often seen variety in California, formed the basis for an ocean of *vin ordinaire*. From the early 1900s through the Prohibition years, Carignane was one of the major grapes of choice because of its extraordinarily high yields when grown in warm and fertile areas such as California's Central Valley and in the warmer, more protected areas of the North Coast. The wine rarely appeared as a varietal; and even now, producers who attempt varietals from the remaining older Carignane vines throughout the state generally end up with lighter ordinary wines. From a peak production during Prohibition approaching 50,000 acres, Carignane has dropped to somewhere in the neighborhood of 11,000 acres today, and will, one presumes, continue to diminish as other grapes, which seem to produce sturdier, better-balanced wines, come into greater favor for the production of jug wines. A half dozen wineries report producing Carignanes, although they are rarely seen beyond the wineries' tasting rooms.

CARNELIAN This University of California–created grape comes from a cross of Cabernet Sauvignon and Carignane crossed again with Grenache. The purpose was to create a grape that would grow in the relatively hotter climates of California's Central Valley, produce high yields, and still carry some of the class and flavor interest of Cabernet Sauvignon. The attempt seems only to have produced vines which over-crop without yielding wines that are more interesting than those from most other grapes grown in intense heat. Carnelian's future thus seems clouded. Unless some new form of vineyard management comes to the rescue, it seems likely to remain among the list of also-rans when it comes to the production of California jug wine. Its release in 1972 was followed by plantings of several thousand acres, but very little new planting has been done since, and the amount standing has slowly dropped to some 1,250.

CHABLIS In California, this is the most broadly used generic name for white table wines. Although a few wineries continue to use the name for dry, crisp offerings that follow the style of wines from France's Chablis region in some modest way, most of the wines under the name Chablis are inexpensive, sweet, and blended primarily to sell in the least demanding white wine markets. Indeed, the name Chablis has been further diluted by the trend lately for North Coast wineries to call their drier generic blends White Table Wine, and to relegate Chablis to even coarser and sweeter offerings. The best of the jug-wine Chablis will use Chenin Blanc and French Colombard in their mix; the lesser will use whatever is on hand, occasionally including such lowly grapes as Thompson Seedless.

CHAMPAGNE   Synonymous with sparkling wine in the U.S. but used less and less by makers of expensive bubbly, this term applies to any wine whose carbonation is derived naturally during a second fermentation in a closed container. There are three ways to produce sparkling wine: the *méthode champenoise,* the transfer method, and the bulk (Charmat) process (see the chapter BASICS OF WINEMAKING).

CHARBONO   If it were not for the 50 acres or so of this otherwise unknown variety now growing in certain Napa and Mendocino vineyards, it is likely that the world would be without Charbono. It tends to produce wines that are high in tannin, thick but stolid in body, acidic, dark in color, and generally lacking in definable or interesting flavors. Fewer than half a dozen California wineries continue to report production of Charbono, perhaps for the fun of trying to make something out of nothing.

CHARDONNAY   (once known as Pinot Chardonnay) This white vinifera grape produces superb dry wines all over the globe, ranging from its premier role in France's Burgundy region and its importance as the white grape of real Champagnes, to its dominant position as California's best dry white and major force in the locally produced sparkling wines. In the U.S., beyond California's borders Chardonnay is the most widely planted vinifera varietal, and is made into wine by some 200 wineries from Massachusetts to Ohio to Washington and Oregon. In recent years, Australian Chardonnays have become somewhat popular in this country, and Italian Chardonnays, although thinner and simpler than those mentioned above, have also sold well.

California Chardonnays are widely regarded as among the best in the world and have been winning tasting competitions on both sides of the Atlantic for more than a decade. Those wines most prized by connoisseurs tend to be fairly fruity, yet carry plenty of balancing acidity and an array of attractive flavor characteristics. These include apple, pineapple, mildly tropical, and sweet or tart citrus among the fruits, while buttery, smokey, spicy, nutty, grassy, or dried-leafy suggestions will often be present in combination with the primary fruit character. In Chardonnay, more than in other white wines, the aromas and flavors derived from oak-barrel fermentation and aging assume a leading role. Indeed, most of the world's great Chardonnays (French Chablis usually being a major exception) sport the toasty, sometimes creamy or spicy character derived from the use of oak barrels in the winemaking process.

Chardonnay seems to produce well in almost all coastal locations, but not so well in warmer inland locales such as Lodi and Fresno. Nevertheless, it has proven itself at home in a wide range of settings, although showing important character variations from one site to another. Many wines are specifically delimited to small geographic areas and carry the stamp of that location. Others, whether identified simply as California in appellation (ZD, Kendall-Jackson among the higher-priced wines; Glen Ellen as an example of the lower-priced offerings), or labeled with a countywide appellation such as Sonoma or Napa, are blends of several areas. Such blends frequently are intended to suit the winemaker's sense of style and complexity; but, as often as not, they are reflections also of economic reality. Most large producers simply cannot limit themselves to one tight geographic area because the grapes are not available in sufficient quantities and at suitable prices for the styles and market niches they have chosen.

In the Napa Valley, where Chardonnay is far and away the leading white wine grape, with 9,600 acres representing some 64% of the white vines in production and 29% of the valley's total acreage, the variety produces exceptional white wines full of flavor and capable of achieving superb balance and aging potential. At the valley's southernmost (and coolest) location, in the Carneros District, the grapes ripen with a high degree of natural acidity. Much of the Carneros harvest is left to hang to full maturity on the vines, and displays the broad spectrum of rich varietal character; but some grapes retain more of the narrow, pineapple-like, and grassy side of Chardonnay. Among the wineries making sparkling wine from Napa Valley grapes, the Chardonnay of Carneros is widely sought because when picked at the desirably low (16–19° Brix) sugar levels, the grapes are perfectly understated in character while very high in the natural acidity that makes sparkling wine such a refreshing beverage.

As Chardonnay plantings move further north in the valley, they tend to yield rounder and richer wines. Some of the best-balanced Napa Chardonnays come from places like the Big Ranch Road area between the city of Napa and Yountville (Chateau Montelena and Trefethen), and in cooler locations, often in proximity to the Napa River, as one moves further up-valley. Hillside-grown Chardonnays in Napa (Sterling's Diamond Mountain bottling, for example) tend to have harder, more angular compositions, but can compensate with deep, often rich character, and good balance.

In Sonoma County (11,200 acres), the range of sites and soils makes Chardonnay even more widely varied in its character. The cooler locations are much like Napa in the character they deliver to Chardonnay, and so are the hillside sites. But flatland-grown Chardonnays throughout Sonoma, especially in the Alexander and Russian River valleys, tend to have more effusive fruitiness, which can border on the tropical and make the wine both extremely easy to like on its own and harder to place with food. Even wines like De Loach and Ferrari-Carano, which are extraordinary winemaking accomplishments by any standard, seem to require service with sweeter fish and shellfish like sole and crab, or with rich or fruit-flavored poultry dishes. The westernmost Chardonnays grown in Sonoma County are usually high in natural acidity and thus tend to a crisper style as finished wines. Chardonnays from these cool-climate areas are also popular in sparkling wine production.

Just to the north of Sonoma, the vineyards of Mendocino County are rapidly becoming a home for Chardonnay. The 3,400 acres planted represent over half of all white grapes there and produce wines much in the fashion of Sonoma. The cool-area grapes (such as those from the Anderson Valley) are high in acidity, and many are picked early for sparkling wine production, while those grown further inland tend to produce fatter, riper-styled wines.

In the last 20 years, as grape growing has moved south of San Francisco in a serious way, Chardonnay has found a happy new home in the Central Coast counties of Monterey (8,400), San Luis Obispo (2,400), and Santa Barbara (5,100). At their best, wines from those areas have exemplary balance and brightly fruit-oriented flavors, often with a slightly floral touch. Within those counties, the districts of Arroyo Seco, Chalone, Edna Valley, Santa Maria Valley, Santa Ynez Valley have been the names most likely to appear on highly regarded Chardonnays. As is true for all cool regions of California, some Chardonnay grown in the Central Coast is sought for sparkling wine production.

The small but important production of Chardonnay undertaken in the Pacific Northwest varies from Oregon's high-acid, piquant wines to Washington's often floral-tinged bottlings, to Idaho's full-bodied, rich, but sometimes underfruited offerings. Adding up to less than 10% of California's outpouring of Chardonnay on a statistical basis, the Northwest wines nonetheless stand shoulder to shoulder with their California brethren for seriousness of intent and adherence to the search for the best the grape can deliver. Total Chardonnay acreage in California continues to increase and now covers some 52,000 acres, up from 29,000 in 85, 17,000 in 81, 11,000 in 76, 2,500 in 69, and 295 in 61. Important plantings (by county): Alameda (800 acres), Mendocino (3,400), Monterey (8,500), Napa (9,600), Riverside (1,200), San Joaquin (4,500), San Luis Obispo (2,400), Santa Barbara (5,100), Sonoma (11,300).

CHENIN BLANC   A native of France, prized in California for its ability to produce clean, balanced wines in hotter climates, this early-budding but late-maturing variety can be marked by delicate, floral, and melonlike characteristics when grown in cooler areas. Chenin Blanc reaches its qualitative peak in France's

Loire region, where in the districts of Vouvray, Saumur, and Savennières its pert fruit and bright acids are employed happily to make a variety of wines, ranging from perfumed sparkling wines (Saumur), to dry and zesty (Savennières), to medium sweet (Vouvray and Mont-Louis), and even to the occasional late harvest wine (Côteaux du Layon) of substantial sweetness.

In Chile, South Africa, and the U.S., there is more Chenin Blanc standing than in France. But in each of those locales, the wines produced tend to be neutral and decidedly ordinary. Over 80% of the 33,000 acres in California are concentrated in the hot Central Valley, and are given over primarily to the production of jug wines. Even a large portion of the 6,200 acres grown in California's cooler locations finds its way into less expensive bottlings because the higher acidities and more attractive aromas are useful when blended into duller wines.

Coastal wineries also produce Chenin Blanc as part of their varietal lines and, like their French counterparts, offer wines ranging from dry to medium sweet. Of the few who offer dry wines, some (notably Chalone) also give extended oak aging to their wines to both deepen and enrich them. The majority, however, favor sweetness ranging from less than 1.0% (barely above threshold—especially if the acidity is slightly elevated) to soda-pop sugars in the 3% to 4% area. On rare occasion, a late harvest version will appear. About 100 wineries make Chenin Blanc, down from 120 in the mid-80s.

CHIANTI   In California, the name Chianti has appeared on generic red wines that have been fairly full-bodied and that have, at least in the early usage of the name, suggested wine to go with Italian foods. Lately the term has pretty much fallen out of use and those Chiantis that remain on the market are, with very few exceptions, the cheapest of the red generic wines, often the sweetest, and usually the dullest. In its current California usage, Chianti shares precious little in common with the Italian Chiantis, grown in the central part of Italy, which have become so deservedly popular over the last several decades in Italian restaurants.

CLARET   In international usage, particularly British, "Claret" refers to the red wines of Bordeaux, and there are those in California who have agitated for limiting its use to wines made in the same style—that is to say, wines based on Cabernet Sauvignon, Merlot, and Cabernet Franc. Unfortunately, the few California wineries that have attempted to upgrade the name Claret have not found a willing and accepting market. Thus, for the most part, the term continues to mean lower-priced generic red wines of no particular origin, and in that sense is fairly well synonymous with the term "Burgundy." In the late 80s, the term "Meritage" was invented by a group of California vintners to refer to wines made from the traditional Bordeaux grapes.

DURIF   A minor variety from the southeastern part of France, where it is now all but abandoned, Durif has found a home in the U.S. under the name Petite Sirah. And, nomenclature aside, the grape performs better in this country than it ever did in its homeland.

EMERALD RIESLING   Like so many other University of California–bred grapes, this cross of Johannisberg Riesling and the lightly regarded Muscadelle was intended to produce wines of interesting quality when grown in hot areas. Up to now, Emerald Riesling grown in California's hot Central Valley has certainly provided acidity, but has never made anybody smile about the quality. The few attempts to grow the grape in coastal areas have met with intermittent success, but its failure to measure up to Johannisberg Riesling has dimmed its prospects. There are some 1,300 acres in California, down from 3,000 just a few years ago, most of which are in the Central Valley. Only a handful of wineries produce Emerald Riesling, and only Paul Masson (which calls its wine Emerald Dry) produces enough to be a force in the marketplace. The wine when offered is typically styled as a poor man's Riesling in a lighter-bodied, sweetish format.

FINO   Fino sherries in Spain are the driest, usually the youngest, wines made in the Jerez area. They derive their unique, sharp and yeasty character from the natural development of a crusty yeast called *flor*. In the U.S., by contrast, Fino sherries derive their character in almost all instances from flor yeast cultures that are artificially introduced into the wine rather than, as in Spain, from naturally occurring surface growths. As a result, U.S. Finos tend to be a little less sharp and at the same time to lack some of the Spanish wines' unique tangy perfume and underlying fruit. Nevertheless, California Finos, like Spanish Finos, are dry and can be very handsomely used with food, especially slightly spicy appetizers. Fino is often served chilled without ice. If the still small interest in the U.S. in Spanish appetizers *(tapas)* should grow, one may eventually see an increased following among the wine-drinking public for both Spanish and American Fino sherries.

FLORA   This white wine–grape cross of Gewurztraminer and Semillon yields, not surprisingly, soft floral wines with an intriguing, somewhat spicy perfume. But it has never fully taken hold in California, because Flora wines have generally proven of less interest than wines produced from the progenitors of the cross. There are fewer than 50 acres currently standing in California, down from 350 acres in the mid-80s. Flora is offered by less than a half dozen wineries, often in slightly sweet to fairly sweet styles, is featured in Schramsberg's sweet sparkling wine "Cremant," and occasionally has raised a good deal of interest when grown in cooler North Coast vineyards.

FOLLE BLANCHE   This unheralded grape produces thin, tart wines of little distinctive character when vinified on its own and has attracted little interest in California. Yet its tendency toward acidity has made it useful to some producers of sparkling wine. Its historical role in the production of French brandies from the Cognac and Armagnac regions also suggests that it may appeal to California brandy producers—although we have seen little evidence of that to date. The few acres of Folle Blanche in California are located in Napa and Sonoma counties.

FRENCH COLOMBARD (also known as Colombard to the French)   This white variety's long and unheralded career in France for the production of dull white table wines and brandy is now coming to an end. But it has found in California a new and happy home, where it has become the single most widely planted wine grape. Its approximately 59,000 acres, concentrated primarily in the Central Valley, gives it 10% more planted area than its nearest pursuer, Chardonnay. Indeed, French Colombard represents about one-third of all of the white wine grapes in California and, given its high-yielding propensities in warmer climates, it is estimated to account for about 40% of all the white wine produced in California in any given year.

Colombard has been propelled into its present popularity by its ability to yield wines of simple but clean, slightly floral fruitiness combined with good acidity in warmer areas. A few coastal wineries also produce French Colombard, generally in a dry style, but frequently with a little sugar left in it, to make softer, more palatable wines which have met with moderate success. There has even been a series of attempts to make Colombard in a ripe, barrel-aged style along the lines of Chardonnay. But, given the wine's inability to improve with age and its fairly narrow and limited flavor range, these efforts at a poor man's white have not met with great public acceptance.

Not surprisingly, French Colombard is also showing up in the newly planted, hot-area vineyards of Texas, as well as other experimental vineyards around the U.S. Indeed, California's handling techniques for French Colombard have led some vineyardists in the warmer parts of France to plant the variety and attempt to follow the California regime of cool fermentations. Initial positive results suggest that Colombard may one day return to France in a more elevated status than when it left.

FUMÉ BLANC   Not a grape variety, Fumé Blanc is, rather, a marketing name for Sauvignon Blanc. It was popularized in the late 60s and early 70s by the Robert Mondavi Winery as a new way of differentiating its Sauvignon Blancs vinified in a dry and oak-aged style from the sweet-finished versions then dominating the marketplace. The success of Mondavi Fumé Blanc has led to the grape becoming the second most popular dry white table wine in California, after Chardonnay, and the adoption of the name Fumé Blanc by a variety of wineries. In the last half a dozen years, however, we've seen the Fumé Blanc cognomen lose some of its standing—especially as the suggestion of sweetness previously associated with Sauvignon Blanc has been forgotten. Government labeling rules now require all wines called Fumé Blanc to show the subtitle "Dry Sauvignon Blanc" directly below in small print.

GAMAY   There have been grapes in California called Gamay (or more specifically Napa Gamay and Gamay Beaujolais) for as long as anybody can remember. But it now appears that both of those names have been applied to grapes which have no relationship to the Gamay Noir à Jus Blanc variety, the Gamay that grows in the Beaujolais region of France. Nevertheless, wines called Gamay here in California have usually been made in the Beaujolais style. Indeed, from time to time, some producers have succeeded handsomely in making wines which are light, fruity, and enjoyable in their youth in the manner of French Beaujolais. It now appears that very little of the true Beaujolais grape exists in California vineyards.

GAMAY BEAUJOLAIS   Until the 70s, the red vinifera grape variety traditionally identified as Gamay Beaujolais was thought by California vineyardists to be the true grape of France's Beaujolais region. Then, it was reidentified as one of the many versions (or clones) of Pinot Noir. It is a productive vine that requires cool growing conditions and can yield either a light or medium-bodied red wine, depending on vineyard management and winemaking choices. Because of historical usage, the vines planted as Gamay Beaujolais have been allowed to retain the name if the proprietor prefers. Another grape, the Napa Gamay, which is also not truly from Beaujolais, took on the standing of the true Beaujolais grape when that which we call Gamay Beaujolais turned out to be Pinot Noir. The wines now made from Napa Gamay may also be called Gamay Beaujolais even though it, like the Gamay Beaujolais, is not from Beaujolais.

   In the midst of all this confusion over grape names, and owing perhaps to the fact that wines identified as Pinot Noir can sell for more money than wines identified as Gamay Beaujolais, the number of wines carrying the Gamay moniker has been steadily decreasing in recent years. Given the fact that almost nothing grown in California is true Gamay, one presumes that the name may in time be phased out entirely as the regulatory authorities bring labeling practices up to date with scientific knowledge. Nomenclature and science notwithstanding, California vineyardists still report some 1,400 acres of Gamay Beaujolais standing and 1,500 acres of Napa Gamay.

GEWURZTRAMINER   Grown in most European countries and having found a home in Australia and New Zealand as well, this highly perfumed white wine grape with the difficult name has succeeded well in California, Washington, and Oregon. Although a native of Italy, but not widely grown there now, its best showing is in the Alsace region of France, where it ripens to near-perfection with somewhat high alcohols and just the right amount of natural acidity. Elsewhere in the world, California included, the grape presents a bit of a trial. Grown too cold, it never gains the intense aromatics that mark it when fully ripe. When grown too warm, it loses acidity in the vineyard before it ripens and also shows a distinct bitter edge. The cooler parts of California (the Anderson Valley in Mendocino County, the Carneros District, and Monterey and Santa Barbara counties), as well as appropriate sites in the Pacific Northwest, have yielded the best-balanced Gewurztraminers grown in the country.

   In spite of—or perhaps because of—its incredibly full and heady perfume that can be reminiscent of roses, cloves, nutmeg, lychee, and wildflowers, the wine has not grown in popularity and instead remains as one of the also-ran "sweet whites" amidst the Chardonnay and Sauvignon Blanc booms. More's the pity, because in addition to having deep and pretty characteristics, the wine, in its just slightly sweet configuration, goes exceptionally well with most pork-based sausages, with chicken prepared with a touch of sweetness or fruitiness, and with most Oriental foods. Though rarely produced to good effect as a dry wine in California or the Northwest, Gewurztraminer in that style, when successful, is absolutely smashing with fresh trout or cracked crab. The medium-sweet, quaffing style is well suited to the wines from middle-warmth vineyards, and allows California wineries to retain some of the grapes' natural sugars as a way of keeping the alcohol lower and at the same time using the retained sugar to buffer any tendency toward bitterness.

In the last few years, the California acreage devoted to Gewurztraminer has dipped to 1,850 (down from 3,900 in 85) and the number of wineries producing it has fallen. But it has retained its place of favor elsewhere in the West and, indeed, in most of the Northern states with wine-producing industries. Important plantings (by county): Mendocino (300 acres), Monterey (700), Napa (100), Santa Barbara (200), Sonoma (400).

GREEN HUNGARIAN   This white vinifera grape of indeterminate origin produces wines of indifferent character for a small but seemingly dedicated band of consumers, most of whom seem to be buying their Green Hungarian under the Weibel label. There are some 160 acres of the grape planted in California. Although a half dozen producers continue to offer the varietal, only one has made it a staple. And, indeed, Weibel even offers it in a sparkling version.

GRENACHE   The second most widely planted variety in the world, Grenache has never really made a home for itself in this country. Here, we use it for blending some fruit into jug wines, for rosés, and now, even for a so-called White Grenache. But, almost without exception, Grenache is not used in the production of cork-finished red table wines, either on its own or as a major blending component. Perhaps one of the reasons is that 99% of all Grenache growing in California is in the Central Valley or in the almost abandoned vineyards of the Cucamonga area. Of late, a few enthusiasts of Rhone-type wines have begun searching out the coastal acreage (about 100 of some 13,000) for blending into their experimental and often successful flirtations with Rhone wines influenced by Grenache.

GREY RIESLING   This popular, modestly priced, simple-tasting white vinifera wine is produced from the grape known as *Trousseau* or *Chauche Gris* in France, and is not, in fact, a member of the Riesling family. The widest-selling Grey Rieslings are offered in a mild, medium-acid style, with light, fruity flavors and no oak-barrel aging. They seem well suited for meals, especially seafood, and have become mainstays on some wine lists. Since the grape has very muted flavors on its own, the better Grey Rieslings on the market are usually blended with a little Sylvaner or Chenin Blanc to uplift their character. A few slightly sweet or medium-sweet versions are offered by the dozen or so California wineries that still put this variety on the market. The 500 acres of Grey Riesling standing in California represent a reduction of 77% in the last 10 years. The Wente Bros. Winery has been, and continues to be, the leading producer of Grey Riesling in California.

GRIGNOLINO   A grape of minor moment in its native Italy, where it produces light, simple red wines that barely hold their own with the most unchallenging foods, frothy reds, and base wines for red bubbly, Grignolino is, in California, the province of three wineries. The best-known Grignolino is the Rosé produced by Heitz Wine Cellars. Total plantings are less than 50 acres.

ICE WINE   Called *Eiswein* in Germany, it is produced from grapes whose juice has been frozen while they are still hanging on the vine (or occasionally nowadays in cold storage). When the frozen grapes are pressed, the resulting juice has a very high concentration of sugar; accordingly, the wines tend to be very sweet, and, one hopes, also carry concentrated aromas and flavors. These wines are a treasured rarity in Germany. We know of only a handful of American Ice Wines that have been produced naturally on the vine, although Bonny Doon Vineyards has been experimenting with Ice Wine from artificially frozen grapes—in refrigerators.

JOHANNISBERG RIESLING (also known as White Riesling in the U.S. and simply as Riesling in Germany) Producing white wines with a distinctively fruity, floral, sometimes peachy, typically delicate varietal character, Johannisberg Riesling is made in every style from bone dry to very sweet, concentrated dessert wine. In the 60s most California wineries produced this white vinifera in a dry, relatively austere, high-alcohol style, sometimes with a hint of oak, usually at the expense of the grape's subtle charms. The trend beginning in the 70s, spurred by consumer demand and improved technology, has been to stress the grape's more delicate qualities and to finish the wine in a slightly sweet to medium-sweet style. Another recent trend has been to allow the grapes to be attacked by *Botrytis cinerea*, the result being a luscious sweet wine. Rapid expansion of Johannisberg Riesling plantings pushed the 1980 acreage over 10,000; but by 1990, the total had dropped back to about 5,000 acres, over half of which is in Monterey County. Important plantings (by county): Mendocino (200 acres), Monterey (2,600), Napa (400), San Benito (200), Santa Barbara (700), Sonoma (400).

MALBEC Aside from its modest standing (122 acres total) as a potential blending grape for Cabernet Sauvignon, Malbec has no following in California. In its own right, it does produce decent, somewhat sturdy wine in some parts of the South of France and in Chile and Argentina. But in California, it has yet to prove itself either on its own or as a blender for Cabernet. Attempts to experiment with Malbec here have been discouraging because of the grape's tendency to yield little or no crop.

MALVASIA BIANCA Something of an alternative to Muscat, the white wines made from this varietal are typically fragrant, sweet, and low in acidity. Most often, Malvasia wines are fortified to keep them from oxidizing quickly and to take advantage of the grape's ability to produce pleasing sweet after-dinner sips. Some 2,100 acres of the grape stand in California, of which the significant majority is in the hot Central Valley. Malvasia's 2,000-year presence in Mediterranean winemaking makes it more interesting as an historical footnote than as a wine.

MARSANNE One of three dominant white grapes in the northern Rhone, Marsanne (along with Roussanne, with which it is sometimes blended, and Viognier) has enjoyed the most popularity because it is the easiest of the three to cultivate. Almost all wines identified as White Hermitage are made with Marsanne exclusively. In this country, Marsanne is an experiment, albeit one that has initially produced wines with a perfumed raciness not typical of the French version.

MATARO This red vinifera variety, long out of favor in California but once planted substantially in the vineyards around Cucamonga, which have been disappearing in the last three decades under housing subdivisions, is in fact the Rhone-variety Mourvedre. In that guise and in the face of an awakening interest in Rhone-type wines, Matero or Mourvedre has begun to show the first signs of a comeback via new plantings in the North Coast. Small, forward-looking wineries like Bonny Doon, Cline, Qupe, and Edmunds St. John have recently used Mataro/Mourvedre in wines of interesting character. There are 270 acres currently standing.

MELON Once a white grape of Burgundy, Melon became the major varietal in the Loire-Atlantique district of France in the 18th century and remains so today, under the more familiar name Muscadet. In California, many of the wines we called Pinot Blanc are, in fact, Melon (or Muscadet).

MERLOT   Long a variety of major importance in Bordeaux, where it is used for blending with Cabernet Sauvignon–based wines in the Médoc and Graves areas and as the primary grape in the red wines of Pomerol and St. Emilion, Merlot is also widely planted in other regions of France, as well as in Italy, in Hungary, and (to a lesser extent) in the Southern Hemisphere. In California, Merlot has come into fashion during the last two decades. Indeed, it was during the Cabernet planting boom of the early 70s that Merlot was first sought and planted as a blending grape to round out, soften, and add some complexity to Cabernet. But, just as some parts of Bordeaux are able to produce better wines based on Merlot than on Cabernet, so the vineyardists and wineries have found the same to be true here. As the vines matured, Merlot proved itself capable of yielding a wine that could stand on its own, and by the latter 70s California wineries had added a new name to their list of offerings.

The most critically acclaimed wines are medium-deep red to dark in color and have openly fruity aromas and flavors, often tinged with herbaceous, tealike, orange-rindy, current, and/or cherryish notes. Merlot wines are almost always softer, rounder, and more supple than Cabernet in their youth, yet retain much of the latter variety's tendencies toward richness and complexity. While it is too early to know volumes about their long-range aging potential in California, initial indications are that most mature earlier than Cabernet (which can last 15 to 30 years), but that the best have appeared to be holding well as they edge into their second decade. Moreover, there is an increasing tendency to add some Cabernet Sauvignon or some Cabernet Franc to Merlot to stiffen its constitution and add complexity, in hopes of pushing the wine into a longer and deeper aging cycle. As a result, Merlot easily challenges Pinot Noir as the second most expensive red varietal wine from California.

Merlot is also grown in the Pacific Northwest and has shown better in the warmer, eastern-lying vineyards of Washington than in Oregon's chilly and often damp settings. In the last few years, we have tasted the occasional Washington State offering from the likes of Chateau Ste. Michelle and Hogue Cellars that augurs well for Merlot in that location as well. The standing acreage of Merlot in California hovered around the 3,500-acre mark until the mid-80s, but has grown to 7,400 in the last five years, with a marked decrease in acreage south of San Francisco and increasing concentration in the North Coast (now almost 65%, up from 40% a decade ago). Important plantings (by county): Lake (100 acres), Mendocino (300), Monterey (700), Napa (2,100), Sacramento (400), San Joaquin (700), San Luis Obispo (200), Santa Barbara (300), Sonoma (1,900), Yolo (100).

MOSCATO   In its many variations, *Moscato* is nothing more than an artistic play on the name Muscat, based on the Italian spelling of the word, also spelled *Muscato* in Italy. The two Muscat grapes used primarily in California winemaking are Muscat Blanc and the Muscat of Alexandria.

MOURVEDRE   Known in California as Mataro, this grape is a major player in the Rhone area of France; now, because there is a burgeoning interest among California vintners in trying to emulate Rhone wines, Mourvedre is making a comeback here. A few hundred acres of old vines remain standing and there is evidence that new plantings, albeit in small lots, are going in. In the hands of a new generation of experimenters, the old thin, tart style of wine is giving way to something deeper, richer, and sturdier.

MUSCAT BLANC   One of the two Muscat grapes used extensively for winemaking in California, the Muscat Blanc is the finer and thus tends to be the predominant grape in most Muscat and Moscato bottlings. Its fragrant perfume of flowers and slight grapiness is best captured by modern, cold-fermentation techniques that also allow the winemaker to retain some of the grape sugars in the finished wine and to maintain a bit of a lively sparkle that furthers adds to the pretty, happy, highly quaffable nature of a well-made Muscat Blanc. Of the 1,400 acres currently planted in California, half are in cooler, coastal vineyards and half in the hotter Central Valley locations. The names Muscat Canelli and Muscat Frontignan are also used for wines made from this variety.

MUSCAT CANELLI   Another name for white, usually sweet-finished table wines made from the Muscat Blanc grape.

MUSCAT FRONTIGNAN   A synonym for the Muscat Blanc grape, it is typically reserved in California for wines that have been fortified by the addition of alcohol to produce after-dinner products. Beaulieu Vineyard makes an especially attractive fortified Muscat de Frontignan that captures the grape's fragrant charms.

MUSCAT OF ALEXANDRIA   A white wine grape in Mediterranean vineyards, it is grown primarily as a raisin grape in California's Central Valley, where it occasionally finds its way into sweet-edged quaffing wines of little distinction. It is not unfair to report that a dollop of this wine is added to other inexpensive quaffers in order to boost and prettify aromas. Of the 5,700 standing acres (down from 11,500 in 76), only a small percentage is converted into wine.

NAPA GAMAY   Once thought to be the grape of the Beaujolais region, this heavy-footed red varietal now turns out to be the lackluster Valdiguié, one of the workhorse grapes in the hot French Midi. As the truth of its heritage has become known in California, and with the Gamay Beaujolais strain of Pinot Noir producing more attractive wines, this mislabeled variety has slowly lost its place. The current 1,500 planted acres (down from 6,000 in 76) appear to be just a way station on this grape's journey to oblivion.

NEBBIOLO   Without question, Nebbiolo is one of the great red wine grapes of the world. In Italy's Piedmont region, Nebbiolo yields wines of depth, complexity, and, with aging, great finesse. The best of Italy's wines from Nebbiolo are called Barolo, Spanna, and Barbaresco. Here in California, Nebbiolo sits near the top of our wish list. We wish it grew here; we wish the few experiments with it had proven to be more successful; we wish more vineyardists would try it in hopes of finding a suitable site that would capture the grape's inherent charms. Once totaling over 500 acres, mostly in the Central Valley, it now covers less than 50 and, aside from an occasional offering having little in common with Nebbiolo-based wines from Italy, has not yet earned a place as a separate varietal wine in California.

PETIT VERDOT   A minor grape in Bordeaux, it is used primarily (and not very extensively) to add color and tannin to red wines that otherwise lack those qualities. In California, a few producers of Cabernet Sauvignon/Merlot blends have planted Petit Verdot in the search for the quintessential locally grown combination of Bordeaux grapes. Only about 100 acres exist here, however, and little has come out of the early experiments with Petit Verdot to create a rush for new plantings.

PETITE SIRAH   During the early 70s, when the world discovered California wine and California winemakers discovered the world, grapes like Petite Sirah, which were capable of producing big, inky, tannic wines, came into vogue. It was California's way of saying, "We have arrived and we can make wines that live as long as any grown anywhere in the world." At the same time, the Central Valley growers of grapes for jug wine began to think that Petite Sirah would perform marvelously in their locales, and thus, thousands of acres were planted in California's warmest vineyards during that time. As a result of this unprecedented wave of new Petite Sirah plantings all over the state, the grape boasted some 13,000 acres by the end of that decade. Now, more than a decade later, Petite Sirah has fallen out of favor and shows but 3,100 acres still standing. Tastes changed away from big, tannic wines, whites replaced reds as the wines of choice; and Petite Sirah did not perform as well as expected in the Central Valley. Acreage in Napa County fell from 1,300 to 450, while acreage in Fresno County fell from 1,200 to 0!

Intriguingly, the vines left standing are producing better wine now than ever before, in part because the winemakers have adjusted to a somewhat more accessible style of wine and in part because those who still work with the grape are the ones who enjoyed the most critical success in the previous decades. Today's wines are still firm and robust, with more than a little tannin, and they match best with sturdy beef and lamb dishes and the occasional piece of cheese. But they are no longer confused by vineyardists with the true Syrah grape of France's Rhone region. Petite Sirah is now widely believed to be the common, and minor, French variety Durif; if so, it performs substantially better in California than it has ever done in France. Important plantings (by county): Mendocino (300 acres), Monterey (800), Napa (500), Sonoma (300).

PINOT BLANC   This white vinifera grape developed in France as a natural variant of Pinot Noir and is planted primarily in the Alsace region there. Both in France and in California, Pinot Blanc usually produces simple, moderately fruity, somewhat steely and narrow wines, although a few producers seem able to coax something richer and riper from the grape. Coupled with its modest flavors, the typical low yield in the vineyard has kept it from gaining popularity, in spite of attempts to cast it as another poor man's Chardonnay. Only a few outstanding examples coming from the dedicated efforts of small wineries achieve even that modest status. A number of wineries are turning to Pinot Blanc as a component in their better sparkling wines because of its brisk natural acidity and clean, almost neutral flavor. There are 1,800 acres planted in California (up from 1,400 in 76), a little more than 60% in Monterey County, but the number of producers offering it as a varietal wine has dropped from 24 to 10 or less in just the last few years. A good deal of Pinot Blanc's changing fortunes seems to be explained by recent research reports that claim much of what is planted here to be Melon rather than true Pinot Blanc.

PINOT CHARDONNAY   Not much more than a decade ago, the Chardonnay grape was thought to be one of the many variants (or clones) of the Pinot family—hence the Pinot prefix. That usage has all but disappeared on California wine labels, consistent with the evidence that Chardonnay is its own variety. Only a few wineries keep "Pinot" Chardonnay around for historical (albeit inaccurate) reasons.

PINOT GRIS   A red, sometimes pink-grey, variant of Pinot Noir, it is planted widely in Europe yet rarely produces memorable wines. Its most widely noted accomplishments have been in Italy, where the grape is called Pinot Grigio and yields simple, clean, inoffensive white wines. It has found a small but growing home in Oregon, where it is offered by about a dozen producers.

PINOT NOIR   The great red Burgundies of France, made from this grape, rate among the finest wines in the world. In vineyards like Romanée-Conti, Richebourg, Bonnes Mares, and Chambertin, Pinot Noir produces rich, lush, complex wines that age into even richer, lusher, and more complex wines having almost no rivals for range and drama. The natural comparisons with wines from Cabernet Sauvignon and its Bordelais associates show the Pinot Noirs as more inviting and more complex, often better suited to richer foods, and given to a much wider range of flavors and levels of performance. By contrast, the better Bordeaux reds, especially those influenced substantially by Cabernet Sauvignon, tend to be sturdier, longer-lived, more direct and more predictable wines.

But not all Pinot Noir is so well favored as the most famous names. And it is sadly true that when Pinot Noir wines are not rich and round, they tend, even in Burgundy, to become thin, mean, and uninviting. There is not much room for a middle ground in Burgundy and almost no middle ground for Pinot Noir outside of Burgundy. It is, some vineyardists and winemakers will tell you, the single greatest challenge of their careers to learn the secrets of this enigmatic grape and find a way to tap its full potential. After all, even in Europe, there is a good deal of Pinot Noir planted outside Burgundy, but none of it makes red wines of real note.

Pinot Noir does, however, play an important role in the making of French Champagnes. For those wines, Pinot Noir is picked at somewhat low sugar levels and with high acids. It is combined with Chardonnay, also picked at lower sugars and higher acids, to make up the base cuvées for sparkling wine. Interestingly, for a grape capable of such dramatic range and complexity as a red wine, its usefulness in Champagnes is based on its ability to show almost no character in that setting, bringing only—but importantly—body and age-ability rather than flavor.

In the New World, Pinot Noir displays all of the problems experienced by European producers. That has not stopped vineyardists from growing it and winemakers from trying to coax the best of red Burgundy out of it. If failure occurs more often than success, there is an increasing number of growers and producers in California and Oregon who are proving that the cause is not lost. Indeed, for most of California's vinous history, Pinot Noir was the number-two red wine at the quality end of the scale. Those early wines, while in no way resembling their French counterparts, always managed to convey a sense of depth and weight as a substitute for the more subtle and complex phrasings that are Pinot Noir's claim to nobility. Then, in the early 70s, first Zinfandel and then Merlot seemed to push Pinot Noir from center stage; as a result, the number of labels offered in California shrank dramatically.

The true Pinot Noir aficionados, however, never gave up on the grape, and even as its market popularity was slipping, its fortunes in the hands of the true believers were rising. For more than a decade now, a dedicated band of wineries has been conducting a wide variety of experiments. Trials with clones, stems in the fermentation, open versus closed fermenters, crop levels in the vineyard, soil types, trellising systems for the vines, and leaf stripping have produced a variety of positive but not always replicable results. So, even today, just as a decade ago and a decade before that, consistently and reliably great Pinot Noir from West Coast vineyards remains as much hope as reality.

Some things have been learned. It is now almost universally recognized that Pinot must not be allowed to get too ripe lest it lose its fruit and its potential for grandeur. This single discovery in itself means that Pinot Noir is a more enjoyable wine now than it was in the past. Another recent finding that produces more fruit in Pinot Noir is to plant it in cooler areas, rather than the mid-valley hotlands where it once grew side by side with Cabernet Sauvignon and other medium-warmth varietals. The Carneros District in southern Napa and Sonoma counties, the near-coastal Russian River Valley, and cool areas south of San Francisco in Monterey, San Luis Obispo, and Santa Barbara counties have all proven to be rewarding places to plant Pinot Noir. To these cool-climate California locations must be added the majority of Oregon locations. Indeed, Oregon Pinots seem to develop color and flavor at excessively low levels of ripeness and, as a result, only in an unusual year will Oregon produce richness to go along with balance and fruit.

Even with all the obstacles, there is plenty to like about locally grown Pinot Noir wines. Smaller producers such as Calera, Chalone, Acacia, and Eyrie have shown the ability to find fruit, balance, and richness in the grape. To their number must be added another two to three dozen small and dedicated establishments that have raised the stakes in the Pinot game. They have brought the grape back to the point where it now challenges the number-two red position in California again, and is already clearly number one among reds in Oregon.

The use of Pinot Noir in French Champagne is paralleled in California. In recent years, the best California bubblies have contained anywhere from 60% to 100% Pinot Noir. By some estimates, in fact, as much as one-third of all the Pinot Noir grown in California goes into the production of sparkling wine. It plays a more important role here than in France, however; the locally grown fruit has more flavor and contributes a positive fresh, bright quality.

Plantings of Pinot Noir in California have remained more or less static for the last decade and now total some 9,500 acres. Important plantings (by county): Mendocino (700 acres), Monterey (1,600), Napa (2,700), San Luis Obispo (200), Santa Barbara (800), Sonoma (3,100).

PORT   In the United States, this term is applied to sweet, fortified, usually red wines made in the style of the Port produced in the Douro region of Portugal. A few U.S. producers (Quady, St. Amant, Ficklin, Masson, among others) attempt to employ the same or similar grapes as used in Portugal and, at their best, achieve a reasonable semblance of the real thing—that is to say that their ports can combine richness, depth, fruit (as opposed to raisins), and aging potential. Most of the local ports, however, are simple, cheap, quickly made, and have little in common with their Portuguese namesakes.

RED TABLE WINE   This title is gaining increased usage for generic wines, usually blended and inexpensive, in substitution for the borrowed handles—Burgundy, Claret, and Chianti. In current practice, the coastal-oriented wineries have been more likely to adopt this term than the big jug-wine producers, for whom Burgundy remains the generic name of choice (and marketplace acceptance).

RHINE   Borrowed from one of the premier wine-growing regions of Germany, this title is often used by American wineries as a generic name for ordinary white wines with lots of sweetness.

RIESLING   Used as a shortened version for any of the grapes (Johannisberg, Grey, Sylvaner) whose last name is Riesling, the term is most often applied to those wines deriving their identity from one of the lesser varieties, since Johannisberg Riesling on the label would seem to carry more prestige than the Riesling title by itself. "Rieslings" usually carry slight to medium sweetness.

ROSÉ   This is the artsy term for pink wine made for early consumption. The best achieve a fresh, fruity taste and carry enough acid to balance the sweetness that most rosés have. Many rosés also possess varietal names (Zinfandel Rosé, Gamay Rosé, for example) but rosés made from blends of grapes are not necessarily less attractive. The wine's color is achieved either by blending red wine into white or by keeping the juice of red wine grapes (which starts out white and acquires color during fermentation) from extensive contact with the grape skins. Either way, the trick is to acquire a pleasing pinkish hue that suggests a lighter body and taste than red wine. Use with food depends on the degree of sweetness.

ROUSSANNE   One of three white wine grapes usually associated with the northern Rhone area (along with Marsanne, with which it has often been blended, and Viognier), Rousanne yields wines of great perfume and a certain delicacy. Its presence in California is strictly on an experimental basis, and it has been seriously pursued mainly by Bonny Doon.

RUBY CABERNET   In theory, Ruby Cabernet should have been the answer. After all, it is a man-created grape that was said to combine the wonderful intensity and beauty of Cabernet Sauvignon with the high yield and heat-withstanding abilities of Carignane. Plant it, the professors said, in the hot Central Valley and we'll be awash in the best low-priced red wine ever to gladden the palate of mankind. Its meteoric rise in the grape-planting extravagances of the early 70s (2,000 acres added in 71; 7,000 in 72; 4,000 in 73) accounted for the greater part of its 18,000 standing acres by 76. But the wines turned out to be dull, soft, and not at all like Cabernet Sauvignon, and that sad result, together with the ensuing white wine boom, has led to the elimination of half the Ruby Cabernet in just 10 years. By the 90s, the grape could claim just 6,900 acres remaining in the Central Valley and less than 30 (down from 350) in cooler locations. Fewer than 10 wineries offer it as a separate varietal wine, and half of those are fledgling efforts in Texas or New Mexico.

SANGIOVESE   The dominant grape in the Chianti wines of Italy's Tuscany region has been almost totally ignored throughout California's vinous history. With the turn into the 90s, a few acres are now in place, but even preliminary judgments are some years away.

SAUTERNE   Bearing no resemblance to the stunning wines from France's Sauternes region, the few cheap white wine blends that appear under this generic moniker are most often overly sweet, dull, and uninviting.

SAUVIGNON BLANC   This very popular white grape is second only to Chardonnay for the production of quality dry white table wines in California (many of which are identified by the name Fumé Blanc). The grape produces wines with a distinctive grassy, herbal quality, usually with a bounty of natural grape acidity. This combination has made Sauvignon Blanc very useful and exceptionally popular for service with fish and shellfish, as well as with herb-seasoned poultry dishes. Its typical price is one-half to two-thirds that of the same producers' Chardonnays, which may also account for its continuing rise in popularity.

Much of the California inspiration for Sauvignon Blanc has come from France, where the grape is planted in the Loire region and produces, especially in Sancerre and Pouilly-Fumé, wines of a refreshingly fruity, sometimes green character. As in California, the Loire's best Sauvignon Blancs can age to gain an added measure of complexity and a certain supple richness they never had when young. Sauvignon Blanc is also grown in Bordeaux, although only a few châteaux try to make truly great wine from it. Rather, Sauvignon is usually consigned to vineyards in which red grapes cannot produce miracles, and that, for the majority of white Bordeaux wines, means areas like Entre-Deux-Mers and other Bordelais regions of less than "classified" standing. In the Sauternes region of Bordeaux, however, Sauvignon Blanc is a minor but important player in the luscious sweet wines of the area.

The predominant style for California's Sauvignon Blanc wines has undergone a change in recent years. The once-sought-after extremes of varietal character, which gave the wine a pungent, almost dandelion-greens quality, have been tempered. Most producers are now trying to make wines that are a bit more subtle in their grassy, weedy aspects. To accomplish this, wineries employ a variety of techniques, including warmer fermentations, more sun exposure for the grapes in the vineyard, and reduced skin contact with the grape skins prior to the initial phases of fermentation.

The inclusion of Semillon in some Sauvignon Blancs has also had a salutary effect in producing less varietally overbearing versions. Winemakers have found that Semillon helps flesh out the somewhat narrow flavors of Sauvignon Blanc, without detracting from its essentially tight-knit structure on the palate. At the same time, it can bring along a note of floral prettiness that fits comfortably with the Sauvignon Blanc personality.

Further testimony to the growth in popularity of the grape is found in the rate at which California growers are planting it in their vineyards. The 7,500 acres of Sauvignon Blanc reported as of 80 have nearly doubled by 90 to 13,500, and the number of wines in the marketplace has kept pace with that expansion. More than 120 wineries in California offer the wine, and another 50 or so Sauvignon Blancs appear under private labels. The most noteworthy producer of the variety remains the Robert Mondavi Winery, with names like Phelps, Dry Creek, Kenwood, Duckhorn, and Chateau St. Jean having important places in the sweepstakes and often winning the highest-quality awards, if not the volume title. Important plantings (by county): Alameda (200 acres), Amador (200), Lake (600), Mendocino (900), Merced (800), Monterey (1,500), Napa (2,900), San Joaquin (1,500), San Luis Obispo (700), Santa Barbara (400), Sonoma (1,600), Stanislaus (600), Yolo (300).

SAUVIGNON VERT   This grape variety can still be found in California, but its 100 acres, down from 1,000 two decades earlier in the face of the near-trebling of planted grape acreage, is dramatic proof of its low standing. Long thought to be a cousin of Sauvignon Blanc and eclipsed by that variety in every regard, Sauvignon Vert is now believed to be, in fact, Muscadelle—a minor and vanishing variety from the Sauternes region of France. The grape has rarely shown up in varietally designated bottlings in the last decade.

SCHEUREBE   One of many German crossbreeds, this one came into being in 1916 when the botanist Georg Scheu crossed Johannisberg Riesling with Sylvaner. The result was a grape with both higher yields and higher natural sugars when grown on the same sites as Riesling. Nonetheless, Riesling has remained king in the high-quality regions (Rheingau and Moselle) of Germany, while the Scheurebe and Müller-Thurgau have found success only in regions where volumes of wine sold at lesser prices (i.e., Liebfraumilch) are produced. It is occasionally made into wine in this country and has its Riesling parent's ability to develop late harvest characteristics.

SEMILLON   Semillon seems to be all over the globe—but where there is Semillon, there is not necessarily exciting wine. Indeed, everywhere it is planted in France, except for Sauternes, as well as in Chile, Argentina, Australia, and South Africa, Semillon almost always seems to produce wines of mediocre character, at best. Yet, attempts to make dry Semillons into something better are now succeeding in California, Australia, and France. The wine's natural sense of weight has allowed it to accept a substantial amount of oak aging with grace, while at the same time those wines grown in cooler climates and fermented at relatively lowered temperatures have shown an attractive floral streak. Whether these directions will take hold and lead to a new generation of Semillons throughout the world and an increase in acreage in California remains to be seen. Certainly, Semillon is at present a minor player on the West Coast. Its 2,300 acres, planted all around the state in both moderate and overheated locations, have remained more or less steady, in spite of the continued increase in acreage of varieties like Chardonnay and Sauvignon Blanc. And while some wineries in the Pacific Northwest have produced very fine Semillons, the wine remains on the second team there as well.

Semillon does enjoy a role as a blending agent for dry-styled Sauvignon Blanc in some parts of the world, including Bordeaux and the U.S., where Semillon may constitute anywhere from 10% to 20% of the Sauvignon Blancs of Joseph Phelps and Sterling to 50% of wines like Haut-Brion Blanc and Vichon Chevrignon. California, however, has not yet found the key to the sweet, late harvest wines made from Semillon-dominated blendings with Sauvignon Blanc which are so successful in the Sauternes region of France (Château d'Yquem being the most famous example). Important plantings (by county): Alameda (100 acres), Monterey (400), Napa (300), Sonoma (200).

SHERRY   In California, and indeed throughout the U.S., the term "Sherry" is used generically for fortified wines, usually sweet, which have been baked, aged, or artificially infused with yeasts, all of which are intended to create a product similar to Spanish Sherry. The dry versions rarely measure up, although occasionally a wine in the rich, sweet style of Cream Sherry can challenge the popular Spanish blends.

SOUZAO   This Portuguese grape is more highly thought of for port production in the U.S. than it is in its native land. It adds a ripe, slightly raisiny, concentrated quality to California port and, in the hands of the Masson Winery, has been made successfully into one-varietal port.

SPARKLING WINE   Any wine with noticeable bubbles (beyond the mild spritz that occasionally remains behind in still table wines) is probably a sparkling wine. In technical terms, it must contain at least two atmospheres of pressure. In layman's terms, this means that it pops and fizzes when opened and has lots of bubbles rising exuberantly in the glass. The gas, carbon dioxide, is the same as that which puts the bubbles into your Pepsi or Perrier, but the method for getting it into sparkling wine is usually a little more complicated than that used with soft drinks and bottled waters. For, while it is legally permissible to inject the fizz into wine, almost no one does it, even for low-end products. The techniques used in this country for putting the bubbles into bubbly, ranging from most complex (expensive) to least, are: *méthode Champenoise*, transfer process, and bulk (Charmat) process. Each is explained in the chapter WINE LANGUAGE. In the U.S., the term "champagne" is a legal alternative, but it has become the custom for the best bubblies to avoid it and instead to be sold as sparkling wines.

SYLVANER (also called Sylvaner Riesling and Franken Riesling) Heading for the endangered species list here in California, this once famous white variety has held on tenaciously although not entirely successfully in Germany, where it has been substantially replaced by the ubiquitous Müller-Thurgau. Never the hit in California that it was for German vineyardists, Sylvaner has now been abandoned by most West Coast producers and growers. Standing acreage has dropped to about 200, about two-thirds in Monterey County, and no new acreage has been reported in any location for almost a decade. Twenty years ago there was as much Sylvaner as there was Chardonnay or Sauvignon Blanc in California.

SYMPHONY This new grape variety, produced from a cross of Muscat of Alexandria and Grenache Gris, was released for commercial planting in 81. Today, some 200 acres are in production, and one winery, Chateau de Baun, has given the grape full opportunity to show its mettle by using it for everything from sparkling wine to dry table wine to sweet dessert wine. Symphony's character varies from mild spiciness at average ripeness for table wine to intense peach-and-apricot qualities at higher levels of ripeness. One wonders, however, whether Symphony will make much of a home for itself in a wine setting that has seen sharp acreage decreases in all of the coastal-grown "sweet whites."

SYRAH California vineyardists have long grown a grape they call Petite Sirah which, until the last decade, they believed to be the Syrah grape of France's Rhone district. Now it turns out that Petite Sirah is almost certainly Durif, and California possesses very little real Syrah (only 350 acres at last count). From this somewhat meager resource, a handful of enterprising vintners are trying, with varying degrees of success, to produce Rhone-like red wines. The occasional triumph captures Syrah's deep, almost dense quality, reminiscent of wild blackberries cast in a slightly drier, less effusively fruity mold than Zinfandel's berryish fruit, and adding in hints of black pepper, tar, saddle leather, cassis, and other vinous exotica. That kind of complexity, taken together with the richness, depth, and sturdiness found in the near 100%-Syrah northern Rhone wines, has allowed French appellations like Hermitage and Côte Rotie to challenge the leading Bordeaux and Burgundies in price and attractiveness. Elsewhere in the Rhone, especially in the southern Rhone, Syrah tends to be blended with other grapes, and in many areas is submerged to the point of losing its identifiable character. Châteauneuf-du-Pape, the most famous southern Rhone red, can legally contain 13 separate varieties; and, while Syrah and Grenache may dominate some wines, others are fully integrated blends.

California vintners are following much the same track in their pursuit of Rhone-type wines. In the absence of all 13 Rhone varieties, Syrah, Mourvedre (under the name Mataro), and Grenache are the most frequently adopted varieties for what must be called "experiments" because of the newness of the attempts and the very limited amounts of fruit with which the winemakers are able to work. With the exception of McDowell Valley Vineyards and the Joseph Phelps winery, whose mid-70s plantings of Syrah in the Napa Valley have yet to produce much wine of distinction, most players in the small but burgeoning Rhone game (sometimes referred to as the "Rhone Rangers") are small establishments like Bonny Doon, Edmunds St. John, and Qupe.

THOMPSON SEEDLESS   Not so long ago, this popular table and raisin grape, which represents almost 35% of all grapes of every type planted in California, was also California's most widely used wine grape. Although no winery in recent memory has called attention to the inclusion of Thompson in its inexpensive jug blends and cheap sparkling wine, many producers still do rely on this low-acid, low-flavor grape for their generic products. Thompson Seedless's number-one position as a wine grape was surpassed in 83 when immense waves of new French Colombard acreage surged into production. One hopes that the ready availability of Colombard, and Chenin Blanc as well, taken together with the demand for raisins, will continue to diminish Thompson's role in winemaking. Much of the current Thompson Seedless crush goes into brandy or into grape concentrate.

TINTA MADEIRA   Claimed as, but not proven to be, a true Portuguese variety, this red grape is grown almost exclusively in the Central Valley for use in the production of port. Its 97% drop in acreage over the last decade (to a total of 52 acres) evidences its fall from grace.

VIN GRIS   Following the custom of a few small regions of France, a winery will occasionally offer a bottle of dry, lightly colored rosé or Blanc de Noirs that carries the name Vin Gris (literally, "Gray Wine") in an attempt to separate its bottling from the mounds of sweeter versions. Many wines labeled Vin Gris are made from Pinot Noir grapes, following the traditional Burgundy practice.

VIOGNIER   One of the rarest (about 100 acres worldwide) and hardest-to-grow varieties, this white grape, with its blossomy and perfumed, somewhat peachy and appley character, produces limited amounts of expensive wine in the northern Rhone under the appellation Condrieu. Although some of the early California efforts have had extremely encouraging results, it is a little too early to know whether Viognier will gain a firm toehold here. Most of the 50 acres here will begin to bear fruit by 92 or 93.

WHITE   Except for the White Riesling, all the so-called "white varietals" (White Zinfandel being most prominent among them) are nothing more than white (or light pink) wines made from the free-run juice of red-skinned (and thus, red wine) grapes. This term, in conjunction with the varietal name of a red wine grape, is synonymous with Blanc de Noirs.

WHITE RIESLING   Some wineries and at least one state (Oregon) have opted to use this name on wines made from the grape more commonly called Johannisberg Riesling in the U.S. or simply Riesling in its native Germany.

WHITE TABLE WINE   Generic white wine blends, often from coastal wineries wishing to find an upscale term as an alternative to the ubiquitous Chablis-labeled jug-wine offerings, are found under this name.

WHITE ZINFANDEL   Not a grape variety, but rather a white wine (usually with a distict pink "blush") made from the Zinfandel grape, it has been around in limited production for most of the century. Only in the last decade, however, has the popularity of White Zinfandel skyrocketed. The Sutter Home Winery, whose brawny Amador County Zinfandels gained prominence in the early 70s, is generally given the credit for initiating the White Zinfandel boom sometime in the latter 70s. And while it is true that Sutter Home White Zinfandel was the first to gain widespread fame and remains today one of the best-selling White Zinfandels, with an estimated 25% of the approximately 6-million-case market, the wine was first made in California by other wineries, including David Bruce.
   The dominant style of White Zinfandel intends to be high in freshness and fruitiness, with 1% to 3% residual sugar, and enough acidity and occasionally a slight spritziness to be light and lively on the palate. At its best, the wine is

a fine quaff and can, in its less sweet styles, accompany most picnic foods. It should be consumed in the bloom of youth and well chilled.

The White Zinfandel phenomenon appears to be a combination of several converging trends, including the white wine boom, the aging of the "Coca-Cola" crowd, and the search for something better by wine cooler aficionados. It has occurred concurrently with a decrease in the popularity of every other sweet white variety, especially including Chenin Blanc, and is probably partly responsible for the latter's current lack of favor.

ZINFANDEL Its origins cloaked in mystery for most of its 130-year history in California winemaking, this red grape now thought to be related to southern Italy's Primativo is used in everything from the production of the trendy White Zinfandel (and its derivative, sparkling White Zinfandel) to hearty, robust red wines filled with fruit, tannin, depth, and semblances of complexity and longevity. It is in this latter guise that Zinfandel came to popularity in the early 70s through the interest shown in stands of old vines by wineries like Sutter Home (now known more for its tidal wave of White Zinfandel) and Ridge. Within a few years, the modern-era boom in California wine took Zinfandel along for the ride; using the enormous standing acreage as a base, this now noble grape was elevated from jug-wine obscurity into something approaching the adored status of Cabernet Sauvignon. By the late 70s, hundreds of wineries were producing Zinfandel (the red version) in a full-bodied, fairly sturdy style, and aging the wine in barrels heretofore reserved for the likes of Cabernet and Pinot Noir. Of course, the price escalated as well, and when the backlash came against red wines in general and California reds more specifically, the expensive versions of Zinfandel took it on the chin.

Along came White Zinfandel to take up the overflow in grape production, and, for a period of time lasting through most of the 80s, wineries found they could often make as much or more money selling the "white" product within months of harvest rather than the barrel-aged, red version two to three years after picking the grapes. During that time, the number of red wines from Zinfandel fell by over 50%. It is only now that robust, red Zinfandel has begun to come back into favor, boosted, in large measure, by the renewed focus on California Cabernet and the resulting price escalation in that variety, which has made Zinfandel in the $7–10 bracket seem a relative bargain.

In medium-warmth coastal locations, especially sheltered hillsides, Zinfandel yields medium-full-bodied, intensely flavored wines with substantial tannin. The best wines of this type show Zinfandel's vigorous, berrylike, sometimes spicy varietal character. Late harvest Zinfandels (a style more associated with the 70s than the 80s) are high in alcohol and frequently contain residual sugar. When well made, they are a fruity alternative to port; but when made poorly or from poor grapes, they take on cooked, desiccated flavors often running in the direction of "pruniness."

Parts of Sonoma County—notably the Dry Creek Valley, the Sonoma Valley, and the Lytton Springs and Geyserville areas—as well as Amador and Napa counties have yielded most of the exceptional Zinfandels of the last decade and a half. The grape is also widely grown in the Central Valley, including the Lodi area, which contains almost 40% of the state's total plantings. Lodi Zinfandels often display the variety's berrylike nature, but tend toward flatter, earthier qualities at the expense of the lively, vigorous character found in other regions. Jug-wine Zinfandels exhibit the same lack of virtue found in most wines of the type.

Zinfandel is a versatile grape, and has proven successful in a variety of other styles, including light fruity red wine, rosé, and Nouveau. Over 200 producers and a substantial number of private bottlers produce Zinfandel from the state's 34,000 standing acres, a number that has held more or less steady for several decades even as the grape's fortunes as a wine grape have changed with some regularity. Important plantings (by county): Amador (1,200 acres), Colusa (1,100), Mendocino (1,800), Monterey (1,900), Napa (2,000), Sacramento (400), San Joaquin (12,700), San Luis Obispo (1,400), Sonoma (4,100).

Wine Geography

Every bottle of wine identifies the source of its grapes—its "appellation"—prominently on its label. For wines of the United States, the appellation shown can be as broad as "American," meaning that the grapes could have come from anywhere in the 50 states, or as limited as "Sonoma Mountain," meaning that the source could only have been those few hundred acres of vines grown on that one particular hill southeast of Santa Rosa, California.

The rules governing the use of appellations in this country are established by the U.S. Bureau of Alcohol, Tobacco and Firearms. Under BATF regulations, any wine produced from grapes grown here can carry the appellations American or United States. Similarly, any wine is entitled to bear the name of the state or states (up to three contiguous), or the county or counties (up to three within the same state), where the grapes were grown. Wine labels may also bear the appellation of a specified delimited area, officially called a "Viticultural Area," which distinguishes itself from surrounding areas by geographic features (including soil, elevation, topography, and climate). Wines labeled with one or more states as their appellations must be made 100% from the named state(s). When one county is named as the appellation, only 75% of the grapes used in its production need come from that county; if two or three counties are specified, all grapes must come from the named counties. Wines from Viticultural Areas are required to have 85% of their contents from the named appellation.

To establish such a delimited Viticultural Area, which may range in size from a few hundred acres to several million (total acreage—not grape acreage), interested parties (usually growers and/or wineries) petition the Bureau of Alcohol, Tobacco and Firearms for recognition by providing evidence that the proposed area is worthy of special consideration by virtue of its unique character for grape growing. BATF holds public hearings and receives evidence from anyone with an opinion on the proposed Viticultural Area, then accepts, rejects, or amends the boundaries as it sees fit. The process moves slowly and often with great difficulty when conflicting views are presented by the various vested interests.

MENDOCINO and
LAKE COUNTIES

0   10 Miles

AREA
OF MAP

San Francisco

Willits

MENDOCINO

REDWOOD
VALLEY

POTTER
VALLEY

Calpella

Lake
Mendocino

Navarro

TALMAGE

ANDERSON
VALLEY

Ukiah

Upper Lake

Philo

MENDOCINO

Talmage

L   A   K   E

Boonville

COLE
RANCH

Lakeport

Clear Lake

VITICULTURAL

Hopland

CLEAR LAKE

AREA

MC DOWELL
VALLEY

Kelseyville

Clearlake

Cloverdale

Lower
Lake

Asti

SONOMA

Russian River

Middletown

PACIFIC
OCEAN

Geyserville

GUENOC
VALLEY

Lytton

MOUNTAINS

NAPA

MAYACAMAS

E. Fork Russian River

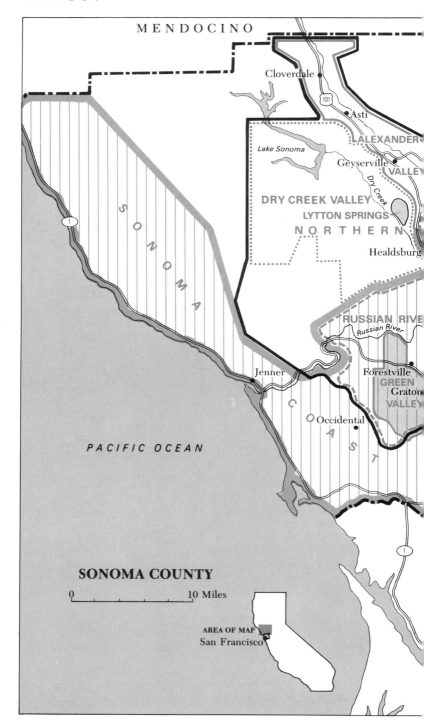

MENDOCINO

Cloverdale

Asti

Lake Sonoma

ALEXANDER

Geyserville

VALLEY

Dry Creek

DRY CREEK VALLEY

LYTTON SPRINGS

NORTHERN

S O N O M A

Healdsburg

RUSSIAN RIVE

Russian River

Jenner

Forestville

GREEN

Graton

VALLEY

Occidental

C O A S T

PACIFIC OCEAN

SONOMA COUNTY

0   10 Miles

AREA OF MAP

San Francisco

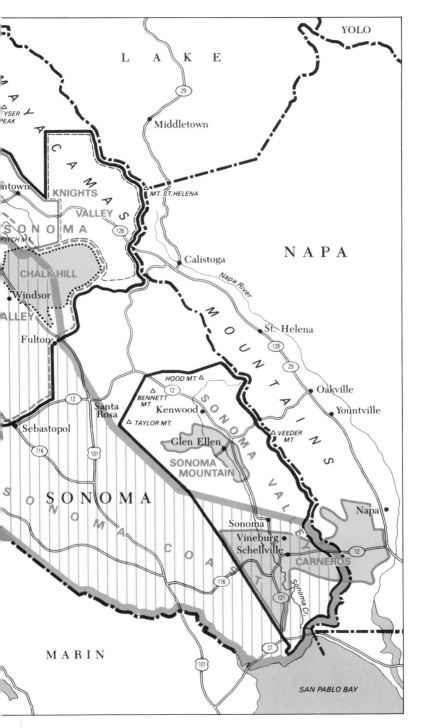

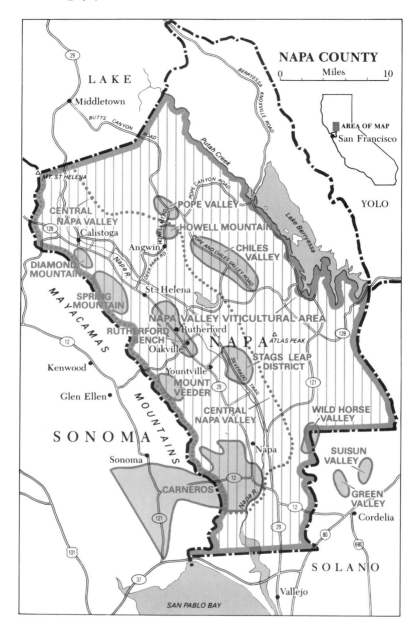

NAPA COUNTY

0 Miles 10

AREA OF MAP

San Francisco

LAKE

Middletown

YOLO

BUTTS CANYON ROAD

Putah Creek

PUTAH CREEK

BERRYESSA KNOXVILLE ROAD

MT. ST HELENA

CENTRAL NAPA VALLEY

Calistoga

POPE VALLEY

HOWELL MOUNTAIN

Lake Berryessa

POPE CANYON ROAD

HOWELL MT RD

Angwin

CHILES VALLEY

DIAMOND MOUNTAIN

Napa R.

DEER PARK RD.

St. Helena

POPE AND CHILES VALLEY ROAD

SPRING MOUNTAIN

M A Y A C A M A S

RUTHERFORD BENCH

Oakville

NAPA VALLEY VITICULTURAL AREA

Rutherford

N A P A

ATLAS PEAK

STAGS LEAP DISTRICT

128

Kenwood

12

Yountville

MOUNT VEEDER

SILVERADO TRAIL

Glen Ellen

M O U N T A I N S

CENTRAL NAPA VALLEY

29

121

WILD HORSE VALLEY

S O N O M A

Sonoma

Napa

SUISUN VALLEY

CARNEROS

12

GREEN VALLEY

121

12

Cordelia

101

80

680

37

S O L A N O

SAN PABLO BAY

Vallejo

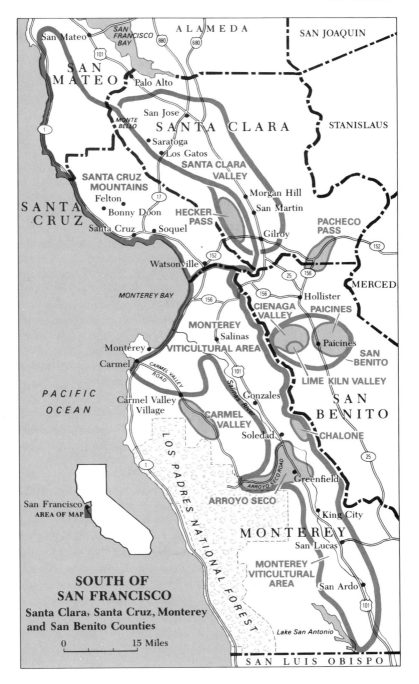

**SOUTH OF
SAN FRANCISCO**

Santa Clara, Santa Cruz, Monterey
and San Benito Counties

0   15 Miles

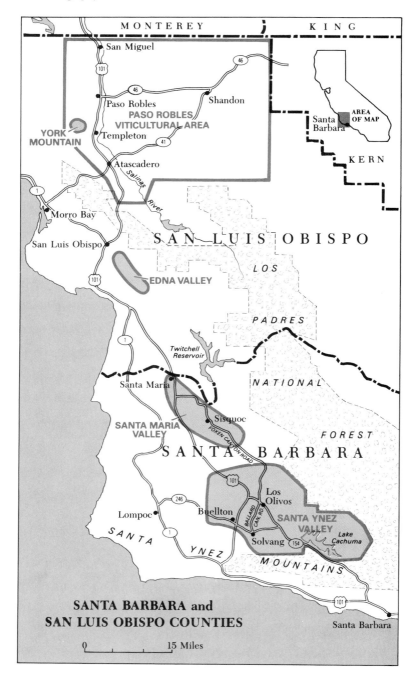

MONTEREY

KING

San Miguel

101

46

46

Paso Robles

Shandon

PASO ROBLES VITICULTURAL AREA

YORK MOUNTAIN

Templeton

41

Atascadero

Morro Bay

AREA OF MAP

Santa Barbara

CALIFORNIA

KERN

San Luis Obispo

SAN LUIS OBISPO

LOS

1

101

EDNA VALLEY

PADRES

Twitchell Reservoir

NATIONAL

Santa Maria

SANTA MARIA VALLEY

Sisquoc

FOXEN CANYON ROAD

FOREST

SANTA BARBARA

101

Los Olivos

246

BALLARD CAN. RD.

SANTA YNEZ VALLEY

Lompoc

Buellton

Lake Cachuma

SANTA

1

Solvang

154

YNEZ

MOUNTAINS

101

SANTA BARBARA and SAN LUIS OBISPO COUNTIES

Santa Barbara

0   15 Miles

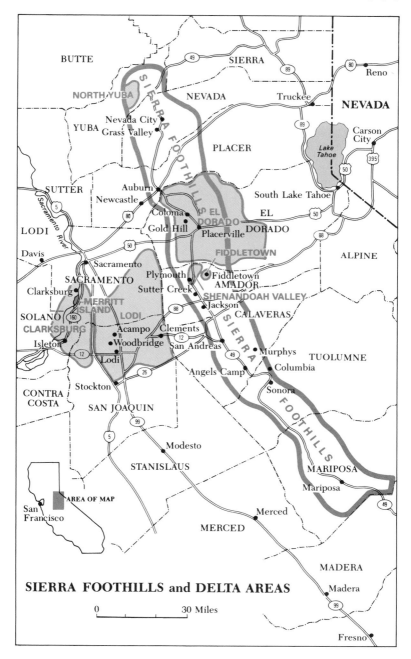

SIERRA FOOTHILLS and DELTA AREAS

0   30 Miles

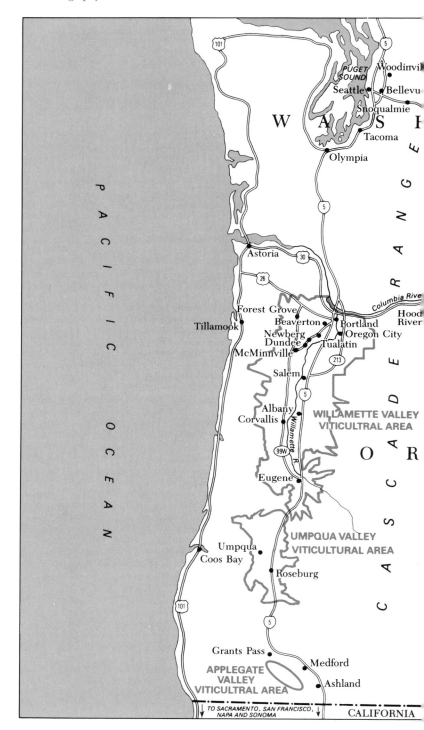

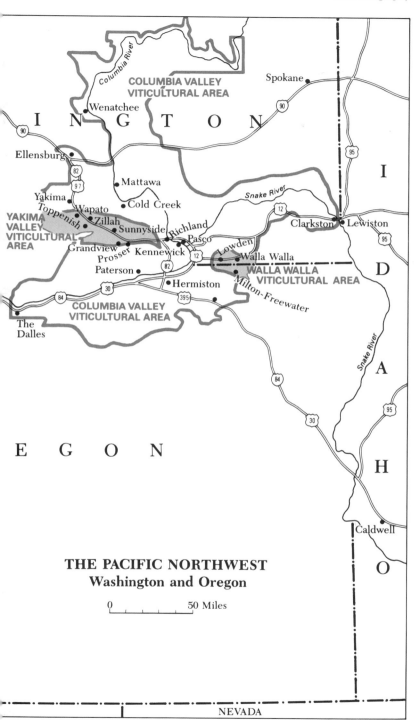

COLUMBIA VALLEY
VITICULTURAL AREA

Spokane

Wenatchee

W A S H I N G T O N

Ellensburg

Mattawa

Yakima
Toppenish
Wapato
Zillah
Cold Creek
YAKIMA
VALLEY
VITICULTURAL
AREA
Grandview
Prosser
Sunnyside
Richland
Pasco
Kennewick

Snake River

Clarkston
Lewiston

I D A H O

Lowden
Walla Walla
WALLA WALLA
VITICULTURAL AREA
Milton-Freewater

Paterson

Hermiston

The
Dalles

COLUMBIA VALLEY
VITICULTURAL AREA

O R E G O N

Snake River

Caldwell

THE PACIFIC NORTHWEST
Washington and Oregon

0   50 Miles

NEVADA

69

Some of the defined Viticultural Area appellations (for example, Howell Mountain or Shenandoah Valley) are small enough and possessed of such uniform soil and weather that their names on the label offer a clear indication of the conditions under which the grapes were grown. Others are either so large (North Coast) or so remote and undeveloped (Willow Creek) that no inference can confidently be drawn or, indeed, needs to be. The one thing that can be said about any approved Viticultural Area appellation on a label is that it defines the source of the grapes. By contrast, most appellation systems in Europe, particularly those used in the most famous wine-growing areas, specify the grape varieties which may be grown within an appellation, the maximum production allowed, the degree of ripeness the grapes must attain in order to be considered representative of the area, and for a few appellations, a minimum level of quality.

In this chapter, we discuss each of the identified Viticultural Areas in California and the Pacific Northwest, with an eye toward giving the reader a sense of the importance each enjoys and why. Other place names are also referenced, either because they are destined to become Viticultural Areas in the future or because they appear frequently on wine labels or crop up in discussions about wine.

In California, a principal distinguishing characteristic of a place where grapes are grown is the amount of heat to which the grapes are subjected during a typical growing year. The conventional measure employed is "degree days," which is arrived at by adding together the average temperature in excess of 50° F. for each day during the growing season (i.e., a day that averages 66° is said to have 16 "degree days"). The total of the degree days during the growing season is used as measure of the warmth of a particular growing area. Cool areas, those with fewer than 2,500 degree days, are referred to as Region I, and are considered to be most suited to grapes like Johannisberg Riesling and Pinot Noir and grapes for sparkling wine. Areas that have accumulations of 2,500–3,000 degree days are called Region II, and are regarded as appropriate for Cabernet Sauvignon, Chardonnay, Sauvignon Blanc, and Merlot.

Region III growing areas, with heat totals in the range of 3,000–3,500 degree days, are on the borderline between temperatures suitable for growing the better (and more difficult) grapes and temperatures best for growing high-volume, jug-wine grapes and inexpensive varietals. Nevertheless, Region III can be hospitable to Zinfandel, Petite Sirah, Syrah, and Chenin Blanc, and is not totally inappropriate for the varieties that thrive in Region II growing conditions. Regions IV and V, with degree days ranging up to and beyond 4,000, are relatively warm for grapes and rarely produce wines of significance from a collector's viewpoint, but do yield the greatest part of the wines produced in California.

ALAMEDA COUNTY   Located directly across the Bay from San Francisco, Alameda County contains 1,700 acres devoted to grapes today, down from 2,000 a decade ago. Almost all of the acreage is found in the Livermore Valley, and about

75% of the total is used to grow white varieties. The Livermore Valley was famous for white wines long before Prohibition. Today, the leading grapes are Chardonnay (760 acres) and Sauvignon Blanc (190). Wente and Concannon, two of the oldest wineries in Livermore, own most of the vineyards. Both worked hard in the 80s to restore the reputation of Livermore Valley. Of the 20 other producers in the county, many can be found in the Oakland-Berkeley area, and the majority tend to be part-time winemakers. Though their production is often only a few hundred cases per year, their performances can surpass many big, well-financed competitors. Rosenblum Cellars and Edmunds St. John are two of the best-known small producers.

ALEXANDER VALLEY *(Sonoma)*   This 12-mile-long inland Viticultural Area follows the course of the Russian River from north of Cloverdale until it flows past Healdsburg in the south. The northern boundary of the area is defined by the Mendocino County border, and its southern boundary, shared with the Chalk Hill Viticultural Area, is found northeast of Windsor. As a landlocked piece of topography, the Alexander Valley is a warm part of the county, with the river offering the primary tempering influence. Summertime fog is an infrequent guest that rarely stays long. The northern pockets from Cloverdale to just south of Geyserville tend to satisfy heat-loving varieties like Zinfandel. For other locales, especially those near the river or along the benchlands, earlier-ripening grapes (Chardonnay, Riesling, Gewurztraminer) fare surprisingly well. Such well-known Chardonnay suppliers as Robert Young Vineyards, Belle Terre, and the Gauer Ranch are located on upper benchlands. In general, the valley's gravelly, sandy loam soils are quite fertile, and vines tend to be vigorous and productive. This vigorous tendency helps to account for the strong, often pungent character of Alexander Valley–grown Sauvignon Blanc.

Of the close to 7,000 acres under vine, the leading varieties are Cabernet Sauvignon and Chardonnay. The Cabernets range widely in style. The best capture a berry, cherry fruit, with herbal notes that avoid a strong bell pepper character and overripeness. Napa's Silver Oak—along with Clos du Bois, Simi, and Lyeth—has coaxed the most depth and charm out of Alexander Valley Cabernet, in our experience. Noteworthy Alexander Valley Chardonnay is more plentiful, and at its best presents ripe apple and spice aromas, fat, ripe fruit flavors that are deep and lush, and typically strong. At their finest, these Chardonnays reach ✸✸✸ levels. Chardonnay from local growers is much in demand, and many wineries outside the region regularly bottle an Alexander Valley Chardonnay.

Close to two dozen producers are located within the Alexander Valley. Among the best known are larger ones such as Geyser Peak, Chateau Souverain, and Clos du Bois, and smaller ones like Jordan, Simi, Lyeth, and Alexander Valley Vineyards.

AMADOR COUNTY   Smack in the middle of the Sierra Foothills grape-growing district, Amador County shares the rich heritage of Gold Rush era winemaking with counties both north and south of it. And, as with its neighbors, the times passed it by, except for the legacy of a few hundred acres of vineyard that remained in production from those halcyon days. Then, in the late 60s, with most of its grapes being sold to the makers of jug wines, Amador got a boost when the notion of making Zinfandel from old vines, including those in Amador County, developed among home winemakers and quickly passed to the commercial wineries. At that point only 450 acres remained in production, mostly Zinfandel, and only one winery of longevity existed.

The first widely recognized wine of the new era for Amador came from Sutter Home, and its first vintages were quickly followed by a rush of coastal wineries that found superb, if somewhat overripe, grapes in the Shenandoah Valley and Fiddletown areas. Almost at the same time came a small but significant rush of new wineries to the area and a tripling of grape production. Now, acreage reaches 1,700, and although Zinfandel still reigns supreme with

1,200 acres, Sauvignon Blanc has become an important second variety at 240 acres. A small planting of traditional port varieties under the auspices of St. Amant has been a noteworthy recent addition to the Amador scene.

ANDERSON VALLEY *(Mendocino)* Tucked away into a 25-mile-long, 2-mile-wide valley halfway between Ukiah and the Pacific, the Anderson Valley is an isolated Viticultural Area. Enclosed by steep mountains on three sides, this cool Region I and Region II area experienced wholesale expansion in the 80s. Most of the dozen or so producers and 1,000 acres of vineyards are located between Philo and Navarro, where vineyards are situated along a series of elevated river terraces. The valley's reputation improved once the area was planted to compatible varieties such as Chardonnay, Pinot Noir, and Gewurz-traminer, now representing 75% of the total acreage. In the early 80s, the French firm of Louis Roederer purchased close to 600 acres and has developed 400 acres to vineyards used exclusively for sparkling wine. A few winemakers cling to the belief that along the high-elevation ridges there is less fog and enough warmth to ripen Cabernet Sauvignon, Merlot, and even Zinfandel. One of the oldest vineyards in the state, the DuPratt Vineyard, noted for its Zinfandel, is located along the Greenwood Ridge.

In 1964, the Edmeades family planted 11 acres to become the valley's first modern-day grape grower. Husch, Lazy Creek, and Navarro soon appeared as wine producers to steadily improve the valley's reputation. Handley Cellars was established in the early 80s, and has become a quality leader. All four producers contribute to the belief that Gewurztraminer may be the most successful wine made in the Anderson Valley. Roederer Estate and Scharff-enberger Cellars (owned by Pommery of Champagne) settled in the Anderson Valley in the 80s to establish the region's credentials for sparkling wine production.

APPLEGATE VALLEY Located in southwest Oregon not far from the California border, this tiny valley enjoys a warmer climate than other parts of Oregon. The main metropolis is the Medford-Jacksonville area. Most vineyards are located at elevations above the 1,000-foot level or higher which look down on those towns. The limited amounts of wines produced from this region over the first decade offer some encouragement for Chardonnay and Cabernet Sauvignon. Valley View Winery is the best-known producer in this area.

ARROYO SECO *(Monterey)* Most of this Viticultural Area falls within a protected area nestled against the foothills of the coastal range. It begins due south of Soledad and extends about a mile south of Greenfield. Shaped somewhat like a triangle, it fans out west from Greenfield and crosses the Arroyo Seco Road, covering a low-lying, gently sloped benchland. Over its first two decades, Arroyo Seco has been the identified source of several late harvest Rieslings and many vintages of superb Chardonnays grown at Ventana Vineyards. Wente is the major grower within the area, along with Jekel, J. Lohr, Hess, and Ventana. Approximately 5,000 acres are located within this appellation. Chardonnay and Riesling are the leading varieties.

CALAVERAS COUNTY Despite the efforts of its one major winery, Stevenot, Calaveras has not made much progress as a wine-growing location in the last two decades. Zinfandel, its leading variety, continues to show but 50 acres, and the other varieties of note (Chardonnay, Cabernet Sauvignon, and French Colombard) range down from there. All told, Calaveras contains some 200 planted acres and has not generally shared in the return to prominence of the Gold Rush counties that brought Amador and El Dorado counties back into the vinous limelight.

CALIFORNIA The number-one state in population, cars per capita, wine and beer consumption, and natural beauty, California is also number one in vineyard acreage, with over 330,000 acres of wine grapes in 45 of the state's 58 counties. Some 80% to 85% of all wine produced in the U.S. is grown in California and, by some estimates, up to 95% of this country's premium wine production is Californian by origin. The approximately 3 million tons of grapes crushed for wine produces over 400 million gallons, making viticulture the third most important agricultural activity in the state.

On wine labels, the appellation California typically means that the grapes came from a combination of areas and thus the wine is not entitled to a more specific appellation. On inexpensive wines labeled with a California appellation, the grapes most often will have their origins in the hot Central Valley, home for 80% of the total California crush. The majority of California's over 700 wineries, however, are located in the coastal counties and are producers of varietal wines, typically using more narrowly defined appellations than California.

CALISTOGA *(Napa)* The northernmost community in the Napa Valley has become its most densely packed tourist center. Calistoga boasts hotels, restaurants, wine bars, glider rides over the vineyards, hot springs, geysers, mud baths, and just about anything else the weary tourist could want at the end of a long day of trekking through vineyards and production facilities. Surrounded by mountains on three sides and vineyards on all four, Calistoga provides a warmer climate for grape-growing than its down-valley neighbors; its best-known products are the fat, rich Cabernets of Chateau Montelena and Robert Pecota, as well as Phelps's Eisele Vineyard bottling. Sauvignon Blanc and Zinfandel also often grow well in the Calistoga area. Among the important wineries located near Calistoga, in addition to Montelena and Pecota, are Sterling, Cuvaison, Clos Pegase, and Stonegate. The area is generally rated medium-warm Region III in heat accumulation, with high daytime temperatures often moderated by cooling winds that blow in at night through the narrow, twisting gap that connects the upper Napa Valley to Knights Valley.

CARMEL VALLEY *(Monterey)* Inland and beginning a few miles southwest of the famous resort town of Carmel, the Carmel Valley Viticultural Area runs parallel to the Salinas Valley, which in turn is several miles further inland. The Carmel Valley is situated at higher elevation than its neighbor and receives considerably more rainfall. The climate within this protected valley is generally warmer and better suited to red varieties than the Salinas Valley. It has three wineries, one of which, Durney Vineyards, is primarily responsible for most of the 200 acres contained in the appellation. Château Julien is located on the flat western end of the valley, and Robert Talbott has its original vineyard located to the southeast on hillsides further inland.

CARNEROS (also known as Los Carneros) *(Napa and Sonoma)* As an appellation, Carneros falls within the counties of Sonoma and Napa where they meet at the northern edge of San Francisco Bay. From a wine-identification standpoint, they are also part of the Sonoma and Napa valleys and are the southernmost appellations of origin within each. Most of the land is low-lying or rolling terrain, almost all within sight of the Bay and moderated climatically by its cooling influence. Heat accumulations are generally thought to be cool Region II, although some of the protected locations and upper hillsides can be somewhat warmer. About three-fourths of the total Carneros acreage (some 4,800 of approximately 7,000 acres planted to grapes) lies within Napa County, while the rest occupies a narrow strip that juts out into and across the bottom of the Sonoma Valley Viticultural Area.

On the Napa side of this justifiably famous area are located vineyards that have yielded the Carneros-identified Pinot Noirs and Chardonnays of Acacia, Bouchaine, Beaulieu, Carneros Creek, and Saintsbury, as well as the highly esteemed Winery Lake Vineyard founded by the iconoclastic art collector and wine lover Rene Di Rosa, and now owned by Sterling Vineyards. Sparkling wine producer Domaine Chandon also draws heavily on grapes from Carneros. On the Sonoma end, Buena Vista has substantial holdings—now reaching toward 900 acres—in which it grows the usual "cool-area" varieties as well as an often-successful Cabernet Sauvignon. Several Sebastiani vineyards are dotted throughout Sonoma Valley–Carneros, and the Sangiacomo Vineyard, whose name appears on numerous Chardonnays, is also here. Tucked in the southwest corner of Carneros are the champagne cellars of Gloria Ferrer, among the first wineries one sees when coming to Sonoma on the Golden Gate Bridge/Marin County approach to the wine country from San Francisco.

CENTRAL COAST   Covering an immense span of territory south of San Francisco, this Viticultural Area includes the following counties: Alameda, Monterey, San Benito, San Luis Obispo, Santa Barbara, Santa Clara, and Santa Cruz. Despite seeming to include every vine between San Francisco and Los Angeles, the Central Coast appellation is frequently used to identify wine produced from grapes grown in two neighboring counties.

CENTRAL VALLEY   California's Central Valley, the most productive agricultural area in the state and one of the most important in the world, dominates Californian grape growing from a quantitative standpoint. In actual fact, the Central Valley consists of two major portions: a northern section, often referred to as the Sacramento Valley, and a southern portion, which is the more important agriculturally and viticulturally, called the San Joaquin Valley. Between the two is the Delta area, whose wetlands contribute to a slight lowering of the otherwise scorching midsummer temperatures experienced throughout the valley. Except for some 9,000 acres of grapes in the northern portion, including about 6,000 acres in or near the Delta, the bulk of the Central Valley's 180,000 acres of grapes (about 55% of California's total planted grape acreage) lie within the San Joaquin Valley. There, spread across some eight valley floor counties, are grown the grapes for the vast quantities of jug wines and inexpensive varietals, including the majority of White Zinfandel, that make up the greatest part of the California wine output.

Until the last decade or so, Central Valley wines were very often bad: low in acid, oversweetened to hide a multitude of faults, and possessing a cooked quality in aroma and flavors. The bad days are not totally past, but things have certainly changed. Varieties with higher natural acidity (French Colombard, Barbera, and Chenin Blanc) have been planted where once Carignane, Mission, and Grenache ruled. Grapes are picked with more care so that balance and ripeness are more nearly achieved. And the modern technology of temperature-controlled, stainless-steel fermentation keeps the fruit cleaner and retains whatever freshness is brought into the winery from the vineyard. Notwithstanding the few failed attempts to make long-aging, pricey (or even mid-priced) wines from the Central Valley, the best wines in their youth are clean, flavorful, and among the highest-quality everyday drinking wines in the world. Of course, at their worst, they remain as unpalatable as before.

CHALK HILL (Sonoma)   Located southwest of Knights Valley, and south of the Alexander Valley, Chalk Hill is a small Viticultural Area that is also a subappellation contained within the western corner of the Russian River Valley. With some 1,000 acres under vine, Chalk Hill covers the hilly terrain due east of the town of Windsor, most of which (but not all) is characterized by white soils. The color actually derives from volcanic ash, not from chalk as was once mistakenly assumed. Chardonnay is the primary variety planted in this almost exclusively white wine region. The terrain consists of gentle hills, which help distinguish it from the rest of the Russian River Valley. These hills discourage the intrusion of fog and cooling marine air, so the climate of Chalk Hill is slightly warmer than the rest of the Russian River Valley. Chalk Hill Winery and Rodney Strong Vineyards are among the best-known vineyard owners in the area.

CHALONE (Monterey)   Home to one winery of the same name, Chalone is a vast span of land located high in the steep hills to the east of Salinas. The area covers a total of 8,600 acres, but only 200 are planted to vines, all owned by Chalone Vineyards. As a Viticultural Area, Chalone enjoys one of the highest elevations in California, averaging 1,650 feet above sea level. The soils are volcanic, with generally rocky topsoil that contains heavy limestone deposits. The cool but extremely dry climate contributes further to generally stressful conditions for the vine. Chardonnay and Pinot Noir are the dominant varieties planted. Both varieties produce small crops of usually intensely flavored grapes. The name Chalone is taken from the North and South Chalone Peaks, which flank the area but are not included within it.

CHILES VALLEY *(Napa)* Located in the hills east of the main body of the Napa Valley and at higher altitude, this small valley has been allowed to call its grapes Napa Valley because of historical precedent. In point of fact, the growing season is shorter, hotter, and less hospitable than the real valley, and very few wines of significance are grown here. Occasionally a Zinfandel from this area will remind us of its existence.

CIENEGA *(San Benito)* Located at the base of the Gabilan Mountain Range, the Cienega Valley separates Monterey County from San Benito County. It is a pretty, hilly region with a moderately warm climate. Almadén Vineyard developed and owned most of the vineyards. After Almadén was sold in 87 and moved its winemaking facilities to the Central Valley, it harvested only a portion of its Cienega holdings. It was in Cienega that Almadén cultivated most of the Grenache used for its once popular rosé wines. In 88, producers such as Bonny Doon and others interested in Rhone varieties were purchasing Grenache from this Viticultural Area. One minor distinction is that the San Andreas Fault line runs across the northeast border of Cienega.

CLARKSBURG *(Sacramento, Solano, and Yolo counties)* Lying almost immediately southwest of the city of Sacramento, the Clarksburg Viticultural Area extends southward through the Sacramento River Delta for some 16 miles and is up to 8 miles wide at its broadest point. In spite of its size, the area contains only a couple of wineries and a handful of vineyards. The water and the occasional cooling breezes blowing up the river from the San Francisco Bay moderate the Clarksburg climate, and allow it to produce grapes with better balance and depth than in the hotter places of the Central Valley. With few exceptions, however, the best wines produced here are marketed as low-priced varietals. Chenin Blanc and Petite Sirah have been the most successful to date.

CLEAR LAKE *(Lake County)* Covering an enormous expanse of land measuring approximately 250 square miles, Clear Lake is a Viticultural Area that incorporates all agricultural land in and around Clear Lake. This includes over 90% of all the vineyards in Lake County with the exception of the Guenoc Valley. To date, the one producer using this place name on many labels is Kendall-Jackson.

COLE RANCH *(Mendocino)* This mountainous area located midway between Ukiah and Boonville became a Viticultural Area in the early 80s, even though it was defined and controlled by a single grape grower. Over 80% of the 60 acres are planted to Cabernet Sauvignon, with Riesling and Chardonnay making up the rest. Much of the tonnage has been purchased by Fetzer over recent vintages.

COLUMBIA VALLEY By far the largest Viticultural Area in the Northwest, this one covers some 18,000 square miles and as an appellation is practically synonymous with Washington State. Located in south-central Washington, it encompasses both the Yakima Valley and the Walla Walla region, the two other major Viticultural Areas of the state. It also includes a big slice of land in northern Oregon facing the Columbia River. The Columbia Valley is a semi-arid valley protected from Pacific marine intrusion by the Cascade Mountains to the west, but its climate overall is quite likely the warmest of any wine region in the Northwest. As a result, there is a range of growing conditions from Region I through III, enabling growers to succeed both with cool-climate Riesling and with warm-weather grapes such as Merlot and, in some sites, with Cabernet Sauvignon. Over a dozen winemaking premises are found within this region.

DAVIS *(Yolo)* Ninety miles northeast of San Francisco, on the doorstep of Sacramento, sits the pretty university town of Davis, home of the University of California, Davis. Its Viticulture and Enology Department, the best in the country, has trained winemakers from more than half of the premium wineries in the state and has contributed substantially to the high-tech orientation of most California winemaking. The university is a world leader in studies of grapevine diseases, vineyard problems, and grape clones.

DELTA *(Sacramento, Yolo, and Solano)* The watery lowlands lying in the triangle formed by the confluence of the San Joaquin and Sacramento rivers is known as the Delta. On some of the many islands, especially those in the eastern Delta, and on the adjoining terra firma to the immediate east, there is a small but increasing wine-growing industry. The Delta is warm (high Region III to Region IV) but more temperate than its Central Valley neighbors to the south because of the San Francisco Bay marine influences. The Clarksburg and Merritt Island Viticultural Areas lie within the Delta, and the Lodi appellation lies immediately to the east.

DIAMOND MOUNTAIN Part of the Mayacamas Range that separates the Napa Valley from the Sonoma Valley, Diamond Mountain forms a portion of the Napa Valley's western hills between St. Helena and Calistoga. Its sunny slopes and rich soils are planted primarily to Cabernet Sauvignon, with some Chardonnay and Merlot also present. The most notable players on Diamond Mountain are Sterling and Diamond Creek, both of which have produced exceptional wines from grapes grown there. The Cabernets are firm, deep in tannin, and somewhat closed-in, but are capable of extraordinary depth and beauty when aged. The steep vineyards of Diamond Mountain are not always deep in soil, making them difficult to farm and frequently stingy yielders.

DRY CREEK VALLEY *(Sonoma)* This northwest-to-southeast-running appellation practically parallels the Alexander Valley. The eastern border stretches from Geyserville down to Healdsburg, while the Warm Springs and Dry Creek intersection defines its northwest boundary. The climate is both wetter and warmer than that of the Russian River Valley, and the growing season tends to be longer. The red soils of Dry Creek are more common in the benchlands and hills in the north, and these sites seem just about perfect for Zinfandel and close to that for Sauvignon Blanc. Zinfandels from the Dry Creek Valley appellation are ripe, rich, with berrylike fruit and peppery nuances. The area's Sauvignon Blanc can often be too exuberant in a pungent, weedy-grassy manner, needing some calming influence from barrel fermentations or from blending with Semillon. The finer Cabernet Sauvignons are very expressive, with a strong bell pepper, green olive, earthy nature. As one moves south toward the Russian River, the plantings begin to favor Chardonnay and Riesling. Vineyards have steadily expanded through the 80s to bring the current total acreage close to 6,000. About a dozen producers are located within Dry Creek, including Dry Creek Vineyards, Preston, Ferrari-Carano, Meeker, A. Rafanelli, Quivira, and the North Coast outpost of Gallo.

EDNA VALLEY *(San Luis Obispo)* Beginning a little southeast of the town of San Luis Obispo, the Edna Valley is a Region I wine-growing valley, granted Viticultural Area status in 1982. Cool marine air from Morro Bay is partially deflected by a low string of hills along the valley's western boundary. Edna Valley is bordered on the northeast by the Santa Lucia Mountains and on the southwest by the San Luis Range. Chamisal Vineyards was the first producer in the area, establishing the first commercial vineyard in the late 70s; it now has 52 acres of Chardonnay. Paragon Vineyards, co-owner of the Edna Valley Vineyards, developed 400 acres in the Edna Valley, planted to Chardonnay and Pinot Noir. With close to 100 acres under vine, the MacGregor Vineyard is the best-known independently owned vineyard, whose Chardonnay grapes have been sold to Leeward, Morgan, Karly, Windemere, and Mount Eden Vineyards. Mount Eden's series of "M.E.V." Chardonnays were made entirely from MacGregor Vineyard. Corbett Canyon is the largest producer in the Edna Valley. The majority of the 1,000 total acres planted are Chardonnay, with Pinot Noir a distant second. Without question, Chardonnays from the Edna Valley can be successful. The best versions have a somewhat distinctive butterscotch character and are deeply fruited and viscous.

EL DORADO *(El Dorado)* Grape growing in El Dorado County is limited to the area of the county lying between 1,200 and 3,500 feet elevation; accordingly, this Viticultural Area is also so delimited.

EL DORADO COUNTY During the 19th-century Gold Rush days, El Dorado County is reputed to have contained 5,000 acres of vineyards. While the current count of 500 acres is not much by comparison, most of it has been planted since the mid-70s and every year seems to see a small but steady growth in the total. El Dorado County's dozen or so wineries also date from the same period. The most plentiful grapes, and the most successful, are Zinfandel (usually made in a ripe, medium-full style) and Sauvignon Blanc. The recognized Viticultural Area of El Dorado encompasses all of the county lying between the 1,200-foot and 3,500-foot levels of the Sierra Nevada Range's western slope. The eight-county Sierra Foothills appellation includes El Dorado County within its boundaries.

FIDDLETOWN *(Amador)* Lying just to the east across the ridge from the Shenandoah Valley, this area yields typical ripe, concentrated Zinfandels in the Amador County style, but possibly a little less forceful in flavor and alcohol than those of the Shenandoah Valley, apparently because of Fiddletown's slightly higher elevations and cooler nighttime temperatures. The Eschen Vineyard is Fiddletown's most notable grape-growing property and is referenced on several wineries' products. Fiddletown was granted Viticultural Area status in 1983. About 100 acres of grapes are planted in the area.

GEYSERVILLE *(Sonoma)* Surrounded by vineyards, Geyserville is a small town located just a few miles north of Healdsburg in the northwest corner of the Alexander Valley. It is the home address of many wineries, including Geyser Peak, Chateau Souverain, Gauer Estate, and Lyeth. However, what also makes it noteworthy is its association with excellent, ripe-style Zinfandels, especially those bottled by Ridge and identified as "Geyserville." The vineyards in this warm region also contribute ripe, full-bodied Cabernet Sauvignons, as well as Zinfandels.

GLEN ELLEN *(Sonoma)* Jack London once had the good sense to live in this enchanting rustic village, and his name adorns many local points of interest. The original vineyard developed by Jack London is now leased by Kenwood Vineyards. Located halfway between the towns of Sonoma and Kenwood, Glen Ellen is home today to several wineries, notably Grand Cru Vineyards, Valley of the Moon, B. R. Cohn, Kistler, Laurel Glen, and Glen Ellen Winery.

GREENFIELD *(Monterey)* Hometown to Jekel Vineyards and to the vineyards owned by J. Lohr, Greenfield falls at the midpoint of the Salinas Valley. The climate, however, is cool and extremely breezy on summer afternoons, best suited, it seems, for early-maturing white varieties. The early leader was Riesling, which remains consistent, but Chardonnay began exhibiting good results in the late 80s. Arroyo Seco is located west of Greenfield.

GREEN VALLEY–SOLANO *(Solano)* One of two Green Valley appellations in California, this is the lesser of the two and is rarely seen on labels. It lies one valley east of Napa County and several valleys east of the true Napa Valley and, accordingly, has hotter, drier, and shorter-season growing conditions.

GREEN VALLEY–SONOMA *(Sonoma)* This subdivision of the Russian River Valley can be found in its southwest corner. The tiny town of Sebastopol fixes its southeastern border, and the area extends a few miles north of Forestville. Located 10 miles inland from the Pacific, Green Valley experiences less intense heat during the growing season than the rest of the Russian River Valley. Therefore, it is planted to cool-climate varieties, primarily Chardonnay and Pinot Noir, which are used for both table and sparkling wines. The most distinctive wines are the medium-bodied Chardonnays, with a typical lively, green apple character. Chateau St. Jean's sparkling wine facility is located here in Graton, and the winery buys the majority of its grapes locally. Iron Horse Vineyards also produces its attractive sparkling wines from grapes grown here. Dehlinger, Laurier Vineyard, and Iron Horse Vineyards are strong supporters as well as residents of this appellation, which is labeled Green Valley–Sonoma County to distinguish it from another Green Valley in Solano County. Total acreage approaches 1,000 today, led by Chardonnay with close to 450.

GUENOC VALLEY *(Lake and Napa counties)*   Located 15 miles north of Calistoga, the Guenoc Valley extends from the upper part of Napa Valley into Lake County. Granted Viticultural Area status in 81, the Guenoc Valley is home to one winery, Guenoc Winery. Encompassing some 23,000 total acres, this valley is currently planted to 350 acres of vines, with about 1,400 acres suitable for planting in the future. The vineyard sites are located at the 1,000–1,400-foot-elevation levels. With widely fluctuating warm days and cool nights during the growing season, the region is categorized as a cool Region III. Spring frosts have turned out to be a serious problem, so all vineyards have frost-protection systems. The leading varieties are Cabernet Sauvignon and Chardonnay, with Sauvignon Blanc a distant third.

HEALDSBURG *(Sonoma)*   If there can be a hub to Sonoma County's dispersed wine-making activities, then the town of Healdsburg is emerging as the logical candidate. This small city's borders touch three important Viticultural Areas: Alexander Valley, Russian River Valley, and Chalk Hill. Immediately to the west of Healdsburg is the Dry Creek Valley. Over 50 wineries call Healdsburg their home, with several—among them Clos du Bois, White Oak, and William Wheeler—operating wineries and tasting rooms within city limits.

HECKER PASS *(Santa Clara)*   The Coast Range Mountains to the west of Gilroy gradually open up to the coastal plain. In this low-lying area, known as the Hecker Pass, about a dozen wineries can be found. Most of them are family-owned, and their wines generally harken back to the old days when heavy but often pleasing generic jug wines were purchased by local folks. The Hecker Pass wineries are popular among the weekend picnic crowd. Sarah's Vineyard has loftier ambitions and targets its efforts outside of the area.

HOWELL MOUNTAIN *(Napa)*   In the hills northeast of St. Helena, this Viticultural Area is found amidst a rolling hillside of vineyards, forest, and brush, at elevations between 1,600 and 2,200 feet. The soils in this near–Region III growing area are volcanic in origin and have a rusty, terra-cotta appearance. The location and moderately warm temperatures make it a hospitable place for grapes like Zinfandel and the Rhone varieties, yet it is the Cabernet Sauvignon, grown here by Dunn Vineyards and La Jota, that has given a special standing to the few hundred acres of vines on Howell Mountain. The area has a long and successful vinous history dating back to the late 1800s, when its four producers, relying on the 600 acres then planted, were winning gold medals for their wines.

IDAHO   The main Idaho wine region is located across the Snake River from Oregon, in the southwestern corner between Boise and Caldwell. Situated at the far western end of the Snake River Valley, most of the vineyards are planted along its slopes above the 2,000-foot level. About 1,000 acres of vineyards have been developed in an area referred to as the Sunny Slope district, where the summer weather is dry and moderate but the growing season is quite short. As a result, most red varieties have difficulties developing full maturity, and some of the whites are tart and overly acidic. Ste. Chapelle is the oldest brand, having established vines in 76 and a winery in 79. It is also the largest, producing over 80,000 cases from 400 acres it either owns outright or leases. A half dozen other wineries perform pioneering work in the state. Early vintages suggest Chenin Blanc and Riesling can be consistently successful. The Chardonnay has yet to come across with the ripe varietal fruitiness needed to complement its otherwise pleasing acidity and body.

KENWOOD *(Sonoma)*   A whistle-stop town located at the midpoint of the Sonoma Valley, Kenwood can also be found on nonwine maps by stopping midway between the city of Santa Rosa to the north and the town of Sonoma to the south. All of this suggests there isn't much there when you find Kenwood, except for three noteworthy wineries—Kenwood, Chateau St. Jean, and St. Francis. Each cultivates vineyards within the town's borders, but only St. Francis relies substantially on home-grown grapes.

KNIGHTS VALLEY *(Sonoma)*   Flanked by Alexander Valley on the north and the Napa Valley on the south, Knights Valley shares warm growing conditions with the Alexander Valley. Most of the approximately 1,000 acres planted belong to Beringer Vineyards. To date the region's most consistent wines are Cabernet Sauvignon and Sauvignon Blanc, both showing ripe fruitiness and modest varietal intensity. Limited amounts of Merlot made by Whitehall Lane Winery have been the most exciting red wine from this region so far. However, several wineries—Peter McCoy Vineyards, Johnson Turnbull, and Peter Michael Winery—have emerged as prominent Knights Valley Chardonnay producers. Completed in 89, the Peter Michael Winery became the first new winery to settle in Knights Valley since Prohibition.

LAKE COUNTY   Located due north of Napa County and directly east of Mendocino County, Lake County is home to a large lake—Clear Lake—and about 3,500 acres of vineyards. Approximately 57% of the total now consists of red varieties, 43% of whites. In 70, only 100 acres contained vines, but tremendous plantings in 73 and 74 brought the total quickly to 2,500. After a lull, expansion resumed in the mid-80s. However, the current total of 3,200 still remains below the 5,000-plus acres that existed during the county's heyday in the 1880s.

Though part of the North Coast appellation, Lake County touches no coasts, and is generally warmer in midsummer than its neighbors to the south and west. It is visited by cooling summer fog only on rare occasions. Many of the vineyards are situated along upper elevations on the mountainous terrain, which allows for a needed cooling evening effect during the summer. The majority of today's vineyards consist of Sauvignon Blanc (600), Chardonnay (550), Cabernet (1,200), and Zinfandel (400), which together represent 80% of the total. Riesling, which was widely planted in 1980, has all but disappeared in favor of Chardonnay and a smattering of Merlot that some growers believe will play a major role in future expansion. So far the most distinctive white varietal has been Sauvignon Blanc. Kendall-Jackson, Guenoc, and Konocti are the major forces among local wineries, but many grapes are sold to wineries outside of the region—often to be blended and sold as North Coast wines. Fetzer buys high percentages of grapes and wines from independent growers in this appellation.

Napa Valley's Louis Martini Winery is developing several hundred acres in Lake County, primarily to Cabernet Sauvignon and other red varieties. Beringer, Sutter Home Winery, Geyser Peak, and Parducci all purchased considerable acreage in the late 80s and have developed vineyards in the county. Geyser Peak has about 300 acres planted in a subregion known as the Benmore Valley, located midway between Lakeport and Hopland. Seven wineries are found in Lake County today.

LIME KILN VALLEY *(San Benito)*   A subregion of the Cienega Valley Viticultural Area, Lime Kiln Valley contains fewer than 100 acres of grapes today. The only producer using it to identify wines at all has been the Enz Winery, which helped define the region and which presently owns 40 acres.

LIVERMORE VALLEY *(Alameda)*   Southeast of San Fransisco, and lying in its own enclosed pocket, is the 15-mile-long, 10-mile-wide Livermore Valley. Settled in the 1880s, this once-famous region has been whittled down by urban expansion until today only about 2,000 acres of vineyards remain. Of the dozen local wineries, Wente and Concannon are the oldest and best-known. Marked by a warm (low Region III) climate and rocky soil, Livermore Valley fares best with Sauvignon Blanc and Semillon.

LODI *(San Joaquin and Sacramento counties)*   Lying between the cities of Stockton and Sacramento, this diverse growing region and designated Viticultural Area starts near the watery Delta area (which forms its western boundary for all intents and purposes) and runs eastward into the hills until it abuts the lower edge of the Sierra Foothills Viticultural Area. For years this has been primarily Zinfandel country, but recent plantings have increased the percentage of whites grown here as well, especially Chenin Blanc, Sauvignon Blanc, and, to a lesser extent, Chardonnay and French Colombard. Although part of the Central Valley, those parts of the Lodi appellation lying nearest the Delta are cooled by its marine-influenced breezes which can lower the average temperature by as much as 10 degrees in midsummer in comparison to the immediately adjoining areas. In addition to being a recognized source of grapes on labels, Lodi is home to a number of wineries. The best known is Robert Mondavi, which makes its generic and inexpensive table wines in Lodi. Lodi is also referred to as the center of California brandy production, which relies substantially on the crush of locally grown Flame Tokay table grapes as the base for the distillation process.

LYTTON SPRINGS *(Sonoma)*   Just north of the town of Healdsburg is a small pocket in the low-lying hills that has been the source of many brawny Zinfandels. This region became famous through Zinfandels made by Ridge Vineyards from grapes grown by the owners of Lytton Springs Winery. The name today appears on red wines made by that winery and also on Ridge Zinfandels, now grown in the general vicinity. This subregion technically belongs to the Alexander Valley Viticultural Area.

MADERA *(Madera and Fresno)*   An appellation in search of a purpose, this 700-square-mile Viticultural Area contains some 33,000 acres of vines, mostly in Madera County, but also some that lie in the northern end of Fresno County. In spite of being given its own special name and the fact that it grows over 10% of the grapevines in California, the Madera appellation is rarely seen on wine labels.

MADERA COUNTY   Its 38,600 acres of wine grapes makes Madera County the most heavily planted county in California. Its mid-Central Valley location marks it mostly as jug-wine country, but several noteworthy ports and dessert wines from the likes of Quady and Ficklin are grown here as well. The major plantings in the county consist of French Colombard (16,600 acres), Chenin Blanc (6,200), Grenache (4,400), Carignane (3,000), and Barbera (2,600). The government-recognized Madera (note the absence of "county") Viticultural Area is located here, as well as in the northern end of adjoining Fresno County. Madera County is now the home of Almadén Vineyards.

MCDOWELL VALLEY *(Mendocino)*   This one-winery Viticultural Area lies in southeastern Mendocino County just east of Hopland. All of the grapes are grown by four independent growers, and by the McDowell Valley Winery, which owns or controls over 600 acres. About 50 acres are planted to Syrah, with the oldest parcel established in 1919. In general, the region is slightly cooler than the Redwood Valley, and is categorized as a Region II. Total acreage now stands at 750, the leading varieties being Chardonnay, Cabernet Sauvignon, and Sauvignon Blanc.

MENDOCINO COUNTY   The northernmost of the coastal regions, Mendocino County established a wine identity of its own by the late 70s. Best known for its rugged, majestic coastline and rough timberlands with giant redwood forests, Mendocino reserves a series of isolated valleys and canyons cut into the hills by the Russian River for vine cultivation. Its primary growing regions are the marine-influenced Anderson Valley, running southeast to northwest in the direction of the Pacific, and the inland Redwood Valley, running south to north with its heaviest concentration of vines around Ukiah. Three small Viticultural Areas in the county—Cole Ranch in the middle, McDowell Valley in the southeast, and Potter Valley in the northeast—help push the total acreage to over 12,000. The majority of the county's wine regions are a warm Region III climate. However, the Anderson Valley directly experiences cooling coastal influences and offers an unusually long growing season. Over 1,000 acres are planted in the Anderson Valley, mostly to cool-climate varieties.

The number of producers within the county now tops three dozen. Among the best known are four of its largest—Fetzer, Parducci, Weibel, and McDowell Valley Vineyards. A relative newcomer that quickly made its presence felt, Roederer Estate, owned by Louis Roederer Champagne, is located in the Anderson Valley. Most of the other producers are small, family-owned enterprises opened for business since 1970.

Historically, the vast majority of grapes in Mendocino were Carignane and Colombard, grown in the Redwood Valley and intended for jug wines. By the mid-70s the county's reputation began to improve with the success of ripe, brawny Zinfandels, powerful Cabernets, and muscular Petite Sirahs. Today, Chardonnay has assumed preeminence with 3,400 acres planted, and Sauvignon Blanc at 900 is more popular than Colombard. Among red varieties, Zinfandel (1,800 acres) and Cabernet Sauvignon (1,300 acres) have edged out Carignane (1,100 acres).

MERRITT ISLAND *(Yolo)*   A part of the much larger Clarksburg Viticultural Area, Merritt Island is located just south of the city of Clarksburg and west of the Sacramento River. The northernmost of the Delta islands, it is cooled by the marine breezes which come up the river from San Francisco Bay but is rarely affected by fog. Its loamy soil separates it from the peaty and claylike soils that are found elsewhere in the Delta. A very warm but not hot growing climate allows Merritt Island to produce passable Chenin Blancs and Petite Sirahs.

MONTEREY *(Monterey County)*   In the Monterey Viticultural Area (formerly the Monterey County Viticultural Area) the primary grape-growing district is an inland valley called the Salinas Valley. Several smaller appellations—Arroyo Seco, Chalone, and the Carmel Valley—are also included within the official boundaries of the Monterey Viticultural Area. In the early 60s the Salinas Valley contained no vines, but university studies identified it as an ideal site for premium wine varieties because of its cool climate and dry summer weather. From less than 5 acres in 1966, the area experienced vineyard expansion to 2,000 acres by 1970. Then a full-scale planting boom got under way, and acreage rose to a peak of 35,000 in 1975. Today, it stands near 28,000.

Over the next few vintages, wines began to appear under the Monterey County appellation. At least some of them, however, were marred by an excessively vegetative character. The most unsuccessful varietal of all was Cabernet Sauvignon, which unfortunately was widely planted; but other red grapes also suffered from an overly aggressive vegetative note.

The problem was eventually traced to highly abnormal growing conditions. The region is extremely dry, with a scant 6 to 8 inches of rainfall per year. Irrigation is a must, and the Salinas Valley was the first wine region in the West to depend entirely on irrigation. The Salinas Valley is also subject to high winds in the summer afternoons, which retard vine maturity. Some vines often had difficulties developing mature grapes with balanced fruit flavors and acids. Growers developed new trellising and vine management techniques to cope with such conditions, or else planted more suitable varieties.

Cabernet Sauvignon, which once covered over 5,000 acres, has been whittled down to 3,400. Today, the Monterey appellation is a region focused on white wine grapes and a more sensible sprinkling of reds in the warmer, southern locations or in a few isolated hillside sites in the north. White varieties represent close to 70% of the total plantings, with Chardonnay topping the list at about 8,500 acres. Chenin Blanc and Johannisberg Riesling are each near the 2,700-acre mark, while Sauvignon Blanc has risen to 1,500 acres. Pinot Blanc, with more than 1,050 acres, claims 58% of California's total; the Riesling acreage represents 52% of all plantings in the state.

Some of the state's most intensely fragrant Johannisberg Rieslings carry the Monterey identity. Though less consistent, Monterey Chardonnays have ranked among the finest and, in the hands of several winemakers, display tremendous varietal intensity and balance. A handful of wineries, notably Monterey Peninsula, and occasionally Smith and Hook, have demonstrated that Cabernet Sauvignon from a few choice sites can result in wines of ✿ ✿ caliber.

Today, the number of wineries located in the area remains over a dozen, ranging in size from Taylor California Cellars and Paul Masson to smaller ones such as Jekel, Morgan, Ventana, and Talbott. Wente, Mirassou, and J. Lohr are all pioneers who own substantial acreage in Monterey and identify many of their wines as Monterey in origin. However, Delicato Vineyards, located in the Central Valley, owns 8,000 acres (most of which is not in vines), which makes it the largest holder of Monterey wine turf. A high percentage of the grape crop still leaves the valley, often destined to be blended.

Chalone Vineyards, though located within the general area, formed the Chalone appellation to separate itself from the Monterey place name.

MONTEREY COUNTY   With over 28,000 acres planted to wine varieties, Monterey County contains several Viticultural Areas. The largest appellation is Monterey, which also includes the Arroyo Seco appellation and contains all but several hundred acres of the county's total wine-grape lands. Chalone in the northeast and the Carmel Valley on the western edge are two other appellations within the county. In the southern area of the county is San Lucas, a Viticultural Area delineated by Almadén Vineyards, but one that has yet to appear on the label of any wine bottle. The number of wineries within the county has grown to 17.

MOUNT VEEDER *(Napa)*   West of Yountville, near the southern extremity of the Mayacamas Mountains, Mount Veeder rises some 2,500 feet above the Napa Valley floor. Dotting its flanks are numerous small vineyards and a few wineries, the best known of which are the Mayacamas Vineyards, long famous for their full-bodied Cabernets and Chardonnays, and the Mount Veeder Winery, whose wines are substantially of the same stripe. Chateau Potelle and Hess Collection are two newer producers on Mount Veeder.

NAPA COUNTY   For all intents and purposes, the Napa County name means Napa Valley when one speaks of grape-growing and winemaking. Virtually every vine standing in the county is, in fact, included within the recognized Napa Valley appellation. Only a small portion of the county, in the upper northeast quadrant, miles removed from the valley itself in distance, climate, and soil type, is not included in this appellation. However, it is the county which is the category employed in measuring such important statistics as grape acreage, number of wineries extant, tonnage crushed, and grape price levels. In addition, some wineries choose to use the Napa County appellation on their labels for a variety of reasons, including philosophical opposition to the use of a "valley" designation for mountain-grown grapes. Within the county, there are about 200 wineries (the most in any county in the U.S.) and some 33,200 acres of wine grapes (fifth highest in California but second among coastal counties). The most widely planted varieties here are Chardonnay (9,600 acres), Cabernet Sauvignon (9,100), Sauvignon Blanc (2,900), and Pinot Noir (2,700). Napa County is the leader in number of wineries and in planted acreage of Cabernet Sauvignon, Sauvignon Blanc, and Merlot; it ranks second in Chardonnay and Pinot Noir acreage.

NAPA VALLEY *(Napa)*   The most famous wine-growing area in the U.S., this land lives up to its Indian moniker as the "Valley of Plenty." As a geographic mass, it begins at the base of Mount St. Helena in the north, dissolving some 30 miles to the south into a floodplain as the Napa River enters San Francisco Bay. From Mount St. Helena to the city of Napa, the valley is defined by two north-south ridgelines of the Coast Range Mountains. The valley floor varies from 3 to 4 miles in width in the south to 1 mile or less in the north. The hills to the west of the valley floor are part of the Mayacamas Range; they contain peaks and watersheds that start with Mount Veeder to the west of Yountville and include Mont St. John, Spring Mountain, and Diamond Mountain as the hills progress up-valley. The hills on the eastern side of the valley are not nearly so important on a winemaking basis or so well known, although Howell Mountain, Pope Valley, and Chiles Valley are all part of that area, and the productive but relatively unknown Gordon and Wooden valleys lie further east again. The bulk of grape growing takes place on the valley floor, and in the gentle slopes adjoining the floor. Indeed, the Napa Valley floor is almost totally committed to vineyards; just as in the developed vineyard areas of Europe, there is little land left that can now be converted into new space for grapes.

From its earliest days, the Napa Valley has been the home of some of California's most famous wine estates, including such well-known producers as Charles Krug, Beringer Brothers, Schramsberg, and Inglenook. Today, the valley boasts upward of 33,000 acres planted to wine grapes and some 200 wineries, most of which offer high-caliber, often expensive wines.

With some notable exceptions, the best California Chardonnays, Cabernet Sauvignons, and Merlots come from the Napa Valley, and the greater part of the valley's worldwide reputation is based on the success of those varietals, which account for over half of its planted acreage. But the valley is large and filled with varied growing conditions that support many varieties with great success. The cool Los Carneros region by San Francisco Bay yields good Chardonnay and Pinot Noir but less frequently produces well-ripened Cabernet Sauvignon. At the other end of the valley, the warm Calistoga area can produce nicely ripe Zinfandel and Petite Sirah as well as near-blockbuster Cabernets, but overcooks Pinot Noir and the other heat-sensitive varieties.

On wine labels, the term "Napa Valley" has historically included all areas within Napa County and now, as a defined Viticultural Area, continues to include all but the most outlying and inhospitable lands of Napa County. Over 20 major sub-areas have been identified within the Napa Valley; 14 have already gained prominence as viticulturally important political subdivisions or recognizable microclimates, and are described in the adjoining pages (see Calistoga, Chiles Valley, Diamond Mountain, Howell Mountain, Los Carneros, Mount Veeder, Oakville, Pope Valley, Rutherford, Rutherford Bench, St. Helena, Spring Mountain, Stag's Leap, and Yountville).

NORTH COAST   Given its somewhat tortured history, once including almost every grape north of Bakersfield, the government-recognized North Coast appellation as now constituted actually makes a good deal of sense. Today it is limited to those coastal and near-coastal counties north of San Francisco which are actually thought of as being north and coastal by the people who live there. Included in this catchall Viticultural Area are the counties of Mendocino, Napa, Sonoma, Lake, Solano, and Marin. While the North Coast's 82,000 acres of grapes form less than 25% of the statewide total, they include about 60% of the state's Merlot, 55% of the Cabernet Sauvignon, and 48% of the Chardonnay.

NORTH YUBA *(Yuba)* Thirty square miles of appellation in the low foothills of the Sierra Nevada Range west of Grass Valley and Nevada City contain a few hundred acres of vines. In granting Viticultural Area status to North Yuba, the government was moved to observe that boundaries define "a region well-suited to viticulture." To date, however, the small acreage of Cabernet Sauvignon, Johannisberg Riesling, and Sauvignon Blanc planted there has yet to prove out that statement.

NORTHERN SONOMA *(Sonoma)* This infrequently used appellation yokes together under one name six Viticultural Areas: Alexander Valley, Dry Creek Valley, Knight's Valley, the Russian River Valley, and its subregions, Chalk Hill and Green Valley. It excludes Sonoma Valley and Los Carneros, along with a series of smaller places within the county. Historically, Northern Sonoma has been used by Bandiera, Foppiano, and the now defunct Cordtz Bros. Winery. In the 80s, only Seghesio Winery has labeled wines as Northern Sonoma with any regularity. However, when the appellation was being proposed, the Gallo Winery argued strongly in its favor. With a winemaking facility in Dry Creek Valley and long-term grape contracts with many growers in this Viticultural Area, Gallo may someday bottle wines at its Sonoma facility that could be identified as estate bottled.

OAKVILLE *(Napa)* Situated in the southern half of the Napa Valley, midway between Yountville and Rutherford, this way station is the home of several wineries (foremost among them the Robert Mondavi Winery) and adjoins some of the Napa Valley's best Cabernet-growing turf. The superb Martha's Vineyard produced by Heitz Cellars and a substantial portion of the Robert Mondavi and Beaulieu Vineyard vines are in Oakville, along the western edge of the valley floor right in the middle of the justifiably famous Rutherford Bench. Other wineries in the area include De Moor and Far Niente on the bench, the Inglenook production facility (but not its visitor center, which is in Rutherford), and Girard, Silver Oaks, and Villa Mount Eden across the valley floor.

OREGON From modest beginnings in the mid-60s, the Oregon wine industry came of age in the 80s to earn international praise by the end of its first quarter century. With 85 wineries in operation, and over 150 independent grape growers located in the state's five small growing regions, Oregon now produces a little under 1 million gallons of vinifera and close to 75,000 gallons of fruit and berry wines. The primary growing regions—the Willamette Valley and the Umpqua Valley—are located 60 miles inland from the Pacific. As a river valley/watershed, the Willamette Valley begins a little northwest of Portland in the Tualatin Valley and extends south through Eugene. The smaller Umpqua Valley is located in the south and is carved out by the Umpqua River. A smaller, warmer region known as the Rogue River Valley is emerging in the south. The Willamette and Umpqua Valley regions in western Oregon are situated on hills overlooking small valleys which form a north-south corridor, and they struggle to ripen fruit in a climate that is cool and wet by California standards. Yet the climate is drier during the growing season than France's Burgundy region. The typical Oregon growing season lasts from April through the end of October. The last three weeks of October often run the risk of early fall rainstorms.

The prime variety is Pinot Noir, which now covers more than 1,000 acres. Pinot Noir, Riesling, and Chardonnay, the three top varieties, account for 75% of the 4,200 acres under vine by 90. Riesling remains the best-selling wine within Oregon. However, a few producers have ignored Riesling in favor of Pinot Gris, a white variety widely believed by some growers to be the third best variety for Oregon after Pinot Noir and Chardonnay. About 150 acres of Pinot Gris have been established to date. Oregon's finest Pinot Noirs tend toward the cherry-berry side of the varietal spectrum, with a sometimes wiry, medium-bodied feel, and relatively high acidity. Most others, even in fine vintages, seem to have a somewhat narrow flavor profile, though the aromas are often beautifully complex. Chardonnays as a rule tend to be austere and hard, though exceptions are frequent enough to hold our attention. Minor initial interest in producing sparkling wine surfaced in the late 80s. At around the same time, several wine companies from both Europe and California were beginning to invest in Oregon vineyards, spurred on by the state's reputation for Pinot Noir and by the relatively low cost of vineyard land.

In the mid-70s, Oregon winemakers imposed a few special regulations governing their labeling. First, learning from California's mistakes, Oregon banned the use of generic names derived from European types—Chablis, Burgundy, Champagne. Second, to carry a varietal name, an Oregon wine must contain at least 90% of the designated variety; Cabernet Sauvignon is an exception and follows the federal varietal minimum of 75%. To warrant an appellation of origin, Oregon law requires that 100% of the wine originate in the region named on the label.

PACHECO PASS *(San Benito and Santa Clara)* Flanked east and west by the hills of the Diablo Mountain Range, Pacheco Pass is a small Viticultural Area—5 miles long, 1 mile wide—where several modest wineries are located. The winemaking emphasis falls upon everyday table wine, sold mostly to locals and to tourists wandering through on their way elsewhere.

PACIFIC NORTHWEST Linked geographically, the burgeoning wine states of Washington, Oregon, and later Idaho banded together in the 70s in order to focus national attention on the area and gain respect for the vinifera wines produced. Climatically, the Pacific Northwest wine regions are generally cooler overall and unlike most of California's growing areas. Therefore, the growers and winemakers are confronted by different problems and situations. However, most of the pioneering winemakers and the current new generation learned their trade in California and are much closer philosophically to California than to Europe or elsewhere. We sense more of a kinship between the Northwest and California vintners than any rivalry, friendly or otherwise. Besides, most of the wines from the Northwest are available in many important wine markets today. Over the last two decades the Northwest has produced much more white wine than red. About two-thirds of the total 17,000 acres is in Washington.

PAICINES *(San Benito)* Located in the relatively warm plains 12 miles south of Hollister, Paicines was once an important growing region for Almadén Vineyards. It is a Region III growing area in terms of climate because during the summer days ocean breezes and an occasional fog roll in, to make it cooler than Fresno, which is located to the southeast. After Almadén was sold in 87, the 2,000 acres under vine remained. The Enz Vineyards and its 40-acre vineyard are located here.

PASO ROBLES *(San Luis Obispo)* With over a century of grape-growing history, the Viticultural Area of Paso Robles is in the northern part of the county, the town of Paso Robles comprising its focal point. It is a large area (over 600,000 acres), consisting mostly of the low-lying land and the foothills, bordered on the west by the Santa Lucia Mountains and extending east to the foothills known as the Cholame Hills. Along the modest elevations the climate is generally Region III, which makes many of its sites well suited to Cabernet Sauvignon and Zinfandel. In the late 80s vineyard acreage approached 7,000 total, with white varieties beginning to enjoy a slight lead. The primary whites grown are Sauvignon Blanc, Chardonnay, and Chenin Blanc. Zinfandel and Cabernet lead the red contingent handily in terms of total acreage, and also in terms of overall quality. However, some success has been achieved by the Syrah variety from the large planting (35 acres) established by Estrella River Winery. After a few wineries experienced financial difficulties in the 70s, renewed interest in the following decade brought the number of wine producers to the two dozen mark. Most are small and family-owned; Arciero and Meridian (formerly Estrella River Winery) are the two largest by quite a margin.

POPE VALLEY   Nestled in the hills east of the main portion of the Napa Valley, this hot and dry depression hosts a few hundred acres of vines that suffer a shorter, hotter growing season than the main valley but are, for financial and historical reasons, still entitled to use its prestigious appellation. Wines from this subsection have generally proven to be as rustic as the setting, but St. Supéry Vineyards, using grapes from the Dollarhide Ranch in Pope Valley, has produced tamer wines.

POTTER VALLEY *(Mendocino)*   The most northerly region in the North Coast, Potter Valley now contains approximately 1,000 acres of wine varieties. Chardonnay, Sauvignon Blanc, and Johannisberg Riesling have historically been the major varieties planted. Pinot Noir was increasing in acreage in the late 80s. Generally, Potter Valley contains deep, rich soils. The climate is characterized by extremely warm days and cool nights, and by early rains which when not excessive often encourage *Botrytis* to occur on Riesling and Semillon. Most grapes are sold to producers outside the region who mix them as part of a Mendocino County appellation. In the late 80s several producers, including La Crema and Hidden Cellars, made successful Pinot Noir from this region. Both Scharffenberger and Shadow Creek use Chardonnay and Pinot Noir from Potter Valley for their sparkling wines. To meet the demand, growers have added Pinot Noir along the higher-elevation sites. Most of the white varieties are grown on the valley floor.

REDWOOD VALLEY *(Mendocino)*   Following the northern meanderings of the Russian River, the Redwood Valley by consensus of Mendocino wine producers begins 15 miles north of Ukiah and continues south until it ends about a mile below Ukiah. North of Ukiah, the region fans out to encompass Lake Mendocino and includes the major grape-growing territory in and around Ukiah—Talmage, the Sanel Valley, and Hopland. More than 8,000 acres are located within the Redwood Valley, a name used primarily by Fetzer and by several others. In the 70s many dry-farmed hillside vineyards in the Redwood Valley produced excellent Zinfandels and Petite Sirahs to help launch Mendocino as a wine region.

ROGUE RIVER VALLEY / APPLEGATE VALLEY   Located in southwest Oregon not far from the California border, this area enjoys a warmer climate than other parts of Oregon. The main metropolis is the Medford-Jacksonville area on the eastern edge. Most vineyards are located at elevations above the 1,000-foot level or higher which look down on those towns. The limited amounts of wines produced from this region over the first decade offer some encouragement for Chardonnay and Cabernet Sauvignon. Valley View Winery is the best-known producer in this area.

RUSSIAN RIVER VALLEY *(Sonoma)*   The Russian River ranks among the longest rivers in Northern California and helps define quite a few wine regions within Sonoma County as it meanders through. As a Viticultural Area, the Russian River Valley consists of the low-lying flat plains between Healdsburg and Sebastopol which extend westward as the river heads toward the Pacific. At Guerneville, the coastal hills close off the area and mark its western boundary. The Russian River Valley includes the western half of Chalk Hill and all of Green Valley–Sonoma. Its total vineyard acreage now approaches 9,000. The soil types are widely varied, with most of the vines planted on benchlands or bottom lands. The region's climate is quite uniform in that it is cooled by fog intrusion and by proximity to the river. In the southwest sector, fog is a frequent intruder in July and August, which makes that portion well suited to Chardonnay, Gewurztraminer, and Pinot Noir. Also, the same conditions make the lower Russian River Valley hospitable to Pinot Noir and Chardonnay grown especially for sparkling wines. Some success has even been achieved in making dry-styled Gewurztraminers and Johannisberg Rieslings from Russian River Valley grapes. However, the crowning achievements of the entire region go to Chardonnay and Pinot Noir.

Over 50 wineries reside within this appellation. Those that use it regularly and that also help define its capabilities include Sonoma-Cutrer, Dehlinger, De Loach, J. Rochioli, Hop Kiln, and Mark West.

RUTHERFORD *(Napa)*   If Napa Valley is the name most likely to be associated with exceptional California wine, then Rutherford must stand next in line, especially for Cabernet Sauvignon. To be sure, Rutherford town as a place is not much. As a political subdivision, it is a swath cut across the Napa Valley from side to side rather than one identifiable and cohesive source of grapes. But Rutherford has lent its name to the western benchland that encompasses areas both north and south of the town and grows Cabernet Sauvignon known round the world. And it is Rutherford which grows some of the best valley floor Cabernet for Caymus, Raymond, and Sterling (a handsome, aromatic wine which becomes a part of Sterling's Reserve bottling). For years, insiders have referred to the special character of wines from the area as "Rutherford Dust." For us, it is closer to a rich, loamy, near-spicy/rooty quality that fits perfectly with the deep, curranty, and sometimes black-cherry fruit of Rutherford Cabernets. In some wines—especially those grown on the Rutherford Bench— this added seasoning can head in the direction of tea leaves, mint, and allspice.

RUTHERFORD BENCH   By now the wine world knows that the benchland of warm alluvial soils lying along the western edge of the Napa Valley floor from Yountville to St. Helena yields much of the best Cabernet Sauvignon in California. It has been doing so for the entire half century since the end of Prohibition and was doing so another half century before that. Whether it was good luck or good thinking that landed Napa Valley pioneers like Captain Gustave Niebaum of Inglenook there around 1880 and Georges de Latour in 1900, their early successes along the Rutherford Bench have led inexorably to the great California Cabernets of today.

Recent work aimed at establishing the Bench as an official Viticultural Area has shown that two adjoining alluvial fans—one near Rutherford and the other near Oakville—extend from just north of Yountville some 6 miles until they run out just south of St. Helena somewhere in the Zinfandel Lane area. With the exception of the area between Rutherford and Oakville, in which the alluvial soils cross the highway by some half-mile or so, all of the land of the Rutherford Bench lies west of Highway 29. This revered expanse of well-drained, gently sloping vineyards is home to grapes that appear in a veritable *Who's Who* of Cabernet Sauvignon. Among the producers who draw grapes from the Bench are Robert Mondavi, Joseph Phelps, Beaulieu, Heitz Wine Cellars (both its Martha's Vineyard and its Bella Oaks bottlings are from the Rutherford Bench), Inglenook, Grgich Hills, Opus One, Far Niente, Sequoia Grove, Cakebread, and Freemark Abbey (Bosche)—to name a few.

Today, there are some 2,500 acres of grapes planted on the Bench, of which Cabernet Sauvignon and its blending partners comprise an estimated 80%, a substantial change in the last 15 years brought about mainly by the increased recognition of the area as a site for high-quality Cabernet and the resulting increase in the value of Cabernet grown there. A smaller amount of Chardonnay also appears, especially in the lower, colder, creekside locations. Recent work by growers and wineries in the area suggests that the Rutherford Bench may be broken into four separate Viticultural Areas—Rutherford Bench, Oakville Bench, Rutherford, and Oakville. There is also a line of argument that all of the land west of the Napa River in this section of the valley should benefit from being called Rutherford Bench. No government ruling has been issued to date and the arguments continue.

SACRAMENTO COUNTY   While not famous for its viticultural achievements or even very often noted on wine labels, Sacramento County has slowly increased its standing as a wine-producing area because the fertile soils south and southeast of the city of Sacramento receive cooling breezes off the nearby water-oriented Delta area. All of this territory is included in the recognized Viticultural Area of Lodi, which also includes portions of northern San Joaquin

County. Cabernet Sauvignon (1,100 acres) and Chardonnay (800) are the leading grape varieties among the county's 4,000 acres planted.

ST. HELENA *(Napa)*   This picturesque town and its environs are host to several dozen wineries, including such historically important producers as Beringer, Charles Krug, Christian Brothers, and Louis Martini. Among important newer properties, St. Helena can boast Heitz Cellars, Joseph Phelps, Duckhorn, and St. Clement. The vineyards surrounding St. Helena range in climate from Region II just west of town to warmer Region III conditions elsewhere. The low-lying, creekside soils often produce above-average to superb Chardonnays, while the hillside slopes along the western edge of the valley floor are earning a reputation for Cabernet. Here, in what seems like an extension of the Rutherford Bench in soil type and exposure, have been grown grapes for such notable producers as Spottswoode, Duckhorn, and Merryvale. Across the valley, the eastern hillsides get the hot late-afternoon sun and are agreeable hosts to Zinfandel and Syrah.

SAN BENITO *(San Benito)*   Just about every vine within San Benito County is part of this Viticultural Area. As such, the appellation begins 2 miles south of Hollister and follows the San Benito River for several miles. Though the landmass encompasses 45,000 acres, only 1,700 are vineyards. Three of the county's other Viticultural Areas—Paicines, Cienega, and Lime Kiln Valley—are within the borders of San Benito. At present, three producers call this one home. Calera is the best known, and it is one of the few producers in recent year to use San Benito as an appellation.

SAN BENITO COUNTY   For years anything involving grape growing and winemaking within San Benito County could be traced directly to Almadén Vineyards. The winery owned most of the acreage, and during peak production period its acreage exceeded 4,500. As Almadén's sales slipped in the 80s, the county's acreage diminished accordingly. The county contains four Viticultural Areas. Almadén was also directly responsible for defining two of them—Paicines and Cienega—where its production facilities were located. Lime Kiln Valley and San Benito are the others. Over the years Almadén offered a range of varietals from San Benito County that rose above average in quality only on rare occasions. Before the 80s ended, Almadén had new owners who immediately closed both facilities in the county and moved all operations to Madera in the Central Valley. Only a portion of Almadén's holdings in San Benito County were harvested after the move. Vineyards here cover 1,800 acres.

SAN JOAQUIN COUNTY   Near the northern end of the grape-growing area within the Central Valley, the very warm vineyards of San Joaquin (especially in the Lodi and Delta areas) benefit from their proximity to the Delta by receiving the cooling marine breezes that flow across it from San Francisco Bay. This may account for the somewhat higher reputation enjoyed by San Joaquin County's wines in comparison to its even hotter neighbors to the south. The plantings in the 37,700 acres of vineyards located here are a mix of rapidly disappearing old-fashioned varieties (Alicante Bouschet, Mission, Palomino), coastal grapes hoping to benefit from the occasional fog, and the typical high-acid choices for new Central Valley plantings. The 12,700 acres of Zinfandel in the county represent about 40% of the statewide plantings and an even greater percentage of the total tonnage. Reportedly, they are the basis for much of the White Zinfandel selling at low prices. Other grapes include: Chardonnay (4,500 acres), French Colombard (4,200), Carignane (3,600), Chenin Blanc (3,300), Cabernet Sauvigon (3,200), and Sauvignon Blanc (1,500).

SAN JOAQUIN VALLEY   The southern portion of the Central Valley running south from the Stockton-Sacramento area to Bakersfield is often referred to as the San Joaquin Valley (to distinguish it from the Sacramento Valley, which runs north from Sacramento). The San Joaquin Valley is one of the world's most fertile agricultural regions and offers hospitable conditions to all but the most tender plants (leafy greens and some citrus fruits, for instance). As a grape-growing area, it tends to be too hot for the prime varieties but suitably productive for grapes that tolerate heat well, and as a result is the source of most of the jug wine produced in California. Within the counties that make up the San Joaquin Valley (San Joaquin, Stanislaus, Merced, Madera, Fresno, Tulare, Kings, and Kern) some 160,000 acres of wine grapes stand in production (about 50% of the statewide total); and because of the higher yields gained from the grape varieties planted, new viticultural techniques, and extra heat, the San Joaquin Valley crush constitutes almost 70% of all wine grapes crushed in California. By contrast, Napa County holds 10% of the state's wine grapevines but crushes just 2% of the statewide total.

Except for the medium-warm area of the San Joaquin Valley, which abuts the Delta and is high Region III in heat accumulation during the growing season, most of the valley is rated as hot Region IV and V and rarely produces noteworthy wine. Nevertheless, most San Joaquin Valley wine, like other California jug wine, is clean, vinous, and made to be palatable when young. As such, it makes up the greatest part of the wine consumed in this country and is beginning to make inroads in the rest of the world.

SAN JOSE *(Santa Clara)*   This fast-growing urban area (population close to 1 million) has seen the number of wineries in the vicinity steadily diminish over recent years. In the 80s longtime resident Almadén Vineyards pulled a disappearing act, and two others with facilities within the city, Paul Masson and Llords & Elwood, have also closed. As a result, San Jose can now claim only Mirassou and J. Lohr as hometown favorites.

SAN LUIS OBISPO COUNTY   This county is a part of the Central Coast region and, in terms of wine activity, really began to come alive in the early 80s. The total acreage now exceeds 8,300, with red and white varieties about equal. The majority of the vineyards can be found in its two principal growing regions, the Viticultural Areas of Paso Robles and the Edna Valley. (Both regions appear as separate entries.)

About 20 wineries are located within the county. Overall, the leading varieties are Chardonnay (2,400), Cabernet Sauvignon (2,400), Zinfandel (1,300), Sauvignon Blanc (700), and Chenin Blanc (300). Other Viticultural Areas are found within its borders—York Mountain and a small portion of the Santa Maria Valley.

SANTA BARBARA COUNTY   Some of the most picturesque vineyards in the entire state can be found in this Central Coast county, along the coast north of Los Angeles. The modern era of winemaking started relatively late here, but grew surprisingly fast. From 11 acres in 69, the county expanded to over 7,000 acres a decade later. Today's total approaches the 9,300 mark, pushed along by the two dozen local wineries. The majority of the plantings are found in two Viticultural Areas north of the city of Santa Barbara: the Santa Ynez Valley and Santa Maria Valley.

White wine varieties cover over 75% of the vineyarded areas, the leaders being Chardonnay (5,100), Johannisberg Riesling (700), Sauvignon Blanc (500), and Chenin Blanc (500). Cabernet Sauvignon and Pinot Noir near 900 acres each top the red varieties. The most successful wines have been Chardonnay and Riesling. Among the reds, Pinot Noir, though erratic, has greatly outdistanced Cabernet Sauvignon, which is usually hindered by a strong herbaceous character.

Firestone, Brander, Byron, Sanford, and Zaca Mesa are among the nationally known brands from the county. In the 80s, however, a nucleus of small, highly experimental wineries and brands appeared, such as Au Bon Climat and Qupe, to add excitement and draw attention to Santa Barbara as a wine region.

SANTA CLARA COUNTY   Once among the leaders for both volume produced and wine quality, this fast-urbanizing area has managed to preserve only small pieces of its immense wine heritage. The once abundant vineyards to the north and east of San Jose have been replaced by homes and malls. Of the 950 remaining acres, the majority is concentrated in the south, in and around Gilroy. Though the number of wineries within the county approaches 30, only Mirassou and J. Lohr are left in San Jose. These two, however, are the county's largest producers. Chardonnay is the leading variety, with 275 acres. All but the smallest producers rely on grapes from outside the county. Hecker Pass and Santa Clara Valley are Viticultural Areas within this county. Both the Santa Cruz Mountain and Pacheco Pass Viticultural Areas lie partly within it.

SANTA CLARA VALLEY *(Santa Clara)*   Most of the still-standing vineyards in Santa Clara County are found within the Santa Clara Valley. As a Viticultural Area, this valley encompasses the present acreage (under 100) in southern Alameda County, from Pleasanton on south through the Sunol Valley. Its western border is shared with the eastern boundary of the Santa Cruz Mountains Viticultural Area. However, most of the vineyards that once existed in the north are history, except for a few mountain vineyards to the north and west of San Jose. Otherwise, grape-growing is largely confined today to the lower part of the valley, south of San Jose. Fewer than 1,000 acres remain, scattered among such quaint areas as Morgan Hill, Hecker Pass, and Gilroy. Chardonnay and Cabernet Sauvignon are the leading varieties in acreage.

SANTA CRUZ COUNTY   A cool coastal county located between Monterey and San Mateo County, Santa Cruz is home to quite a few wineries (over 20) for a region with a total of only 100 acres planted. However, many of the winemakers are part-time and work in either San Jose or other parts of Silicon Valley within commuting distance. The region has a cool Region I climate, and the leading varieties planted are Pinot Noir, Cabernet Sauvignon, and Chardonnay. Most wine producers regularly purchase grapes from outside the region, often from the Central Coast, to supplement the local supply. But even those wines made exclusively from county-grown acreage are usually identified as originating in the Santa Cruz Mountains appellation.

SANTA CRUZ MOUNTAINS   This Viticultural Area begins in the coastal mountain range rising south of San Francisco and extends south well beyond San Jose. Since the early 19th century, it has been collectively referred to as the Santa Cruz Mountains. It officially includes part of southern San Mateo County, and the mountainous area on the Santa Cruz side of the ridge, as well as the entire ridgeline through Santa Cruz County. The predominant varieties planted in this generally mountainous region are Chardonnay, Pinot Noir, and Cabernet Sauvignon. The region's two dozen wineries are generally small in output but boundless in ambition. The best known include Ridge Vineyards, David Bruce, Roudon-Smith, Santa Cruz Mountain Vineyard, and Bonny Doon.

SANTA MARIA VALLEY *(Santa Barbara)*   Except for a tiny bit of its northern boundary which slips over into San Luis Obispo County, this Viticultural Area is located within Santa Barbara County. It is a pretty valley, lying south and east of Santa Maria and extending south toward Los Alamos. The climate is regarded as a cool Region II, but a few isolated pockets in the west are cooled directly by ocean breezes and are a Region I. The soil tends to be sandy loam, but it becomes light sand in those vineyards close to the ocean. Such sandy soil heats up quickly and holds heat for a long time to compensate for cool weather. Of the present 7,000 acres under vines, the best and most consistent results have been achieved with Chardonnay. Some exciting though erratic results have come from Pinot Noir. In the late 70s–early 80s, many vintners from both the Central Coast and North Coast regions purchased grapes from Santa Maria. Several outsiders like Beringer, Robert Mondavi Winery, ZD, and Kendall-Jackson were among the first major buyers of Santa Maria white varieties, mainly Chardonnay.

By the late 80s, many producers both within and outside of the area, fearing a shortage of Chardonnay, became interested in purchasing well-regarded, independently owned vineyards and vineyard sites within Santa Maria. Robert Mondavi and Kendall-Jackson joined forces to purchase the large (1,400 acres) Tepusquet Vineyard. Jackson acquired 1,000 acres; Robert Mondavi took possession of 340 acres. Beringer's parent company, Wine World, Inc., acquired several vineyards in the area, including the 2,000-acre Rancho San Antonio, planted predominantly to Chardonnay. Two other prominent vineyards whose grapes are highly regarded are the Sierra Madre Vineyards (670 acres) and Bien Nacido Vineyards. Both names have appeared on several noteworthy Pinot Noir bottlings. Bien Nacido is also the source of Syrah bottled by Qupe and Bonny Doon Vineyards. Founded in 84 and producing 15,000 cases a year, Byron Vineyards was the region's first major winery and also its largest until Cambria produced close to 50,000 cases in 90.

SANTA YNEZ VALLEY *(Santa Barbara)*   Having its western border defined by the ocean front, the Santa Ynez Valley enjoys the cooling influence dictated by the flow of fog and offshore breezes. The valley itself surrounds the Santa Ynez River and extends east until it meets the Los Padres National Forest. The climate is a cool Region II. Most of the county's wineries are clustered within the Santa Ynez Valley, which also is home to the colorful Danish community of Solvang. In the early 70s, the Firestone Vineyard was among the first to establish extensive acreage and it has, ever since, assumed the pioneering role. Zaca Mesa, Brander, and Au Bon Climat have all helped bring national recognition to this area. Overall, the consensus is that white varietals led by Chardonnay and Riesling enjoy success and consistency among white wines. Chardonnay has risen above ✿ ranking on a regular basis. Though recent vintages of Cabernet Sauvignon show improvements over their predecessors, Cabernet Sauvignon continues to vary widely in styles but usually contains vegetal notes. However, by the mid-80s the number of attractive Pinot Noirs began to increase. On some occasions, Pinot Noirs from this appellation have been standouts. The Los Alamos Vineyard, now owned by Corbett Canyon, and the Benedict Vineyard were often identified in the 80s as the source for several noteworthy Pinot Noirs.

SHENANDOAH VALLEY *(Amador)*   Despite its grape-growing history dating from the 1880s, the Shenandoah Valley is in some ways a discovery of modern times. Until the late 1960s, the grapes grown there, mostly Zinfandel, were sold under contract to jug-wine producers or in the smallest of lots to home winemakers. Then, building on the reputation being garnered by the intrepid amateurs, the Sutter Home winery gave Shenandoah Valley Zinfandel a try and put the region back on California's wine map. Soon, a dozen Zinfandel makers were making the trek to the Sierras and offering Shenandoah, and other foothill, wines. Plantings were tripled (now in the range of 1,200 acres), still mostly Zinfandel along with a noticeable amount of Sauvignon Blanc (now the area's number-two grape), and new wineries were founded. In the early 80s, when Zinfandel—especially the heavy, jammy style prevalent in the Shenandoah Valley—went temporarily out of fashion, most of the coastal-based winemakers abandoned the area. Now most of the grapes grown in the area are vinified there as well. Formal Viticultural Area status was granted in 1983.

SIERRA FOOTHILLS *(Amador, Calaveras, El Dorado, Mariposa, Nevada, Placer, Tuolomne, and Yuba)*   East of Sacramento and Stockton, which lie on the floor of the Central Valley, rise the majestic Sierra Nevada Mountains. Partway up this 10,000-foot-high range, about an hour's drive from the lowlands, runs a belt of foothills at 1,000- to 3,000-foot elevations that have a long, if uneven, history for winemaking. During the Gold Rush era, places like El Dorado, Placer, Calaveras, and Amador counties were reported to have contained up to 10,000 acres of grapes. By 1970, when the area was rediscovered by makers of varietal wines, there were fewer than 1,000 acres standing. Most of that was in Amador County and was purchased by jug-wine makers. In the ensuing two decades, acreage has grown to approximately 3,200. Some two dozen wineries have established themselves throughout the 160-mile-long swath of the recognized Sierra Foothills Viticultural Area, which extends from Yuba County in the north to Mariposa County in the south. Amador County with 1,800 acres and El Dorado County with 500 acres are the most active regions within the Sierra Foothills area, and Zinfandel (1,400 acres) and Sauvignon Blanc (400 acres) the favored varieties.

SOLANO COUNTY   Though its 1,200 acres of grapes do not make much of a splash in the California wine pool, and the places where grapes are grown lie mostly at the fringes of the county rather than at its heart, Solano County nonetheless can claim three separate and distinct Viticultural Areas within its borders. Solano's Green Valley and Suisun Valley areas lie on the western edge of the county, near the eastern borders of Napa County, while the Clarksburg appellation sits astride the Delta area at Solano County's easternmost boundaries, where it runs into Yolo and San Joaquin counties. There are about 400 acres of Chardonnay and 200 acres each of Cabernet Sauvignon and Sauvignon Blanc.

SONOMA COAST *(Sonoma)*   This large (750-square-mile) Viticultural Area was created to include only those sections of the county categorized as a Region I or cool (under 2,800 degree days) Region II. It excludes the Alexander Valley, the Dry Creek Valley, and the western, hilly portion of Chalk Hill. Sonoma Coast does overlap other Viticultural Areas such as Green Valley–Sonoma, Los Carneros, Sonoma Valley (but only from the south to the town of Sonoma), and the lower end of the Russian River Valley known as the Santa Rosa plain. The coast serves as its western border beginning a few miles north of Bodega Bay and Fort Ross. To the southwest, Sonoma Coast ends at the Sonoma-Marin border. As a result, potential vineyard areas in and around Penngrove, Petaluma, Lakeville, Cotati, and all along the coastal ridgetops which had been excluded from other Viticultural Areas became part of this place name. All told, close to 12,000 acres of vineyards are included. Sonoma-Cutrer and Sea Ridge Winery were among the first to use this appellation.

SONOMA COUNTY   Prior to 1970 Sonoma County was a rural, tranquil wine region, best known for its generally pleasing, modestly priced red jug wines. In fact, except for a brief period in the mid-1800s when Sonoma Valley was the hub of winemaking activity in Northern California, Sonoma County had always run a distant second to its neighbor, Napa County. But within the last two decades, Sonoma County has emerged as home to many fine wines, to numerous high-energy, well-financed producers, and to several significant Viticultural Areas. Today, the county has closed the gap, and is regularly well represented among the highest-ranked wines, especially Zinfandels, Sauvignon Blancs, and Chardonnays.

Sonoma County awakened to the wine boom a few years after Napa Valley had come alive. Despite the late start, it eventually experienced dramatic growth and change. Before 1970, most of the planted grape acreage consisted of the hearty red jug-wine varieties—Petite Sirah, Carignane, and Zinfandel. The primary white grape at the time was French Colombard. Of the 33 wineries within Sonoma at that time, the majority were longtime family-owned producers turning out a range of wines, sometimes under their own brands, but more often selling them as bulk wines to neighbors in Napa Valley. In the vineyards the emphasis fell generally on tonnage, as growers favored high-yielding varieties and methods.

Today, however, Sonoma County is a far different place on the wine map. In areas where the primary crops were once walnuts, pears, peaches, almonds, and prunes, grapevines now predominate. The total acreage has shot up to over 33,000, which places it in just about a dead heat with Napa County. The major change within Sonoma is in the mix of varieties cultivated. The county experienced such a rapid conversion to premium wine varieties that, at the start of the 90s, over 70% of its plantings consisted of Chardonnay, Cabernet Sauvignon, Zinfandel, Pinot Noir, and Sauvignon Blanc. More significantly, the breakdown of grapes grown in this one-time red jug-wine county shows whites nearly as plentiful as reds. Today, the primary white varieties planted in terms of acreage are Chardonnay (11,300), Sauvignon Blanc (1,600), Colombard (700), and Gewurztraminer (400). The leading reds are Cabernet Sauvignon (6,500), Zinfandel (4,200), Pinot Noir (3,000), and Merlot (1,900). By 90, Sonoma County had become the leading county for both Chardonnay and Pinot Noir cultivation, and it is the leader in the North Coast for Zinfandel.

The county of Sonoma covers more territory than Napa County and contains a wide range of climatic zones. As a result, the growers and winemakers agreed to define those places and push for their recognition as federally approved Viticultural Areas. By the mid-80s over a dozen such Viticultural Areas had been identified. Among the first to be defined were the county's cooler zones, such as Los Carneros, Sonoma Valley, and the Russian River Valley, as well as warmer inland regions such as Alexander Valley, Dry Creek Valley, and Knight's Valley. A number of other Viticultural Areas have been delineated since 1983, such as Chalk Hill, Green Valley, Northern Sonoma, Sonoma Mountain, and Sonoma Coast. Despite the numerous narrowly defined regions, most of Sonoma County's 180 wineries identify their wines as Sonoma County.

Sonoma County has built a strong reputation for Chardonnay, Sauvignon Blanc, and Gewurztraminer among white varietals. Both ✿ and ✿✿ Chardonnays have originated in the Alexander Valley, Dry Creek Valley, and Russian River Valley. Among red wines, Zinfandels from Dry Creek Valley, Alexander Valley, and Sonoma Valley are some of the most flavorful and distinctive. Both Merlot and Pinot Noir from the cooler regions are showing steady improvement. Cabernet Sauvignon can be excellent, but as yet has not equaled the consistency and excitement of Napa Valley Cabernet Sauvignons. However, some fine Cabernets have emanated from the Alexander Valley, Sonoma Mountain, and the Sonoma Valley in particular. Sparkling wines have started to come on strong through a cluster of producers relying on Russian River Valley grapes for their cuvées.

The number of wineries and vineyards within Sonoma County is likely to continue growing. Two of the oldest wineries in Sonoma County, Sebastiani Vineyards and Korbel, are its two leaders in terms of volume.

SONOMA MOUNTAIN *(Sonoma)*   This Viticultural Area, a subregion of the Sonoma Valley, is located along the mountain range just to the west of Glen Ellen. It includes east-facing vineyards at the 400- to 600-foot elevation, and west-facing land located at the 1,200- to 1,600-foot elevation. These slopes share similar soils identified as Spreckles-Felta. By virtue of being above the fog line this appellation enjoys a climate that is warmer than the valley floor, but also it is an unusual climate because the daily temperature does not fluctuate widely during the growing season. The total acres planted now stand at close to 650, the majority being Cabernet Sauvignon and Zinfandel. Laurel Glen Vineyards is the best-known winery within this appellation.

SONOMA VALLEY *(Sonoma)*   Nestled between the gentle Sonoma Mountain Range on the west and the towering Mayacamas Mountains on the east, the Sonoma Valley is a picturesque wine valley with a rich history. It was in this valley, also known as the Valley of the Moon, that North Coast winemaking began back in 1825 when the missionary fathers established Mission Sonoma. By the 1850s, thanks to the dealings and accomplishments of Agoston Haraszthy, who started the valley's first winery, Buena Vista, Sonoma Valley had evolved into a winemaking center, better known to the world than Napa Valley. However, by the end of the 19th century the Sonoma Valley was eclipsed by its neighbor to the east. As an appellation, it did not call attention to itself until the early 1970s.

Today the Sonoma Valley, with 6,500 acres planted to wine grapes, actually stretches for some 40 miles as one traces it from the San Pablo Bay in the south to just below Santa Rosa in the north. The generally welcomed summer fog enters the valley from points both north and south. But the cooler regions by

93

far are located toward the south, primarily in the Los Carneros District. In the valley's midsection between Glen Ellen and Kenwood, the climate along the valley floor warms. However, Sonoma Valley's grape acreage, though quite compact, covers such a wide array of soil types, elevations, and topography that the viticultural conditions probably vary as much in this small space as in other larger wine regions of California.

Some general patterns have emerged. In the southern Sonoma Valley from Los Carneros on up to the town of Sonoma, the best wines come from early-maturing varieties: Chardonnay, Gewurztraminer, Pinot Noir, and, from some producers, Merlot. On the hillsides and along the hilltops both eastern and western, so long as the elevation is above the frost line, Cabernet and Zinfandel usually fare the best. The two most widely cultivated grapes in the valley, Chardonnay and Pinot Noir, perform better than average along the benchlands between Sonoma and Kenwood. Cabernet and Zinfandel are the next two popular varieties.

Most of the 30 wineries in the valley were founded after 1970, except for Sebastiani and Buena Vista, the two oldest. Most of the producers remain small to mid-sized. Sebastiani is larger than any of them by a wide margin.

SOUTH COAST   Similar in concept to North Coast and Central Coast, South Coast is a multi-county Viticultural Area bringing together a portion of southwestern Riverside County, the west coastal region of San Diego County, and a tiny grape-growing parcel in Orange County. Included in the South Coast are two primary subdistricts, Temecula and San Pasqual. As the first new winery to settle here, Callaway focused attention on this area in the mid-70s and eventually set the tone by specializing in white varietals. The climate varies slightly, but for the most part is categorized as a warm Region III, despite the cooling assist from frequent fog intrusion. Today, close to two dozen wineries and 3,000 acres are within this Viticultural Area. Together, Sauvignon Blanc and Chardonnay account for over 50% of the total acreage, with Johannisberg Riesling a distant third in popularity. Fewer than 500 acres are planted to red grapes.

SPRING MOUNTAIN (Napa)   A distinctly identifiable watershed area known as Spring Mountain lies west of St. Helena and forms part of the Mayacamas Mountain Range, the boundary between the Napa and Sonoma valleys. This picturesque stretch of hillside has a long and fabled history of grape growing that dates back to the 19th century. It maintained itself fitfully after Prohibition, but many of Spring Mountain's great estates have only been put back into wine-making in the last two decades. Soils and exposures vary considerably on Spring Mountain, with most vineyards seemingly favoring later-maturing red grapes like Cabernet Sauvignon. The York Creek Vineyard, which has been providing grapes to the Ridge winery (among others) for almost two decades, has earned a reputation for its gutsy Cabernets, Zinfandels, and Petite Sirahs. In some vineyards, however, it is the early-ripening varieties such as Chardonnay and Pinot Noir which have earned the better reputations. Among important wineries on Spring Mountain are Keenan, Smith-Madrone, and the aptly named Spring Mountain Vineyards.

STAGS LEAP (Napa)   About a mile east of Yountville is the picturesque Stags Leap area. Known primarily for its rich, supple, balanced, often mouth-filling, usually expensive Cabernet Sauvignon, this superb viticultural pocket has distinctly red soil and gets its name from a prominent knoll of red rocks that marks its eastern boundary. According to legend, the promontory is the home of the cavorting antlered quadruped. In recent history, the name has been applied to the limited area of land near the eastern hills thought to be influenced by reflected sunlight and warmth from the rocks. However, wineries from as far south as the Chimney Rock area to as far north as S. Anderson on the Yountville Cross Road have managed to slip within the shadow of the stag and the borders of the defined Viticultural Area. The early leader in the revival of this area was Warren Winiarski's Stag's Leap Wine Cellars. Important followers include Clos du Val, Stags' Leap Winery, Pine Ridge Winery, and Steltzner Vineyard. All told, 10 wineries and 1,400 acres of grapes are found in the Stags Leap area. (Note that in the name of the Viticultural Area "Stags" has no apostrophe).

SUISUN VALLEY *(Solano)*   Like its neighboring appellation to the immediate west, Green Valley–Solano, this little-heard name is of almost no vinous consequence in spite of having 24 square miles within its government-recognized boundaries. The few grapes that grow here suffer through a relatively hot and dry summer and are nobody's prize when it comes to reputation.

TALMAGE *(Mendocino)*   Extending east and south of Ukiah and occupying the foothills is a region referred to by local growers as Talmage. About half of the Redwood Valley's grape acreage is located here, and most of the plantings were established in the early 70s. The primary varieties are Zinfandel, Cabernet Sauvignon, and Chardonnay.

TEMPLETON *(San Luis Obispo)*   Located 8 miles south of Paso Robles, Templeton is a small town included within the Paso Robles appellation. The York Mountain Viticultural Area, 9 miles due west of Templeton, is home to several wineries, including old-timers such as York Mountain, Las Tables, and Pesenti, as well as newcomers such as Mastantuono and Wild Horse Winery. Most of the 400 acres within Templeton are planted today to red varieties. Zinfandel and Petite Sirah dominate the old plantings, but Cabernet, Merlot, and Chardonnay are definitely on the increase.

UKIAH *(Mendocino)*   Ukiah is the urban center of the county and home to three of the county's oldest and largest producers: Parducci, Cresta Blanca (now Mendocino Estates), and Weibel. Most of the vineyards within sight of Ukiah are located directly to the north.

UMPQUA VALLEY   In the early 60s the Umpqua Valley was the location for Oregon's wine awakening when the state's oldest winery, Hillcrest Vineyards, opened its doors. Located due south of the Willamette Valley, Umpqua extends south for another 70 miles and ends at the Klamath Mountains. Sharing a similar Region I climate with its northern neighbor, the Umpqua Valley has more frost threats but less rainfall than the Willamette Valley. About 600 acres of vines are located both along the hillsides and on the valley floors. The leading varieties are Pinot Noir and Chardonnay. Hillcrest is the oldest, and, along with Bjellend, the best known of the six establishments within this Viticultural Area.

WALLA WALLA   Like the larger Columbia Valley which contains it, this Viticultural Area falls chiefly within Washington State but also takes in a tiny portion of northern Oregon. It can be found west of the city of Walla Walla along the river of the same name. About a half dozen producers are located in the region. Several of the more successful Washington Cabernet Sauvignons have originated here. Woodward Canyon and Leonetti are the best known of the locally based wineries.

WASHINGTON STATE   With over 11,000 acres of vinifera grapes, Washington has become the second-largest premium wine–producing state. The total amount of wine produced annually exceeds 6 million gallons. Washington ranks fourth in the U.S. in terms of per capita wine consumption and is the ninth-largest wine market. The primary growing regions are located east of the Cascade Mountains and they consist of three Viticultural Areas—the Yakima Valley (Yakima and Benton counties), the Walla Walla Valley, and the Columbia Valley area to the east, where the Columbia, Snake, and Yakima rivers converge. These regions are semi-arid, with long, dry, moderately warm summer days and cold winters. Vineyardists rely on irrigation throughout the growing season. Located at the northerly 47° latitude, these wine regions are characterized by a growing season that is generally longer than in California, but with somewhat lower heat totals. However, the summer days experience longer daylight hours, and most varieties with the possible exception of Cabernet Sauvignon have adapted well and ripen more than adequately in most years. We should note that in western Washington, some vineyard activity and small-scale winemaking take place in and around Puget Sound. Most of the state's wine activities, however, are centered in eastern Washington.

Washington's first serious vinifera vineyards were planted in the Yakima Valley in the 60s. Because there was no history of *Phylloxera* in the region, all of the vines are planted on their own root systems. The region soon proved to be unusual in several ways. On the positive side, over the first two decades vinifera vines have carried more quality fruit per acre than many of their counterparts around the world. The one risk encountered is that winter weather can be too tough on the sensitive vinifera vines, and fall frosts have on occasion also taken their toll. When damage has occurred, it has usually been the newly planted vines that suffer.

Gewurztraminer, Riesling, and Grenache were among the first varietals made by pioneers in the late 60s, and those wines were judged good enough to encourage expansion. Since 75 the vinifera acreage has increased fivefold. White varieties enjoy the lion's share and represent 75% of the total, led by Johannisberg Riesling (2,600) and Chardonnay (2,000). Among reds, Cabernet Sauvignon, Merlot, and Pinot Noir are the most popular, and respective plantings of each are increasing slightly. Labrusca varieties, primarily Concord, have been grown for decades in Washington to supply producers of grape juice and sacramental wines. Some 19,000 acres of labrusca remain.

The number of producers approaches 90 and the industry continues to expand. Chateau Ste. Michelle remains the largest in terms of volume and the most visible in terms of national availability.

Over recent vintages Hogue Cellars has emerged as a quality leader as well as a volume leader. Columbia Crest joins Ste. Michelle and Hogue as wineries making more than 100,000 cases a year.

While Washington Chardonnays are often pleasingly fruity, they generally lack the depth and intensity found in California's finest. The most successful varietals to date have been Riesling, Chenin Blanc, and Semillon—all with pert, lively fruitiness. Merlot, however, may with greater maturity achieve consistently high marks. Over the first two decades it has proven to be far more exciting here than Cabernet Sauvignon or any other red grape.

WILD HORSE VALLEY *(Napa and Solano)*   100 acres of grapes reside in this little-known Viticultural Area on the border between Napa and Solano counties.

WILLAMETTE VALLEY   Beginning just north of Portland, the Willamette Valley traverses the state from north to south for 170 miles until it ends near Eugene. Classified as a Region I, it is Oregon's principal wine region and home to a majority of the wineries and vineyards. Most of the plantings are in the hills on the west side of the Willamette River, and as a rule the vineyards are located at elevations between 300 and 1,000 feet. The most extensive plantings fall within the central section from Salem to the Chehalem Mountains. In the foothills along the eastern side, the newly emerging Eola Hills region (a row of low hills stretching from just north of Amity 15 miles south to the Bethel gap) was the site of modest expansion in the 80s. At the north end of the Eola Hills, just west of Amity, William Hill Winery purchased 200 acres in 89. In the late 80s the southern part of the Willamette near the town of Monroe was being viewed as yet another location suitable for establishing Pinot Noir acreage. Napa Valley's Girard Winery acquired land in this region in 88 for the purpose of making Pinot Noir.

From the mid-70s onward, Pinot Noir has been the leading variety in terms of acreage and performance. Chardonnay and Riesling are also widely planted. The Viticultural Area could undergo considerable expansion, with potential sites estimated to be in the neighborhood of 20,000 total acres, if demand continues to grow. Throughout the rough formative days and in the early glory era, Eyrie Vineyard has been recognized as the pioneer and the most influential local winery. Eyrie's Pinot Noirs were the first to win international recognition. Three producers noted for Pinot Noir—Eyrie, Sokol Blosser, and Knudsen Erath—own vineyards in the Dundee Hills, a subregion noted for its red soils and steep hillsides. Australian winemaker Brian Croser founded his Dundee Wine Co. in 86 to produce sparkling wines under the Argyle label. In 87, the influential Burgundy producer Robert Drouhin bought land in Dundee. Drouhin purchased additional land since then and now owns 180 acres. In 89, Laurent-Perrier of Champagne acquired 80 acres in the Willamette's Valley's Dundee Hills area for the purpose of making sparkling wine.

Until the 140,000-case-capacity Montinore Vineyard was built in 87, the largest wineries—Knudsen Erath, Oak Grove, Tualatin, and Rex Hill—were in the 30,000- to 40,000-case range. Most of the wineries in the Willamette Valley are small and family-owned.

WILLOW CREEK *(Humboldt and Trinity)*   This Viticultural Area is located east of Eureka, near the confluence of the Trinity River with its south fork. Since fewer than 10 acres of grapes grow in both counties combined, Willow Creek is more name than reality.

YAKIMA VALLEY   The first officially recognized Viticultural Area in the Northwest, the Yakima Valley is 75 miles long and 22 miles wide, and is heavily planted to both labrusca and vinifera grapes. Though semi-arid, this region was among the nation's first to become a prosperous agricultural center with total reliance on modern irrigation systems. It grows over 18,000 acres of Concord and related labrusca varieties for grape juice, some of the country's most desirable hops, and has yielded some of the Northwest's most distinctive vinifera wines, especially Riesling, Chenin Blanc, Semillon, and Grenache. It experiences the coolest weather in the Columbia Valley and the coldest, most dangerous winter temperatures. Ste. Michelle, Hogue, and Covey Run are among the leading producers within the area. According to estimates, the potential vinifera acreage could grow to 20,000 if and when demand warrants expansion.

YAMHILL COUNTY   This county contains the midsection of the Willamette Valley, including the vinous triangle with apexes at Newberg, Salem, and McMinnville. Though still responsible for growing the majority of Oregon grapes, Yamhill County appears far less frequently on labels today than it did in the 70s. It has given way to the Willamette Valley and other smaller appellations contained within the county.

YOLO COUNTY   Lying west of Sacramento in an area that is technically part of the warm Central Valley, Yolo County vineyards (2,000 acres) experience slightly cooler growing conditions because of the coastal marine influences that push up from San Francisco Bay across the Sacramento River Delta. The majority of vineyards are planted in the eastern part of the county, within the Clarksburg and Merritt Island Viticultural Areas. A newly developing grape-growing area lies in the county's western hills near Dunnigan. Chardonnay is the most widely planted variety (600 acres), with Chenin Blanc (400) and Sauvignon Blanc (300) coming next. Cabernet Sauvignon (200 acres) is the leading red.

YORK MOUNTAIN *(San Luis Obispo)*   Situated on the eastern side of the Santa Lucia Mountains and west of Paso Robles, this Viticultural Area is one of the smallest on the West Coast. The average elevation is about 1,500 feet, and the area contains 23 acres of vineyards and one producer, York Mountain Winery. Compared to its neighboring Viticultural Areas, York Mountain is cooler, but also receives more rainfall, especially during the late summer. The varieties planted are a mix of reds, led by Pinot Noir and Zinfandel.

YOUNTVILLE *(Napa)*   Lying just 6 miles north of the city of Napa, the little but no longer sleepy, increasingly tourism-oriented town of Yountville is the first true wine community one encounters when entering the Napa Valley. Surrounding Yountville are a variety of important growing areas and wineries. To the south, in relatively cool growing conditions, are Chardonnay vineyards that supply Chateau Montelena, Trefethen, Beringer, Rutherford Hill, and others. To the west, in the midst of what might be considered prime Cabernet country, sits the dramatic home of Domaine Chandon, while the eastern side of the valley contains the Stags Leap area, renowned for its rich, generally elegant Cabernet and Merlot from such vinous stars as Stag's Leap Wine Cellars, Clos du Val, Pine Ridge, Shafer, and Chimney Rock.

Vintage Commentary

As vines, regions, and winemakers have all continued to mature quickly throughout the last decade, it has become increasingly obvious that vintages indeed play a role in California wines. One year may not vary as much from the next as is often the case in Europe, but there are differences, and those differences can be significant. A solid knowledge of California vintages can—and should—affect buying decisions.

Climatic differences are primarily responsible for defining vintage differences. The amount of rainfall, frosts, hail, heatwaves, cold spells, droughts, floods, and what-have-you are all part of the general climate. In the 80s, California experienced just about every extreme and possibility. Rain—or the lack of it—certainly influences the quality of grapes a vine yields. But certain climatic variables are also important. A cold spell, heavy rains, or hail during the period of bloom and set (usually in May, when flower blossoms convert into fruit) may hinder both quantity and quality. A cold spell during the harvest, on the other hand, often provides welcome relief because it slows the ripening process, which in turn slows the pace of harvesting.

The sum total of climatic conditions during one growing season, usually April 1 through the end of September, constitutes the vintage conditions and helps define the wines made that year in two ways. The first is the most obvious, and the one most people associate with the word "vintage." That refers to the overall *quality* of a specific wine from a specific region, categorizing it as excellent, above average, average, weak, or poor.

The second relates to the character or the general *style* of a particular wine from a given year. For instance, Cabernet Sauvignons grown in Napa Valley in 85 and in 86 are both categorized as excellent, but the wines are definitely not of the same style. They vary in varietal intensity, depth of flavor, and aging potential. A similar important distinction will be made between California Chardonnays from 86 and 87—they differ slightly in overall quality and in the general vintage style. The vintage assessments that follow highlight, when appropriate, both the qualitative and the stylistic distinctions.

Our assessments are derived from two sources. First, we observe the climatic drama from the day it begins to unfold with budbreak to the time it ends with the last grape of the season being crushed. We do not base our judgments of vintages solely on what happens in the vineyards, however. Many Europeans rely almost exclusively on the climatic conditions and patterns, which is why you may have heard or read someone declaring "a vintage of the century" in Europe as early as October or November when the wines are still fermenting.

We, on the contrary, perform "blind" (meaning objective) tastings of all the wines we are able to locate before passing final judgment on a vintage or, for that matter, on a producer. Neither the winemaking process nor the winemaker can be relied on to follow a predictable and infallible path once the grapes have been harvested. Thus over the last 20 years, no two vintages have yet to be carbon copies in our experience. Producers and winemakers have to prove themselves each and every year.

In this section, we concentrate on five varietals: Cabernet Sauvignon, Merlot, Pinot Noir, Zinfandel, and Chardonnay. These five are the most sought after by consumers and collectors, and they also are the five most likely to reward cellaring. The data presented here range from specific climatic information to generalized stylistic commentary. They relate only to vintages. For well-informed buying decisions, we urge you to consider this section together with the one on Geography, and of course the guide to individual producers and brands.

Cabernet Sauvignon

Exceptional earlier, ageworthy vintages: 1947, 1949, 1951, 1954, 1958, 1966

1968 A copious vintage that surprised many with full-flavored, tannin-laden wines that developed slowly. The most exceptional wines produced were Napa Valley in origin. With aging the finest wines began to display a classic, ripe style. The majority peaked by the early 80s. However, a few show some signs of surviving well into the 90s. Beaulieu's Private Reserve and Heitz Martha's Vineyard will make it into the next century alive.

1969 Starting out from an underrated vintage, the wines were viewed as short-lived because they lacked the ripeness of 68. Those that were properly cellared responded well and evolved into soft, likable wines with straightforward character. Those made from hillside plantings were often the pick of the bunch. Apart from the Cabernets purchased in large-bottle format, most are past prime.

1970 This was a vintage that eventually aroused national excitement and became highly sought after. It began with a mild, wet winter, followed by severe spring frosts that reduced the crop by close to half. Ideally warm late-summer weather brought the grapes to full, intense ripeness. The wines ranged from ripe and balanced to overripe, slightly raisined, and heady. With aging, many became less balanced and barely survived their 10th year. Others made with some restraint developed normally—and by the mid-80s were magnificent. A vintage with many great to excellent wines, but not quite a classic style. The best vintage of the 70s.

1971 A year that began with a cool spring, and a long, cool growing season that lacked real warmth and distinction. Most of the wines, mirroring the weather, possess a thin, simple character. The major exceptions came from low-yielding mountain vineyards, such as Ridge Monte Bello. Beaulieu's Reserve stood out. Most were over the hill by the early 80s.

1972 A much-troubled vintage. Heatwaves in July reduced the crop. Persistent late-season rains created mold problems and diluted flavors. Most versions were soft in body and often light in varietal character. Overall quality was average to below average. Few wines lived very long.

1973 The winter began wet and cold and finally gave way late in the spring to warm, lovely weather that remained through most of the growing season. This one was classified as a cool year. The crop turned out to be bountiful, and early reports on quality were cautious and doubt-ridden. After some aging, many wines began to blossom and display fine character, balance, and harmony. A tannic undercurrent provided structure that aided long-term aging. Above-average to excellent quality overall.

1974 A cool spring, moderate summer weather, and a warm harvest made this year seem textbook perfect. The crop was large, and the grapes ripened steadily and well. The number of producers was beginning to increase. The best wines were dark, concentrated, tannic in their youth, and seemed long-lived. A few of the tannic versions turned out to be fat and ponderous. But the other big wines were developing inner beauty and complexity within a decade. Many of the medium-priced, moderately tannic wines matured nicely and peaked around their 10th year, with good holding ability. A few of the better-structured Reserve bottlings are just beginning to shed their tannins and may last well into the next century. Ridge Monte Bello and Heitz Martha's Vineyard, both stellar, will outlive all others. Some disappointments mar this vintage. Still, it is an excellent one.

1975 Early frosts and early rains were followed by a cool, unusually long, growing season. This was a difficult and unusual vintage, leading to a wide array of styles. By a thin margin, the majority were short on fruit and underfilled, though occasionally elegant. Some superb examples emerged with forthright character, moderate intensity, and balance. Only a few, mostly Reserves, aged beyond a decade.

1976 The first drought year caught producers ill-prepared. After prolonged dry, warm weather throughout the summer, the only consolation was periodic harvest rains. The grapes were tiny, with high sugar, low acidity, and thick skins. As a result, the wines were dark, dense, high in alcohol, and lacking balance or the structure to bring them into balance. The best of an odd year peaked by 1986; the majority were uninteresting or dead long before then.

1977 The second drought year was handled by better-prepared winemakers who, with the help of dry but relatively cool summer weather, achieved better-balanced wines. Sporadic harvest rains provided a little lift to the vine and enabled the grapes to avoid dehydration. Overall, the vintage was average in quality, with good varietal character and short-term aging.

1978 This banner warm year produced many ripe, occasionally overripe, wines. A heatwave arrived at the beginning of the harvest and remained to the end, necessitating round-the-clock picking. The crop was larger than normal, but many wines were fat, tannic, and high in alcohol. The finest were well stuffed with varietal fruit, with an ability to age beyond one decade. Those less well balanced have faded. The number of producers expanded in this vintage. Well above average quality.

1979   A difficult vintage. Frequent late-season heatwaves sent sugar levels soaring and acidity readings falling, sometimes out of control. Then the hot spells were followed by heavy rains that tended to dilute flavor and lower tannins of the remaining grapes. Some wines turned out flavorful and balanced, often those made from grapes picked before the rains. These exceptions aside, most of the wines turned out to be on the austere and tight side. Most peaked within a decade. The primary long-agers were the Reserve bottlings. An average-quality year.

1980   Heavy winter rains persisted into early spring. A cool early season led to warm conditions as the harvest neared. The grapes developed an unusual combination of high sugar content and high acidity which created widespread anticipation of high quality during the harvest. But the harvest was over quickly, indicating grape maturity was achieved too rapidly. Most wines, as a result, never lived up to their early promise of long aging. However, many wines offer generous fruit, moderate tannins, some depth, and high alcohol levels. Similar in style to 78, yet with accessible fruit and depth, this vintage scored for early appeal and produced many ✻✻ and a few ✻✻✻ bottlings. Well above average.

1981   An intense early heatwave reduced the crop and resulted in an extremely early harvest in the North Coast. Both varietal intensity and aging potential were question marks at first. Most wines appealed early on, with an open, fleshy style that invited near-term consumption. However, they have an inner balance that responds well to aging, and are turning out to be moderately complex. From the beginning, this underappreciated vintage offered numerous fine values and gave us a reasonable share of ✻ and even a few ✻✻ wines. Slightly above average.

1982   A wet winter, a mild summer, and a rainy harvest season yielded a mixed bag of wines. The successes offered plummy, jammy fruit, with moderate tannins. Generous, solid, and substantial, the best of the 82s should live a decade, possibly two. Dunn and Spottswoode were among the biggest critical hits. Most ✻✻ bottlings were along Reserve lines. Average to above average.

1983   Moderate weather during the growing season was followed by persistent harvest rains, causing numerous difficulties. Harvesting was slowed by the rains, which led to diluted, out-of-balance grapes. The number of ✻✻ wines was small, primarily restricted to Reserve types. Newcomer Forman Winery debuts with ✻✻✻ results. Most of the ✻ wines offer modest varietal character and moderate aging potential. The majority of others are on the heavy, muscular side and lack integration of fruit and tannin. Average quality.

1984   Early budbreak, and a virtually rain-free, persistently warm growing season, resulted in a relatively early harvest. Though similar to the conditions of 74 and 78, the hot weather during the vintage forced many wineries to harvest quickly to avoid overripeness and high alcohols in their wines. Despite these precautions, the majority of the wines are big, ripe, and tannic. Early excitement encouraged the first successful attempt to sell on a futures basis. The style tends toward ripe, well-stuffed fruit, with ample tannins for support and for long-term cellaring. Many Reserves and a few regular bottlings are likely to age for 20 years or more. Overall, the best vintage since 78. Well above average to excellent.

1985   This year began with early budbreak. A warm early spring was followed by a cool late spring. Then pleasant warm weather in June and July set the stage for one of the most incredible years, even for California Cabernet Sauvignon. The steady warm weather led up to a cool August, resulting in one of the longest growing seasons ever. Dry September weather allowed for an evenly paced crush. The grapes matured with full flavors and good acidity at somewhat lower than normal Brix. The resulting wines were often ripe, yet many managed to possess an inner balance without being heavy. The 85s are compressed and compact, their varietal personality and balancing acidity giving them great aging potential. In style they are the most likely Cabernets in recent memory to invite comparison with the finest from Bordeaux. An excellent vintage, possibly the best since Prohibition.

1986   The year began with winter floods. Then heavy warm February rains once again encouraged early budbreak. The spring weather was hot, but turned cool in late July to slow down maturity and enhance flavor development. Warm weather returned in September to increase sugar and occasionally to contribute less than desirable acid balance. Light rainfall in September caused few problems. The best of the vintage combine the fatness of 84 with the fragrant, inviting, deep fruitiness of 85. With ample tannins, the successes should age for a decade or more, but may not live as long as their counterparts from 85. Many ** and *** wines. Above average to excellent.

1987   The winter was extremely dry; the North Coast received only 60% of normal rainfall. Cool early spring weather was followed by a brief heatwave in May that occurred during bloom and caused a crop reduction of about 15%. The summer weeks were mild but dry, which resulted in small berries with intense flavors. A brief harvest-time heatwave forced wineries to pick rapidly to avoid overripeness. The wines are ripe and deep, but many tend to be soft and lack the backbone needed for aging. A few turned out to be overripe, and aging is not likely to bring them into balance. The Cabernets from this vintage are best enjoyed relatively young, allowing those from the preceding three vintages to be cellared. Average to slightly above-average quality.

1988   Another dry winter, with rainfall again only 50% of normal. The dry weather encouraged early budbreak. A short hot spell in mid-May caused significant crop reduction due to berry shatter. The spring and early summer weeks were warm. A cooling trend in July started what turned out to be a cooler-than-normal summer. The berries were small, but maturation of the fruit was slow and even, boding well for quality. The Cabernet harvest began in mid-September and was completed prior to October 14, when heavy rains arrived. Too many wines, however, have modest varietal intensity, with a ripe, jammy fruit character. Aging potential for all but the best is less than a decade. Average quality.

1989   Favorable springtime weather extended through the bloom and set period, resulting in a potential bumper-sized crop. From June through August the weather was mild and ideal, and grape development was slow and even. By mid-September, when the first rains arrived, few producers had harvested any Cabernet. In the North Coast another storm dumped more rain a week later, setting the sugar levels back. A wait-and-see attitude was rewarded by the hoped-for Indian summer weather. Warm days, cool nights over the last three weeks of October allowed the remaining Cabernet to recover and to develop to maturity, thereby salvaging some of the crop. Harvesting extended over several weeks, as the last grapes in the North Coast were picked in the first week of November. In general, the successes display above-average flavors and good potential. The disappointments, unusually numerous, came from over-crop vines or from plantings in marginal areas. Average.

1990   Heavy rains in late May arrived during bloom in the North Coast and reduced the crop by 20% to 30% overall. June and July provided mild summer weather. Except for one hot spell in early August, the season allowed grapes to ripen evenly. Most of the Cabernet was harvested before light rains came in late September. The small grapes possessed intense flavors. A small crop, but definitely well above average in quality.

Merlot

1978   This generally highly regarded warm vintage was the first in which Merlot was produced in significant numbers. The lengthy warm spell in September caused quick ripening. Most wines, made from grapes harvested without delay, were fruity and rich, in a full-bodied, luscious style. Duckhorn, Rutherford Hill, and Clos du Val led the way. Most peaked by the end of the first decade.

1979   A cool year, with late rains occurring after most Merlot was picked. The typical wines were subdued, closed when young; the best developed slowly. With an elegance and balance gained in the cellar, several now seem capable of lasting longer than the 78s.

1980   Another warm year, especially during the harvest, brought fruity, forthright wines, lush and rich, but sometimes overly ripe and powerful. Rutherford Hill and Stonegate rise to ✿✿ levels.

1981   An early harvest for all varieties, especially Merlot. Many more wineries became involved. The general vintage style leaned toward suppleness and, at their best, a few achieved complexity. Duckhorn, Jaeger, and Clos du Val are standouts.

1982   The abundant winter rains gave way to a cool, damp spring, and the result was later than normal budbreak in the North Coast. The growing season was mild and grapes matured very slowly, but most of the Merlot was picked before the rains arrived. The crop from Napa Valley was large. Keenan and Gundlach Bundschu were among the early standouts. A dozen others entered the expanding competitive arena. The number of ✿✿ bottlings increased dramatically. Well-focused varietal character and generally restrained tannins characterize this vintage. Excellent.

1983   Overall, an uneventful, mild growing season from the beginning until a warm spell arrived in September. Indian summer weather prevailed during the Merlot harvest, and the resulting wines were opulently fruity and rich. With numerous ripe and racy versions made, this was a classic vintage, made doubly important in the way Merlot had outperformed Cabernet for depth, extract, and appeal. Aging potential was also good, with quite a few most likely to peak at the 8- to 10-year range. Excellent.

1984   Wet winter months were followed by unusually warm spring weather. The grapes ripened fast, and Merlot was harvested about two to three weeks early as September remained hot for close to three weeks. Rather variable quality, with some Merlots overripe and raisined; most lean more toward power than finesse. The finest, such as Cuvaison and Whitehall Lane, offered a voluptuous ripeness. Not quite as well balanced overall as the 84 Cabernets. Above average.

1985   A warm early spring, consistently cool, even summertime temperatures, and just slightly warm harvest weather all added up to a classic vintage for Merlot. The wines are not as universally successful as Cabernets, and a few have not quite lived up to their promises at the crushers'. Markham, Ravenswood, Dehlinger, and Inglenook bid for top honors of the vintage. Hogue and Ste. Michelle demonstrate Washington State's competency with Merlot. Well above average.

1986   The winter floods were forgotten by the time of early budbreak for Merlot. The summer was mild, with numerous foggy mornings and warm afternoons. Most Merlot was picked by mid-September. The wines are often wonderfully concentrated, well stuffed with fruit and buttressed by tannins, but there is a wide range in quality. The successes are intense, with deep, ripe fruit in a plump style. A few others are light and simple. Above average, but variable.

1987   Low rainfall in the winter tended to stress the Merlot vine. Then two weeks of unseasonably warm May weather played havoc with the berry development, and the shattered berries reduced the crop by 30% to 40%. The remainder of the summer was temperate and stretched out the growing season. The slow maturation resulted in rich, focused, and in some cases incredibly fruity wines. The crush in the North Coast was uneventful for Merlot. A small crop. Above-average quality in general, with several wines achieving greatness.

1988   The dry winter conditions led to a difficult bloom period, which stretched out over three weeks. Merlot emerged with heavy berry shatter and a resulting light crop. With relatively warm weather during the summer, the reduced crop (in parts of Napa Valley by as much as 40% to 50%) reached maturity early. On their own, most Merlots have good color and good balancing fruit. Those producers who had the resources available blended more than usual amounts of Cabernet Sauvignon and Cabernet Franc for depth. Most wines generally lack the depth of 87, but offer well-knit structure and balance. Slightly above average.

1989   The almost textbook-perfect spring encouraged a big crop during bloom and set in mid-May. The vines were able to develop their fruit through the long, relatively mild summer weeks. Dry-farmed vineyards and others picked before the rains yielded rich, intensely flavored fruit. After the mid-September rains, Merlot from the North Coast varied widely, with some degree of *Botrytis*-affected fruit and even rotten loads reaching wineries. Those culling out the problematic fruit succeeded. Wide-ranging quality, with the best achieving the status of excellent. Most are average.

1990   In most warm growing regions, the May rains arrived during bloom to reduce the crop. Cooler regions enjoyed a normal yield. The summer weather was moderately warm, and the growing season progressed to a quick, easy harvest. In many areas, however, sustained drought conditions helped produce high-pH, low-acid grapes, raising questions about balance and longevity. Generally, the wines are slightly more concentrated than the 89s, but a mixed bag. Average to slightly above average.

Chardonnay

Exceptional earlier vintages: 1972, 1975, 1977

1980   During the crush, winemakers were excited about the unusual combination of high sugar and high acidity in the grapes, but first signs of problems came with reports of difficult fermentations, and more than a few "stuck fermentations" in the North Coast. Ripe, heavy wines were the norm there, with what turned out to be an early-maturing vintage. The Central Coast fared much better in terms of both initial balance and ultimate longevity. Most of the wines are now past prime.

1981   The summer temperatures set record highs, and the intense sunshine diminished the crop size. The crush began early. The wines, however, turned out to be rich, with excellent varietal personality, if a trifle low in acidity. From most regions, the wines were lovely, youthfully appealing, with the Central Coast yielding a high percentage of the ✸✸ and ✸✸✸ bottlings. Fairly good agers, most reaching their peak in 87–88.

1982   This turned out to be the first of two problematic vintages, with parts of Sonoma County ending up with the most erratic results. Heavy fog and late-season rains created mildew and even rotten fruit in many areas. Then intermittent harvest rains only encouraged increases in rot. Few wines from this vintage aged well, and most are now over the hill.

1983   All conditions were reasonably good until the harvest began and was greeted by rain, which was followed by hot, humid days. Napa Valley fared well, though some lots were overripe, creating high-alcohol wines. In parts of Sonoma, the grapes developed unwanted *Botrytis* and sometimes less noble bunch rot. The results were fat, dull, not always clean Chardonnays. Bottlings from the Carneros and from southwest Sonoma County were general exceptions in this average vintage. The Central Coast, primarily Monterey and Santa Barbara, also contributed several ✻✻ wines. Average quality.

1984   This is known as an early-ripening warm vintage. It began with a dry spring that led to a warm summer. Warm days continued through mid-August. September was one of the hottest ever in the North Coast, and most wineries were finished picking by mid-month. As a result, Chardonnay was harvested at ripe, occasionally overripe, levels. North Coast Chardonnays were heavy, sometimes coarse, but often with rewarding richness along with hotness in their flavors. The Central Coast had more than its fair share of ✻✻ and ✻✻✻ bottlings, with characteristic acidity to balance their full flavors. Above average.

1985   Early budbreak and a warm spring set the stage for a large, healthy crop. After a warm summer, August was cooled by persistent coastal fogs, and grape maturation was slowed to the point where a balance of sugar and acidity was often achieved. The small berries held intense flavors, with firming acidity. Many wines were stunning in varietal character. But with a tight and steely structure due to crisp acids, they needed short-term cellaring before revealing their true potential. Likely to rank with 75 for longest-lived Chardonnays. Excellent.

1986   A cold winter; late rains continued and developed into flood conditions in the North Coast. The early spring weather was warm and it prevailed through June. By July the fog's return restored slow, normal development of the fruit, and cool conditions continued into September, creating one of the longest growing seasons for Chardonnay. Generally, the pleasantly intense character without the high acidity of 85 gives 86 an accessible, pretty, deeply fruited personality. The best are forward, concentrated, and balanced. They should reach a high peak around 91–92. Excellent.

1987   A tough vintage on the nervous system that began with a wet spring in which April brought 2 inches of rain. Budbreak was early, but was followed by many cool, dry summer weeks that finally ended with a hot spell in late August. Chardonnay began to ripen quickly, competing for attention with Merlot in the North Coast. The crop size was a little below expectations. The medium-intensity wines offer pretty, blossomy aromas, and deeply fruited, well-focused flavors. As a rule, the wines are more accessible in their youth than the 85s because of tamer acid levels, yet they should age well. Wines from the Central Coast have shown especially well in this vintage. Well above-average quality.

1988   This second year of drought conditions caused vintners to be concerned about vine stress, particularly among the new plantings. Chardonnay in both the North and Central Coasts withstood the relatively wet conditions during bloom to set a relatively good-sized crop. The warm spring and mild summer weather matured the fruit evenly. The crush began in late August in the North Coast, and then because of regular foggy mornings was stretched over the following three weeks. For quantity, this year turned out to be normal. The quality for this fruity, forthright, medium-intense vintage is generally above average.

1989 Because the crop was big and the growing season cool, the harvest was behind schedule when rain arrived in mid-September. It left 2 inches of rain in most coastal regions, with the Russian River area in Sonoma County receiving twice as much. Another rainstorm a week later left its mark on the North Coast to create genuine problems in the form of mold and *Botrytis*. Growers aiming for a big crop with vineyards in fog-prone regions never fully recovered. Though 10% to 33% of the Chardonnay (depending upon region and exposure) was picked before the rains, the remainder was picked over the following four to five weeks. Before the rain, the quality was excellent; afterwards, it varied. The Carneros region suffered crop loss to mold and rot. Parts of the Russian River Valley were hard hit. In the Central Coast, the quality was more consistent and slightly above average. Most wines lack intensity, and tend to be clean but dull. Below average to average quality overall.

1990 Most coastal-grown Chardonnay had set before the May rains, and thus the quantity was only down slightly. The cool summer weather and warm mid-August days enabled the grapes to develop good flavor and balance. Harvested under cool, mild conditions, most North Coast Chardonnay was in the cellars by the third week of September. The Central Coast fared just as well, with the harvest completed a week later. Generally above average with some excellent results.

Pinot Noir

Exceptional earlier vintages: 1971, 1975, 1977

1979 The late-season rains arrived after all or most of the Pinot Noir had been harvested in the North Coast. Some grapes were overripe from August hot spells. The quality overall was a little above average. Two newcomers, Acacia and Calera, showed impressive first wines to bring the average up.

1980 An extremely warm vintage for Pinot Noir. The cool weather in the early season slightly slowed grape maturation to salvage the vintage. Even the finest wines are full-bodied and high in extract. Carneros Creek, Chalone, ZD, Hanzell, Beaulieu joined Acacia and Calera with above-average performances. Most other wines were ripe and flavorful, but often too high in alcohol to make long-term cellaring rewarding. Average.

1981 A warm, dry season culminated in an early harvest. Both color and flavor intensity are good, and most wines manage to avoid being overripe. Crisp acidity made many versions lively and pleasant. The Robert Mondavi Winery showed a quantum leap in quality. The most consistent versions originated in the Carneros. Overall, a mixed vintage, with not much aging potential.

1982 The weather was mild well through August, which is ideal for maturing Pinot Noir. Though it rained, the better versions were made from grapes harvested prior to the September rains. In this vintage, however, a big increase in tonnage went into sparkling wine production. The rest went into what turned out to be an exciting, above-average vintage for Pinot Noir. Quite a few ✿ and several ✿ ✿ efforts emerged from the Carneros and Russian River as overall quality was above average. The Central Coast region and its producers began to make a mark. Calera, however, was the vintage standout. Above average.

1983 After a difficult harvest bothered by late rains, this turned out to be a watershed year for the varietal. The old, brawny style finally gave ground to a new one favoring medium-depth varietal fruitiness and finesse. The total of ✿ wines again showed a dramatic increase in a ripe, open, but under-control style. The Carneros region enjoyed the greatest success in this above-average vintage.

Several wines from Russian River Valley were among ❋ bottlings. In Oregon, mild dry weather throughout the harvest helped make 83 one of that state's finest years. Well above average.

1984   A generally warm, dry growing season. Two dozen or more wineries, however, managed to make well-stuffed wines with depth but also with focused varietal intensity. As more and more marginal brands dropped out of this division, the overall quality again improved as many ❋ ❋ and a few ❋ ❋ ❋ versions came along. Exciting efforts from newcomers—Au Bon Climat, Wild Horse, and Byron—joined Calera to improve the Central Coast's reputation. Well above average, with good aging prospects. Oregon's vintners, however, suffered through a rainy crush after a marginal growing season.

1985   This cool, long, problem-free vintage was kind to Pinot Noir just about everywhere in the West, with good wines from Oregon as well as from Carneros, Russian River, and the Central Coast. The style favored well-ripened, pretty fruit, with often fleshy but balanced flavors. The standouts were numerous and included newcomers like Byron, Etude, Caymus, and La Crema. Above-average vintage. In Oregon, the weather was both pleasantly warm for most of the growing season and dry during the harvesting. The result was an unusual vintage with many successes.

1986   The rainy winter and warm spring returned Pinot Noir vintners to reality. However, the growing season was cool enough and also long enough to allow the grapes to develop cherry-spicy flavors, deep color, and moderate aging abilities. A few wines from the Carneros and other cool locales are often deeper in color and more intense in flavor than the 85s. Above-average quality.

1987   The hot, dry summer months put Pinot Noir vines under stress. An intense heatwave in August caused grapes to ripen quickly and early. The crop size was down in quantity, and the quality was average. Generally, the wines have average color, and a light, simple, fruity character. Limited aging ability. In Oregon, many Pinot Noirs showed good aromas, but extremely hard acidity and insufficient flavors made for a generally disappointing year.

1988   Poor berry set in late May reduced the crop by 10% to 20% in most regions. Temperatures were moderate during the season, with a slightly warm July and cool August. The drought condition contributed to small berries, which combined with the shot berries intensified color. The harvest began early in the Carneros and Russian River Valley, but proceeded smoothly. The character of the vintage is slanted toward jammy fruit of medium-full intensity. Many of the North Coast wines are relatively rich but soft, owing to low acidity. Aging potential is the only question mark. Most wines offered early appeal and accessibility. Above average overall. Sustained warm weather before and during the harvest was the norm in Oregon.

1989   Planted more selectively than Chardonnay, Pinot Noir by its nature also tends to carry a smaller crop. Thus it enjoyed the long, relatively cool growing season; but because the crop was smaller, the majority of its vines were picked before the mid-September rains, more than 75% in the Carneros region and in the Russian River Valley. In most of the Central Coast, Pinot Noir went unscathed and was picked at normal sugar and acidity. However, most North Coast vintners harvested the remaining crop right after the rains, even though some of the fruit had been diluted. The overall quality is good. The higher-quality exceptions come from the Central Coast, where the wines developed greater intensity.

1990   In the North Coast, the May rains reduced the crop by 20–30%, but a cool August following two warm months led to a harvest in full swing by mid-September. The Central Coast harvest was late and interrupted by rains which diluted all remaining grapes. In both regions, quality ranges from excellent to awful, with the best wines possessing deep color and more depth than most 89s. Generally, slightly above average, with average ageability.

Zinfandel

Exceptional earlier vintages: 1970, 1973, 1974, 1976, 1977

1978   This year had the kind of warm conditions that bring out many of Zinfandel's best features—ripe fruit, ample tannins and power, and reasonable balance. Amador was not its usual strapping, brawny style, and thus aged better. Popularity of the varietal, however, was on the decline. Above average.

1979   The persistent late-season rains in Amador and the North Coast regions resulted in widely mixed quality. Most versions lacked adequate tannin and balance to age well. Only the best, especially those from Sonoma County, lived beyond their first decade. Most are past their prime today.

1980   A warm vintage with periodic heatwaves that played havoc with Zinfandel. The style of the vintage ranged from dense and concentrated to overripe and coarse. Most reached the market priced too close to Cabernet and at a time when White Zin was beginning its ascendance. Zinfandel was receiving sparse attention from consumers. Amador wines were better than the majority. Slightly above average.

1981   Early hot weather caused erratic ripening and September rains made quality uneven. Napa Valley was hurt the most as most wines lacked depth. Sonoma County fared slightly better, but the few major exceptions originated in Amador County, where ripeness was controlled. Average quality.

1982   As many contenders dropped out of the competition, the remaining Zinfandel producers tried to redesign and/or revive the varietal. Rains forced early harvesting, which encouraged many streamlined, fruity, slightly tannic versions. Burgess and Grgich Hills excelled. Newcomer Storybook Mountain captured ripe fruit and power. Slightly above average.

1983   Uneven ripening and late-season rains again imposed limits and encouraged better-integrated, accessible, ripe-berry style. Many ** wines were made, with Sonoma County rapidly building a strong reputation as the leader. Quivira, Lytton Springs, and Ravenswood earn high praise. Ridge completed its return to top form, and Kendall-Jackson entered the competition with attractive Mendocino bottlings. The best will age well up to a decade. Well above average.

1984   A warm year, free from harvesting difficulties, enabled Zinfandel to complete its comeback as a bona fide, quality red wine. The favorites are rich, ripe, and hearty without being overripe or overly coarse. Sonoma, led by bottlings from Dry Creek Valley, became unchallenged leader, but Napa's microclimate Howell Mountain emerged in this vintage. Several *** wines, led by Ridge, Quivira, Haywood, and Rosenblum. Well above average.

1985   The all but perfect vintage helped advance Zinfandel's fortunes by accentuating the variety's deep, ripe-berryish fruit. Many producers earned * or more by capturing a dense fruity core without any unpleasant excesses. Clos du Val joined Ridge and Ravenswood as *** leaders in what turned out to be a star-studded vintage. Most will be at their peak around 91–92. Excellent.

1986   A long-drawn-out growing season saw a high proportion of the crop go into White Zinfandel. The red versions possess amicable fruit, variable depth and flavor interest, and many are suited for near-term drinking. However, some superb Zins emanated from old, dry-farmed vineyards in the Dry Creek Valley, northern Napa Valley, and Mendocino. Storybook Mountain in Napa and Mazzocco in Sonoma County were true ✱✱✱ standouts. The Ridge "Gerserville" bottling returned to form to lead a pack of ✱✱ wines. In this year the Dry Creek Valley is validated as the leading source of distinctive Zinfandels. Well above average.

1987   With limited water available because of the drought, the vines were under stress early in the season. Then the heatwave in May further reduced the crop. By the time of the harvest, the berries remained tiny. They yielded intense varietal fruit and high-extract wines in Sonoma, Napa, and Amador. The style is on the coarse side, but similar otherwise to 84. The Russian River Valley joined Dry Creek Valley as a source of distinctive Zinfandels. The best versions of Sonoma County and Napa wines will age 7 to 10 years or more. Average to slightly above average.

1988   Beginning with abnormally warm weather in January and February, which encouraged early budbreak, this year remained unusual in most respects, including a disastrous bloom period. By mid-June, the Zinfandel crop was reduced by 25% to 50%. The rest of the growing season was cooler than normal. From mid-September to harvest, foggy mornings and cool evenings stretched out the growing season in the North Coast and in the Sierra Foothills. As a result, the sugar levels were kept under control and the acidity often remained ideal. With much of the marginal plantings picked to produce White Zinfandel, what remained by late September/early October was often spectacular. Dry Creek Valley, Sonoma Valley, Howell Mountain in Napa, and Amador generally yielded Zinfandels in a ripe, lush fruit style with balance. Though riper, this year is similar to 85. Excellent overall quality, possibly the best of the 80s.

1989   This year began as ideal for Zinfandel. Berry set was outstanding and the crop was large. The early summer weather seemed just right to bring the large crop to full maturity. By early August unusual cool weather set in, and grape development slowed. Only a few vintners in Sonoma and warmer parts of Napa and Mendocino had picked any Zinfandel before the September rains. With its full, compact clusters and relatively thin skins, Zinfandel began to disintegrate in some North Coast vineyards after the rains. In the Sierra Foothills, only 5% of the Zin was in before the rains came. Growers waited and ended by picking in October. Amador County Zins are moderately fruity, without being high in alcohol and tannins. Overall a mixed bag, with few notable high spots. Average quality.

1990   Most vines escaped damage from the May rains, and the crop size was close to normal in key regions. Growers who thinned out excess clusters were rewarded with grapes of good varietal character and balance. A few vineyards were over-cropped and ripened unevenly. Quantities were normal in Amador and Sonoma County, where ripeness levels in the Dry Creek Valley were close to ideal. Cool, dry weather in late September allowed for an evenly paced harvest. Well above average.

Wineries and Wines

Great—or good—wines are not merely grown, they are made. One need only look at the differences in quality and style that result when two wineries make wines from the same vineyard to realize the importance of the winery's hand in the production process. In this section we consider, both descriptively and critically, the wineries and labels most likely to appear on the shelves of wine merchants and on restaurant wine lists. Some are second labels for front-line wineries and some are the products of individuals or organizations acting as buyers/blenders/packagers of ready-made wine. They are an ever-changing, ever-increasing group whose number has more than doubled in the last decade.

The winery entries follow a standard format. We first focus on ownership, intent, acreage controlled, varietal wines produced, and wine quality. In addition, for those producers with intelligible track records, we offer vintage-by-vintage evaluations of their leading varietals. Each of the wines reviewed is rated for quality and for current drinkability. Overall, some 15,000 individual bottlings of Chardonnay, Cabernet Sauvignon, Merlot, Pinot Noir, and Zinfandel are assessed in this manner. Comparative rankings of winery performance on all the main varietals and on sparkling wines will be found beginning on p. 352.

The wine ratings and descriptions that appear in this book are based substantially on evaluations that have appeared in *Connoisseurs' Guide to California Wine,* a monthly newsletter edited and published by Charles Olken and Earl Singer. For subscription information, please see the beginning of this book.

Symbols used here are as follows:

82 below-average quality, a wine to avoid

85 a wine of average quality

✽ a fine example of a given type or style, an
above-average wine

✽ ✽ a very fine wine, likely to be memorable

✽ ✽ ✽ an exceptional wine, worth a special search

81 a wine now past its peak

83 ready to drink now

85 drinkable now, but will improve with further aging

88 needs further aging before drinking

Examples:

83 an average-quality wine, drinkable now

84 ✽ an above-average wine, drinkable now

85 ✽ ✽ a very fine wine that can be drunk now, but will
improve even more with age

88 ✽ ✽ ✽ an exceptional wine that should be held before
drinking

California

ACACIA WINERY   *Napa 1979*   Born in Texas, soft-spoken Mike Richmond worked
for several years at Freemark Abbey before making his own first vintage of
Pinot Noir and Chardonnay in a corner of the St. Francis Winery. Then,
putting together a group of investors including vineyardists Paul Perret, Robert Sinskey, and Ira Lee, he constructed a winery in the Los Carneros region
in 82. The partnership developed the 50-acre Marina Vineyard to supply
Chardonnay. Acacia purchased fruit from its partners and other growers, most
of whom own vineyards in Los Carneros. Its focus fell on vineyard-designated
Pinot Noirs and multiple Chardonnay bottlings.

Acacia's wines in the early 80s were often exceptional in quality, and just
about always provided lessons in the effect of different microclimates. Of the
two varietals, Chardonnay was much more consistent, and on occasion the
Winery Lake, Marina Vineyard, and Carneros bottlings soared to ✽ ✽ ✽ levels.
However, with Pinot Noir, Acacia offered six vineyard-designated bottlings—
Carneros, Madonna Vineyard, Winery Lake Vineyard, St. Clair, Lee Vineyard,
and Iund Vineyard—and in the process generated more excitement for that
varietal than anyone else.

In 84, Acacia developed a separate facility for a line of Bordeaux-type wines.
Joe Cafaro was hired as winemaker for the winery's Cabernet Sauvignon,
Merlot, and Sauvignon Blanc. Apparently, this project created a philosophical
rift in the partnership or aggravated financial problems. In 86 the partnership

was dissolved and Acacia was sold to Chalone, Inc. Both Richmond and long-time winemaker Larry Brooks remained. The winery's production has increased from 30,000 cases in 86 to 50,000 in the 90s. Chardonnay accounts for 80%, and the Pinot Noirs for 20%. The winery has experimented with sparkling wine and in the mid-90s will be marketing about 1,000 cases of Brut a year.

Chardonnay

(Marina Vineyard)   84   85*   86***   87   88*   89

(Carneros)   84*   85*   86***   87**   88*   89*

Both wines are crisp, appley, toasty, and somewhat lean in character, and both need the ripe, rich fruit of good vintages to succeed

Pinot Noir

(St. Clair)   80**   81**   82   83**   84**   85**   86***   87**   88*

(Madonna)   80***   81   82*   83**   84   85*   86**   87   88*

(Carneros)   84   85*   86*   87   88   89*

All of the Acacia Pinot Noirs (including those which are no longer offered—Iund, Lee, and Winery Lake) have steered a fairly consistent line toward cherryish, moderately bright fruit, restrained tannins, and a shorter rather than longer ageability; the St. Clair is often the deepest and frequently shows a roasted herb, dried-bark note

ADELAIDA CELLARS   *San Luis Obispo 1983*   Owner-winemaker John Munch worked in the cellars of Estrella Winery before starting his own line of wine. Leasing space in the Estrella facility, Munch began making Cabernet Sauvignon and Chardonnay. He also served as winemaker and project manager for Tonio Conti, a short-lived line of sparkling wines owned by the Swiss-backed company Chat Bott. For Adelaida, Munch purchased grapes from within the county and had production up to 5,000 cases a year by 87. When Estrella Winery experienced financial difficulties and went on the sales block, Adelaida Cellars moved into other facilities, including Castoro Cellars and Wild Horse. Syrah from Munch's own 2-acre vineyard has joined the line.

ADLER FELS   *Sonoma 1980*   Precariously situated on the northwestern slope of the Mayacamas Mountains in Sonoma Valley, Adler Fels makes 10,000 cases of wines a year. The volume leader is Fumé Blanc, followed by Chardonnay and Gewurztraminer. The winery also makes Pinot Noir and an unusual sparkling wine labeled "Mélange à Deux," a 50–50 blend of Gewurztraminer and Riesling. After several erratic vintages, the winery began to settle down, and by the 86 vintage started showing significant quality improvements pretty much across the line. The Fumé Blancs tend to be on a strong, bold scale, with assertive herbal character. When balanced, they can be of * quality. The winery's Gewurztraminer in a slightly sweet style is also effusively varietal and on occasion has merited ** ratings. Owner David Coleman is a graphic artist who became familiar with the wine business when he began designing labels. Among the many he has designed are those for Far Niente, Château St. Jean, and Hidden Cellars. Adler Fels has no vineyards. All wines originate in Sonoma County.

Chardonnay

84   85   86*   87   89

An inconsistent performer, showing toasty oak, ripe but somewhat restrained fruit

AHERN WINERY   *Los Angeles 1978*   In 78 Jim Ahern, an engineer by trade, opened a winery in part of an industrial complex, and produced a modest line of varietals from several well-known vineyard areas. His style favored intense, barrel-fermented Chardonnays and usually heavy, highly extracted Sauvignon Blancs. Zinfandels from Amador County have been sometimes over-oaked, but with plenty of varietal intensity. The white wines have come from different sources in the Central Coast. Ahern's Chardonnays, from Edna Valley and Paso Robles, were consistently rich and oaky. Despite its modest success, Ahern ceased making wines after 88.

AHLGREN VINEYARD   *Santa Cruz 1976*   Though still tiny, this family-run winery finally outgrew the Ahlgren family basement where it began and now makes 1,500 cases a year. Doing all of the winemaking by hand, the Ahlgrens have made a range of varietals from purchased grapes. What they do best most of the time are red wines. Their Cabernets from Napa Valley and from the Santa Cruz Mountains are usually ripe and highly extracted, and designed for long aging. Chardonnays from the Santa Cruz Mountains and some of the more prestigious vineyards in Santa Barbara and Monterey County (Ventana Vineyards is a regular offering) have yet to rise above average. Barrel-fermented Semillons from Santa Cruz appellations are among the richest made by anyone, and the most consistent of the winery's whites. Most wines are made in quantities ranging from 80 to 600 cases.

ALDERBROOK VINEYARDS   *Sonoma 1982*   In the early 80s partners John Grace, Phil Staley, and Mark Rafanelli converted an old ranch and prune orchard located in the southernmost corner of the Dry Creek Valley into a winery and 55-acre vineyard. They believe that their vineyard site has a microclimate best suited to white varieties, and as a result they grow only Sauvignon Blanc, Semillon, Chardonnay, and Muscat Blanc. Grace, a former dentist, assists with the winemaking, and Rafanelli (from the winemaking family) oversees the vineyard operation. The winery's style emphasizes straightforward varietal fruit and a subtle use of oak. Often bright in fruit and unusually rich, their Semillon has been a standout on occasion. In their price range, Alderbrook's consistently attractive Chardonnays are usually singled out for their youthful appeal, and can in some vintages achieve ✷ results. A Reserve Chardonnay, aged longer in barrel, is sometimes produced. A slight degree of erratic performances characterized the winery's Sauvignon Blancs. By the mid-80s the winery began using more grapes from its own vineyards, developed in 81–82. By 90, Alderbrook was making only estate-bottled wines as its production reached the maximum of 30,000 cases a year.

Chardonnay

84   85✷   86✷   87✷   88✷   89

Lots of pretty fruit in a fresh, appley, almost blossomy vein, supported by creamy, quietly stated oak, medium-full body

ALEXANDER VALLEY FRUIT & TRADING CO.   *Sonoma 1984*   The name, along with the colorful label, suggests that this producer makes more than just wines. In fact, the owners began as growers selling their crop from 55 acres planted in the Alexander Valley. But when a few disagreements arose between grower and buyer over grape prices and payment policies, owner Steve Sommer and his family ventured into winemaking. It was soon decided to market their wines in combination with other locally grown foods and gift items made in Sonoma County. They now run a full-scale enterprise designing and marketing special gift packages and baskets that usually feature wine as the centerpiece. By 87 they were selling the majority of their 10,000 cases of wine to individuals and to businesses which offered them as gifts. The wines regularly made are White Zinfandel, Cabernet Sauvignon, Chardonnay, and a dry-style (under 1% residual sugar) Chenin Blanc. Overall, the wines tend to be light in intensity and average in quality.

ALEXANDER VALLEY VINEYARDS   *Sonoma 1975*   This well-manicured 120-acre estate vineyard in the warm midsection of the Alexander Valley is the pride of the Wetzel family, which purchased the site in 63. Harry Wetzel, the patriarch, also is a major partner in another 120-acre vineyard adjacent to the winery. The winery was expanded in 86, and produces seven varietals, with Chardonnay and Cabernet Sauvignon the major emphasis. Annual production is level at 50,000 cases. This winery has at one time or another performed well with each wine, but at best has lacked consistency and real distinction. Its prices, however, have remained on the modest side. The winery started off well with Chardonnay, but it experienced some disappointing vintages in the 80s. Occasionally, its Pinot Noir earns ✿ status when it avoids a tendency toward overripeness. A dry (under 1% residual sugar) Chenin Blanc enjoys some popularity in restaurants, a segment of the market to which the Wetzels devote considerable attention. Overall, the winery's most reliable wine has been Cabernet Sauvignon, blended with Merlot. After beginning with plenty of promise, the winery strikes us as having been somewhat of a disappointment in the 80s.

Cabernet Sauvignon

80   81✿   82✿   83✿   84✿   86   87

Usually high in ripeness with black-cherry fruitiness, sometimes a touch of herbs or brush, sweet oak

Chardonnay

83✿   84✿   85   86   87

Blossomy fruit in best years, drier and less pretty in others

Pinot Noir

81✿   82   **84✿**   85   86   87

Ripish, usually fairly deep, sometimes muddled

ALMADÉN VINEYARDS   *Madera 1852*   Almadén Vineyards occupies a special place in the history of California winemaking and, until the early 80s, Almadén wines were a real force in the wine market. At that time, Almadén was selling over 13 million cases a year and had three large facilities producing an assortment of table, sparkling, and dessert wines from 6,000 acres of vineyards and purchased grapes. In the 60s Almadén's Grenache Rosé became a best-seller, and many claim it created America's once passionate love affair with rosé wines. But when the rosé market began to sag, Almadén was left with an image as a jug-wine producer, and all efforts in the 80s to change that image failed. Sales slipped badly, and Almadén was sold to Heublein in 87.

To consolidate production, Heublein closed the former facilities, sold most of the vineyards, and moved Almadén to its own vast all-purpose facility in Madera in the Central Valley. Almadén brought to Heublein its established "Le Domaine" sparkling wine label, as well as its ill-fated upscale brand, Charles Lefranc. Almadén is now one of several labels produced and bottled in the Heublein-owned facility. The current roster contains a typical range of low-priced varietals, including White Zinfandel and White Barbera and a host of generics. With its generic line Almadén seems to be aiming toward the mass audience with such items as Blush Chablis and Blush Rhine. Almadén appears now to be just another brand sent out to the low end of the varietal and jug-wine markets.

ALPEN CELLARS   *Trinity 1988*   Trinity County's first and only winery, Alpen is owned by Mark and Keith Groves. Located in a mountain valley in the Trinity Lakes region well within view of the Trinity Alps, Alpen's vineyards are situated at 2,600 feet above sea level. From observations of their original experimental grape-growing parcel, the owners concluded that the altitude and the latitude created conditions suitable for planting early-maturing varieties. Their 7-acre vineyard contains Riesling, Gewurztraminer, Chardonnay, and Pinot Noir. Using an old ranch house as his winery, winemaker Keith Groves works without benefit of refrigeration or electricity to make about 600 cases a year. With the maturity of his vineyard, the output is expected to double.

ALTAMURA VINEYARDS   *Napa 1985*   After working in the cellars of Caymus Vineyards for five years, Frank Altamura decided to produce estate-bottled wines from his own vineyard. In 80 his family purchased a 70-acre vineyard on the Silverado Trail, just north of the town of Napa. Chardonnay is the leading variety planted, but the winery also grows Cabernet Sauvignon, Merlot, and Cabernet Franc. Only Chardonnay, partially barrel-fermented, was produced over the first three vintages. The Cabernet varieties were first crushed in 88. Trying to keep the winery as a one-man operation, Altamura makes about 2,000 cases of Chardonnay, and plans to produce about 1,000 cases of a Cabernet-based red.

AMADOR FOOTHILL WINERY   *Amador 1980*   Located east of Plymouth, Amador Foothill specializes in Zinfandel, Red and White. The red is made from older vineyards, frequently from the Eschen, Esola, or Grand Père vineyards. The winery has bottled each under vineyard designations. In 1980 10½ acres were planted to Cabernet Sauvignon, Sauvignon Blanc, and Semillon. Owners Ben Zeitman and Katie Quinn, the winemaker, decided there was enough Zinfandel available within Amador, so they planted other varieties. The winery enjoyed sales success with its first vintages of White Zinfandel, and by 87, White Zinfandel accounted for 75% of total production. Today, the output from Amador Foothill Winery consists of the two types of Zinfandel plus Fumé Blanc. Oak-aged and blended with Semillon, the Fumé Blanc offers fresh fruitiness in a lean, tart style. Having reduced its production of White Zinfandel to one-third of its total, the winery currently is at the comfortable 10,000-case annual level. Only one wine, an 82 Zinfandel, has ever earned so much as ✿ to date.

AMIZETTA VINEYARDS   *Napa 1984*   In 79, Spencer and Amizetta Clark purchased 40 acres of bare land in Napa Valley from his brother-in-law, Charles Shaw. On extremely steep hillsides that require extra-wide terraces, they began planting 10 acres to Sauvignon Blanc. Another 10 acres were later planted to Cabernet Sauvignon. A winery was finished in time for the 84 crush. Amizetta produced only Sauvignon Blanc in 84, adding Cabernet in 85. Facing a mixed reaction from the trade and the media to the Sauvignon Blanc, Clark decided after 87 to graft all of the vines over to Cabernet Sauvignon, with lesser amounts of Merlot and Cabernet Franc. From 20 acres, Amizetta presently makes only a Cabernet Sauvignon and will gradually expand to the 3,500-case-a-year level. Aging is in a combination of French and American oak for an average of two years.

S. ANDERSON VINEYARD   *Napa 1979*   Dentist Stanley Anderson and his wife, Carol, a dental hygienist, purchased a vineyard site in 71 located in the Stags Leap District, planting it in 73–74 to Chardonnay. By 79, the Andersons had constructed a small winery near their home and produced about 1,000 cases combined of Chardonnay and *méthode champenoise* Brut. In 84 they decided to expand the winery operation and built underground aging facilities. Their 7,000-square-foot caves are used for aging 250,000 bottles of sparkling wine and for the barrel aging of their estate Chardonnay. The sparkling wine line now consists of Brut, the mainstay, along with limited amounts of Blanc de Noirs, Blanc de Blancs, Rosé, and a Reserve. Production continued to grow in the 80s, and topped 15,000 cases in 90. Tivoli is the name attached to a Brut sparkler made from press juice. The estate vineyard contains 32 acres of Chardonnay. The Andersons also own 70 acres in the Carneros, which they began developing in the late 80s.

Chardonnay

84✿   85✿   86   87✿✿   88✿

Typically well balanced between rich, toasty oak and focused varietal fruit directly suggestive of apples and less so of fresh, citrusy influences

ARCIERO WINERY *San Luis Obispo 1986* Frank and Phil Arciero operate a construction and development company in Southern California, and together with their families run this winery located 6 miles east of Paso Robles. Starting their vineyard in 83, they now have close to 600 acres planted. The leading varieties are Chardonnay (200 acres), Cabernet Sauvignon (100 acres), and Zinfandel (99 acres). Experiments with Nebbiolo encouraged the planting of 5 acres. Arciero's winery and tasting-room complex is the largest wine facility in San Luis Obispo County, and at its peak capacity the winery will be able to turn out 500,000 cases a year. At the end of 90, Arciero was making about 100,000 cases, with Chardonnay and Cabernet Sauvignon combining for half of the total. A second label, "Monte Verde," was developed to market Chardonnay and Cabernet Sauvignon in a lower price niche. To date, even though all wines have been priced competitively, the overall quality has often struggled to reach acceptable levels or better.

ARGONAUT WINERY *Amador 1976* This winery started small and stayed small. Its owners are all engineers on a full-time basis and winery owners on a more casual basis. Zinfandel and Barbera are made every year, with the Barbera from the 2-acre estate vineyard. The only white produced on occasion has been a Sauvignon Blanc. Total annual production is just under 2,000 cases.

ARIEL VINEYARDS Developed in 86 by J. Lohr Winery, Ariel is a line of de-alcoholized wines now owned and operated in the Napa Valley independently of J. Lohr. The process used was a revolutionary one at the time, known as reverse osmosis. Of the many known procedures for removing alcohol (centrifugation and distillation are the two most common), reverse osmosis was thought to be the most gentle to the beverage. From a few thousand cases in 86, Ariel has grown to the 100,000-case-a-year level. It offers a variety of products with the so-called "Blanc" the best-seller, followed by a Sparkling Brut, and a White Zinfandel. A sparkling Blanc de Noirs is also available, as are Chardonnay, Cabernet Sauvignon, and Merlot. The wines used have generally come from Napa Valley and the Alexander Valley.

ARROWOOD WINERY *Sonoma 1988* Dick Arrowood, one of the best-known winemakers in the state, started construction of his own winery in 86, while continuing work at Chateau St. Jean (which he joined in 74) until 90. Located in the Sonoma Valley and perched on a knoll, Arrowood Winery emphasizes Chardonnay and Cabernet Sauvignon. Merlot is offered in some vintages when it is not entirely given over to the Cabernet Sauvignon blend. Arrowood's barrel-fermented Chardonnays are blends from three Sonoma County appellations—Russian River Valley, Alexander Valley, and Chalk Hill. The Cabernets are made from vineyards in Knight's Valley, Alexander Valley, and the home acreage. In the first offering, the winery's production was close to 10,000 cases. By the end of the 80s it was making 16,000 cases, evenly divided between Cabernet and Chardonnay. The Merlot debuted at ❋❋❋ with the 88 vintage. The winery has 4 acres planted to Merlot, Cabernet Franc, Malbec, and Petit Verdot. Most grapes crushed are purchased.

Cabernet Sauvignon
85❋ 86❋❋❋ 87❋

Ripe, rich style, deep in curranty and black-cherry fruit; good aging potential

Chardonnay
86❋ 87❋ 88❋ 89❋

Nicely focused, appley fruit, with sweeter pearlike overtones well supported by oak

VINCENT ARROYO WINERY *Napa 1984* Seeking an alternative to the electronics business, Vincent Arroyo bought an old vineyard in Calistoga. At the time, the mature 37-acre vineyard contained Petite Sirah, Gamay, and Cabernet Sauvignon. During the first few years Arroyo sold most of the fruit to the large Co-op Winery in St. Helena. Encouraged by Bob Pecota, a neighbor and longtime advocate of Petite Sirah, Arroyo began making wine in 84, and the mainstay has been Petite Sirah, aged for one and a half years in French oak. Having purchased another vineyard in the area containing 22 acres, Arroyo still sells most of his fruit to other producers. As his production grows to the 3,000-case-a-year target, he is offering Cabernet Sauvignon and Chardonnay, along with Petite Sirah.

DAVID ARTHUR VINEYARDS *Napa 1985* After running a restaurant in Colorado, David Arthur Long returned to his family's 920-acre ranch in the eastern hills of Napa Valley. In the same general area as Chappellet, 40 acres of vineyards were planted there in the early 80s. The winery's name avoids the family's last name in deference to Long Vineyard, a neighboring winery owned by Bob Long. Chardonnay and Cabernet Sauvignon are the leading varieties grown, plus a few acres of Cabernet Franc, Merlot, Petit Verdot, and Sangiovese. After gradual growth the winery will level off at 3,000 cases a year, with Chardonnay representing two-thirds of the total.

HUNTER ASHBY *Napa 1985* This spin-off brand is owned by the Jaeger family, involved in Rutherford Hill Winery, Freemark Abbey, and Jaeger Cellar, as well as other brands outside of Napa Valley. Using grapes from the Ashby block of Jaeger's Vineyard, located just north of Napa, Hunter Ashby has been trotted out a few times, but misses a vintage here and there. In general, the line consists of Chardonnay, Merlot, and Pinot Noir. The only discernible pattern is that each varietal is marketed at a somewhat older age than its competition, though they are not made in a particularly ageworthy style. So far the wines have not been remarkable for either quality or value.

ATLAS PEAK VINEYARDS *Napa 1989* This wine company was created by Whitbread, one of the largest British brewers, in partnership with two prestigious wine firms—Antinori of Italy and Bollinger of Champagne. Buying land, vineyards, and a winery facility from William Hill, the owners spent considerable time and money developing vineyards on Atlas Peak in the southeastern hills of Napa Valley, ending with 460 acres planted. The vineyards' first crush was in 89, and the roster was headed by Cabernet, Chardonnay, Semillon, Sauvignon Blanc, and Sangiovese. With over 30 acres planted to Sangiovese, the largest single planting of that red grape, Atlas Peak seemed likely to be closely followed by the critics. However, before the next crush was under way, Whitbread's interest was bought out by an even larger British corporation, Allied-Lyons, the owners of Hiram Walker, which in turn owns Callaway, Clos du Bois, and William Hill. The Atlas Peak project, with Antinori still owning 5% and Bollinger still a stockholder, slowed to an almost complete stop. In recent vintages, it has crushed only Sangiovese and Cabernet Sauvignon—enough to make 10,000 cases of each.

AU BON CLIMAT *Santa Barbara 1982* While working for the Zaca Mesa Winery, Adam Tolmach and Jim Clendenen decided to form a small company dedicated to producing Chardonnay and Pinot Noir. Au Bon Climat began life in a corner of the now defunct Los Alamos Winery, where they made wines from the adjacent vineyards. In 89 they moved into a larger facility on the Bien Nacido Ranch, which is a primary source of Chardonnay and Pinot Noir. For each varietal, the partners prefer making vineyard-designated bottlings, and over their first several vintages they worked with a number of vineyards in the Central Coast and even one in Oregon. In recent vintages, they have settled on three Chardonnay bottlings—Bien Nacido Vineyard, the Benedict Vineyard, and Reserve. For Pinot Noir, they are now relying on two vineyards—Benedict and Bien Nacido. Fairly consistent high praise has been bestowed on the Chardonnays, especially the Reserve, fermented entirely in new French oak. The Pinot Noirs are often among the most highly extracted versions offered, but are also of erratic quality. Chardonnay accounts for 75% of their annual output, Pinot Noir the remainder. Steady expansion has taken the brand close to its goal of 10,000 cases per year. Nebbiolo and small lots of other Italianate wines are bottled under the "Il Podere dell'Olivos" label. Partner Clendenen is also co-owner of the Vita Nova (see entry) label, and Tolmach owns the Ojai Winery (see entry) outright.

Chardonnay

(Los Alamos Vineyard/Santa Barbara County)　84 ** 　85 * 　86 *
88 * 　89 *

Ripe, oaky, complex, but fruit is sometimes underplayed relative to barrel and winemaking influences

Chardonnay

(Reserve)　85 ** 　86 ** 　87 * 　89 **

Fruit is the key here; when there is enough, the wine shows all the balance needed to carry its heavily oaked, rich style

Pinot Noir

(Los Alamos Vineyards)　8̶3̶ 　84 ** 　86 * 　87

(Rancho Viñedo)　87 * 　8̶8̶

Always deep, always complex, not always able to keep its herbal and tobacco characteristics in check

---

AUDUBON CELLARS　*Alameda 1988*　In 83 Ralph Montali, an elder statesman in the wine-marketing field, took over the ailing Richard Carey Winery along with the inventory and built a facility in Berkeley. Operated later as Montali Winery, it was acquired in 86 by a group headed by Hubertus Von Wulffen, onetime president of Buena Vista. In 86, while still operating it as Montali Winery, Von Wulffen offered a series of limited-production wines identified as the Audubon Collection, with each label displaying one of the Audubon "Birds of America" paintings. In 88 the winery changed its name to Audubon Cellars, and since then has offered a line of varietals and two generics, Audubon Blanc and Audubon Rouge. Made entirely from purchased grapes, Audubon Cellars' varietal line consists of Chardonnay from Sonoma-Carneros, Cabernet Sauvignon from Napa Valley, Zinfandel from San Luis Obispo and other sources, and Sauvignon Blanc from Napa Valley. Audubon's annual production is around 30,000 cases. The 200,000-gallon-capacity facility also custom-makes wines for several independent brands.

AUSTIN CELLARS　*Santa Barbara 1981*　Founder-winemaker Tony Austin came to Santa Barbara County as the first winemaker for Firestone Vineyards. After leaving in 80, he started his own brand by leasing space in another facility. At the time, Austin vowed to remain a small producer buying grapes in the area and making whenever possible at least one late harvest white wine per year. By 84, Austin Cellars had its own winery, and within the next few years was developing its own vineyards. Located in the Los Alamos area, the 20-acre vineyard is planted to Chardonnay and Cabernet Franc. The winery is targeted for a maximum annual output of 25,000 cases. Halfway to its goal, it now offers an array of wines headed by Chardonnay, Pinot Noir (conventional and "White"), Sauvignon Blanc, Gewurztraminer, Cabernet Franc, Johannisberg Riesling, and late harvest Riesling. Austin has regularly offered Sauvignon Blanc in a pronounced, grassy vein and a Pinot Noir which, though usually rich, is often on the overly exotic side.

BABCOCK VINEYARDS　*Santa Barbara 1983*　The Babcock family became interested in wines by way of the restaurant business. Along the western edge of the Santa Ynez Valley, they developed 50 acres to five varieties—Chardonnay, Johannisberg Riesling, Gewurztraminer, Sauvignon Blanc, and Pinot Noir. The first few vintages were on the erratic side as the production team apparently learned on the job. With experience the winery emerged as one to watch for Gewurztraminer, made both in a bold, barrel-fermented, bone-dry style and in a slightly sweet style. In the best years, the opulent, varietally intense dry Gewurztraminer reaches ✿✿✿ performance. Babcock is also becoming reliable for Johannisberg Riesling in a light, lively, slightly sweet style. In more recent vintages, the winery's Eleven Oaks Ranch and regular Sauvignon Blanc have stood out in a rich, brisk style. As it approaches its annual production goal of 8,500 cases, Babcock shows signs of settling into a fine groove.

Chardonnay

84   85   86   87✿   88✿   89

Decently fruity and crisp in balance with oak for richness

Chardonnay (Reserve)

86   87✿✿✿   88✿✿

More oak and richness than the regular bottling and lots of fruit in top years, when it reaches near-classic dimensions

BAILY VINEYARD & WINERY   *Riverside 1986*   A lover of German wines, computer expert Phillips B. Baily, with his wife, Carol, in 81 acquired land in Temecula and developed a 7-acre vineyard; 6 acres were planted to Riesling, 1 to Semillon. Baily buys Chardonnay, Cabernet Sauvignon, and Sauvignon Blanc from neighbors in Temecula. At present the winery's annual output is at the 2,400-case level, with production consisting of White Riesling, White Cabernet, and Sauvignon Blanc. Long term, Baily hopes to expand production to 15,000 cases a year.

BALDINELLI VINEYARDS   *Amador 1979*   Retired engineer Ed Baldinelli and his wife, Kay, acquired the old Dickson vineyard located in the Shenandoah Valley. Their estate-bottled Zinfandel originates in the parcel planted in 23. The original vineyard has been gradually expanded to 70 acres, with Zinfandel (38 acres) and Cabernet Sauvignon (15 acres) the major varieties planted and produced. In 79, with vineyard manager John Miller, they founded a winery which now makes three Zinfandels—a long-aging Reserve from the estate vineyard, an Amador County bottling, and White Zinfandel. In the 80s the production of White Zinfandel represented about one-third of the winery's 16,000-case total output. Cabernet Sauvignon is the second most important wine by volume, with limited amounts (under 1,000 cases) of Sauvignon Blanc and even less of Chardonnay.

BALLARD CANYON WINERY   *Santa Barbara 1978*   Just a few miles outside of the town of Solvang, dentist Gene Hallock founded Ballard Canyon, planning to grow grapes for sale. In the early 70s he established a 50-acre vineyard (over half to Cabernet Sauvignon), only to find that the market for grapes was poor. By 78 the decision was made to build a winery to crush the estate-grown grapes. The winery has gradually expanded its production and has reached its 12,000-case-per-year target. Cabernet Sauvignon, Johannisberg Riesling, Chardonnay, and Muscat Canelli are the primary varieties planted. Each is made as a varietal, and the Cabernet Sauvignon is converted into both a traditional and a "White" version. Made in two styles, a medium-sweet and a *Botrytis*-affected sweet version, Johannisberg Riesling represents about one-third of the winery's production. Ballard Canyon has enjoyed sales success with a deliberately sweet-style Chardonnay nicknamed "Dr.'s Fun Baby," sold mostly at the tasting room. The greatest critical achievement goes to the estate Chardonnay, barrel-fermented and aged *sur lie;* but only a few hundred cases are made a year.

BALVERNE VINEYARDS   *Sonoma 1979*   With 200 acres of vines spread over beautiful hillsides and valleys in the Chalk Hill area, northeast of Windsor, the founders of Balverne decided to market their wines primarily to the restaurant trade, holding them back at the winery for greater age and maturity. Balverne specialized in two reds, Cabernet Sauvignon and Zinfandel, and two whites,

Chardonnay and Sauvignon Blanc. The quality was higher for the reds than the whites. Zinfandel was the most noteworthy, and like all of the wines was from a specific parcel, the Quartz Vineyard. By the mid-80s, Balverne was experiencing financial difficulty and its production was reduced. Today, the winery, owned by over 1,000 shareholders and under new management, has dropped Zinfandel and emphasizes three vineyard-specific varietals—Chardonnay (Deerfield), Cabernet Sauvignon (Laurel Vineyard), and Sauvignon Blanc (Stonecrest Vineyard). Balverne's annual production had dipped to 18,000 cases, but its new owners hope to return it to the 30,000-case level by the mid-90s.

BANCROFT VINEYARDS   *Napa 1988*   Jim Bancroft, a San Francisco attorney, fell in love with the Howell Mountain area in the late 60s. In 69 he purchased 275 acres with the idea of building a weekend retreat. A few years later he acquired a neighboring 90-acre parcel. Though he had no intention of becoming involved with wine, he sold some 40 acres to Bill and Joan Smith, who went on to establish La Jota Vineyard. Randy Dunn, who assisted the Smiths through their first vintages, also encouraged Bancroft to develop a vineyard. By the early 80s he had a 90-acre vineyard planted to Cabernet Sauvignon, Merlot, Cabernet Franc, and Chardonnay. Over the years Bancroft sold grapes to several producers and developed long-term arrangements with Beringer Vineyards, among others. Beringer has relied heavily on Bancroft Cabernet Sauvignon in several vintages of its Private Reserve, and made its first Merlot from Bancroft's vineyard. In 86 he sold Chardonnay to Stony Hill, which produced a wine labeled "SHV." In return, Stony Hill began making Chardonnay from Bancroft Vineyards for the Bancroft label which, in 88, its first vintage, amounted to 200 cases. Long term, Bancroft expects to level off at 1,500 cases a year of Chardonnay only.

BANDIERA WINERY   *Sonoma 1977*   This was one of Sonoma County's old jug-wine producers (founded in 37), revived and reopened in 77 to bottle decent-quality jug wines. Chris Bilbro operated it for a few years, then it changed hands again in 80. Its current owner, known as the California Wine Company, modernized the rapidly decaying old plant. Drawing from 200 acres of vineyard in Sonoma and in Napa Valley, it offered a range of table wines under several labels (Bandiera, Sage Creek, John B. Merritt) until settling on the Bandiera label. By the end of the 80s Bandiera was focusing on four varietals: White Zinfandel, Chardonnay, Cabernet Sauvignon, and Fumé Blanc. The annual production had grown to 150,000 cases and White Zinfandel accounted for just over half of the total. Owning 57 acres of Cabernet Sauvignon, Bandiera produces 30,000 cases of Cabernet from the Napa Valley. Chardonnay from the Carneros, where the winery has 42 acres, is the second significant wine in terms of volume, at 32,000 cases. The winery's Chardonnay and its Fumé Blanc, also from Napa Valley, have achieved little critical acclaim to date. Prices are generally on the lower end of the scale.

BAREFOOT CELLARS   This is a privately owned label whose wines are aged and bottled in leased space. It began in 88 with the acquisition of the trademark, "Barefoot" wines, from the Davis Bynum Winery in Sonoma, which for years bottled wines under the Barefoot Bynum label. The primary standard wines sold under the label are Cabernet Sauvignon and Sauvignon Blanc, both bottled in magnums only. In 90, the owners added a new line (California Beau) that played upon the Barefoot name. It is a line of 5% alcohol wines bottled under the California Beau designation. This line of partially de-alcoholized beverages includes Cabernet Sauvignon, Chardonnay, Sauvignon Blanc, and Gamay Beaujolais. Counting the Barefoot Cabernet Sauvignon and Sauvignon Blanc line together with the low-alcohol products, this company has been bottling about 200,000 cases a year.

BARGETTO WINERY   *Santa Cruz 1933*   One of the oldest wineries in the area, Bargetto has made a graceful shift from old-style wines to those with contemporary appeal. Located on the main street in Soquel, it developed a reputation years ago through its tasting room for its fruit and berry wines and a specialty wine named Chaucer's Mead. In the late 70s, under the direction of the third generation, it began shifting to the classical varietals and purchasing grapes from better vineyards in the Central Coast and in Napa Valley. In its 35,000-case-a-year line, it places major emphasis on Chardonnay (12,000), Cabernet Sauvignon (6,500), White Zinfandel (5,000), and Gewurztraminer (3,000). Lower-priced Chardonnay and Cabernet Sauvignon intended for early enjoyment have been produced from varying appellations, but are united under the "Cypress" designation. The least expensive bottlings are its Red and White Table Wine. Purchasing all of its grapes, mostly now from the Central Coast and Santa Cruz Mountain appellations, Bargetto has targeted 55,000 cases a year as maximum. Best success has been enjoyed with the Chardonnay and Gewurztraminer, with both the low-end Cypress Chardonnay and the regular bottling offering good value in their better vintages. Bargetto owns no vineyards.

Chardonnay

(regular bottling)   84   85*   86   87*   88   89

Medium-bodied wines with direct fruit, sometimes floral and tropical in tone, and moderate oak

---

BARROW GREEN WINERY   A private label owned by ex-restaurateur Melvyn Master, Barrow Green has been attached to bottles of Chardonnay, Pinot Noir, and a proprietary Bordeaux blend. Master buys Chardonnay and Pinot Noir from several growers, and the first vintages were aged and bottled at La Crema, a company with which he was affiliated as marketing director. The red blend named Chartrons contains generally equal portions of Merlot, Cabernet, and Cabernet Franc. Early vintages amount to 5,000 cases total.

BAY CELLARS   *Alameda 1982*   Richard Rotblatt, a structural engineer living in Berkeley, decided in 82 to make wines professionally when a vacant wine facility in nearby Emeryville became available. For five years, Bay Cellars, a part-time operation, shared the facility with St. George's Spirits and Rosenblum Cellars. In 87 it moved to a larger facility in Berkeley. Rotblatt produces a small line of table wine, with emphasis on Pinot Noir, Chardonnay, Cabernet Sauvignon, and in some vintages, Merlot. Buying from a range of growers, Bay Cellars has regularly produced a Pinot Noir from Los Carneros and Cabernet Sauvignon from Napa Valley. The barrel-fermented Chardonnay is most often produced from Napa Valley grapes. Most wines are offered in 400–500-case lots, with annual output holding steady at 1,500 cases. The most noteworthy wines have been the Reserve Pinot Noirs.

BEAUCASTEL ESTATE   *San Luis Obispo 1990*   After a long and fairly well-publicized search for a vineyard site within California, the Perrins, owners of the famous Château Beaucastel of Châteauneuf-du-Pape in the Rhone Valley, acquired a 120-acre ranch about 10 miles west of Paso Robles. The winemaking facility is operated as a joint venture between the Perrins and Robert Hass, owner of Vineyard Brands, a wine importer and wholesaler. The first trial plantings were under way in 90. With a Rhone Valley blend in mind, the owners planted four reds—Syrah, Grenache, Mourvedre, and Counoise—and three whites—Marsanne, Roussanne, and Viognier.

BEAULIEU VINEYARDS   *Napa 1900*   The pride of Napa Valley for several decades, Beaulieu contributed mightily to the recognition of Napa Valley Cabernet Sauvignon, which in turn had a dramatic impact on the emergence of Napa Valley and the reputation of the entire California wine industry. In 1900 founder Georges de Latour, a man of meticulous standards, planted the winery's original vineyards on the western edge of Rutherford, a region recognized by others decades later as prime Cabernet turf. Beaulieu was the leading Cabernet producer, along with Inglenook, prior to Prohibition, and Latour kept his vineyards so well maintained that Beaulieu easily resumed winemaking in 34, the first vintage after Repeal.

In 38, Latour succeeded in convincing the Russian-born, French-taught André Tchelistcheff to become winemaker at Beaulieu. Though Latour died in 40, Tchelistcheff proved to be a wise choice, successfully guiding Beaulieu until early 73. One special lot of 36 Cabernet Sauvignon made from the two oldest vineyards was separately bottled and dedicated to Georges de Latour. That wine began a fabled series of "Private Reserve" Cabernets that came to be the most prestigious and sought-after California wine in many vintages from 36 through the early 70s. In 69, the heirs of Latour sold Beaulieu to Heublein; over the following years the product line was expanded, along with production. Heublein added a low-end Beau Tour Cabernet bottling and a line of generic wines in magnums, and doubled production within a decade.

In the 90s Beaulieu is holding steady at the 450,000-case annual output level, focusing on four varietals—Cabernet Sauvignon (50% of total production), Chardonnay, Pinot Noir, and Sauvignon Blanc. The line includes Johannisberg Riesling, Muscat Frontignan, and sparkling wines made by the *méthode champenoise*. From its 300 acres in the Carneros District, Beaulieu offers a regular and Reserve of both Chardonnay and Pinot Noir. In Napa Valley, the winery owns or controls 385 acres of Cabernet Sauvignon, apportioned among three bottlings—Private Reserve, Napa Valley–Rutherford, and Beau Tour. Except for the Beau Tour, which is blended with Merlot, Beaulieu's Cabernets have been 100% Cabernet and have been aged in American oak barrels. The quality of Beaulieu wines is generally acceptable, with ❋ performances registered occasionally by its Private Reserve Cabernet, the Carneros Reserve Pinot Noir, and Carneros Chardonnay. The scarcity of ❋❋ ratings indicates that Beaulieu is no longer a leader, and even in the high-priced Cabernet sweepstakes, its Reserves are no longer among the finest. In the last decade and a half of releases, its Private Reserves have registered more than their share of disappointments: 1972 (a disaster), 74 (short-lived), 83 (a lightweight), and 84 (an average wine from a superb Cabernet vintage). Tchelistcheff returned to Beaulieu in 1991 to oversee production.

Cabernet Sauvignon

(Private Reserve) 68❋❋❋ 69❋❋ 70❋❋❋ 71❋ 72 73❋ 74❋ 75❋ 76❋ 77❋ 78❋❋ 79❋ 80❋ 81 82❋❋ 83 84 85❋ 86 87❋

Once the holiest name in California Cabernet, this wine has endured a decade of less than outstanding performance and, at its best, now offers medium-intensity currant, tea leaf, and vaguely dusty and peppery character that, in too many recent vintages, has lacked intensity relative to the wine's usually firm structure and its bold oakiness

Cabernet Sauvignon

(Rutherford) 80 81❋ 82❋ 83 84 85 86 87 88

Generally clean, unchallenging wines of medium weight, moderately intense cherry and vaguely curranty flavors, and light tannins

Chardonnay

(Carneros Reserve) 84 85 86❋ 87❋ 88 89❋

(Napa Valley Beaufort) 84❋ 85 86❋ 87 88

Though offering comparable records of success, these wines differ in character. The Carneros Reserve is the oakier and crisper of the two, while the Napa Valley bottling is a bit more open, in a clean, uncomplicated, well-balanced style

Pinot Noir

(Carneros Reserve) 84❋ 85❋ 86❋ 87❋ 88❋

(Napa Valley Beaumont) 84 85 86 87 88

The Reserve, the most consistently likable wine from Beaulieu in the last several years, generally focuses on direct, ripe bright cherrylike fruit, with a dollop of toasty oak for enrichment; even the lighter-styled 88, somewhat strawberryish in tone, turned out well. The Beaumont is a lightweight wine intended for early consumption

BEAUREGARD RANCH   *Napa 1989*   Grape grower Jim Beauregard ventured into winemaking in 87. In his debut vintage, using part of the Swanson winery in Napa Valley, he made 3,500 cases of Chardonnay. His production combines grapes from three vineyards. He favors 100% barrel fermentation and extended *sur lie* aging.

BEL ARBORS VINEYARDS   (FETZER VINEYARDS)   Fetzer's original winery is located on Bel Arbres Road in Hopland, and for many years the Fetzers used the name for a second label. The product line under Bel Arbres changed with the fads. In the mid-70s it was led by three low-priced generic table wines: Blanc de Blancs, Red Table Wine, and White Table Wine. Although the output under this label grew as it was targeted for supermarkets and chain stores, it was not until the blush wine blitz, when Fetzer decided to label all of its blush wines as Bel Arbres, that this line took on great importance to the owners. By 87, in order to keep pace with the demand for low-priced Chardonnay, the Fetzers began buying grapes and wines from Washington to blend with California wine. By law, the appellation then had to be "American." With the addition of a large volume of American wines to Bel Arbres, Fetzer decided to simplify the line and rechristened it "Bel Arbors," the way most consumers were said to pronounce it. The leading wines so labeled are White Zinfandel, Chardonnay, Cabernet Sauvignon, Merlot, and Sauvignon Blanc. The two reds are well above the others in terms of quality. Bel Arbors was selling over 500,000 cases in 90. The long-term goal is 3 million cases a year.

BELLEROSE VINEYARD   *Sonoma 1979*   Charles Richards holds a master's degree in music, and played the classical guitar professionally. In 78 he and his wife decided to change careers and bought 35 acres of vines in the southern part of Dry Creek Valley. Richards, the winemaker, was among the first in California to specialize in a Bordeaux-style Cabernet blend. He labels his version "Cuvée Bellerose," a blend of Cabernet Sauvignon, Merlot, Cabernet Franc, and, in most years, Petit Verdot and Malbec. Richards also makes a Sauvignon Blanc–Semillon blend in a style that is varietal in a weedy-grassy note and on the coarse side. With the 83 vintage, Bellerose added a varietal Merlot, containing lesser amounts of the other red Bordeaux varieties. Both red wines are aged 18 months in oak barrels, and they are usually given only a light egg-white fining for clarification. A blended red wine labeled "Work Horse Red" is bottled on occasion: most of the winery work is performed by hand, with assistance from two Belgian horses kept on the ranch. Production of the Cuvée Bellerose is about 3,000 cases, and the Merlot is near 1,000. Having expanded his vineyard to its present 52 acres, Richards sets 10,000 cases as the maximum annual output when the vines are fully mature.

Cuvée Bellerose

83   84   85*

Complex, herbal, sometimes slightly earthy, smokey, usually fairly tannic and in need of long aging

Merlot

83   84   85*   86   87*

Much like the above wine in range and toughness, and, for that reason, taking a different road from most Merlots

BELVEDERE WINERY   *Sonoma 1979*   Peter Friedman, co-founder of Sonoma Vineyards/Rodney Strong Vineyards, manages the operation, and Bill Hambrecht, a financial adviser and investor in several wineries and vineyards, remains behind the scenes. "Belvedere Winery" is a label usually employed for vine-yard-designated varietals or Reserve wines at the top of the line; it should be distinguished from "Belvedere Discovery," which consists of a line of négo-ciant wines on the low end of the price spectrum. Belvedere's vineyard-designated varietals were once marketed under the grandiose and confusing moniker "Grape Maker Series," which highlighted each grower's name in such a way as to make each seem like a separate brand. Today, Belvedere's top varietals remain single-vineyard wines. One is the Robert Young Vineyard in the Alexander Valley, which supplies both Cabernet Sauvignon and Merlot to Belvedere. The Bacigalupi Vineyard, a 45-acre spread in the Russian River Valley, provides grapes for separate bottlings of Pinot Noir and Chardonnay. Cabernet Sauvignon also comes from the 100-acre York Creek Vineyard in Napa Valley. Another Belvedere Chardonnay regularly offered is a Reserve from the Carneros appellation.

To summarize, the portfolio is made up of two Chardonnays (Bacigalupi and Carneros Reserve), two Cabernets (Robert Young, York Creek), the Bacigalupi Pinot Noir, and the Robert Young Vineyards Merlot. Each is made in approxi-mately 4,500-case batches.

Cabernet Sauvignon

(Robert Young Vineyard)   82   83   **84***

Cherryish fruit, firm but accessible flavors, herbal leanings, quiet oak

Cabernet Sauvignon

(York Creek Vineyard)   **82****   **83***   **84***

Deep, strongly constituted, briary, curranty, tannic

Chardonnay

(Carneros)   86*   **87***   88

Appley and tropical fruit, spicy oak, direct flavors

BENZIGER OF GLEN ELLEN   *(Glen Ellen Winery)*   By 88 the family-owned Glen Ellen Winery had become so successful (sales topped 3.2 million cases) with its low-priced, highly visible line that its owners, the Benziger family, decided to use the family name for a line of upscale varietals. Benziger wines, unlike those in the Glen Ellen line, are all made at the winery, in part from grapes grown in their adjacent 85-acre vineyard, planted to Cabernet Sauvignon, Merlot, Chardonnay, and Sauvignon Blanc. A Meritage Red, White, and occa-sionally a Semillon have been bottled. The quantities average about 2,000 cases for each primary Sonoma Valley bottling. In addition to these home-grown wines, Benziger of Glen Ellen produces a line of Sonoma County varietals from grapes purchased throughout the county. Made in 10,00–15,000-case lots, the wines offered are Cabernet Sauvignon, Chardonnay (partially barrel-fermented), an oak-aged Fumé Blanc, and Pinot Blanc. Generally, the estate-grown Sonoma Valley varietals offer more intensity, and in the early rounds the quality leaders have been Merlot, Cabernet Sauvignon, and Char-donnay. To date, all Benziger offerings are definite improvements over wines labeled Glen Ellen Winery.

Chardonnay

(Sonoma County)   86   **87***   88

Simple, clean, direct in approach, the wines have shown moderate fruit and quiet oak

Cabernet Sauvignon

85   86   **87***

Fruity, moderately tannic, accessible wines

Merlot

86   **87****

Round and rich with good fruit

BERGFELD WINE CELLARS *Napa 1986* The original winemaking facility, a stone structure built in 1885, is now contained within a larger processing plant. The property was acquired in 34, enlarged, and operated for many years as the Napa Valley Cooperative Winery. As a cooperative run by hundreds of grape growers, it crushed and fermented wines that were sold in bulk, primarily to the Gallo winery. In the 80s, as Gallo developed its own winemaking facility in Sonoma County, it came to rely less and less on the Napa Valley Co-op. As a result, in 86 125 remaining growers of the Co-op made the decision to bottle and market their wines themselves; they reorganized the group into what they called "an agricultural processing and marketing cooperative." All grapes crushed are supplied from 2,000 acres in Napa Valley owned by members. Among numerous varieties made, the leaders are Chardonnay, Sauvignon Blanc, Cabernet Sauvignon, Merlot, and Zinfandel. All contribute to a line of table wines that has grown to 25,000 cases a year. As the winery has expanded, it has set 400,000 cases a year as its production goal. "Bergfeld 1885" was the brand name chosen to establish a link to the origins of the facility. Located between Inglenook and Sutter Home on the main wine road, Bergfeld has built a hospitality center with the hope of selling many wines on the premises.

BERINGER VINEYARDS *Napa 1876* Jacob and Frederick Beringer, the brothers who founded this winery, would have little trouble identifying their estate, their home (the Rhine House), and the old stone winery behind it carved into the hillside. However, everything else has changed. Operated by the Beringer family until 71, this grand old name had run into serious problems by the 60s. The winery was making a range of dull, nonvintaged wines that undermined the reputation gained by the better vintaged versions bottled through the 40s. In 71, the winery and its old, worn-out cooperage (mostly redwood tanks and large German oak ovals) and equipment along with some 800 acres were bought by Wine World, Inc., a division of the Swiss-based conglomerate Nestlé. The new owner invested millions of dollars in renovating the Rhine House and the old aging caves, turning them into a popular visitors center. Construction of a large production facility across the road was finished in 74, and the winery acquired and developed prime vineyard lands in Napa and Sonoma counties. Winemaking was turned over to Myron Nightingale, who was later succeeded by his apprentice, Ed Sbragia.

Signs of quality improvements were first noticed with the release of the 73 Napa Valley Chardonnay and Cabernet Sauvignon. Gradually but persistently, Beringer worked to remove the tarnish left from the 50s and to counter the corporate image. In 77, Beringer made a Private Reserve Cabernet Sauvignon from the Lemmon Ranch (renamed Chabot Vineyard) that caught our attention. Building upon that Private Reserve Cabernet base, Beringer toiled away to improve its overall track record and image. Today, Beringer draws from the 3,100 acres it owns, 2,300 in Napa Valley and the rest in Knight's Valley. Beringer has substantial Napa Valley Chardonnay vineyards in Napa, Yountville, and Oakville, adding up to 620 acres, while 520 acres in both Napa and Sonoma counties are devoted to Cabernet Sauvignon. Chenin Blanc remains an important grape for the winery, with 260 acres, followed by Sauvignon Blanc at 240 acres.

To fill out its large line of table wines, Beringer still purchases grapes from growers in the Napa Valley or other North Coast regions. The current volume leaders are White Zinfandel (over 750,000 cases), Chardonnay (150,000 cases) and Chenin Blanc (100,000 cases). In terms of prestige, Cabernet Sauvignon is Beringer's leader, represented by three bottlings—Private Reserve, Chabot Vineyard, and Knights Valley. Second is Chardonnay (Private Reserve and Proprietor Grown). Other noteworthy offerings include its Napa Valley Fumé Blanc, its oak-aged Knights Valley Sauvignon Blanc (blended with Semillon), and its remarkably attractive Gewurztraminer, a well-kept secret. A Zinfandel partially made by carbonic maceration, and a late harvest Semillon/Sauvignon Blanc blend bottled as "Nightingale," are also worthy of attention. In the late 80s Beringer added Merlot from Howell Mountain. Today, the winery bottles about 1.3 million cases a year. Nestlé also owns Chateau Souverain, Meridian, Napa Ridge, Los Hermanos, and, in part, Maison Deutz Champagne.

Cabernet Sauvignon

(Private Reserve—Lemmon Ranch)   77 *   78 *   80 * *

(Private Reserve)   81 *   83 * *   84 * *   85 *   86 * *

(Lemmon-Chabot; Chabot Vineyard)   81 * *   83   84 * *

This group of wines, under their varied and changing nomenclature, represents the evolution of Beringer into a producer of top-quality Cabernet; the wines have been medium-full-bodied and fairly tannic, usually with enough ripe, curranty fruit to achieve satisfactory balance for medium- to long-term aging

Cabernet Sauvignon

(Knights Valley)   82 *   83 *   84   86   87

A medium to medium-full-bodied wine, with direct, moderately ripe, accessible cherry and quietly herbal flavors supported by light-medium tannins

Chardonnay

(Private Reserve)   85 *   86 * *   87   88   89 *

(Proprietor Grown—Napa Valley)   84 *   85   86 *   88 *   89

Generally well-made wines, showing appley and sometimes citrusy fruit with toasty oak, especially in the Private Reserve, and good acid balance

BIANCHI VINEYARDS   *Fresno 1974*   Also known as Villa Bianchi, this family-owned winery divides its attention between bottling its own wines and selling directly to other producers. From its 1.5-million-gallon-capacity facility, it offers a line of varietals made primarily from its 580-acre vineyard and a line of generics. The still-evolving varietal roster consists of Chardonnay, Sauvignon Blanc, Chenin Blanc, Cabernet Sauvignon, and Zinfandel. Blush wines, almost as numerous, include Blush, White Cabernet, White Grenache, and White Zinfandel. Bianchi's specialty wines are its two proprietary whites, "Casa Bianca" and "Cosa Nostra," and one red, Lambrusco. With strong sales in Italian restaurants, Bianchi offers some of its wines in screw caps and also has a line of wines, known as "canteens," packaged in cans. Annual sales are close to 100,000 cases.

BLACK MOUNTAIN VINEYARD   *(J. W. Morris Winery)*   Acquired in 76 by Ken Toth, who once was president of Sonoma Vineyards, Black Mountain Vineyard is a 275-acre estate with 100 acres under vine. Most of the crop goes to Toth's other brand, J. W. Morris. Located in the Alexander Valley, Black Mountain Vineyard straddles the Russian River and extends east up the hillsides. The primary varieties planted are Chardonnay, Sauvignon Blanc, Cabernet Sauvignon, and Zinfandel. The specific sites where these varieties are respectively grown are each said to enjoy a microclimate, and each is given a vineyard designation that appears on the label. Most of the Zinfandel is planted on a knoll named Cramer Ridge. The parcel of Sauvignon Blanc is situated midway up the slopes and is called Laurelwood. Located closer to the river one Chardonnay patch is Gravel Bar, and another one surrounded by fir trees is Douglas Hill. The name given to Cabernet Sauvignon is Fat Cat. From the early vintages onward, both Chardonnays have aimed for size and richness through barrel fermentation and *sur lie* aging. The other varietals have not shown any kind of distinction or consistency. The total output for the four wines is about 10,000 cases a year.

Chardonnay

(Gravel Bar)   84 *   85 * *   87

Bigger, richer (and pricier) than its stablemate, with very obvious toasty, buttery qualities when successful

Chardonnay

(Douglas Hill)   85**   87   88

Less expensive and less complete, this one, aside from its initial success, has been mildly fruity and a bit angular

---

BLACK SHEEP VINTNERS   *Calaveras 1987*   Formerly known as Chispa Cellars, this old winery was acquired in 86 by its present owner, Dave Olson, onetime winemaker for Stevenot. He promptly changed the name to Black Sheep. Chispa had produced limited amounts of often tanky, old-style Zinfandel. Black Sheep's current production consists of Zinfandel and Cabernet Sauvignon from Amador County and Sauvignon Blanc from Calaveras County. Zinfandel is the major wine in the annual output of 1,000 cases.

BLOSSOM HILL WINERY   *(Almadén Vineyards)*   In early 89, two years after Heublein acquired Almadén Vineyards, this spin-off brand of table wines was introduced. Blossom Hill offers low-priced varietals and generics in magnums only as an upscale jug-wine line. Bottled at Heublein's main production facility in Madera, Blossom Hill wines consist of two reds, Cabernet Sauvignon and Gamay Beaujolais, along with Chardonnay, Sauvignon Blanc, and White Zinfandel, the volume leader. Red Table and White Table bottlings complete the line. All are vintaged and display the California appellation.

BOEGER WINERY   *El Dorado 1973*   As the first winery established in El Dorado County after Prohibition, Boeger quickly became the best known and also the biggest in the county. This family-owned producer has led the way for others in El Dorado through its many experiments with numerous varietals. In 73 the Boegers established a 35-acre vineyard on an old, pre-Prohibition winery site. They planted Cabernet Sauvignon, Chardonnay, and Sauvignon Blanc in significant acreage along with parcels of Semillon, Zinfandel, and Merlot. This estate vineyard is a series of beautiful terraces situated at the 2,000- to 3,000-foot elevation. The Boegers also lease a nearby 20-acre vineyard, the Peek Vineyard, which they planted to Johannisberg Riesling, Flora, Symphony, Cabernet Franc, and Petit Verdot.

The neighboring Walker Ranch supplies Boeger with Chenin Blanc and Zinfandel. In most vintages the winery offers estate-bottled Cabernet Sauvignon, Chardonnay, and Merlot, and each has risen to * level on occasion. On the basis of consistency, Chardonnay is its most noteworthy wine. In addition to its popular blends—Hangtown Red and Hangtown Gold—Boeger makes a light, refreshing slightly sweet Johannisberg Riesling and a sweet-tasting Sauvignon Blanc. The winery has reached its maximum level of 12,000 cases a year. The volume leaders are Chardonnay, Cabernet Sauvignon, White Zinfandel, and Sauvignon Blanc.

Cabernet Sauvignon

75*   76*   77*   78*   79   80   81*   82   83   **84***   85   86*
87

Usually made in a ripe, not overblown style, with curranty, sometimes jammy or tarry notes, moderate tannins, all adding up to good value when it succeeds

Merlot

82*   83*   **84***   85   86   87   88

Seemingly deeper wine in its first vintages, now showing enjoyable ripish, briary character and good oak richness, but less distinctive fruitiness

---

BOGLE VINEYARDS   *Yolo 1979*   In the Delta region of Clarksburg, the Bogle family has long been involved in agriculture. Although they have entered grape growing in a big way with more than 600 acres under vine, the Bogles remain diversified farmers, and continue to sell many crops as well as a major portion of their grape crop. In the mid-80s, like many other growers, they removed several varieties such as Chenin Blanc and Grey Riesling in favor of Chardonnay and more Chardonnay. Cabernet Sauvignon is the second most widely planted variety. Under their own brand, they are making about 100,000 cases. Most of their output consists of low-priced varietals in 1-liter bottles, the top-selling wines being Chardonnay, White Zinfandel, Cabernet Sauvignon, and Fumé Blanc. In the traditional 750-ml bottle labeled with the Clarksburg appellation, Bogle makes Zinfandel, Petite Sirah, Merlot, and Semillon, all of which are moderately priced.

BONNY DOON VINEYARD   *Santa Cruz 1981*   A former philosophy instructor, Randall Grahm purchased land on Bonny Doon Road in 81. He planted Pinot Noir and Chardonnay, and proclaimed himself a Burgundian. His first wine to appear was a Vin Gris from Pinot Noir that met with a mixed reception. Then in 84, turning to Rhone Valley wines, he created a proprietary wine, "Le Cigare Volant," to replicate a red Châteauneuf-du-Pape. (The wine's name, French slang for a flying saucer, was an inside joke poking fun at a proclamation in the 50s prohibiting UFOs from landing in the region of Châteauneuf-du-Pape.) That wine, made from Grenache and Syrah, was of high quality. Not long afterwards, Grahm made a Nouveau-style wine from Grenache grown in Gilroy, known as the garlic capital of the world, and bottled it under the name of Clos de Gilroy.

By the end of 86, Grahm was marketing a range of wines, from Syrah originating in Paso Robles, to Chardonnay from Monterey County, to Pinot Noir grown in Oregon. Shortly thereafter, he cast his lot with the Rhone. His vineyard now covers 27 acres and consists of roughly 5 acres each of Syrah, Marsanne, Rousanne, Mourvedre, and Viognier. (Pinot Noir and Chardonnay were long since removed.) Beginning in 87, his Vin Gris was made from Mourvedre.

As production hits the 15,000-case-a-year level, the three leading wines are Vin Gris, Cigare Volant, and Chardonnay made from purchased grapes. Since 88, the Syrahs have been made entirely from the 6 acres in the estate vineyard. The winery has also developed a line of fruit infusions—grape juice blended with brandy. And in 89, the first spirits from Bonny Doon appeared. Grahm makes Grappa from Muscat and Grenache grapes, but also from two popular labrusca varieties, the Isabella and the Niagara. His interest in Grappa led to an interest in traditional Italian grapes and wines. A small vineyard in Monterey County was chosen as a site for experimentation with a wide range of Italian grapes, from Sangiovese to Nebbiolo and numerous others. In the 90s, Bonny Doon's maximum production could grow to 30,000 cases, and Grahm will continue to be something of a character.

Chardonnay

(La Reina Vineyards)   83*   84**   **85***   86   **87***   88   89*

Always deep in toasty oak, usually with sufficient fruit for balance, these are consistently wines of medium-full body and broad character

---

BORRA'S CELLAR   *San Joaquin 1975*   South of Lodi on property farmed by his grandfather in the early 1900s, Steve Borra has been busy replanting the old vineyard and reviving winemaking. The 35-acre vineyard contains 12 acres of Barbera, the rest consisting of Zinfandel and Flame Tokay, the pride of Lodi. From a first crush that yielded under 200 cases, the winery focused on Barbera in the 80s, making both a red and a blush version. With the offering of Zinfandel, production has edged to the 1,000-case level. However, Borra began removing some of the Barbera in favor of Cabernet Sauvignon, which he will emphasize in the 90s. To date, the quality has been variable.

BOUCHAINE VINEYARDS   *Napa 1980*   When it started, this winery seemed to have everything going for it: financial backing (the owners were an heir of the DuPont dynasty and a member of the Kiplinger family) and its location in Los Carneros. After renovating the old Garetto Winery (founded in 1899), Bouchaine made its initial vintage in 81, and also started a strong custom-crush business. The early vintages of Pinot Noir and Chardonnay consisted of a variety of vineyard-designated bottlings. The quality often seemed to lag behind the reputation of the vineyard and the competition. In 82 Jerry Luper, formerly of Chateau Montelena, was brought in as winemaker, staying until 86. Since then, the winery has placed emphasis on its estate-bottled Chardonnay, and on the Pinot Noir from its own 31-acre vineyard in Los Carneros. On average it makes 10,000 cases of Chardonnay and 5,000 cases of Pinot Noir. Additional grapes from Carneros or the Yountville area have been purchased. The Chardonnays, including an occasional Reserve, are 100% barrel-fermented and undergo partial malolactic fermentation. For Pinot Noir, the winery uses the old open-top rectangular fermenters made of concrete. During fermentation, the Pinot Noir has whole clusters added, and a special system is used for frequent punching down of the cap. By 90 Bouchaine's quality was on an even course.

Chardonnay

(Napa Valley)   84*   85*   86*

(Carneros)   84**   86*   87**   88*

Throughout its twists and turns, Bouchaine has produced Chardonnays that are crisp, oaky, well fruited, and moderately rich

Pinot Noir

82*   83*   84   85   86   87*

Direct, sometimes thinly fruited, cherrylike qualities come with moderate oak enrichment, hints of herbs, and mild tannins

RICHARD BOYER WINES   *Monterey 1985*   Like several other full-time winemakers, Rick Boyer branched out to start his own limited-production specialty wine company. In the beginning he traded services for goods as he made Chardonnay from Ventana Vineyards, his normal place of work. Since then, he has developed an 8-acre Chardonnay vineyard. With vineyard maturity, Boyer will switch sources from Ventana to his own grapes. In any event, Boyer's Chardonnays are barrel-fermented and aged *sur lie*. His production has been steady at 1,500 cases per year. By the end of the 90s he plans to reach the 2,000-case maximum level. Already showing well, this winery seems poised to grab the brass ring with upcoming Chardonnay vintages.

Chardonnay

(Ventana Vineyard)   85   86*   87*   88*   89

Fairly bright fruit and creamy oak are combined in well-balanced, medium-depth wines

BRANDBORG CELLARS   *Marin 1986*   A longshoreman in San Francisco, Terry Brandborg lives in the quaint town of Fairfax in the middle of Marin County. At first, he only wanted to produce a few hundred cases to sell locally. However, as he experimented with small batches of varietals from different microclimates, he found himself making 1,200 cases a year, the facility's absolute capacity. The varietals he enjoys producing are Zinfandel, Charbono, Riesling, Pinot Noir, and Sauvignon Blanc. He has come to prefer Zinfandel from Mount Veeder and from Mendocino, Charbono from Napa Valley, Sauvignon Blanc from Mendocino's Potter Valley, and Pinot Noir from many sources, including Anderson Valley, Sonoma Valley, and Santa Barbara. One wine he continues making despite sluggish sales is Riesling from the Anderson Valley.

BRANDER VINEYARD   *Santa Barbara 1980*   Fred Brander, owner and winemaker, came to Santa Barbara County to work initially for the Santa Ynez Winery. After three vintages he left to make wines under his own brand and from his own vineyard. From 79 through the 84 vintage, Brander specialized in Sauvignon Blanc (blended with Semillon) from his vineyard. Other wines were made from his vines, such as several blush wines, but they were marketed under St. Carl, his second label. In 85 he added Chardonnay and upgraded the Cabernet Blanc (blush Cabernet Sauvignon) to the Brander line. The Cabernet Blanc from 85 ranks as one of the finest, most flavorful of the blush type. Though it was produced in limited volume, a Cabernet Franc from Brander's vineyard was among the first California wines sold with that varietal identity. His Cabernet Franc from 85 in a blush style was another wine marketed that created some early interest in Cabernet Franc as a varietal. Then from the 84 vintage, Brander released another new wine in 86 called Bouchet, a blend of Cabernet Franc and Merlot.

This wine and subsequent vintages were intended to present Cabernet-type wines in a much better light than their counterparts from other wineries in Santa Ynez. However, we find Bouchet (fewer than 1,000 cases made) to be on the overly jammy-fruity side, without complexity, and tending toward the overripe and ponderous. So far, Brander Chardonnays have been erratic and unimpressive. Its mainstay is Sauvignon Blanc, which in its best vintages captures bold, varietal character in a crisp, slightly fruity, lean style. We peg it as a ✿ performer. With annual production at the 10,000 level, Brander is at its optimum. The Sauvignon Blanc represents about 50% of the total.

BRAREN PAULI WINERY *Sonoma 1979* Partners Bill Pauli and Larry Braren are longtime friends who decided to combine their talents in this small winery. Pauli is a vineyardist who owns part of the Richetti Vineyard in Mendocino County, which has supplied Fetzer with its Richetti Vineyard Zinfandel for many years. Braren oversees the winery, located in Petaluma. The two owners are also partners in a vineyard in the Potter Valley that grows their Chardonnay. Cabernet Sauvignon and Merlot are made from vineyards they lease under long-term contract. By the end of the 80s, they were producing 9,000 cases a year, evenly divided among Chardonnay, Cabernet Sauvignon, and Merlot. The style of wine has leaned a little toward the heavy-handed, excessively wood-aged for the two reds. For the moment, good intentions have outstripped results.

BRITTON CELLARS *Riverside 1984* After purchasing a 20-acre vineyard in Temecula as an investment, the Britton and Freestone families, longtime friends, soon decided to ease into wine production. Their vineyard contains Chardonnay, Riesling, Sauvignon Blanc, and Cabernet Sauvignon. The winery was set to reach 10,000 cases a year, but that plan derailed, and the winery was sold in 89. It has been renamed Clos du Muriel (see entry) by its new owners.

DAVID BRUCE WINERY *Santa Cruz 1964* In his first decade of winemaking, David Bruce accomplished enough to deserve a special place in the history of post-Prohibition wine. While he was earning his medical degree at Stanford, Bruce became acquainted with Martin Ray and volunteered to work with him. He shared Ray's enthusiasm for the Santa Cruz Mountains appellation and for mountainside vineyards. Setting up a dermatology practice in San Jose in 60, Bruce began making wines at home. In 61, he built a winery and planted 25 acres on terraces high in the hills of Los Gatos. In contrast to his quiet demeanor, Bruce made wines that were bold, sometimes bizarre, and often highly experimental. Among his many curious wines, he made a White Zinfandel in 64, forerunner of the blush wines of the 80s. He also made a range of late harvest wines, including both dry and sweet late harvest Zinfandels, and a late harvest Grenache. Bruce expressed an interest in making Petite Syrah and Grenache long before the Rhone Valley trend arrived in the 80s.

But it is the Chardonnays that elevated Bruce to special status. Believing in extremely ripe grapes, barrel fermentation, high extraction, plenty of new oak, and in the complexity achieved by malolactic fermentation, Bruce began cranking out Chardonnays in 67, 68, and 69 that were big, powerful, sometimes overwhelming—and unlike any others of the era. His 72 and 73 Chardonnays added to his reputation for big, controversial, and unusual wines. In 73, half of the Chardonnay harvested was labeled Late Harvest. With Zinfandels made into a variety of styles, often big and portlike, and with Pinot Noirs made with the minimal handling approach, David Bruce wines from 67 to 77 were the center of attention.

By 82, Bruce's wines had turned toward a more conventional style, and he yielded the chores to his staff. Today, Bruce maintains that his winemaking style has not changed, but rather that other winemakers have adopted it and made it seem more conventional. The estate vineyard, located at the 2,000-foot level in a Region I climate, contains 16 acres of Pinot Noir, 12 of Chardonnay. Production is steady at 30,000 cases a year. The flagship wines are the estate-bottled Chardonnay and Pinot Noir. Included in the line are Cabernet Sauvignon, a "California" Chardonnay, and blended wines under the Shandon name.

Chardonnay

(Santa Cruz Mountains) 84* 85 87 88

More ripe than fruity, yet always with plenty of acid and oak, these wines have seemed short of richness and center in most years

Pinot Noir

82 83 84 85 86 88*

Herbal, dried-leaf qualities are the predominating characteristics, with somewhat thin, cherrylike fruit in quiet support

---

BUEHLER VINEYARDS *Napa 1978* Starting with a vineyard site purchased in 72, the Buehlers have nurtured 61 acres of vines. Both vineyard and winery are in the remote mountainous terrain along the eastern edge of Napa Valley near Lake Hennessey. John Buehler, Sr., is an engineer who retired as vice president from the Bechtel Corporation in 72. John Buehler, Jr., developed the vineyard and now oversees the entire operation. The vineyard was planted to 27 acres of Zinfandel, 26 acres of Cabernet Sauvignon, and 8 acres of Pinot Blanc. The winery has earned plaudits for its robust Zinfandels and its rich, highly distinctive, but sometimes controversial Cabernet Sauvignons. Aged in French oak for 18 months, Buehler Cabernets display to some degree an earthy, tarry component, and their success depends on how well that characteristic is controlled. Buehler's Zinfandels are ripe in style, with a deep blackberry fruitiness. With regard to Pinot Blanc, however, the Buehlers, after a valiant struggle to convince consumers of its merits, threw in the towel after the 88 vintage. This defeat was made less painful by the success enjoyed by White Zinfandel. After testing the market for Zinfandel Rose, Buehler consolidated its pink wine efforts into White Zinfandel. With sales of White Zinfandel growing each year, that wine now represents two-thirds of Buehler's annual 30,000-case output. A new line of low-priced varietals (led by Chardonnay and Cabernet) is labeled Bon Marché.

Cabernet Sauvignon

80 81 82** 83* 84* 85* 86*** 87*

Opulent, deep, curranty, leathery, sometimes earthy and tarry, and always loaded with character and tannin, this series of wines possesses all the stuffing for long aging, but sometimes seems a little too heavy and ripe to stay on course

Zinfandel

82* 83 85** 86* 87 88

Not unlike the Cabernet in its emphasis on full-blown character, this wine is usually ripe and tannic, with suggestions of tar thrown in

---

BUENA VISTA WINERY *Sonoma 1857* This old, historically significant winery was established by the flamboyant Count Agoston Haraszthy and is now owned by the West German firm of A. Racke. It was acquired in 79 from Young's Market of Los Angeles, and under the Racke regime the winery has been given a new and more vigorous direction. The original stone winery (Haraszthy Cellars) in the Sonoma Valley has been restored, caves and all, and serves as a visitors center and picnic grounds. The modern working winery sits amidst a 1,700-acre estate in the Carneros, where the owners have planted 900 acres of vines. With the annual production of table wines in excess of 190,000 cases, the owners use the Buena Vista name for the top varietals and "Domaine Buena Vista" for the highly popular proprietary blends. Most varietals are from the Carneros appellation, with the exception of Sauvignon Blanc, which generally hails from Lake County and sometimes from Alexander Valley.

Throughout the 80s the winery and its winemaker, Jill Davis, have worked hard to develop a small line of Private Reserve wines. We often like the Reserves of Chardonnay, Pinot Noir, and Cabernet. The winery also enjoys periodic critical success with Sauvignon Blanc and Chardonnay. Perhaps the varietal it will someday be known for is Cabernet Sauvignon, based on its Carneros and a Reserve bottling offered. Working in a region not hospitable to Cabernet, the winery is making close to 20,000 cases of friendly, fruity Cabernet Sauvignon and a bold, highly laudable, but not always successful Reserve. Its proprietary wines are spearheaded by "Spiceling" (Gewurztraminer and Riesling), and "Steelhead Run" (a blush Pinot Noir), which combine to represent close to half of total sales.

Cabernet Sauvignon

78 79* 80* 81 82 **83** **84** 85 **86** 87

Balanced, low-key, cherryish, medium-bodied, often herbal

Cabernet Sauvignon

(Special Selection) **78**** **79**** **80*** 81* **83** 86

Balanced, ripe, aromatic, cherry and currant fruitiness

Chardonnay

83 84 85 86 87* 88 89

Fruity, lean, simple, brisk acidity

Chardonnay

(Reserve) 84* 86** 87* 88

Riper and richer, with oak filling out appley fruit; acidity remains ample

BURGESS CELLARS *Napa 1972* Occupying a site used for winemaking since 1880, Burgess Cellars is located along the steep hillsides on the western edge of Howell Mountain. Former Air Force and private corporation pilot Tom Burgess purchased the property originally known as Souverain Cellars, founded by the legendary winemaker Lee Stewart. After selling the winery, Stewart retained the Souverain name, which eventually was bought by Pillsbury. Burgess began replanting the hillside vineyard to Cabernet Sauvignon and Cabernet Franc. Over the first several vintages Burgess purchased grapes from hillside locations, and before long his winery had developed a good reputation for Zinfandel, Cabernet Sauvignon, and a dry, oak-aged Chenin Blanc. Though it ranked among the finest in most vintages, the Chenin Blanc was discontinued in 84. From 72 to 76, Burgess also made some incredibly rich Petite Sirahs, before removing the old vines near the winery. In 79, he acquired a 50-acre vineyard in Yountville and planted it to Chardonnay. From 83 on, he has produced Chardonnay entirely from his Trière Vineyard. Until 81, a Napa Valley Cabernet Sauvignon from purchased grapes was offered in addition to a Reserve bottling.

Beginning with the 82 vintage, Burgess has produced only one Cabernet Sauvignon, labeled "Vintage Selection." Made entirely from nonirrigated, low-yielding hillside grapes, and blended with Merlot and Cabernet Franc, the Vintage Selection Cabernet is aged for two years in French oak. The Zinfandel, also made from hillside grapes partly from the Burgess vineyard, has long been a favorite of ours, and over recent years has become more refined and polished without sacrificing any of its lovely ripe-berryish flavors and tannic backbone. Burgess Chardonnays are barrel-fermented in small oak vessels made exclusively by the Damy cooperage in Meursault.

Burgess had reached his optimum production of 30,000 cases a year by 90. Over half consists of Chardonnay, with his Cabernet Sauvignon Vintage Selection falling in the 6,500- to 7,000-case range. From time to time, the second label, Bell Canyon, appears on wines that did not make the primary label.

Cabernet Sauvignon

(Vintage Selection) 73 ** 74 *** 75 * 76 * 77 * 78 * 79 * 80 ** 81 82 ** 83 * 84 *** 85 ** 86 * 87

Typically tight and closed-in when young, yet full of promise, these curranty and well-oaked wines seem to age slowly and with a certain firmly structured refinement; they are among the top tier of California Cabernets

Chardonnay

84 * 85 *** 86 ** 87 * 88 89 **

Sophisticated aromas of toasty oak and crisp apples remind some of French Burgundies, and the ample acidity that adds firmness to the wine's backbone follows suit, while also making it a little on the hard, unyielding side in some vintages

Zinfandel

81 ** 82 *** 83 ** 84 85 ** 86 ** 87

Tight in the Burgess mold, these slowly unfolding, berryish, and richly oaked wines are among the firmest and best-aging Zinfandels

BUTTERFLY CREEK WINERY *Mariposa 1987* Owned and operated by John Gerken, this is the largest winery in Mariposa County. The 20-acre vineyard, planted to Pinot Blanc, Merlot, and Chardonnay, is expected to yield about 7,000 cases of estate-bottled wine a year when in full production.

BYINGTON WINERY & VINEYARD *Santa Cruz 1989* On hillside property between Los Gatos and Boulder Creek, William Byington, owner of Byington Steel, has developed a chateaulike winery and visitors complex. The facility was completed in time for the 90 harvest, but from 87 through 89 Byington made wines from purchased grapes in rented space. The first vintages consisted of Chardonnay, Cabernet, Pinot Noir from Napa Valley, and Fumé Blanc from Monterey. Recent emphasis falls on Napa Valley Chardonnay, Dry Creek Valley Cabernet Sauvignon, and—until the winery's 8 acres of Pinot Noir reach full production—on Santa Barbara Pinot Noir. The winery is producing 12,000 cases a year with a long-term goal of 25,000 cases.

DAVIS BYNUM WINERY *Sonoma 1975* After operating a storefront winery in Berkeley for a decade, Bynum moved to his present location in the Russian River Valley area, where he expanded production. The line has steadied at 25,000 cases a year and consists primarily of Pinot Noir, Chardonnay, and Fumé Blanc. Today, most of the wines are made from Sonoma County vineyards owned by shareholders in the winery. In its early history the winery enjoyed success with Zinfandel and Fumé Blanc. In recent years it has achieved some distinction with Pinot Noir. Bynum's Chardonnay has been consistently average, except for the occasional higher rankings earned by the Reserve-type bottlings. After many years of erratic performances, the winery hired Gary Farrell as winemaker in 86, and he brought stability to the brand. Today, Bynum's top-of-the-line wines carry either the Reserve or Limited Release designations and account for 20% of the total output. To produce Pinot Noir, the winery uses relatively small, 2-ton capacity fermenters, which are said to facilitate punching down and extraction during fermentation. In 88 Bynum sold the once highly successful label "Barefoot Bynum," which included a line of generics and low-priced varietals. The buyers use the Barefoot Vineyards name.

Pinot Noir

83 * 84 * 85 86 87 * 88 *

Light cherry fruit, moderate oak, medium body, and herbal-toned in some years

BYRON VINEYARD & WINERY *Santa Barbara 1984* Byron Ken Brown, better known as Ken Brown, was the first winemaker at Zaca Mesa. After six crushes, he formed a small corporation and moved a few miles north in the Santa Maria Valley to establish this winery. The winery grew quickly to the 15,000-case level, with Chardonnay, Sauvignon Blanc, and Pinot Noir representing over 80% of the total. Small amounts of Cabernet Sauvignon and Pinot Noir Blanc were added to the line. However, the partnership began to weaken, and in early 90 the winery was sold to the Robert Mondavi family, with Brown remaining in charge. A 5-acre Chardonnay vineyard surrounds the winery, and it owns an additional 120 acres in the Santa Maria Valley.

The new owners inherited a winery with an interesting, if uneven, track record. At times the barrel-fermented Reserve Chardonnay and both Pinot Noir bottlings, regular and Reserve, have earned ✷. However, the most note-worthy wine of all is the Sauvignon Blanc, which tends to be soft and round, yet balanced, with only a pleasurable trace of herbaceousness to it. At its best, Byron's Sauvignon Blanc is of ✷✷ caliber, and one of the finest from Santa Barbara County. The winery's current output of 20,000 cases is due to expand gradually under Mondavi ownership to 50,000 cases a year.

Chardonnay

84✷   85   86   87   88   89✷

Oaky, appley, fully expressed but not always pretty

Pinot Noir

84✷✷   85   86   88✷✷

Sometimes rich, supple, complex, balanced, sometimes less so

Pinot Noir

(Reserve)   86✷   87   88✷

Now exhibiting the fruit, range, depth, velvety texture found in the winery's 84 regular bottling

CAFARO CELLARS *Napa 1988* Well-known winemaker and consulting enologist Joe Cafaro added his own label to his impressive résumé in 86. Cabernet Sauvignon and Merlot are the primary wines offered by Cafaro, who has made wines for Chappellet Vineyards, Keenan Winery, Acacia Winery, and Sinskey, as well as working with numerous other brands on a part-time basis. Cafaro's Cabernets and Merlots are made in part from grapes grown by Hess Collection and Spottswoode. Using only Nevers oak barrels, Cafaro ages both reds for about 18 months. To date, an average production consists of 250 to 300 cases of Cabernet Sauvignon and a like amount for Merlot. The initial releases of both varietals have possessed highly admirable character (✷✷ and ✷✷✷) and good aging potential.

CAIN CELLARS *Napa 1983* After selling his electronics business, Jerry Cain purchased a 540-acre parcel along the Mayacamas Mountain Range in 80. Over the next few years the terraced vineyards were planted with 120 acres of the five Bordeaux red varieties. The stunning winemaking facility and home, located close to a ridgetop overlooking St. Helena, were completed in 85. Forced to make wines in the first vintages entirely from purchased grapes, Cain Cellars was a little slow out of the gate, but when it tapped its own vineyards in 85, making both a Cabernet Sauvignon and a proprietary blend, "Cain Five," the winery made heads turn. In 86, Cain turned out attractively styled Merlot. Usually blended with 10% Cabernet Sauvignon and 5% Cabernet Franc, Cain Merlot captures the grape's sought-after aroma and suppleness in most vintages. Two white varietals are offered. Sauvignon Blanc generally displays fruit and freshness in a ✷ package.

In the late 80s Cain settled on producing two Chardonnays, one from Napa

Valley, and a second from Carneros that is 50% barrel-fermented. With a production goal of 30,000 cases a year, Cain had reached 24,000 by 90. As the vineyard matures, production of its flagship wine, Cain Five, is expected to approach 6,000 cases.

Cabernet Sauvignon

82 83* 84* 85*** 86* 87*

An attractive mix of currant fruit and sweet oak is seasoned with background notes of herbs and mint in a wine that is generally medium in depth and moderately tannic; in strong vintages, it seems capable of aging for a decade or more

Cain Five

85** 86** 87*

Seemingly a little richer and a bit stiffer-structured than the Cabernet Sauvignon, this blended wine combines currants and hints of berries with creamy oak, in a style that appears to promise substantial improvement with extended bottle age

Chardonnay

(Napa Valley) 84 85 86 87

(Carneros) 85 87 88

Typically made in a clean, crisp, somewhat narrowly fruited style, with toasty oak in the background

Merlot

82 83 84 86***

The deep, rich 86 set a new standard for Cain Merlots, which, until then, were low in fruit, high in tannin, and frequently lacking in appeal

CAKEBREAD CELLARS *Napa 1973* In the late 60s Jack Cakebread was operating the family auto-repair business in Oakland, studying photography with Ansel Adams, and working as a professional photographer himself. In 71, on a two-week assignment in the Napa Valley to illustrate a wine book, he suddenly decided to buy 60 acres and a house in the Rutherford area. A 22-acre vineyard was planted with Cabernet Sauvignon, Sauvignon Blanc, and Chardonnay. Though he made wines in 73, Cakebread had intended to sell most of his grapes, but the general slump in grape prices in 75–76 pushed him further into winemaking. By 78, the winemaking facility was enlarged, and Cakebread Cellars began growing to its present 40,000-case-a-year capacity. Vineyard holdings were expanded to 75 acres, including the major planting of Cabernet Sauvignon on their Hill Ranch on the western edge of the valley. The Chardonnays, made in part from purchased grapes, are partially barrel-fermented.

Cakebread was among the first to produce barrel-fermented Sauvignon Blancs aged *sur lie* and imbued with French oak character. The better-balanced Sauvignon Blancs merit **, but overall Cakebread's Sauvignon Blancs have earned fairly consistent * rankings. In the mid-8os, Cakebread added a Rutherford Reserve Cabernet Sauvignon to accompany its regular Napa Valley Cabernet Sauvignon, Chardonnay, and Sauvignon Blanc. Zinfandel made from the Howell Mountain appellation was discontinued after 82.

Cabernet Sauvignon

(Napa Valley) 76* 77 78* 79 80* 81* 82 83* 84* 85 ** 86* 87*

(Reserve) 84** 85*

Ripe cherries and hints of currants, lots of sweet oak, and plenty of tannin; sometimes tar and herbs are evident as well

Chardonnay

84 85 86 87 88* 89

Always ripe and oaky, but frequently lacking adequate fruit for the wine's size

CALAFIA CELLARS   This label is owned by Randle Johnson, a Napa Valley wine-maker. When not making wines for the Hess Collection, Johnson buys Cabernet Sauvignon from a vineyard on Mount Veeder to produce about 1,000 cases a year. Until recent years, Calafia offered several varieties, but the line was whittled down to one as Johnson's responsibilities with Hess increased.

CALERA WINE COMPANY   *San Benito 1976*   Owner Josh Jensen came to winemaking by the unlikely route of Yale and Oxford. Fascinated by French wines, he spent two years working the harvests in Burgundy and the Rhone Valley. In 72, determined to specialize in California Pinot Noir, he began searching for a site whose soil was thin and overlying limestone, like that of the Côte d'Or, and in 74 he ended up in the hills of the Gavilan Mountains near Hollister. A lime kiln had been built there around 1900 (*calera* is Spanish for lime kiln). The nature of the soil justified planting 24 acres to Pinot Noir. Three microclimates near the peak were identified, and have since always been treated individually. They are the Jensen Vineyard (14 acres), Reed Vineyard (5 acres), and Selleck Vineyard (5 acres). A rock-crushing facility on the property was converted into a gravity-feed winery, and in 78 Jensen made 700 cases total, all in half bottles.

Serving as his own winemaker for the early vintages, Jensen established a traditional regime. Using small open-top fermenters, he ferments with the natural, native airborne yeast, including a high percentage of stems and, during the fermentation, whole uncrushed berries. After a long, warm fermentation, the wines are clarified by racking and egg-white fining. In 84, Jensen planted a fourth Pinot Noir vineyard, the 14-acre Mills Vineyard. Jensen also buys Santa Barbara grapes and produces Pinot Noir labeled "Central Coast."

Always barrel-fermented and almost always an adventure to taste, Calera Chardonnays originate in two appellations. The estate or Mount Harlan Vineyard contains 6 acres planted in 84. The first vintage offered was 87. A second bottling is from the Central Coast area. Viognier, also first made in 87, is the third varietal offered. With 2 acres planted to Viognier in 83, Calera was among the first wineries to work with this difficult-to-grow Rhone variety. The vineyard has since been expanded to 5 acres. When his 47-acre estate vineyard reaches full maturity, Jensen envisions leveling off production at 17,000 cases a year. Based on its performance to date, Calera deserve a place as one of the genuine leaders in the emergence of Pinot Noir.

Chardonnay

(Central Coast)   84   85*   86   87   88*

(Mount Harlan)   87***

Both wines are marked by extensive reliance on rich oak, but the greater depth of the estate wine handles its heavier oak better than the less complete fruit of Calera's high-volume wine

Pinot Noir

(Reed)   79**   81*   82*   84*   85**   86*   87*   88**

(Selleck)   79**   80   81*   82***   84***   85**   86***

(Jensen)   79*   80   81*   82**   83   85***   86***   87**   88*

From the mid-80s onward, this trio of ripe, rich, complex, supple wines has set the standard for California Pinot Noir; their balance and underlying tannins help contribute to their considerable aging potential

CALLAWAY VINEYARD & WINERY   *Riverside 1974*   The long-departed founder, Ely Callaway, one-time president of Burlington Industries, might not recognize his old Temecula winery and vineyards today. Hiram Walker bought the property in 82 and set the winery on a fast-paced expansion course, quickly abandoning all attempts to produce red wines and concentrating instead on whites. Today, one proprietary wine, the "Calla-Lees" Chardonnay, represents half of the winery's total production. Made without any oak aging and instead aged *sur lie,* Calla-Lees quickly became a sales success. Other wines made today are Sauvignon Blanc (slightly sweet), Fumé Blanc (dry-finished, oak-aged), Chenin Blanc, and two blends, Vin Blanc and Spring Wine. Land owned or controlled by the winery now totals 720 acres, with 500 planted to Chardonnay alone. In the late 80s a *méthode champenoise* Blanc de Blancs was introduced, along with a Reserve Calla-Lees Chardonnay. Callaway is moving toward a maximum annual output of 250,000 cases.

Chardonnay

(Calla-Lees) 85* 86 87 88 89

Tropical and floral fruit qualities exhibit less complexity than the wine's proprietary name implies, thus leaving it on the simple and fruity side even when successful

CAMBRIA WINERY *Santa Barbara 1988* Jess Jackson, owner of Kendall-Jackson, bought Chardonnay grapes from several vineyards in order to keep pace with the demand for his Chardonnay in the 80s. One of his major suppliers was the Tepusquet Vineyard, a 2,000-acre ranch in the Santa Maria Valley. In 88 Jackson bought the lion's share (the Robert Mondavi Winery bought the rest) of Tepusquet, and now has 1,400 acres planted, over 1,000 to Chardonnay and 100 to Pinot Noir. Having built a winery on the property, Jackson is using Cambria as the primary brand for Santa Barbara–grown Chardonnay and Pinot Noir. He also has retained the rights to the Tepusquet name. Located 12 miles southwest of Santa Maria, the 84,000-square-foot winemaking facility was operating by late 90. It has a capacity of 100,000 cases a year. In 89, Cambria made 50,000 cases, and it will grow to its maximum by the end of the decade. Cambria's early Chardonnays show lots of promise.

Chardonnay

86* 88* 89*

Appley, somewhat citrusy from ample balancing acidity, toasty oak, a bit obvious in style but pleasing

J. CAREY CELLARS *Santa Barbara 1978* Named after its founder, James Carey, this winery was operated by the Carey family from 78 to 87. During the first decade, Carey's wines were uneven in quality. By 86 the winery, looking a little worn and in need of capital, was producing more Cabernet Blanc (blush) than anything else. Now owned by the Firestones of Firestone Vineyards, the winery has been upgraded and new cooperage installed. The winery has three vineyard parcels covering a total of 46 acres. The original 25 acres, developed in 73, are planted primarily to Sauvignon Blanc and Cabernet Sauvignon. One 12-acre parcel containing Cabernet Sauvignon and Merlot is known as the La Cuesta Vineyard. Under the Firestone ownership, it is responsible for a vineyard-designated Cabernet Sauvignon and Merlot. As the winery grows from 6,000 cases to the 8,000-case mark, the La Cuesta Vineyard will become more prominent. Chardonnay and Sauvignon Blanc (often blended with Semillon) are regular items, joined on occasion by a Semillon and a Pinot Noir made from purchased grapes. Over its first decade, the winery experienced uneven quality across the board, but Chardonnay has been the top performer to date.

Chardonnay

83** 84 85 86* 88* 89

Delightfully fruity, almost floral in cast in good years, with judicious use of oak to provide a bit of breadth

CARMENET VINEYARD *Sonoma 1982* Owned and managed by Chalone, Inc., Carmenet is a picturesque winery perched high in the eastern hills above the

Sonoma Valley. It was intended to produce Bordeaux-style red and white wine blends. Along steep terraced hillsides, 55 acres are planted to Cabernet Sauvignon, Cabernet Franc, and Merlot. With vineyard maturity, Carmenet grows all of the red varieties needed for its 10,000-case production goal. The winery was designed to replicate the winemaking conditions and to encourage the same winemaking practices traditional in Bordeaux. During the crush, the red wines from 15 separate blocks are handled separately. In the spring the master blend is composed, and the blend is then barrel-aged for two years. Racking is the primary clarification method and is strictly handled barrel to barrel. Carmenet was one of the first companies to dig into the hillsides and create aging caves.

Carmenet's red wine (typically 85–87% Cabernet Sauvignon, with up to 10% Merlot and 5% Cabernet Franc) tends to be rich and multi-faceted, and its frequent ✻ ✻ performance justifies all of the hand labor involved in making it. A white wine counterpart—a blend of Sauvignon Blanc and Semillon—is also provided, but with less consistency. Over its first vintages, Carmenet made an Edna Valley Sauvignon Blanc that was one-dimensional. A Sonoma County Sauvignon Blanc has also been made, and has been agreeable and often quite complex enough to be awarded ✻. For some reason, the owners every now and then put out a rare, but not exciting, barrel-fermented French Colombard from Napa Valley. In the future, the winery intends to cease making Sauvignon Blanc and other whites in order to specialize in its red wine. All told, Carmenet produces 30,000 cases a year.

Cabernet Sauvignon

82 ✻✻ 83 ✻✻✻ 84 ✻✻ 85 ✻ 86 ✻ 87 ✻

Capable of offering deep and broad fruit, suggestive of currants and cherries always enriched by obvious oak, the wine has become exceptionally tannic and unyielding in recent vintages, sometimes at the expense of fruit

---

CARNEROS CREEK WINERY *Napa 1972* This winery has made a major contribution to the improved quality of California Pinot Noir and has played a vital role in the development of the Carneros appellation. Native San Franciscan Francis Mahoney became interested in wine, and particularly Pinot Noir, while working as a clerk in a wine retail shop. In the late 60s he studied enology at U.C. Davis and in 73, with his former employer Balfour Gibson joining him as a partner, Mahoney purchased 30 acres in the Carneros and planted 10 of them to Pinot Noir. Over the next several vintages Carneros Creek made a variety of wines from purchased grapes, including Amador County Zinfandels in a late harvest style. It was not until the 76 Pinot Noir was released that the winery signaled its commitment to that varietal. Its production of Pinot Noir steadily rose to the 4,000-case mark.

Chardonnay from the Carneros appellation is still the major wine offered in terms of volume. Partially barrel-fermented, the Chardonnays emphasize varietal fruit and usually hit the ✻ level. Having made Cabernet Sauvignon from many appellations, including Stags Leap from 76 to 82, Carneros Creek began working with the Truchard Vineyard in the Carneros, which is now the only source of its Cabernet Sauvignon. Carneros Creek limits the quantity of this wine to about 2,000 cases a year.

A fascinating and potentially far-reaching viticultural experiment is being conducted jointly by Carneros Creek Winery and U.C. Davis. Beginning in 74, they selected 20 different clones of Pinot Noir, and planted a few vines to each on 9 acres at the winery. In 80 they began harvesting each clone, making wines under identical conditions, and monitoring the quality level achieved. Beginning in 87, the winery added a "Signature Reserve" limited-edition Pinot Noir, and this top-of-the-line bottling is now offered along with a mid-level Carneros version and a light-bodied, early-maturing Pinot Noir labeled Fleur de Carneros. The winery's annual production is steady at 20,000 cases.

Chardonnay

84 85 ✻ 86 87 ✻ 88 89 ✻

Tending toward the lean, wiry side of the spectrum, the wine succeeds when it manages enough fruit to fill out its frame and balance its oaky, buttery aspects

Pinot Noir

83**   84*   85**   86*   87**   88*

Usually moderately rich in oak, and filled with ripe, cherryish fruit, backed by sufficient tannins for backbone and mid-term aging potential

CARRARI VINEYARDS   *Santa Barbara 1985*   South of Los Alamos, the Carrari family tend to their long-established 125-acre vineyard. Primarily grape growers, Carrari ventured into winemaking on a small scale when a few of their long-time clients were cutting back on production in 84 and 85. However, today most of their grapes are sold to wineries within the Central Coast. Among the numerous varieties they grow, the three most in demand are Chardonnay, Cabernet Franc, and Nebbiolo. Both Arciero and Au Bon Climat have made Nebbiolo from the Carraris' vineyard. The primary varietals they produce from their own fruit are Cabernet Sauvignon, Chenin Blanc, Muscat Canelli, and Chardonnay. Annual production holds steady at 4,000 cases.

MAURICE CARRIE VINEYARD & WINERY   *Riverside 1986*   Using grapes from the mature 45-acre vineyard that came with their retirement property, Budd and Maurice Van Roekel entered winemaking by building a facility with a 150,000-gallon capacity. After expanding their vineyard to 80 acres, they leased a further 110 acres in the Temecula region. Blush Wines—White Zinfandel and a White Cabernet labeled "Sara Bella"—represent 40% of the annual output. Another 40% consists of white wines with varying degrees of sweetness—Chenin Blanc, Muscat Canelli, and Johannisberg Riesling. Conventional, dry-finished Chardonnay (partially barrel-fermented), Merlot, Cabernet Sauvignon, and Sauvignon Blanc fill out the extensive line. Production jumped from 7,000 in 87 to 12,000 in 89, with steady growth planned to take the winery to the 30,000-case-a-year level.

CARTLIDGE & BROWNE   *(Stratford)*   In 81 Tony Cartlidge, a wine broker in Napa Valley, with financial help from Glen Browne, a friend and neighbor, ventured into winemaking and produced 1,000 cases of Napa Valley Chardonnay. The next year, they teamed up with others to develop the Stratford label (see entry) with the stipulation that Cartlidge & Browne would continue to be used for Chardonnay. Today, Cartlidge & Browne and Stratford are under the same ownership. Except for the 89, all Chardonnays have been from Napa Valley. Over recent vintages, Cartlidge & Browne Chardonnays have become less exciting than some of the early vintages, but remain acceptable for the price.

Chardonnay

84*   85   86   87   88

Suggestions of apples show in the low-intensity, mildly oaked character

CASA NUESTRA VINEYARDS   *Napa 1979*   In the early 70s, San Francisco attorney Gene Kirkham and his wife, Cody, purchased an old farm and 8 acres of vineyards south of Calistoga. After renovating the house on weekends, the family moved to Napa Valley. By 79 they had opened a winery and begun specializing in Chenin Blanc, made from the 10-acre estate vineyard. Over the years, the Chenin Blanc has always been kept in stainless-steel tanks and the residual sugar has been below 1%. Occasionally, a *Botrytis*-affected Chenin Blanc is made and marketed as "Dorado." In 86 the Kirkhams bought 4 acres of Cabernet Franc located next door to their vineyard and began making a varietal Cabernet Franc. In an average vintage, Casa Nuestra makes 800 cases of Chenin Blanc and 400 cases of Cabernet Franc. Just about all of the wine is sold direct by the owners, either at the tasting room or via a mailing list.

CASTORO CELLARS *San Luis Obispo 1983* Having worked in the cellars for several wineries, Niels Udsen branched out to start his own brand in 83. All of his wines originate either in the Paso Robles appellation or other regions in San Luis Obispo County. Now at the 12,000-case level, the winery is emphasizing three varietals—Zinfandel, both White and Red, Chardonnay, and Cabernet Sauvignon. Limited amounts of Sauvignon Blanc and Pinot Noir are occasionally produced. Overall, the wines have been more than acceptable, and they are often candidates for good value. The winery's ultimate production goal is 25,000 cases per year.

CASWELL VINEYARDS *Sonoma 1981* A diversified farming approach best describes Caswell Vineyards, located in eastern Sebastopol. The Caswell family is probably best known for its hard cider and fruit wines, marketed under the "Winter Creek" label. It also produces a popular line of jams and jellies sold as "Caswell Farms." The family has been almost too successful with these other ventures to develop the wine side of the master plan. There are 20 acres planted to Chardonnay, Cabernet Blanc, Pinot Noir, and Zinfandel. Two acres of Zinfandel were planted in 02, and its wine is a source of pride to the Caswells. The winery has averaged close to 3,000 cases of wine per year. Sales are primarily at the winery gift shop and through a mail-order catalogue.

CAYMUS VINEYARDS *Napa Valley 1972* Longtime Napa Valley grape-grower Charlie Wagner had been selling most of his grapes before venturing into winemaking in 72. At the time, the family simply converted an old barn into a functioning winery. Produced from their 65-acre vineyard situated in Rutherford, Caymus's estate-bottled Cabernets from 73 to 86 established themselves as benchmarks of Napa Valley Cabernet. The estate vineyard contains 40 acres of Cabernet Sauvignon, but its annual production averages only about 4,000 cases. In the 75 vintage, Caymus offered its first Special Selection Cabernet, a pick-of-the-bunch bottling given extended wood aging. It averaged 500 to 600 cases a year until in the late 80s it grew to about 1,000. Randy Dunn served as winemaker for Caymus from 75 to 82, developing a sufficiently outstanding reputation to form his own winery. However, Chuck Wagner, the owners' son, has performed well as winemaker since Dunn's departure, and now supervises the operation.

In 84, blessed with an excellent reputation and a growing demand for Cabernet, Caymus added a Napa Valley bottling made from grapes purchased within Napa Valley, labeled "Napa Valley Cuvée." Beginning with the 87 vintage, Caymus has been combining its estate-grown Cabernet with its Napa Valley Cuvée, and the result is a single "Napa Valley" bottling. Caymus was among the first to produce a blush wine; named "Oeil de Perdrix," its debut vintage, made in a lively, dry style, was 75.

Even though they are growers, the Wagners have always preferred buying Zinfandel from old hillside vineyards to produce Zinfandels that are often *performers. Other Caymus wines produced today include Sauvignon Blanc, Pinot Noir Special Selection, and a proprietary white blend, "Conundrum." As growers, the Wagners are proud of the plaudits earned by their home-grown Special Selection Pinot Noir, made from grapes planted in a region assumed to be inhospitably warm. Chardonnay has been dropped from the Caymus line, and is now sold under the winery's second label, Liberty School. Led in volume by Cabernet Sauvignon and Sauvignon Blanc, Caymus is averaging 50,000 cases a year.

Cabernet Sauvignon

(Special Selection) 78 ** 79 *** 80 *** 81 ** 82 ** 83 **
84 *** 85 *** 86 *** 87 **

Almost universally ranked among the top few Cabernets made in California, the wine is consistently ripe, broad, deep, supple, intense, loaded with rich, creamy oak, and backed up by a decade's worth of tannin. If too weighty and viscous ever to achieve much refinement or elegance, it still manages to remain well blanced and highly inviting

Cabernet Sauvignon

(Estate)　72**　73***　74***　75**　76**　77*　78*
79**　80***　81**　82**　83**　84***　85**　86**
87**

Only slightly less rich and broad than the Special Selection, although decidedly less oaky, this set of wines, selling at near-average prices for Napa Valley Cabernets, has consistently been among the best values. Its curranty, spicy, and rich character is firmed up by noticeable but never harsh tannin, and the wine tends to age exceptionally well

Pinot Noir

(Special Selection)　81**　82**　83**　84**　85**　86**
87**　88*

Ripe black-cherry character is enriched by pushy oak in this fairly deep and velvety-textured wine; like the upscale Cabernet, this one holds little in check and turns out to be almost as good

Zinfandel

80　81　82*　83*　84*　86*　87*

Usually medium-full-bodied, with medium-depth berryish fruit and moderate oak richness; it has tannin for several years of bottle aging

---

CECCHETTI-SEBASTIANI CELLAR　*Sonoma 1985*　As his political career was winding down, Don Sebastiani decided to return to the wine business and eventually started this brand with his brother-in-law, Roy Cecchetti. At that time Sam Sebastiani was struggling to retain control of the family winery, Sebastiani Vineyard, and did not welcome his politically controversial brother's involvement. The creation of Cecchetti-Sebastiani probably exacerbated the power struggle within the family. Cecchetti-Sebastiani began by having Cabernet Sauvignon, Sauvignon Blanc, and Pinot Noir custom-made from purchased grapes, adding Chardonnay to the line in the second vintage. As production levels off at 6,000 cases a year, they are making Cabernet from Sonoma County, the two white varietals from Napa Valley, and Pinot Noir from Santa Barbara County. Don Sebastiani is now involved with the larger family winery, but Roy Cecchetti remains at the helm. In 88, the brand was extended to imported extra-virgin olive oil; sales of olive oil grew quickly to 2,000 cases a year. To market a much larger line of low-priced varietals that would not be confused with Sebastiani Vineyard, the partners created the "Pepperwood Grove" brand. Initial output of this line of wines was 20,000 cases.

CHAINE D'OR　*(Congress Springs Winery)*　"The Chaine d'Or"—literally, "the golden chain"—was a pet name given by Paul Masson to the vineyarded area in the Santa Cruz Mountains appellation, and then widely used by Martin Ray, one-time director of Paul Masson Winery. Dan Gehrs, founder of Congress Springs, got his start by working at Paul Masson Winery, and later revived the term for a line of *méthode champenoise* wines. Using grapes from both the Santa Clara Valley and the Santa Cruz Mountains, the winery favors barrel fermentation prior to assembling the cuvée, and aging *en tirage* for an average of two years. Three types are produced: Blanc de Blancs (Chardonnay and Pinot Blanc), a Rosé Royale (Pinot Noir), and a Blanc de Noirs (80% Pinot Noir, 20% Chardonnay). On occasion, limited amounts of Blanc de Blancs are given extended aging *en tirage* and receive an "R.D." (recently disgorged) designation. The early total production level was 2,000 cases. Gehrs departed in 90, leaving the fate of this brand uncertain.

CHALK HILL WINERY　*Sonoma 1980*　In 74, attorney Fred Furth bought a 650-acre ranch and began developing 260 of those acres to vineyards. The vineyards fall within the Chalk Hill Viticultural Area. The winery itself used the name Donna Maria Vineyards for its primary wines, and Chalk Hill for its second-label wines until 86, when Chalk Hill became the only name used. The production grew quickly to the present 60,000-case level, all grown on the estate. Chardonnay accounts for over 50% of the total output, with the other half equally divided between Sauvignon Blanc and Cabernet Sauvignon. On those occasions when climatic conditions encourage it, the winery makes a late harvest, *Botrytis*-affected Sauvignon Blanc. In the late 80s, it added a varietal Merlot to the line. Given the financial commitment of its owner and the location of its vineyards, in our opinion Chalk Hill was a great underachiever of the 80s, offering a decade of not terribly interesting wines. In early 90, Fred Furth hired David Ramey, formerly of Matanzas Creek, as the winemaker, and Ramey brought with him a strong record for Chardonnay and Sauvignon Blanc.

CHALONE VINEYARD *Monterey 1960* Located on a ridge in the hills east of Salinas, with the Pinnacales National Monument as a dramatic backdrop, this much-revered winery has contributed mightily to the present reputation of California wine. The site and the old winery saw several owners come and go until Richard Graff and partner Phil Woodward took over in 69. The vineyard by then covered 32 acres, consisting of Pinot Noir, Chardonnay, Pinot Blanc, and Chenin Blanc. In 72, after making noteworthy vintages of powerful barrel-fermented Chardonnay and rich, often exotic Pinot Noir (the 69 and 71 still rank among the greatest ever), the owners added 50 acres of Chardonnay and 25 acres of Pinot Noir. To cultivate and tend the vines, workers at Chalone have had to truck water in from the valley for irrigation, and it was not until the mid-80s that the facility had electricity. As production grew gradually, Graff and Woodward formed a management company and eventually had 150 private investors involved in Chalone.

In 82, a new facility got under way, aiming to handle a production increase to 12,000 cases in 85. Today, with close to 200 acres planted, the winery is moving toward a goal of 25,000 cases per year. Made from the 125 acres planted, Chardonnay is the mainstay and is produced in a full-blown style—barrel-fermented, and aged in new oak barrels. From its 30 acres of Pinot Noir, Chalone has been making an estate bottling from the newer vines and a Reserve from the old block. Pinot Blanc is barrel-fermented and oak-aged, and Chenin Blanc, also barrel-fermented and full-bodied, completes the line. Gavilan Vineyards, (see entry) is a second label used in random fashion for years. Now incorporated, Chalone offers most of its Reserve Pinot Noir bottlings to its stockholders. Chalone, Inc., also owns Carmenet and Acacia, and co-owns Edna Valley Vineyards.

Chardonnay

84 *** 85 * 86 88 89 **

Immensely toasty in its combination of charry oak and sur lie *yeast-aged character, this wine can be among the best Chardonnays when its fruit measures up to the rest of its personality, but tends to be overdone and overwhelmed when the fruit fails to bring it into balance*

Pinot Noir

73 *** 78 *** 79 ** 80 *** 81 * 82 ** 83 ** 84 85 86 *
88

Ripe and dense wines of effusive black-cherry and cassis character in the best vintages, they also can turn out poorly in years when the fruit is not as bold as the wine's structure; some of the older wines, including the stunning 73 and the still-strapping 78, continue to show extremely well

CHAMISAL VINEYARD *San Luis Obispo 1980* The 60-acre Chamisal Vineyard owned by the Goss family is the oldest in the Edna Valley. At present, it consists of 52 acres of Chardonnay; the other few acres are planted to Cabernet Sauvignon and Pinot Noir. Beginning with its first vintage of Chardonnay made in 79, the winery was highly erratic until the 86 vintage, when the winemaking team changed. Since then, the quality has steadied. Most of the 3,000 cases made each year consist of its big, ripe, oak-influenced style of Chardonnay.

Chardonnay

~~84~~ 86 * * 87 * * 88 ~~89~~

Fleshy, yet balanced by good acidity, with plentiful oak balanced by fairly deep fruit in best vintages

CHANDON *Napa 1973* This beautiful winery, restaurant, and tourist complex, situated in Yountville, opened in 77 after four years of construction. Chandon was the first French-owned sparkling wine company in California. Its parent Moët-Hennessy owns and operates three producers of Champagne—Moët & Chandon, Ruinart, and Mercier—and when it merged in 87 with Louis Vuitton, its sparkling family was extended to include Veuve Clicquot, Canard Duchêne, and Henriot. The same company also owns Hennessy and Hine Cognac, Christian Dior perfume, and Simi Winery. Napa's Chandon outpost concentrates primarily on three sparkling wines—Brut, Blanc de Noirs, and Reserve. Using the *méthode champenoise,* Chandon prefers multi-vintage blends, adds 20% to 30% of aged Reserve wines from previous harvests, and relies heavily on traditional Champagne varieties, Chardonnay, Pinot Noir, and, to lesser degrees, Pinot Blanc and Pinot Meunier.

From a modest beginning in 77 of 20,000 cases, Chandon quickly exceeded its original target of 100,000 cases. Its vineyard holdings have been augmented considerably and the winery owns 1,600 acres of land with over 1,000 in vineyards. Its biggest vineyard site consists of close to 500 acres in the Carneros. Chandon believes in using hillside-grown grapes in all cuvées and developed 150 acres on Mount Veeder for that purpose. Within sight of the winery west of Yountville, Chandon established 220 acres. In its sparkling wine production, Chandon generally relies on Pinot Noir as a key component. Chandon's Brut, its best-seller, blends Pinot Noir, Chardonnay, and Pinot Blanc in proportions that usually are 65%–25%–10%, respectively. The Blanc de Noirs cuvée is 100% Pinot Noir and has always displayed a deep reddish hue despite its cool-climate origins. Made in marketable quantity since 88, the Reserve is a Brut cuvée aged for about four years *en tirage,* or twice as long as its two others. The latest addition is the "Club Cuvée," a long-aged bubbly made from Chardonnay grown on hillside sites. "Panache," an aperitif wine, made by adding pot-distilled brandy to still-fermenting Pinot Noir juice, is another item in the line.

Overall, for sparkling wine, quality has been admirably well maintained. Chandon's Blanc de Noirs has reached * * levels at times, and its Brut is a frequent * performer. Occasionally, the Brut in magnum has hit * * * level, with the Reserve often earning * reviews. Chandon's annual output is close to 500,000 cases. Future growth is limited to availability of grapes from the Napa Valley appellation. Chandon also owns Shadow Creek, another brand of sparkling wine, made from non-Napa Valley–grown grapes.

CHANTICLEER VINEYARDS *Sonoma 1982* For a few years when both grapes and readymade wines were in need of a home, Dennis Hill, the enterprising owner of Chanticleer, took advantage of the situation and bottled wine. He bought enough to produce close to 6,000 cases in 85. Most wines came from Sonoma County, where Hill serves as a consulting enologist. For a time—88 to 90—he was the winemaker for de Lorimier, before moving to his present post with Mill Creek Vineyards.

CHAPPELLET VINEYARD *Napa 1969* In a rustic setting, this beautiful winery with its unique pyramid design remains something of an enigma to us. In 67, when he was in his early 30s, Donn Chappellet left a highly successful career in the industrial food-vending business to become a vintner in the eastern hills of the Napa Valley. His terraced vineyards cover 110 acres and cling to the steep hillsides up to the 1,700-foot level. The puzzling aspect is that after making such a successful first-ever Cabernet Sauvignon in 69, the winery has rarely fulfilled that early promise. Instead, its Cabernets have been surprisingly erratic, ranging in quality from one of the finest 73s to one of the weakest 74s. On average the winery produces 7,000 cases of Cabernet, which is usually blended with Merlot from its 35 acres.

Beginning with the 84 vintage, all Chappellet Cabernet has carried the Reserve designation. Early on, Chappellet began making a bone-dry, oak-aged Chenin Blanc and, despite the decline of the varietal's popularity, the winery continues making 6,000 to 7,000 cases a year of what turns out to be a very slow seller. Chardonnay has been more consistent, in a barrel-fermented, ripe fruit style. The average annual production for Chardonnay is 3,500 cases. Finished with 1% sugar or less, Chappellet Johannisberg Riesling was often a wonderful, pert, attractive wine. However, Riesling was dropped from the lineup after 88. In its first 25 vintages, Chappellet produced five Merlots, usually in 500-case lots, but without any real distinction. The winery has been operating at its full capacity of 20,000 cases a year.

Cabernet Sauvignon

69***   70***   73**   74   75*   76*   77*   78*   79*   80*   81
82   83**   84**   85*   86

After the first several vintages, in which vibrant fruit accompanied the firm, tight structure, this series of wines began to show less intensity from the mid-70s to the present, leaving it more tannic than fruity, and de-manding long aging that seems likely to prove unrewarding in weaker years

Chardonnay

84   85   86   87   88

Firm, tight wines, lacking fruit intensity and roundness, have turned out low on overall appeal

---

CHARIS VINEYARDS   *Sonoma 1981*   Content to lead the life of grape growers, the Florence family makes just enough wine under the Charis name to keep its options open. From the 30-acre vineyard in Dry Creek Valley, it produces Fumé Blanc and Cabernet Sauvignon. The wines are custom-made in another winery. On average, about 750 cases of each varietal are made each year.

CHASE-LIMOGÈRE   (GUILD)   The folks at Guild who bring us Cook's Imperial de-cided in 88 to move up a notch in price, with a Brut and Brut Rosé labeled "Chase-Limogère." Though both brands of bubbly are made by the Charmat process in Guild's Lodi facility, Chase-Limogère Brut is given 18 months' aging with the yeast in relatively small tanks. An old, oak-aged, pot-distilled brandy used for the dosage is said by the winemaker to add distinction. Aged for less than a year, the Rosé, much like the Brut, is also among the most likable of the genre. Both modestly priced sparklers offer plenty of clean, fruity charac-ter and are generally well balanced. Annual sales are 40,000 cases today.

CHATEAU CHEVRE   *Napa 1979*   Former airline pilot Gerry Hanzen bought 21 acres in Napa Valley in 73, about a mile south of Yountville along the western edge of the valley. The place was once a goat farm. Hanzen contracted with the owner of Franciscan Vineyard to plant 8.5 acres of Merlot under a 25-year agreement to sell his grapes to that winery. When Franciscan was sold, Hanzen found himself on his own, and decided to make wine himself. Bob Mueller, an enologist for the Robert Mondavi Winery, assisted with the wine-making. In 83 Mueller became a partner in Chateau Chevre, and his vineyard contributes Cabernet Franc, Cabernet Sauvignon, and Sauvignon Blanc grapes to the partnership.

It is Merlot that places the winery on the map. The 80 bordered on the spectacular for intensity and richness, only excess tannins holding it back. Blended with Cabernet Franc, the 84 and the 85 showed more restraint and suppleness. Unfortunately, Chateau Chevre hit a serious snag on its upward path when defective frost-protection systems allowed most of the 86 crop to be wiped out by May frosts and the output was low.

The typical aging regime for Merlot is close to two years in French oak and six months in bottle. The winery has produced limited amounts of varietal Cabernet Franc on an experimental basis. Its production of Merlot in a good year is close to 2,000 cases. The winery is designed to produce no more than 4,000 cases a year. Hanzen is once again sole proprietor.

Merlot

80 ***   81   82 *   83 *   85 **   86 *

More supple now than in its first vintages, the wine remains ripe in character, with oak and tannins as major elements in its makeup

CHÂTEAU DE BAUN   *Sonoma 1986*   The winery is owned by Ken de Baun, an engineer who was once given 20 acres of land in lieu of payment for services. Being the adventurous type, he decided to start a vineyard, and chose to work with Symphony, a spicy white variety with a Muscat parent, developed by U.C. Davis. At one time, with 84 acres under development, de Baun had the largest single planting of Symphony. That one variety had been made into as many as six wines, each of which carries a proprietary name based on some musical reference or pun. For a few vintages Jamie Maves produced Symphony from de Baun grapes, selling them under his Matrose label, and when de Baun himself began making wines. Meves came in as general manager and has diversified the roster.

Today, the winery bottles four table wines—Symphony, in a slightly sweet style, "Finale," in a late harvest style, Chateau Blanc, and Chateau Rouge. Two sparkling wines made by the *méthode champenoise* have been added under the names of Romance Brut and Rhapsody Rosé. During the blush wine craze, the winery offered its version under the moniker of "Jazz." A large new facility located just off the main highway north of Santa Rosa was finished in 90. The wines made from Symphony are well made and generally capture the refreshing, forthright appeal of the varietal. De Baun has added Pinot Noir and Chardonnay in the 90s, to bring the total production close to 30,000 cases a year.

CHATEAU DIANA   *Sonoma 1979*   This is a family-owned company that has become successful as blender and bottler of a variety of table, fortified, and flavored wines. Tom Manning is the owner, and directs traffic at the facility in the Dry Creek Valley. The business began by emphasizing varietals blended from the bulk wine market, and it grew at one time to about 250,000 cases a year. It was not unusual for Chateau Diana to be marketing Chardonnays bottled under four appellations and an equal number of Cabernets. In the mid-80s the Mannings introduced a peach-flavored product, and its sales took off. Although it still offers an array of varietal and generic wines, Chateau Diana has done well with its flavored wines. By 90, much of the facility was giving over to bottling private-label wine, often destined for supermarket and chain-store outlets.

CHATEAU JULIEN   *Monterey 1982*   Five miles inland from the Monterey Peninsula, Chateau Julien stands next to the main road taking you through the Carmel Valley. Named after and modeled upon châteaux in the St. Julien district of Bordeaux, Chateau Julien has from the start emphasized Merlot and Cabernet Sauvignon, but Chardonnay has always been important. Originally buying grapes from other parts of the Central Coast, it has relied more and more on Monterey County for Chardonnay (both the regular and Reserve are barrel-fermented), as well as for Merlot, Cabernet Sauvignon, and Semillon and Sauvignon Blanc. The latter two go into a proprietary blend called "Platinum." Riesling and Gewurztraminer remain as minor players on the roster. Aged longer than usual in barrel and bottle, a Reserve Cabernet Sauvignon was made for the 86 vintage, turning out to be one of the most noteworthy versions ever from the Monterey appellation. Two separate brands of wine are also under the same ownership. Great American Wineries, Inc., is the owner of Chateau Julien, and also produces two other brands of wine, Emerald Bay and Garland Ranch (see entries). All told, the facility with its three labels is producing 40,000 cases a year. Chateau Julien itself accounts for an average of 10,000 cases a year.

CHATEAU MONTELENA *Napa 1972* Built in 1882, the medieval-looking old stone winery and its vineyard were abandoned or ignored for decades until the present owners acquired the property in early 69. Directed by attorney and general partner Jim Barrett, the owners restored and expanded the winery, and brought the old estate back to life. Rather than create a tourist center, Barrett kept the winery functional and invested in vineyard development. He also made special efforts to locate and buy the best grapes available while his own vineyards were nonbearing. In early 72, Mike Grgich, then an unknown, was hired as winemaker. Under Grgich's direction, the winery made Chardonnay by blending grapes from Napa and the Alexander Valley, and it was the 73 Montelena Chardonnay that won first place in a well-publicized tasting held in Paris in 76. That victory advanced Montelena's reputation, but it also sidetracked its plan to become known as an estate Cabernet producer.

After Grgich departed in 77 to start Grgich Hills, his successor was Jerry Luper, who had gained a solid reputation with Freemark Abbey. The understudy to both Grgich and Luper was Bo Barrett, the owner's son, who was destined to advance to the winemaking position. Luper's final vintage with Montelena was 81, then Bo Barrett took over. At that point the 95-acre estate vineyard, planted to 72 acres of Cabernet Sauvignon in 69–70, was being used by Montelena. Through the 77 vintage, Montelena augmented its grape supply by buying Cabernet from Sonoma County. From 78 on, it has made only one Cabernet Sauvignon, the 100% estate vineyard. The winery produced several vintages of outstanding Cabernet Sauvignon, developing and maintaining an outstanding record for ripe, full-bodied wines. With its two Chardonnays—Alexander Valley and Napa Valley—Montelena continues to be among the very top performers in most vintages. The third noteworthy wine is Zinfandel, made in a ripe, berryish style that has been successful since the mid-70s. Montelena's total annual production remains at the 30,000-case peak, with Cabernet Sauvignon steady at 10,000 cases. The two Chardonnays combine for 18,000 cases, and Zinfandel averages 1,500 annually.

Cabernet Sauvignon

77 ** 78 * 79 ** 80 81 82 ** 83 84 ** 85 *** 86

Ripe, curranty, and black-cherry fruit with occasional leanings toward overripeness, lots of sweet oak, and fairly massive tannins add up to a series of wines that make up in boldness for what they lack in finesse

Chardonnay

(Napa Valley) 83 *** 84 ** 85 ** 86 * 87 * 88 ** 89 *

(Alexander Valley) 83 84 ** 85 *** 86 ** 87 88 **

The Napa bottling is more consistent and is fairly classic in its focus on ripe, balanced appley fruit, with nuances of butter amidst the toasty oak; the Alexander Valley wine is more tropical and opulent in good vintages, but can become lean and wiry in lesser years

---

CHATEAU NAPA BEAUCANON *Napa 1986* Owned by the de Coninck family of Bordeaux, France, the winery is situated 3 miles south of St. Helena, west of the main wine road. De Coninck operates the second-largest négociant firm in Bordeaux, J. Lebegue, headquartered in St. Emilion. After buying the 65-acre Napa Valley estate in 86, the family subsequently purchased another 190 acres, in two parcels. The larger parcel, 117 acres, is located north of St. Helena, and is now planted half to Chardonnay and half to Cabernet Sauvignon, Merlot, and Cabernet Franc. The second parcel, near the town of Napa, is planted predominantly to Chardonnay. The 86 and 87 vintages were made at other wineries (Domaine de Napa, Vichon) pending completion of its own ultramodern facility. From 88 on, the three primary wines—Chardonnay, Cabernet Sauvignon, and Merlot—have all been estate bottled. Once the winery was completed, the production increased to the desired 45,000- to 50,000-case level. About half is devoted to Chardonnay, with Cabernet Sauvignon at about 15,000 cases, and Merlot around 10,000 cases a year.

CHATEAU POTELLE *Napa 1985* Raised in Bordeaux, where their families were involved in wine, owners Jean-Noël and Marketta Fourmeaux du Sartel were sent by the French government in 80 to study the California wine business. They were impressed enough by its opportunities to decide to join in. In 83, they moved to California and soon began blending and bottling wines under their private label. Most of the first few vintages were aged and bottled at Souverain. Their lineup, then and now, consists of Cabernet Sauvignon, Chardonnay, and Sauvignon Blanc. Overall, quality was good, with an occasional vintage of Alexander Valley Cabernet Sauvignon (last made in 88) worthy of ✳ and offering good value. A second line of less expensive wines marketed under the Domaine Potelle name has been dropped.

As the annual output approached 20,000 cases, they decided to make the full commitment by purchasing land and a facility. First, they acquired a 90-acre vineyard on the Silverado Trail of Napa Valley, and developed that site to Cabernet Sauvignon and related Bordeaux grapes. In the same year they purchased the former Vose Vineyard facility and land, amounting to 270 acres. Situated in the Mount Veeder hills, the winery has 45 acres under vine, mainly Chardonnay, Cabernet Sauvignon, and Zinfandel. Once that vineyard has been expanded, Chateau Potelle will focus its efforts on estate-grown Napa Valley Cabernet Sauvignon and Chardonnay, and Sauvignon Blanc made from purchased grapes. In the 90s, the annual production is expected to grow to 35,000 cases.

CHATEAU ST. JEAN *Sonoma 1973* St. Jean was the first ultra-modern, multi-million-dollar winery to be developed in the Sonoma Valley, perhaps in all of Sonoma County. The wines offered immediately justified the attention to detail as the winery quickly built a strong reputation for vineyard-designated, limited-production white wines. Among its several early successes were Chardonnays from the Robert Young Vineyard and the Belle Terre Vineyard, along with Fumé Blancs from several individual vineyards, particularly La Petite Etoile. Before leaving in 90, winemaker Dick Arrowood also helped expand the late harvest category of dessert wines through a range of *Botrytis*-affected Rieslings and Gewurztraminers.

After several vintages of smooth sailing and critical success, by 82 the winery's production had expanded to over 100,000 cases. The first offering of the long-awaited sparkling wine disappointed for quality and value. The founders, table grape growers from the Central Valley, decided to sell in 84, and after a spirited bidding war, the buyer was Suntory, Ltd., of Japan. The new owners have reinstated Cabernet Sauvignon, which had been discontinued after 81, and have maintained the winery's white wine emphasis. Annual production has grown to 175,000 cases, with the white wines representing 90%. The now acceptable sparkling wines continue to be made at a separate facility in Graton, located in southwestern Sonoma County. After producing an intensely varietal, often pungent style of Fumé Blanc from the independently owned Petite Etoile Vineyard for many years, St. Jean bought the 62-acre vineyard in 88. The St. Jean Vineyard noted on labels refers to the 55-acre vineyard of Sauvignon Blanc and Chardonnay adjacent to the winery. Overall, St. Jean remains an important Chardonnay producer, even though the wines may not be as outstanding after 82 as they were before. However, after a poor start, the Brut and Blanc de Blancs sparklers have recently been earning ✳.

Cabernet Sauvignon
  (Laurel Glen)   75   76✳   77✳✳

Cabernet Sauvignon

(Glen Ellen) 76 77* 78*

Cabernet Sauvignon

(Wildwood Vineyard) 78* 79 80*

Cabernet Sauvignon

(Alexander Valley) 85* 86*

Older wines were typically bold, tannic, briary, alcoholic, and heavily extracted. Some have aged well; none is especially refined. The newer wines are more restrained, still have plenty of weight, and show more black-cherry fruitiness than before

Chardonnay

(Sonoma County) 84* 85* 86 87* 88* 89

Crisp, fruity, moderately oaked style, medium depth

Chardonnay

(Robert Young) 79** 80*** 81** 82 83* 84** 85* 86 87* 88*

Once among the very best Chardonnays, and still quite good. Many older wines have aged very well. The newer wines show somewhat less depth, but the ripe, luscious, tropical-floral-tinged appley fruit, rich oak, and crisp balance remain in evidence

CHATEAU SOUVERAIN *Sonoma 1973* Modeled architecturally upon a hop kiln, this handsome facility has survived several dramatic ownership changes. It was built by Pillsbury in the northwestern corner of the Alexander Valley, and named Souverain of Alexander Valley because Pillsbury was operating another winery in Napa Valley called Souverain of Rutherford. When Pillsbury decided to get out of the wine business, the Sonoma County winery was sold in 76 to a partnership of grape-growers and renamed Souverain Cellars. The close to 300 growers owned acreage in Sonoma, Mendocino, and Napa counties. They agreed to use the appellation North Coast for all their wines, but, as it later turned out, they could agree on little else. Annual production approached 500,000 cases of table wine as the undercapitalized winery struggled into the 80s. A good portion of the large facility was rented to other producers and private brands, who either made and/or stored wines there. Winemakers left, and by the mid-80s, it became apparent that the facility and the brand were in serious trouble.

In 86, Souverain Cellars was purchased by Wine World, Inc., the wine division of Nestlé, which immediately renamed it and poured millions of dollars into restoration and modernization. The new owners converted the operation into a line of Sonoma County varietal wines. Vineyard sources had to be lined up through lease or other arrangements, and the owners began developing vineyards adjacent to the Colony facility they had bought earlier.

By 90, close to 200 acres were under development in the Alexander Valley and Dry Creek Valley. The wines offered are Cabernet Sauvignon, Zinfandel, Merlot, Chardonnay, and Sauvignon Blanc. Zinfandel is made from the Dry Creek Valley appellation, and the Carneros region supplies Chardonnay. All other bottlings are from the Alexander Valley. Both white wines and the Cabernet have been bottled in a Reserve version. The initial production of 40,000 cases had increased threefold by 90. Chardonnay and Cabernet Sauvignon represent close to two-thirds of the annual production, which is growing toward a maximum of 250,000 cases. Both quality and availability have varied all over the lot, but seemed to take a step in the right direction with the early vintages of the Carneros Chardonnay and Merlot.

CHATEAU WOLTNER *Napa 1985* Occupying the plateau of Howell Mountain, the historic (ca. 1886) Brun and Chaix building remained inactive from Prohibition until 80. Then the old winery and its 181-acre estate were bought by Francis and Françoise DeWavrin-Woltner of Bordeaux. Until 83 their family owned the prestigious Château La Mission Haut-Brion. In 82–83, as the old Howell Mountain winery was being restored, the nearby land was cleared and 35 acres were planted to Chardonnay. A total of 55 acres are under vine, with the eventual goal set at 120 acres.

Given the viticultural history of Howell Mountain and the background of the owners, the decision to focus exclusively on Chardonnay surprised most observers. Having worked with Chardonnay as a winemaker in Meursault, Ted Lemon arrived at Wolfner with impressive credentials. Over the first few vintages, the winery produced three vineyard-designated Chardonnays—an estate, the Titus Vineyard, and St. Thomas Vineyard. Each, made in small quantities, was offered to the wine trade on a futures basis. This was an unheard-of practice in California for white wine. Additionally, the first vintages of Chardonnay were priced at levels much higher than the quality merited. It was not until 87 that the wines showed greater depth of flavor and balance. But even now they are among the highest-priced California Chardonnays and are not usually among the best in quality. The Frederique Vineyard bottling was added in 89. The winery is presently producing around 3,500 cases a year.

CHATOM VINEYARDS   *Calaveras 1986*   Situated 8 miles from Angels Camp, the tiny town made famous by Mark Twain, Chatom was in the vineyard business exclusively until 85. Its vineyard, one of the oldest in Calaveras County, has been expanded recently to 60 acres, the leading varieties being Chenin Blanc, Sauvignon Blanc, Zinfandel, and Cabernet Sauvignon. Its first vintages were custom-made, and the total annual production has been averaging 2,000 cases. With the completion of its own facility in the mid-90s, Chatom has the capability for producing 10,000 cases.

CHIMNEY ROCK WINERY   *Napa 1986*   Native New Yorker Sheldon "Hack" Wilson was an executive with Pepsi-Cola International, and for several years was associated with the brewing business in South Africa. When he decided to join the wine world, he searched Napa Valley for an available site and, as an avid golfer, was attracted to property in the Stags Leap District known as the Chimney Rock Golf Course. Buying the land in 80, Wilson removed nine holes, or about 75 acres, and is said by those who play the game to have improved the remaining nine. The vineyard was developed in 81–82, with major emphasis on Chardonnay, Cabernet Sauvignon, and Sauvignon Blanc. Merlot and Cabernet Franc were planted as blenders for Cabernet. The winemaking facility was completed in late 89, when the winery was in its fourth vintage. Most of those wines, made in a temporary facility, captured varietal character, but were not complex. Now, under the steady hand of winemaker Doug Fletcher, the wines are on a solid course and seem headed for distinction. To date, Chimney Rock's Fumé Blanc is among the few coastal versions not aged in wood at all. A Reserve (Meritage Red) was bottled in 89. The winery's maximum total-production goal is 22,000 cases.

Cabernet Sauvignon

84   85**   86   87

Rich, firm, moderately tannic wines, they need to capture enough fruit extract to balance their somewhat tight and reserved style

Chardonnay

84*   85   86*   87   88

Medium-depth appley fruit and good crisp acidity, with oak in support; can be somewhat lighter in lesser years

CHOUINARD VINEYARDS   *Alameda 1985*   Former civil engineer George Chouinard decided to settle down in one place after years of traveling. He and his family bought 100 acres of steep, hilly land a few miles west of Pleasanton. After planting a small (3-acre) vineyard and building a winery, George turned the project over to his son, Damian, who is now the winemaker. Chardonnay and Cabernet Sauvignon grow in the estate vineyard. Additional grapes are purchased from both North Coast and Central Coast appellations. Making most varietals in 200–400-case lots, the winery has reached the 1,000-case-a-year level. About 300 cases of apple wine are also produced by the winery.

THE CHRISTIAN BROTHERS *Napa 1882* In mid-89 the wine world, including many Napa Valley residents, was shocked to learn that Grand Metropolitan, the British conglomerate and parent company of Heublein, had purchased the venerable Christian Brothers winery. Run by the teaching order since 1882, the Christian Brothers had moved to the Napa Valley from Martinez in the 20s, devoting winery proceeds to the order's many schools and colleges. The operation at one time included three facilities in Napa and a large winery and brandy-making facility in the Central Valley. The first Napa Valley facility (part of the Novitiate) was located in a pastoral setting in the hills east of Napa. That facility, known as Mont La Salle, closed in the 80s and was soon acquired by Donald Hess, owner of the Hess Collection Winery. In the 50s, with their winemaking operation growing, the Brothers purchased the Greystone Winery just north of St. Helena. This striking facility quickly became one of the top tourist spots in Napa Valley.

As winemakers, the Christian Brothers produced a large line of varietal and generic wines, along with a line of sparkling wine by the Charmat process. They also owned a large facility in the Central Valley where they produced a credible line of sherries, ports, brandy, and their once best-selling proprietary wine, Chateau La Salle. At the height of their winemaking operation, the Brothers produced about 1 million cases of wine a year and a like amount of brandy, making them the best-seller in the U.S. at that time.

With about 1,500 acres of vineyards in Napa and another 1,000 acres in the Central Valley, this winery was a major producer. Under the direction of winemaker Brother Timothy, the Christian Brothers emphasized nonvintage blends for varietals, but by the late 70s that approach had lost its appeal. Throughout the late 70s and the 80s, the Christian Brothers attempted to catch up with the more recent developments in the wine world by introducing vintaged varietals, small oak, and even a jazzier label. The efforts paid off in some instances, as their 84 and 85 Cabernet Sauvignon offered a new look, and their white wines showed some intensity.

In the late 80s, Christian Brothers slowly began taking on laypeople to run the marketing program and later to work in wine production. When the firm was sold in 89, the new owners acquired over 1,000 acres of Napa Valley Vineyards, the Greystone Winery, and a fermentation facility south of St. Helena. However, the winery's annual production had slipped considerably by 89, with its primary wine, White Zinfandel, representing more than 100,000 cases. For now, the brand remains in a state of flux.

CHRISTOPHE VINEYARDS Christophe is a negociant label owned by French producer and negociant Grands Vins Jean-Claude Boisset of Burgundy. Boisset owned vineyards in Napa Valley which he sold to Skalli (now St. Supéry). In 85, under the direction of Ginny Mills, the Christophe Vineyards brand was created. She selects and blends all wines, which are aged and bottled in a Sonoma County winery. The line of modestly priced wines consists of Chardonnay, its mainstay, along with Sauvignon Blanc and Cabernet Sauvignon. Limited-volume Reserve bottlings of Chardonnay, Cabernet Sauvignon, and more recently Pinot Noir are also offered. Generally, the quality leaders are Sauvignon Blanc and Chardonnay, both frequently earning ✿ ratings, and winning their share of "good value" plaudits. A trio of blends (red, white, blush) are labeled "Joliesse," a proprietary name. Over 75% of Christophe California appellation varietals are made from Napa and Sonoma counties.

Overall sales of Christophe have steadily increased to its present plateau of 85,000 cases.

CILURZO VINEYARD & WINERY *Riverside 1978* Originally this winery was the Cilurzo Piconi Winery, but when the partnership dissolved in 80, Vincent Cilurzo remained on the site and Piconi founded his own wine venture. On his 52-acre estate, Cilurzo had developed 10 acres of vineyard in 68, making it the oldest in the Temecula area. As in many of the early vineyard developments in Temecula, the favorite variety planted was Petite Sirah. A wide range of varietals is now produced from grapes grown within Temecula. Of the 10,000-case annual production, the leaders by volume are White Zinfandel (3,000), Petite Sirah (1,000), Chenin Blanc (1,000), Chardonnay (1,000), Cabernet Sauvignon (1,000), and Sauvignon Blanc (1,000). In recent vintages Petite Sirah has been made in a Nouveau style (once labeled "Full Moon Nouveau") and a regular oak-aged version. A Muscat Canelli labeled "Reindeer Reserve" is bottled in time for the Christmas season. One of the most popular tourist stops, the winery sells much of its production to visitors. Long term, Cilurzo wants to expand his winery's production to 20,000 cases a year.

CINNABAR VINEYARDS AND WINERY *Santa Clara 1986* On a hilltop overlooking Saratoga, Tom Mudd and Melissa Frank built a small winery and started a vineyard nearby. Mudd, who was in the mining profession, named his wine venture after the heavy, deep, almost blood-red mercury ore, cinnabar. The steep mountain vineyard covers 24 acres, equally devoted to Cabernet Sauvignon and Chardonnay. The first estate-grown Cabernet was made in 86, the first Chardonnay in 88. Early output consisted of a few hundred cases of each wine. The winery also made small amounts of Cabernet from the Woodside region labeled Fox Hollow Vineyard. The owners, favoring 100% barrel-fermented Chardonnay and 100% Cabernet Sauvignon, are emphasizing estate-grown wines with the Santa Cruz Mountains appellation. The winery, complete with three aging caves, was ready for the crush of 87. Production is expected to grow gradually to the 3,500-case level.

CLAIBORNE & CHURCHILL VINTNERS *San Luis Obispo 1983* Claiborne (Clay) Thompson and his wife, Fredericka Churchill, are behind this brand, which specializes in white wines. From 83 to 86, Thompson made wines in space leased from Edna Valley Vineyards, where he worked on a part-time basis. Now in its own production facility, this winery offers Riesling, Gewurztraminer, and a Muscat Canelli in a dry style. A blend of the three makes up the fourth wine bottled, "Edelzwicker." Chardonnay completes the line. Both the Riesling and the Gewurztraminer succeed more often than not, and the Gewurztraminer is often round and smooth. Annual production is at the 2,500-case level. Thompson is also a part-time enologist for Chamisal Vineyard.

CLINE CELLARS *Contra Costa 1982* Located in the town of Oakley, northeast of Berkeley, Cline Cellars is operated by Fred Cline, who entered the wine business as manager on a farm growing almonds, walnuts, and wine grapes. In 82 he purchased the defunct Firpo Winery, the oldest in the region, and began crushing three red varieties—Carignane, Zinfandel, and Mataro. Until 89, the winery had no refrigeration system, the tanks were redwood, and the fermenters were open-topped redwood vats. White wine production was limited to a few hundred cases. In 87 several wineries working with Rhone varieties discovered that the old California red called Mataro was none other than the prestigious French Rhone variety, Mourvedre.

Holding long-term contracts for 180 acres of the suddenly in-demand variety, Cline began selling Mourvedre to the likes of Bonny Doon and Edmunds St. John. Cline Cellars also began blending and marketing Rhone Valley types, and two bottlings in particular were attractive blends of Mourvedre, Zinfandel, and Carignane. One labeled "Oakley Cuvée" contains over 50% Mourvedre, and the second, "Côtes d'Oakley," is made with about 60% Carignane, 20% Zinfandel. By 90, Cline Cellars was turning out 10,000 cases total. Varietal

Mourvedre and Zinfandel are both made, sometimes in a late harvest style. In the 90s the Cline family will develop acreage in the Sonoma Carneros. A small portion has been planted to Syrah and Viognier. Long term, Cline intends to move the production facility to Carneros to make wines from both the Carneros and Oakley appellations. When that happens, he sees 30,000 cases a year as the maximum.

CLONINGER CELLARS *Monterey 1989* A partnership of four families from the Salinas Valley who have all been involved in local agriculture, Cloninger is specializing in Chardonnay and Cabernet Sauvignon. Barrel-fermented and aged *sur lie*, the Monterey County Chardonnays represent the bulk of the winery's 2,500-case production. Early vintages showed promise.

CLOS DU BOIS *Sonoma 1976* As a modest investment, Frank Woods purchased 100 acres of vineyard land in the Dry Creek Valley in 70. The following year he formed a partnership with a college buddy, Thomas Reed, and additional acreage was purchased in the Alexander Valley. When the grape market dipped in 74, the partners decided to try their hand at winemaking. At the Sonoma Vineyards/Rodney Strong facility, they made 2,000 cases of a 74 Chardonnay from Dry Creek Valley. Still in leased space in 77, their first wine from the Alexander Valley pushed production to 6,000 cases. With an improving market for varietal wine in 80, they abandoned their original plan to sell grapes and moved into their own facility, a renovated warehouse in Healdsburg. By then Clos du Bois had 590 acres under vine in the Alexander Valley. In 81, John Hawley became winemaker and Clos du Bois was off and running.

The winery now offers six varietals: Chardonnay, Sauvignon Blanc, Gewurztraminer, Cabernet Sauvignon, Pinot Noir, and Merlot. A series of vineyard-designated wines include two Chardonnays ("Calcaire" in Alexander Valley, "Flintwood" in Dry Creek Valley) and two Cabernet Sauvignons ("Marlstone," a Bordeaux blend, and "Briarcrest," 100% varietal). Chardonnay is the volume leader, with over 100,000 cases produced, most of that represented by the barrel-fermented version from Alexander Valley. Both Calcaire and Flintwood Chardonnays are 100% barrel-fermented—the former in lightly toasted Limousin oak, and the latter in heavily toasted Nevers oak.

Clos du Bois has become a leader in the production of Merlot, owning more acreage than any other winery and making one of the most consistent Merlots from 82 on. Among other noteworthy wines offered is the Gewurztraminer, made in an early harvest style that has been a frequent success. The winery had gained acceptance from critics and consumers by 88. It was then that the owners sold to Hiram Walker, Inc., owner of Callaway Winery. A line of low-priced table wines labeled River Oaks Vineyard has been dropped. A new facility in Geyserville is planned for the 90s which will enable production to expand from its present annual level of 350,000 cases. A new winemaking team began work in 91.

Cabernet Sauvignon

81* 82 83 84** 85 86* 87

Ripish, open, juicy, cherry and black-cherry fruit, medium depth, lightly tannic

Cabernet Sauvignon

(Briarcrest) 80 81* 83 84** 85* 86*

Deeper, slightly tougher, with medium aging potential

Chardonnay

84 85 86* 87* 88 89

Clean, straightforward, blossomy fruit, light oak

Chardonnay (Calcaire)

83 84* 85 86* 87 88*

Peachy fruit, slight spice hints, creamy oak, firm balance

Marlstone

78 79 **80*** 81* 82* 83 **84**** **85**** **86*** **87****

Mild-mannered in early vintages, the latest efforts are deep, tasty, round, with lots of cherryish and herbal-tinged fruit, filled out by sweet, rich oak

Merlot

82 83 **84*** 85* **86***** 87* **88***

Lots of bright fruit and wonderful balance; elegance in best vintages, but in others wine can be thin, evanescent

CLOS DU MURIEL *San Diego 1989* Local developer Joe Pavelich was looking for a new challenge when he heard that Bretton Cellars was for sale. In May of 89, he purchased the winery, much of its inventory, and some 30 acres of vines. Renamed Clos du Muriel, the winery presently produces in the range of 22,000 cases. The lineup features Cabernet Sauvignon, Chardonnay, Sauvignon Blanc, White Zinfandel, and Riesling, all from the estate vineyard. Muscat Canelli from Paso Robles completes the line. The barrel-fermented Chardonnay is the major wine by volume, representing over 25% of the total. Long term, the winery could expand to the 40,000-case-a-year level.

CLOS DU VAL *Napa 1972* Owned by John Goelet and managed by Bernard Portet, Clos du Val was an accidental discovery. Goelet, a New York businessman whose family was once involved in the Bordeaux wine trade, asked Portet to search out and study potential winemaking sites. On a brief visit to the Napa Valley one hot summer day in 70, Portet felt a cool breeze as he drove through a particular spot on the Silverado Trail, and realized he had discovered a significant microclimate. A site within that area was for sale, and before long it became Clos du Val.

The winery was up and functioning by 72, producing Zinfandel and Cabernet Sauvignon. The owners developed 140 acres and helped pioneer what is now known as the Stags Leap District. That vineyard contains 100 acres of Cabernet Sauvignon, 20 acres of Merlot, 10 acres of Zinfandel, and 10 acres of Semillon. Merlot, blended with Cabernet, was first offered as a varietal in 77, and Chardonnay joined the winery roster in 78. In 79–80, Clos du Val developed a 105-acre vineyard in the Carneros, containing Chardonnay and Pinot Noir. A third winery-owned vineyard consists of 20 acres of Chardonnay. Cabernet Sauvignon and Chardonnay represent close to two-thirds of the winery's 65,000-case annual output. Zinfandel, Pinot Noir, and Semillon remain on the roster. Between 72 and 78, Clos du Val's Zinfandels were produced from an old hillside vineyard; in every vintage since then, the Zinfandels have been made entirely from the winery's grapes. Regardless of origin, the winery's Zinfandels have earned plenty of * ratings and more than a few ** and *** have been awarded. Since 86, when the winery made its first estate-bottled Carneros Chardonnay, all wines except its Pinot Noir have been estate bottled. In 87, the winery started a second line, "Joli Val," that consists of Chardonnay and Cabernet Sauvignon made from grapes not 100% winery-owned. Low-priced, blended red and white table wines are labeled "Le Clos."

Cabernet Sauvignon

73 **74**** **75*** 76* 77* 78 79* **80*** 81 82 83 **84***
85* 86*

Tight wines, even when not overly tannic, these refined and somewhat low-keyed efforts carry nicely focused curranty fruit and a generous dollop of creamy, almost milk-chocolatey oak

Chardonnay

(Carneros) 86* 87 88 89

Very well balanced, clean and crisp wines, they show only moderate intensity and can be low in fruit

Merlot

80 *   81 *   82   83 *   85 * *   86   87 *   88 *

Inconsistent to a fault, these wines have ranged from rich, curranty, and well oaked to earthy and vegetal; sweet, creamy oak is always evident

Pinot Noir

80 * * *   81 *   82 *   83   84 *   85 *   86 *

Medium-weight, firm, well-constructed, sweetly oaked wines, with moderate-intensity cherry fruit; capable of half a dozen years or more of aging

Zinfandel

78 *   79 *   80 *   81 *   82 *   83 *   84 *   85 * * *   86 *
87 * *

Ripe and fleshy wines, firmed up by imposing tannins, they show the rich oak and keen varietal focus of other Clos du Val reds while carrying greater intensity

---

CLOS PEGASE   *Napa 1984*   The tone for this brand was fixed at the outset in 84, when owner and art collector Jan Shrem selected the controversial postmodernist architect Michael Graves to design the winery. Construction of the multi-million-dollar facility in Calistoga was delayed for a time owing to strong objections from town residents over the building's size and appearance. Since its completion, Clos Pegase has been offering Chardonnay, Sauvignon Blanc, Cabernet Sauvignon, and Merlot. Cabernet Sauvignon comes from the winery's 42-acre Palisades Vineyard north of Calistoga. Planted primarily to Sauvignon Blanc, and Merlot, another 50 acres are located at the winery site.

In 90, Clos Pegase purchased a 365-acre parcel in Carneros and began planting 70 acres to Chardonnay. The winemaking style over the first several vintages emphasized varietal fruit in its Chardonnays, which were fermented in stainless steel and aged for only a few months in oak. Aged briefly in used or neutral oak, the winery's Sauvignon Blancs were also rather straightforward in character and modest in intensity. Although the early vintages of Cabernet Sauvignon aroused little excitement, the winery's Merlots showed considerable promise. With vineyard maturity, Clos Pegase winery will become self-reliant for Chardonnay, Cabernet Sauvignon, Cabernet Franc, and Merlot. By 90, it was producing 35,000 cases on its way to a 50,000-case-per-year goal. Quality to date has been average or better for most wines.

CLOS ROBERT   This is a brand owned by Première Wine Merchants, the importing company owned by the prestigious French firm Rémy Martin. Rémy became active in California when it formed a partnership with Schramsberg Vineyard to produce a pot-still brandy in Napa Valley. A magnificent facility was built and outfitted in the Carneros, and production of RMS brandy got under way; but then the partners decided to split. In the amicable settlement, some of the wines in inventory went to Rémy Martin, which had them bottled under the Clos Robert brand. Enjoying some success in the low-end price spectrum, Première Wine Merchants has continued with this line, which now consists of a somewhat thin version of a Napa Valley Chardonnay and a simple Cabernet Sauvignon.

CLOS STE. NICOLE   (Domaine St. George)   Around 88, the availability of readymade wine for sale had declined in California. Some wineries and negociants reached out to Washington State to secure gallons of bulk Chardonnay, Merlot, and Cabernet Sauvignon, among others. A few wine-marketing companies looked to Europe or South America. Clos Ste. Nicole took another approach to the supply deficiency by shipping French wines to California for blending with California wines. Identified as French-California cuvées, the wines are blended and bottled by the Domaine St. George facility in Sonoma County. Under the Clos Ste. Nicole label, Chardonnay, Merlot, and Cabernet Sauvignon are offered. Priced on the low end, they are adequate in quality.

CODORNIU NAPA *Napa 1990* The Spanish firm Codorniu, Spain's largest producer of *méthode champenoise* sparkling wine, purchased a 350-acre vineyard and winery site in the Carneros region in 85. By 91, when its first Brut reached the market, Codorniu Napa had developed 50 acres, with a long-term planting goal of 225 acres. Chardonnay and Pinot Noir are the primary varieties planted, but several Spanish white grapes are being grown on a trial basis. With the production of *méthode champenoise* cuvées expected to hit 60,000 cases by 95, the non-vintage Brut remains the major item, joined by a limited-volume Carneros Cuvée. Eventually, the winery plans to expand annual production to 180,000 cases.

B. R. COHN *Sonoma 1984* Owner Bruce Cohn managed several successful rock groups, and by 74 was wealthy enough to purchase a mature 65-acre vineyard in the Sonoma Valley. From this estate vineyard, known as Olive Hill, the winery has moved relatively quickly to its maximum capacity of 8,000 cases a year. Cohn's 85 Cabernet Sauvignon was one of the first from that great vintage to earn critical praise, and certainly helped the winery's growth. Just over half the output is devoted to Chardonnay. The regular bottling is partially barrel-fermented, and a Reserve is 100% barrel-fermented in new French oak. Though made in a ripe, full-bodied style, the Chardonnays have been less impressive than the Cabernets. The first attempt to produce *méthode champenoise* sparkling wine consisted of a few hundred cases of a Brut labeled "Platinum." The quality was not much of a hit. Pinot Noir is also made, but in such small quantities (under 100 cases) that it is only available locally.

Chardonnay

(Olive Hill)   85   86   **88**   89   **88** * *

Lots of oak tends to dominate the ripe fruit, but future vintages from this well-situated vineyard could show better balance and earn higher ratings

Cabernet Sauvignon

(Olive Hill)   **84** * *   **85** *   **87** *

Like the Chardonnay, the Cabernet seems to follow in the no-holds-barred direction, but here the ripe, dense fruit maintains its flavor in the face of the plentiful oak and coarse tannins; the results are long-aging wines of considerable depth

COLONY Known for close to a century as Italian Swiss Colony, this once famous name was reduced to a slow-moving line of jug wines by the late 70s. In the mid-50s, Colony was the largest-selling wine in the U.S., thanks to its "little ol' winemaker" advertising theme. Italian Swiss Colony began in 1881 in Asti, at the northern end of Sonoma County, as a cooperative employing immigrants from abroad. After Prohibition it became the leading producer in the county and the most popular tourist attraction north of the Golden Gate Bridge. This all began to unravel in 68 with the acquisition of Italian Swiss by Heublein. The tasting room was closed, and the product emphasis changed. Sales slipped steadily. Eventually a partnership of growers bought the winery and renamed it Colony. It never regained its lost ground or prestige, and by the end of 88 the brand was bought by Erly Industries, who then sold the winery and the land in Asti to Wine World, Inc., owner of Chateau Souverain, Beringer Vineyards, and other wineries. Erly Industries sold the brand Colony to the Wine Group, which is now making Colony wines in its Central Valley facility. Along with Colony, the Wine Group keeps alive numerous other brands once used by Colony, including Lejon, Jacques Bonet, and North Coast Cellars.

CONCANNON VINEYARDS *Alameda 1883* Nestled just outside the city limits of Livermore, Concannon was once a cornerstone of the California wine industry. Owned and operated by the Concannon family until 1982, the winery built a sound reputation for both red and white wines. In 62 it bottled the first varietal Petite Sirah, and for many vintages thereafter the Concannons emphasized estate-bottled Petite Sirah and Cabernet Sauvignon. However, by the late 70s, the winery's antiquated facility began to hinder its winemaking, and the winery's staid image did not help. After financing a badly needed renovation program, Jim Concannon sold the winery and vineyard to Distillers Company, a large international corporation. That parent company experienced problems of its own and sold Concannon in early 88 to a partnership headed by winemaker Sergio Traverso and Deinhard of Germany. Traverso, formerly with Domaine Chandon and Sterling Vineyards, has reworked the 180-acre estate vineyard to make Sauvignon Blanc and Cabernet Sauvignon the winery's two leading varietals. Deinhard has since become the majority partner.

With over 100 acres consisting of Sauvignon Blanc and Semillon, Concannon is making both a varietal Sauvignon Blanc and "Assemblage," a proprietary blend of Semillon and Sauvignon Blanc. Petite Sirah, aged in small French oak barrels, and Cabernet Sauvignon Reserve are also estate bottled. The winery's Chardonnays are labeled "Selected Vineyards," and are blends of grapes grown in several Central Coast vineyards. Total annual production at Concannon is 65,000 cases, with Chardonnay accounting for 20,000 cases.

Cabernet Sauvignon

81   82*   83   85   86

Soft, ripe cherry and herb-tinged fruit, light tannins, mild oak

Chardonnay

84*   85   86**   87

Usually fruity, with citrus and floral elements giving the wine an alluring prettiness in better vintages

---

CONGRESS SPRINGS VINEYARDS   *Santa Clara 1976*   Founded by Robin and Dan Gehrs, Congress Springs occupies a historic winery site near Saratoga, in the Santa Cruz Mountain appellation. Run successfully for many years as a small (5,000 cases a year) winery, Congress Springs expanded in the late 80s after an infusion of capital from Anglo American Agriculture, a minority shareholder until 90, when it acquired a controlling interest. At the 30,000-case-a-year level, the winery, with the Gehrs departed and now directed by Anglo American, Inc., devotes over half of its output to Chardonnay. Before expansion, the winery enjoyed a good reputation for Semillon, Pinot Blanc, Sauvignon Blanc, and Zinfandel. The Zinfandels are still made from the winery's old unirrigated mountain vineyard, now named "Monmartre." The Zinfandels from the 70s were ripe, brawny, and sought after. The current lineup features several wines—Chardonnay, Pinot Noir, Pinot Blanc, and Riesling, all from the San Ysidro Vineyard, which is owned by the winery's parent company. Congress Springs also makes Cabernet Franc from the Santa Cruz Mountains, and in 86 started offering sparkling wines made by the *méthode champenoise*. A trio of Chardonnays consists of a partially barrel-fermented Santa Clara County, a barrel-fermented Reserve, and a barrel-fermented estate-bottled version from the "Monmartre Vineyard."

Chardonnay

(Santa Clara County)   84**   86*   87   88   89

(barrel-fermented Reserve)   86**   88*   89

(Monmartre Vineyard)   87*   88*

While generally successful in the case of Chardonnay, the changes in production require a bit of patience to see if quality and stylistic range continue apace; current wines run the gamut from moderately oaked and directly fruity to heavier oak and more expressive fruit, but all are balanced toward briskness

---

CONN CREEK WINERY   *Napa 1974*   Founder Bill Collins was in the electronics industry in Silicon Valley in the late 60s when he bought 55 acres just north of St. Helena. The vineyard contained Zinfandel planted in the 30s. Collins sold grapes and also increased his vineyard holdings until venturing into winemaking. Luck was on his side when he rented the old Ehlers Lane Winery in 75, a winery later used to launch Saintsbury Cellars and Vichon. He had the good fortune to buy 73 and 74 Cabernet Sauvignon from the ill-fated Lyncrest Vineyards, and also acquired the services of winemaker John Henderson as part of the deal. The two Cabernets issued under Conn Creek's label were among the best from each vintage and, along with Zinfandel made from the old vineyards, Conn Creek was off to an excellent start.

In 79 the owner decided to construct a new winery adjacent to Conn Creek. Bringing financial assistance to this project were the former owners of Château La Mission–Haut-Brion, who once owned 25% of Conn Creek and who later founded Chateau Woltner.

Despite continued good fortune with Cabernet Sauvignon, the winery expanded beyond its marketing ability. Before long wines were being sold at low prices under the Chateau Maja brand, a second label used first for Chardonnay and soon after for Chenin Blanc and Zinfandel. With inventory threatening to swamp the facility, the winery was sold to Stimson Lane (owners of Chateau Ste. Michelle and Villa Mount Eden). Since then, the winery has been on a even course, and both Merlot and Sauvignon Blanc added to the roster. The flagship wine, Cabernet Sauvignon (both Napa Valley Barrel Select and Private Reserve bottlings) is being gradually expanded to the 20,000-case level.

Cabernet Sauvignon

(regular bottling/Barrel Select) 79** 80* 81* 82* 83* 84* 85 86

(Private Reserve) 84*** 85* 86**

Always rich and ripe, with fairly prominent oak and a slight tendency toward briariness in some vintages, the Conn Creek Cabernets have been generally consistent performers and have shown an ability to age well; the new Private Reserve picks up the extra oak and richness that marked the mid-70s efforts from Conn Creek

R & J COOK   *Yolo 1979*   Roger and Joanne Cook grew up in families owning diversified farms in the Clarksburg region of the Delta. After they were married in the late 60s, they developed 115 acres of vineyards on their large ranch, with the intention of selling all their grapes. By the 78 vintage the market for their grapes weakened, and the following year they built a winery to crush and bottle wines from their vineyards. For a few years, the Cooks enjoyed enough success as producers of a line of table wines to grow from 7,000 cases to 55,000 cases a year. Part of their success lay in the fact that Chenin Blanc from the Delta appellation was slightly in vogue. At one time R & J Cook produced Chenin Blanc in three styles, including a barrel-fermented version. However, by the mid-80s, as White Zinfandel came into fashion, Chenin Blanc sales slipped. The Cooks did not grow Zinfandel, so to compete in the blush wine category they made a Merlot Blanc. The wine roster was cut back in the late 80s as the Cooks began selling more of their own grapes as well as grapes they controlled on a lease basis. Production is steady at 55,000 cases a year, including wines custom-made for others. Chestnut Hill and Chateau Joanna are brands bottled at R & J Cook's facility.

COOK'S CHAMPAGNE CELLARS   Owned by the Guild Winery based in Lodi, Cook's was an old, neglected brand, kicked around for years. Guild bought it in 71, and in 78 decided to use Cook's Imperial as a label for a line of low-priced Charmat process sparkling wines to compete with the enormously successful and seemingly unbeatable André line. From a modest 10,000-case production in 78, Cook's enjoyed smooth sailing and was selling over 500,000 cases by 85. In addition to the popular Imperial Brut, Cook's kept expanding its product line, which now includes Extra Dry, Blush, Spumante, White Zinfandel, and its upscale product (closed with a cork), the Grand Reserve. All sparklers have been identified as "American Champagne," a fact that may or may not lie behind the brand's success. Cook's is now selling more than 1.6 million cases annually. To capitalize on the name, the winery is now offering varietal wines under the name of "Cook's Captain Reserve."

CORBETT CANYON VINEYARDS *San Luis Obispo 1979* The biggest winery in the county, Corbett Canyon did not find smooth sailing in its first decade. Owned since 88 by the Wine Group (Franzia, Summit), the winery was originally named the Lawrence Winery after its founder, Jim Lawrence, who sold it to Glenmore Distillers in 82. Winemakers changed with even greater regularity than owners. The facility remains tucked away in the middle of the Edna Valley, and buys a considerable percentage of locally grown grapes. To assure itself of a supply, the Wine Group purchased the 350-acre Los Alamos Vineyard in Santa Barbara. For many years that property had sold grapes, and today is the primary source of Corbett Canyon's estate-bottled Chardonnay and Pinot Noir. Most of the winery's 300,000-case output now consists of a line identified as "Coastal Classics," low-priced varietals in 1-liter bottles. The volume leaders in this line are White Zinfandel and Chardonnay. A line of Reserve bottlings consists of five varietals from the Central Coast appellation, led by Chardonnay, partially barrel-fermented, Merlot, and Cabernet Sauvignon blended with Merlot, the latter two, as of 89, coming from Napa Valley. Given the vineyards owned, Corbett Canyon is a brand to follow for both Pinot Noir and Chardonnay.

CORISON WINES *Napa 1987* Longtime winemaker Cathy Corison launched her own brand after serving as winemaker for Chappellet Vineyards for 10 years. Her first vintage was 87. She specializes in Napa Valley Cabernet Sauvignon. All grapes are purchased from vineyards situated in the mid-Napa Valley, from Yountville to St. Helena. Annual production is about 1,800 cases.

COSENTINO WINERY *Napa 1980* One-time wine wholesaler in the Central Valley region, owner-winemaker Mitch Cosentino began making small batches of wine in a rented corner of a warehouse in Modesto. During the first few years, he produced a wide assortment of table wines under the Crystal Valley Cellars brand and sparkling wines labeled "Robin's Glow." Beginning with the 85 vintage, Cosentino began focusing on Bordeaux varietals—Cabernet Sauvignon, Merlot, and Cabernet Franc—and a Bordeaux blend called "The Poet." He earned critical praise for all four, and his pioneering efforts on behalf of Cabernet Franc paid off with an outstanding 86. That year the primary name switched to Cosentino Winery and plans were made to move the facility to Yountville in the Napa Valley. By mid-90, Cosentino had finally settled into his new home.

To date all wines have been produced from purchased grapes, but Cosentino plans to plant 4 acres of Merlot next to the winery. The majority of the reds are grown in Napa, Sonoma, and Lake counties, explaining the frequently used North Coast appellation. Two Chardonnays have been regularly produced, North Coast and a Reserve type from the Napa Valley labeled "The Sculptor." The quantities of each wine offered fall into the 600- to 1,200-case range, with the North Coast bottlings on the high end. Total annual production is at 12,000 cases.

Cabernet Sauvignon

(North Coast) **85** * **86**   **87**
(Reserve) **84** * * **85** * * **86**   **87** *

Both wines rely heavily on sweet, creamy oak to lift light- to medium-density, currant, and herbal fruit past noticeable tannins; the Reserve is usually a little riper and richer, but not necessarily more ageworthy

Chardonnay

(The Sculptor) **84**   **85**   **86** * **87**   **88**

Toasty, over-oaked wines have often lacked the fruit to bring them into a balanced package

Merlot

85* 86** 87* 88

Medium-depth cherry and subtle orange-rind fruit notes are enriched by sweet oak and firmed by light-medium tannins

The Poet

85** 86 87

Cosentino's blend—typically about half Cabernet Sauvignon, the rest split between Cabernet Franc and Merlot—is moderately rich in oak, fairly tannic, and occasionally a little on the heavy side and in need of great fruitiness

---

COSTELLO VINEYARDS *Napa 1982* In 78, John Costello and his wife bought a small ranch located a little north of the town of Napa. The site had been partly converted from prunes to vines by the previous owner. Costello expanded his vineyard to its present 40 acres by planting Chardonnay, Sauvignon Blanc, and Gewurztraminer. At first all grapes were sold, but Costello built a small winery and made wines from a portion of his crop. Within a few years he had converted the entire 40-acre vineyard into Chardonnay. Now focusing on estate-bottled, partially barrel-fermented Chardonnay, Costello has increased his annual output and is moving toward a maximum of 12,000 cases.

COTTONWOOD CANYON *San Luis Obispo 1988* In 88, wine wholesaler and distributor Norman Beko purchased 78 acres of an established larger vineyard in Santa Maria Valley called Santa Maria Hills Vineyard. Using rented space, consulting enologist Gary Mosby (formerly of Edna Valley Vineyards) has been producing barrel-fermented Chardonnay and Pinot Noir for Cottonwood Canyon. The annual production in the early vintages averaged 4,000 cases, 80% of which was Chardonnay.

H. COTURRI & SONS *Sonoma 1979* One of the first producers to emphasize the natural, no-chemicals approach to winemaking, Coturri seems to have filled a modest need. This is a family-owned venture, using a slightly expanded shed behind the family home to produce about 2,500 cases a year. Zinfandel and Cabernet Sauvignon are regular items, joined on occasion by Chardonnay and Sauvignon Blanc. The family farms 10 acres, and most of its wines are identified as Sonoma Valley in origin. The reds have generally attracted the most notice, though all too often for the wrong reasons. They are often high in volatility, with dirty characteristics; the Zinfandels in particular tend to be heavy-handed and close to late harvest in style.

CRESTON MANOR VINEYARDS & WINERY *San Luis Obispo 1982* In the hills in the La Planza Mountain Range, Creston Manor has the distinction of being located at the highest elevation in the county. After a rather flashy beginning when the winery was partly owned by Christina Crawford, daughter of the famous actress, ownership changed in 87 to the Rosenbloom family of Los Angeles. The 450-acre estate was planted to 140 acres of vineyards in the early 80s. The major varieties contained are Chardonnay, Cabernet Sauvignon, and Sauvignon Blanc. Pinot Noir, Semillon, Chenin Blanc, and Zinfandel are planted in small amounts. As it expanded to 30,000 cases a year, the winery has enjoyed good sales success with Pinot Noir made by carbonic maceration. Cabernet Sauvignon (regular and Winemaker Selection bottlings) and Chardonnay together account for over 50% of total output. White Zinfandel and Chevrier Blanc (Semillon) fill out the roster. We have found the Sauvignon Blanc (blended with Semillon) to range from average to * occasionally, depending on the level of fruit intensity. Though well made, the majority of the Cabernets have displayed excessive vegetal notes. Winemaker Victor Hugo Roberts estimates that 50,000 cases is the maximum production goal.

Chardonnay

84* 85* 87 88*

Pleasantly fruity, with appley and occasionally tropical highlights, toasty oak in the background, and good balance

CRIBARI WINES   This historic name is now a label owned by the Guild co-operative. The original Cribari Winery, located near Morgan Hill in Santa Clara County, was founded in 1904. It was one of a handful allowed to produce wines during Prohibition, but in the 50s the Cribari family became members of the Guild. As part of the multi-label Guild, Cribari has always been associated with a large line of generic wines and inexpensive bulk process sparkling wines, and it was not until the 70s that a line of varietals appeared. With the inclusion of a White Zinfandel, Cribari saw sales top 2 million cases in the mid-80s, only to decline gradually to about 1 million today. In 87, Cribari took a chance and began marketing generics in a 1.5-liter easy-pour wine pack, a container that was aluminum-lined and looked very much like a milk carton. It was received better in Japan than in the U.S. Most of the wines are made and bottled in Fresno or in Woodbridge.

CRICHTON HALL VINEYARD   *Napa 1985*   Richard and Judith Crichton left their respective careers in merchant banking and teaching behind them in 79 to settle in the Napa Valley and develop their vineyard. The 17-acre spread, planted entirely to Chardonnay, is located on the western foothills of Napa Valley about 3 miles north of Napa. To date, the wines are made in rented space, but aging takes place in barrels owned by the Crichtons. Producing only estate-grown Chardonnay, the Crichtons favor 100% barrel fermentation, partial malolactic fermentation, and aging *sur lie* for approximately eight months. From a first-year production of 1,500 cases, they have now reached their annual production goal of 4,000 cases. After a rough first vintage, the winemaking has settled into a better groove.

Chardonnay

85   86   87   88*

In their short history, these wines have ranged from citrusy and pinched to peachy and appley; toasty oak fills in the background

CRONIN VINEYARDS   *San Mateo 1980*   Dwayne Cronin is one of several Silicon Valley computer executives who make wine in their spare time. What sets him apart from the others is that Cronin wines, most particularly the Chardonnay, are among the very best made in California, year in and year out. If we had only one Chardonnay to choose, chances are we would select one of Cronin's. The bad news is that Cronin has yet to top the 2,000-case-a-year level, and most of his wines are made in lots of only 150 to 350 cases. As a rule, four Chardonnays are offered—one from Ventana Vineyards in Monterey, another from Napa Valley, a third from Sonoma's Alexander Valley. The fourth bears the Santa Cruz Mountain appellation, and it joined the roster in the late 80s when Cronin's own 1-acre vineyard began bearing. All Chardonnays are barrel-fermented, and given extended *sur lie* aging. Though a little less dramatic, Pinot Noir has also responded well to the Cronin treatment, earning * on virtually every outing. The weak link from this relatively fine producer is its red wine, a 2/3–1/3 blend of Cabernet Sauvignon and Merlot, which is rich in style but sometimes only average in quality. Currently, Cronin bottles two versions—Santa Cruz appellation and Napa Valley Stags Leap District. Located in the quaint town of Woodside, the winery is actually in the basement of the Cronins' home. It is not open to the public.

Chardonnay

(Sonoma County/Alexander Valley)   84**   85*   86***   87***   88**   89*

(Napa Valley)   83*   84*   85**   86***   87***   88**   89

(Ventana Vineyards) 83*** 84*** **85***** 86* 87** **88*****
89

*Each is complex, toasty, buttery, rich, mouth-filling, and filled with fruit,
and each carries the stamp of the winemaker in its combination of depth,
range, and balance. In rough generalizations, the Sonoma is often the most
fruity, the Napa the deepest, and the Monterey the most complex*

JOHN CULBERTSON WINERY *Riverside 1981* When he owned Martech International, a Houston-based company supplying diving and exploration services to
the oil industry, John Culbertson made wines as a hobby. In 75 he invested
in an 80-acre avocado ranch, located in Falmouth, a small town in the remote
northern corner of San Diego County. Not long afterwards he decided to build
a small sparkling wine facility on the ranch and make the wines himself. By
85, with production of over 7,000 cases of *méthode champenoise* wines, he was
beginning to enjoy the recognition of the wine world and wanted to expand
the facility. Culbertson purchased a 20-acre site located directly across the
street from Callaway Winery in Temecula, the premier South Coast grape-
growing region. With key investors from Los Angeles, he built a large (250,000-
gallon-capacity) showcase facility, along with a restaurant, Chez Champagne,
and a gift shop/tasting room.
   The Culbertson facility opened in 88 and soon became the entertainment
center of Temecula. Producing primarily *méthode champenoise* sparkling
wines, Culbertson now has a winemaking staff and is moving toward a 60,000-
case-a-year goal. The line of sparklers includes Brut, Brut Rosé, Natural, Blanc
de Noirs, Cuvée Rouge, and a Cuvée Frontignan made in a demi-sec style. A
small line of table wines—Cabernet Sauvignon, Chardonnay, and Pinot Noir—
went on direct sale from the winery in 87. Culbertson distribution is largely
in Southern California. The overall quality of its sparkling wines is generally
agreeable, but only an occasional bottling reaches ✿ level.

RICHARD CUNEO *(Sebastiani Vineyards)* Dick Cuneo was hired by his father-in-
law, Gus Sebastiani, and is now the general manager of the large family winery
run by his brother-in-law, Don Sebastiani. In 86, when Don took control of the
wine company, he rearranged many lines and added this one-wine line as an
upscale sparkler. The first offering bearing the Richard Cuneo name was
purchased from Sonoma-Cutrer; all subsequent vintages have been custom-
made. The wine is made 100% from barrel-fermented Chardonnay, produced
by the *méthode champenoise.* It averages three years *en tirage* before being
released. The early vintages were uneven in quality.

CUTLER CELLAR This is a Cabernet Sauvignon–only label, owned by Lance Cutler,
the longtime winemaker for Gundlach Bundschu Winery. In the mid-8os,
when the owners of Gundlach Bundschu wanted to emphasize estate-grown
wines, they decided to cease production of a Cabernet Sauvignon from the
neighboring Batto Ranch. Beginning in 85, Cutler took over the contract and
has since produced Cabernet Sauvignon that in some years has earned ✿ for
its rich cassis and herbal character, balanced by sweet oak. A Merlot-
dominated proprietary blend is named "Satyre." Production is under 1,000
cases total.

CUVAISON WINERY *Napa 1970* During its first decade, this attractive winery on
the outskirts of Calistoga seemed to attract confused and confusing owners.
Started by two partners from the engineering world of Silicon Valley in 69,
it was left in the hands of one partner within its first year. Owner/winemaker
Tom Cottrell made nine wines his first year, including a Beaujolais-style
Gamay named "Vivace" and other oddities. Within a few years Cuvaison was
purchased by a publishing company, Commerce Clearing House, which actu-
ally built the present-day winery before selling out in 79 to a Swiss company,
Isenhold. Among the primary stockholders of Isenhold was the Alexander
Schmidheiny family, which since 86 has owned Cuvaison.

The wine roster of today bears no resemblance to that of the past. In the 70s, Cuvaison became notorious for big, bold, often tannic Cabernet Sauvignons and Zinfandels, both made from old hillside vineyards. Later in the 70s it enjoyed some success with Chardonnay from Winery Lake Vineyard in Carneros. In 79, under the new ownership, Cuvaison acquired 400 acres of prime land in the Carneros and planted more than 300 acres over the next few years. The major varieties established are Chardonnay, Pinot Noir, and Merlot. At one time the owners had considered making sparkling wine and had also thought of building a facility within the Carneros. These ideas were dropped when Cuvaison's Chardonnays from the 85 vintage onward enjoyed unexpected critical and sales success. A Merlot produced in 84 was also among the top ranked of its type, and the winery's planting of Merlot expanded to 20 acres.

By 90 Cuvaison was making 35,000 cases of Chardonnay a year (with further expansion anticipated), 4,000 cases of Cabernet Sauvignon, and about 2,000 cases of Merlot. It occasionally bottles 2,000 cases of Carneros Reserve Chardonnay. In the 90s, Cuvaison will introduce limited-production Pinot Noir from its Carneros holdings.

Cabernet Sauvignon

84 ** 85 86 ** 87 *

Owing all of its reputation for Cabernet quality to wines dating from 84 onward, Cuvaison has now established a house style of firm, tight, curranty wines that are high in oak and exhibit a tannic edge in need of many years of aging

Chardonnay

85 ** 86 * 87 * 88 ** 89

Crisp, appley, and slightly citrusy fruit is supported by rich and toasty oak in this series of moderately deep, exceptionally well-balanced wines

Merlot

84 ** 85 ** 86 * 87 * 88 **

Well-made, rich wines, high in sweet, ripe-cherryish fruit, and loaded with sweet oak; they seem likely to need fairly long aging on the basis of balance and youthfully coarse tannins

DALLA VALLE VINEYARDS *Napa 1986* On a knoll overlooking the intersection of the Oakville Crossroad and the Silverado Trail, the Dalla Valle winemaking facility was completed in the fall of 86. Four years earlier, Gustav Dalla Valle and his wife Naoko developed a 25-acre vineyard in the Oakville area. Dalla Valle had previously been a manufacturer of diving equipment, and was a deep-sea diver himself before entering the wine business at the age of 70. His hillside vineyard, situated on the slopes east of the Silverado Trail, is planted predominantly to Cabernet Sauvignon with a few acres of Cabernet Franc and Merlot for blending. The first vintages were made with the assistance of consulting enologist Joe Cafaro. In addition to Cabernet Sauvignon, the winery bottles "Maya," a proprietary blend of Cabernet Sauvignon and Cabernet Franc. The winery was designed to handle a maximum output of 4,000 cases a year.

D'ANNEO VINEYARD *Napa 1986* The D'Anneo family owns a vineyard in Calistoga, opposite Sterling and adjacent to Clos Pegase. Its 10 acres of Zinfandel were planted in 24. Andrew D'Anneo decided to test the wine market and made 300 cases of Zinfandel in 83. Since then his production has been on again, off again. The quality has been good, with long wood aging and tough tannins giving the wines a slightly rustic note.

DAUME WINERY *Ventura 1982* John Daume was a home winemaker and a dealer in winemaking supplies before turning professional. His store, the Home Wine Shop in Woodland Hills, also serves as headquarters for an amateur winemaker club. In a modestly equipped winery, with assistance from club members, he makes varietal wines, most of which are from two appellations, Mendocino County and Paso Robles. Over 50% of his 2,200-case annual output consists of Mendocino County Chardonnay. The winemaking approach is traditional—barrel fermentation and extended *sur lie* aging. The rest of his line is usually derived from Paso Robles fruit, and is pretty evenly divided among Zinfandel, Cabernet Sauvignon, and Fumé Blanc.

DE LOACH VINEYARDS *Sonoma 1975* One-time San Francisco fireman Cecil De Loach took early retirement in 75 to concentrate on his small vineyard operation in the Russian River Valley. The old 24-acre Zinfandel vineyard he had acquired in 70 was in full production, but a weak demand for grapes in 75 forced him to venture into winemaking. After making only Zinfandel during his first three vintages, De Loach has become one of the leading Chardonnay producers as well as one of the most reliable brands around. Located west of Santa Rosa, the De Loach winery is surrounded by the 120-acre estate vineyard. Another 75-acre vineyard in the same cool subregion of the Russian River Valley is under long-term lease, and in 90, De Loach purchased an additional 80 acres in a warmer region near Windsor suited to Cabernet Sauvignon and related Bordeaux varieties.

Over the first several vintages De Loach developed a modest reputation for ripe Zinfandels and spicy Gewurztraminers. In 79, the winery started making White Zinfandel that proved to be a style-setter and a wild commercial success, and it also began earning high marks for Chardonnay in a style combining juicy fruit flavors and early drinkability. By the end of the 80s De Loach was making 25,000 cases of Chardonnay and at least as much White Zinfandel each year. Partially barrel-fermented and aged in French oak for nine months, De Loach Chardonnays have always managed to offer ripe apple appeal and modest depth and complexity when first released. Gewurztraminer is another highly successful varietal produced by De Loach. An early harvest version typically captures varietal intensity in a clean, crisp finish. In some vintages the early harvest ranks among the very best Gewurztraminer of all. Small quantities of late harvest Gewurztraminer are made in certain vintages, and they too are often of ✿ or ✿✿ caliber.

De Loach has been making Pinot Noir from his own 9-acre parcel, but the quality and style have varied widely. Sauvignon Blanc of generally average quality and Cabernet Sauvignon fill out the roster. Special lots of limited-production, high-priced, estate-bottled Chardonnay, Cabernet Sauvignon, and Pinot Noir are identified as "O.F.S.," ostensibly standing for "Our Finest Selection." The total annual production at De Loach is close to 85,000 cases.

Chardonnay

83 ✿✿ 84 ✿✿✿ **85 ✿✿✿** 86 ✿ 87 ✿✿ **88 ✿✿** 89 ✿

Immensely fruity, almost juicy in its concentrated, bright style, with pert acidity and toasty oak in support; medium-long aging potential

DE LORIMIER WINERY *Sonoma 1985* In the early 60s Dr. Alfred De Lorimier, a San Francisco surgeon, purchased a home in the Alexander Valley and began developing a vineyard adjacent to it. Located in the northern end of the valley near Geyserville, De Lorimier's vineyard has been expanded to 64 acres, growing mainly Cabernet, Merlot, Chardonnay, Sauvignon Blanc, Semillon, and Cabernet Franc. De Lorimier produces a partially barrel-fermented Chardonnay and four proprietary blends. "Mosaic" is the name given to its red Bordeaux blend; "Spectrum" is the white Bordeaux blend (typically 65% Sauvignon Blanc, 35% Semillon). A late harvest blend of the same two wines fashioned along Sauternes lines is named "Lace." Even the winery's Chardonnay sports a proprietary name, "Prism." Initial production was close to 5,000 cases a year. The winery has the capacity to expand output to 25,000 cases a year, a goal its owner hopes to reach by the end of the decade.

DE NATALE VINEYARDS *Sonoma 1985* The De Natale family owns 7 acres of vineyards on Eastside Road in Healdsburg. With annual production below 1,000 cases a year, the winery is entirely family-run. In small batches averaging between 200 and 300 cases, they have in one vintage or another produced Chardonnay, Pinot Noir, Cabernet Sauvignon, Zinfandel, and Riesling, the latter in a slightly sweet style. The first vintages of Chardonnay were impressive, and speak well for the family's winemaking abilities.

DEER PARK WINERY *Napa 1979* This beautiful old stone winery, built in 1891, went through several ownership changes before it was acquired by two families, the Knapps and the Clarks, refurbished, and put back in operation by the fall of 79. Most of the 48-acre property is steep, rocky hillside, 6 acres of which have been planted to Chardonnay and Sauvignon Blanc. The winery buys Zinfandel and on occasion Chardonnay and Petite Sirah from various growers in Napa Valley. As winemaker, David Clark prefers Zinfandels in a big, ripe style, and usually gives them two years of oak aging. His Napa Valley Zinfandels are generally supple and woodsy, with a hint of fruit. Every now and then he produces a bigger, bolder style of Zinfandel from the Beatty Ranch on Howell Mountain. The winery's total production is about 3,000 cases, with 6,000 set as the maximum level.

DEER VALLEY (PAUL MASSON WINERY) This was a second label used by Smith & Hook until it was acquired by Paul Masson in 88. In an effort to enter the competitive low-price end of the varietal wine market, Vintners International, Masson's owner, decided to make Deer Valley its major weapon. All wines are vintaged, and the line presently consists of Chardonnay, Cabernet Sauvignon, Sauvignon Blanc, and White Zinfandel, the number-one-volume wine. The market was tested with an 86 Cabernet Sauvignon, which led to a full series in 88. Sales have reached 70,000 cases a year.

DEHLINGER WINERY *Sonoma 1976* Located in the Forestville corner of the lower Russian River Valley, Dehlinger has quietly risen to first-class status. With assistance from his father and brother, Tom Dehlinger planted 14 acres adjacent to the winery. By 80, the winery was producing over 5,000 cases a year. Tom Dehlinger took a degree in biochemistry and went on to study enology at U.C. Davis. Early on, his winery developed a strong reputation for Zinfandel, but was soon performing well with all varietals. In 85 Tom Dehlinger became the sole owner, and the 85 vintage, a highly successful one for the winery, signaled the end of a rough and rustic note and the beginning of a polished, refined winemaking style. At that time the decision was made to produce only estate-grown wines. Unable to buy a suitable vineyard or to grow Zinfandel in his cool-climate locale, Dehlinger ceased making Zinfandel after 83.

Steadily expanding the home vineyard in the 80s, he now has 50 acres planted, mainly to Pinot Noir (20 acres) Chardonnay (15 acres), Cabernet Sauvignon (7 acres), and Merlot (3 acres). Each is made as a varietal. From 4 acres of Cabernet Franc, Dehlinger is making 200 to 400 cases a year of a varietal (available only at the winery) and also using the grape to blend with Cabernet Sauvignon. For barrel fermentations of his successful Chardonnays as well as for aging all of his wines, Dehlinger prefers using the 135-gallon puncheon oak container. In the 90s, the winery is holding steady at the 8,000-case-a-year level. About one-third of the total is sold directly at the winery through a futures program.

Cabernet Sauvignon

78* 79* 80* 82* 83* 84* 85* 86* 87

Ripish, curranty, somewhat plummy fruit, with occasional cedary or herbal undertones, medium-rich oak, generally 10-year aging potential

Chardonnay

84   85**   86*   87*   88*   89*

Nicely focused appley fruit, frequently with pretty, pearlike overtones, is buoyed by toasty oak and balanced by brisk acids

Pinot Noir

82*   83*   84**   85**   86**   87***   88**   89**

Medium- to full-intensity cherryish fruit, sometimes with black cherry and orange rind, is enriched by oak, firmed by medium tannins, tends to age well

---

DELICATO VINEYARDS   *San Joaquin 1935*   Located in Manteca and the ninth largest wine producer in the country, Delicato supplied wines to other brands for many years until it also began bottling its own wines in the early 70s. Until recently, all wines have been made from Central Valley grapes. In the 80s, Sutter Home began buying White Zinfandel from Delicato, and as sales increased dramatically, both companies benefited from the relationship. In the early 80s Delicato, intending to upgrade its quality, had developed close to 300 acres in Clements, not far from Lodi. Then, in 88, it acquired the 13,000-acre San Bernabe Ranch in Monterey County, which contained 8,000 acres of established vineyards.

After that bold move of buying what is probably the world's largest contiguous vineyard, Delicato has expanded production for both its own line and the bulk business. Its Manteca facility now has a storage capacity of 30 million gallons. In 88, a crushing facility was built in Monterey where the grapes are processed, and the juice then transported to Manteca for fermentation. Plans call for a fermenting and aging facility in Monterey by the mid-90s. Today, most Delicato generic wines are from the California appellation. At over 100,000 cases, White Zinfandel is the volume leader among cork-finished wines. For the on-premise market, Delicato sells a range of generics and White Zinfandel in 18-liter containers, and that side of the business brings its total production to 2 million cases a year. To date, Monterey County is used for Chenin Blanc, White Grenache, Zinfandel, Sauvignon Blanc, and Chardonnay. This line of Monterey County varietals is expected to grow significantly by the end of the 90s.

DEMOOR WINERY   *Napa 1973*   Known from 73 to 83 as Napa Wine Cellars, this winery was often described as the one in the geodesic dome. Despite a favored location along the main wine road in Oakville, the founders had a rough time of it before selling to the Belgian wine merchant family of DeSchepper-DeMoor. They expanded the winemaking and aging facility, changed the name, and converted the dome into a tasting room that is overflowing with merchandise and often crowded with tourists. By the end of the 80s DeMoor was among the most popular tourist stops. In 90, DeMoor Winery was acquired by Sky Court Corporation of Japan. As in the past, the winery purchases all grapes crushed. It focuses on Cabernet Sauvignon, Chardonnay, and Zinfandel, and these three account for most of the winery's 20,000-case annual output. In addition, it produces Sauvignon Blanc and Chenin Blanc. The winemaking style has emphasized about 50% barrel fermentation for Chardonnay, and the Cabernet Sauvignons undergo extended (25-day) maceration prior to pressing. Usually full-bodied and made for long aging, DeMoor's Cabernets have varied in quality and have not aged as well as they promised in their youth. A limited-volume sweet Sauvignon Blanc named "Fie Doux" is available only at the winery. Napa Cellars is used as a second label for wines sold at the winery.

Cabernet Sauvignon

81*   82**   83*   84**   86

Ripe, fairly concentrated character, often with a suggestion of dried fruit, enriched by omnipresent oakiness and tending toward an herbal streak in some vintages

Chardonnay

84   85*   86   87   88*

Ripe, not especially fruity wines, high in oak but low in inviting varietal character

Zinfandel

84*   85   86   88

Following the "house" style of emphasized ripeness, these wines have been fairly tannic and well oaked, but not always carrying sufficient fruit

---

DEUX AMIS WINERY   Owners Phyllis Zouzounis and Jim Penpraze are indeed two friends who combine their talents to produce a limited line of wines. Both have worked for wineries in Dry Creek Valley. To date all wines have been made in leased space and are from the Dry Creek Valley appellation. The offerings include Sauvignon Blanc, Zinfandel, and Cabernet Sauvignon. Each at times has displayed good medium-intense character. Total annual production is around 500 cases.

DEVLIN WINE CELLARS   *Santa Cruz 1979*   Located in Soquel, just south of Santa Cruz, Devlin Wine Cellars sells most of its wine from its tasting and sales room. Owner/winemaker Chuck Devlin produces a range of varietals from purchased grapes. In a roster subject to change from year to year, Devlin emphasizes Santa Cruz Mountains Chardonnay, Cabernet Sauvignon, and Zinfandel. The Central Coast appellation is frequently seen on Devlin's Sauvignon Blanc and Merlot, and the Merlots have enjoyed * success in the mid-80s. A barrel-fermented Santa Cruz Mountain Chardonnay, "Beauregard Vineyard," is Devlin's prestige bottling. However, White Zinfandel is the volume leader in the annual output of 8,000 cases.

DIAMOND CREEK VINEYARDS   *Napa 1972*   This Cabernet Sauvignon–only winery is a great study in making the most from the smallest financial stake. In 67, Al Brounstein left his prospering pharmaceutical business in Los Angeles and moved to Napa Valley. He bought 79 acres of steep, forested land along the mountain ridge west of Calistoga known as Diamond Mountain. He then planted the land to 20 acres of Cabernet Sauvignon with Merlot for blending. Because of the configuration of the site, Brounstein set the vines on three separate blocks which, when each block was made into wine, revealed three distinct personalities. He kept each separate for bottling. Volcanic Hill was the largest parcel, named after the volcanic soils. The parcel opposite it was on red soils and was named Red Rock Terrace. The third, on extremely rocky soil, Brounstein called Gravelly Meadow. For many years, Brounstein used the services of a part-time winemaker and had his wines crushed and fermented in rented facilities. Once it was in barrels, the wine would be transported to his mountain location. This "aging room" might better be described as a lean-to shed under the trees.

From 72 to 78, the yields were small, and Diamond Creek did not make more than 1,000 cases total. Over the years Brounstein wisely developed a clientele, and by 80 was able to sell every drop bottled through a mailing list. A fourth vineyard, less than 1 acre, is the Lake Vineyard named after the manmade pond on the property. Usually blended into the Gravelly Meadow, the Lake has been bottled separately on occasion. In the 80s Diamond Creek averaged 2,500 cases a year. It is among the more expensive Cabernets.

Cabernet Sauvignon

(Red Rock Terrace)   73*   74*   75**   77*   78*   79*
80*   81*   82*   83*   84**   85***   86***   87*   88

(Gravelly Meadows) 74** 75* 76** 77* 78* 79* 80*
81 82* 83 84*** 85** 86** 87** 88*

(Volcanic Hill) 73 74* 75̶ 76* 77 78** 79** 80**
81* 82* 83* 84* 85** 86 87* 88

In the early to mid-70s, these were brutally tannic, overmade wines, whose complexity and depth was often joined by a host of earthy, loamy characteristics. But toward the 80s, the style became moderated just enough to produce cleaner wines, whose somewhat lowered but still mouth-puckering tannins now seemed more reasonably fitted to the rest of the wines' character. Red Rock Hill is often the most fruity of the wines; Gravelly Meadows tends to be as intense but sometimes slightly less complete; the Volcanic Hill bottling can be a bit drier and thus not quite as able to fight through its bold tannins in lesser vintages. Nonetheless, this trio of wines is fully deserving of the high esteem it has won

DION VINEYARDS *Sonoma 1986* In 78 the Dion family purchased an old vineyard located in the western hills of the Sonoma Valley and immediately replanted 7½ acres to Chardonnay. In the early 80s they sold grapes to Adler Fels and other neighboring producers. After making wines as a home winemaker for several years, Jerry Dion, a commercial pilot, used his own grapes to produce Chardonnay. The first vintages here were made at Mark West vineyards, owned by fellow pilot Bob Ellis. Zinfandel purchased from a Sonoma Valley neighbor has been Dion's only red wine to date. The estate vineyard, situated in the Sonoma Mountain appellation, has been expanded to 13 acres. Dion's annual production remains below 2,000 cases, and is evenly split between Chardonnay and Zinfandel.

DOLAN VINEYARDS *Mendocino 1980* Paul Dolan has been the winemaker for Fetzer Vineyards since 77. In 80 he began making wines for his own label, using a small facility behind his home. Cabernet Sauvignon and Chardonnay are the primary wines produced, and the 100% barrel-fermented Chardonnay has been made from the Lolonis Vineyard. In the late 80s, when Fetzer production was growing rapidly, Dolan cut back the production of his own wines to the 200–300-case level. After 88, he quit using his own label for a year or two. The style of Dolan wines was no-holds-barred, and a few vintages of his Chardonnay rank among the heavyweights of all time.

DOMAINE CARNEROS *Napa 1987* The prestigious name Taittinger appears prominently on the Domaine Carneros label, which is in fact a partnership between Champagne Taittinger, the Kobrand Corporation, a wine importer, and Peter Ordway, who owns the vineyards. Its large chateau-style facility is modeled upon the 18th-century Taittinger residence in Champagne. Located in the Carneros and relying exclusively on fruit grown in that area, Domaine Carneros makes only sparkling wine by the *méthode champenoise*. To date its primary wine is a nonvintage Brut. Initial output of 3,000 cases grew to 25,000 cases by 89. The winery's capacity is 60,000 cases a year, a goal it expects to reach by the end of the decade.

About 110 acres adjacent to the imposing winery are planted to vines; the owners favor Pinot Noir and Chardonnay, but have also planted Pinot Blanc and Pinot Meunier. The initial cuvées were made from 60% Pinot Noir, 35% Chardonnay, and 5% Pinot Blanc. Like Taittinger Champagne, its French relative, Domaine Carneros, under the direction of Eileen Crane, also hopes to become known for a light-bodied, delicate style of sparkling wine. Crane apprenticed at Domaine Chandon and was in charge of winemaking operations at Gloria Ferrer before joining Domaine Carneros.

DOMAINE DE LA TERRE ROUGE *Amador 1987* Longtime San Francisco Bay wine merchant Bill Easton began developing vineyards in 85. Located in Fiddletown where he resides, the primary vineyard of 8 acres is planted to Rhone varieties—Syrah, Mourvedre, Marsanne, and Viognier. Easton purchases grapes from the Sierra Foothills to produce a proprietary red blend from Grenache, Syrah, Mourvedre, and Cinsault. Production has grown from 400 cases in 86 to 1,200 cases in 90. Easton also makes 400 to 500 cases of Vin Gris from Zinfandel, which he barrel-ferments and ages *sur lie.* Long-term annual production of Domaine de la Terre Rouge is expected to be 3,000 cases.

DOMAINE KARAKASH *Napa 1983* Owner Miles Karakasevic left his native Yugoslavia in 62. After a stint in Canada as a chemist and in Michigan as an enologist, he began his wine career in California in 70 by working for United Vintners. Moving on to the enology department of Beringer Vineyards, he next became a consultant and bought property in Napa Valley's Spring Mountain area in 82. Karakasevic began by making wine at wineries that used his consulting services. He often buys grapes from his clients, most of whom are now in Mendocino and Sonoma counties, and plans to build a winery next to his home. Meanwhile, renting space in a Mendocino County winery, he produces Chardonnay, Sauvignon Blanc, and Charbay, a proprietary wine. The latter is a blend of Chardonnay and brandy liqueur that at 18% alcohol is best suited as a dessert beverage. On average, Domaine Karakash makes 3,500 cases a year, with Chardonnay predominating at 2,000 cases.

DOMAINE LAURIER Now known as Laurier Vineyards. See entry under that name.

Cabernet Sauvignon

82　83＊　84＊　85＊

Medium intensity, spicy-earthy aroma, supple but with tannins to age out

Chardonnay

83＊＊　84　85　86＊

Appley, lemony aroma; medium-bodied, direct; oak is a major component

DOMAINE MICHEL *Sonoma 1987* Owner Jean-Jacques Michel is an investment banker originally from Switzerland. In 79 he purchased land and began developing 50 acres of vineyards in the western Dry Creek Valley. About half of the total acreage is devoted to Chardonnay; the rest is planted to Cabernet Sauvignon (14 acres), Merlot (8 acres), and Cabernet Franc (4 acres). The rather elaborate Mediterranean-style wine facility and adjoining estate were fully operative by the 86 harvest, while wines from 84 and 85 were made at another winery. Despite being compared by many to Jordan Vineyard, Domaine Michel's first vintages were not well received by the wine trade. A change in winemakers occurred in 89, not long after the winery decided not to market its 85 Cabernet Sauvignon. A barrel-fermented Chardonnay from 86, however, was of ＊ quality. When the 86 Cabernet Sauvignon attained a similar level, Domaine Michel was once again a winery to be carefully watched. By the early 90s it was making close to 15,000 cases of Cabernet Sauvignon and 10,000 cases of Chardonnay.

DOMAINE MONTREAUX *Napa 1987* Represented by its owners as a separate brand and company, Montreaux is run by Jay Corley, owner of Monticello Cellars, his marketing director, and other partners involved with Monticello in some capacity. The only product is sparkling wine made by the *méthode champenoise;* Montreaux produced its first commercial batch in 83. A separate facility was in place by 87. About 32 acres of Chardonnay and Pinot Noir in the Oak Knoll area are set aside to supply grapes for this brand. The wines used in the cuvée are barrel-fermented and oak-aged. Once selected, the cuvée is given about three years' aging *en tirage.* Typically, the cuvées for the Brut style consist of 60% Pinot Noir, 40% Chardonnay. The early vintages did not in fact live up to all the winemaking attention bestowed upon them. Production is moving toward a goal of 3,500 cases per year.

DOMAINE MUMM Until late 90, Domaine Mumm was the label for a line of sparkling wines now known as Mumm Napa Valley (see entry).

DOMAINE NAPA *Napa 1985* French-born Michel Perret built a winery just north of Rutherford in 85. He has 10 acres under vine adjacent to the winery and has access to 180 acres of vineyards which he manages for other owners. During the first several vintages, the winery specialized in three varietals—Chardonnay, Cabernet Sauvignon, and Sauvignon Blanc. The official name in the beginning was Domaine de Napa. Production by 90 reached 9,000 cases, equally divided among the three wines. Early vintages struggled to rise above the mediocre.

DOMAINE ST. GEORGE *Sonoma 1986* The old Cambiaso Winery which had muddled along for decades was rechristened Domaine St. George in 86 and began moving on a fast track. A batch of 85 oak-aged Chardonnay purchased from another producer was the first wine issued under the Domaine St. George label. The immediate sales success inspired the winery name change and led to its expansion into the low-priced varietal wine market. The facility, located in the northern Russian River Valley, has been upgraded and expanded to handle over 300,000 cases of varietals and proprietary blends. Some of the wines are crushed and fermented at the Sonoma winery, and a bigger portion is bought. Domaine St. George regularly offers Chardonnay, Cabernet Sauvignon, Fumé Blanc, Zinfandel, Chevrier, and blended white and red wines. Confirming its emphasis on the popular and trendy, the winery was the first to bottle a blush Chardonnay. Overall, its quality varies, depending on what is available on the bulk market. But the quality rarely rises above average, save for a Reserve Chardonnay from 87 that earned ✻. Otherwise, the results have been erratic.

DOMINUS ESTATE *Napa 1982* This one-wine producer comes with an exciting cast of characters. Dominus Estate is the name of a Bordeaux-style blend made by a partnership, the John Daniel Society. The partners are the daughters of John Daniel, Robin Lail and Marcia Smith, and Christian Moueix, the winemaker-director for the legendary Château Pétrus of Pomerol. John Daniel owned Inglenook Vineyard during its prime years—the 30s to the late 60s. Many of California's most fabled Cabernets, such as the Inglenook Cask Cabernets of 41, 49, 52, 54, 55, 57, 58, and 59, were made entirely or in part from a vineyard that came to be known as Napanook Vineyard.

Now owned by Robin Lail and Marcia Smith, the 125-acre property dates to the 1880s and is located on the western hills near Yountville. In an area proven to be excellent Cabernet turf, Napanook has 50 acres planted to Cabernet and its blending cousins, 20 acres to Chardonnay, and 20 additional acres suitable for planting. Dominus is made by Moueix, who visits Napa Valley regularly, exclusively from Napanook Cabernet Sauvignon (75–80%) with Merlot and Cabernet Franc filling it out. The first vintage was 83, a wine that was released a year after the 84, and met with some controversy. While some critics proclaimed Dominus to be an instant legend, we found that the first vintages approached the ✻ to ✻✻ quality, but were neither classic nor the best of their class in the high-priced division. The owners have used a second label, Daniel Estate, on occasion. The annual output of Dominus is moving toward an ultimate 10,000 cases.

Cabernet Sauvignon

83✻ 84✻✻ 85✻ 86✻

Immense wines that are bold in curranty fruit, high in rich and creamy oak, and very tannic, they are among the leaders for intensity and drama. But in the early vintages, they also have been bothered by background earthy notes that raise troubling questions about how well they will hold up in the long run

DONATONI WINERY *Los Angeles 1980* In 68 when United Airlines pilot Hank Donatoni purchased a home north of Los Angeles, the property contained a few Zinfandel vines. That same year he made several gallons of Zinfandel "just for fun." Over the next few years he made more wine at home, encouraged by John Daume of the Daume Winery. In 80, in an industrial complex within walking distance of LA International, in a small area exempted from Los Angeles ordinances forbidding the production of wine inside city limits, he began making wines professionally. His annual production holds steady at 1,000 cases. Chardonnay from Monterey and Cabernet from the Paso Robles appellation have been his mainstays.

DRY CREEK VINEYARDS *Sonoma 1972* Owner Dave Stare deserves considerable credit for his pioneering efforts in founding the first small, premium-quality winery in Sonoma County since the end of Prohibition. He was also among the first proponents of the Dry Creek Valley Viticultural Area, and his winery played a key part in the evolution of Fumé Blanc as a varietal, thanks to its pungent, aromatic version. Now, after two expansion stages, Dry Creek is functioning at its maximum capacity of 75,000 cases annually. Fumé Blanc is the major wine, with 28,000 to 30,000 cases made a year, followed by Chardonnay (8,000–20,000 cases), and Cabernet Sauvignon (10,000 cases). Chenin Blanc, Zinfandel, and Petite Sirah fill out the line. Both Gewurztraminer and Johannisberg Riesling have been provided, but were discontinued in the late 80s. Dry Creek Vineyards' Fumé Blanc, tending toward a grassy, pungent style, has succeeded in some years and gone too far in that direction in others. Of late, the winery's Chardonnay has been the best performer. Ironically, the only minor disappointments have come from the Reserve wines, which for a few vintages were labeled "David S. Stare" wines. Recently, the much improved Reserve program has consisted of about 3,000 cases of Chardonnay, 100% barrel-fermented, and 2,000 cases of a Meritage red. The winery draws from 50 acres surrounding it and another 40 acres in the Dry Creek Valley. It also buys from growers in the Alexander Valley, and growers in the Delta region supply most of its Chenin Blanc.

Cabernet Sauvignon

80 81 82 83 84 85* 86 87* 88

Always containing Merlot and lately a dollop of Cabernet Franc, the wine can be fruit-focused and clean, with good depth in its best showings, but less complete and a bit too rough at other times

Chardonnay

84** 85* 86** 87 89

Tightly focused fruit, of good intensity and firm balance, is enriched by toasty oak

DUCKHORN VINEYARDS *Napa 1976* A limited partnership of ten families, including Dan and Margaret Duckhorn, this winery is run by the Duckhorns. A banker by profession, Dan Duckhorn became involved in Napa Valley when he was an expert witness in a case involving grape growers. Never much to look at by Napa Valley standards, the winery is located northeast of St. Helena on the Silverado Trail. Ever since its inaugural release of 78 Merlot, Duckhorn has been the most in-demand producer of Merlot, and as a result its usually fine accomplishments with Cabernet Sauvignon and Sauvignon Blanc have taken a back seat. Only the white wine is made from winery-owned grapes, and Duckhorn's 6½ acres of Sauvignon Blanc and Semillon now contribute to its annual production of about 7,500 cases of Sauvignon Blanc, about 50% barrel-fermented and often blended with 20% Semillon. They have been rich and attractive enough to earn ** often.

Merlot is bought from several vineyards, including the Three Palms Vineyard in Calistoga and Vine Hill Vineyards in Rutherford, both of which have been individually bottled. The Three Palms Merlots are often the best of the class. The more plentiful Napa Valley Merlot combines fruit from five or six vineyards as a rule, and is usually blended with Cabernet Sauvignon and Cabernet Franc. Duckhorn's Cabernet, derived from as many as eight vineyards scattered about Napa Valley, is often blended with Cabernet Franc and occasionally contains a pinch of Merlot. A Meritage red from Howell Mountain was added to the roster in 89.

For over a decade, Duckhorn's Cabernets, limited to about 2,000 cases per year, were among the highest rated of the vintage, and the quality was a little more consistent than was that of its Merlots. In the last few vintages of the 80s, Duckhorn's production increased to about 20,000 cases of red wine—55% Merlot, 45% Cabernet Sauvignon. "Decoy," a second label originally used for a Pinot Noir from Three Palms Vineyard, is kept alive to use for Sauvignon Blanc and Semillon not used in the master blend, and for Pinot Blanc that is occasionally made. Decoy's output is under 1,000 cases.

Cabernet Sauvignon

78** 80** 81*** 82** 83** 84** 85** 86** 87**
88*

Medium-full-bodied wines, high in curranty Cabernet fruit and rich oak, are seasoned with brushy, briary notes and come with fairly tough tannins; they are tasty, deep, and long aging

Merlot

(Napa Valley) 79** 80** 81** 82** 83** 84* 86**
87*** 88**

(Three Palms Vineyard) 78*** 81*** 83* 84*** 85**
86*** 87* 88**

(Vine Hill Vineyard) 85* 86 87*

With a decade of outstanding performance behind it, Duckhorn clearly stands as the leading producer of Merlot in California; its Three Palms Vineyard bottling is typically robust and complex, with deep curranty and cherryish fruit emerging as the wine ages through a decade or more of development; the Napa Valley bottling is more directly fruity, less complex but occasionally outperforms its more expensive stablemate when its focused ripe cherry fruit is at its most intense

---

DUNCAN PEAK VINEYARDS *Mendocino 1987* San Francisco Bay Area attorney Hubert Lenczowski decided to develop a small vineyard on his family's ranch. In the early 80s he laid out 4 acres total to Cabernet Sauvignon, Merlot, and Cabernet Franc on a hillside in an area of Hopland known as the Sanel Valley. By the time of his first crush in 86, Lenczowski had refurbished a two-story barn on a hilltop on the edge of Duncan Peak and converted it into a small winery. The facility has a capacity to ferment and age 500 cases a year.

DUNN VINEYARDS *Napa 1982* As the winemaker for Caymus Vineyards in the 70s, Randy Dunn established a reputation for outstanding Cabernet Sauvignon. In the late 70s he and his wife, Lori, began reviving an old Cabernet vineyard on their home property west of Angwin in the Howell Mountain appellation. The old 5-acre vineyard was returned to productivity and from it about 500 cases were made in 79. Encouraged by the owners of Caymus, Dunn bonded his winery in 82 and began a distinguished series of Cabernet Sauvignons. His Howell Mountain bottling, produced from his own and a neighboring 5-acre vineyard he manages, started to develop a cult following when the 81 was offered. In the next vintage, Dunn added a Napa Valley Cabernet Sauvignon made from purchased grapes. Dunn's Cabernets have usually been 100% Cabernet and are aged for about two and a half years in small French oak. By the end of the 80s, the annual production of each bottling was 2,000 cases. Dunn has also been an active consultant, and in the 80s his talents were brought to bear on the early vintages of Cabernet Sauvignons bottled by La Jota, Grace Family, Livingston, Pahlmeyer, and others.

Cabernet Sauvignon

(Howell Mountain) 81 82*** 83*** 84*** 85** 86***
87***

(Napa Valley) 82*** 83** 84*** 85*** 86*** 87***

Deep, ripe, concentrated, immensely fruity wines, broadened by gobs of rich, sweet, creamy oak and carrying the structure and depth for long aging, Dunn Cabernets are arguably the best of breed in recent years. The Howell Mountain is the tougher, more briary wine, while the Napa Valley is somewhat smoother and richer

---

DUNNEWOOD (Mendocino Vineyards) Introduced in 88 by its parent, Guild, as an upscale brand, Dunnewood began with some excitement, but has not been able to sustain the initial level of interest. In the first rounds, Dunnewood offered an 84 Reserve Napa Valley Cabernet Sauvignon and an 88 Napa Valley Chardonnay, and the Cabernet was an attention-getter. Today, all wines are from either the North Coast or California appellation, and the quality is generally indifferent. The line includes Cabernet Sauvignon (blended with Merlot), Chardonnay, Sauvignon Blanc, Gamay Beaujolais, and White Zinfandel. All but the White Zinfandel are made and bottled by Mendocino Vineyards in Ukiah. The generics consist of a Reserve Red and Reserve White. Production is close to 50,000 cases a year.

DURNEY VINEYARD *Monterey 1977* William Durney and his wife, author Dorothy Kingsley, were the first to establish vineyards in the Carmel Valley. Situated on a series of ridges in a woodsy, remote sector of the valley, the vineyard was started in 67 and now covers 140 acres. The principal varieties planted are Cabernet Sauvignon, Riesling, Chardonnay, and Chenin Blanc. Slightly over half of the winery's 15,000-case production is Cabernet Sauvignon, blended with Merlot as a rule. In exceptional vintages a Reserve Cabernet is made. Several winemakers have come and gone during the winery's existence. The ultimate production goal is 25,000 cases a year. Since the death of William Durney in 89, the winery continues to be operated by his family.

Cabernet Sauvignon

78** 79* 80* 81* 82* 83* 84

Consistently good, usually rich in sweet oak, sometimes too much ripe fruit; light-medium tannins and good depth combine to give aging potential

---

DUXOUP WINE WORKS *Sonoma 1981* Named after the Marx Brothers movie *Duck Soup,* this winery makes only red varietals. It owns no vineyards, so all grapes are purchased, with most of the wines originating in the Dry Creek Valley. Over recent vintages it has made Syrah, Zinfandel, Napa Gamay, and Charbono. The Zinfandel has been quite erratic and sometimes unpleasant. The others, notably the Charbono from Napa Valley and the Dry Creek Valley Syrah, offer solid character in a ripe, fruity style. The Gamay is the one wine rising above average in some vintages. Total annual production is at the maximum 2,000-case level.

EAGLE RIDGE OF PENNGROVE *Sonoma 1982* This is the only winery located in Penngrove, a small town in southern Sonoma County near Petaluma. Winemaker and general partner Barry Lawrence planted 5 acres adjacent to the winery to a rare cross between Sylvaner and Riesling named "Ehrenfelser." Most wines made at Eagle Ridge are from purchased grapes. For a few vintages the winery, focusing on Sauvignon Blanc, offered both a Fumé Blanc aged in oak and a Sauvignon Blanc without oak aging. In 87 it changed to emphasize Zinfandel from Sonoma County and Amador County, and Chardonnay from Napa Valley. With production level at 3,000 cases, the winery has been expanded recently and now has a capacity of 12,000 cases a year.

EBERLE WINERY *San Luis Obispo 1982* Gary Eberle came to Paso Robles in 77 to serve as winemaker for Estrella River Winery, the ambitious winery and vineyard project founded by his stepbrother. After the 81 vintage, Eberle left to start his own much smaller winery about 3 miles away. For several vintages, Eberle's wines were made from his former winery's vineyards. Now, he has 35 acres of his own, planted primarily to Cabernet Sauvignon and Chardonnay. From purchased grapes, Eberle makes "Paso Robles" Cabernet Sauvignon and Chardonnay, along with a sweet-finished Muscat Canelli. He favors unblended Cabernet Sauvignon, while his Chardonnays are fermented in stainless-steel tanks with about 50% going through malolactic fermentation. Annual production is close to the stated goal of 10,000 cases. Chardonnay and Cabernet (a Reserve has been occasionally bottled) account for all but a few hundred cases of the total.

EDMUNDS ST. JOHN *Alameda 1985* Located in Emeryville, this winery operated for two years as the East Bay Wine Works before assuming its present name. Former wine retailer Steve Edmunds began his professional winemaking career by blending a white wine, "Melange," and a red, "Petit Rouge." In 86 he began applying his blending skills to Rhone Valley grapes and wine types, and became one of the key members of the so-called Rhone Rangers. Edmunds ferreted out Syrah from Sonoma, Mourvedre from Oakley in Contra Costa County and Mount Veeder in Napa, and Grenache from Mendocino and Washington State. He has experimented with numerous combinations, only a few of which have been marketed. His small regular production consists of Zinfandel, "Côtes Sauvage" (a proprietary blend of Syrah, Grenache, and Mourvedre), and from time to time, varietally bottled Syrah and Grenache. In the late 80s he began developing 20 acres in the southern part of El Dorado County, a region supplying Grenache and Syrah for his label. The annual production will remain under 2,000 cases until the El Dorado plantings come into full production.

Zinfandel

86 * * 87 * * 88

Ripe, brawny, deeply flavored wines capable of aging for half a decade or more; 88 was an overripe anomaly

EDNA VALLEY VINEYARDS *San Luis Obispo 1980* A joint venture between Chalone, Inc., and Paragon Vineyards, Edna Valley has come on strong in the late 80s. Paragon Vineyards is owned by the Nivens family, which planted 650 acres in the Edna Valley appellation in the early 70s. Today, the vineyard is predominantly Chardonnay, with less than 100 acres of Pinot Noir planted. As a wine producer, Edna Valley Vineyards made both the 79 and 80 vintages in leased space, then set up its own winery by 81. Its Pinot Noirs were highly erratic in the 80s, plagued on many occasions by a vegetal note. As of 90, the winery was producing only 1,000 cases of Pinot Noir. Its Chardonnays are barrel-fermented and made in a ripe fruit style. The expansion program completed, most of the winery's energies are now focused on Chardonnay, with an annual production of 50,000 cases of that one varietal. In its most successful vintages, the Chardonnay has been one of the best values available in the upscale range.

Chardonnay

84 * * 85 * 86 * 87 * * 88 * * * 89 *

Ripe fruit comes superbly balanced by ample acidity, and the wine can be both rich and complex in its combination of oak and roasted-grain elements

ELIZABETH VINEYARDS *Mendocino 1987* In the middle of the Redwood Valley, Betty Foster and family planted 40 acres of vines in the 70s. The name Elizabeth is that of her first granddaughter. While selling the crop to numerous Mendocino producers as well as to the Robert Mondavi Winery, Simi, and Souverain, the owner began testing the winemaking world in 87. Only Sauvignon Blanc, Zinfandel, and Chardonnay are made, and the Chardonnay is partially barrel-fermented. After making the first vintages at Greenwood Ridge in Philo, a new winery was planned for the 91 harvest. Until the winery is in full swing, the production will be confined to 200 cases of each varietal.

ELLISTON VINEYARDS *Alameda 1983* The name Elliston is taken from the historic 17-room mansion located in the Sunol Valley, south of Pleasanton, purchased by the current owners in 69. After refurbishing the house and grounds, the Awtrey family converted the carriage house into a small winery, planted 3 acres to Chardonnay, hired a winemaker, and ventured into the wine business. Selling wines directly to visitors, the winery produces 2,000 cases per year. Over the first several vintages, it made Chardonnay, Pinot Blanc, Pinot Gris, and, for its red wine, Merlot. All are from the Sunol Valley appellation. Elliston was the first California producer of Pinot Gris, a variety sparking some interest in Oregon. The winery currently plans to emphasize that variety along with Chardonnay and Pinot Blanc.

ELYSE WINE CELLARS *Napa 1987* This small winery is owned by Nancy and Ray Coursen of Napa, who are making Zinfandel from a single vineyard in West Rutherford. The Morisoli Vineyard was established in 15, and today it remains a field blend of Zinfandel, Petite Sirah, and miscellaneous reds. Produced from this vineyard, Elyse Zinfandel is aged for one year in a combination of French and American oak. The production is averaging 300 cases a year. For such a small, part-time operation, this label's quality level has been impressive.

EMERALD BAY CELLARS *(Chateau St. Julien)* Made and bottled by Chateau St. Julien, Emerald Bay represents the owners' notion of a highly competitive, low-priced line of varietals. With most carrying the California appellation, Emerald Bay covers a line of varietals headed by Cabernet Sauvignon, Chardonnay, and White Zinfandel. Over recent vintages, the brand's annual production has been averaging 25,000 cases.

ENZ VINEYARDS *San Benito 1973* Located in the Lime Kiln Valley of San Benito, Enz is a family-owned and -operated company. One-time engineer Robert Enz built the small winery, and has little by little replanted the 30-acre vineyard. Among five varieties cultivated, Enz has one of the largest plantings of Pinot St. George, and one of the oldest parcels of Orange Muscat. The other varieties planted are Zinfandel, Chardonnay, and Sauvignon Blanc. Production has edged up to the optimum of 10,000 cases a year.

ESTANCIA VINEYARDS *(Franciscan Vineyards)* Around 86, following its umpteenth reorganization, Franciscan Vineyards introduced Estancia as the label for wines made exclusively from its holdings in the Alexander Valley. Ever since then Franciscan Vineyards has been used only for Napa Valley wines from its Oakville Estates. To start with, the Estancia lineup consisted of Alexander Valley Cabernet Sauvignon, Chardonnay, and Fumé Blanc, grown in the winery's 240-acre vineyard. Presented in a handsome package, the three varietals were marketed as "values for the money." Estancia achieved its goal most often with Cabernet Sauvignon made in a moderately fruity, soft, slightly herbaceous style. Somewhat less successful, the Fumé Blanc was renamed Sauvignon Blanc, but remains inconsistent. As of 88, Estancia's Chardonnay originates in Monterey County. Estancia has emerged in the 90s to offer Monterey Chardonnay, Cabernet Sauvignon (blended with Merlot), and a Meritage red. All Alexander Valley acreage is now planted to Cabernet Sauvignon, Merlot, and other red varieties. Total output is currently at 95,000 cases, including 2,000 cases of Meritage and 60,000 cases of Chardonnay. The annual production is expected to reach 125,000 cases by 1995.

ESTRELLA RIVER WINERY *San Luis Obispo 1977* Estrella River was the first major winery and vineyard development in San Luis Obispo County. The original partners included Gary Eberle, who started his own winery later on, and one-time football hero Rocky Bleir. By the early 70s the partnership had developed over 700 acres of vineyards for the purpose of selling the vast majority of the crop and making limited amounts of wine themselves. When the vineyards reached full productivity in the late 70s, the demand for their grapes, most of which were red wine varieties, was weak. Increasing the production of wine, by 80 Estrella River was making close to 100,000 cases. After many further ups and downs, the facility and 560 acres of mature vine-yards were acquired in 88 by the Nestlé Corp., owner of Beringer, Chateau Souverain, Deutz, and other brands, from then owner Cliff Giacobine. Giaco-bine retained the name—Estrella River Winery—and about 300 acres of vine-yards. For a few years he rented space at his former facility, renamed Meridian by Nestlé, and produced wines. Throughout its shaky history, Estrella River made several successful Syrahs, selling grapes to Bonny Doon and others who went on to generate greater recognition for Syrah. Today, it is building back up to 30,000 cases, led by Cabernet Sauvignon and Chardonnay. Quality has been consistently average.

ETUDE *Napa 1985* Tony Soter, a highly regarded consultant and former wine-maker for Chappellet and others, owns Etude. To date he has produced only Pinot Noir and Cabernet Sauvignon. All fruit for Etude is purchased from Napa Valley growers, with Pinot Noir made from three vineyards in the Carneros, and Cabernet from several vineyards in mid–Napa Valley. Soter, who serves as winemaker for Spottswoode, blends about 12% Merlot and 10% Cabernet Franc into Etude's Cabernets. Renting space in another facility, Soter has been making about 2,000 cases of each wine a year. Etude's sturdy, ageworthy Pinot Noirs have attracted more interest and have earned ✳✳ in several vintages.

Cabernet Sauvignon
85　86✳✳　87✳

Fleshy wines, high in extract and tannin, and fairly direct in their dense, ripe cherry and sweet oak character; they should age well but will always be more bold than refined

Pinot Noir
84✳　85✳✳✳　86✳　87✳✳　88✳✳

Like the Cabernets, these wines are deep in character and appear to have the balance and backbone for long aging; their Pinot Noir heritage shows in the rich, broad fruit and supple, almost velvety texture, set within fairly bold tannins

EVENSEN VINEYARDS & WINERY *Napa 1979* Located on winery row in Oakville, this winery is operated by the Evensen family as a part-time project. For many years they sold the fruit from their 5 acres of Gewurztraminer. In 79, working in the basement of their home, Dick and Sharon Evensen produced a few hundred cases of dry-styled Gewurztraminer. Over the years, the production of Gewurztraminer has averaged about 700 cases. In 86–87, Evensen made Chardonnay from the Howell Mountain area. The Evensen home vineyard now has 1 acre of Chardonnay, which will yield about 200 cases a year.

FALLENLEAF VINEYARDS *Sonoma 1986* Planted in the early 80s, Fallenleaf's 15-acre vineyard falls partly within the Carneros appellation and partly within Sonoma Valley. The winery's first several vintages were custom-crushed at Bouchaine, and only Chardonnay and Sauvignon Blanc have been produced.

Because the appellation boundary runs through its vineyard, the winery bottles two Chardonnays—Sonoma Valley and Carneros. By 90 production was at the 3,000-case level, with equal emphasis on Chardonnay and Sauvignon Blanc.

FAR NIENTE WINERY *Napa 1979* Founded in 1885, the Far Niente Winery was abandoned at Prohibition, and remained a hollow shell until Gil Nickel came along in 78 to revive it. With neighboring vineyard owner Dick Stelling, and John Nickel, his brother, Nickel completely restored the original winery, which is set back from the wine road just south of the Robert Mondavi Winery. During its first three vintages Far Niente produced its wines in a rented facility and released only Chardonnay in a ripe, well-oaked, sometimes heavy-handed style. In 82 its first Cabernet Sauvignon was rich, ripe, and also tannic. However, as production of Chardonnay grew to 25,000 cases, and Cabernet (blended with Cabernet Franc and Merlot) grew to 10,000 cases, the quality has improved. On occasion, the winery produces a sweet dessert wine named "Dolce," made from *Botrytis*-affected Sauvignon Blanc and Semillon. In 90, Far Niente added 15,000 square feet of man-made aging caves, which completed the restoration and expansion of this showcase facility.

Cabernet Sauvignon

82   83   84   85*   86***   87

Marked by inconsistency, these wines are always ripe and oaky, with medium tannins, but have only delivered a full measure of ripe cherry and currant fruit in some recent vintages

Chardonnay

84   85*   86   87*   88   89

Always high in toasty oak character and medium-full-bodied, the wines have often been low in vitality and, as a result, have sometimes carried an exaggeratedly dry, smokey quality

FARELLA-PARK VINEYARDS *Napa 1985* The Farellas, Frank and Annie, own a 28-acre vineyard in the eastern hills of the Napa Valley. It consists of 12 acres of Chardonnay, 7 of Sauvignon Blanc, and 9 of Cabernet Sauvignon and Merlot. After planting the vineyard in 79, they sold most of the crop to the Robert Mondavi Winery, keeping a few tons to produce wine. Their son, Tom, is an enologist (formerly of Preston Vineyards) who assists with the family operation. At full capacity their small winery can handle 500 cases a year. Starting with a first vintage in 85 that totaled 200 cases, Farella-Park had not quite reached its peak production level by 90. The mainstays bottled are Chardonnay, Sauvignon Blanc, Cabernet Sauvignon, and Merlot. After a shaky first vintage, the winery has offered good-quality products.

GARY FARRELL WINES *Sonoma 1981* Starting in the cellars of Davis Bynum in 78, Gary Farrell worked his way up the ladder and has toiled as winemaker for both Bynum and J. Rochioli. Now, while winemaker for Davis Bynum, he continues making wines under his own brand as he has since 82. Using his own barrels and a corner of the Bynum winery, Farrell produces small batches of varietals from specified vineyards in the cool sectors of the Russian River Valley appellation. He has shown flashes of brilliance with Chardonnay and with Pinot Noir. In 87, he stopped making Sauvignon Blanc and added Cabernet Sauvignon and Merlot. Both varieties are grown in the Danielik Vineyard east of Santa Rosa. Pinot Noir from the Howard Allen Vineyard, bordering Rochioli's property, usually shows more earthiness than the Russian River Valley bottling. Farrell's production is holding steady at 3,500 cases a year. He has set 4,500 cases as the maximum.

Pinot Noir

(Howard Allen Vineyard)   85   86*   87*   88***

(Russian River Valley)   82**   84***   85*   86   87*   88*

Ripe grape aromas redolent of cherries and enriched by oak, together with mouth-filling flavors, good balance; the lesser efforts have shown foresty, mushroomy notes

FARVIEW FARMS VINEYARD *San Luis Obispo 1979* This winery evolved from what was originally intended to be a vineyard operation only. In the early 70s the owners developed 50 acres to Zinfandel (36) and Merlot (14) in the Templeton area. In 79, they began making wines in rented space, and by 84, without a proportional increase in demand, the output was close to 7,000 cases. In the following year the vineyards and business were acquired by Ray Krause, one of the partners. He has added 10 acres of Chardonnay and trimmed the production to a manageable level of 3,000 cases. White Zinfandel, Merlot, and barrel-fermented Chardonnay are the major wines offered, together with limited amounts of a Botrytised white dessert wine and an occasional batch of Cabernet Sauvignon. Opened in 89, a renovated Victorian farmhouse serves as the headquarters and tasting room.

FELLOM RANCH VINEYARD *Santa Clara 1987* In the early 80s Roy Fellom decided to redevelop an old vineyard owned by his family since 20. Located on Montebello Ridge in the Santa Cruz Mountains, the 12-acre vineyard, contiguous to the famous Ridge Monte Bello Vineyard, had contained Zinfandel and other red varieties. Fellom planted Cabernet Sauvignon, and restored the old winemaking facility just in time for the 87 crush. In addition to its estate-grown Cabernet, Fellom Ranch produces both Zinfandel and a Cabernet Sauvignon from an old vineyard in the Santa Clara Valley. Early total output was under 1,500 cases. Over the long haul, Fellom expects to make about 2,000 cases of estate Cabernet.

FENESTRA WINERY *Alameda 1976* A family-owned brand without vineyards, Fenestra remains small and competitive. Owners Lanny and Fran Replogle made wines in several locations prior to setting up their present facility in the Livermore Valley. Replogle, a chemistry professor at San Jose State, finds the time to make 4,000 cases a year. His production includes numerous small batches of as many as eight varietals. Buying grapes from three primary appellations—Livermore Valley, Monterey County, and Santa Clara County—he regularly offers Cabernet Sauvignon, Merlot, Chardonnay, and Sauvignon Blanc among the varietals. A generic red is named "True Red" in honor of George True, founder of the now historic winery. The long-term production goal is 10,000 cases a year. An 84 Cabernet Sauvignon was quite good (❋ ❋), but most other wines have generally been less so.

FERRARI-CARANO VINEYARDS *Sonoma 1981* In 79, Don Carano, owner of the El Dorado Hotel in Reno, bought vineyard land in the Alexander Valley near the town of Geyserville. He later purchased additional vineyard sites in the middle of Alexander Valley and in Dry Creek Valley, where he eventually built the winery. After his first two vintages, Carano acquired more vineyards in the Knight's Valley and in the Carneros, where he now has 39 acres of Chardonnay. All told, the winery has 450 acres under vine in twelve separate sites. The primary varieties planted are Chardonnay, Sauvignon Blanc, Cabernet Sauvignon, and Merlot. With the release of its first vintages of Fumé Blanc and Chardonnay, the winery got off to an excellent start. The barrel-fermented Chardonnay was an immediate success, and it has been joined by a Reserve version (strongly oaked) limited to about 300 cases total. Made in a brisk, floral-weedy, youthful style, the Fumé Blanc is of ❋ caliber. Both Cabernet Sauvignon and Merlot are varietals blended with other Bordeaux varieties. A Meritage red, first produced in 88, is given four years' aging before release. The initial output of 10,000 cases grew quickly to the 45,000-case level by 90. In the 90s, production will grow to 100,000 cases.

Chardonnay

(regular bottling) 85** 86** 87 88 89*

(Reserve) 86*** 87* 88*

Bright, fresh appley fruit and lots of toasty oak are combined in wines that are balanced, lively, and deeply flavored; the Reserve is the richer of the two

---

GLORIA FERRER *Sonoma 1982* The owners of Freixenet, the popular Spanish sparkling wine, launched this brand of *méthode champenoise* sparkling wine in 86. The cuvées were produced at other facilities, until the new winery and large aging cellars located in the Sonoma-Carneros region were ready in mid-88. On 160 acres of former pastureland, the winery, headed by the eldest son of Freixenet's owners, Jose Ferrer, and his wife, Gloria, now has 50 acres planted to Pinot Noir and Chardonnay. The winery's list of offerings, each of which finds Pinot Noir the dominant grape, is keyed on the nonvintage Brut and a vintaged Brut dubbed "Royal Cuvée," aged longer on the yeasts and made from 60% Pinot Noir. A third but limited-volume sparkler is the vintaged Carneros Cuvée, made exclusively from grapes grown in the Carneros District. The annual production was near 65,000 cases by the end of the 80s, with 80,000 cases a year as the facility's maximum capacity.

FETZER VINEYARDS *Mendocino 1968* Former lumberman Barney Fetzer planted a few acres of vines on a ranch he bought in 58. After selling the crop for several years, he decided to produce Zinfandel and Cabernet Sauvignon in 68. With his sons John and Jim, he restored an old stone winery northwest of Hopland, and the Fetzers were in the wine business. They soon outgrew that tiny facility and kept on expanding production throughout the 70s. After their father died, the entire family became involved in the winery operation. Fetzer earned an early reputation for sturdy red wines, especially Zinfandels from the Scharffenberger Vineyard, Ricetti Vineyard, and their own vineyard. The winery also made heavyweight Petite Sirahs in the 70s. As the overall production grew, the Fetzers shunned advertising and concentrated upon marketing through a strong national network of wholesalers. They also kept prices below their competition during the expansion years.

In the early 80s, with winemaker Paul Dolan at the helm of a separate facility for white wines, the winery made remarkable improvements in the quality of its Chenin Blanc, Riesling, and Gewurztraminer. Each was made in a slightly sweet to sweet style, but with such forthright fruitiness and balancing acidity that the wines succeeded. When the blush wine era began in California, Fetzer was flexible enough to seize the opportunity, and before long was making four blush wines, including an ever popular White Zinfandel. The blush wine sales grew to such a volume that they were given the winery's second label, Bel Arbres Vineyard, changed in 89 to Bel Arbors (see entry).

By the late 80s Fetzer was operating three winemaking facilities and Valley Oaks, a vineyard as well as a garden/entertainment center. With over 2,000 acres owned, and another 2,000 acres under long-term contract, the winery was making wines from many California growing regions. Fetzer was also among the first to use wines from Washington and Oregon in its Bel Arbors line. Two varietals took on proprietary names—Valley Oaks Fumé Blanc and Sundial Chardonnay—and the sales success of the latter soon exceeded the supply from the Fetzer Sundial Ranch. Though many other producers had given up on Gewurztraminer, Fetzer began pushing it in the late 80s and now makes over 160,000 cases of a frequent * version.

For several vintages the Fetzers focused on what is now the "Barrel Select" line of Chardonnay and Cabernet Sauvignon. Entirely barrel-fermented, the Barrel Select Chardonnay is a blend of grapes from four regions. In 86, the Barrel Select Cabernet Sauvignon was aged entirely in small French oak and won plaudits for quality and value. The flagship wines are labeled

Reserve and include Cabernet Sauvignon, Chardonnay, Pinot Noir, and Petite Sirah. By the end of the 80s, Fetzer's annual production was over 2 million cases.

Cabernet Sauvignon

(Barrel Select)   82   **83   84*   85*   86***

Ripish, cherryish fruit with sweet oak, supple texture with moderate tannins for moderate ageability

Chardonnay

(Sundial)   84   85*   86   87   88   89

Low-priced, broadly distributed, changeable stylistically from year to year, but always keyed on direct fruit; brisk acidity rather than oak or complexity

Chardonnay

(Barrel Select)   84   85*   86*   87   88*

(Special Reserve)   85*   86**

The upscale models, ranging from the moderately oaked, usually dependable Barrel Select to the fairly oaky and rich Reserve, have both offered good value when in peak form

Zinfandel

(Ricetti Vineyard / Special Reserve)   81*   **82*   83****   85*   **86***

Usually tough, tight, hard, concentrated, deep blackberryish fruit, substantially oaked, long-aging

---

FIELD STONE WINERY   *Sonoma 1977*   With its tasting room built into the underground cellars and the winery itself surrounded by oak trees, Field Stone is one of the more picturesque wineries in the Alexander Valley. The winery began by focusing on white and rosé wines, but by 82, when under new management, it began stressing red wines, mainly Cabernet Sauvignon and Petite Sirah. Cabernet Sauvignon represents 70% of the 130 acres planted, Petite Sirah accounts for 10%, and the remaining 20% consists of several white varieties, including recently planted Viognier. Once bottled under several vineyard designations, Cabernet Sauvignon production has been trimmed to a regular and a Reserve. However, throughout the 80s the quality has been uneven, sometimes below standard. In the most recent vintages Field Stone has shown improvement with both Gewurztraminer and Cabernet Sauvignon. Sauvignon Blanc and Chardonnay complete the line. Since the late 80s, Chardonnay has been obtained from Carneros and the Russian River Valley areas. Visitors and regular mailing-list customers purchase about one-third of the 12,000 cases produced per year. The winery is gradually expanding to the 20,000-case level.

FILSINGER WINERY & VINEYARDS   *Riverside 1980*   This is a family-owned and -operated winery. In the early 70s, Dr. William Filsinger purchased property in Temecula and eventually developed 32 acres of vineyards. The production emphasis varied during the first decade, but the leading varieties now are Chardonnay and Sauvignon Blanc. Lesser amounts of Gewurztraminer, Cabernet Sauvignon, and Zinfandel are also grown and produced. In the late 80s, Filsinger added a line of *méthode champenoise* sparklers—Brut Blanc de Blancs, Brut Rosé, and Extra Dry. The annual production is at 7,000 cases, with 12,000 viewed as the absolute maximum.

FIRESTONE VINEYARD   *Santa Barbara 1974*   Early vinous settlers in the Santa Ynez Valley, the Firestones began developing their estate vineyard in 73. A stunning facility and visitors center were ready, though incomplete, in time for the 75 harvest. Both the name Firestone and the scope of the investment (265 acres of vineyards) in an unknown region meant that the winery would be closely watched from the start. In 76 and 77, its Pinot Noirs were highly successful, but then and long after, its Cabernet Sauvignon and Merlot contained damaging degrees of vegetal character. As the winery grew to its present 80,000-case-a-year level, Firestone worked hard to develop a reputation for Johannisberg Riesling in a medium-sweet style. Floral and fruity, with medium-deep flavors and excellent balance, its Rieslings are frequently in the ✿ category, occasionally rising to ✿✿.

Beginning in 85, Firestone's Merlots started to earn recognition for early enjoyment and an infrequent ✿ as the vegetal component was brought under control. A similar over-grassy-weedy streak to the Sauvignon Blanc has been toned down by barrel fermentations and by the addition of about 8–10% Chardonnay. Generally, the winery's Sauvignon Blancs offer exotic aromas, but lack a little vitality. A similarly disconcerting muddled impression marred the Chardonnays up to the late 80s. From the mid-80s, the Cabernets, unlike their heavy-bodied, often overly herbal predecessors, have turned out to be enjoyable in a soft, undemanding style. A slightly sweet Rosé of Cabernet, first produced in 75, enjoys some popularity. The production breakdowns of the premium wines are Johannisberg Riesling (25,000 cases), Chardonnay (12,000), Cabernet Sauvignon (8,000), Merlot (7,000), and Sauvignon Blanc (5,000). The Firestones also own the neighboring J. Carey Winery (see entry) and are co-owners in a brand of nonalcoholic beer, Firestone & Fletcher.

Cabernet Sauvignon

78✿   79   81   82   83✿   84✿   85   86   87

Now made in a lighter style that preserves fruit and acid and avoids vegetal and soft-structured tendencies

Chardonnay

84   85   86   87   88

Fruity, firm, noticeable oak, somewhat low in intensity

Merlot

82   84   85   86✿   **87**   **88**

Like the Cabernet, this one is now lighter, fruitier, better

FISHER VINEYARDS   *Sonoma 1979*   Fred Fisher, a descendant of the automotive "Body by Fisher" family, established his winery on the Sonoma County side of the Mayacamas Mountains. In 73 the hillside vineyard was developed and now covers 25 acres. The winery owns another 50 acres situated at the northern, warmer end of the Silverado Trail in Napa Valley. In both locations, Cabernet Sauvignon and Chardonnay are the only varietals planted. The winery's primary Chardonnays carry the Napa/Sonoma appellation and are a blend of hillside and valley floor grapes. The reserve versions of Chardonnay, labeled "Coach Insignia," have ranged in quality from excellent to ordinary. The Coach Insignia Cabernet Sauvignon, made exclusively from the Sonoma hillside acreage, was also introduced with the 84 vintage. It is the only Cabernet Sauvignon offered and its output is about 1,500 cases a year. By the mid-80s the yearly production reached the winery's 8,000-case maximum.

Cabernet Sauvignon

(Coach Insignia)   **84✿**   **85✿✿**   86✿   87✿✿

Deep in handsomely rendered varietal fruit, and showing lots of rich oak, the wine can be high in tannin and very tight when young

Chardonnay

(Napa/Sonoma)   85   86✿   87   88   89

Medium-depth fruit, with toasty oak in better vintages, but showing less focus and depth in other years

Chardonnay

(Coach Insignia)   84✿   85✿   **86✿✿**   87   **88✿**

Usually rich in ripe appley fruit, and rich in toasty oak, the wine lives up to its special billing in most years

FITCH MOUNTAIN *Sonoma 1985* A negociant brand operating in Sonoma County, Fitch Mountain is owned by Greg Smith, who is also co-owner of Optima. Using his own cooperage and a rented facility, Smith blends, ages, and bottles wines he purchases. His output depends on the availability of grapes, and therefore has varied from year to year from as many as 20,000 cases to as few as 2,000. Given a choice he prefers offering Zinfandel, Cabernet Sauvignon, and from time to time, Chardonnay and Merlot. Most wines have come from Sonoma County, a few from Napa Valley. In better years, Fitch Mountain wines offer good value. The brand is named after a real Fitch Mountain, visible from the barrel-aging cellar/warehouse in Healdsburg.

FITZPATRICK WINERY *El Dorado 1980* Situated in the southern end of the county, Fitzpatrick was known originally as Somerset Vineyards. It was renamed Fitzpatrick in 85. Over the first several vintages, the winery produced a range of table wines. In the late 80s the owners of this small winery decided to diversify and developed a popular bed-and-breakfast complex. Directed by Brian Fitzpatrick, the winery has a 15-acre vineyard, which yields Cabernet Sauvignon, Chardonnay, and Sauvignon Blanc. Its Zinfandels originate in Amador's Shenandoah Valley. Over its early history, the winery has bought Zinfandel from many individual growers. Additionally, it makes White Zinfandel and a blend of Zinfandel and Petite Sirah named "King's Red." By the end of the 80s, the winery's annual output reached 4,500 cases. In the long term, the winery has set 7,000 cases as its target maximum.

FLAX VINEYARDS *Sonoma 1986* This is a Chardonnay-only brand that has distinguished itself primarily by having one of the most unusual labels ever used. Owner Phil Flax, who runs a chain of art-supply stores, made wine initially to help publicize his business. By 88, Flax was intrigued enough by wine to be developing a 12-acre vineyard in Sonoma. The quality of the early vintages has been unexciting.

FLORA SPRINGS WINERY *Napa 1978* In 77 Jerry and Flora Komes purchased an old winery (ca. 1888) and vineyard once used by Louis Martini for barrel-aging sherry and other wines. Komes had retired from Bechtel Industries and looked on the Napa Valley acquisition as a means of producing retirement challenges. When Julie Komes Garvey, her husband, Pat, and her brother John became interested in moving to Napa, the family's plan changed. Julie and Pat Garvey purchased additional vineyard land, and the family winemaking venture began. They restored the old stone winery nestled against the western Rutherford hills, and replanted the adjacent 50-acre vineyard to Cabernet Sauvignon, Merlot, and Cabernet Franc. Now known as the Komes Ranch, this vineyard is responsible for the winery's upscale Meritage red, "Trilogy." The winery has other vineyards in Napa Valley, bringing the total to 400 acres.

Close to 75% of the crop is sold, making the grape business an important part of this operation. Both the Komes Ranch and the Garvey Ranch are in the Rutherford Bench region and grow mostly Cabernet Sauvignon and Merlot. In the cooler growing area of Yountville, the Crossroads Ranch grows most of the winery's Sauvignon Blanc. North of Rutherford and along the Napa River, is the winery's primary Chardonnay vineyard, the P. & J. Ranch. In the late 80s the owners picked up the Cypress Ranch, north of Pope Valley. As an important grape grower, Flora Springs owns 119 acres of Cabernet Sauvignon, 72 acres of Chardonnay, 69 acres of Sauvignon Blanc, and 36 acres of Merlot. Two Chardonnays have been offered since 1980—the "Barrel Fermented" limited edition is consistently in the ** category, and a Napa Valley estate bottled is often at the * level. In most vintages, the Sauvignon Blanc takes on a forward herbal-weedy personality, in a style that combines depth with firm crisp acidity, a wine of ** caliber. The varietal-labeled Cabernet Sauvignon (blended with Merlot and Cabernet Franc) has performed on a higher level than its more expensive stablemate, "Trilogy." Given long "sur lie" aging, a small batch of Sauvignon Blanc is bottled under the "Soliloquy" name. By 90, the annual production had reached 25,000 cases, two thirds of which are white wines, one third reds.

Cabernet Sauvignon

80 *   81 *   82   83   84 *   85 * *   86

Capable of possessing deep fruit, well supported by rich oak, and made ageworthy by fairly bold tannins

Chardonnay

(regular bottling)   84 * *   85 *   86 *   87 *   88   89
(Barrel Fermented)   84 * *   86 * *   87 * *   88 * *   89 * *

Both wines have good fruit and good balance; the Barrel Fermented is richer, deeper, and oakier, and has been consistently well rated

Merlot

85 * *   86   87 *

Typically possessed of ripe cherry fruit, buttressed by oak, the wine can be rich and supple in top vintages

Trilogy

85 *   86 *   87 *

A blend of equal parts Cabernet Sauvignon, Merlot, and Cabernet Franc, it is medium in depth and tough in structure; in spite of the above-average quality, this wine has not yet fully lived up to its pedigree or price

---

THOMAS FOGARTY WINERY   *San Mateo 1981*   The winery, perched on the northern end of the Santa Cruz Mountains appellation, is owned by Thomas Fogarty, a cardiovascular surgeon practicing in Palo Alto. He purchased 300 acres of land in 68 in what is locally known as the Portola Valley, began planting vineyards in 78, and added to them in 80. His 24-acre estate vineyards consist of Chardonnay (18) and Pinot Noir (6). The winery was built in 81, and winemaker Mike Martella has been involved since then. Fogarty emphasizes Chardonnay and Pinot Noir, and has produced numerous versions from many regions and vineyards. Among his regular offerings are Chardonnay from Santa Cruz, from Ventana Vineyards in Monterey, and from the Edna Valley, along with Pinot Noir from Santa Cruz, Ventana Vineyard, Carneros, and Edna Valley. For many years Fogarty made Pinot Noir and Chardonnay from Winery Lake Vineyards, but the series ended when Seagram bought the vineyard. From a neighboring Santa Cruz Mountains vineyard, the winery has regularly produced a slightly sweet Gewurztraminer. Though made in smaller quantity, Cabernet Sauvignon and Sauvignon Blanc have been produced. At times, the Santa Cruz Gewurztraminer is a * * stunner, and the Ventana Vineyards bottling has reached * *, with rich varietal spice, depth of flavors, and balanced, firming acidity. Total production is close to the 7,500-case maximum, about half devoted to Chardonnay.

Chardonnay

(Edna Valley–Paragon Vineyard)   84 * * *   86   87   88 *   89
(Santa Cruz)   84 *   85   86   87   88
(Ventana Vineyards)   84   85 *   87 * *   88

Always oaky and typically trying for richness and complexity, these wines have all too often been overdone and lacking in the fruit depth needed to keep them in balance

---

FOLIE À DEUX WINERY   *Napa 1981*   Both the name and the whimsical label helped to focus immediate attention on owners Larry and Eva Dizmang's shared fantasy. As the director of the Mental Health Department of St. Helena Hospital in search of some diversion, Larry planted a few acres adjacent to their home north of St. Helena. Eva, a psychological counselor, designed the label, and now organizes sales and marketing. For the first few years, the annual production was fewer than 2,000 cases. The winery began to be taken seriously with the release of its lovely 83 Chardonnay, balanced to ✺✺✺ quality. From that time on, the winery expanded production with the help of an assistant winemaker. With 30 acres owned—the original 15 acres beside the winery and 15 in Yountville—Folie à Deux specializes in Chardonnay and Cabernet Sauvignon. With production to level off at 20,000 cases annually, Chardonnay represents over half, and Cabernet about one fourth. Always a favorite of the owners, Chenin Blanc was made into a dry, oak-aged serious wine for several years. Recent vintages opt for freshness in a lighter style. Muscat Canelli is purchased, and the Dizmangs make both a table and a sparkling wine ("Fantasie") from it. A second label, "Pas de Deux," was introduced to market a lower-priced Chardonnay.

Chardonnay

83 ✺✺✺   84   85 ✺   86 ✺   87 ✺   88 ✺

After starting out with near-perfection, this wine has settled into a pattern of offering satisfying, somewhat appley, medium-depth fruit, and slightly toasty oak

FOPPIANO VINEYARDS *Sonoma 1896* This historic family-run winery produces close to 200,000 cases a year under three labels. Located southwest of Healdsburg, the old facility has been significantly modernized, though from the outside it still looks like a remnant of a bygone era. Beginning in the late 60s, the Foppiano brand moved away from its jug-wine emphasis and entered the varietal wine market under the Louis J. Foppiano label (now Foppiano Vineyards). The first varietals to earn modest critical praise were Petite Sirah and to a lesser degree, Cabernet Sauvignon. The white table wines lagged behind the reds by a good margin until the mid-80s. Today, the Sauvignon Blanc has reached ✺ quality more than once. Though usually in the average-quality range, Foppiano Chardonnays are aged in small oak and occasionally offer decent value. A limited-volume Reserve Petite Sirah, aged entirely in French oak barrels, was joined by a limited-production Reserve Zinfandel in 87.

The Foppiano family owns 160 acres under vine, the leading varieties being Chardonnay (30 acres), Cabernet Sauvignon (24 acres), and Petite Sirah (20 acres). With all its vineyards situated in the Russian River Valley region, Foppiano's estate-grown wines carry that appellation. A separate line of upscale Chardonnay and Cabernet Sauvignon is named Fox Mountain (see entry). To also help sever the association of the Foppiano name with jug wines, the winery markets close to 150,000 cases a year of low-priced varietals and generics under the Riverside Farms label (see entry). The total amount of wine made and named Foppiano Vineyards is close to 30,000 cases a year.

FOREST HILL VINEYARDS *Napa 1987* David Manace, a plastic surgeon in San Francisco, purchased a vacation home in St. Helena in 1982. After making wines as an amateur for a few years, he decided to specialize in barrel-fermented Chardonnay. Buying grapes from two local vineyards, he made 200 cases his first year, and has gradually increased production each year, setting 1,000 cases a year as the maximum. The bottle chosen for Forest Hill Chardonnay is an unusual crystal-clear Burgundy bottle and, for an added touch, each is offered in a custom-made wooden box.

FORMAN WINERY *Napa 1983* In 68 the newly formed Sterling Vineyards picked 24-year-old Ric Forman as its first winemaker. Heading Sterling's wine program until 77, Forman became known for a series of barrel-fermented Chardonnay, Cabernet Sauvignon, and for his contributions to the styling of Sauvignon Blanc and Merlot. When Sterling was sold to Coca-Cola of Atlanta in 77, Forman became partners with Sterling's founder, Peter Newton, helping to develop vineyards and making the first few vintages of a winery that reportedly was to be named Forman Winery, but ended up as Newton Vineyard.

Forman left Newton in early 82 to start his own winery on Howell Mountain. He planted 6 acres to Cabernet on the hillsides near the winery, and has expanded that initial block to 47 acres. His Chardonnay is obtained from a vineyard in the valley floor area of Rutherford. He and Charles Shaw jointly own the vineyard. All Forman Chardonnays are barrel-fermented. With Cabernet Sauvignon, Forman almost always adds Merlot and sometimes Cabernet Franc. Aging in French oak for close to two years, Forman's Cabernets have been among the richest made in the 80s. He produces a maximum of 2,000 cases each of Chardonnay and Cabernet. A second label, "Chateau La Grande Roche," has been set aside for a Grenache and any lower-priced wines he might wish to produce.

Cabernet Sauvignon

83 *** 84 ** 85 *** 86 * 87 88 **

Deep, handsomely crafted fruit is set with a solid framework of tannins in a wine that seems capable of aging well for a decade or more

Chardonnay

84 * 85 ** 87 * 88 * 89

Always complex in its far-ranging, toasty, roasted-grain qualities, this appley, citrus-tart wine sometimes founders, due to a shortage of essential fruit to balance its diverse and demanding character

---

FOX MOUNTAIN *(Foppiano Vineyards)* Fox Mountain represents Foppiano's entry into the upscale, Reserve wine world. Only a Reserve Cabernet Sauvignon and Chardonnay are offered, and each consists of about 2,000 cases. Aged in French oak and blended with Cabernet Franc and Merlot, the Cabernet is released five or six years after the vintage. Over the first few vintages its quality has been several notches above that of Fox Mountain's Chardonnay.

Cabernet Sauvignon

(Reserve) 81 ** 82 84 ** 85

Usually ripe, black-cherryish, often somewhat chocolatey, with sweet oak adding to the richness, tannin for aging, and the depth to justify in most years

Chardonnay

(Reserve) 84 85 86

Not up to the competition in depth, focus, or prettiness

FOXEN VINEYARD *Santa Barbara 1987* This winery is a joint effort between partners Bill Walthen and Richard Dore. One-time vineyard manager for Rancho Sisquoc and Chalone, Walthen is the grape buyer for the joint venture. Dore (a member of the Foxen family) managed the large Foxen cattle ranch in the northern corner of Santa Barbara County. Over the first vintages, an assortment of wines were made from purchased grapes grown in several Santa Barbara County appellations. The winery's emphasis falls on two wines, Cabernet Sauvignon and Chardonnay, but it also has produced small quantities of Pinot Noir and Chenin Blanc. The owners have established a 10-acre vineyard in the Santa Maria Valley adjacent to their winery, with 5 acres of Chardonnay and the rest planted to Cabernet Sauvignon, Merlot, and Cabernet Franc. From Foxen's first vintage of 800 cases, the annual production has grown to 2,000 cases. With vineyard maturity, the owners plan to level off at 3,000 cases per year.

FRANCISCAN VINEYARDS *Napa 1973* Now on solid footing after what still ranks as one of the roughest starts by any winery in memory, Franciscan sits in the middle of Rutherford on the main wine road. The founders, now long forgotten, went out of business before their first wines were bottled, and Franciscan continued on a roller coaster until 79, when its fifth ownership began. Now in the hands of its sixth owner, a 50–50 partnership between the Peter Eckes firm of Germany (the fifth owner) and Augustus Huneus, who also owns Mount Veeder Vineyards, Franciscan's five wines—Chardonnay, Cabernet Sauvignon, Merlot, Zinfandel, and a Meritage red—also bear an "Oakville Estate" designation. The owners have 204 well-established acres under vine in Oakville. In 90, they bought 270 acres on the western side of the Silverado Trail, of which about 200 acres will be planted to the five red Bordeaux varieties. This vineyard will eventually supply most of the fruit for Franciscan's Meritage Red. Chardonnay (50% barrel-fermented) and Cabernet Sauvignon (blended with 10%–15% Merlot) are the mainstays in the line. Estancia (see entry) is another name under the same ownership that appears on non–Napa Valley–grown wines. The annual production of Franciscan Vineyards is steady at 40,000 cases.

Cabernet Sauvignon

83 84 85* 86 87

Soft, ripe, cherry and herb-tinged fruit; moderate tannin; occasionally attractive in the short term

Chardonnay

84 85 86 87* 88* 89*

Direct, presentable wines with medium-depth fruit and just enough oak for a suggestion of richness

Merlot

83* 84 85** 86* 87*

Generally attractive, ripe and round fruit, with sweet oak creaminess and moderate tannins combined in wines of short- to medium-term appeal

FRANZIA *San Joaquin 1906* The Franzia family, which founded the winery and operated it until 73 as Franzia Brothers, sold both winery and name to Coca-Cola of New York. Today's parent company is the corporation named the Wine Group, which owns Corbett Canyon among other wine properties. Franzia covers a broad line of table wines, varietals and generics, along with low-priced sparkling wines and wine coolers. Ripon is the hometown of the primary production facility, which bottles over 4 million cases a year. Much of that total goes into the world with the Summit label attached, and most of Summit's business is the bag-in-the-box trade. Franzia's line of varietals is led in volume by White Zinfandel, White Grenache, French Colombard, and Chenin Blanc. In the late 80s Franzia expanded its wine cooler production to include a Chardonnay cooler, but today only a White Zinfandel cooler remains in that program.

FREDERICO WINES *Sonoma 1985* This small family winery was established to satisfy the owner's love for late harvest Rieslings. The winery has a capacity of 2,000 cases per year. On occasion it makes Chardonnay from Edna Valley.

FREEMARK ABBEY WINERY *Napa 1967* This site was first home to a winery in 1886, and the original Freemark Abbey sign went up in 39. That operation continued until the late 50s, with the official door-closing taking place in 62. By 67, however, it had been revived and the winery restored by a partnership of seven, most with deep Napa Valley roots. Longtime resident Chuck Carpy headed the group, which included the well-known vineyardist Laurie Wood, and the now legendary winemaker Brad Webb. A fourth partner, Bill Jaeger, later became better known for running Rutherford Hill Winery and Jaeger Cellars. Webb, who had been with Hanzell, guided the early winemaking at Freemark Abbey as a consultant. Among many of his contributions, Webb was a proponent of French oak aging for Chardonnay, was among the first to use Nevers oak, and began blending Merlot in Cabernet Sauvignon as early as 68.

By the late 60s and early 70s, Freemark Abbey had become a quality name to every wine lover. Petite Sirah rose to prominence in that era due largely to such highly praised versions as the 69 and 71 made from the York Creek Vineyard. From the Bosché Vineyard in the Rutherford Bench, the winery has since 70 produced a noteworthy series of Cabernets. Among its other credits, Freemark Abbey made an enormously appealing dessert-style Riesling in 73 called "Edelwein" that ranks even today among the finest of its late harvest type.

By 80 the winery slipped back a little with its Cabernets, but has been turning out generally successful Chardonnays from 71 onward. As production edged toward the full-capacity level of 30,000 cases, the winery trimmed its line to Chardonnay (Napa Valley and a 100% barrel-fermented Carpy Ranch) and three Cabernet bottlings (Napa Valley, Bosché, and Sycamore Vineyard), with limited amounts of Riesling. Normally, the winery makes a slightly sweet Riesling with about 1.5% residual sugar. In years when *Botrytis* concentrates the grapes, Freemark Abbey makes the late harvest wines called Edelwein for residual sugar near 10%, or Edelwein Gold when the sweetness level is close to 20%.

Cabernet Sauvignon

(Napa Valley) 78* 79 80 81 82* 83 84* **85** 86

(Bosché) 70** 78* 79 80 81 82* 83 84* **85** **86**

(Sycamore) **85****

Over two decades of making Cabernet Sauvignon, Freemark Abbey has garnered precious few high ratings for its stable of light-to-medium-depth, cherry and herb-flavored wines; the addition of the Sycamore Vineyard wine to the roster starting in 85 may signal a change in fortune

Chardonnay

(Napa Valley) 84* 85 86** 87 **88***

In the early to mid-70s, Freemark Abbey Chardonnays were considered among the best in California; but following a spectacular wine in 75, things went somewhat downhill, and the wines rarely were able to recapture the bright, luscious fruit that had been their early hallmark. Now, even in their better performances, they tend to be stiff and green appley, with toasty oak in the background

FREMONT CREEK WINERY *Mendocino 1988* Owner Andy Beckstoffer is a grape grower who currently owns 1,500 acres of vineyards. In the late 60s Beckstoffer was part of the Heublein team that negotiated the acquisition of United Vintners, which at the time included Inglenook and Swiss Colony. In 69 he was involved in the purchase of Beaulieu Vineyard. He came west to work for Heublein and eventually formed a vineyard management division for them. In 71 Beckstoffer arranged a leveraged buyout of the vineyard management subsidiary, and by 78, as the sole owner, he changed the name to Beckstoffer Vineyards.

With the addition of 225 acres acquired from Beaulieu Vineyard in 89, Beckstoffer now owns 1,000 acres in Mendocino and 500 in Napa Valley. Most of his energies go to growing and selling the crop to a range of well-known producers. For several vintages Schug Cellars has bottled a Beckstoffer Vineyard Chardonnay. Beckstoffer began producing Fremont Creek wines from his own vineyards in 88. With the help of a consulting enologist, he makes about 20,000 cases in a rented facility in Mendocino County. Three wines—Chardonnay, Cabernet Sauvignon, and Sauvignon Blanc—have been produced to date under a dual appellation of Mendocino/Napa County. About half of the output consists of Chardonnay, with Cabernet Sauvignon accounting for 30% and Sauvignon Blanc 20%. Over the first vintages, all wines were of average quality.

FREY VINEYARD *Mendocino 1980* Owned by the large (12 children at last count) Frey family, this winery is located in the northern end of the Redwood Valley. Patriarch Dr. Paul Frey was a physician at the Mendocino State Hospital when he purchased the old ranch in 61. A few years later he planted a 40-acre vineyard, and little by little the family edged into the grape business, using organic farming methods. After a few wineries earned plaudits for wines made from Frey's grapes, in 80 they decided to produce wines. Frey wines are made without sulfur dioxide, and all grapes fermented by the winery are grown organically. The winery is a collection of used equipment; many of the fermenting tanks were once used and abandoned by dairies. Though the quality has been quite uneven, the Freys have enjoyed the advantages of good timing. An interest in organic wines pushed their production from 5,000 cases in 86 to close to 15,000 in 90. The current lineup includes Zinfandel, Syrah, and several vineyard-identified and one Reserve-type Cabernet Sauvignon. The white wines, fluctuating more widely in quality, include Grey Riesling, Colombard, and Gewurztraminer.

FRICK WINERY *Santa Cruz 1977* After making their first two vintages in an abandoned gas station in Bonny Doon, Bill and Judith Frick moved into their first "real" facility in the city of Santa Cruz. They produced wines at this location through 88, made entirely from purchased grapes. Their major emphasis fell on barrel-fermented Chardonnay and Pinot Noir, both from the Central Coast, and on Zinfandel and Petite Sirah. A small batch of Grenache plus blended generic wines often filled out the 3,500-case-a-year line. After a long search for a new location, the Fricks moved in late 88 to a vineyard and winery site purchased in the Dry Creek Valley of Sonoma County. The hillside vineyard contained 5 acres of mixed reds such as Zinfandel and Gamay, and the Fricks have added 4 acres of Syrah. During the transition, they greatly reduced production. They expect to work back up to 3,000 cases a year after the vineyard matures.

FRISINGER CELLARS *Napa 1988* The Frisinger family owns 20 acres in the southwestern corner of Napa Valley, in the town of Napa. After retiring as senior vice president of John Morrell & Co., James Frisinger, Sr., established the vineyard in 83, and James Jr. is now in charge of the winemaking side. Only Chardonnay is produced, and the wine is partially barrel-fermented in French Nevers puncheons. Given short-term aging *sur lie*, Frisinger Chardonnay does not undergo malolactic fermentation. From an initial crush of 600 cases, the winery will gradually grow to its capacity of 2,400 cases by the mid-90s.

J. FRITZ CELLARS *Sonoma 1979* Set back into the hillside, J. Fritz Cellars is a charming winery with an underground aging cellar. It is located in Cloverdale at the northern end of Dry Creek Valley. The Fritz family owns three separate vineyards in the Dry Creek Valley that combine for 90 acres and has another 35 acres in the Russian River Valley under long-term lease. Over the first several vintages, the production of Fritz wines has fluctuated widely. To varying degrees, the facility has been involved in custom-making wines for others, and has sold some of its grapes, depending on the demand. Normal production is 25,000 cases a year, with Chardonnay representing 65% of the total. Chardonnays appear under two appellations—Russian River Valley and Dry Creek Valley. In some vintages Fritz makes a Reserve Chardonnay from the Russian River region. The second most prominent varietal is Sauvignon Blanc from Dry Creek Valley. Generally, the Sauvignon Blancs have captured direct varietal aroma and are of good quality. Small amounts (under 1,000 cases) of Dry Creek Zinfandel and Cabernet Sauvignon complete the roster, with the Zinfandel, a medium ager, proving the winery's only consistent success to date.

Zinfandel
83* 84* 86 87* 88**

Medium ripe, with black-cherryish fruit and reasonable depth, moderate tannins for ageworthiness; 88 was near-classic

FROG'S LEAP WINERY *Napa 1981* Owner Larry Turley, a physician in the trauma ward at a nearby hospital, bought property in Napa Valley once used to raise frogs whose legs were destined for the restaurant trade. In 78 he planted 1 acre to Sauvignon Blanc, and converted the old livery stable into a winery, choosing a name and a label design aimed at poking fun at the highly successful Stag's Leap Wine Cellars. The joke happily backfired when the overall quality of Frog's Leap Sauvignon Blanc, along with the artistic merits of the label, brought considerable recognition to the winery. Within a few years winemaker John Williams (ex–Spring Mountain) became a partner, and through his full-time efforts the winery was able to grow in size and expand its varietal roster.

Williams and his wife, Julie, now have an 8-acre vineyard supplying Zinfandel and Cabernet Sauvignon. The lineup today, much of which is made from purchased fruit, consists of Sauvignon Blanc, representing 50% of the total production; Chardonnay (Napa Valley and Carneros bottlings); Zinfandel; and Cabernet Sauvignon. Both Chardonnays are 100% barrel-fermented. Cabernet Franc is blended into the winery's highly appealing Cabernet Sauvignons. Total annual production has reached the facility's capacity of 22,000 cases.

Cabernet Sauvignon

82   83 * *   84 *   85 *   86 *   87 * *   88

Not the most elegant wine around, this one impresses for its intensity, breadth, and aging potential, as well as for the value it offers when it occasionally earns very high ratings. Its character favors black cherry and faint notes of herbs, with tinges of orange rind and mint showing up from time to time, while noticeable astringency suggests several years of cellaring

Chardonnay

(Napa Valley) 84   85   86   87 *   88

Straightforward, mild, appley fruit, often with citrusy and blossomy aspects, carrying background notes of toasty oak in wines that are usually low to medium intensity

Zinfandel

85 *   86   87 * *   88 *

In its best showings, the wine has managed to find admirable balance between ripeness and black-cherry fruitiness; sweet oak and medium tannins are constants

GAINEY VINEYARDS *Santa Barbara 1984* The Gainey family, like many of their neighbors, live on a large ranch in the Santa Ynez Valley. Their 1,800-acre spread is home to a variety of crops and farm animals. Gainey Vineyards began to receive attention in the early 80s, and today the winery has 60 acres planted to several varieties. Winemaker Rick Longoria, one of the best known in the Central Coast region, has taken the winery to the 12,000-case-per-year level, with most wines bearing the Santa Barbara County appellation. About one-third of Gainey's output is Chardonnay, its most consistently good wine, with Johannisberg Riesling accounting for 22%. As the winery grows to its targeted annual maximum of 15,000 cases, Cabernet Sauvignon and Merlot together represent 30% of the annual emphasis. Both Pinot Noir (from the Benedict Vineyard) and Sauvignon Blanc are regularly made, but in small quantities. In some vintages, Gainey's Pinot Noir is a distinctive wine earning * *. The winery sells a significant portion of its wines from the tasting room or through its mailing list.

Cabernet Sauvignon

84   85   86

> *Ripe and soft, with distinct herbal leanings at the best of times and bothersome, earthy qualities at others*

Chardonnay

85 86* 87 88* 89

(Reserve) 85* 88**

> *Usually showing lots of fruit, the Reserve has an extra measure of aging potential*

E. & J. GALLO WINERY *Modesto 1933* Brothers Ernest and Julio Gallo started out in 33 with a $500 bank loan to purchase winemaking equipment. Today, Gallo is the largest wine company in the world, operating five facilities in California and selling about 70 million cases a year. Headquartered in Modesto, the Gallos rose to prominence on the strength of generic wines in jug bottles with screw caps, promoted—as with their extensive lines of table, sparkling, and dessert wines—by savvy marketing techniques. In the 60s and early 70s, Gallo's Hearty Burgundy was a perennial best-seller, while in the mid-70s its Chablis Blanc took over the top spot. Though the Gallos own over 4,000 acres of vineyards, they are the biggest customers for grapes grown in Sonoma County, Mendocino County, Napa Valley, and Monterey County. Milestones for the Gallos include the debut of varietal wines with cork closures in 75, and the completion in 78 of a massive aging cellar housing thousands of 3,000-gallon-capacity oak uprights. This cellar enables Gallo to offer Chardonnay, Cabernet Sauvignon, and Zinfandel under the "Reserve Cellars" designation. At their Modesto winery, the Gallos manufacture their own bottles, averaging about 2 million per day.

In addition to the Modesto facility, Gallo Winery operates others in Fresno, in Livingston, and in the Dry Creek Valley of Sonoma County. In the 80s the Gallos began paving the way for an eventual shift of emphasis, not of volume, to Sonoma County. After buying the former Frei Brothers Winery in 77, they have expanded that facility in Sonoma County to its present capacity of 9 million gallons. New vineyards have been developed in several Sonoma locations. To date, Gallo has established 800 acres in the Dry Creek Valley with emphasis on Cabernet and Zinfandel, and 400 acres in the Russian River Valley planted primarily to Chardonnay, Riesling, and Gewurztraminer. It has also developed a 200-acre site north of Geyserville that will contain Cabernet and Zinfandel. Eventually, Gallo plans to produce estate-bottled wines in Sonoma County.

However, Gallo's strength is in generic wines with California as their appellation. With a combined storage capacity of 330 million gallons, Gallo has a 27% share of the entire U.S. wine market and, in the generic wine category, its sales represent 45% of the jug-wine business. These figures take into consideration the myriad of labels used in addition to Gallo Winery. The most significant of these are Carlo Rossi (Chablis, Rhine, and Rosé), André and Tott's for sparkling wine, Livingston Cellars for a good Cream Sherry and other fortified wines, and Ballatore Spumante. Bartles & James reigns as the best-selling cooler, and E & J is the best-selling brandy. All are owned by Gallo.

From time to time, we have found Gallo's Reserve Sauvignon Blanc, made in an accessible, light style, to be pleasant and a good value. And in the low-priced sparkling wine category, Tott's Reserve is sometimes a cut above the competition.

GAN EDEN WINERY *Sonoma 1985* Located within the Green Valley appellation of Sonoma County, Gan Eden Winery was designed to produce certified Kosher wines. Its line of varietals is made from Sonoma County grapes, primarily from the Alexander Valley. The fairly broad line consists of Cabernet Sauvignon, Chardonnay, Chenin Blanc, Gewurztraminer, and Gamay Beaujolais. Over its early history, the quality leaders to emerge are Cabernet Sauvignon and Chardonnay. With dense black-cherry fruit and deep, yet soft flavors, the Cabernet Sauvignons, which can be erratic, have at times earned up to **. In a style accentuating lemony fruit, vanillin oak, and bright acidity, its Chardon-nays have been of ✿ caliber. Annual production has grown to 40,000 cases, the winery's full capacity. Continuation of its initial quality performance could place Gan Eden within the top echelons of California wineries, as well as making it the world's leading producer of high-caliber Kosher wines.

GARLAND RANCH *(Chateau Julien)* Presented by the owners of Chateau Julien as a line to compete in the mid-priced category, Garland Ranch wines are usually from the Central Coast appellation. As a rule Garland Ranch offers Cabernet Sauvignon, Chardonnay, and Merlot. The annual output has been about 10,000 cases over recent years.

GARRIC-LANGBEHN WINERY *Sonoma 1988* Larry Langbehn was winemaker for Freemark Abbey from 76 to 85. After leaving there, he served as a consultant to several producers, including Lamborn Family Winery. In the meantime, he and his wife, Lynn Garric, moved to a hillside location on the Sonoma side of the Mayacamas Mountains where they built a small winery. With a game plan of making only Chardonnay from the Sonoma Mountain region, they plan to grow to a maximum of 2,000 cases a year. The early vintages were uneven in quality.

GAUER ESTATE VINEYARD *Sonoma 1988* In the early 70s Ed Gauer, owner of Roos Atkins clothing stores, purchased over 5,000 acres in the Alexander Valley. Part of the land was used for cattle grazing, and sites more suited to agricul-ture were devoted to vineyard development. Within a decade, the Gauer ranch had 550 acres planted to wine varieties. For many years, all grapes were sold, and a few wineries produced vineyard-designated Gauer Ranch Char-donnays. In 86, with the thought of producing wines, Gauer purchased the relatively new and capacious facility named Vinwood, which custom-makes wines for many labels and wineries. Slowly, Gauer eased into production, starting with 2,000 cases of 87 Chardonnay. In 88 came the first Gauer Estate red wine, a proprietary blend of Cabernet Sauvignon, Merlot, and Cabernet Franc. A few years later, Merlot joined the line.

In early 89 Gauer, who was then in his 80s, sold the winery and vineyards to Huntington Beach Associates, a division of the Chevron Corporation. Main-taining a low profile, the owners of Gauer Estate wines continue to custom-crush for many labels and are gradually increasing their own production toward a target of 25,000 cases a year. When that goal is reached, Gauer Estate's barrel-fermented Chardonnay will represent 60% of the annual out-put, the red Bordeaux blend 30%, and Merlot 10%.

GAVILAN VINEYARDS *(Chalone)* Over its history this second label has been at-tached to a wide variety of wines from numerous appellations. For several years, the wines were bottled at Carmenet (part of the Chalone group of wineries) in Sonoma Valley. Currently they are bottled at the Chalone winery in Monterey County, and the label appears on wines made by Chalone that for one reason or another are not used for the primary label. The line includes Chardonnay, Chenin Blanc, Pinot Noir, and Pinot Blanc. On average, about 2,000 cases of Gavilan are bottled a year.

GEORIS WINERY *Monterey 1989* Walter Georis owns the highly praised Casanova restaurant in Carmel, and in the early 80s decided to develop a vineyard near his home in the Carmel Valley. On a site northeast of Durney Vineyards, Georis planted 15 acres to Merlot, Cabernet Sauvignon, and the three other Bordeaux red varieties. In 86 he made about 400 cases of Merlot at Morgan Winery. A small winery was built by 89, and Georis intends to specialize in Merlot and a proprietary red Bordeaux blend. When his vineyards are fully productive, he anticipates an annual production of about 2,000 cases.

GERWER WINERY *El Dorado 1983* The Gerwers presently occupy land that was the site for a test plot and experimental vineyard for El Dorado County set up by the University of California in 67. Encouraged by the results, Vernon Gerwer and his family began developing their own 12-acre vineyard in 79. On a 40-acre parcel south of Somerset at the 2,600-foot level, they planted Ruby Cabernet, Sauvignon Blanc, Semillon, and Petite Sirah. Chenin Blanc and Zinfandel (for White Zinfandel) are made from grapes grown by their neighbors. The winery, known for a few years as Stony Creek, changed to the family name in early 83. Since then, its production has reached 5,000 cases; with the expansion of their vineyard to 20 acres, the Gewers intend to level off at 8,000 cases a year.

GEYSER PEAK WINERY *Sonoma 1972* This ancient bulk wine producer, founded in 1880, was brought back to life when Schlitz of Milwaukee acquired it from the Bagnani family in 72. The beer company modernized and expanded the facility, located a mile north of Geyserville. Within three years, the winery was cranking out 200,000 cases of varietals and generics. Under Schlitz ownership, this winery was the first to make and sell wines in a can, wines in the bag-in-the-box, and wines in a plastic container. Its line of cheap generics expanded to the point where it was finally given its own name and label, "Summit." With Summit leading the way, the winery was making over 1 million cases by the end of the 70s. Geyser Peak acquired 600 acres of vineyards and a reputation for making wine almost as bland in character as most beer. In 83, after Schlitz was taken over by another major brewery, the winery became the property of the local Trione family, which gradually discontinued the novelty packaging and eventually disposed of the Summit brand. Vineyard acreage grew to 1,150 acres, including 650 acres in the Alexander Valley, 200 acres in the Russian River Valley, and 300 in Lake County.

Under the Trione leadership, the winery began to focus on a line of varietals, most of which were in the mid-price range or lower. A limited-volume line of upscale varietals under the Trione Vineyard label offered only modest improvement. In 89, the next chapter opened as the winery entered into a 50–50 partnership with Penfolds, the largest and most widely distributed brand of Australian wines. Penfolds owns the facility and the Geyser Peak brand, and has contracted to purchase Trione grapes. A new winemaker was brought in from Australia, and the Trione Vineyards line phased out. Geyser Peak today is producing 800,000 cases a year, the volume leaders being a trio of generics. The primary varietals made are White Zinfandel, Chardonnay, and "Soft Johannisberg Riesling." This third, most popular varietal is made in a relatively low-alcohol, medium-sweet style. Geyser Peak's Soft Riesling is often pleasant and balanced enough to win ✿ status in most vintages. With the 84 vintage, Geyser Peak revealed its desire to move up the prestige ladder with a Bordeaux blend named "Reserve Alexandre," a limited-volume wine.

Cabernet Sauvignon

82 83 84 85

Ranging from light and fruity to light and uninteresting, this one can be a good value in its better years

Chardonnay

84 85 86 87 88 89

Light and vaguely floral, but usually lacking substance

Reserve Alexandre

84 ✿ 85

Containing about 40% each of Cabernet Sauvignon and Merlot, the remainder made up of Cabernet Franc and Malbec, this wine tries, by content at least, to make a quality statement missing in most Geyser Peak releases to date

GIRARD WINERY *Napa 1980* The family-owned and -operated winery was founded by Stephen Girard, Sr., and has been run by Stephen Jr. from the beginning.

Stephen Sr., a vice president of Kaiser Industries, took his cue from Gene Trefethen, a previous retiree from Kaiser, and looked into vineyard land in Napa Valley. In 74 the Girards bought 60 acres with 44 planted to vines surrounded by an oak grove. Located on the midsection of the Silverado Trail in Oakville, the site contained Cabernet Sauvignon established in 68. Retaining the Cabernet and a small Chardonnay planting, the Girards improved the old vineyard and added Chenin Blanc in 77. For several years the Cabernet Sauvignon was sold to the Robert Mondavi Winery. By 80, the Girards were building a winery, and two years later they bought over 400 acres of hillside property on Mount Veeder, eventually planting 35 acres to Cabernet Sauvignon, Cabernet Franc, Chardonnay, and Semillon.

With emphasis on Chardonnay, Cabernet Sauvignon, and Chenin Blanc, Girard was making about 17,000 cases by 90. Sauvignon Blanc, made through 85, has been dropped. A Reserve Cabernet Sauvignon, a Reserve Chardonnay, and a regular Semillon are each made in 500-case quantities. The winery's Napa Valley Cabernet Sauvignon is made in an accessible style, and totals about 3,000 cases a year. The dry-oak-aged Chenin Blanc is holding steady at 4,000 cases a year. In an average harvest, Girard makes about 7,500 cases of partially barrel-fermented Chardonnay. With vineyard maturity, all Chardonnay bottled will be estate-grown. In the mid-80s, Girard planted 25 acres of wine grapes on land it owns in southern Oregon. Girard's first Oregon Pinot Noir was made in 87, and now with Carl Doumani, owner of Stags' Leap Vintners, as his partner, Girard will have an Oregon winery in operation by the mid-90s. The California winery will reach its peak production of 21,000 cases by then.

Cabernet Sauvignon

(regular bottling) 80 ** 81 ** 82 * 83 **84** * 85 * 86 87 *

(Reserve) 83 **84** ** **85** * 86 *

High in ripeness and oak, these well-stuffed wines rarely lack personality but can become overblown, over-oaked, and too tough in tannin; the hillside-grown Reserve goes in the same direction but is generally the bolder of the two

Chardonnay

(regular bottling) 84 85 86 * 87 **88** **

(Reserve) 86 ** 87 *

The Reserve bottling carries the richness and depth of grand Chardonnay, although at times it can be almost too oaky

---

GIUMARRA VINEYARDS *Kern 1974* This is one of California's largest wine producers, but most people today, including those drinking Giumarra wines, will never see its label. In 46, the Giumarra family began grape growing and winemaking in the town of Edison, located in fertile Kern County. The company concentrated on bulk wine production until 74, when it decided to change its approach. Within a few years it was using all of the grapes from its own vineyards and buying from the Central Coast region to offer a typical full line of varietals and generics in bottles. By 80 the winery had pushed sales up to 500,000 cases a year of modestly priced wines. Then, in late 85, Giumarra changed its approach again. It began offering a program of wines in the bag-in-a-box for the house wine, on-premise trade. That program became so successful that by the late 80s the Giumarra family decided to specialize. Today, Giumarra owns over 6,000 acres planted to wine grapes and produces 13 million gallons of wines each year. Its line consists of White Zinfandel, French Colombard, and Rosé, along with Chablis, Blush, and Red Table Wine. The bulk of it is sold is the 4-liter and 18-liter containers, but a growing segment of the winery's business is also in disposable 60-liter kegs. The Giumarras remain the largest producers and shippers of table grapes in the world.

GLEN ELLEN WINERY   *Sonoma 1980*   Within the borders of the quaint town of Glen Ellen, the Benziger family updated an old facility in the western hills of the Sonoma Valley. On beautifully terraced hillsides, they established an 85-acre vineyard. The first wines offered under the Glen Ellen Winery name were inexpensive Cabernet Sauvignon and a red generic blend bought readymade, only to be blended and bottled. Both wines were adorned with a folksy-looking label and given the designation "Proprietor's Reserve." Patriarch Bruno Benziger, a successful importer and marketing executive with the Park-Benziger spirits importing company in New York, soon proved equally adept at building a wine brand through clever merchandising. As the demand for the first two wines increased, Glen Ellen Winery added a low-priced Chardonnay which enjoyed extremely rapid sales growth. Unintentionally, the winery had created a new industry category called "fighting varietals," which are inexpensive and designed for popular appeal. With the addition of a White Zinfandel to the Glen Ellen line, total sales topped 1.6 million cases by 87. Before long, Sauvignon Blanc was added and labeled "Proprietor's Reserve."

By the end of the decade, Glen Ellen Winery had developed an elaborate network for buying, blending, and bottling bulk wines, which allowed its annual sales to grow to over 3 million cases. All of the Proprietor's Reserve wines are blends of wines and grapes purchased from numerous sources and regions throughout California. Each bottling is made totally or in part from purchased wine. The estate-bottled line of varietals offered under the Glen Ellen Winery label for a few years grew slowly to 30,000 cases a year. However, the success the winery enjoyed with cheap wines made it difficult to sell higher-priced wines. Before long, the owners decided to label the estate-grown line Benziger of Glen Ellen (see entry). In 85–86, the family slowly introduced wines under yet another brand, M. J. Vallejo (see entry), covering a line similar to those under the Glen Ellen Winery. And finally, the parent Glen Ellen Winery also puts out a small-volume line of varietals from selected growers and regions under the Imagery Series label.

Under the Glen Ellen Winery "Proprietor's Reserve" label, the wines offered are White Zinfandel, Chardonnay, Chenin Blanc, Sauvignon Blanc, Gamay Beaujolais, and Red Table and White Table wine.

GOLD HILL VINEYARDS   *El Dorado 1986*   Gold Hill is located in the town of Coloma, a mile south of Sutter's Mill, where gold was discovered. Owner Hank Battjes acquired part of an experimental vineyard planted in the mid-60s and has since expanded it to 35 acres. Chardonnay at 15 acres is the prime variety, followed by Cabernet Sauvignon at 13 acres. A few acres each are planted to Merlot, Cabernet Franc, Chenin Blanc, and Riesling. Chardonnay represents 70% of the total annual output. Limited amounts of Cabernet, Merlot, and Cabernet Franc are offered. With vineyard maturity, Gold Hill will build to the 8,000-case level. Some wines are sold under the Coloma Gold label.

GOLDEN CREEK VINEYARD   *Sonoma 1983*   Owner-winemaker Ladi Danielik was born in Czechoslovakia and emigrated to the U.S. in 68, coming to California in 77, where he bought 70 acres of land a few miles northeast of Santa Rosa. On steep hillsides he planted 12 acres to Merlot and Cabernet Sauvignon, and two white varieties, Sauvignon Blanc and Gewurztraminer, which were eventually budded to more Cabernet and Merlot. Unfortunately, the first wines to be marketed were the whites which, due to a lack of cooling equipment in the winery, were not of acceptable quality. The Cabernet and Merlot have been more successful, as has been a blend of the two termed "Caberlot." Production has varied from 500 cases a year to just over 1,000, depending upon sales. When the production is low, the owner has a ready market for his grapes.

GOLDEN STATE VINTNERS   *Tulare 1936*   An old facility that was once a grower co-operative, this one has been responsible for many different wines under many different labels in its history. Among the more notable brands produced here have been Growers Winery, Le Blanc Vineyards, and Bounty Vineyards. In the late 80s, after being modernized and upgraded under new management, the facility was dubbed Golden State, and that name has recently been attached to a line of varietals offered in both 375 and 750 ml bottles. They are Chardonnay, Cabernet Sauvignon, and White Zinfandel, all priced at the low end. With a storage capacity of over 30 million gallons, the facility devotes considerable attention to selling wines to other brands, and the Golden State wines represent a fraction of the total production.

GOOSECROSS CELLARS *Napa 1985* Goosecross is owned by the Gorsuch family, whose name in Old English literally translates into "when the goose crosses." In the early 80s Ray Gorsuch bought a vineyard on State Lane in Yountville and developed the family's 10½-acre Chardonnay estate. Until 85 all grapes were sold, and Far Niente and Burgess Cellars were among the several buyers. His son, Geoff Gorsuch, runs the winery operation and manages the vineyard today. Only Chardonnay is produced, the flagship wine being the estate-bottled version. From three growers in the nearby area, Goosecross buys Chardonnay for a Napa Valley bottling. Both wines are partially barrel-fermented. The winery's production goal is 8,000 cases. To date it is making 2,500 cases of the estate Chardonnay and 3,500 of Napa Valley.

GRACE FAMILY VINEYARD *Napa 1978* Planning to move his brokerage business to the country, Smith Barney stockbroker Dick Grace and his wife, Ann, bought a home in St. Helena in 74. Two years later they planted 1 acre of Cabernet Sauvignon adjacent to their home, making their first small crop into wine at Caymus Vineyard in 78. From then until 83 the Grace Family Cabernet was bottled as a vineyard-designated wine under the Caymus label. Because the wine made was of good quality and extremely scarce, Grace Family Cabernet attracted strong interest from collectors. Dick Grace also knew how to obtain remarkable publicity from the Napa Valley wine auction and, as a result, his wine developed a coterie following. From his 2-acre planting, Grace now makes at most about 250 cases a year in the small winery he built in 87. Aged close to three years in French oak, Grace Family Cabernet is 100% varietal. By the end of the 80s, when it was priced at $50 a bottle, it was selling primarily through a mailing list.

Cabernet Sauvignon
  84* 85** 86*
  *Very rich, highly oaked wines, offering curranty fruit, complexing sugges-
  tions of loam, and light to medium tannins*

GRAESER WINERY *Napa 1985* Richard Graeser inherited an old estate and 45 acres of mountainous property in 84. His parents had purchased the property in 58 and used it for many years as a summer home. With years of experience as a farmer in the Bakersfield area, Graeser decided to try his hand at grape-growing and winemaking. Intending to specialize in a Cabernet Sauvignon blend from the mountain vineyard, he planted 9½ acres in 84–85 to Cabernet Sauvignon, Cabernet Franc, and Merlot, and will gradually plant 7 additional acres to the same varieties in the 90s. Located on the Petrified Forest Road about a mile north of Calistoga, Graeser Winery began by making Cabernet Sauvignon, Semillon, and Chardonnay from purchased grapes. The facility allows for gradual production increases to a maximum of 8,000 cases a year.

GRAND CRU VINEYARDS *Sonoma 1970* When it began, this winery located in a quiet section of Glen Ellen intended to specialize in carbonic maceration Nouveau Zinfandel. When that wine type failed to generate enough demand, it started making a variety of other table wines, including late harvest Zinfandels and white wines that accentuated youthful fruitiness. By the end of the 70s, Grand Cru had developed a good reputation for Gewurztraminer finished with about 2% residual sugar. It was also making a slightly sweet Chenin Blanc from the Delta region. With the 75 vintage, Grand Cru introduced a long-aged Cabernet Sauvignon from the Alexander Valley, and labeled the wine "Collector's Reserve." In the early 80s a Sauvignon Blanc joined the line. Throughout many changes in focus, including a short-lived sparkling wine program, the 20,000-case winery survived largely on the energy of co-founder Bob Magnani. By 81, however, it was in need of improvements, and Magnani decided to sell it.

The new owners, Walt and Tina Dreyer, one-time owners of Oroweat Bread, retained Magnani as winemaker through 88. Under their ownership, production increased to over 50,000 cases, with the addition of a White Zinfandel, and a low-priced Sauvignon Blanc and Cabernet Sauvignon under the California appellation. Its other varietals are united under the subtitle "Premium Selection." As the winery became better known nationally, it increased the production of Chenin Blanc from the Delta to 10,000 cases, and steadied the quality of its upscale Sauvignon Blanc. Its Alexander Valley–grown Gewurztraminer is often moderately intense and balanced for the medium-sweet style, and steadily earns ❋. In 88 the winery produced its first Chardonnay, from Carneros, and early offerings emphasized fruit and simplicity. The winery obtains grapes from its 17-acre vineyard as well as from growers throughout the state.

Cabernet Sauvignon

(Collector's Reserve) 78❋ 79 80❋❋ 85❋ 86❋

On again, off again, this wine usually favors a ripe cherry, somewhat herbal direction, and boasts medium depth and moderate tannins

Cabernet Sauvignon

(Premium Selection) 84 85 86

Medium-bodied and more accessible in style, the wine offers cherryish fruit with suggestions of oak, but has not yet risen above average in quality

GRANITE SPRINGS WINERY *El Dorado 1981* With a name reflecting the granitic soils prevalent throughout its vineyards, Granite Springs is a family-owned winery. In 79, owner-winemaker Les Russell developed a 24-acre vineyard planted to Cabernet Sauvignon, Sauvignon Blanc, and Zinfandel, with small amounts of Chenin Blanc, Petite Sirah, and Muscat Blanc. The first vintage, 81, consisted of Zinfandel and White Zinfandel, Cabernet Sauvignon and Chenin Blanc. Beginning with an annual production of 2,700 cases, the winery has grown to its maximum of 10,000 per year. Within its first decade, Granite Springs established solid winemaking credentials by turning out well-made White Zinfandels and Chenin Blancs, both in a slightly sweet style. Its estate-bottled Petite Sirah also ranked as one of the better versions of the varietal available. Port production has been given attention by winemaker Russell, who has experimented with both Zinfandel and Petite Sirah, individually and combined. A Sierra Reserve Red and a Sierra Reserve White are low-priced blends rounding off the line.

GREEN & RED VINEYARD *Napa 1977* Jay Heminway abandoned the teaching profession and moved to the Chiles Valley in 70, purchasing a 160-acre farm that had fallen into neglect. By 72 he had developed a 16-acre vineyard on a site that ranges in elevation from 900 to 1,500 feet, and where, Heminway believes, two distinct microclimates exist. On the lower levels he planted 9½ acres of Chardonnay, and along the higher contours 7½ acres of Zinfandel. The soils also vary, red iron mixed with green serpentine being the most common; these soil types explain the vineyard's name. Heminway also decided to plant Zinfandel on its own root system rather than using grafted vines. In the mid-80s a White Zinfandel made from purchased fruit was added. However, the winery's main focus is its regular Zinfandel, usually made in a tannic style, and estate-grown Chardonnay. They represent 80% of the winery's annual output, which will level off at 5,000 cases a year. The Zinfandel occasionally rises to ❋ rating.

GREENSTONE WINERY *Amador 1980* The Greenstone Winery rests on a gentle knoll in the middle of a 40-acre ranch in a part of Amador County known as

Jackson Valley. A partnership of two families, Greenstone offers a range of table wines and fortified wines. Beginning in 80, a 30-acre vineyard was planted to French Colombard, Chenin Blanc, Zinfandel, Sauvignon Blanc, Cabernet Sauvignon, Muscat Blanc, and Palomino (used for sherry). Slightly sweet, picnic-style White Zinfandel and Colombard account for over 50% of the annual 10,000-case production. Most wines are made from Greenstone's own vineyards, with the exception of a Zinfandel Port from Calaveras County. Long term, the winery will level off at 20,000 cases a year.

GREENWOOD RIDGE VINEYARD *Mendocino 1980* On an isolated southern ridgeline at the 1,200-foot level, the Greenwood Ridge winemaking facility can be found in a pretty, pastoral setting. A tasting room was later built on the floor of the Anderson Valley to connect the winery to the world. Owner Allan Green left the graphic arts profession and bought an old vineyard, once owned by Husch, not far from the Dupratt Zinfandel vineyard which sells to Kendall-Jackson. Green redeveloped his vineyard and now has roughly 4 acres each of Riesling, Cabernet Sauvignon, and Merlot. He purchases Chardonnay from the Redwood Valley, Zinfandel from Sonoma County, and Sauvignon Blanc from Mendocino County. The winery has produced a string of excellent White Rieslings in a slightly sweet style. Most of the other wines fall in the average-quality grouping. Green continues to work with Cabernet and Merlot, even though both often display a strong degree of herbal character. The winery is at its full production level of 3,000 cases.

GRGICH HILLS CELLAR *Napa 1977* The partners behind this successful winery are Mike Grgich, the winemaker, and Austin Hills, the vineyard owner and developer. Though not as well known in wine circles as Grgich, Austin Hills comes from a San Francisco family that once owned Hills Bros. Coffee, and was involved in the family business until it was sold in 76. At that time he decided to expand his small vineyard located in Rutherford and to venture into wine production. In early 77 he and Grgich, who had been with Chateau Montelena, became equal partners. Born in Desne, Croatia, in Yugoslavia, Grgich emigrated to the U.S. in 58. He began his California winemaking experience with the original Souverain as Lee Stewart's apprentice. He later worked for the Christian Brothers, Beaulieu Vineyard, and the Robert Mondavi Winery, where he remained until going to Montelena as head winemaker in 72. It was during his tenure that Montelena produced the 73 Chardonnay that bested its French counterparts in the now famous 76 tasting held in Paris.

The new Grgich Hills winery was barely finished in time for the 77 harvest. The wines produced were Chardonnay, Zinfandel, and Johannisberg Riesling in a slightly sweet style. A Fumé Blanc was added to the line in 81, and the first Cabernet Sauvignon vintage was 80. Using Chardonnay from the Hills vineyard in Rutherford, Grgich was performing at the ✶ level from the beginning. Changes in winemaking have been implemented gradually. In 85, Grgich introduced partial barrel fermentation; by 87 he was fermenting 100% of the Chardonnay in Limousin barrels. Malolactic fermentation has just about always been prevented in Grgich Chardonnays, as it also is in Zinfandels. The grape sources for Chardonnay are four vineyards in Napa Valley: Rutherford, Yountville, north of Napa, and Los Carneros. The Fumé Blanc is made primarily from the winery's Olive Hills Vineyard in Napa. Grgich plays down the grassy-herbal side of Fumé Blanc to emphasize ripe fruit, balanced and substantial flavors in an oak-enriched style that varies between ✶ and ✶✶ performances. Aging his red wines in a combination of American and Nevers oak barrels, Grgich also prefers Zinfandel from old, nonirrigated hillside vineyards, and he has found an appropriate source in the Alexander Valley. The quantity of Cabernet Sauvignon was small in 80 and 81, but with the 84 vintage grew to 10,000 cases a year. Grgich Cabernets are grown in the winery's Yountville vineyard and blended with Merlot before being aged for two years in both French and American oak. By 90 the winery was at its capacity level of 30,000 cases. Chardonnay accounts for over 30% and Fumé Blanc for 20%, with Zinfandel and Riesling combining for 15%.

Cabernet Sauvignon

81 ** 82 * 83 84 * 85 **

Fairly full-sized Cabernet sometimes showing more ripeness, tannin, and oak than restraint; the wine succeeds when its fruit is able to match up with its ambitions

Chardonnay

84 ** 85 ** 86 ** 87 ** 88 *

High in oak and high in appley fruit, with somewhat stiff acidity in the background, this wine is among the standard-setters for California Chardonnay

Zinfandel

78 *** 79 80 *** 81 ** 82 *** 83 * 84 * 86 87 **

Always a wine heading toward overripeness, it has seemed to lose its massive berryish center in recent years and no longer is able to command top ratings or be worthy of lengthy cellar aging

GROTH VINEYARDS & WINERY *Napa 1982* One-time president of Atari and former accountant Dennis Groth decided to invest in the grape and wine world in 81. He bought two vineyards in Napa Valley, the Oakcross Vineyard in Oakville containing 68 acres of Cabernet Sauvignon (all planted in 74) and 32 acres of Chardonnay, and the Hillview Vineyard just south of Yountville, with 28 acres of Sauvignon Blanc, 12 acres of Merlot, and 3 acres of Chardonnay. Construction of a winery in Oakville was finally completed in 89. Until then, the wines were fermented in one location, aged in another, and bottled in a third. In 90, all winemaking was brought together under one roof and the winery was close to its production capacity of 40,000 cases. Making only estate-grown wines, Groth produces 20,000 cases of Cabernet Sauvignon (with about 10% Merlot), and 10,000 cases each of Sauvignon Blanc and Chardonnay. Winemaker Nils Venge (formerly of Villa Mt. Eden) has been with Groth since 82. Cabernet Sauvignons, regular and limited-volume Reserve, have been the winery's best performers. The regular is building a * track record.

Cabernet Sauvignon

82 * 83 * 84 * 85 ** 86 87

(Reserve) 85 *** 86 **

Loaded with sweet oak, sometimes at the expense of the fruit, this wine is usually well proportioned, otherwise with medium tannins adding to the notion that it will age well

Chardonnay

84 * 85 86 * 87 88 * 89

Omnipresent, heavy-handed oak often outdistances the appley fruit; but when the wine is in balance, it is attractive to fans of the toasty, fleshy style

GUENOC WINERY *Lake 1981* This winery and estate are owned by the Magoon family, which acquired 23,000 acres in the early 60s in exchange for land in Hawaii it gave to the University of Hawaii. The winery is in Middletown, about 20 miles north of St. Helena. Part of the Magoon property, approximately 4,000 acres, was once owned by the famous Victorian actress Lillie Langtry, who lived there from 1888 to 1906. The Magoons restored the Langtry House, and have used the historical connection in their publicity. Beginning in the late 60s they developed vineyards in and around the former Langtry estate, and also in a part of their ranch that falls within Napa County.

The Guenoc Winery today has 320 acres of vineyards; the leading varieties are Chardonnay (120 acres), Cabernet Sauvignon (70 acres), and Sauvignon Blanc (38 acres). Walt and Roy Raymond of the Raymond Vineyards in Napa Valley helped develop the vineyards, and the first vintage produced, the 76, was made by Walt Raymond. By 80 the Magoons had built their own winery and begun making a line of varietals, mostly from their own grapes. Magoon defined the Guenoc Valley well enough to have it become approved as a Viticultural Area in 81. Most of his vineyards are in the Lake County part of Guenoc Valley, but Magoon decided to plant Cabernet Sauvignon and all related varieties in a lower-elevation site in the northern corner of Napa County.

Over the years, Guenoc Winery has frequently altered its wine roster. For a few vintages it made a name for itself with its Petite Sirahs and heavy-bodied Zinfandels. Its Chardonnay has earned * but has been highly variable. When the tannins are under control, the winery's Zinfandel can rise above average. Its most recent releases of Sauvignon Blanc and Cabernet have been well made, and represent good values. Several different Reserve designations have been tried and discarded, and the Reserves are currently labeled under vineyard designated names. Currently, the Meritage red and white blends are identified by the Langtry moniker. Modestly priced Chardonnay, Zinfandel, and Sauvignon Blanc are bottled under the "Le Breton" label. Guenoc's annual production is 85,000 cases, with 110,000 set as the target maximum.

EMILIO GUGLIELMO WINERY *Santa Clara County 1925* Located in the Morgan Hill area, this family-owned winery is now in the hands of the third generation. In the 60s and into the early 70s, under the Emile's Private Stock brand, it produced large quantities of jug wines for many restaurants in Northern California. Since then it has developed three distinct levels of wine. The Emile's label is used only for a line of generics, sold mostly in jug containers. Under the name Mount Madonna, it offers a line of varietals, most from purchased grapes, and others, such as Zinfandel, from its own 125-acre vineyard. The family name, Guglielmo, is often highlighted on a limited line of Reserve varietals. The most consistently successful wine is a Reserve bottling of "Claret," blended from family-grown Zinfandel and Petite Sirah. Though the winemaking style retains a rustic touch, the red varietals—Zinfandel, Cabernet Sauvignon, and Petite Sirah—are often more than decent wines in a relatively inexpensive price range. Total annual output is around 75,000 cases.

GUNDLACH-BUNDSCHU WINERY *Sonoma 1973* This family-owned winery can trace its history back to 1858. Prior to Prohibition, the name was well regarded for a range of table and fortified wines, and from the time of Repeal until it reopened as a producer, Gundlach-Bundschu's vineyard was a favorite of many producers within the area. Under the direction of Jim Bundschu, the winery started on a small scale in 73. Growing steadily each year, it has leveled off at 40,000 cases a year. The Bundschus own 375 acres of vineyards and still sell a portion of their crop to others. The original 125-acre family vineyard, referenced on labels as "Rhinefarm," is located in the Sonoma-Carneros appellation. Another family-owned vineyard with 150 acres is located east of the town of Sonoma. The winery has preferred to use Sonoma Valley as the appellation. In its initial vintages, it promoted an obscure white varietal, Kleinberger, and gained some critical attention for its ripe, brawny Zinfandels.

Quality rose higher in 80, a year in which the winery began producing Merlot in a big, rich style and Gewurztraminer that in some vintages was intense in character and balanced. Throughout the 80s Gundlach-Bundschu performed well, with the exception of a Zinfandel wandering to the overripe end of the spectrum. Cabernet Sauvignon from the neighboring Batto Vineyard was bottled from 77 to 84. Today, the winery concentrates on estate-grown wines, making a Rhinefarm and a Rhinefarm Reserve Cabernet Sauvignon. Chardonnay in a fruity, moderately oak-influenced style has been consistently solid and often represents good value. Occasionally, Gundlach-Bundschu's vintages of Pinot Noir display some finesse and rise to * levels. Finished in a relatively dry style, Gewurztraminer ranks in the * range in most vintages. A barrel-fermented, full-bodied Chardonnay labeled "Sangiacomo Ranch" is the only wine made from purchased grapes. Two low-priced blends, Sonoma Valley White and Sonoma Red, complete the line. Overall, Gundlach-Bundschu is a reliable brand offering good value in many of its wines.

Cabernet Sauvignon

80* 81* 82* 83 84* 85* 86

Typically showing ripe, cassislike fruit, medium-full body, and herbal leanings in a medium-aging style

Chardonnay

83* 84* 85 86** 87 88

Straightforward, somewhat appley fruit, moderate oakiness, medium depth, good balance; good value in best vintages

Merlot

80* 81** 82** 83* 84* 85** 86** 87* 88*

Very ripe style that skirts the boundaries of acceptability, but is kept in check by enormous fruit, rich oak, and tannic structure

HACIENDA WINERY *Sonoma 1973* This picturesque Sonoma Valley winery is located within a mile of Sonoma town. It occupies the site where in 1862 Agoston Haraszthy is said to have planted the first vines in Sonoma County. The vineyard and the original winery were restored in 73 by Frank Bartholomew, who from 41 to 68 had revived and run Buena Vista Vineyards. The present owners have 50 acres adjacent to the winery that include Chardonnay (14 acres), Cabernet Sauvignon (13 acres), and Pinot Noir (6 acres). Another 70-acre vineyard is located in Cloverdale, supplying the winery with Zinfandel and several other varieties. It contains 25 acres of Zinfandel used for White Zinfandel and at times for Port. The winery now favors partial barrel fermentations for its Chardonnay, subtitled "Clair de Lune," a wine that reaches * levels fairly frequently. The winery's Reserve Pinot Noir is said to be made from vines propagated from the famous Romanée-Conti clone. Though sometimes too rough and out of balance, Hacienda's Pinot Noir is capable of rising above the ordinary. Its Chenin Blanc, usually made with under 1% sugar and not always consistent, was among the first to carry the Clarksburg appellation.

In the 70s Hacienda produced a series of successful * Cabernet Sauvignons exclusively from 50-year-old vines. By the early 80s Cabernet production was bumped up to 5,000 cases and the wine from the old vines was lost in the blend. In the 84 vintage, Hacienda introduced an estate Reserve Cabernet Sauvignon from that old block of vines, and offered a Sonoma County Cabernet Sauvignon from several sources. In 86, "Antares," its high-priced Bordeaux blend, was first made, but the quality has yet to rise above *. The winery has leveled off at the 27,000- to 30,000-case range. The volume leader is Chardonnay, accounting for roughly 33% of the total, with Chenin Blanc at about 20%, Cabernet Sauvignon at about 15%, Sauvignon Blanc at 10%, and Gewurztraminer just below 10%. Varying widely in quantity with each vintage, Pinot Noir has been averaging about 1,000 cases a year. The winery has at one time or another succeeded with each varietal, but consistency became a real problem in the 80s. Steve MacRostie, the winemaker from the beginning, left in 86 to start his own brand.

Cabernet Sauvignon

80 82 83 84 85*

Usually containing around 10% Merlot and lately a smaller proportion of Cabernet Franc, this hearty but often briary wine has won few plaudits

Chardonnay

84* 85 86** 87* 88

Medium-intensity fruit is well supported by toasty but not overpowering oak in most vintages of this likable, reliable wine

Pinot Noir

81** 82* 83* 84* 85* 86 87*

Often ripe in emphasis and usually rich in oak, this wine seems frequently to be on the verge of stardom and, in many vintages, it can age fairly well

HAFNER VINEYARD   *Sonoma 1982*   Primarily vineyardists, with 95 well-regarded acres under vine in the Alexander Valley, the Hafners regularly sell about two thirds of their crop. Gary Farrell, among others, makes Chardonnay from their vineyard for his brand. The Hafner family began developing the vineyard in 67, and 90% of the acreage consists of Chardonnay and Cabernet Sauvignon. In 82 the Hafners built a small winery with the intention of making modest quantities of wine. By 85, they expanded the facility and developed a direct-marketing mailing-list program. Hafner's annual production has reached the maximum of 7,500 cases of Chardonnay and 2,500 cases of Cabernet Sauvignon. Occasionally, a late harvest Riesling is made with varying levels of *Botrytis*.

HAGAFEN WINERY   *Napa 1980*   In Hebrew, *hagafen* means "the vine," and Hagafen was the first Kosher wine specialist in the North Coast. Founded by Zach Berkowitz and Ernie Weir, who has always served as winemaker and is now sole owner, Hagafen also had a famous silent partner, Rene di Rosa, once owner of the best-known single vineyard in Napa Valley, Winery Lake Vineyards. For three or four years, Hagafen attracted some media attention, but the quality was a little uneven. A Pinot Noir-Blanc failed to capture a significant portion of the blush wine audience. From a high mark of 5,000 cases, the winery's production has dipped to below half of that and now seems settled on 3,000 cases a year. Chardonnay, Riesling, and about 1,000 cases of Cabernet Sauvignon account for virtually all of the output. The Cabernet remains the most noteworthy.

HALLCREST VINEYARDS   *Santa Cruz 1976*   After Repeal, one of California's best-known vineyards was Hallcrest, owned by Chaffee Hall. Until that winery was closed in 69, the Hallcrest vineyard was noted for Cabernet Sauvignon and Riesling. The property was renovated and reopened in 76 under the name of Felton-Empire Vineyards. After 10 years the partnership involved began to unravel, and the winery and vineyard were sold in 88 to the Schumacher family. They had previously made wines under the brands of Davis Wine Cellars and Schumacher Cellars. Having revived the Hallcrest name, they are making estate-bottled Riesling from the 5½-acre vineyard, as well as Sauvignon Blanc from Napa Valley, Gewurztraminer from Mendocino, and a proprietary light-style red, "Clos de Jeannine." In batches of 200–400 cases, Schumacher has produced Chardonnays and Cabernet Sauvignons from growers in Napa and in El Dorado County. Over the first several vintages, Hallcrest achieved the best results with its Dry Gewurztraminer and Riesling. A secondary label, Organic Wine Works, has been formed to market a line of organically grown wines. Total production of 12,000 cases a year is expected to double before leveling off.

HANDLEY CELLARS   *Mendocino 1978*   After gaining winemaking experience first at Chateau St. Jean and next at Edmeades Vineyard, winemaker Milla Handley went on to start her own winery in Philo, at the western edge of the Anderson Valley. The first few vintages of barrel-fermented Chardonnay from her parents' vineyard in Dry Creek Valley received considerable critical praise. Her father owns 20 acres in southern Dry Creek Valley, planted mostly to Chardonnay and Sauvignon Blanc. A 20-acre vineyard surrounding the winery was planted to Chardonnay and Pinot Noir. By the mid-80s the winery was producing two Chardonnays (Dry Creek Valley and Anderson Valley), Gewurztraminer, and Sauvignon Blanc, also from Dry Creek Valley. The overall quality level is above average. A small-scale sparkling wine program is under way as Handley makes both a Brut and a Rosé sparkling wine by the *méthode cham-*

penoise. Total production for the sparklers remains under 1,000 cases a year. The winery's maximum production capacity is 12,000 cases.

Chardonnay

(Dry Creek Valley)   83*   84*   85**   86*   87**   88

Medium-intense fruit, floral notes, and toasty oak are presented in a firmly structured, medium-long-aging wine

---

HANNA WINERY   *Sonoma 1985*   Owner Dr. Elias Hanna, a heart surgeon, established his winery on his 35-acre estate a few miles west of Santa Rosa. After developing 10 acres of Chardonnay adjacent to the winery, he purchased 100 acres in the Alexander Valley and over time 60 acres were planted to Chardonnay, Sauvignon Blanc, Cabernet Sauvignon, and Merlot. The first crush in 85 amounted to 8,000 cases, and within its third harvest the winery has grown to the 25,000-case level. Until the mid-90s, when his own vineyards reach maturity, Hanna will purchase most of his grapes from several subregions within Sonoma County. All wines, including the barrel-fermented Chardonnay, Sauvignon Blanc, and Cabernet Sauvignon (blended with Merlot), were of above-average quality. While each was relatively impressive, the early vintages of Cabernet Sauvignon and Chardonnay have led the way. Hanna's annual production will level off at 30,000 cases.

Cabernet Sauvignon

85   86**   87

Capable of being ripe and fruity, with good depth and aging potential, this is one to watch in future years

Chardonnay

85*   86**   87   88**

Fruity, with some hints of juiciness; rich oak

HANZELL VINEYARDS   *Sonoma 1956*   This was the original showcase winery, and one of the few successful small wineries after Repeal whose wines inspired many others to follow in its path. Hanzell was designed by the late Ambassador James Zellerbach, who modeled it on Clos de Vougeot in Burgundy. Located in what is still a remote hillside region along the eastern edge of the Sonoma Valley, Hanzell has 33 acres planted to well-established Chardonnay and Pinot Noir and a few to relatively young Cabernet Sauvignon. Among its many accomplishments, the Hanzell winery emphatically introduced French oak barrels for aging and also for barrel fermentations of Chardonnay. It was also a technical leader for Pinot Noir in its small-batch approach, with frequent punching down of the cap for extraction.

For many years Hanzell's wines set high standards. The Chardonnays have always been made in a ripe style, with considerable oak influence. Though less consistent by far, Hanzell Pinot Noirs are big, ripe, and intense, with varying degrees of complexity and balance. The full-blown, large-scale style of both wines reflects the microclimate, which has always seemed best suited to Cabernet Sauvignon or possibly Zinfandel. Since the early 80s the winery has made about 500 cases of estate Cabernet, with highly variable results. Total annual output is fixed at 3,000 cases. The winery and beautiful grounds are closed to the public. They are owned by the Barbara de Brye estate of Canada.

Cabernet Sauvignon

82   83**   84   85*   86*

Potentially the best wine to come from Hanzell, it follows the winery's expansive style in its ability to offer ripe, deep character; but inconsistent results somewhat dampen our enthusiasm

Chardonnay

83**   84*   85   88**

Near to overdone in every vintage, at its best it manages sufficient fruit to balance its ripeness and heavy oak

Pinot Noir

78** 79* 80* 81* 82 83 84* 85* 86*

Almost always too ripe to be called classical Pinot Noir, the wine can be deep in character, if often somewhat wanting in fruit

HARRISON VINEYARD *Napa 1988* In 87 Lyndsay Harrison purchased a mature 17-acre vineyard located on the eastern hills of the Napa Valley. Encouraged by neighbor Bob Long of Long Vineyards, Harrison arranged to have the first vintages custom-made by Pecota Winery. Harrison's Chardonnay is barrel-fermented, undergoes complete malolactic fermentation, and ages six months *sur lie*. Grown on the steeper hillsides near Pritchard Hill, Harrison's Cabernet is 100% varietal and is given two years' aging in small French oak. Early vintages averaged 1,000 cases of Chardonnay and 600 of Cabernet a year.

HART WINERY *Riverside 1980* Both Travis and Nancy Hart taught in the Carlsbad school district west of Temecula for several years. In 73 they purchased a site close to the Callaway winery and began developing their 11-acre vineyard. After selling their first few harvests, they built a winery in 79 and have edged up to their present 5,500-case-a-year level. Sauvignon Blanc, Chardonnay, Cabernet Sauvignon, and Cabernet Blanc are the primary wines offered.

HAVENS WINE CELLARS *Napa 1984* Between 84 and 89, owner-winemaker Mike Havens rented space in other facilities to produce his wines. Havens, a former English professor at UCLA, transferred to U.C. Davis in order to learn more about enology and viticulture. In 83 he purchased property next door to the Truchard Vineyard in the Carneros, and has been purchasing grapes from Truchard to supplement his own crop since the first crush in 84. The Havens wine roster consists of Sauvignon Blanc, Chardonnay, and Merlot, the latter representing two-thirds of the winery's total annual production of 4,500 cases. Havens blends as much as 20% Cabernet Franc into his Merlot. In the 90s Havens is moving toward a trio of vineyard-designated Napa Valley Merlots—Truchard, Hazen Vineyard, and Veeder Springs. The winery's quality performance has been uneven over the first few vintages.

HAWK CREST *(Stag's Leap Wine Cellars)* This second label first appeared in 74 on a bottle of Riesling, and by 76 was being used for Cabernet Sauvignon that did not make the cut for the primary brand. It lurched along in no particular direction until the early 80s, when it became a full-fledged line of competitively priced, ready-to-drink varietals. Made from purchased grapes or purchased wines, and often a combination of the two, Hawk Crest wines have carried many appellations. The majority are California and North Coast. The present lineup consists of Chardonnay, Sauvignon Blanc, Cabernet Sauvignon, and Gamay Beaujolais. Annual output of about 50,000 cases is led by Chardonnay and Sauvignon Blanc in terms of volume and consistent quality.

HAYWOOD WINERY *Sonoma 1980* Between 76 and 78, Peter Haywood developed a 90-acre vineyard on steep terraces and hilly terrain in a secluded valley northeast of the town of Sonoma. A decade later he planted 18 additional acres of Cabernet Sauvignon and Merlot. The primary varieties cultivated are Chardonnay, Riesling, Cabernet Sauvignon, Zinfandel, and Sauvignon Blanc. All five are produced as varietals, and since the appearance of the first estate-grown Sauvignon Blanc in 87, Haywood has been making only estate-bottled wines. In its early history Haywood's reputation was largely based on its Rieslings. When that varietal wine failed to enjoy any kind of enduring popularity, Haywood began exploring other wines. Before long, he was offering a blended red named "Spaghetti Red" whose label was designed to show a splash of red sauce in one corner. Success with that wine encouraged Haywood to blend and bottle a "Linguine White." At times, the winery has made a Zinfandel in a ripe style that has earned our strong praise. Both Cabernet Sauvignon and Chardonnay have recently been well received, and Fumé Blanc has, from time to time, been among the best in California. Los Chamizal Vineyard, the original estate vineyard, is the origin of most of Haywood's present annual production of 30,000 cases. Racke, Buena Vista's owner, acquired a controlling interest in Haywood in 91.

Cabernet Sauvignon

81   82   83*   84*   85*   86   87

Typically blended with a portion of Merlot (12–18% in most recent vintages), the wine tends toward tannic toughness that can all but cover the underlying black-cherryish fruit

Chardonnay

84*   85   86   87   88   89*

Mixed results from a wine that can be coarse and closed-in if the fruit is not up to snuff

Zinfandel

81**   82*   83**   84***   85   86   88**

After a string of hits, the wine has fallen off in some recent years but, at its best, is full of ripe and rich, well-focused Zinfandel fruit

---

HEITZ WINE CELLARS   *Napa 1961*   This winery is located to the east of the Silverado Trail in an isolated area in mid–Napa Valley. Originally housed in the small building in St. Helena that now serves as its sales room, Heitz Wine Cellars began as a bottler of an assortment of wines, some purchased and blended and finished by winemaker Joe Heitz. Heitz made his first Cabernet in 65, and the next year had the good fortune of being offered the opportunity to make Cabernet from a single vineyard located in Oakville named Martha's Vineyard. It is the series of Martha's Vineyard Cabernets that placed Heitz Cellars at center stage. The 68 vintage was the first highly acclaimed bottling, and the 70 received even better reviews. Martha's Vineyard, a 34-acre parcel in the foothills west of Oakville, is sold only to Heitz, who makes about 4,000 cases of Cabernet from it each year. Over the years he has also made Cabernet fron the Fay Vineyard (now owned by Stag's Leap Wine Cellars), and from Bella Oaks (owned by Belle and Barny Rhodes, who developed the first 12 acres of Martha's Vineyard in 60).

A Napa Valley bottling is a regular part of the roster, first made from purchased grapes but since 86 from a newly acquired 75-acre vineyard on the Silverado Trail. The winery now owns a total of 115 acres. Heitz believes in making 100% Cabernet Sauvignon, and all of his bottlings age in French and American oak. In the late 60s and early 70s, he was highly regarded for Chardonnay, but many vintages have come and gone since a Heitz Chardonnay has earned a kind word.

Heitz once blended and bottled attractive Barbera, but in the 80s that wine was dropped. Nor has he enjoyed much success with Zinfandel, added in recent years. The only Heitz wine worthy of any notice after Cabernet is Grignolino, made into a pleasing regular bottling and a rosé. By the end of the 80s the winery's annual production was 35,000 cases. From its sales room in St. Helena, Heitz offers a lengthy list of older vintages, and every February makes its first offering of a new vintage of Martha's Vineyard. Many people, ourselves included, maintain that the 68 and 74 Martha's Vineyard Cabernets are among the best wines ever produced in California. Characteristically, the independent-minded Mr. Heitz thinks the 69 is his top effort.

Cabernet Sauvignon

(Martha's Vineyard)   68***   69**   70***   72**   73**   74***
75***   76**   77**   78**   79**   80**   81**   82*   83**
84**   85*   86*

*Clearly among the stars in California's Cabernet galaxy, this deeply cur-
ranty, always minty/eucalyptus-toned, long-aging wine has earned a
strong following for its two-decade record of outstanding performance; a
slight fall-off has been noticeable as the vineyard has aged, and the 85 was
less than stellar*

Cabernet Sauvignon

(Bella Oaks) 76** 77*** 78 80** 81* 82 83 84* 85
86

*Softer and focused on ripe cherry fruit, with hints of herbs and occasion-
ally of brush and dried bark, this wine can be round and rich in some
years, but has recently lacked the depth and prettiness that characterized
its early vintages*

HERBERT VINEYARDS *El Dorado 1982* In 74 Frank Herbert began developing a
14-acre vineyard on the hills south of Placerville. For several years, his crop
was sold to neighbors. In the early 80s Herbert tried his hand at making
Zinfandel, Sauvignon Blanc, and White Zinfandel. Annual output reached
1,000 cases. By 88 Herbert decided to back away from winemaking and sell
most of his grapes to Sierra Vista Vineyards. A year later, the winery was closed
after Herbert died.

HERITAGE CELLARS *Fresno 1984* Part of the Old Master Winery, a gift store and
restaurant complex in Fresno, Heritage Cellars produces a line of table wines
and brandies that win a fair share of medals and awards. Buying all grapes
from the North and Central Coast districts, Heritage Cellars regularly offers
Alexander Valley Cabernet Sauvignon, Sauvignon Blanc from the Central
Coast, Chardonnay from Monterey County, and California White Zinfandel.
Its annual production is close to 7,500 cases, including a small amount of
brandy under the "Old Master Cellars" label.

THE HESS COLLECTION *Napa 1982* Swiss-born Donald Hess came to California
seeking new sources of mineral water to expand Valser, his mineral water
business. Wine caught his attention, and in 78 he purchased 550 acres of
land on Mount Veeder from William Hill. Over the next several years he
developed vineyards that now cover 275 acres, equally divided between
Chardonnay and the Cabernet complex—Cabernet Sauvignon, Merlot, Cabernet Franc, Malbec, and Petit Verdot. Hess now owns 900 acres in Napa
Valley, with another 180 acres plantable. Part of his expanded holdings
came in 86 when he purchased the historic Mount La Salle Winery, owned
and operated by the Christian Brothers, who had decided to consolidate
their winemaking operations. After renovating the large facility, Hess chose
to build up his brand slowly, and until 88 sold most of the production to
other wineries. Hess's present intention is eventually to make 50,000 cases,
half Chardonnay and half Cabernet Sauvignon. The winemaking style favors 50% barrel fermentation for the Chardonnay, and extended maceration and long barrel aging (two years) for the Cabernet. On occasion the
winery offers a Reserve Cabernet.

The "Collection" in the brand name refers to the 13,000-square-foot art
gallery that Hess built in the winery to display his hundreds of paintings to the
public. The track record for Hess wines has so far been uneven, with Cabernet
Sauvignon occasionally earning * ratings. Chardonnay has not performed as
well.

HESS SELECT *(The Hess Collection)* Created in 1989, Hess Select is a second label
first used for Chardonnay made by the Hess Collection winery in Napa Valley.
Cabernet Sauvignon has been added to the line recently. These wines are
identified by a California appellation, but most of the grapes used originate in
Hess's 350-acre vineyard near Soledad in Monterey County. Simple, fruity,

and given short-term aging, the Hess Select wines are produced in the large Napa Valley facility.

HIDDEN CELLARS   *Mendocino 1981*   The winery once known primarily for its intriguing, artsy wrap-around label made strong quality strides in the late 80s. Located in Talmage east of Ukiah, Hidden Cellars is now making close to 15,000 cases of table wines for its label and conducts a busy custom-crush business as well. In the beginning, owner Dennis Patton emphasized white wine production. Over the first few vintages the results were somewhat uneven, and only the occasional dry-finished Gewurztraminer and dessert-style Riesling caught our attention. Starting in 86, Hidden Cellars began to improve as its Sauvignon Blanc and Chardonnay displayed better character and balance, and the 86 Zinfandel confirmed the upward course when it was released.

Nowadays, Patton buys all grapes from within Mendocino County and is offering a medium-intense Sauvignon Blanc of ✻ caliber. He ferments 75% of his Sauvignon Blanc in oak, and ages the wine *sur lie* for about nine months. Chardonnays are also partially barrel-fermented. Zinfandel from the old-vine Pacini Vineyard has offered deep berry fruit and solid varietal character. Among the lighter white wines, Hidden Cellars makes Riesling from the Potter Valley, which also supplies the winery with *Botrytis*-laden Semillon and Sauvignon Blanc for its dessert wine, "Chanson d'Or." Cabernet Sauvignon and Pinot Noir, both made in small quantities, fill out the line.

Chardonnay

84✻   85   86   87✻   88✻   89

Now showing solid middle-of-the-road varietal character, backed up by oak and ample acidity

Zinfandel

(Pacini Vineyard)   82   **83**   **84**   85   **86**✻✻   **87**✻   **88**✻

After a wobbly start with good grapes, quality has come up, and the latest efforts have shown admirable fruit and depth

WILLIAM HILL WINERY   *Napa 1976*   After graduating from the University of Oklahoma, William Hill earned an MBA at Stanford and by 74 was deeply involved in vineyard development. Always fascinated with precipitous mountain vineyards, Hill began by developing a steep site high in the mountains west of Calistoga, planting 120 acres to Cabernet Sauvignon and Chardonnay. In 77 this property, now known as Diamond Mountain Ranch, was sold to Sterling Vineyards. From 500 acres he owned on Mount Veeder, Hill developed 200 acres of vineyards, selling them to the Hess Collection in 78. Hill has always been in the process of selling this, buying that, putting together a partnership here, there, and everywhere. He retained another Mount Veeder parcel known as Veeder Peak and planted 70 acres. By the end of the 80s he owned 100 acres on the slopes of Atlas Peak, and another 120 in the Soda Canyon pocket. Further up the slopes, on a 1,200-acre parcel, Hill developed and then sold 170 acres under vine to an international group, now known as Atlas Peak Vineyards.

Hill started producing wines in rented facilities in 76, specializing first in Cabernet Sauvignon and then in 78 in Chardonnay from vineyards developed in southern Napa Valley—Mount Veeder, Atlas Peak, and the Carneros. By the end of the 80s he was making over 45,000 cases a year of Chardonnay and 20,000 cases of Cabernet Sauvignon. Two separate bottlings of each are made—a Silver label and a Reserve, once identified by a gold label. The Chardonnays are barrel-fermented in new French oak, while the Reserve Chardonnay is oak-aged for at least eight months prior to bottling. The Silver-label Chardonnay is partially barrel-fermented and bottled sooner.

All of Hill's Cabernets have been from the Mount Veeder area. The Reserve Cabernet, picked as the best from the vintage, is aged in small oak for close to two years. The Silver-label Cabernet is given one year of barrel aging. In the late 80s Hill's vineyard development instincts took him to Sonoma County, where he owned vineyard sites on Sonoma Mountain and on Sugarloaf Mountain, both in Sonoma Valley. He and partners bought 500 acres of bare land in Mendocino's Anderson Valley in late 89. The following year, Hill accepted an offer to sell William Hill Winery and its Napa Valley vineyards to the Wine Alliance, the wine division of Hiram Walker, which also owns Callaway and Clos du Bois.

Cabernet Sauvignon

(Gold Label/Reserve)   82 * *   83 * *   84 * *   85 *   87 *

Ripe and briary with solid tanning, the wine usually has sufficient fruit for balance

Chardonnay

(Gold Label/Reserve)   84   85   86 * *   87 * *   88 *

Oaky and ripe with appley fruit at the center

HMR   *San Luis Obispo 1972*   Originally known as Hoffman Mountain Ranch, this wine venture actually began in 62 when Dr. Stanley Hoffman and family purchased the large ranch (1,002 acres total) and began developing the estate vineyard. Located in the foothills west of Paso Robles, the vineyard was expanded to 63 acres, and at one time the wines made from the 24 acres of Pinot Noir were looked upon as the great hope for that varietal. In its first several vintages the winery produced Chardonnay, Cabernet Sauvignon, Zinfandel, Chenin Blanc, Franken Riesling, several Rosés, and small amounts of Pinot Noir. When properly balanced and avoiding overripe, raisiny character, the Pinot Noirs justified the excitement, but they were not made frequently enough and in large enough quantities to carry the winery. By 80, Hoffman Mountain Ranch was experiencing financial problems. It expanded production and that tactic worked, but the Hoffmans were forced to sell in 82.

An investment firm from Los Angeles bought the company and renamed it HMR, Ltd. They managed to keep afloat through 85. For reasons now buried in history, they decided to market wines under a second label, Santa Lucia Cellars. The label, a too-close-for-comfort copy of that used by the legendary French producer Domaine de la Romanée-Conti, led to a lawsuit. HMR did not win, and not long afterwards, the company went belly up. The Wells Fargo Bank took possession of the property and determined during receivership that it did not want to make wine. Instead, grapes from the HMR estate were sold to several wineries. By 89, the property was sold to an international corporation, with one owner from Japan, and it began doing business as the San Luis Obispo Winery, Inc. Its first crush was in 90.

HONIG CELLARS   *Napa 1980*   In 66 Louis Honig bought a 67-acre ranch and old vineyard from Charlie Wagner of Caymus. The vineyard was renamed HNW and the Honigs ventured into the grape-growing business. By 80 Bill Honig, Louis's son, and Daniel Weinstein, his son-in-law, began guiding the project into winemaking. Bill Honig is known to many as California's Superintendent of Public Instruction, a role he assumed in 82. A few hundred cases of 80 Sauvignon Blanc were made and bottled under a garish HNW label. Both the name and the label soon changed to the present versions. The Honig vineyard is highly esteemed for Sauvignon Blanc, and has sold grapes to Vichon every year. Honig Cellars made only Sauvignon Blanc, until adding Chardonnay and Cabernet Sauvignon in 87. The 67-acre vineyard, after several changes, now consists of 29 acres of Sauvignon Blanc, 18 acres of Cabernet Sauvignon, 4 acres of Merlot, and 6 acres of Chardonnay. With close to 10,000 cases a year of Sauvignon Blanc, Honig has steadily improved its performance and in recent vintages has been a consistent * version with excellent depth. With vineyard maturity, Cabernet Sauvignon production should level off at 3,000 cases and Chardonnay at a little over 1,000 cases a year. Since it opened, the 30,000-case-capacity facility has custom-made wines for many clients. For their own brand, the Honigs see 13,000 cases as maximum.

HOP KILN WINERY *Sonoma 1975* Located in the Russian River Valley, this winery, a converted hop kiln, is a state historical landmark. Surrounded by its 65-acre vineyard, Hop Kiln produces eight varietals, two blends ("Marty's Big Red" and "A Thousand Flowers White"), and an unusual sparkling wine named "Verveux." Even since it began, the winery has been best known for sturdy reds, particularly its intense, heavy-bodied Petite Sirah and its compact, ripe Zinfandel. Both red varietals are produced from nonirrigated vineyards planted around 20. A medium-sweet Riesling is often appealing at an average-quality level. Occasionally, a dry-finished, assertive, and unusually full-bodied Gewurztraminer rises to the * level. However, sustained success with red wines prompted Dr. Marty Griffin, Hop Kiln's owner, to expand its production of Cabernet Sauvignon. In the late 80s, the winery planted 10 acres to Cabernet, and purchased enough grapes from growers to produce over 1,000 cases of Cabernet. Currently, the winery's total production is 9,000 cases a year. It remains one of the more rewarding wineries to visit.

Zinfandel

83 84* 85* 86* 87** 88*

More power than finesse is packed by this very ripe, gutsy wine, which is not designed for the faint of heart

HOUTZ VINEYARDS *Santa Barbara 1984* Near Los Olivos in the Santa Ynez Valley, this small winery is owned and operated by the Houtz family. After leaving the real estate business in Los Angeles, Dave Houtz was ready for the first crush in 84, which yielded 1,000 cases. From its 16-acre vineyard, Houtz offers Chardonnay, Sauvignon Blanc, and Cabernet Sauvignon. Both its Chardonnay and Sauvignon Blanc are barrel-fermented. Houtz also makes an oak-aged Chenin Blanc from a neighboring vineyard, and a pink Blanc of Cabernet Sauvignon in a slightly sweet style. Both the Chenin Blanc and Sauvignon Blanc offer straightforward varietal character. The winery's annual production has reached the optimum 4,000-case level.

ROBERT HUNTER *Sonoma 1980* Robert Hunter owns 45 acres of Chardonnay and Pinot Noir in the Sonoma Valley. He has sold grapes to many wineries over the last two decades, one of the best known being Chateau St. Jean, which made vineyard-designated Robert Hunter Chardonnay in the late 70s. In 80, Hunter decided to use part of his vineyard to make sparkling wine by the *méthode champenoise*. One version was a Brut de Noirs, made predominantly from Pinot Noir with small amounts of Chardonnay and Pinot Blanc. Though the quality was somewhat variable, Hunter enjoyed modest success as the brand grew to about 8,000 cases. Production took place in rented space, but that arrangement began to deteriorate in 87. Hunter ceased production in 88, pending the establishment of his own facility.

HUSCH VINEYARDS *Mendocino 1968* As the first winery after Prohibition to open in the Anderson Valley, Husch struggled through its early few pioneering vintages. Founder Tony Husch worked hard and achieved moderate success, but decided to sell the winery in 79 to the Oswald family, longtime grape growers who owned the 110-acre La Ribera Vineyard near Ukiah and another 50 acres in Anderson Valley. The Oswalds invested in winery equipment and improved the facility. Under their ownership, Husch steadily improved, and today puts out a line of varietals ranging from average to * without wide variations.

From the Anderson Valley appellation, Husch offers Gewurztraminers which are often superb, along with an increasingly enjoyable Pinot Noir. Sauvignon Blanc, Cabernet Sauvignon, Chenin Blanc, and Chardonnay are from the Mendocino appellation, usually made entirely from the winery's La Ribera Vineyards near Ukiah. Made in a slightly sweet style, both Gewurztraminer and Chenin Blanc are usually reliable. One of the most consistent wines on a * track is Husch's always likable Chardonnay. Partially barrel-fermented, Husch Sauvignon Blanc has earned *. The most variable wine is

Cabernet Sauvignon. La Ribera Vineyards is a name used for a second level of Cabernet Sauvignon and blended white. All told, Husch makes 25,000 cases a year.

Chardonnay

84*   85*   86*   87*   88*

Consistently fruity and firmed by perky acidity, medium-bodied, quietly okay; a good value in every vintage to date

---

INGLENOOK–NAPA VALLEY *Napa 1879* From the time Gustave Niebaum founded Inglenook until his grandnephew John Daniel, Jr., sold it in 64, Inglenook was known as a pioneer and as a producer of high-quality wines, particularly Cabernet Sauvignon. Under the direction of the Daniel family (J. Daniel, Jr.'s heirs now operate Dominus and Merryvale), Inglenook offered a regular and a Special Cask Cabernet Sauvignon (introduced in 49) from its holdings adjacent to the winery located on the west side of the wine road in Rutherford. Up until the early 60s, Inglenook's Cabernet's competed head-on with those from Beaulieu and Charles Krug.

In 64 the winery and most of its acreage (except for the 100 acres known as Napanook) was purchased by Allied Grape Growers. In 69, they were in turn bought by giant Heublein, which expanded production throughout the 70s. The name Inglenook was extended to cover three lines of wines: Napa Valley varietals, the main group; a lengthy list of varietals and generics lumped together under the "Inglenook Vintage" label; and a line labeled "Inglenook Navalle," which relied on grapes grown in the Central Valley where the bottling occurred. This volume-oriented Navalle jug line all but ruined the once proud Inglenook name.

In 79, faced with a faltering image, Heublein's wine division decided to reverse the direction and begin a major revitalization program. This included restoring the old winery, replanting the original vineyard, and improving the quality of the wines bottled. The new label emphasizes Inglenook–Napa Valley to differentiate it from Inglenook Navalle. The roster was trimmed to six varietals, but has grown since with the expansion of a Reserve program that includes Cabernet Sauvignon, Merlot, Chardonnay, and Sauvignon Blanc. In 83, "Reunion," a new proprietary wine made primarily from Cabernet Sauvignon, appeared. Made from the original vineyards used by John Daniel, Jr., to produce Inglenook's fabled vintages, Reunion has earned * and ** in its early issues. In 85, Inglenook added "Niebaum Reserve Claret," a limited-production, ageworthy red Bordeaux blend. To complete the renewed emphasis on Bordeaux wines, Inglenook has been bottling "Gravion," a proprietary blend of oak-aged Semillon and Sauvignon Blanc. With 72 acres owned in Rutherford and the Carneros, along with long-term leasing arrangements on 270 acres in the Napa Valley, Inglenook currently produces about 150,000 cases annually. Close to 50,000 cases are Cabernet Sauvignon; Chardonnay is the second most important wine by volume.

Cabernet Sauvignon

80*   81   82*   83*   85*   86

A direct, ripe cherry and curranty offering, with moderate oak, and evident but unimposing tannins

Chardonnay

(regular bottling)   84   85   86*   88   89

(Reserve)   84*   85*   86*

Straightforward, presentable wines, with citrus, apple, and oak qualities; medium depth at best for the regular bottling and more obvious oak in the Reserve

Merlot

(Reserve)   83**   85**   86

Save for the 86, which was out of form, this has been a fruity, rich, firm wine, which has handsomely combined moderately deep cherry and currant character and creamy oak

INGLENOOK NAVALLE, NAVALLE SELECTIONS *(Inglenook)* Since the mid-70s Inglenook has used Navalle in some form for a line of wines priced on the low end. Rather belatedly, Heublein, the parent company, sensed that Inglenook Navalle, the first label used, was harming the name Inglenook more than helping the sales of the Navalle line. Today, the primary label for a line of inexpensive varietals is "Navalle Selections." It covers Chardonnay, Sauvignon Blanc, Cabernet Sauvignon, and White Zinfandel, all from the California appellation and all bottled in 750-ml and 1.5-liter containers. Navalle Selections is headquartered in Madera, where Heublein operates a large facility also used for Almadén Vineyards, Blossom Hill, Sylvan Springs, and others. However, Heublein continues using the Inglenook Navalle name, primarily for generics in magnums and for a line of varietals and generics sold in 18-liter bag-in-the-box containers. Brands with Navalle in their name represent annual sales of 2.5 million cases.

INNISFREE *Napa 1984* This winery is located on the property of Joseph Phelps Vineyards, and though not owned by Joe Phelps, it surely owes much to him. Innisfree belongs to Steve Carlin, a longtime employee of Phelps who is now the national sales director for Phelps Vineyards. When Carlin expressed a desire to leave and start his own winery, Phelps offered to back him and assist in any other ways needed. Making Chardonnay and Cabernet Sauvignon, Innisfree buys in all its grapes, usually from Phelps-owned vineyards. Its Chardonnays are a blend from Yountville, Carneros, and the Stags Leap regions. The Cabernet Sauvignons are made from grapes grown adjacent to Phelps Vineyards, with Merlot used in the blend originating from Stags Leap. Total production is now at the optimum 22,000 cases a year. Chardonnay, including a limited-volume Carneros bottling, accounts for 80%, and Cabernet for 20%. Carlin's desire is to keep Innisfree wines priced slightly below the competition, which has made them attractive values when they succeed.

Cabernet Sauvignon

86   87   88 *

Generally showing cherryish fruit, sometimes lacking in depth and excitement

Chardonnay

84 *   85   86   87   88 *   89

Direct and nicely focused fruit of medium depth lifts this quietly oaked wine in better vintages

IRON HORSE VINEYARDS *Sonoma 1978* This winery is known more for its sparkling wines than for its agreeable but not quite as successful table wines. In 76 owners Audrey and Barry Sterling purchased an old estate and 300-acre ranch that was once a railroad stop named Iron Horse. A corporate attorney, Barry Sterling took on one-time vineyard manager Forrest Tancer as a partner in the establishment. Situated in a cool growing region near Sebastopol in Sonoma's Green Valley, the surrounding vineyards, first developed independently by Tancer, now cover 110 acres, evenly divided between Chardonnay and Pinot Noir. Another vineyard in the warmer Alexander Valley contains 44 acres and is planted to Cabernet Sauvignon (20 acres), Sauvignon Blanc (12 acres), Cabernet Franc (3 acres), Viognier (6 acres), and Sangiovese (3 acres).

In its first decade, Iron Horse developed a strong following for its barrel-fermented, rich, balanced Fumé Blanc, a frequent * performer that rises to * * on occasion. Introduced with the 80 vintage, the winery's sparkling wines started on a small scale but have grown in quantity and in quality. Both the Brut and Blanc de Blancs have been in the * * category on several occasions. It offers two other sparklers in significant quantities—a Blanc de Noirs labeled

"Wedding Cuvée" and a deeply hued Brut Rosé. After the 84 vintage, Cabernet Sauvignon was replaced in the roster by "Cabernets," a blend of Cabernet Sauvignon and Cabernet Franc. For volume, Chardonnay is the winery's major varietal. Barrel-fermented, it displays apple character in a crisp, lemony style. Though fairly successful, Zinfandel was dropped from the line after 82. Pinot Noir, made in small quantities, completes the line.

Total production at Iron Horse is 32,000 to 34,000 cases a year, equally divided between table wine and sparkling wine. Lesser-quality, early-maturing Pinot Noir is bottled under the "Tin Pony" second label. In the 90s, Iron Horse and Laurent Perrier of Champagne hooked up in a joint venture to produce sparkling wine from vineyards in the Sonoma Green Valley.

Cabernet Sauvignon/Cabernets

80   81   82 *   83   84   85   86 *   87 * *

Now containing about 35% Cabernet Franc, this tight, black-cherryish wine has needed more depth of character to measure up, regardless of title and blend changes

Chardonnay

84 *   85   86 *   87 *   88 *   89 *

Blossomy fruit with citrusy overtones and background oak are carried in a typically medium- to medium-full-bodied wine, whose crisp acidity usually takes an extra year or two to soften

---

JAEGER CELLAR   *Napa 1979*   Starting in 68, Bill Jaeger developed a vineyard adjacent to his home south of St. Helena. Named Inglewood Vineyard, it is a 20-acre parcel planted primarily to Merlot, with Cabernet Sauvignon and Cabernet Franc also grown. Jaeger, an owner of Freemark Abbey and managing partner of Rutherford Hill Winery, sent the first several crops to those wineries until deciding to bottle Merlot under the Jaeger Cellar label. Crushed and fermented at Rutherford Hill under the supervision of Joe Cafaro, Jaeger Merlot (usually blended with 15% Cabernet Sauvignon and 5% Cabernet Franc) ages two years in Nevers oak barrels and receives two years of bottle aging in Jaeger's cellars near the home and vineyard. The production of Jaeger Merlot grew steadily until peaking at 5,000 cases. Generally, Jaeger Merlot, offering considerable depth and rather tough tannins, has been on a * track.

THOMAS JAEGER WINERY   *San Diego 1989*   Owned by the Jaegers (owners of Rutherford Hill Winery and Jaeger Cellar) and their youngest son, Paul Thomas, this winery is the former San Pasqual Vineyards, which the new owners took over in 89. Before its sale, San Pasqual had grown in production to a peak of 25,000 cases. By the mid-80s the founders were losing interest and their 20-acre vineyard was losing its battle against a vine pest. The first Thomas Jaeger wines to appear, made from the old vineyard and purchased grapes, consisted of Chardonnay, Sauvignon Blanc, and White Zinfandel. Initial output of 5,000 cases is about half of what the owners view as their long-term goal.

JEKEL VINEYARDS   *Monterey 1978*   One of the first wineries to commit itself to Monterey County, Jekel began by developing vineyards in the Greenfield area in 72. Founded by twins, Bill and Gus Jekel, the winery and vineyards have been under the control of Bill and his wife, Pat, since 86. The winery continues to enjoy a reputation for consistency with Johannisberg Riesling if not its other wines. Now made in three styles—a medium-sweet (2%) bottling, another labeled "Sweet Styled," and, when possible, a late harvest—Rieslings represent over one-third of Jekel's annual output and 125 acres in its 327-acre vineyard. Chardonnay, made in regular and Private Reserve bottlings, is the next major variety, planted at 116 acres, while at 80 acres Cabernet Sauvignon and its consorts (Merlot and Cabernet Franc) follow in importance. These three varietals—Riesling, Chardonnay, and Cabernet Sauvignon—account for 90% of the winery's production. Limited amounts of Muscat Canelli and Cabernet Franc are regularly offered. After working with Pinot Noir and

Pinot Blanc as varietals for almost a decade, Jekel has dropped both. All wines carry the Arroyo Seco appellation. The winemaking facility has a capacity of 85,000 cases a year. In early 90, the Jekels agreed to sell the entire operation to Vintech, but regained ownership a year later.

Chardonnay

84* 85* 86 87* 88* 89

Fighting a tendency to be over-oaked and lacking in fruit, the wine succeeds best when it is able to capture elements of brightness and balance that keep its ripe, appley fruit at the center of attention

JEPSON VINEYARDS *Mendocino 1986* Banker and entrepreneur Robert Jepson bought the winery, inventory, and vineyards of the former William Baccala Estate (founded 82) in 86 and was able to have Jepson wines on the market within a few months of the purchase. The winery is situated between Hopland and Ukiah, with its 108-acre vineyard located across the road to the east. Chardonnay and Sauvignon Blanc represent about 90% of the total acreage and are the primary wines produced. A Reserve Chardonnay, 100% barrel-fermented, is made in small volume. About 10 acres of French Colombard, used for a generic white table wine, are adjacent to the winery. In 88 the winery introduced its line of *méthode champenoise* sparkling wine. Made 100% from Chardonnay, the winery's Brut Blanc de Blancs has been of * quality. Jepson also produces a brandy made by the pot-still method. This Cognac-style brandy is well worth seeking out, but the annual output is small (less than 500 cases). Its Blanc de Blancs production averages 3,500 cases. Jepson's Chardonnay and Sauvignon Blanc remain the mainstays and currently account for most of the 17,000 cases produced each year. With expansion of the facility, annual total production could grow to 30,000 cases.

Chardonnay

85* 86 87*

Straightforwardly fruity, tending toward apples, with hints of blossoms, quietly oaked, well balanced

JOANNA VINEYARD *Napa 1984* Richard and Jack Ryno are partners in this small winery, located in Yountville. They have been buying all grapes to produce a range of varietals, each made in small (150- to 300-case) lots. The roster regularly includes Chardonnay, Cabernet Sauvignon, and Sauvignon Blanc. White Zinfandel and Muscat Canelli have also been produced. Annual production is expected to double in the 90s to 2,000 cases total.

JOHNSON TURNBULL VINEYARDS *Napa 1979* Longtime friends and associates Bill Turnbull and Reverdy Johnson purchased a dilapidated farmhouse and a neglected 20-acre vineyard in 77. Turnbull had been an architect who helped design the Sea Ranch community on the North Coast, and Johnson served as the project's lawyer. Their plan was to sell grapes and use the remodeled farmhouse as a weekend retreat. The vineyard, originally planted in 67, was in the middle of prime Cabernet Sauvignon turf just north of Oakville. Johnson and Turnbull began replanting, ending up with four separate blocks covering 20 acres (18½ of Cabernet, 1½ of Cabernet Franc). In 78 their neighbor Cakebread Cellars made a Cabernet from their grapes, identifying the wine with a "JT L-1" label. The grapes came from the oldest block, a 5-acre parcel since used by Johnson Turnbull for its occasional "Special Reserve" bottling.

From time to time the winery bottles each vineyard separately, identifying the bottlings by the date the vineyard was planted. Most of the time, its Cabernet is a blend of all vineyards. Aged an average of nine months in large American oak uprights, followed by a year in small French oak barrels, the winery's Cabernets often display a distinctive minty-eucalyptus character, possibly due to the presence of eucalyptus trees bordering one vineyard. When their Cabernet vineyards are in full production, Johnson Turnbull will level off at 5,000 cases. This total will eventually be matched by Chardonnay made from the 18-acre Teviot Springs Vineyard situated at the southern end of Knights Valley. This vineyard was planted to four Chardonnay clones in 83, and four years later the winery's first Chardonnay was made. Partially barrel-fermented, with only a small portion undergoing malolactic fermentation, the Chardonnays are aged in French oak puncheons and barrels.

Cabernet Sauvignon

80 * *   81 * *   82 *   83 *   84 *   85   86 (Lot 67) *   86 (Lot 82)
87 (Lot 67) *

Always enormously minty, and backed by lots of sweet oak, the wine often delivers satisfactory amounts of fruit to bring itself into balance

---

JOHNSON'S OF ALEXANDER VALLEY WINES   *Sonoma 1975*   Back in the late 60s the Johnson brothers converted 50 acres of pears and prunes to vineyards. After selling grapes for a few years, they branched out into winemaking, building a small winery next to the vineyards in the heart of the Alexander Valley. Within a decade, they were producing a fairly wide range of varietals. Blush wines—White Zinfandel and Pinot Noir Blanc—were added to bring their annual output close to 10,000 cases by 85. Now, after some reorganization, Tom Johnson is the manager and his daughter Ellen is the winemaker. They focus production on White Zinfandel, Cabernet Sauvignon, Chardonnay, and Johannisberg Riesling. Most of the current production is sold direct from their tasting room. To date, the winery's quality record has generated very little acclaim.

JORDAN VINEYARDS   *Sonoma 1976*   The imposing Jordan Winery and family estate are situated on a hilltop east of Healdsburg. The winery, which is not open to the public, draws from its 200 acres of Cabernet Sauvignon and Merlot, and 50 acres of Chardonnay. All varieties are planted in the Alexander Valley and contribute to an annual production of 85,000 cases. The winery's mainstay, Cabernet Sauvignon, accounts for 60,000 cases. Owned by Tom Jordan, a geologist specializing in oil exploration, the winery had developed a special cachet even before it marketed its second vintage. At first, only Cabernet Sauvignon was to be produced. Debuting with a well-reviewed 76 Cabernet, the winery was able to make its first estate-bottled offering in 1978. From that time on, Jordan has followed a relatively long aging program, in which a new vintage is released about four years after the harvest. Situated in a low-lying area close to the river's edge, the estate vineyards have to be carefully cultivated to try to control excessive vigor, which can contribute a herbal-vegetal character.

Over the first 10 vintages, Jordan's Cabernet did not quite live up to the high early expectations. Even though most Cabernet vintages have, with the exception of the dismal 82, been enjoyable, only a few standout vintages have been awarded * *. The caveat among those who fault Jordan Cabernet is its early appeal and lack of ageability. The majority of Jordan's Chardonnays, moreover, have been heavy and oaky, and not always clean. Neither the Cabernet Sauvignon nor the Chardonnay, even in better years, has been good enough to stand at the top of its class. Jordan has been experimenting with sparkling wine for years and its first offering, labeled "J," appeared in 91.

Cabernet Sauvignon

80 * *   81   82   83 *   84 *   85 *   86 *

Soft, ripish, black-cherryish, and cedary character, sometimes high in herbal notes, lightly tannic, and supple on the palate

---

JORY WINES   *Santa Clara 1986*   Occupying space in a large defunct winery in Los Gatos, Jory makes the majority of its wines from the local Santa Clara area. The specialties are Chardonnay (regular and Reserve) and Pinot Noir, which account for over 60% of its 5,000-case output. In small lots of 300 to 500 cases it also offers Gamay Beaujolais, Pinot Blanc, Merlot, Mourvedre, and a *méthode champenoise* Champagne. Labeled "Mistral," the sparkling wine is made from barrel-fermented Pinot Blanc. Jory Chardonnays are frequently produced from the San Ysidro Vineyard. On occasion, it bottles wines deemed to be of lesser quality as "Vin Jory." To date the wine quality has been inconsistent.

JOULLIAN VINEYARDS *Monterey 1987* Located in the Carmel Valley, Joullian is neighbor to Durney Vineyards. Co-owner and winemaker Ray Watson is a former wine merchant whose brother is the pro golfer Tom Watson. Inspired by early vintages of Durney Cabernet, Watson purchased the large ranch in 82, and since then has developed 40 acres of vineyards. The leading varieties are Cabernet Sauvignon, Merlot, Chardonnay, Sauvignon Blanc, and Semillon. After producing experimental-size quantities its first two vintages, Joullian managed its first substantial crush in 88, when it produced 1,000 cases of barrel-fermented Chardonnay, 1,000 cases of Sauvignon Blanc (blended with 15% Semillon), and 600 cases of Cabernet Sauvignon (blended with Merlot and Cabernet Franc). With vineyard maturity, Joullian is expected to produce 10,000 cases a year, 50% consisting of Cabernet Sauvignon, 25% of Chardonnay, and 25% Sauvignon Blanc. Over the early vintages the winery used the "Cepage" label for small-batch bottlings.

JUSTIN VINEYARDS & WINERY *San Luis Obispo 1987* An investment banker for two decades, Justin Baldwin branched out into the grape and wine business in 82, acquiring 165 acres of land in the Paso Robles appellation. His 65-acre vineyard, located 15 miles west of the town of Paso Robles, is the most westerly of any in the area. Specializing in two wines—Chardonnay and a red Bordeaux blend—he planted 30 acres of Chardonnay, 25 acres of Cabernet Sauvignon, and 5 acres each of Merlot and Cabernet Franc. Baldwin prefers wines that are ripe and full-bodied, and his Chardonnays are 100% barrel-fermented in new oak. Over the first several vintages, the production held at 3,500 cases, with 60% consisting of the Bordeaux blend and 40% of Chardonnay. From time to time the winery bottles small amounts of Cabernet Sauvignon, Merlot, and Cabernet Franc. When the estate vineyards are mature, production will grow to 12,000 cases a year.

KALIN CELLARS *Marin 1976* Owner Terry Leighton is a microbiologist at U.C. Berkeley, and a winemaker in his spare time. Using a warehouse in the town of Novato, he produces Chardonnay, Pinot Noir, Semillon, Cabernet Sauvignon, and sparkling wines. In a typical year Kalin bottles several Chardonnays, and in recent vintages the recurring appellations have been Livermore Valley, Potter Valley, Russian River Valley, and Sonoma Valley. In addition, he identifies the grower by a system of lettered cuvées. Kalin Chardonnays, often highly rated and earning ✺ ✺ in 87 for both Cuvée "LV" and Cuvée "W," are barrel-fermented, and are put through malolactic fermentation. Usually they display a strong oak component and depth, and often are successful, albeit in a weighty, viscous style. Pinot Noirs from Potter Valley and Sonoma Valley are highly variable. Barrel-fermented Semillons from the Livermore Valley are often among the most noteworthy efforts with the varietal. Production, including a few hundred cases of sparkling wine made by the *méthode champenoise*, is at the facility's capacity level of 6,000 cases.

KARLY WINES *Amador 1979* A family-owned and -operated winery, Karly developed a 17-acre vineyard in the 70s. Larry "Buck" Cobb and his wife, Karly, planted Zinfandel and Sauvignon Blanc, with a small amount of Petite Sirah. The latter, sometimes blended into the winery's Zinfandel, is most often bottled as a limited-volume varietal. Over its first decade, Karly produced Chardonnay from different sources within the Central Coast region and then shifted to Napa Valley for Chardonnay. More recently, it has been offering an Edna Valley Chardonnay under the quaint "Mr. MacGregor's" label. Karly's Amador Sauvignon Blancs, big-bodied wines with a creamy oak texture and a figgy character, have risen on occasion to ✺ level. Though somewhat erratic, Karly's Zinfandels (about 2,500 cases per year) belong to the big, brawny, no-holds-barred school. This also holds true for the vineyard-designated "Sadie Upton" Zinfandel. White Zinfandel rose to prominence in the middle of the 80s and brought the winery's annual output close to the 9,000-case maximum.

Zinfandel

80** 81* 82* 83* 84 85 86* 87 88

Ripe, brawny, full-bodied, sometimes tarry and bordering on the overripe, usually rich in creamy oak

---

ROBERT KEENAN WINERY *Napa 1977* In the early 70s, Robert Keenan purchased the defunct Conradi Winery, a 180-acre estate located at the 1,700-foot level on Spring Mountain. Conradi began operating in 1904, but did not recover after Prohibition. Some 47 acres were planted by Keenan to Cabernet Sauvignon, Chardonnay, and Merlot. A stone winery was set into the hillside for natural cooling. In 78, because his own vineyard was not then in full production, Keenan was purchasing grapes from Winery Lake Vineyard, a famous vineyard in the Carneros region. To obtain that grower's Chardonnay in sufficient quantity, Keenan took more Merlot than was needed for blending with Cabernet Sauvignon. As a result of the surplus, he reluctantly bottled Merlot as a varietal, but the quality of that first bottling earned such high praise that Merlot became a regular and successful part of the line. Always a blend of Merlot from Carneros and hillside locales, the wine today represents 25% of the winery's 12,000-case output. Two Chardonnays are bottled, one from the estate vineyard, Ann's Vineyard, which is fermented in stainless steel, and another from Napa Valley (a blend of Carneros and estate-grown fruit) that is partially barrel-fermented. The Chardonnays account for 5,000 cases a year, and Cabernet Sauvignon remains steady at 3,000 cases a year.

Cabernet Sauvignon

78* 79** 80** 81 82* 83** 84* 85* 86** 87

Medium-density cherry, currant, and quietly herbal fruit is firmed by noticeable tannin in this series of ageworthy wines

Chardonnay

(Napa Valley) 84* 85** 86* 87 88* 89*

(Ann's Vineyard) 86* 87

The Napa Valley bottling is the bigger, richer, of the two, while the Ann's Vineyard wine offers tighter, more wiry fruit

Merlot

82** 83*** 84** 85* 86* 87

Rated among the top Merlots in many vintages, the wine is rich, round on the palate, and fairly deep in ripe cherry fruit; its medium tannins have helped it to age well

---

KENDALL-JACKSON VINEYARDS *Lake 1982* Starting out with modest goals, San Francisco attorney Jess Jackson bought a vineyard near Clear Lake in the early 70s. His grapes were sold for a few years, until he decided to make wine under the Chateau du Lac brand. Shortly after changing the name to Kendall-Jackson, Jackson started on a course to make this producer one of the major stories of the 80s. With the assistance of well-known winemaker-consultant Ric Forman, Jackson entered the battlefield with an 81 Chardonnay, a blend of grapes from several regions that carried the California appellation. Produced even before the winery was completed, this first Chardonnay was widely appealing and a critical success. With the 83 vintage, Jackson hired Jed Steele as winemaker, and the combination clicked. From that year on, the brand grew, the success stories multiplied, and Jackson began expanding his vineyard and wine empire. Steele, formerly of Edmeades Vineyards in Mendocino's Anderson Valley, proved to be a master blender, maker of larger and larger blends of Chardonnay from North Coast and Central Coast grapes. At the same time, he produced an array of small-batch Zinfandels (Dupratt-DePratie Vineyard, Mariah Vineyard, Zeni, and Ciapusci Vineyard). In 85 he elevated Kendall-Jackson Cabernet to the big time with a Cabernet-Bordeaux blend named "Cardinale." In 86 a limited-volume Syrah from the cool-climate Durell Vineyard was added to his credits.

The only challenge left was Sauvignon Blanc. In 88, the winery made a highly popular, well-focused Sauvignon Blanc, Lake County, Vintner's Reserve, and paired it with a barrel-fermented stablemate from the Jackson Vineyard to win still more critical plaudits. While Steele was crafting an array of often-exciting wines, owner Jackson was off shopping. After failing to acquire Corbett Canyon, he bought 1,000 acres of Tepusquet Vineyard in the Central Coast, a region that had been contributing to Kendall-Jackson's Chardonnays. Later he purchased the winery and vineyards in Sonoma County once known as Zellerbach Vineyards. In 88 he bought the defunct Edmeades Vineyards in Anderson Valley, Steele's old haunt. Cambria Winery & Vineyard was the name of his facility in Santa Maria Valley. In Lake County, Jackson owns 80 acres of vineyards; in Sonoma County, he has 200; and in Santa Maria, he has 1,000 total acres under vine. Under the Kendall-Jackson label, he produces over 400,000 cases a year. Close to half of that is Chardonnay, led by the partially barrel-fermented Vintner's Reserve, presently accounting for 175,000 cases. Jed Steele left in 91.

Cabernet Sauvignon
(Cardinale)   83   84*   85*   86*

Ripe, herbal, sometimes loamy and tarry, fleshy and fairly full-bodied, with moderate tannins; only moderate aging

Cabernet Sauvignon
(Lake County and other titles)   83   84   86   87*

Throughout changes in appellation and nomenclature, Kendall-Jackson's other Cabernets have been fruitier, firmer, less ripe than Cardinale in orientation. The 85 Proprietor's Reserve was stunning

Chardonnay
(Vintner's Reserve)   84*   85*   86*   88*   89

The quintessential "popular-styled" Chardonnay, it is always fruity, a little on the blossomy side, usually slightly sweet-tasting without being cloying, and meant to be drunk young

Chardonnay
(Proprietor's Reserve)   83*   84*   85*   86*   87***   88

Barrel-fermented and often showing more depth and range than the Vintner's Reserve, as well as more aging potential, the wine is nonetheless oriented to appley and lightly floral fruit, with oak showing up in a supporting role

---

KATHRYN KENNEDY WINERY   *Santa Clara 1979*   Originally the vineyard was established by Kathryn Kennedy to discourage developers in the area who wanted to build a road through an open field adjacent to her home. In 1973, 8 acres were planted (now it is 9½) to Cabernet Sauvignon, and the first wine was made in 79. The small winery is located close to the original Paul Masson Winery in Saratoga. The annual production of Cabernet Sauvignon from the nonirrigated vineyards varies widely, but averaged 500 cases a year in the 80s. Approximately 1,000 cases a year is the maximum production goal for the Santa Cruz Mountains appellation Cabernet Sauvignon. "Lateral," a Bordeaux blend of Merlot and Cabernet Franc from purchased grapes, is the only other wine produced. The quality for the estate Cabernet has been generally above average, and most vintages seem capable of medium-term aging.

KENWOOD VINEYARDS   *Sonoma 1970*   Within its first decade, the present owners transformed an old jug-wine facility in the Sonoma Valley town of Kenwood into a modern winery offering a range of varietals. In the early years, wine-maker Bob Kozlowski was responsible for many top-notch reds. Partners Mike and Marty Lee, along with John Sheela, their brother-in-law, kept plugging away and over the next few years transformed Kenwood into a first-class, full-range winery, offering good- to excellent-quality red and white varietals. With the release of its 83 Sauvignon Blanc, a ✻✻✻ classic, Kenwood entered a new era. From then on, the winery began making more white wines than reds, and is now holding the ratio at a desired 60/40. Its best-selling varietal is Sauvignon Blanc, which continues to be among the best of each vintage even as annual production approaches 50,000 cases. The second leading wine is now Chardonnay, with over 25,000 cases made, spread out over three bottlings (Sonoma Valley, Beltane Ranch, and Yulupa Vineyard).

A sentimental favorite among the owners, Zinfandel (the 70 vintage was the first Kenwood wine to gain wide critical praise) has been produced every year. Two Zinfandels are offered today, one from Sonoma Valley and the other from Jack London Ranch. In 75, Kenwood made a special batch of ageworthy Cabernet Sauvignon and commissioned an artist to design a label for it. This "Artist Series" of Cabernet Sauvignon became one of the most sought-after of its type; however, production is limited to 2,500–3,000 cases. As of 89, Merlot has joined the roster, and its output will grow to 10,000 cases. Buying most grapes from Sonoma County, Kenwood recently prefers Sonoma Valley as its source. The winery has expanded its own holdings to include 135 acres of estate vineyards. However, Kenwood enjoys an exclusive relationship with the 110-acre Jack London Ranch, from which it makes vineyard-designated Pinot Noir, Cabernet Sauvignon, and Zinfandel. All told, the winery has 450 acres under long-term contract. Its annual production is close to 175,000 cases.

Cabernet Sauvignon

(Sonoma Valley) 78✻ 80 81 82 83✻ 84✻✻ 85✻✻ 86✻ 87✻✻

The most variable of Kenwood's Cabernets tends to be big, ripe, black-cherryish, moderately dense in warm years and a little on the understuffed side in others

Cabernet Sauvignon

(Jack London Vineyard) 78✻✻ 79✻✻ 80 81 82 83✻✻ 84✻✻ 85✻ 86✻ 87✻

Usually bold, brawny wines, full of briary, brambly spice and tight, black-cherryish fruit, wrapped in long-aging tannins, this one is the toughest of the three Kenwood Cabernets

Cabernet Sauvignon

(Artist Series) 78✻ 79✻✻ 80 81 82✻ 83✻✻ 84✻✻ 85✻✻✻ 86✻✻✻ 87✻✻

The rich and deep centerpiece of the Kenwood line, this wine matches the Jack London in aging potential but surpasses it in pure Cabernet-focused, balanced, youthful fruit

Chardonnay

(Sonoma Valley) 84✻ 85✻ 86✻ 87✻ 88✻

(Yulupa Vineyard) 84✻ 85 89

(Beltane Ranch) 84✻ 85 86 87 88✻✻

In spite of their above-average record of success, and even though they collectively are the number-two varietals in terms of volume, this collection of Chardonnays does not constitute Kenwood's strong suit; the wines have a tendency to ripeness and pushy oakiness, which sometimes combine to crowd out the fruit

Zinfandel

79✻✻ 80 81✻ 82✻ 83✻ 84✻✻ 85✻✻ 86✻✻ 87✻ 88

Always ripe, deeply fruited, well focused, solidly structured, and proven to be ageworthy—no wonder Kenwood Zinfandels rank among the handful at the top

KENWORTHY VINEYARDS   *Amador 1979*   The Kenworthy family specializes in Zinfandel grown in its 8-acre estate vineyard. Made by John Kenworthy, the heavy-duty Zinfandel accounts for over half of the winery's 2,000 case-a-year maximum output. Chardonnay and Cabernet Sauvignon, made from El Dorado grapes, represent the remainder of the production.

J. KERR WINES   *Santa Barbara 1986*   After stints with Chalone, Jekel, and Ventana Vineyards, John Kerr returned to his hometown area of Santa Barbara to work as a consulting enologist. He is the winemaker at Houtz Vineyard, a consultant for other wineries, and is developing his own brand. After producing 130 cases of Chardonnay in his first vintage, Kerr added Syrah to the line in 88 to bring the total production to 500 cases. Johannisberg Riesling and Pinot Noir from local growers have also been produced. Over the long term, with the completion of his own facility, Kerr would like to expand to 5,000 cases.

KISTLER VINEYARDS   *Sonoma 1978*   Perched on an isolated ridge of the Mayacamas Mountains some 2,000 feet above the Sonoma Valley, Kistler is truly far from the madding crowd. This first-class producer has emphasized small-batch, vineyard-designated Chardonnays and Pinot Noirs from its own vineyard and numerous other sources. In its short history, seven different vineyard Chardonnays have been produced. After an excellent beginning, Kistler fell back for a few years as if to repent for an ill-fated 80 Chardonnay. By 85 it was again in top form and has become one of the outstanding Chardonnay producers. Owned by Steve and John Kistler and winemaker Mark Bixler, the winery adheres to the traditional, minimal handling school of winemaking. Its Chardonnays are barrel-fermented and undergo complete malolactic fermentation.

The current roster of vineyard-designated Chardonnays consists of Dutton Ranch, Durell Vineyard, McCrea Vineyard, and Kistler Estate. Pinot Noir is increasing in importance as the winery expands production from the McCrea Vineyard and its estate vineyard. In 84 Kistler made its first estate Cabernet (fewer than 100 cases), and since then production has grown to about 1,000 cases a year. The winery's mountaintop vineyard is now planted to 15 acres of Cabernet Sauvignon, 17 of Chardonnay, and 3 of Pinot Noir. In 86 Kistler purchased a mature 20-acre vineyard in southwestern Sonoma County that brings 18 acres of Chardonnay and 2 of Pinot Noir into the fold. With Chardonnay production over 10,000 cases, the winery is close to its 12,000-case capacity.

Cabernet Sauvignon

(Kistler Vineyard)   85**   86**   87*

Seemingly destined to make its place among the top Cabernets grown in California, this one is deep in curranty and black-cherryish fruit, tight in structure, and loaded with aging potential

Chardonnay

(Dutton Ranch)   84   85**   86**   87**   88**   89

(Durell Vineyard)   86***   87***   88*   89**

(Kistler Vineyard)   86***   88***   89*

(McCrea Vineyard)   88***   89**

With its recent vintages, Kistler has reestablished its place among the top handful of Chardonnay producers in California. All of its wines have possessed depth of fruit, complexity, and aging potential. The Dutton often follows a more floral line than the others, while the Kistler seems to be the most durable

KONOCTI WINERY *Lake 1975* Originally, this winery was a co-operative venture run by three dozen growers in the county who owned or controlled close to 500 acres of vineyards. By 79, they had completed construction of their winery between the towns of Lakeport and Kelseyville. In 83 the Parducci wine family acquired an interest, other new partners own 50%, and the growers, now 24 in number, retained a 25% interest in the winery. Those growers own 300 acres. The winery's early history was an up-and-down course, and for several years it conducted a strong bulk wine business. By the end of the 80s, however, Konocti was moving toward an annual case production of 60,000, with an expected gradual growth to the maximum of 100,000 cases. As early as the 85 vintage, Konocti established itself as a producer of true-to-type varietals, particularly of Fumé Blanc and Riesling. It has been building from that base since, and has improved its record for Chardonnay, which tends to highlight appley fruit and light oak. The 88 vintage signaled the beginning of barrel fermentation for Konocti Chardonnay. The winery makes a consistently likable Cabernet Sauvignon and a Merlot in a fruity, balanced style. Meritage red and white blends were added in the 90s.

Cabernet Sauvignon

83✻ 84✻ 85✻ 86

Directly fruity, with cherryish and slightly plummy character and hints of richness, light tannins; a great value to date

Chardonnay

85 86 87✻ 88✻

Like the Cabernet, this one is approachable, fruity, nonchallenging, and a good value when successful

---

KORBEL CHAMPAGNE CELLARS *1862* California's leading volume producer of *méthode champenoise* sparkling wine, Korbel is approaching its production goal of 2 million cases. The beautiful old winery is located along the western edge of the Russian River Valley a few miles west of Guerneville. In the distant background one can see part of Korbel's 600-acre vineyard, which supplies a small portion of the winery's crush needs. Grapes are contracted from throughout the state as the winery concentrates on making its line of sparkling wines—Brut Natural, Brut, Blanc de Blancs, Blanc de Noirs, and Rosé. The Brut is the top seller, and accounts for over 700,000 cases a year. By contrast, the winery's Blanc de Noirs (100% Pinot Noir) and Blanc de Blancs (100% Chardonnay) are each made in quantities of about 10,000 cases.

The quality of Korbel's line has recently been disappointing and even the once highly touted Natural and Blanc de Blancs have suffered from a diffuse, muddled impression in some recent releases. The Brut Rosé (not to be confused with the sweeter Rosé) has been consistently enjoyable, however. The winery's Blanc de Noirs along with the Brut Rosé were the quality leaders at the end of the 80s, each achieving ✻ ratings. Between 75 and 85 Korbel enjoyed such tremendous growth in the sparkling wine field that it reduced its line of table wines to a few thousand cases, mainly for sales at the winery gift store. Korbel is also a leader in the field of California Brandy, with annual sales in excess of 350,000 cases.

HANNS KORNELL CHAMPAGNE CELLARS *Napa 1952* Born and raised in Germany's Rhine Valley, Hanns Kornell left in 1939 and after a stay in England arrived in California in 40. His experience as a sparkling wine producer in his native land was put to use at several California wineries before he made his own bubbly in a makeshift cellar in Sonoma County. In 58 he purchased the defunct Larkmead Winery north of St. Helena, and settled in to make a range of sparkling wine. Following German practice, Kornell purchased readymade batches of wine, usually from the Riesling grape, and made them sparkle by the *méthode champenoise*. Some historians maintain Kornell was the first in

California to adopt this traditional French method. From the 50s to the late 70s, Kornell produced a range of generally popular sparklers, all displaying their Riesling parentage. But with the appearance in California of Schramsberg Vineyards and Domaine Chandon, who were leaders focusing California's sparkling wine on a more "French" style, Kornell began to lose ground in the marketplace. Making around 80,000 cases, Hanns Kornell Cellars was out of sync with the times by the mid-80s.

Eventually, the Kornells realized their winery needed to crush grapes in order to have more control over quality and also to use more traditional "champagne" grapes in the cuvées to appeal to a more sophisticated market. It was not until the 87 vintage that Kornell was able to offer a Blanc de Noirs (from Pinot Noir) and a Blanc de Blancs (from Chardonnay). Neither showed any trace of Riesling. However, its once popular house speciality, "Sehr Trocken" (meaning Very Dry) continues to be made from Riesling. Annual production is running at the cellar's capacity of 90,000 cases.

CHARLES KRUG WINERY *Napa 1861* Charles Krug, a Prussian emigrant, arrived in San Francisco in the 1850s. He married Caroline Bale of Napa Valley, whose dowry included the Oak Grove Ranch where the winery now stands in what is now St. Helena. He started a vineyard and built the winery bearing his name in 1861. Charles Krug died in 1892, and though his winery was relatively large, the quality achievement during his reign is unknown. The winery was operated by his daughters, but as Prohibition approached it fell on quiet and then idle times. In 43, Cesare Mondavi, who was running a successful winery in Lodi as well as in St. Helena at the Sunny St. Helena Winery, purchased the Krug property in order to expand his family enterprise. The next year the Mondavi era began as their first wines were made in the original cellar and aged in the carriage house. Cesare Mondavi ran the Krug Winery with his two sons, Peter, who focused on winemaking and production, and an older brother, Robert, who handled marketing and promotions. Krug is usually credited with introducing temperature-controlled fermentation and sterile filtration during this period, and for performing breakthrough research into oak aging and the use of French oak barrels. The California style of slightly sweet, fruity Chenin Blanc is said to be a Krug innovation that was introduced in the mid-50s.

In 59 Cesare Mondavi died, leaving the winery in the hands of his wife, Rosa, their two sons, and one daughter. This working relationship began to unravel as the brothers, both strong-minded, collided on many issues. The well-documented account has Peter Mondavi gaining control, while Robert, eased out, left in 66 to start his own winery. A long legal battle followed, and when finally resolved in the late 70s, Robert won on almost every count and was awarded money, wine, and vineyards from the Krug Winery. For the next several years Krug was forced to work on a frugal budget and the winery failed to keep up with the fast-moving competition.

Prior to 70 the Charles Krug Winery had developed a strong reputation for both its line of white wines and its Cabernet Sauvignons. Its Cabernets, including a Reserve wine identified as "Vintage Selection," were standouts in the 50s and 60s. We find that Krug's Cabernets diminish in intensity and appeal after 71. Recent efforts to reinstate this special Cabernet to its former glory have not yet succeeded.

Currently, the winery owns or controls 1,200 acres of vineyards scattered throughout Napa Valley. Two vineyards in the Carneros grow Chardonnay and Pinot Noir, and the winery is surrounded by over 100 acres on the original ranch. Krug is currently developing vineyards on 600 acres it owns in Yolo County. Krug's wine roster in addition to two Cabernet bottlings now includes Chardonnay, Fumé Blanc, Chenin Blanc, Johannisberg Riesling, and Pinot Noir. In the 80s the winery's output varied from one year to the next, but more recently it has made approximately 125,000 cases of varietals a year, of which 30% is Cabernet Sauvignon and another 30% Chenin Blanc. In the early 80s, Chenin Blanc, the flagship wine, accounted for close to 50% of production, but the demand weakened quickly with the success of White Zinfandel.

After years of neglect, the winemaking facility has been renovated and brought up to contemporary standards. However, across the board Krug wines have been disappointing and often below average quality. Recent Special Selection Cabernets top the list of disappointments. The only wine to earn a star has been an occasional vintage of Carneros Chardonnay. C. K. Mondavi & Sons (see entry) is Krug's line of jug wines.

LA BELLE *(Raymond Vineyards)* Introduced in the early 80s, this second label consists of modestly priced varietals. Having worked as consultants for a number of growers, the Raymonds took advantage of their contacts to create this brand. Made from grapes purchased from vineyards in the North Coast and Central Coast, the La Belle roster features Chardonnay, Cabernet Sauvignon, Sauvignon Blanc, and White Zinfandel, all bottled with the California appellation. Chardonnay represents 60% of the 40,000 cases bottled in an average year.

LA CREMA *Sonoma 1979* This winery started out located in a dreary warehouse in Petaluma, where it made only Pinot Noir and Chardonnay. The winery's name then was La Crema Vinera, and its emphasis was on small-batch, vineyard-designated wines made with minimal clarification. The wines made varied widely in quality, and by 83, winemaker-manager Rod Berglund was confronted by bad reviews and reports of sagging sales. In 84 the winery was acquired by Jason Korman, who implemented many changes and began by destroying much of the inventory. With a new winemaking team and a new name, La Crema, the winery continued purchasing Pinot Noir and Chardonnay from several vineyards. However, it simplified its line by offering only a regular and Reserve version of each varietal. Pricing its wines competitively to reestablish itself, the brand grew quickly to the 60,000-case-a-year level. A badly needed larger facility was found in Sebastopol, where the winery owns 70 acres planted to Pinot Noir and Chardonnay. The top-of-the-line Chardonnays are 100% barrel-fermented. Sauvignon Blanc has joined the line, and it has occasionally risen to ❋ level with its balance of fruit flavors and creamy oak character.

After some experimentation, the winery introduced an oak-aged blended white named "Crème de Tête," a moderately priced blend of Chenin Blanc, Semillon, and barrel-fermented Chardonnay. With expected increases in the Crème de Tête sales, the winery is aiming at 80,000 cases a year.

Chardonnay

(regular bottling) 85 ❋ 86 87 ❋ 88
(Reserve) 85 ❋❋ 86 ❋❋❋ **87 ❋❋** 89

Both wines are balanced, somewhat appley, and well oaked in composition, but the Reserve seems to find extra measures of depth and richness that have been wanting in the regular edition

Pinot Noir

83 ❋ 84 ❋ **85 ❋** 86 ❋ 87

Relatively direct cherry and herb style, with moderate depth and short-term aging potential

LA JOTA VINEYARD CO. *Napa 1985* Encouraged by his home winemaking experiences, Bill Smith began looking for a vineyard where he could grow grapes and continue his amateur winemaking. As an executive with an oil exploration company, Smith and his wife, Joan, wanted to be weekend vineyardists. In 74 they discovered the remains of the pre-Prohibition La Jota Winery, on Howell Mountain, and bought it along with the surrounding property. Abandoned during Prohibition, the original stone winery was built in 1895 by Frederick Hess. Starting gradually with a few acres of Cabernet Sauvignon, the Smiths developed 30 acres to Cabernet Sauvignon and Zinfandel. Dissatisfied with the grape market, they began making wine with the help of a neighbor, Randy Dunn.

In 82 they produced their first estate-grown Cabernet, and a year later they made their first estate-grown Zinfandel. Aged for close to 2 years in Nevers oak, the Cabernets are blended with 5% to 10% Merlot and Cabernet Franc. Over the years their Zinfandel vineyard was converted to Cabernet Franc and to Viognier. Among the first to make Viognier, the Smiths produced a few hundred cases in 86, and are now up to about 400 cases from their 3 acres. Zinfandel production ceased after 88, replaced to some degree by Cabernet Franc. After experimentation, Bill Smith is making Cabernet Franc in two styles—one light and fruity, the other full-bodied and ageworthy. The winery's mainstay, Cabernet Sauvignon, is made from the estate 20 acres, and production is level at 3,000 cases.

Cabernet Sauvignon

82* 83** 84* 85* 86* 87* 88*

Firm, ageworthy, tightly bound wines, these ripe and rustic offerings have been more notable for their perceived aging potential and Howell Mountain appellation than for their depth of fruit

LA REINA WINERY *Monterey 1984* The brainstorm of the McFarland brothers, who have developed many vineyards and several wineries in Monterey County, La Reina is now owned outright by the Chrietzberg family, one of the founding partners. The McFarlands also own a vineyard named La Reina which is planted primarily to Chardonnay, but there is no longer any association between that vineyard and this winery. Barrel-fermented Chardonnay made from Monterey County grapes is the only wine La Reina produces. Over the first several vintages the winemaking took place in rented space. By 90 the annual production had reached 5,000 cases. Twice that amount is the goal.

Chardonnay

86 87*

Classic Monterey fruit (rich but a little bit stiff) comes wrapped in toasty oak

LA VIEILLE MONTAGNE *Napa 1981* Owner-winemaker John Guilliams is a full-time employee of a cooperage firm in Napa Valley. Beneath his home, in a modified basement/wine cellar built into the hillside, he produces fewer than 1,000 cases a year. After refurbishing the property on Spring Mountain Road, he replanted the steep, hillside vineyards to 7 acres of Cabernet Sauvignon and White Riesling. His first vintage—81—was made with grapes from a neighboring vineyard, but all wines have since been made from the home vineyard. Blended with small amounts of Cabernet Franc and Merlot, the winery's Cabernet Sauvignon is both the more plentiful and the better-crafted.

LAKE SONOMA WINERY *Sonoma 1977* Originally known as Diablo Vista Vineyards, this winery was founded in Benicia in Contra Costa County. The winery was purchased in 82 by the Polson family, which owned vineyards in the northern part of Dry Creek Valley. From 82 to 86 Robert Polson made wines in Benicia, but by the next year he had moved the operation to Sonoma County. A winemaking facility was built in stages and was finally completed in 90. Beginning with the 86 vintage, Polson changed the winery's name to Lake Sonoma. The family-owned 10-acre vineyard is located near Lake Sonoma Dam, and the primary varieties grown are Zinfandel, Sauvignon Blanc, Cabernet Sauvignon, Merlot, and Chenin Blanc. Zinfandel and Sauvignon Blanc are the mainstays in the present output of 3,000 cases. From its own vineyards and purchased grapes, Lake Sonoma could grow to its capacity of 6,500 cases.

LAKESPRING WINERY *Napa 1980* This winery is owned by the Battat family, and run by the three Battat brothers—Frank, Harry, and Ralph—and their families. Adjacent to their winery, which is located a few miles southwest of Yountville and operated by Frank and his wife, Lee, they have planted 10 acres to Chardonnay. For other varietals, they purchase grapes. In addition to its

Chardonnay, Lakespring produces Cabernet Sauvignon, Merlot, and Sauvignon Blanc. As of 89, Lakespring's Sauvignon Blancs are from Napa Valley. Earlier vintages were a blend of Napa and Central Coast wine, labeled "California." As a rule, the winery prefers making Cabernets that are unblended, and the Cabernet is grown in the Stags Leap and the Yountville regions.

Though the style has varied over the years, the quality has been generally above average. Big, often assertive in varietal character, the Sauvignon Blancs do sometimes reach ✻✻ levels, but are extremely erratic. With a similar inconsistent record, Lakespring's Chardonnays are usually 100% barrel-fermented. All told, Lakespring has been a better performer with red wines. By the 85 vintage its Merlot was beginning to show promise.

As of now, the winery has yet to demonstrate continuing success with any varietal. Annual production is about 20,000 cases, with the winery's capacity at 24,000 cases.

LAMBERT BRIDGE *Sonoma 1975*   Located in the Dry Creek Valley, Lambert Bridge began in 69 when proprietor Jerry Lambert purchased the present 119-acre site. By 73, with his vineyard established to Chardonnay and Cabernet Sauvignon, and a fraction to Merlot, Lambert began construction of a winery that was finished in 76. The vineyard has been expanded to 76 acres divided into three parcels. Over its first decade, the winery specialized in three varietals—Chardonnay, Cabernet Sauvignon, and Merlot—and prided itself for producing only estate-grown wines. But both its Chardonnay and Cabernet Sauvignon met with extremely mixed reviews. The winery has made some changes in winemaking direction, and today buys some grapes from within the county. It also added Fumé Blanc to its line. Chardonnay remains its primary wine, accounting for over one-third of the 25,000-case annual output. Since the mid-80s it has become more consistent. Of late the Cabernets and Merlots range from very good to below average. Recent additions to the line are Reserve-type wines—Chardonnay "Tête de Cuvée" and "Library Reserve" Cabernet Sauvignon, both from the Dry Creek Valley appellation. The Reserve Cabernet began on a high note of ✻✻ quality.

Cabernet Sauvignon

84   85✻   86✻✻

Black-cherry fruit is combined with ample oak in a medium-full-bodied wine of supple, moderately tannic structure

Chardonnay

85✻   86✻   88   89✻

Floral and direct apple tones are presented in a crisp, firm style, amenable to a few years of development in the bottle

LAMBORN FAMILY VINEYARDS *Napa 1982*   Bob Lamborn, a private investigator in the Oakland area, bought 30 acres of secluded land on Howell Mountain in 73, intending to use the property as a rural retreat. Upon hearing from his neighbors that a famous vineyard once occupied the site, he cleared the land and planted 9 acres to Zinfandel. In 79, with his neighbor Randy Dunn acting as winemaker, Lamborn produced 100 cases. A decade later he was making 1,100 cases a year in his own tiny winery. As production expands to the 2,200-case level, he purchases Zinfandel from the neighboring Beatty Ranch. Aged in a combination of French and American oak for an average of 18 months, Lamborn Zinfandels are ripe and jammy, in a style typical of the area. With another 10 acres plantable, Lamborn has considered adding Nebbiolo or Sangiovese.

Zinfandel

84✻✻   85✻   86✻   87   88✻✻✻

Ripe-berry fruitiness, with briary and spicy notes, comes in a firm, full, and tannic package that is not always up to its brusque exterior; the 87 was a bit of a clinker; the 88 was one of the finest

LANDMARK VINEYARDS *Sonoma 1974* Now a self-proclaimed Chardonnay special-ist, Landmark tried out a number of wines over its first decade. Founded by the Mabry family, owners of several vineyards in Sonoma, the winery was located in Windsor until 88, when it finally fell victim to urban encroachment and real estate developers. Bill Mabry, who remains as managing partner and winemaker, decided he could not stop progress, and relocated to a site north of Kenwood in the Sonoma Valley where a new 40,000-case winery was read-ied for the 90 harvest. Now owned by Demaris Ethridge and the Mabrys, Landmark boasts 56 acres of Chardonnay in the Alexander Valley and 17 acres in the Sonoma Valley. An additional 20 acres surrounding the winery were planted to Chardonnay in 90. Focusing on Chardonnay, Landmark bottles three barrel-fermented versions—Sonoma County, Demaris Reserve, and "Two Williams," from a vineyard in Sonoma Valley. The current annual pro-duction of 18,000 cases is expected to increase gradually to a maximum of 40,000 cases by the mid-90s. "Cypress Lane," a second label used for a low-priced line of wines prior to 1988, has been dropped.

Chardonnay

83* 84* 85 86 88

Showing appley and somewhat floral fruit in good years, this wine contin-ues to have a spotty track record

LAS MONTANAS WINERY *Sonoma 1982* Literally a one-woman show, Las Montanas is a small (1,500 cases a year) winery located on the steep hillsides overlooking the Sonoma Valley. Owner-winemaker Aleta Apgar is adamant about making only natural (chemical-free) wines from grapes farmed organically. She has 3 acres adjacent to the winery, and they provide most of the fruit needed to produce 400 cases each of Cabernet Sauvignon and Zinfandel. Though the quality is slightly erratic, the Zinfandel has on occasion been extremely attrac-tive in a ripe-berry style.

LAS VINAS *San Joaquin 1986* The Cotta family (John, Jim, and Joe) own 800 acres of vineyards within the Lodi region. With John as the winemaker, they are producing a line of varietal wines from their vineyard. Most of their crop is sold to wineries within the general vicinity. The major varietals produced, in order of importance, are: Cabernet Sauvignon, Sauvignon Blanc, Symphony, Chardonnay, and Zinfandel. A medium-sweet blended blush wine goes by the proprietary name of "Amorosa." On occasion, Symphony is produced in a late harvest style. By 90, the winery's annual output was 8,000 cases, about halfway to the goal of 15,000 cases a year.

LAUREL GLEN VINEYARDS *Sonoma 1980* Owner and winemaker Patrick Campbell makes Cabernet Sauvignon from 35 acres located on the rocky slopes high above the Sonoma Valley. His vineyard falls within the Viticultural Area he identified and promoted as Sonoma Mountain. Campbell made wines as an amateur in the 70s, and also sold some of his grapes to Chateau St. Jean and others before going professional in 81. He began developing his vineyard in 68, and with gradual expansion the vineyard now consists of eight distinct blocks, all east-facing at the 1,000-foot-elevation level. So situated, the vine-yards are above the frost line, and the eastern exposure protects the vines from intense late-afternoon heat during the growing season. Both Cabernet Franc and Merlot are grown, but mainly as blending candidates, should they be needed.

For his Cabernet Sauvignon, Campbell begins by harvesting the crop from each block separately, and then uses open-top fermenters and allows the temperature to approach 90°F. Clarification is accomplished in most vintages by frequent rackings. For aging, he uses mostly new Nevers oak, and allows the wine to spend close to two years in small oak. As a rule, Laurel Glen Cabernets are impeccably made, and offer deep, intense fruit. Batches of wine not used in the final master blend are sometimes bottled and sold as "Counter-point." The maximum annual production is 5,000 cases. From time to time

Campbell has bottled "Terra Rosa," a Cabernet he purchases and ages before bottling.

Cabernet Sauvignon

81*   82   83*   84*   85***   86**   87*

Deep black-cherry fruit, hints of cocoa and herbs, rich oak, and a tannin-firmed, supple texture combine in wine of good aging potential

LAURIER VINEYARDS (FORMERLY DOMAINE LAURIER) *Sonoma 1978* This compact winery is located just north of Forestville and is within the Sonoma Green Valley appellation. Under the direction of the Shilo family, its founders, the winery gradually expanded over its first decade to produce 12,000 cases by 88. The winery's best-known wine was an estate-grown Cabernet Sauvignon from the 30-acre vineyard next to the winery. However, in early 89 the winery was sold to the Vintech Group, also owners of Lyeth in the Alexander Valley. Later that year the well-known winemaker Merry Edwards (justifiably famous for her Chardonnays at Mt. Eden, Matanzas Creek, and Merry Vintners) joined the winery. Under her direction, the winery is specializing in Chardonnay (Sonoma County and Reserve) and Pinot Noir. Edwards's style of winemaking is based on 100% barrel-fermented Chardonnay, and the small-batch method with frequent punching down for Pinot Noir. She has overseen the subsequent expansion of the winemaking facility to its present 60,000-case capacity. However, the winery was again under new ownership in late 91.

LAVA CAP VINEYARD *El Dorado 1986* Situated northeast of Placerville on a rocky ridge that is unusually rich in volcanic soils, Lava Cap is family-owned and -operated. Its 23-acre vineyard located at the 2,600-foot elevation was developed in 81. The vineyard contains four varieties which are made into six wines—Chardonnay, Sauvignon Blanc, Cabernet Sauvignon (both red and Blanc), and Zinfandel (both red and white). A generic wine, Lava Cap Red (a blend of Cabernet Sauvignon and Zinfandel), and Riesling complete the line of this 5,000-case producer. Overall quality is average.

LAZY CREEK VINEYARDS *Mendocino 1973* Founded by former restaurateur Hans Kobler and his wife, Theresia, Lazy Creek is located in the Anderson Valley just west of Philo. The small, cozy winery is surrounded by 20 acres planted to Gewurztraminer, Pinot Noir, and Chardonnay. The winery is best known for its first-class Gewurztraminers, which usually rank among the very best in the state. The style of recent vintages has been opulently spicy and flowery and finished with a slight sweetness. Its Pinot Noir in the mid-80s began to earn * in a style that displays cherry-berry characteristics with moderate intensity. In a fruity, well-made style, Lazy Creek Chardonnays are usually pleasant, if lacking in complexity. A Red Table Wine made from left-over Pinot Noir is made in most years to accompany the three varietals. Total production approaches 4,000 cases.

LE DOMAINE (ALMADÉN VINEYARDS) This once highly visible line of moderately priced sparkling wine was acquired in 87 by Heublein Wines, which also owns Inglenook, Beaulieu, and the Christian Brothers. At one time Le Domaine's offerings were produced by the transfer process and the quality was decent and remained so for several years. The two current bottlings, Brut and Extra Dry, are made by the Charmat process and tend toward the dull, sweet side of their respective categories.

LEEWARD WINERY *Ventura 1979* After some success as home winemakers, partners Chuck Brigham and Chuck Gardner decided to go commercial in 79. However, until they moved into a full-scale winery in 82, they continued to make wine in their basement. From the very first vintage, Chardonnay has been the major wine by volume. Stressing barrel fermentations, French oak aging, and malolactic fermentations, Leeward built a reputation for full-blown Chardonnays. After producing Chardonnay from numerous Central Coast appellations, it settled down to make three versions on a regular annual basis—Edna Valley (MacGregor Vineyard or Paragon Vineyards), Monterey (Ventana Vineyard or Sleepy Hollow), and Central Coast, a regional blend. In the past the winery has produced Zinfandel, Merlot, and a Blanc de Noirs termed "Coral." Today, 90% of its annual 15,000-case production is Chardonnay. Cabernet Sauvignon from the Alexander Valley, Coral, and a few hundred cases of Pinot Noir round out the line.

Chardonnay

(Edna Valley) 84 85 86 87 88

(Central Coast) 84* 86* 87 88 89*

Always oaky, and typically full of winemaking nuances, these wines have all too often lacked the necessary core of fruit to balance their other parts

CHARLES LEFRANC CELLARS Charles Lefranc founded Almadén Vineyards in 1852, and when National Distillers, Almadén's owner until 1987, tried to compete in the premium-quality wine market in the late 70s, it created the Charles Lefranc line. After Almadén was sold to Heublein, Lefranc became just another line of ordinary wines intended for mass appeal. Bottled in Madera along with Almadén, Blossom Hill, and Inglenook Navalle, Lefranc Cellars offers a blush trio of White Zinfandel, White Cabernet, and White Grenache. Its other wines are Chardonnay and Sauvignon Blanc among whites, and Cabernet Sauvignon, Merlot, and Gamay Beaujolais for red. All are vintaged and carry the California appellation.

LIBERTY SCHOOL *(Caymus Vineyards)* Introduced by Caymus in 75 as a way to sell left-over Cabernet Sauvignon, Liberty School evolved into a full-scale brand. The name derives from the nearby schoolhouse attended by owner Charles Wagner as a schoolboy. Made primarily from bulk wine purchased throughout the coastal counties, Liberty School's line now consists of Chardonnay (the volume item), Cabernet Sauvignon, and Sauvignon Blanc. In 88 Liberty School reached out to include Cabernet Sauvignon and Sauvignon Blanc made in Chile, but that program lasted just one vintage. Now, with its line of "California" wines trimmed to three varietals, Liberty School is bottling and selling 80,000 cases a year. Overall, its quality performance has been among the best of the many low-priced second labels.

LIMUR WINERY *Napa 1988* This is one of those instances in which the owners never intended to make wine commercially. The de Limur family planted 2 acres to Chardonnay adjacent to their summer home in the easternmost edge of Rutherford. The original idea was to sell the grapes, but contracts were never arranged. When a neighboring winery agreed to custom-make wines, only to ask too much for the service, Charles de Limur made his own wines in 86 and 87 for home consumption. By 88 he was granted a winemaking bond which allows him to make no more than 350 cases a year. This Chardonnay-only winery is likely the smallest licensed producer in Napa Valley.

LIPARITA WINERY *Napa 1988* On a site said to have been the home of a winery prior to Prohibition, San Franciscan Robert Burroughs has revived the Liparita brand and developed a vineyard. Located on Howell Mountain, the vineyard, now covering 80 acres, is planted to Chardonnay, Cabernet Sauvignon, Merlot, and Sauvignon Blanc. Grapes from the first few harvests were sold, with Chardonnay being purchased by Chateau Montelena and Grgich Hills. In 87 the owner asked winemaker Merry Edwards to make an experimental batch of Chardonnay to officially reinstate the Liparita name. After passing on 88, Burroughs made 300 cases in 89 in a rented facility. Plans call for increasing production slowly and eventually building a winery.

LIVERMORE VALLEY CELLARS *Alameda 1978* About midway between Livermore and Pleasanton, this family-owned operation sold grapes to Wente and others for several years. By 78, owner Chris Largis began making wines from a portion of his mature, 34-acre, dry-farmed vineyard. All grapes are white, but the varieties represented a mix of old and contemporary, obscure and common. Golden Chasselas and other museum pieces grow alongside Grey Riesling, French Colombard, and Chardonnay. One vineyard parcel is a mixed planting of Chenin Blanc, Pinot Blanc, and other varieties, picked and crushed together to produce a generic white. Chardonnay and dry-style Colombard are mainstays in this 3,000-case winery.

LIVINGSTON VINEYARDS *Napa 1987* John and Diane Livingston own a 10-acre vineyard on the western edge of the Rutherford Bench. The pre-Prohibition vineyard was replanted to Cabernet Sauvignon in 69. Named Moffett after Diane's family, the vineyard supplied grapes to many Napa Valley wineries until the Livingstons decided to custom-crush in 84. Overseeing the winemaking process is Randy Dunn of Dunn Vineyards. A small winery has been built on the property. First vintage in 84 yielded 900 cases. The optimum annual output for Moffett Vineyard is pegged at 2,000 cases. Both Cabernet Franc and Merlot have been used in the blend. Livingston prefers to age the Moffett bottling at least two years in small oak barrels. In 89 a Napa Valley Cabernet from purchased grapes was added, and about 2,500 cases of it are produced each year.

Cabernet Sauvignon

(Moffett Vineyard) 84✶✶ 85✶✶ 86✶✶✶ 87

Deep, curranty, often somewhat loamy, and rich in creamy oak, the wine is supple and inviting at the center but also has plenty of tannin for backbone and ageworthiness

LLORDS & ELWOOD *Napa 1984* This is a relative old-timer among California brands, having been founded in 1955 by Mike Elwood, a wine merchant in Beverly Hills. Elwood started the label for special wines he would sell to customers, but by 61 he was enjoying enough success in the wine-producing business to devote full time to it. The original winery was located in the Santa Clara Valley, and though it offered a wide range of wines, Llords & Elwood became best known for its sherries and ports. The best-sellers were his "Dry Wit" Sherry and the "Judge's Secret Cream Sherry." After Mike Elwood died in 74, his son, Richard, ran the wine operation until 84, renting a corner of the Weibel Winery in San Jose. In early 84 the Llords & Elwood name and inventory were purchased by Jay Corley of Monticello Cellars. He relocated the small-scale operation to Napa Valley. In addition to its line of ports and sherries, Llords & Elwood once again is offering a range of varietals. Most are modestly priced, the quality leaders being Chardonnay and Sauvignon Blanc.

LOGAN WINERY *(Talbott)* Not long after the Talbotts saw a sufficient demand for their over-$20-a-bottle Chardonnay, they introduced a less expensive Chardonnay under the Logan name. Grown in the same vineyards of Monterey's Salinas Valley, Logan Chardonnay is also barrel-fermented. It receives about half as much aging in the barrel as the Talbott brand and is as a rule available within a year after the vintage. Owner Robb Talbott named this label after his son, Logan. Annual output has ranged from 4,000 to 5,000 cases. The quality has been surprisingly erratic, especially in view of the success enjoyed by the main brand.

J. LOHR WINERY *Santa Clara 1974* Taking over an old brewery site in downtown San Jose, owner Jerry Lohr and a since departed partner, Bernie Turgeon, built a winery and tasting room. In the early 70s, they were both successful in the custom home construction business and invested in a vineyard site in the Greenfield area of Monterey County. When the 280-acre vineyard was reaching maturity, they began producing a hit-or-miss line of wines, led by a slightly sweet Johannisberg Riesling. After 84, when Lohr took charge of the operations, the winery changed direction with the help of a marketing partnership with the Wine Trust. By 90 many changes were being felt.

With vineyards in four regions, J. Lohr now owns or controls 1,100 acres. A line of upscale varietals has evolved, a few featuring vineyard designations and others being marketed under the "J. Lohr Estates" banner. In Napa Valley it has 34 acres near St. Helena planted to Cabernet Sauvignon, and the resulting wine has been bottled individually as Carol's Vineyard. In Monterey County, the winery's 55-acre Cypress Vineyard gives birth to its Reserve Chardonnay. The major J. Lohr Estates wine is the "Riverstone" Chardonnay from Monterey. The original 335-acre Greenfield holding grows several varieties and contributes to the regular J. Lohr Winery bottlings of Chardonnay, Gamay, and Johannisberg Riesling. Its popular Chenin Blanc originates in the Clarksburg region in the Delta where the winery's Pheasant's Call Vineyards of 225 acres was developed in the mid-80s.

With plantings beginning in 80, the fourth vineyard, Seven Oaks, is in Paso Robles, and its 280 acres will be dominated by Cabernet Sauvignon, Merlot, and Cabernet Franc. J. Lohr's vineyard-designated wines added an emphatic note of seriousness to a winery enjoying success with its simple, drink-now "California" Cabernet Sauvignon, its consistently zesty, fruity, and popular Monterey Gamay that earns ✲, and White Zinfandel. Today, J. Lohr's production is about 230,000 cases a year. Ariel, a line of wines with no alcohol, was developed by the same company. Wines under the various Lohr brands are expected to expand as its vineyards mature in the 90s to the maximum of 400,000 cases a year.

Chardonnay

(Greenfield/Riverstone)   **84**   85   86   87   88✲   89

Floral-toned fruit and candied flavors make this an unusual entrant in the Chardonnay field

---

LOLONIS WINERY   *Mendocino 1982*   The Lolonis family established a vineyard in the Redwood Valley about 2 miles north of Lake Mendocino in 21. Situated on the slopes at the 1,000-foot elevation, Lolonis Vineyard sold its grapes to home winemakers during Prohibition and for many years afterwards. Grapes were sold to wineries and blended until Fetzer Vineyards began producing a vineyard-designated Lolonis Zinfandel in the early 70s and continued throughout the 80s. These Zinfandels by Fetzer were often big, intensely flavored, and powerful versions that were well received. Over the years the dry-farmed Lolonis vineyard was expanded to its present 300 acres, and the major varieties planted are Chardonnay, Zinfandel, Cabernet Sauvignon, and Sauvignon Blanc. Many wineries buy Lolonis grapes, among them Fetzer, Parducci, and Kendall-Jackson Vineyards, which often bottles a Lolonis Chardonnay. In the early 80s Lolonis began producing wines from its own vineyard; while emphasizing Chardonnay and Fumé Blanc, it also made Cabernet Sauvignon and Zinfandel. Using their own equipment and barrels, the Lolonis family oversees the winemaking process in leased space. The quality overall has been average, and the Chardonnays have been ripe in fruit and full-bodied, typical of the vineyard. Total production is level at 8,000 cases a year, led by Chardonnay and Fumé Blanc.

LONG VINEYARDS   *Napa 1977*   When Zelma Long was a winemaker at the Robert Mondavi Winery, she and her husband Bob lived near the town of Angwin in the northeastern corner of Napa. As a weekend project, they planted 12 acres of Chardonnay and 4 of Riesling along the rocky hillside. Early vintages were sold to Mount Veeder Vineyards, which produced superb Long Vineyard Chardonnay in the mid-70s. As they eased into wine production, the Longs made excellent Chardonnays from their own fruit. In 81, Zelma Long became head winemaker for Simi Winery, and shortly thereafter the couple divorced. Still co-owners of this winery, they now have 16 acres of Chardonnay and 4 of Riesling planted. The production is still headed by Chardonnay (barrel-fermented) and Riesling in a medium-sweet style, both from the home vineyard. Sauvignon Blanc (blended with about 20% Chardonnay) comes from the Carneros District. In addition, Long occasionally offers about 200 cases of Cabernet Sauvignon from the University of California's Experimental Vineyard in Yountville.

The decision to bottle the wine depends on the quality of the Cabernet resulting from each year's experiments in grape growing. Long is currently bottling about 2,500 cases a year, with Chardonnay accounting for three quarters of the total. When the vines are fully developed, Long plans to make 3,000 cases annually. Each of the wines produced has been among the best from time to time.

Cabernet Sauvignon

83* 84* 85* 86

Well-fruited wines, high in oak and massively tannic, they may last for decades but seem a little overdone

Chardonnay

84** 85* 86* 87* 88*

The first vintages (going back to the mid-70s) from this vineyard were more fruity than recent efforts, which are clean, well-oaked, somewhat complex, yet also somewhat stiff and citrusy

---

RICHARD LONGORIA WINES   *Santa Barbara 1982*   Rick Longoria has been making wines in Santa Barbara County since 76. After working for J. Carey Cellars, he is now winemaker for Gainey Vineyard. As a sideline, he and his wife work together on this family wine venture. Production has been limited to 100 cases or so of Pinot Noir from Santa Maria Valley. In the future, the Longorias intend to offer Chardonnay and Merlot, and to bring their annual production slowly to a target of 2,000 cases. Quality to date has been all over the board.

LOS HERMANOS   *(Beringer Vineyards)*   Created as Beringer's second label in the late 70s, Los Hermanos became a popular brand for low-priced generics and varietals mostly bottled in jug containers. Over the first several years its quality was usually in line with its very modest prices. During the brief time when light, low-calorie wines were in vogue, Los Hermanos was a leader with its Light Chablis and Light Rosé. It still bottles Light Chablis, along with popular White Zinfandel, White Cabernet, Chenin Blanc, French Colombard, and several generic wines. Sales in the 90s are holding steady at 225,000 cases, mostly blush and light wines.

LUCAS WINERY   *San Joaquin 1978*   Among a handful of family-owned wineries in Lodi, Lucas Winery specializes in Zinfandel. In 77, the Lucas family (Dave and Tamara Lucas) acquired property that included a 30-acre vineyard. About 18 acres consisted of old Zinfandel, with the remainder planted to Tokay. In 79 their first Zinfandel was made, and ever since they have been using the oldest vines to make about 1,000 to 1,200 cases a year. The owners field-crush the fruit, and ferment in small stainless-steel tanks. As a rule, the Zinfandel is aged in French oak for about a year and a half. During the White Zinfandel boom period, the winery's output varied. In 88, for example, the demand for Zinfandel was so strong that most of the Lucas crop was sold. The old Tokay acreage was removed in the late 80s to make room for other wine varieties.

LYETH WINERY   *Sonoma 1981*   The Lyeth Winery, named after founder Chip Lyeth, was among the first to apply the estate wine concept as it is defined in the region of Bordeaux to California winemaking and labeling. Before the word "Meritage" was coined, Lyeth was making a red and a white wine from the standard Bordeaux varieties and identifying and marketing them both with "Lyeth" displayed in gold silk screen and no varietal name or wine explanation given on the label. Located in the northern end of the Alexander Valley, Lyeth established 150 acres. About 100 are planted to red varieties—

Cabernet Sauvignon, Merlot, and Cabernet Franc—which yielded 16,000 cases a year. The other 50 acres are planted to Sauvignon Blanc, Semillon, and Muscat Blanc, which, until the entire vineyard was sold in 91 to Gallo, yielded 12,000 cases of Lyeth's white wine. Generally, the white is a ✳ wine, offering fresh fruit with a figgy aroma in a firmly structured, smooth style with a hint of oak. The red is aged for two years in barrel and two in bottle before being marketed. In 88 the winery was sold to the large corporation named Vintech which also owns Laurier Vineyard, Jekel Vineyard, and Mazzocco Vineyard. Vintech filed for bankruptcy in 90. Lyeth and the surrounding 18 acres were sold in late 91. Production remained in limbo.

Lyeth Red

81 ✳✳   82   83 ✳   84 ✳   85 ✳   86 ✳✳

More complex in the telling than in the the bottle, this blended wine is typically fruity in a cherryish, slightly herbal vein, and has good structure for several years of aging potential

---

LYON VINEYARD   *Napa 1987*   Owner Fred Lyon, a professional photographer, specializes in the field of wine and food. He is best known to many as the photographer for the Time-Life cookbook series, which had him traveling to many places, including the Napa Valley. In 71, after several visits to Napa, he bought vineyard land in Rutherford and began developing it to Cabernet Sauvignon; 10 years later he acquired property in the Carneros District which has since been planted to Chardonnay. The first several harvests were sold off, and it was not until 82 that Lyon made his first wine, a Cabernet Sauvignon released in 88. In the same year he also marketed his first Chardonnay. All vintages have been made in leased space, and production remains below 1,000 cases as Lyon continues to sell the major share of his grapes.

LYTTON SPRINGS WINERY   *Sonoma 1975*   Located on the northwestern edge of Healdsburg that separates Dry Creek from the Alexander Valley, Lytton Springs was known first as a vineyard. It has 150 acres, including 50 of Zinfandel planted in the early 1900s. This parcel of old vines, possibly the oldest in Sonoma County, is known as the Valley Vista Vineyard. Ridge brought Lytton Springs to our attention in 72 when it made a vineyard-designated Zinfandel. The vineyard's owners, inspired by the recognition, established their own winery in 77, and have always made Zinfandel their mainstay. As a producer, Lytton Springs turned out Zinfandels that were often intense, sometimes close to late harvest in style, and brawny but not always cleanly made. In the early 80s the winery had developed a full line, including White Zin, Chardonnay, Cabernet Blanc, and an ill-advised blended red named "Weinburger."

In the 90s the winery is once again concentrating on Zinfandel and produces on average 6000 to 7,000 cases of a regular bottling and 1,000 cases of a Private Reserve from the old vines. Traditional winemaking practices are still followed as the Zinfandels are neither fined nor filtered prior to bottling. When all goes well, Lytton Springs appeals to lovers of potent, full-blown Zins. Cabernet Sauvignon from a vineyard owned near Hopland in Mendocino County has recently been added to the line. Ridge Vineyards has resumed making a vineyard-designated Lytton Springs Zinfandel, but from an adjacent parcel.

Zinfandel

79 ✳✳   80   81   82 ✳✳   83 ✳✳✳   84 ✳✳   85 ✳   86   87 ✳✳✳   88 ✳✳

Full-blown, ripe, dense, rich, oaky, tannic, alcoholic; incredible when right and disastrous when not

---

MACROSTIE WINERY   *Sonoma 1988*   After leaving his post as winemaker at Hacienda Winery, where he served from 75 to 87, Steve MacRostie formed his own family wine company. His focus is on Chardonnay grown by Sangiacomo, one of the biggest independent vineyards in the Carneros District. His approach is to whole-cluster press the grapes and then ferment the juice entirely in oak barrels. The wine is aged for several months *sur lie*. As he expands the annual output to 3,000 cases of Chardonnay, MacRostie is looking into production of a Pinot Noir from the same region. In 89 he was a consultant to several winemakers, and moved his own operation into the Roche Vineyards in the southern Carneros. He became the consulting enologist for Roche before its first harvest. MacRostie Chardonnay started off at a high quality level in its first few vintages.

Chardonnay

87 ✷   88   89 ✷

Firm fruit and suggestions of complexity in early vintages show promise for the future

MADRONA VINEYARDS   *El Dorado 1980*   With 35 acres planted along a ridgetop at the 3,000-foot level, Madrona can claim to have vines growing at the highest level in the state. Located 5 miles east of Placerville, the vineyard is owned by Dick Bush, who established it in 73 with the intention of selling all of the crop. When the grape market proved difficult, he built a winery and began making wines in 80. Most of the winery's production is from his own vineyard, which contains Cabernet Sauvignon, Merlot, Cabernet Franc, Zinfandel, Chardonnay, Johannisberg Riesling, and Gewurztraminer. All are made as varietals. On occasion a portion of his Riesling develops *Botrytis* and a late harvest version is produced. Overall the winery has had limited distribution of its wines and has enjoyed limited success. Its highlights include an 85 Chardonnay that earned ✷✷, and in 86 Madrona made an outstanding ✷✷ White Zinfandel. The winery's annual production target is 7,500 cases.

MAISON DEUTZ WINERY   *San Luis Obispo 1981*   A joint venture between Deutz Champagne of France and Wine World, Inc., owner of Beringer Vineyards, et al., Maison Deutz is located in the Arroyo Grande area of San Luis Obispo County. Originally, the winery was to use grapes from the Edna Valley and other parts of the county. Today, through subsequent acquisitions of Wine World, Inc., it owns 150 acres in Santa Barbara County. The holdings consist primarily of Pinot Blanc (49 acres), Pinot Noir (44 acres), and Chardonnay (40). French winemaker Christian Roguenant also originally wanted to follow the same process he used as assistant winemaker for Deutz Champagne in France: all grapes are hand-picked, and pressed by hand in a basket press. The base wines are barrel-fermented and undergo 100% malolactic fermentation. The cuvée selected is composed of roughly equal parts of Pinot Blanc, Chardonnay, and Pinot Noir. The second fermentation is activated with "prise de mousse" yeast. Held *en tirage* for an average of 18 months, the wines are complexed by older "Reserve" wine in the dosage.

Like its French parent, Maison Deutz focuses on nonvintage wines, primarily a Brut and to a lesser degree, a Rosé. Made in limited amounts (500 cases) and only in unusual years, a Reserve Vintage Champagne (first made in 86) completes the line. Also, consistent with Deutz of Champagne, Maison Deutz plans to grow to the modest production level of 30,000 cases by the mid-90s. For the Brut, the quality level over the first few years has been ✷.

MANZANITA   *Napa 1980*   This is a label owned by Steve Koster, a longtime resident of Napa Valley who has designed numerous wineries. Using leased space and operating part-time, he has regularly made Napa Valley Chardonnay and Cabernet Sauvignon. Manzanita Chardonnays are 100% barrel-fermented, and about one-third goes through malolactic fermentation. The Cabernet Sauvignon, usually softened with Merlot, is aged for two years in small French oak barrels. On average, Manzanita makes about 1,500 case of Chardonnay and close to 1,000 cases of Cabernet Sauvignon per year.

MARIETTA CELLARS   *Sonoma 1980*   Heavyweight red wines are the major focus of this owner-operated winery. Winemaker Chris Bilbro, whose family once owned Bandiera, buys grapes from within Sonoma County to produce 10,000 cases a year. The mainstays are Zinfandel and Cabernet Sauvignon, both made in a somewhat rustic style, and a country-style blend, "Old Vine Red." Zinfandel has occasionally earned ✻ and more. When Bilbro feels he has a special batch, he bottles it as a Reserve Zinfandel.

Cabernet Sauvignon
81 ✻ 82 ✻ 83 84 85 87 ✻

Following the house style, this wine is typically rough, ripe, sometimes hinting at tar, and best suited to burgers and steaks hot off the barbecue

Zinfandel
82 83 ✻✻✻ 84 ✻ 85 ✻ 86 ✻ 87 ✻

A berryish version of the Cabernet, it has been enjoyable and attractively priced for the last several vintages

---

MARILYN MERLOT This play on words, which may seem a tasteless joke to some, is in fact a private label owned by Nova Wine Partners in St. Helena. First made in 85, so far each vintage uses a different photograph of Marilyn Monroe on the label, and the name is written across the label in a lipstick-smear script. Part of the proceeds go to her estate. For the first two vintages, all grapes originated in Napa Valley. When it became difficult to find sufficient Merlot from Napa in 87, wines from the French region of Aude were used. The annual output has increased from 1,500 in the first year to over 5,000 cases.

MARION WINERY Started in 1980, this private label belongs to Dennis Marion, who until 89 used the Domaine Marion and M. Marion label identities. A former wine retailer and importer specializing in French Burgundies, Marion began in 80 as a negociant offering a range of varietals from ready-made wines he blended and bottled. In the mid-80s, he decided to lease space in the old winery owned by the Novitiate of Los Gatos and began crushing, fermenting, and bottling a line of varietals and generics. Dealing in the low end of the price spectrum, Marion was bottling about 100,000 cases in 88. However, the operation was not cost-efficient, and in 89 Marion moved north to Sonoma County, reentered the negociant field, and started over at the 50,000-case-a-year mark. The Marion line consists of Chardonnay, Cabernet Sauvignon, White Zinfandel, Fumé Blanc, and Pinot Noir, all labeled with the California appellation. Generic red and white table wines are sold under the Pacific Coast label.

MARKHAM VINEYARDS *Napa 1978* Founder Bruce Markham bought an old, defunct winery north of St. Helena along with some choice acreage in the Yountville area. Within a year the large (1-million-gallon-capacity) winery was cleaned up and ready to crush, both for Markham's own brand and for others on a custom-crush basis. Despite his background in the advertising profession, Markham never really generated much publicity for his own winery. He may have gotten off on the wrong foot by offering high-priced Muscat de Frontignan and Gamay Beaujolais Blanc as his first releases. His first red wine, a Merlot, was sold under the second label, Vin Mark, and the quality was not high.

One of the primary vineyards Markham purchased was a 100-acre plot in Yountville that came with a rich history. It once belonged to the Van Loben Sels family, who owned Oakville Vineyards (now defunct) and produced a few exciting Cabernet Sauvignon vintages during its tenure from 68 to 77. Even though Markham is located between the frequently visited Charles Krug Winery and Sterling Vineyards, the plain-looking Markham facility did not attract the attention of tourists until its major facelift in 89. By then Markham was gone, having sold his winery in early 88 to Sanraku of Japan. Markham's annual output had reached 18,000 cases by 80, and stagnated at that level until 88. By the mid-80s, however, the winery was beginning to earn ✻ and ✻✻ for its Merlots and Cabernet Sauvignons, and by 87 was heading on a positive course.

Under the new ownership, the vineyards have been redeveloped and expanded. The winery draws from three locations within Napa Valley. The largest planting is in Yountville, with all 100 acres now devoted exclusively to Cabernet, Merlot, and Cabernet Franc. In Napa, the winery has a 70-acre parcel called Hopper Creek Ranch, with Chardonnay and Sauvignon Blanc predominating. In a sector of Calistoga at moderate warmth and high elevations, the winery has 60 acres under vine, with 49 acres of Cabernet and 11 of Merlot. In order to meet the demand for Merlot, it has been buying grapes from within Napa Valley. As its annual output hit the 30,000-case mark, halfway to its projected maximum, Markham focuses attention on Merlot (blended with Cabernet Sauvignon), Cabernet Sauvignon, and Chardonnay (100% barrel-fermented from 87 onward). It offers limited amounts of Muscat Frontignan, Sauvignon Blanc, and a red Meritage wine. Sanraku, the parent company, has developed a global network, with wineries in Australia, Bordeaux, Italy, and in Japan, where it is the largest producer.

Cabernet Sauvignon

78* 79* 80** 81** 82* 83** 84** 85** 86**

Here is our candidate for the best-kept secret among high-quality Cabernet Sauvignons; the consistent results from year to year and the very good aging potential exhibited by this wine make it one to look for, especially in view of its relatively moderate price level; in every vintage it has delivered nicely focused cherry and cassis fruitiness, filled out by rich oak, with medium tannins that firm but do not overwhelm the wine

Chardonnay

84 85* 86 87 88

Never one of our favorites, it has been clean, oaky, but limited in range even in its better years

Merlot

81** 82 83* 84* 85*** 86** 87 88*

Attractive ripe, bright, cherrylike fruit, sweetened by a nice touch of oak, comes with just a bit of tannic coarseness to encourage a few years of cellaring without interfering with the wine's early drinkability

---

MARTIN BROTHERS WINERY *San Luis Obispo 1981* Located east of Paso Robles, the Martin winery has grown from a tiny renovated dairy barn to a mid-sized, modern facility. Run by the entire Martin family, the winery is surrounded by the family-owned 70-acre vineyard. Chardonnay at 35 acres and Chenin Blanc at 15 are the prime varieties, but the vineyard also contains 8 acres of Nebbiolo and 1 acre of Dolcetto. Though the volume emphasis has fallen on White Zinfandel, Chenin Blanc, and Chardonnay over the first several vintages, the Martins have tried hard to generate interest in Nebbiolo and other Italian grape varieties. After making their first Nebbiolo in 84 from Amador County grapes, they switched to a Central Valley source until their own acreage came into maturity. They have increased the production of Nebbiolo to 3,500 cases, and from grapes purchased they also produce small amounts (500 cases) of Aleatico. In the late 80s they offered even smaller quantities of a Grappa made entirely from Nebbiolo. Most of the varietals are of standard quality, with the exception of the bone dry, oak-aged Chenin Blanc, which is lean, tart, and on occasion worthy of special attention. Annual total output of 14,000 cases is expected to increase to 20,000.

Chardonnay

84 86 87

Made in a lean, direct style, usually with noticeable tart acidity evident, the wine gains a bit of range and softness from oak

Zinfandel

83 84 85 86

Dilute fruit, hints of brush, and a lack of varietal focus keep this one from being attractive

MARTINELLI VINEYARDS *Sonoma 1987*   In the grape-growing profession since 05, the Martinelli family began producing small amounts of wines in 87. Zinfandel, Gewurztraminer, and Chardonnay are the primary varieties found in its Russian River Valley vineyard. Planted in 19, the 4 acres of Zinfandel are located on the steepest hillside, and part of the Zinfandel crop is made into wine by Williams & Selyem. Z Moore has purchased Martinelli Gewurztraminer and Chardonnay. Under its own label, Martinelli focuses on Chardonnay, Gewurztraminer, and Zinfandel, and its annual production is approximately 2,000 cases.

MARTINI & PRATI *Sonoma 1951*   Though this large (2½-million-gallon-capacity) old winery is an integral part of Sonoma County's wine history, it produces little wine under its own label. Most of its production is made under contract for other large wineries. The majority of what it makes for itself from its 250-acre vineyard is sold under the historic Fountain Grove label, Cabernet Sauvignon and Chardonnay being the two primary items. The quality pays homage to a bygone era noted for its rustic-style, over-aged wines.

LOUIS M. MARTINI WINERY *Napa 1922*   One of the most revered wine families, the Martinis have always seemed to pride themselves on a low-keyed, no-frills approach to the wine business. From 34, when Louis M. Martini made his first vintage in Napa Valley, to the early 70s, Martini enjoyed a following for its red wines, Cabernet Sauvignons, Zinfandels, and Barberas. In 57 Louis M. turned the reins over to his son, Louis P. Martini, who operated the winery in much the same fashion. Today, his two children, Carolyn and Michael, have taken on full responsibilities as president and head winemaker, but the senior Martini remains active in the winery's daily operation.

Prior to 80, the winery was producing about 400,000 cases, with strong emphasis on red wines, but to many people it seemed to be resting on its laurels. Martini Cabernet Sauvignons from the 40s, 50s, and 60s—Special Selection and/or Private Reserve—were held in the same high esteem as Inglenook's and Beaulieu's Cabernets. Martini Cabernets tended to be less intense than the competition, but responded exceptionally well to bottle aging, and in our experiences Martini Cabernets in 51, 57, 58, and 68 Lot 4 rank among the finest tasted. The winery offered three bottlings of Cabernet Sauvignon, the California appellation being the mainstay. For the Special Selection, the winery would set aside the best 10% from a given vintage, while the Private Reserves through the mid-50s often came from the Monte Rosso Vineyard in Sonoma Valley, and thereafter were often Cabernets given extended bottle aging by the winery. After the 70 vintage, the winery's Cabernets failed to keep pace. Martini was also highly regarded for Barbera, an occasional vintage of bone-dry Gewurztraminer, a white varietal known as "Folle Blanche," and for Moscato Amabile, a semi-sparkling wine sold at the winery. The winery produced and bottled the first commercial Merlot (a blend of 68–70) from California.

Despite its record and its honest pricing, the Martini Winery failed to sustain interest after the early 70s. The style of many red wines, derived from aging in large redwood vats, was out of sync with the times. By the end of the 80s, needed changes had been made. All the old redwood cooperage had disappeared, and small oak barrels aging both red and white wines lined the walls. Although Cabernet Sauvignon is still the volume leader, Chardonnay follows right behind it, and Sauvignon Blanc has been added to the line. The new Martini offers three categories of table wine. Its modestly priced varietals from Napa Valley, Sonoma County, or North Coast appellations now number a dozen. The Reserve program consists of three Napa Valley varietals—Cabernet Sauvignon, Petite Sirah, and Chardonnay. A series of vineyard-identified varietals is at the top end of the price scale and includes Chardonnays, two Pinot Noirs (La Loma Vineyard, Las Amigas Vineyard), Cabernet Sauvignon from Monte Rosso in Sonoma Valley, and Merlot from Los Vinedos del Rio Vineyard.

Of the winery's 1,000 acres established to vines, over 50% fall within Napa Valley, about 35% in Sonoma County, and the remainder in Lake County. The annual output of varietal wines is 225,000 cases. Even with a new label and changes in the lineup, Martini's recent wines remain low in intensity and in quality usually rank only as acceptable.

Cabernet Sauvignon

(North Coast)   80   81   82   **83**   84   85   86

(Vintage Selection)   82 *   **83**   84 *   **85**   87 *

Martini's regular bottling is light, fruity, directly but not very boldly cherrylike, and geared to immediate drinking; the Vintage Selection wines are much fuller in body, wider-ranging in character, with briary and spicy notes added to ripe cherry flavors, more evident oak, and long-lasting tannin

Chardonnay

84   85   86   87 * *   **88 ***   89

Aside from the rich and deep 87, Martini Chardonnays have been crisp and green appley, with occasional citrus or floral overtones, but without the depth or richness to lift them to higher ratings

Zinfandel

82 *   83   84 *   85   86   87

Thin but generally fruity; light in tannin; immediately drinkable

MASSON VINEYARDS   *Monterey 1852*   Paul Masson founded his winery in Saratoga, part of today's Santa Cruz Mountain appellation. He developed a brand that was among the best known in California, both during his reign and long after his death. Known as Paul Masson Vineyards, the original mountain winery was purchased by Joseph E. Seagram in 43, and under its ownership production was expanded to a full line of table (varietal and generic), fortified, and sparkling wines. Concentrating on nonvintaged table wines in the 60s, Masson offered consistency but rarely great quality. Annual output grew to close to 8 million cases, as Seagram augmented production by operating a large facility in Soledad in Monterey County, even larger facilities in the Central Valley, and maintained both its modern Champagne Cellars and historic mountain winery in Saratoga.

By the mid-80s, Masson owned 4,500 acres of vineyards in Monterey County, and was turning out a line of varietals from Monterey that lacked consistency and failed to win any kind of following. In 87 Vintners International acquired Masson, along with Taylor California Cellars and Taylor of New York. Shortly thereafter, all Masson operations were shifted to Soledad and to a large production facility in Madera. The new owners decided to focus on separate lines of wines. The top of the line is known as Masson Vineyards, a name attached to five Monterey County varietals: Chardonnay, Sauvignon Blanc, Johannisberg Riesling, Cabernet Sauvignon, and Merlot. Second is a line identified as Paul Masson that includes generics, sparkling wines, blush wines, and a few once popular items such as Emerald Dry, Rare Souzao Port, and Rhine Castle. By the end of the 80s, the management had gone through some reshuffling and had sold all of the original vineyards. The winery purchases most grapes under contract, and the present Vintners International partnership brings 1,500 acres in Monterey into the fold. The lion's share of the business remains generic bottlings, including 600,000 cases of wines in Masson's carafe container. Overall, annual sales were moving close to 5 million cases.

MATANZAS CREEK WINERY   *Sonoma 1977*   From very modest beginnings (3,000 cases made in a converted barn in 77) Matanzas Creek has grown moderately in size and exponentially in reputation. In 74, 22 acres were planted to Chardonnay and Merlot in what was then a remote part of Sonoma County called the Bennett Valley, midway between Santa Rosa and Kenwood. Initial success with Chardonnay encouraged the owners, Sandra and Bill MacIver, to add 20 acres of Chardonnay and some Cabernet Sauvignon. After a few vintages and a change in winemakers, Matanzas Creek dropped its erratic Pinot Noir and by 84, with production up to 8,000 cases, it constructed a new, ultra-modern winery with a much greater production capacity. Having earned ✳✳✳ for its Chardonnays and critical acclaim for its Sauvignon Blancs, the winery, to the surprise of many, made a major commitment to Merlot by phasing out of Cabernet production to devote all efforts to Merlot. Today, three varietal wines are made. Chardonnay, in a barrel-fermented style, is the most important, with 15,000 cases produced. Sauvignon Blanc (about 5,000 cases), aged in oak and usually blended with Semillon, is a trendsetter with the complexity and balance to earn ✳ regularly and ✳✳ on occasion. It also has some aging potential. Merlot (1,500 cases) is usually blended with Cabernet Franc and Cabernet Sauvignon, and then aged in new French oak. Future increases in annual output will likely be in Merlot.

Chardonnay

84 ✳   85 ✳   86 ✳✳   87 ✳✳✳   88 ✳✳   89 ✳

Enormous depth of flavor, showing ripe, appley fruit, augmented by rich, toasty oak with balance provided by ample acidity; medium-length aging potential

Merlot

82 ✳   83 ✳✳   85   86 ✳   87 ✳✳   88 ✳

Marked by inconsistency in its early vintages, the wine is typically on the very ripe side and often adds nuances of brush, herbs, and cocoa to deep fruit

MAYACAMAS VINEYARDS   *Napa 1941*   A good choice as the prototype of the modern boutique winery, Mayacamas began to assume its present shape in 41, when Jack and Mary Taylor bought a long-abandoned stone winery and distillery, both built in 1889. Jack Taylor was an executive with Shell Oil, and he and his wife wanted a simpler lifestyle. An old vineyard was planted to Pinot Noir and Chardonnay along extra-wide terraces on the steep hillsides. Situated on the slopes of Mount Veeder at the 2,000-foot elevation level, the vineyard proved difficult to farm and experienced low yields owing to deer and bird damage. After some success with their Chardonnays, the Taylors gave up on Pinot Noir and planted Cabernet Sauvignon. For several vintages in the 60s, Philip Togni was the winemaker at Mayacamas.

By 68, weary of the pace, the Taylors sold the winery to Bob and Elinor Travers, owners ever since. The winemaker for them in 68–72 was Bob Sessions, who went on to work at Hanzell. The Traverses have expanded the vineyard to 55 acres and concentrate on Cabernet Sauvignon and Chardonnay, along with limited amounts of Sauvignon Blanc, Pinot Noir, and Zinfandel. A late harvest Zinfandel appears every now and then. About 2,000 cases of Cabernet Sauvignon are made each year. Mayacamas Cabernet is 100% varietal and usually tannic. During the 70s its Cabernets enjoyed a well-deserved following, but they have not been among the quality leaders in recent vintages. Mayacamas also makes about 1,000 cases of barrel-fermented Chardonnay. Most of the winery's production is sold through a mailing list.

Cabernet Sauvignon

70 ✳✳   73 ✳✳   74 ✳✳   78   79 ✳   80   81 ✳   82   84

Even now, older Mayacamas wines are among the best of their vintages; sadly, the more recent efforts have lacked the fruit to bring the wine into focus and, as a result, it has lost a good deal of standing among top producers

MAZZOCCO VINEYARDS *Sonoma 1984* Dr. Thomas Mazzocco is a famous eye surgeon practicing on the West Coast who acquired an 18-acre vineyard in the Alexander Valley. This vineyard is named River Lane, and contains 18 acres of Chardonnay. Another vineyard in the Dry Creek Valley has 13 acres planted to Cabernet Sauvignon and its blending varieties. Chardonnay accounts for 75% of the winery's total production. Mazzocco offers two versions: a limited River Lane Chardonnay, and a Sonoma County Chardonnay, three times more plentiful. Zinfandels from Dry Creek Valley were an immediate hit in a big, richly fruity style. Mazzoco also produced noteworthy Cabernet Sauvignon. The winery was on course to produce 35,000 to 40,000 cases a year before it was dragged down by the financial problems of Vintech, an investment firm that bought it in 90. Dr. Mazzocco bought his winery back in 91. A Bordeaux blend labeled "Matrix" is also produced.

Cabernet Sauvignon

   86* 87**

   Following a ripe, rich style, with both depth and tannins for medium-term aging, the wine leans toward fullness without sacrificing balance

Chardonnay

   (River Lane Vineyard)   86   87*   **88****
   (Sonoma County)   85   86*   87   **88***

   Both wines feature well-balanced, appley fruit, and noticeable oak; the latter is the oakier of the two

Zinfandel

   86***   87***   88**

   Ripe, lots of concentrated berryish fruit, tannic, and capable of being among the best and longest-aging Zinfandels made in California

PETER MCCOY VINEYARDS *Sonoma 1984* McCoy, a CPA in San Francisco, has reserved a place for himself in history as the first to make Chardonnay from the Knight's Valley appellation. Beginning in 80, he planted 15 acres on rocky soils and dubbed that vineyard Clos des Pierres. A very good Chardonnay is the primary variety, followed by small amounts of Cabernet and Merlot. The Chardonnays are 100% barrel-fermented in French oak. When the vineyard reaches full maturity, McCoy's production will peak at 3,500 cases.

Chardonnay

   84*   86**   87*   **88****

   Lots of toasty oak from barrel fermentation is positioned atop solid, deep varietal fruit, while ample acidity assures both balance and ageworthiness

MCDOWELL VALLEY VINEYARDS *Mendocino 1979* In 70 Richard and Karen Keehn purchased a large ranch situated 4 miles east of Hopland. It was their intention to develop a vineyard and sell the fruit. Within a few years they had not only developed the original vineyard site but had also expanded it to over 300 acres. For several years they sold their grapes, but in early 79 they decided to start their own winery. A mechanical engineer, Rich Keehn constructed a 40,000-case winery operated by solar energy. The varieties grown and made into wines changed with the times, as the once popular Chenin Blanc, French Colombard, and Zinfandel (since reinstated) were dropped from the line. With the addition of Chardonnay, Cabernet Sauvignon, and Sauvignon Blanc, the Keehns expanded their vineyard to a total of 600 acres. Throughout the changes in focus, the winery continued making Grenache and Petite Sirah.

In 81 the Petite Sirah, which consisted of 36 acres, was identified by experts as the French Syrah, giving McDowell one of the oldest and largest plantings of Syrah in the state. In 82 they began labeling their wine "Syrah." A new winemaker hired in 85 experimented with Grenache and Syrah, and with newly planted Rhone varieties—Mourvedre, Marsanne, and Viognier. By 89

McDowell was producing modest amounts of wines made from Rhone varieties collectively identified as "Les Vieux Cépages." This group is made up of Syrah, a Grenache Rosé, and a Syrah-Grenache blend named "Le Trésor."

By the end of the 80s McDowell Valley winery had helped to define the McDowell Valley as a Viticultural Area. By then, the winery was making a range of estate-grown varietals which includes a Fumé Blanc that has achieved ✳ ✳ ranking, a rich, ripe Syrah, and an erratic Chardonnay. As its annual output grew to over 125,000 cases, McDowell was also offering a White Zinfandel, low-priced bottlings of California Chardonnay, and Cabernet Sauvignon.

Cabernet Sauvignon

81 ✳   82 ✳   83 ✳   86

Early vintages showed good fruit and depth, but later wines have been more ordinary

Chardonnay

(McDowell Valley)   84 ✳ ✳   86   87   88

(California)   87   88   89

The winery has experienced limited success with wines that are thin and mildly fruity with floral overtones; the home-grown version is noticeably oaky

---

MCHENRY VINEYARD   *Santa Cruz 1980*   After retiring in 74 from his position as Chancellor of the University of California at Santa Cruz, Dean McHenry tended to his 4-acre vineyard adjacent to his home in the Santa Cruz Mountains. Beginning in 77, with the help of his family, he became a home winemaker and won several awards. With his son Henry McHenry, a professor from U.C. Davis, serving as winemaker, they went pro in 80, making a total of 300 cases. At 3.3 acres of Pinot Noir and 1 acre of Chardonnay, the winery's maximum annual output will remain below 500 cases. Most of the output is sold at the winery located on Bonny Doon Road or at retail in the San Francisco Bay Area. Both wines reach ✳ status on occasion.

MCLESTER WINERY   *Los Angeles 1980*   At the eastern end of the runway of LA International, McLester occupies a small building in an industrial area. Another home winemaker turned pro, Cecil McLester retained his position as sales manager for a semiconductor firm in Los Angeles. Grapes are trucked in from Amador County for Zinfandel and from Paso Robles for Cabernet Sauvignon, Merlot, and Sauvignon Blanc. The best-selling wines are the blends "Runway Red" and "Runway White," both depicting a 747 on their labels. A small quantity of medium-sweet Muscat Canelli named "Suite 13" is occasionally offered. Total production is at the 1,000-case-a-year mark, with 5,000 set as the maximum.

THE MEEKER VINEYARD   *Sonoma 1984*   On a 215-acre ranch in the Dry Creek Valley, Los Angeles attorney and investor Charles Meeker has set up his small winery. With a 60-acre vineyard on the hillsides in northwestern Dry Creek, Meeker is producing Zinfandel, Cabernet Sauvignon, and Chardonnay. Zinfandel was the volume leader over the five vintages. With vineyard maturity, however, Meeker's production of Cabernet Sauvignon blended with Merlot and Cabernet Franc will top 4,000 cases. Chardonnay and Zinfandel are each at 3,000 cases a year. Meeker's first vintages of Zinfandel were on the brawny, high-alcohol side. His Cabernets display more tannin than fruit. The winery's production will level off at the 10,000-case-a-year mark.

Cabernet Sauvignon

84 ✳   85 ✳

Bold, ripe, immensely tannic wines requiring long aging are the rule here, but the fruit seems unlikely to measure up to the demands of a decade or more of cellar aging

Chardonnay

84   86   87*   88

Ripe and loaded with oak, the wine often lacks the brightness and depth to carry its aggressive style and tends at times to become a little ragged and heavy-handed.

Zinfandel

84**   85*   86*   87

Like the other Meeker wines, this one is made in a no-holds-barred style featuring ripeness and oak in abundance; it can be among the better examples of Dry Creek Zinfandel, but occasionally needs more depth to match its abrasive tannins

---

MELIM VINEYARDS *Sonoma 1986* In 73 Cliff Melim bought a 140-acre ranch in the Chalk Hill region of the Alexander Valley which contained 50 acres planted to grapes. After selling his Cabernet Sauvignon to many neighboring wineries for a dozen years, Melim decided to venture into the winemaking business. His vineyard has been expanded to 80 acres and now consists of Chardonnay and Cabernet Sauvignon. Having produced Sauvignon Blanc for two vintages, he replaced that variety with Chardonnay. Melim makes only two wines, Chardonnay and Cabernet (blended with Merlot) and markets them as "Melim Reserve." Odd lots of Cabernet Sauvignon that are not used in the primary wine are bottled and sold under Maacama Creek, Melim's second label. The winery's current production of 8,000 cases is equally divided between Chardonnay and Cabernet Sauvignon. Melim intends to keep that ratio as he grows toward the 12,000-case-a-year target.

MENDOCINO VINEYARDS *Mendocino 1986* In a facility in Ukiah once known as Cresta Blanca, Mendocino Vineyards is one of seven wineries belonging to the Guild co-operative of growers. The old winery built in 46 was upgraded in 79, and today is home to Mendocino Vineyards, which offers a line of generic and varietal table wines. In the 80s the facility has been used by many smaller brands such as Fremont Creek and Lolonis. The Mendocino Vineyards lineup consists of Cabernet Sauvignon, Chardonnay, Zinfandel, Johannisberg Riesling, and White Zinfandel. Favoring proprietary names, the winery offers three generics—"Eagle Creek White," "Timber Ridge Red," and "Salmon Point Blush." The overall quality for this line of low-priced wines is at best barely acceptable. Dunnewood, a sister label, is produced in this facility.

MERIDIAN CELLARS *San Luis Obispo 1984* Chuck Ortman, one of the first young winemakers to make a name for himself in the 70s, owned this brand before selling it to Nestlé in 88. After buying the former Estrella River Winery facility, but not the brand, and 560 acres of vineyards, Nestlé hired Ortman to be the winemaker and acquired the name Meridian in the deal. In the 60s, Ortman began his career at Heitz Cellars, and then moved on to become winemaker for Spring Mountain Winery. With them, he was responsible for several fine vintages of Chardonnay, Cabernet Sauvignon, and unusually rich Sauvignon Blancs. Ortman left Spring Mountain and then consulted to several wineries—Far Niente, Shafer, Fisher, Keenan, and Cain—before starting Meridian in 84. Napa Valley Chardonnay and Sauvignon Blanc were produced by Meridian in Napa Valley until Ortman joined the Nestlé company in Paso Robles, the site of the present Meridian. With the new Meridian, Ortman began by making two Chardonnays, Edna Valley and Santa Barbara County. The first vintages yielded close to 30,000 cases total. As the name gains recognition, the winery will expand production to 100,000 cases a year. Chardonnay dominates the volume, but both Syrah and Pinot Noir are also being made by Meridian.

MERLION WINERY *Napa 1985* After Vichon Winery was sold to the Robert Mondavi Winery, half of the Vichon team remained together to start Merlion.

George Vierra and winemaker John McKay are equal partners in Merlion, and they have been emphasizing the same wine trio as they did at Vichon. Chardonnay, Cabernet Sauvignon, and Sauvrier (an equal blend of Sauvignon Blanc and Semillon) top the roster. Lesser amounts of Pinot Blanc labeled "Coeur de Melon," Pinot Noir, and late harvest-style whites have been made. Using leased space and buying all grapes, Merlion came roaring out of the chute and made close to 15,000 cases in each of its first few vintages. However, sales were unable to keep pace, and in recent vintages Merlion's production has been averaging about 7,000 cases, with "Sauvrier" accounting for over half of the total. Except for a wonderful but limited-production 86 Cabernet Sauvignon that earned ❋❋, Merlion wines have not generated much interest, nor have they risen above the level of acceptable quality.

MERRY VINTNERS *Sonoma 1984* The Merry in the winery name belongs to well-known winemaker Merry Edwards. After three years as Mt. Eden's winemaker (74–76), she moved to Matanzas Creek Winery in 77. Then, having supervised seven vintages there, she started her own winery. Her husband, Bill Miller (the winery's sales manager), and her parents are all partners in this winery, located a few miles northwest of Santa Rosa. The focus has been Chardonnay, with as many as three different versions in one vintage. Several label designations have been used in an effort to distinguish among them. More recently, the winery favors the "Reserve" tag for its riper style of completely barrel-fermented Chardonnay. A less expensive bottling once labeled "Vintage Preview" is now identified as Sonoma County, and the third, first bottled in 87, is a vineyard-designated wine called Sylvan Hills Vineyard.

The winery's first three vintages met with mixed reviews. A more consistent quality level began in 86, but we have yet to witness much consistency in style in any one Chardonnay from one year to the next. The total production is close to the 7,500-case capacity of the winery. In 89, Merry was named winemaker for Laurier Vineyards, a post that allows her to continue making Merry Vintners wines.

Chardonnay

    (Sonoma County) 84 85 87 ❋ 88 ❋

    (Reserve) 86 87 ❋ 88 ❋

    (Sylvan Hills) 87 ❋

    Each of these wines, regardless of the extra oak showing in the Reserve and the Sylvan Hills, is oriented toward lean, appley fruit, and is crisp and tight on the palate

MERRYVALE VINEYARDS *Napa 1983* Owned by five partners, three in real estate and two in the wine business, Merryvale burst onto the scene with great promise. The same partnership owns the Sunny St. Helena Winery (see entry) and since 86 Merryvale wines have been produced and bottled there. Merryvale was the brainchild of partner Bill Harlan, who in addition to developing and owning offices in San Francisco also owns the Meadowood Club in St. Helena, a resort which is home to the annual Napa Valley wine auction. Ric Forman served as the consulting winemaker when early vintages were made at the Rombauer Winery. Bob Levy, formerly of Rombauer, has since joined Merryvale as winemaker.

Only two wines are made, Chardonnay and a Red Table Wine that combines Cabernet Sauvignon with lesser amounts of Merlot and Cabernet Franc. All grapes are purchased, with Spottswoode and the Napanook Vineyard supplying some of the Cabernet. Merryvale's Chardonnays, made in part from Napanook grapes, are barrel-fermented and aged in new oak. About 2,500 cases of each are produced.

Chardonnay

    84 ❋ 85 ❋ 86 87 88 ❋ 89 ❋

No shrinking violet, this brashly oaked, tight, but solidly fruity wine will appeal to fans of expansive Chardonnays

Red Table Wine

83 * * *   84   85 *   86

Somewhat inconsistent to date but never lacking for size, this one can be wonderfully fruity and full of rich oak at its best; even in lesser years, it has the capability to improve for up to a decade in the bottle

---

PETER MICHAEL WINERY *Sonoma 1988* In the early 80s, London-born business-man Peter Michael acquired vacation property on a knoll overlooking the Knight's Valley. In 84 he was encouraged to develop a vineyard which is located at the 1,700–2,000-foot-elevation level. Cabernet, Merlot, and Cabernet Franc were the main varieties planted in the 23-acre site. In 88, 25 additional acres of the same varieties were developed. Chardonnay from the Gauer Ranch in the Alexander Valley, the first wine to be released, has been produced each year. Made in the traditional Burgundian manner—barrel fermentation in new oak—the inaugural Chardonnay release was a * * * success. A new winemaking facility with several unusual touches was fully operational by 89. The winery was divided into two separate sections, one for red winemaking, the other for Chardonnay. A special barrel-fermentation room controls both the temperature and the humidity for Chardonnay production and aging. With vineyard maturity, the winery plans to grow gradually to about 12,000 cases a year, equally divided between Chardonnay and a Cabernet blend that is named Les Pavots.

Chardonnay

(Gauer Ranch) 87 * * *   88 * *

Debuting with one of the best Chardonnays in years, and following with an impressive second wine, this producer will be one to watch; the wines to date have been rich, complex, deep, and fairly pretty

---

MICHTOM VINEYARDS *Sonoma 1982* Back in 71 the Michtom family acquired a large ranch in the Alexander Valley to the east of Healdsburg. Lying along the Russian River, the original vineyard contained Cabernet Sauvignon, which was later increased and joined by Chardonnay. The total acreage today stands at 130. In 82, Michtom began using part of the crop to produce its own wine. Though a large percentage of the crop is still sold, Michtom's production has grown to 12,000 cases combined of Cabernet and Chardonnay. A blended white wine is marketed under the second label, Bethune Street.

Chardonnay

84   85   87

A thin, citrusy, and boring wine at best, it offers little attraction in spite of its moderate price

---

MILANO WINERY *Mendocino 1977* Located in Hopland, Milano is a compact winery that is a refurbished hop kiln. Over its first few vintages, the winery offered an array of wines from Mendocino and Sonoma County appellations with variable quality results. In 80 the ownership was restructured, and the winery came into the control of the Milone family. Jim Milone is both director of operations and winemaker and is emphasizing Chardonnay, Cabernet Sauvignon, and Zinfandel. In 85 the winery was still making numerous wines, including four separate Chardonnay bottlings. That year the annual output reached 10,000 cases. Production, due to slow sales, has since been reduced to 2,000 cases, though the owners plan to work their way back to 5,000 cases a year. All wines offered are produced from the family's 60-acre vineyard, located a short distance from the winery. Chardonnay has been the only wine hinting of success in the last few vintages.

MILAT VINEYARDS   *Napa 1986*   Brothers Bob and Mike Milat, longtime residents of St. Helena, own a 22-acre vineyard established in the late 40s. They were content to sell their grapes to local wineries until the mid-80s. After seeing so many of their BMW-driving customers become successful wine producers, they decided to join in. A cozy winery and tasting room were built close to the wine road a little south of St. Helena. Their marketing plan was to sell all wines direct from the centrally located winery. As the output grew to 2,500 cases, they focused on White Zinfandel, Chenin Blanc (below 1% sugar), Sauvignon Blanc, Chardonnay, and Cabernet Sauvignon.

MILL CREEK VINEYARDS   *Sonoma 1974*   Located at the southern end of the Dry Creek Valley 5 miles due west of Healdsburg, Mill Creek is owned and operated by the Kreck family. The Krecks first planted vines in 65, and the family vineyard, always weighted toward Cabernet Sauvignon, now covers 75 acres. In 77 the first harvest from young Cabernet vines yielded a wine so light in color that it was bottled and dubbed "Cabernet Blush." When the blush wine era arrived in full, Mill Creek had the trademark rights to the Blush name and was paid royalties by those using it. By 82 the winery had been expanded to include a visitors facility and picnic grounds. The winery sells a high percentage of its 15,000-case annual output direct from the tasting room.

A full line of table wine is made, including four reds (Cabernet Sauvignon, Merlot, Pinot Noir, and Gamay Beaujolais) and three whites (Chardonnay, Sauvignon Blanc, and Gewurztraminer). Though it was among the pioneers of a Merlot, Mill Creek has not been among the leaders. The Sauvignon Blancs, however, are among the most herbaceous and aggressive versions of the varietal, and represent the winery's best performance. To market wines at the low-priced level, Mill Creek uses the Felta Springs brand as its second label. Overall, Gewurztraminer and to a lesser extent, Chardonnay have been the winery's other occasionally praiseworthy offerings in a generally lackluster performance.

MIRASSOU VINEYARDS   *Santa Clara 1966*   A family winery that is now run by the fifth generation, Mirassou produced bulk wines for decades. Since entering the bottled-wine world in 66, the winery has grown to the 350,000-case-per-year level. It has not reached that level easily or without experiencing serious setbacks along the way. With the winemaking facility located in the Evergreen area south of San Jose, the winery maintains 200 acres of vineyards within Santa Clara County and has another 600 acres under vine in northern Monterey County. Most of the vineyard land once owned or leased by the winery was giving over to houses in the early 60s. In 66–67, the Mirassou began developing vineyards in Monterey to supply anticipated needs. Many of the early vintages were derived from Monterey County, and as the largest, most visible brand using the Monterey appellation, Mirassou became identified with the "Monterey veggies." This condition derives from a strong vegetative component in the red wines, especially Cabernet Sauvignon and Zinfandel. Throughout the 70s and even into the early 80s, the Mirassous continued making red wines that were not always acceptable and correct.

In recent years the winery has changed its vineyard focus by removing Zinfandel and some of its Cabernet from Monterey. Buying some fruit from Napa Valley, it has begun to offer Cabernet Sauvignon with a California appellation. Its production level breaks down into 70% white wines, 20% reds, and 10% sparkling wine. The volume leader is White Zinfandel, followed by Chardonnay, Monterey Riesling, and White Burgundy. The latter, often a good value, is made predominantly from Pinot Blanc. The *méthode champenoise* sparkling wines are beginning to earn recommendations after years of erratic performance.

Beginning in 89, Mirassou sparkling wines have been made in a separate facility. Over the years the special designation for limited-volume table wines has been "Harvest Reserve," but no wine in the last several years has lived up to that title. The name "Pastel" first appeared attached to a proprietary blush wine, but now has been elevated to a separate line of low-alcohol wines. The winery has set 500,000 cases a year as its maximum production level for all wines. With the few exceptions mentioned, Mirassou wines have rarely garnered many recommendations.

Chardonnay

84 85 86 87 88*

Light in intensity and low in character, this wine carries quiet suggestions of flowers and pears in a balanced but rarely inviting presentation

---

C. K. MONDAVI WINES *(Charles Krug Winery)* This label covers a large-volume line of once popular jug generics that have failed to keep pace with the times. All the wines are made primarily from Central Valley–grown grapes and are labeled with the California appellation. A line of low-priced varietals—Chenin Blanc, Sauvignon Blanc, Chardonnay, Zinfandel, and Cabernet Sauvignon—appeared in 91, representing an attempt to add some needed zest and interest. The roster is still headed by Chablis and Burgundy. Annual sales, which topped 1 million cases in the early 80s, are now level at 700,000 cases.

ROBERT MONDAVI WINERY *Napa 1966* After being forced out of Charles Krug Winery, a winery owned by his family, Robert Mondavi formed his own company in 66 and built a new winery in Oakville. At first he worked with his son Michael, but within a year he was joined by his other son, Tim, now in charge of enology, and his daughter Marcie. Robert was able to finance the development and start-up operation through a 50–50 partnership with Rainier Brewing Company of Seattle. The winery at the time was the first new one built in Napa Valley since Prohibition, and was also to become known as an ultramodern, highly experimental, high-tech facility. All tanks for fermentation and storage have always been monitored by computer, and Mondavi conducted untold experiments in what evolved into a winery within a winery experimental lab.

The use of oak was a subject of endless experiments, and the winery was soon overflowing with barrels of all sizes from every known cooper in the world. Early in its history, the Robert Mondavi Winery rescued Sauvignon Blanc from oblivion by popularizing a dry, oak-aged style under the name Fumé Blanc. In 78, Rainier's interest was purchased and the winery became a wholly owned family project. Shortly thereafter the winery's production reached 350,000 cases, and it owned 1,000 acres of vineyards adjacent to the winery and in other Napa Valley sites. In 79 Mondavi revamped an older winery in Woodbridge, near Lodi, and transferred the production of his lower-priced line of Cabernet Sauvignon, Sauvignon Blanc, and White Zinfandel. These wines evolved from a trio of table wines (red, white, and rosé) introduced in 75. Opus One (see entry) was yet another Mondavi project that became a reality in 79.

Amidst amazing expansion marked by the uncanny promotional knack of its proprietor, Robert Mondavi Winery earned worldwide recognition for its wines, especially the Cabernet Sauvignon. Now making both a regular and Reserve (the initial vintages were labeled "Unfiltered"), Mondavi has fiddled with the style of each Cabernet bottling over the years. By the mid-80s the regular Cabernet was styled to be varietally correct, early maturing, and attractive to restaurateurs, whereas the Reserve Cabernets had become fatter and more ageworthy. However, Pinot Noir, both regular and Reserve versions, demonstrated great improvement in the 80s. Robert Mondavi Chardonnays have been generally consistent, but ironically, Fumé Blanc, once the winery's flagship, has been less successful of late, although the Reserve Fumé Blanc remains among the very best of the type.

Completing the winery's line are Johannisberg Riesling, Chenin Blanc, and a sweet, dessert wine, Moscato d'Oro. The winery's leading wine in volume is Chardonnay at 200,000 cases, followed by Cabernet Sauvignon at 100,000 cases. With annual production close to 650,000 cases, Mondavi purchases about half of all the grapes it crushes. A vineyard in the Carneros was established in 88, and when fully developed will bring 480 acres (mostly of Pinot Noir and

Chardonnay) into the fold. All told, Mondavi now owns about 1,500 acres in the Napa Valley and controls another 1,000 acres. Included in its Napa holdings are 400 acres of Cabernet Sauvignon. Mondavi also owns close to 500 acres in Santa Barbara County. Other California wineries owned by Robert Mondavi or his family are Vichon Winery, Byron Winery, Opus One, Montpellier, and Robert Mondavi–Woodbridge.

Cabernet Sauvignon

(regular bottling) 68** 70** 73* 74** **75*** 76 77 78 79* 80 81 82 **83*** **84*** **85*** **86*** **87***

Among the best Cabernets in the early 70s, this wine has been made in a softer, more drinkable style for over a decade now; it retains generally attractive fruit, has a softly oaky veneer, and carries moderate tannins

Cabernet Sauvignon

(Reserve) **71**** **73***** **74***** **75**** **76**** **77**** **78*** **79**** **80**** **81**** **82**** **83**** **84**** **85**** **86***** 87**

Rich, refined, balanced wines, deep in curranty and ripe cherry fruitiness and sporting lots of creamy oak, these attractively supple wines are buttressed by plentiful but never overwhelming tannins, and are among the most elegant offerings within Cabernet's upper echelons

Chardonnay

84** 85 86* 87* 88 89

Stressing toasty oak, this wine succeeds when its appley fruit is able to bring the composition into balance

Chardonnay

(Reserve) 84** 85** 86 **87***** **88***** 89*

Round, mouth-filling, deeply drawn wines, these complex Chardonnays combine appley fruit with oaky and roasted-grain notes; superb balance will keep the best efforts in good shape for many years of cellaring

Pinot Noir

(regular bottling) 80* 81* 82* 83** **84**** **85*** 86 87* 88 89*

(Reserve) 80* **81**** **82**** 83** 84* 86 87** **88**** 89*

Somewhat closer in character and style than the other Mondavi pairings, these wines are supple, somewhat velvety, and balanced; both have cherry and black-cherry fruit and rich oak. The Reserve is clearly the deeper and longer-lasting, often with more range

MONT ST. JOHN CELLARS *Napa 1979* The Bartolucci family, owners of the Mont St. John Cellars and the estate vineyard known as Madonna Vineyards, is one of the old and most important families in Napa Valley. In 22, the family acquired a winery and 24 acres of vineyards offered through an auction. After Prohibition, it operated the Madonna Winery, which at one time was the 12th largest in California. In 71, confronted by "an offer they could not refuse," the Bartoluccis sold the winery and vineyard in Oakville, and the buyers started the ill-fated but often exciting Oakville Vineyards. Afterwards, Buck Bartolucci used his share of the proceeds to buy 160 acres in Los Carneros. Over the next few years, he developed new vineyards, and ended up with 140 acres planted.

By 79 Buck and his father had built a small winery in Los Carneros. During the 80s the Bartoluccis sold most grapes, notably their Pinot Noir and Chardonnay, to the likes of Acacia, Robert Mondavi, and Joseph Phelps. For years both Acacia and Bargetto have made a Pinot Noir, Madonna Vineyard, from Bartolucci's grapes. As its own wine producer, Mont St. John Cellars expanded gradually, and by 90 was at the 15,000-case-a-year mark. It has shown promise at times with Pinot Noir and with recent vintages of Cabernet. Chardonnay represents over 60% of the winery's total production, with Cabernet Sauvignon at 20%. All other varietals—Pinot Noir, Sauvignon Blanc, Gewurztraminer, Johannisberg Riesling, and Muscat—are made in lots of 500 cases and are available primarily at the winery. For any wines bearing the California appellation, the owners use their second label, Poppy Hill. All told, the annual output will level off at 22,000 cases.

MONTEREY PENINSULA WINERY *Monterey 1974* Owned by two dentists in the Monterey Bay area, this winery developed something of a maverick reputation during its first five vintages. The original building serving as its winery until 86 was a slightly restored restaurant, and along with the basic equipment within, the overcrowded premises added to the "devil-may-care" feel. However, Monterey Peninsula made several exceptional wines, and for many years it was the only producer of first-rate Cabernet Sauvignon from Monterey County. In the 70s it was also highly involved in the Zinfandel revival, and for many vintages produced as many as eight separate bottlings.

After moving into a bigger, more efficient facility in 86, the winery began emphasizing Monterey-grown wines, led by Cabernet Sauvignon, Merlot, Chardonnay, and Pinot Blanc. It uses "Doctor's Reserve" as a designation for the best Cabernet, Merlot, and occasionally best Zinfandel from a particular vintage. Directed By Dr. Roy Thomas, the winery regularly makes Chardonnay (barrel-fermented) from the Sleepy Hollow Vineyard in Monterey, Pinot Blanc (barrel-fermented in neutral oak) from the Cobblestone Vineyard in Monterey, and Zinfandel from the Ferrero Ranch in Amador County. Its often praiseworthy Cabernet Sauvignon (2,500 cases) and an usually exceptional Merlot (1,000) represent close to half of the winery's production. An unusual, long-aged, blended red (Petite Sirah with Zinfandel) is called Black Burgundy. The winery's more conventional, jug-style blended white and red table wines are sold under the Big Sur label. In some years, small quantities of Barbera and Pinot Noir are made. With production today at 10,000 cases, the winery has a capacity to expand to 20,000 cases.

MONTEREY VINEYARD *Monterey 1973* Now an elaborate 2-million-gallon-capacity winery, the Monterey Vineyard began with a well-known winemaker and great aspirations for varietal wines from Monterey, an unproven growing region. Winemaker Dick Peterson arrived from Beaulieu Vineyard to direct production, and the erudite Gerald Asher, author and essayist for *Gourmet,* joined him as marketing director. However, over the first few vintages the wines were not well received. The whites were excessively grassy and intense; the reds bordered on the vegetal. The whole venture never really got off the ground and was beginning to disintegrate fast. Peterson soon found himself the sole owner and winemaker until Coca-Cola of Atlanta came along to buy the winery in 77. The Coke team used Peterson to create many wines for their new low-end brand, Taylor California Cellars. Slowly, they made changes in the product line, bringing respectability to Monterey Vineyard.

In 83 Coca-Cola of Atlanta sold its various wine interests to Joseph E. Seagram, and in 86 a new winemaker, Cary Gott, was brought in. Amidst many changes, all the varietal wines still originate in Monterey County, and the Classic Red and Classic White, developed and highly promoted during Coke's reign, remain its best-sellers. The winery now owns or controls 1,200 acres of vineyards, with Cabernet Sauvignon, Chenin Blanc, and Chardonnay the most widely planted. Its two best-selling varietal wines are Chardonnay and White Zinfandel. Two lines of varietals are offered. The primary one consists of Cabernet Sauvignon, Chardonnay, Sauvignon Blanc, White Zinfandel, Chenin Blanc, and Riesling. A limited-volume, pricier line of "Limited Reserve" wines is composed of Chardonnay, Cabernet Sauvignon, and Pinot Noir. Annual production is around the 750,000-case mark. The maximum goal is 1 million cases. In 91, Gott moved to Sterling Vineyards.

Cabernet Sauvignon

(Limited Release)   85*   86*

Medium-depth fruit, cast in a bright, zesty vein, is firmed up by moderate tannins and makes the wine worthy of a few years in the cellar

Chardonnay

(Limited Release)   **84**   85   86   87   88

Ripe but narrow, and sometimes showing a hard, lean quality; rarely with enough depth to justify bottle aging

MONTEVINA WINERY   *Amador 1973*   A key player in the revival of Amador County, Montevina was the first new winery established in the Sierra Foothills after Prohibition. Between 72 and 74, it developed its 80-acre vineyard in the Shenandoah Valley, consisting of Sauvignon Blanc (29 acres), Zinfandel (22), Cabernet Sauvignon (15), and Semillon (10). Trial parcels of Ruby Cabernet, Nebbiolo, and Barbera were also planted. (Of the latter, only 4½ acres of Barbera survived.) From 73 to 82, the winery was directed by winemaker Cary Gott, who developed a reputation for several types of Zinfandel along with an innovative streak. Montevina was among the first to make a Nouveau-style Zinfandel (labeled "Nuevo") by carbonic maceration, and also a White Zinfandel, made in a bone-dry style.

   In the 80s production increased as the winery attempted to emphasize whites such as Chardonnay from purchased grapes and Sauvignon Blanc and Semillon from the estate vineyard. After a family dispute, Gott left, and for a time the winery lost any sense of direction. In late 88 the winery and vineyard were bought by the Trinchero family, owners of Sutter Home Winery in Napa Valley. They have since added 50 acres of red grapes, primarily Zinfandel, with 10 acres each of Barbera, Refosco, and Sangiovese. As the annual production holds at 60,000 cases, the winery is again focusing on Zinfandel. Time will tell whether the latest ownership change will stabilize the winery and return it to the quality level achieved during its first decade.

Zinfandel

84*   **85**   87

Changes in style have made this one hard to follow through its many variations in name, depth, and tannin levels; the 87 is the first under new management, and is both lighter and shallower than the typical Amador County Zinfandel

MONTICELLO CELLARS   *Napa 1980*   Thomas Jefferson happens to be one of Jay Corley's personal heroes, so when Corley ventured into the grape-growing business, he named his company Monticello. In the early 70s, Corley was operating a successful real estate and insurance business in Los Angeles, and among several investments he bought a former prune orchard in Napa Valley located just north of the town of Napa. He planted the site to vines, and sold all of the first several harvests from the 125 acres. However, by 80 Corley began easing into winemaking, producing his first two vintages at a neighboring facility. His own winery was built in time for the 82 crush. As a grower, Monticello initially specialized in white varieties—Chardonnay, Sauvignon Blanc, and Gewurztraminer. While still selling many tons of grapes, it now buys some Cabernet Sauvignon and Merlot to use in its expanding red wine program. Cabernet Sauvignon now accounts for half of the winery's production. The "Jefferson Cuvée" Cabernet is a fruit-oriented version softened with Merlot. Another Cabernet, made in a riper and longer-lived style, is named "Corley Reserve." Its two Chardonnays follow the same terminology—the stainless-steel-fermented, fruity Chardonnay is labeled "Jefferson Cuvée," and the barrel-fermented, new-oak-influenced Chardonnay is "Corley Reserve."

   Monticello was first known for its dry-styled Gewurztraminer, and at times this dry (under 1% residual sugar) wine earns *. Most of the time its Sauvignon Blanc is extremely grassy and herbal, almost to a fault. The same is often equally true of its Chevrier (made from Semillon). Experimental batches of Pinot Noir are light in color but promising. Monticello made 24,000 cases in 90, but some of the 40,000-case-capacity facility is used to custom-make wines. Corley is also actively involved in Domaine Montreaux and Llords & Elwood.

Cabernet Sauvignon

(Corley Reserve)   82*   84*   85*   86*   87**

(Jefferson Cuvée)   82**   83***   84   85   86**   87

Proving that bigger is not always better, the Jefferson Cuvée has turned out to be the more attractive wine over the years for its better fruit; if not as tough as the Corley, it will age perfectly well for up to a decade or more

Chardonnay

(Corley Reserve)   84   85*   86**   87   88

(Jefferson Cuvée)   84*   85*   86*   87   88

Though not exhibiting the range of its oakier sibling, the Jefferson is capable, in most years, of being an accessible, fruity, crisp, and clean Chardonnay, while the Corley, when it succeeds, relies on wood and ripe grape character

---

MONTPELLIER VINEYARDS, *Stanislaus 1988*   Members of two prominent wine families are behind this winery. The joint venture brings together the Franzia brothers, operators of the once gigantic Bronco Wine Co., and Robert Mondavi's son, Michael, and Robert's wife, Margrit. Part of the wine production takes place in Ceres, the home facility for Bronco, but in the first few years, the wines were aged and bottled in Woodbridge, home to Robert Mondavi's low-priced line of Woodbridge wines. The owners bring to the Montpellier brand 300 acres of mature vineyards, and another 700 acres of land that will be developed into vineyard. The winery focuses on five varietals—Cabernet Sauvignon, Chardonnay, White Zinfandel, Sauvignon Blanc, and Merlot. The annual production of White Zinfandel, Cabernet, and Chardonnay amounts to 50,000 cases. All were 100% varietal in composition, and priced at the low end.

MORGAN WINERY   *Monterey 1982*   As winemaker for Durney Vineyards in Carmel and Jekel Vineyards in the Salinas Valley, Dan Lee had the opportunity to acquire first-hand knowledge of many vineyards within Monterey County. In the early 80s when working for Durney, he began developing his own brand. In the beginning Morgan was to be a Monterey County Chardonnay–only label. Enjoying critical success for his Chardonnays, Lee added Sauvignon Blanc from the Alexander Valley and bottled it under the now abandoned St. Vrain name. By 86 Lee decided to make Morgan his full-time project and opened a small facility in Salinas. Purchasing grapes for all wines, Lee produces a Monterey Chardonnay by blending fruit from six separate vineyards. Barrel-fermented in heavily toasted French oak from Burgundy, Morgan Chardonnays undergo partial malolactic fermentation before being aged for close to a year *sur lie*. An occasional Reserve Chardonnay is given longer barrel and bottle aging. Partially barrel-fermented in less toasty oak, Morgan's Sauvignon Blanc (blended with 5–10% Semillon) originates in the Alexander Valley. A low-yielding hillside vineyard in Carmel Valley remains the source for Cabernet Sauvignon, which Lee ferments at relatively warm temperatures and confines to 100% varietal composition. Bottled with the California appellation, Morgan's Pinot Noir is from grapes grown primarily in the Carneros, with a small portion from Monterey. Using open-top fermenters, Lee adds 10% whole clusters and believes in a warm fermentation for Pinot Noir.

Overall Dan Lee has turned out such magnificent Morgan Chardonnays (up to ***) that his other wines often go unnoticed. However, this talented winemaker has been successful with all wines. The Sauvignon Blanc, rich and creamy, is usually varietally precise and elegant enough to earn **. The 86 Cabernet, the first offered, began on a ** level. As production edges toward the 20,000-case annual goal, 50% consists of Chardonnay and 25% is Sauvignon

Blanc. From wines purchased and blended, Lee bottles low-priced Chardonnay under the Del Mar label.

Cabernet Sauvignon

86** 87*

Impressively stuffed, medium-full-bodied, rich and ripe wines which, from all indications, should age well

Chardonnay

84** 85*** 86*** 87* 88** 89*

This wine's impressive track record has been crafted with a string of deeply fruited, pineappley, and sometimes citrusy efforts, buttressed by toasty oak and hints of roasted grains. It places Morgan among the top 10 Chardonnay producers in the state

J. W. MORRIS WINERY *Sonoma 1975* Ken Toth owns the 275-acre Black Mountain Vineyard in the Alexander Valley. His grapes were sold to many wineries in the 70s, but one of the bigger buyers was J. W. Morris Port Works, located 100 miles south in downtown Emeryville. Morris began life as a port wine specialist and branched out to offer a range of table wines. By 83, the winery was in financial trouble, and it was taken over by one of its major creditors, Toth of Black Mountain. The winery—tanks, barrels, and wine—was moved to Black Mountain in July 83. The name was changed to J. W. Morris Winery and still appears on port as well as a range of inexpensive varietal and generic wines.

Wines currently produced by Morris are Sonoma County Chardonnay, Sauvignon Blanc, and Cabernet Sauvignon, as well as red and white blended table wines identified as "Private Reserve." Upscale vineyard-designated varietals from Toth's vineyard are bottled under Black Mountain Vineyard (reviewed separately). J. W. Morris Ports are produced in limited volume and include a Vintage Port and a late-bottled Vintage Port. Total output of all products is just in excess of 70,000 cases, which includes close to 20,000 cases of the red and white generic wines. The prices are generally on the lower end, and the quality is often acceptable for the money.

MOSBY WINERY AT VEGA VINEYARDS *Santa Barbara 1979* Owned and operated by the Mosby family, this winery used the name of Vega Vineyards until the family name was added recently. The facility occupies a renovated carriage house in the Santa Ynez Valley. With 34 acres developed on two separate parcels in the area of Buellton, the winery produces Gewurztraminer, Johannisberg Riesling, Chardonnay, and Pinot Noir in both a conventional and "Blanc" style. The Mosbys label the Pinot Noir-Blanc "Pineau." Every now and then a late harvest, *Botrytis*-affected Riesling is produced. Throughout the winery's history, the overall quality has varied considerably. At times, the slightly sweet Gewurztraminer earns ❀, but in some vintages it is unattractive. Its other offerings seldom rise above the acceptable level. Over its first decade, as Vega or as Mosby Winery, the wines have been made by owner Bill Mosby. The annual production goal is 10,000 cases.

MOUNT EDEN VINEYARDS *Santa Clara 1972* In the early 40s, Martin Ray left Paul Masson Winery and developed vineyards and a winery which he operated until 72 as Martin Ray Vineyards. Ray was a strong-minded individual, who was often involved in controversy over finances and winery control. After protracted legal battles among investors which culminated in the removal of Ray from the winery, the property was split by a court order. The bigger vineyard parcel and the original winery on the steep mountainside overlooking the Santa Clara Valley were renamed Mount Eden Vineyards. The lower, smaller portion was taken over by the Ray family and operated as Martin Ray Vineyards. Since 72 the Mount Eden winery, also no stranger to controversy, has made three wines from its 36-acre vineyard. Both Chardonnay and the Pinot Noir (originally planted in 43) are located at the highest elevations—1,800- to 2,000-foot level. Cabernet Sauvignon is established in the lower parcel at the 1,400-foot level. The crop from these old, unirrigated vines planted on thin mountain soil is usually extremely small.

In the 80s, the acreage of Cabernet Sauvignon was expanded to 20. At times Mount Eden has made spectacular, rich vintages of Chardonnay in a ripe, barrel-fermented vein, and highly extracted Cabernet Sauvignon. Pinot Noirs have performed erratically. However, after a slump in the early 80s, the winery, under the guidance of winemaker Jeffrey Patterson, began returning to form in 84. In a typical year it makes 500 cases of estate-bottled Chardonnay and Pinot Noir. The production of Cabernet should double to 1,000 cases with vineyard maturity. Following a traditional approach, its Cabernets are aged two years in French oak and two years in bottle before being sold. The volume wine (3,000 cases) is a Chardonnay from the MacGregor Vineyard in Edna Valley sold through 87 under the winery's second label, MEV, and now offered as a second Mount Eden Chardonnay. It too is a full-blown, barrel-fermented wine, though usually less rich than the winery's estate Chardonnay.

Cabernet Sauvignon

73 *** 74 ** 75 * 76 ** 77 * 78 ** 79 * 80 81 82 83
84 ** 85 * 86 ** 87

Gone are the days of waiting 10 to 15 years for this wine to become somewhat accessible (although the still-evolving 73 ranks as one of our all-time favorites) and now one can taste the deep, curranty, briary, somewhat rooty and bell-peppery fruit through the tannins at an earlier age

Chardonnay

(Estate) 84 *** 85 * 86 *** 87 *** 88 ***

An enviable track record in the last few vintages has lifted this deep, rich, toasty, appley, fleshy, and well-balanced wine to stardom

Chardonnay

(Edna Valley) 85 86 * 87 * 88 * 89 *

In the rich Mount Eden style, the wine is both oaky and nicely fruity, but has less range and substance than its more expensive running mate

Pinot Noir

80 81 82 83 84 ** 85 87 ***

At its inception, in 72, this was one of the few true standouts among California Pinot Noirs, but lately it has had a difficult time and more often than not fails to deliver the ripe, deep, black-cherryish fruit and rich, loamy, slightly leafy nuances that have been its hallmark in the best vintages

MOUNT PALOMAR WINERY *Riverside 1975* One-time merchant seaman, tuna fisherman, and U.S. Army officer John Poole owned and operated the popular radio station on Catalina Island, KBIG, before entering the wine business. He left radio in 69, attracted by the opportunity to buy vineyard land in Temecula. His vineyard, the Long Valley Vineyard, was among the first in the area. Once covering 150 acres, it now contains about 100 acres. Poole acted as winemaker for the first vintage in 75, and for the next hired Joseph Cherpin. In the early vintages the winery's line was slanted toward slightly sweet table wines (including a Cabernet Sauvignon) and sherries, selling many wines directly from the tasting room. In 81 the owner revamped the vineyards, removing several varieties that performed poorly and replacing them with Chardonnay and Sauvignon Blanc. A few acres have been planted to Sangiovese.

With 32 acres planted, Chardonnay is the volume leader, followed by Johannisberg Riesling, Cabernet Blanc, and Chenin Blanc. As the winery moves toward its ultimate production goal of 30,000 cases, its white wines represent 80% and blush wines 10% of the total. Its large visitors center is one of the most popular in the area, and several wines—Cream Sherry, Gamay Beaujolais Nouveau, and the occasional late harvest Riesling—are sold only at the winery. Every so often, wines are bottled under a second label, Long Valley Vineyards.

MOUNT VEEDER WINERY *Napa 1973* In the mid-1960s, founders Mike and Arlene Bernstein planted 20 acres on the steep slopes of Mount Veeder. Among the first vintages, the winery offered rich, brawny Cabernet Sauvignons, often on the weedy-green olive side, and an often fantastic, rich, barrel-fermented Chenin Blanc. Enamored of immense, ripe Zinfandels (73 was a classic that remains alive), Bernstein also went out of his way to make them in both standard and late harvest styles. Chardonnay from the Long Vineyard was made for several vintages, and there were several successes. By 80, when its annual production had reached 4,000 cases, the winery was more of an artistic success by virtue of its "interesting" wines than a commercial success. The low-yielding vineyards turned out to be extremely labor-intensive to farm.

In 82 the winery and the 80-acre estate were sold to the Matheson family. The vineyard was expanded to 23 acres, with 6 to Chardonnay, 12 to Cabernet Sauvignon, and the remainder to other Bordeaux red varieties. Buying additional grapes, the winery was making 5,000 cases by 85. It remained at that level until June 89, when the winery was sold again, this time to Agustin Huneeus and the Eckes family, owner of Franciscan Vineyards. From its 40-acre vineyard and additional grapes purchased, the winery has set 15,000 cases as its annual goal, with a Cabernet Sauvignon and a red Meritage blend representing 75% and Chardonnay 25% of the total.

Cabernet Sauvignon

74** 75** 76 77 78 79* 80* 81** 82 83 84 86 87

The deep and long-lasting fruit captured in the early vintages seems to have been lost in the more recent offerings; as a result, the wines of the mid-80s have turned out stiff, hard, and ripe, without the necessary center of fruit to bring them into balance

Chardonnay

84 85* 86 87 88

Firmly structured but sometimes lacking in depth, the wine tends toward apples and citrus, with more of the latter quality in lesser years, and typically carries an oaky component

MOUNTAIN VIEW VINTNERS A negociant brand for a line of table and sparkling wines, Mountain View is owned by Vinformation, a wine-marketing company in San Francisco. The wines first appeared in 80, after which the annual output grew to a peak of 100,000 cases. Chardonnay (50,000 cases) from Monterey County and White Zinfandel (15,000 cases) are the volume leaders. Generic red and white blends account for 25,000 cases. Small batches of other varietals (Sauvignon Blanc, Cabernet Sauvignon, Pinot Noir) are offered from various regions. Quantities each year depend upon availability. To date, no wine in this line has stood out in any special way.

MUMM NAPA VALLEY *Napa 1985* In 83 Mumm of Champagne and Seagram Classic Wine of California started this sparkling wine company as a joint venture. Until 90 the label was Domaine Mumm. In 84 it was producing a range of cuvées in a facility adjacent to Sterling Vineyards, and the first bubbly from Domaine Mumm hit the market in 86. By 88, it was fully ensconced in its present location on the Silverado Trail. From 50 acres in the Carneros and Rutherford areas and another 200 acres available to it through Sterling Vineyards, Mumm produces four styles of sparkling wine. Its most important wine in terms of volume is labeled "Cuvée Napa, Brut Prestige." In presumably exceptional years it makes a Vintage Reserve. The third wine, a vintaged Winery Lake Cuvée, is limited to about 2,000 cases a year and was likely the first vineyard-designated sparkling wine made in California. A Blanc de Noirs, the fourth sparkler, was added in 90.

For its Brut, Mumm has been using about 10% Reserve or older wine, and each year the winery directs more of its production into increasing its supply of older wines. With winemaker Greg Fowler (formerly with Schramsberg Vineyards) directing the operation, the winery harvests its grapes at the 19.5 Brix target, slightly higher than its French parent. In the early going, Mumm performed extremely well, with a wonderful fruity, slightly yeasty Brut displaying the sought-after delicacy of Pinot Noir, and a richer, complex Reserve presenting a creamy, toasty impression. By 90, Mumm's annual sales were close to 65,000 cases. Long term, the output will level off at 200,000 cases.

MURPHY-GOODE ESTATE VINEYARDS *Sonoma 1986* Two of the principals in this winery are longtime, highly regarded vineyardists. Tim Murphy developed vineyards in the Alexander Valley in the mid-60s; his partner Dale Goode is a vineyard manager for several wineries, and a partner in the Alexander Valley Vineyard, for which he serves as vineyard manager. Their combined holdings represent 300 acres of vineyards in the heart of the Alexander Valley. All wines are made from their estate vineyards. The winery focuses on four varietals—Chardonnay, Fumé Blanc, Cabernet Sauvignon, and Merlot. As production grows from the present 25,000 cases a year to its targeted 50,000-case level, Chardonnay accounts for close to 50% of the total. Fumé Blanc represents about 30%, with the reds at the 15% mark. The Chardonnays are 100% barrel-fermented and aged *sur lie*. The Fumé Blancs have been extremely varietal, with brisk acidity, and have been awarded ❊. A small amount of Reserve Fumé Blanc, made in a barrel-fermented, *sur lie*-aged style, is also available. Merlot has been the best performer to date.

Cabernet Sauvignon

86❊   87

Medium-intensity black-cherry fruitiness is combined with sweet oak in a wine of moderate tannins and moderate aging potential

Chardonnay

85   86❊   87   88❊   89

Straightforward, fairly bright fruit, redolent of apples, pears, and flower blossoms, is enriched by supporting notes of sweet oak in a wine noteworthy for its immediate appeal rather than its aging potential or complexity

Merlot

86❊❊   87   88❊❊

Round, open cherry and black cherry fruit, moderately tannic and medium aging

NALLE WINERY *Sonoma 1984* Doug Nalle gained winemaking experience at Jordan and Souverain before going on to become winemaker at Quivira. Like a number of winemakers working within Sonoma County, Nalle came to be fascinated by Zinfandel grown on benchlands in the Dry Creek Valley. To produce wines under his own label, Nalle insists upon Zinfandel from relatively old, low-yielding vines. Using grapes purchased from growers, he has developed a style of Zinfandel that exudes a rich, berrylike fruit but also offers finesse in place of tight tannins. He uses open-top fermenters, and ages his wines in small French oak barrels for close to two years. As a result, his wine has depth of flavor but is ready to enjoy in its youth. His Zinfandel production is steady at 2,000 cases a year. A short time after the 89 harvest, Nalle decided to devote all of his efforts to his own brand, which now includes Cabernet Sauvignon.

Zinfandel

84❊   85   86❊❊   87❊   **88❊❊**

Sent to market young and presentable, this wine is oriented to berryish fruit, often with a touch of ripeness adding an extra dimension of sweetness to its oak-enriched aspects

NAPA CREEK WINERY *Napa 1980* Renovating a former meat-packing plant located on the Silverado Trail, owner Jack Schulze's winery got off to a poor start as some of the wines from the first vintages displayed serious problems. New equipment was eventually installed to avoid repeating history, but the winery's production reached 13,000 cases a year without many successful wines. However, by 86 it was on a much-improved course. Relying on a 50-acre vineyard in Napa Valley under long-term contract, Napa Creek produces Chardonnay, Merlot, Cabernet Sauvignon, Riesling, and Gewurztraminer. About half of its 10,000-case output consists of Chardonnay; Merlot and Cabernet Sauvignon combine for 40% of the total. In the 90s Schulze intends to take production up to 18,000 cases a year.

NAPA RIDGE *(Beringer Vineyards)* In 85 Wine World, Inc., owners of Beringer Vineyards, established this label to compete in the then-burgeoning low-priced end of the varietal market. Beginning with bottlings of Chardonnay and Cabernet Sauvignon blended from readymade wines, Napa Ridge was well received in the marketplace and expanded. Within a year, the parent company bought Souverain Cellars in the Alexander Valley with the idea of using that facility for Napa Ridge wines. It did so for about one year and added Sauvignon Blanc, White Zinfandel, and Chenin Blanc to its roster. Before long, the blending and bottling operations shifted to the old Colony facility in Asti, acquired by Wine World. Today, Napa Ridge is also offering Merlot, along with a Red Table and White Table Wine. All wines carry the California appellation. Annual sales are led by White Zinfandel and are approximately 750,000 cases.

NAPA VALLEY PORT CELLARS *Napa 1984* Specializing in Vintage Port, this brand is owned by a Napa Valley wine retail company. The Vintage Port, a blend of Cabernet Sauvignon, Petite Sirah, and Zinfandel, is aged two years in French oak before being bottled. Production of 500 cases could expand to a maximum of 1,500 cases a year, if demand is sufficiently strong. Most of the wine is sold within Napa Valley.

NAPA VALLEY WINE CO. *Napa 1978* Founder Donald C. Ross has changed brands on a fairly regular basis. Making a range of varietals from purchased grapes, he has at different times identified his company as Napa Vintners, Don Charles Ross, and Napa City Cider. At one time in the early 80s he made Sauvignon Blanc from Lake County. At other times he has made Chardonnay, Cabernet Sauvignon, and Zinfandel. Production of wine reached 13,000 cases a year. In the late 80s Ross began cutting back on wine production in favor of cider making.

NAVARRO VINEYARDS *Mendocino 1974* On a 900-acre ranch formerly used as pastureland, Ted Bennett and Deborah Cahn built a beautiful winery which currently enjoys a solid reputation for quality wines. At their Anderson Valley winery, they developed 50 acres of terraced vineyards with Gewurztraminer, Chardonnay, and Pinot Noir predominating. The winery buys Riesling and Cabernet Sauvignon from within the county. Navarro's reputation was founded on Gewurztraminer, usually finished with under 1% sugar, and on the occasional and sometimes outstanding *Botrytis*-affected late harvest Gewurztraminer. The winery now produces two versions of Chardonnay. One is a limited-volume, barrel-fermented wine labeled "Premiere Reserve," and the second is a stainless-steel-fermented, oak-aged Chardonnay with a Mendocino appellation. Both have earned ✿ ratings.

Since its beginning, Navarro has tried many approaches with Pinot Noir, and by the end of the 80s had settled on two production methods. The estate-bottled Pinot Noir is made by the traditional method of punching down, stem retention, and the addition of whole clusters during fermentation. The second

version is produced by carbonic maceration. Both have proven to be successful in most vintages. Over one-third of the winery's 12,000 cases are sold direct
through the winery's twice-a-year mailings.

NEVADA CITY WINERY   *Nevada 1980*   This northernmost winery in the Sierra Foothills produces a variety of wines from local vineyards and from North Coast
counties. The owners, avid skiers as well as wine lovers, built a small winery
in the center of Nevada City where they sell to locals and the ski crowd. The
most popular wine is a proprietary blush, "Alpine Glow." From locally grown
grapes they make Zinfandel, Chardonnay, Pinot Noir, and Charbono, all bottled with the Nevada County appellation. They also offer Napa Valley Chardonnay, Sonoma County Gewurztraminer, and, when *Botrytis* conditions
allow, late harvest Sauvignon Blanc and White Riesling. Both of these late
harvest wines have earned ✷ and are exotically rich, but usually limited in
production to 200 cases or less. Otherwise, Zinfandel is the most conventional
wine made, and the Pinot Noir the most promising. Total production is edging
close to the 7,000-case-a-year goal.

Chardonnay

(Napa)   86✷   87✷   **88**

(Nevada Co.)   88

*Ripe grape and slightly toasty oak have been featured in a wine that has
sometimes lacked depth of fruit*

NEWLAN VINEYARDS & WINERY   *Napa 1981*   Bruce Newlan was an engineer for
Lockheed before deciding to become involved in a vineyard project. In the
mid-60s he was both a grape grower and a part-time winemaker in Napa
Valley. By 77 he became a partner in the Alaterra Vineyards, which lasted
until 80. Relying on his own 30-acre vineyard, he launched his own brand the
following year. From his 16-acre Pinot Noir vineyard south of Yountville,
Newlan makes 600 to 1,000 cases a year. The wine ferments with 15% whole
clusters added at the start. A special batch of Pinot Noir labeled "Vieilles
Vignes" comes from the famous pre-*Phylloxera* School House Vineyard on
Spring Mountain. Another parcel of this old vineyard—a field blend of Zinfandel, Petite Sirah, Carignane, and other reds—is made into a wine Newlan calls
"Century Selection."

From his own 14-acre Cabernet vineyard, Newlan makes about 1,500 cases
of estate-bottled wine and on occasion about 750 cases of Reserve. From
purchased grapes, he makes 2,000 cases a year of Chardonnay, preferring
partial barrel fermentation. Also from grapes bought from neighbors, he will,
when *Botrytis* is prevalent, make a few hundred cases of late harvest Riesling.
Today the winery produces 5,000 cases, and Newlan sells a portion of his
grapes. By selling less and using more of his own grapes, he intends to level
off at about 10,000 cases a year.

Cabernet Sauvignon

84   85   86✷

*Medium-bodied and somewhat skimpy in their cherryish fruit, these wines
have a lean, angular feel on the palate, but will soften with age*

Chardonnay

84✷✷   85✷   86   88✷   89

*Expressively toasty in oak and roasted, nutty qualities, with citrusy and
appley fruit in support; angular in structure*

NEWTON VINEYARD   *Napa 1979*   After selling his interest in Sterling Vineyards in
77, Peter Newton and his wife, Su Hua, began developing the 650 acres of
untamed land they acquired on Spring Mountain. On steep terraces, the
Newtons planted 62 acres to Cabernet Sauvignon, Merlot, Cabernet Franc,
and Sauvignon Blanc. The early plantings and the first vintages were assisted

by Ric Forman, the well-known winemaker whose partnership role in this winery did not work out. In 79 the winery made 2,000 cases of Merlot, and added Cabernet Sauvignon the following year. Despite some successes, the quality of the first few vintages was inconsistent. John Kongsgaard has been in charge of winemaking since the 83 crush. The winemaking facility is a visual delight, as are the surrounding grounds. A barrel-aging room is housed in an underground cellar. Today, the winery makes Merlot, Cabernet Sauvignon (blended with Merlot), and Chardonnay produced from purchased grapes. Sauvignon Blanc, an inconsistent item, was dropped after 87. The annual output is about 25,000 cases.

Cabernet Sauvignon

80 81 82* 83* 84* 85** 86*

Moderately rich in oak and exhibiting ripe black-cherry fruit; somewhat coarse tannins; half a decade or more of aging potential, especially in top vintages

Chardonnay

84* 85** 86 88

Medium-full-bodied wines, usually carrying a nice balance of oak and appley fruit; medium intensity

Merlot

81* 82* 83* 84* 86* 87* 88*

Ripe cherry and subdued herbal and briary notes are buttressed by a bit of sweet oak in moderately tannic wines

NEYERS WINERY *Napa 1980* Bruce Neyers, a research chemist, became interested in wine when he was stationed in San Francisco toward the end of his Army stint. In 71 he started his wine career as a cellar worker at Mayacamas Vineyard. When winemaker Bob Sessions left to become the head winemaker at Hanzell, Neyers found himself wearing many different hats at Mayacamas, including that of winemaker. By 75 he had become acquainted with Joe Phelps, and was hired to establish a marketing program and run the new winery, Joseph Phelps Vineyards. The urge to produce his own wines resurfaced, and with the financial support of Phelps, Neyers began making wines in 80 at the Rombauer facility while he has continued to work at Phelps.

Buying all grapes needed for his wines, Neyers has maintained fairly consistent, if unspectacular, quality, though his grape sources have changed. His Cabernets are from Napa Valley—a blend of grapes from Stags Leap and the Oakville region—and containing lesser amounts of Merlot and Cabernet Franc. Many of his Chardonnays are blends of Napa Valley floor fruit with grapes from Sonoma County, initially from the Alexander Valley, now from Los Carneros. As of 88 he began producing two Chardonnays, one labeled Carneros and the other Napa Valley. The overall quality is certainly acceptable in a straightforward, medium-intense style. By 90 the production was at the optimum level—6,000 cases of Chardonnay and 2,500 of Cabernet Sauvignon. A varietal Cabernet Franc has been bottled from time to time.

Cabernet Sauvignon

80* 81* 83* 84 85 86

Firmly structured in most vintages, but seemingly lacking just a bit of stuffing to match its structure

Chardonnay

84 85 86 87 88

Oaky but somewhat underfruited wines always seem a bit short of achieving higher rankings, but they possess the good balance and firm structure to make them very useful alongside dishes such as broiled fish or pastas in cream sauces

GUSTAVE NIEBAUM COLLECTION *Napa 1989* An offshoot of Inglenook Vineyards, this brand covers a line of limited-production wines, most of which are vineyard-designated. All wines are made at Inglenook, which was founded by Gustave Niebaum. Rather than expand the Inglenook line into a series of vineyard-designated wines, Heublein (the owners) decided to create a separate brand with its own winemaker, Judy Matulich-Weitz. To date the Carneros appellation wines offered are Chardonnays from the Laird Vineyard and the Bayview Vineyard, and in some vintages a "Special Reserve" Bayview Vineyard. Cabernet Sauvignon is bottled from three separate vineyards— Tench in Oakville, Reference in Rutherford, and Mast Vineyard located at the base of Mayacamas Mountains in Yountville. Chevrier (Semillon blended with Sauvignon Blanc) from the Herrick Vineyard is also offered. Total annual production is about 15,000 cases.

NIEBAUM-COPPOLA ESTATE *Napa 1978* Francis Ford Coppola, the famous movie producer, acquired the historic Niebaum home, built by Gustave Niebaum, Inglenook's founder. He purchased an adjacent vineyard of 10 acres, said to be among the oldest in Napa Valley, and developed an additional property into a total of 120 acres of vines. The primary varieties planted and used to produce a Bordeaux blend are Cabernet Sauvignon (60 acres), Cabernet Franc (20 acres), and Merlot (10 acres). "Rubicon," the proprietary name under which the wine is marketed, is aged at least three years in oak and two or more years in bottle before reaching the market. The initial vintage, the 78, did not appear until 85, leading to rumors of dissension between owner and cellar staff. The winery, soon settling into a pattern, grew quickly to the 5,000-case level. In its formative years Niebaum-Coppola bottled a Cabernet Franc and a wine labeled "Claret," but only Rubicon is now regularly made. As of 88 the output of Rubicon was limited to 2,000 cases a year. Its quality level has been ✴, in a style that tends to be hard, tannic, and in need of cellaring. For unknown reasons, the winery has maintained a low profile, despite the fame of its owner and the pedigree of its vineyard.

Rubicon

79 80✴ 81✴ 82✴

This blended wine is always tough in construction and oaky more than fruity; yet it manages in most vintages to be fairly attractive and to promise long-aging improvement

NOBLE HILL VINEYARDS *Santa Cruz 1986* One of many engineers in the computer and software design field jumped ship in 84 to develop a vineyard and prepare for a career in the wine business. On a 24-acre mountain site (1,600-foot elevation) overlooking Los Gatos, owner-winemaker Russ Schildt planted 5 acres to Chardonnay. He also designed his winery, which specializes in white wine production. Barrel-fermented Chardonnay and stainless-steel-fermented Sauvignon Blanc are the only wines produced. The first several vintages of Sauvignon Blanc came from Sonoma County. Chardonnay from both Sonoma County and the Santa Cruz estate appellation are made on a regular basis. The first efforts displayed more than adequate winemaking ability. With vineyard maturity, the winery will grow to 5,000 cases a year.

Chardonnay

(Sonoma)   86   87✴

(Santa Cruz)   87

The winery style emphasizes toasty oak in league with pert fruit and plenty of balancing acidity

OAK RIDGE VINEYARDS *San Joaquin 1934* An old-time co-operative winery in Lodi named East-Side introduced Oak Ridge in the mid-80s as its upscale brand of varietal wines. The large winery still uses Royal Host for its line of low-priced dessert wines. The grower-members behind East-Side own about 3,000 acres in Lodi, and the most widely planted wine varieties are Zinfandel (1,000 acres), Chardonnay (600 acres), and Cabernet Sauvignon (600 acres). Today, thanks to sales of 60,000 cases of White Zinfandel, Oak Ridge is producing about 175,000 cases a year. Red Zinfandel covers 40,000 cases, with Chardonnay and Cabernet Sauvignon each averaging 20,000 cases yearly. Priced on the low end, the Oak Ridge wines are made in a popular, light style, but are generally acceptable for their type and price range.

OAKFORD VINEYARD *Napa 1988* One-time oil explorer Larry Ball decided to slow down and change careers, so he purchased a mature 8-acre vineyard in 86 and moved to Napa Valley. Located on the slope along the Oakville Grade Road, the vineyard is planted entirely to Cabernet Sauvignon. All vintages from 86 to the present have been custom-made for Ball at the Sunny St. Helena Winery. Early production of 800 cases has grown to 1,000 a year.

OBESTER WINERY *Mendocino 1977* After 10 years of planning, the Obesters moved their wine headquarters from their original site in Half Moon Bay to Mendocino's Anderson Valley in 89. A new tasting room and 45 acres of vines have been added adjacent to the winery in Philo. Making a range of table wines from purchased grapes, the Obesters had been most successful with Johannisberg Riesling from Ventana Vineyards in Monterey County and Gewürztraminer from the Anderson Valley. Two Chardonnays are produced, one from the Anderson Valley and a second from the Nelson Ranch in Mendocino County. A Mendocino County Sauvignon Blanc fills out the line.

Sandy Obester is the granddaughter of John Gemello, an historic winemaking figure who founded Gemello Winery in 34. In the same facility she and her husband, Paul, use for Obester wines, she continues the Gemello line of wine, now limited to Cabernet Sauvignon and Zinfandel from purchased fruit. The Obesters still operate the tasting room and gift shop in Half Moon Bay, where they produce enough wine to keep their permit active. Total annual production of the Obester line is close to 10,000 cases.

Chardonnay

84   85   86   87   88   89

Mildly fruity wines with subtle oak, but often exhibiting suggestions of dried brush, and sometimes of cardboard, in the background, the 89 was barrel-fermented and shows more oak

OBSIDIAN VINEYARD *Napa 1984* Over the first few vintages, this small winery was known as Macauley Vineyard and made only a late harvest Sauvignon Blanc. Marketed as "Topaz," a proprietary name, the Sauvignon Blanc was made from 2 acres planted on Spring Mountain. Beginning in 87, owner George Grant Watson added Cabernet Sauvignon from his 5-acre vineyard in St. Helena and changed the brand name to Obsidian. As the winery expands to the 2,000-case level a year, Cabernet Sauvignon accounts for 85% of the total.

OJAI VINEYARD *Ventura 1984* Adam Tolmach is a vineyardist by training and an adventurer when it comes to making wines. He is co-owner of Au Bon Climat, specializing in Chardonnay and Pinot Noir. In 84 he started his own winery, and began developing a 6-acre vineyard. From the beginning, Ojai has made a Syrah and an intriguing blend of Sauvignon Blanc–Semillon. After working with Zinfandel, Tolmach has returned to focus on Syrah and the other Rhone varieties—Viognier and Mourvedre in particular. The Sauvignon Blanc–Semillon blend has sometimes been too pungent in aroma and too soft in texture to make it consistently praiseworthy. It is now joined by a limited-volume bottling of a 100% Sauvignon Blanc labeled "Cuvée Spéciale." Annual production is a modest 1,500 cases, with close to half consisting of Syrah. Ojai is a small town in Ventura County. Even when the wines originate entirely from the winery's estate vineyard, Tolmach opts for the California appellation, because Ventura is unknown to wine lovers.

Syrah

86   87 *

Fruit suggestive of cherries and raspberries carries a noticeable herbaceous edge and moderate tannins

---

OLD CREEK RANCH WINERY   *Ventura 1981*   The historic 850-acre Old Creek Ranch was purchased in 76 by Mike and Carmel Maitland. Having recently retired from the MCA Record Company, Mike wanted to preserve the ranch, which also included the remnants of a pre-Prohibition winery. By 81 the old winery was renovated and producing a few hundred cases of wine. The winery now has 5 acres planted to Sauvignon Blanc and Chenin Blanc, and buys grapes from Santa Barbara County to produce Chardonnay, Pinot Noir, and Riesling. An estate-grown Sauvignon Blanc joined the line in 86. Carmel Maitland has run the operation since the death of her husband in 88. Most of the 1,200 cases made each year are sold at the winery.

OLIVET LANE ESTATE   *Sonoma 1986*   On Olivet Road in the Russian River Region west of Santa Rosa, the Pellegrini family planted 65 acres to Chardonnay and Pinot Noir in 75. For 20 years after the repeal of Prohibition, the Pellegrinis made wine in Sonoma, only to ease away from it by 56 in order to concentrate on their major business at the time, wine wholesaling. They resumed wine-making on a limited basis primarily to supply house wines to restaurant accounts. By the end of the 80s they were making a line of wines under the Pellegrini Bros. brand, and Olivet Lane was used for their estate-grown wines. The brand has grown to the 10,000-case-a-year mark, 60% consisting of Chardonnay, which is partially barrel-fermented, and 40% of Pinot Noir.

Chardonnay

87   88   89

Somewhat understated throughout, with brisk, green appley fruit played off against mild oak, and firm acidity

---

OLSON VINEYARDS   *Mendocino 1982*   Northeast of Ukiah on a ridge that overlooks Lake Mendocino, the Olson family built a small winery and a tasting room. Because of the setting and breathtaking view, they had hoped to sell most of their wines at the winery. A few years later they opened up a second tasting room in tiny valley east of the Anderson Valley. However, the winery, which had enjoyed sporadic success, was sold in 89 to the Konrad family. The Konrads phased out the second tasting room and expanded the original site. The winery has 14 acres of old Zinfandel and Petite Sirah vines which are farmed organically. By 90, all grapes crushed were being farmed organically. With primary emphasis on red wines, the winery is making estate-bottled Petite Sirah and Zinfandel, and buys grapes from Mendocino County for its Cabernet Sauvignon and Merlot. Two white wines are made—Chardonnay from the Redwood Valley and a proprietary wine made from Colombard named "Glacier White." With expansion, the winery will increase its annual output from 8,000 cases in 90 to 20,000 cases, and the wines will be labeled Konrad Estate.

Chardonnay

84   85   86   89

In the absence of adequate fruit, oak has become the dominant element in these somewhat understuffed wines

---

OPTIMA   *Sonoma 1984*   This company is a two-man operation that began on a shoestring budget. Behind it are Mike Duffy, who has been winemaker for Balverne and Field Stone, and Greg Smith, who gained winemaking experience with Lytton Springs and currently owns the Fitch Mountain Winery. They combined talents to create Optima, with the first wine being a Cabernet Sauvignon–Merlot blend. Starting off with 400 cases, the output has grown to 3,000 cases. In some years the red blend contains Cabernet Franc, Petite Sirah, or Zinfandel. Aged for over three years before its release, Optima tends to be a full-bodied, amply endowed red in need of long cellaring. In 88 the owners produced 200 cases of variable-quality Chardonnay from the Carneros region. Long term, the owners hope to expand their total annual output to 6,000 cases.

Cabernet Sauvignon

84 *   85 *   86 *   87 * * *

Ripe and full-bodied, with a mouthful of tannin, these brooding wines barely let their black-cherry fruit show in the first five years and will likely require at least twice that to come into their own

OPUS ONE   *Napa 1979*   One of the most widely publicized wine projects ever, Opus One is a joint venture between the Robert Mondavi Winery and Château Mouton-Rothschild. In 68 the two respective patriarchs, Robert Mondavi and Baron Philippe de Rothschild (who died in 88), agreed to work together on this project. All grapes are grown in Napa Valley, and the winemaking responsibilities are shared by winemakers from both companies. The release of the first vintage sent shock waves through the wine world for both the fanfare involved and the $50-a-bottle price tag. Though no longer the most expensive California wine, Opus One—a blend of Cabernet Sauvignon, Cabernet Franc, and often Merlot—has been consistently successful. Its annual production grew steadily to reach 12,000 cases by 90. The wines, through 90, have been made and aged in space rented from the Robert Mondavi Winery. Opus One, however, has its own 110-acre vineyard in Oakville, where a winery has been constructed. Located within a mile of the Robert Mondavi Winery, Opus One's uniquely designed facility is shaped as a hemispherical structure placed in a shallow, specially excavated crater, and the 60,000-square-foot building is not visible from the nearby wine road. In the 90s, Opus One will reach its peak production of 20,000 cases.

Red Table Wine

79 * *   80 * * *   81 * *   82 * *   83 * *   84 * * *   85 * *   86 * *   87 * * *

Owing most of their character to the substantial Cabernet Sauvignon component, blended with lesser portions of Merlot and Cabernet Franc, these wines are deep in curranty and black-cherry fruit that balances, sometimes somewhat precariously, the generously laid-on creamy oak; bold tannins provide a firm, long-aging quality to this full-bodied wine

ORLEANS HILL VITICULTURAL ASSOCIATION   *Yolo 1980*   Located in Woodland, a few miles away from Davis, Orleans Hill is headed by Jim Lapsley, who taught in U.C. Davis's Department of Agriculture before heading the series of wine classes offered through the university's extension program. As the winemaker, Lapsley relies on grapes grown by the major stockholders who among them own 76 acres of vines in Yolo County. The leading varieties are Sauvignon Blanc (22), French Colombard (17), Zinfandel (13), Chardonnay (12), and Cabernet Sauvignon (12). Close to 90% of the annual output is white wine. In order to sell wines from this appellation, the winery has emphasized labels with none-too-subtle seasonal themes and lighthearted names. The leading labels are "Noel Blanc," "Bunny Blanc," "Sunday Chardonnay" (for Mother's Day and summer), and the "Grape Pumpkin." An attempted culinary motif— "Cajun Red," "Cajun White"—failed to develop a following. The annual output by 90 was halfway to the goal of 22,000 cases a year.

PACHECO RANCH WINERY   *Marin 1979*   In the town of Ignacio in northern Marin, the Rowland family occupies a 100-acre ranch, all that remains of a large land grant. In the early 70s, the Rowlands were encouraged by an owner of Cuvaison Winery (and resident of Marin) to plant Cabernet Sauvignon on the steep hills by first establishing terraces. The vineyard now consists of 12 acres of Cabernet Sauvignon and Cabernet Franc. The first few harvests yielded extremely small amounts of fruit, but Cuvaison made wine from them up until

76. From 77 on, the Rowlands have made wines under their brand. Ann Rowland, a daughter, married Jamie Meves, whose winemaking experience at Paulsen Vineyards and Chateau de Baun makes him a perfect unpaid consulting enologist for Pacheco Ranch. Aged for close to two years in French oak, the Cabernets are blended with an average of 10% Cabernet Franc. The dry-farmed vineyard yields a light crop, and the production of Pacheco Ranch Cabernet Sauvignon has been averaging 750 cases a year.

PAGE MILL WINERY *Santa Clara 1976* Working in a basement in his Los Altos home, owner-winemaker Dick Stark manages to produce a variety of wines in small batches that are almost always noteworthy. Most wines are vineyard-designated, including multiple Chardonnays and Cabernet Sauvignons in most vintages. Among the regular offerings are a barrel-fermented Sauvignon Blanc from San Luis Obispo, Cabernet Sauvignon from the V. Eisele Vineyard in Napa, and Chardonnay from the Dimick Vineyard, also in Napa Valley. Most wines are sold directly by the winery, thanks to a well-attended series of preview tastings presented by the owners. Typically, it releases new vintages in November, and in that month alone the winery hosts two dozen special events. What is not sold directly is targeted for the local retail market. By the end of the 80s Page Mill was operating at its full capacity of 2,500 cases per year. Quality has varied widely.

PAHLMEYER WINERY *Napa 1987* Jason Pahlmeyer is a trial attorney who confesses to having spent more time reading wine journals than law journals. In the early 80s he began developing a 25-acre parcel planted to the five red Bordeaux varieties. The terraced vineyard, named Caldwell Vineyard after the vineyard manager and partner, John Caldwell, is situated in a cool region to the east of the town of Napa. In 86 he hired Randy Dunn of Dunn Vineyards to oversee wine production. In the making of Pahlmeyer's proprietary red, each variety is picked, fermented, and aged separately, with aging taking place in Nevers oak barrels for an average of two and a half years. After the final blend has been determined, the wine is bottle-aged for six months. Total red wine production is steady at 1,000 cases a year. A barrel-fermented Chardonnay has been added. The winery's impressive initial vintages have made Pahlmeyer a name to watch.

PALISADES ESTATES WINES *Napa 1984* Originally, Palisades was a joint venture between winemaker Robert Pecota and San Francisco attorney Bill Lukens. Both are fans of Petite Sirah wines, and in the early 80s they bought an old vineyard planted to that variety. Now Lukens is sole owner, but the wines are custom-made at the Pecota winery. Petite Sirah from an old (ca. 1900) vineyard located north of Calistoga remains the mainstay. Lukens owns or controls 50 acres in the northeastern end of the Napa Valley. From his own vineyards he also offers Sauvignon Blanc in a typically lean, high-acid style. Cabernet Sauvignon from purchased fruit completes the roster. Annual production is averaging 3,500 cases, with Petite Sirah accounting for 1,500 cases.

PARADISE VINTNERS *Butte 1982* One of the few wineries found in Butte County today, Paradise has few other distinctions. There are 6 acres under vine, producing red wines, both varietal and generic. Most of the 2,500-case output is sold locally. Overall, the quality record has not been good.

PARDUCCI WINE CELLARS *Mendocino 1932* For many years this was a family-owned and -operated winery. Today, the management team is drawn from the Parducci family, but the owner is an investment group known as TMI. In wine circles, Parducci is a highly regarded pioneering name as well as a driving force within Mendocino County viticulture. Owning close to 400 acres, the winery offers a line of table wines, varietals, and generics. Parducci was the first winery to bottle a varietal French Colombard in the 50s, and a leader in the evolution of slightly sweet Chenin Blanc. When Petite Sirah came on as a varietal in the 60s, Parducci was in the forefront with its versions.

Like many of his colleagues, winemaster John Parducci avoided using small oak barrels until recent vintages. In the 70s he made a series of no-oak Chardonnay and Sauvignon Blanc that often were exceptionally attractive. For red wines, he preferred large redwood tanks for aging. Many aspects of the winery have changed over time. It uses small oak barrels and went into the White Zinfandel market with gusto in the 80s. The Reserve wines are labeled "Cellarmaster Selection," which consists of Cabernet Sauvignon, Pinot Noir, and Chardonnay. Chenin Blanc remains a frequent ✿ performer. Although rarely rated above average, Parducci wines are priced moderately and are often good value. The winery's production is 400,000 cases per year.

Cabernet Sauvignon

81   82   83   84   85   **86**   87

If never getting high marks, this moderately fruity, slightly berry-flavored wine can be a good value in some years when its fruit takes the lead over earthy, woodsy suggestions

Chardonnay

83   84✶   85   86   87   88   89

Quietly fruity, somewhat green-appley in character, and showing stiff acidity played against hints of a fresh juicy character

Pinot Noir

84   85✶   86   87   **88**

Youthful, simple, direct fruit, with little tannin or oak in the way of its immediate quaffability

Zinfandel

86   87

Following a simple, moderate-tannin approach, the wine has average fruit in some years but less than that in others

---

PARSONS CREEK WINERY   *Mendocino 1979*   This winery had just survived the difficult first few vintages and was beginning to make a name for itself as a white wine specialist when a devastating fire destroyed the facility and most of the inventory in July 85. Owner-winemaker Jess Tidwell gradually put it all back together again to produce about 12,000 cases of white wines and sparkling wines. In 88 his perseverance was rewarded when a Canadian company acquired the controlling interest and retained Tidwell as winemaker. Cabella Wines of Canada owns 500 acres in the Alexander Valley and has planted 150 acres to Cabernet Sauvignon and Merlot. Chardonnay from the Carneros appellation was added to the winery's line by the new owners, who had expanded the original winery in Ukiah. Parsons Creek made its first Cabernet Sauvignon in 85, and today it specializes in Cabernet Sauvignon (blended with Merlot), Chardonnay, and sparkling wine by the *méthode champenoise*. A Brut and a Tête de Cuvée sparkler are the mainstays. The winery is moving close to the 25,000-case-a-year mark. However, the owner's ambitious plans call for expansion to 50,000 cases by 95.

Chardonnay

(Sonoma)   **84**   85   86   87   88

Lean fruit of a distinct citrusy bent is trimmed with quiet oak in a wine of limited excitement

---

PATZ & HALL   *Napa 1988*   James Hall is the winemaker for Honig Cellars and Donald Patz is sales director for Flora Springs Winery. They produce some 500 cases of barrel-fermented Napa Valley Chardonnay. To date, the quality has varied. The winemaking takes place at Honig Cellars.

PAT PAULSEN VINEYARDS   *Sonoma 1980*   In 70 comedian and one-time presidential candidate Pat Paulsen bought a large ranch just south of Cloverdale in a warm area of the Alexander Valley. Over the next few years he planted 37 acres to Cabernet Sauvignon, Sauvignon Blanc, and Chardonnay. Paulsen's name first appeared on a wine label when Chateau St. Jean made a vineyard-designated Sauvignon Blanc in 74. Paulsen hired a winemaker in 80 when he built a winery next to the vineyard and opened a tasting room in Asti. Production started slowly at 1,600 cases in 80, but gradually expanded as the winery offered a range of table wines consisting of Sauvignon Blanc, Chardonnay, Gewurztraminer, Muscat Canelli, and Cabernet Sauvignon. The quality was erratic, only the Gewurztraminer being noteworthy. The winery added two blended wines that finally aroused some excitement as Paulsen unleashed a little wry humor on his back labels. The two wines, "Refrigerator White" and "American Gothic Red," brought the winery's total annual output up to 25,000 cases. By the end of the 80s Paulsen's career as an entertainer enjoyed a modest revival; the winery did not receive as much attention afterwards. Paulsen went through two divorces, and before long both winery and vineyards were for sale.

ROBERT PECOTA WINERY *Napa 1978* Bob Pecota began working for Beringer Vineyards in the early 70s, where he was involved in land acquisitions and later with vineyard management as well as public relations. When the opportunity came up to buy a 35-acre vineyard near Calistoga, Pecota purchased it, and in 78 built a small winery. Originally the vineyard was planted entirely to Petite Sirah. Pecota replanted half to a combination of Cabernet Sauvignon and Sauvignon Blanc. In the early years, in order to stay afloat as the vineyard matured, Pecota produced wines like Grey Riesling and Flora. Eventually his vineyard holdings expanded to 50 acres, led by Sauvignon Blanc (20), Cabernet Sauvignon (18), and Merlot (12). Since 78, he has been buying Gamay to make Nouveau Gamay by carbonic maceration.

Each year Pecota makes about 3,000 cases of Muscat Blanc, with varying degrees of residual sugar. Named "Sweet Andrea" after his daughter, Pecota's Muscat is on occasion a lush, opulent, dessert-style wine. For many vintages the winery made a small lot of Chardonnay from Canepa Vineyard in the Alexander Valley. Of the 20,000 cases produced a year, Sauvignon Blanc represents about 7,000 cases, Cabernet Sauvignon—since 84 made only from the estate (Kara's Vineyard)—is around 3,000 cases. Merlot was added to the line in 89, and accounts for 1,000 cases. The rest is evenly divided between Gamay and Muscat.

Cabernet Sauvignon

(Kara's Vineyard) **84** * **85** * * **86** * 87 *

Ripe, sweet, fairly concentrated cherryish fruit, backed by lots of rich oak, but tending sometimes to be burdened by coarse and drying tannins

PEDRIZZETTI WINERY *Santa Clara 1945* The second generation of the Pedrizzetti family took over this operation in 63. The winery, a pre-Prohibition site located east of Morgan Hill, was originally acquired by the Pedrizzettis in 45, and for years produced a line of generic wines in large bottles. The winery was upgraded in the 60s as the line expanded to include a range of varietals. All grapes crushed are purchased, the majority originating from San Luis Obispo County and the Mandeville Island in the Delta region. Among the wines offered, the best-sellers are Barbera made in a rustic style and Chablis. In the 80s the winery began developing what is now a busy private labeling business, supplying house wines to many restaurants and stores. Annual production is steady at the 75,000-case level. Wine quality is adequate at best.

J. PEDRONCELLI WINERY *Sonoma 1904* This remains a family-run winery and Jim and John Pedroncelli have quietly developed a solid reputation for good value. They currently have 135 acres next to the winery in the Dry Creek Valley. Over the years they have bought grapes from neighboring growers and others in the Alexander Valley to reach a production level of 130,000 cases a year. In the late 60s the winery began to slough off its jug-winery, rustic-wine image and moved into the varietal wine world. For a time Pedroncelli was best known for its reds, Zinfandel and Pinot Noir in particular, but by the 70s it was earning praise, and ❋ on occasion, for Chardonnay, while its other white wines showed signs of improvement. Since then it has settled into a groove to offer generally straightforward wines that if a little light in intensity make up for that by being honestly priced.

Pedroncelli's Chardonnay is its quality leader and has grown in quantity (15,000 cases), but Cabernet Sauvignon remains its volume leader. In some vintages, Pinot Noir represents a remarkable value. Both Zinfandel and Cabernet Sauvignon are involved in a modest Reserve program in which the winery will release them some six to seven years after the vintage. A consistent, slightly sweet Chenin Blanc, a fruity and frequently highly rated Fumé Blanc, and a floral, slightly sweet–style Gewurztraminer fill out the reliable, attractively priced line.

Cabernet Sauvignon

(regular bottling)   81   **82**   83   84   **85   86   87**

(Reserve)   80   82❋   **85**❋

Cherry and blackberry fruit is combined with oaky richness and often with an herbal streak, while the late-released Reserve is oakier, more tannic, and less fruity

Chardonnay

84   **85**❋   **86**❋   **87**❋   88   89

Usually fruity, with hints of pears and blossoms, this light and pretty wine is often one of the true Chardonnay bargains when right

Zinfandel

84❋   85   **86**   87   **88**❋

Berryish fruit of medium depth is roughened by tannins in a wine that ranges from ripe to shallow, depending on the year

PEJU PROVINCE   *Napa 1983*   While running his nursery business in Los Angeles, Tony Peju visited the Napa Valley in 79. Not long afterwards, he purchased an established vineyard in the Rutherford region. Retaining the old parts planted to Cabernet Sauvignon, he added new acreage of Chardonnay to bring the total planting to 30 acres. In his first vintage, Peju made a pink wine dubbed "Karma," a blend of Cabernet, Chardonnay, and Colombard. By 85 he was ready to build a winery, but then became involved in a battle with Napa County officials over the right to sell wine from a tasting room, and construction was held up for close to two years. By 89, the winery was completed. Cabernet Sauvignon, Chardonnay, and "Carnival," a blended white, are the primary wines offered in its 5,500-case annual output. Carnival, made predominantly of French Colombard, is the best-seller. On occasion, a Reserve Cabernet Sauvignon is made. The oldest acreage of Cabernet is named HB Vineyard.

Cabernet Sauvignon

(HB Vineyard)   **85**❋   **86**❋   **87**❋❋

Well-constructed, medium-depth wines, showing black-cherry and cassis fruit, oak, and supporting tannins, and seemingly capable of aging for up to a decade or more

ROBERT PEPI WINERY   *Napa 1981*   Robert A. Pepi was in the fur-dressing business in San Francisco when he began looking for a country place for eventual retirement. In 66 he found a 70-acre site in the middle of Oakville, which included 15 acres of Cabernet Sauvignon. Over the next few years, as he expanded the vineyard, he developed a keen personal interest in Sauvignon Blanc, despite the fact that Cabernet Sauvignon was much more in demand at the time. Pepi eventually built a home and a small winery on a knoll overlooking his vineyards. By 81, he had removed all Cabernet Sauvignon, and his 65-acre vineyard consisted of Sauvignon Blanc, Semillon, and Chardonnay. Most of the winery's day-to-day operations are now in the hands of Pepi's son Robert L. Pepi, who helped develop the vineyard and now oversees wine production.

Close to 80% of the winery's 22,000-case output is Sauvignon Blanc, blended with Semillon. In most years the winery makes 1,000 to 2,000 cases of Semillon, a seldom-seen Napa Valley varietal. One of the unusual aspects of Pepi's style of winemaking is the avoidance of traditional small oak barrels. For fermentation and often for aging, the winery uses 90-gallon puncheons for Chardonnay. For aging Sauvignon Blanc and Semillon, it uses 1,600-gallon-capacity French oak tanks. The primary red wine, made since 81, is Cabernet Sauvignon, from the Vine Hill Ranch in Yountville next to the well-known Martha's Vineyard. Pepi ages its Cabernets for four years prior to their release. Made in a consistent style, with 10% to 15% Semillon, the Sauvignon Blancs typically offer spicy, herbal qualities with a touch of oak and a crisp, lively flavor. They often are at the ✣ quality level. In 88 the winery made the first Sangiovese in the U.S. and labeled it "Colline di Sassi."

Cabernet Sauvignon

(Vine Hill Ranch)   **81**✶✶   **82**✶   **83   84   85**✶   **86**✶   87✶

Nicely focused curranty fruit—medium-depth in most vintages—quietly enriching oak, moderate tannins, but occasional earthy, mushroomy notes

Chardonnay

84   **85**✶   **86**✶   **87**✶   **88**✶   89

More rich in early vintages, now it is firm, bright, balanced, and moderately oaked

---

PEPPERWOOD SPRINGS VINEYARDS   *Mendocino 1981*   This small winery is situated along the beautiful rolling hills at the 1,000-foot level in the Anderson Valley Viticultural Area. At present, its vineyard consists of 4 acres of Pinot Noir and 3 acres of Chardonnay. The vineyard had to be redeveloped following a few years of noncultivation. The present owners, Gary and Phyllis Kaliher, bought the property a few years after the winery's founder and winemaker, Larry Parsons, died in an auto accident. Parsons had produced several fine vintages of Pinot Noir and one unusual vintage of late harvest Chardonnay. Blind from birth, Parsons printed his label information in Braille, which may have added to the collectibility of his wines. The Kalihers took over in 87, and produced only a few hundred cases of Pinot Noir. With their vineyard back in full production, they intend to make about 1,000 cases a year, equally divided between Pinot Noir and Chardonnay.

MARIO PERELLI-MINETTI WINERY   *Napa 1988*   From the Central Valley wine dynasty family, Mario Perelli-Minetti was the manager of his family's once gigantic winery in Delano, the California Wine Association. As the winery and its numerous labels gradually lost their market share in the early 80s, he left to relocate in the Napa Valley. Owning 8 acres planted mostly to Cabernet Sauvignon, Perelli-Minetti had his first few vintages custom-made at Rutherford Hill. In 88 he built a winery on the Silverado Trail and crushed his first vintage there. The wines from 87 were aged and bottled at the new location. Buying Chardonnay from within Napa Valley, the winery made 5,000 cases in 90, 60% Chardonnay and 40% Cabernet Sauvignon (blended with Cabernet Franc). Long term, the annual production goal is 10,000 cases, following the same 60–40 breakdown.

PERRET VINEYARDS   *Napa 1982*   Attorney Paul Perret owns 20 acres of Chardonnay in Los Carneros. In addition to serving as corporate counsel for several clients, including Chalone, Inc., he has run a successful vineyard management program. His own vineyard is situated close to the Marina Vineyard, which he once managed for its owner, Acacia Winery. At one time Perret had a financial interest in Acacia, and until 82, his Chardonnay was crushed by that winery and blended into its Carneros bottling of Chardonnay. Perret has recently been custom-making his wines at Monticello. Annual production is around 3,000 cases.

JOSEPH PHELPS VINEYARDS *Napa 1973* As a highly successful contractor-developer in Colorado, Joseph Phelps visited the San Francisco area in 71 to establish an office for his expanding business. There he met the Sangiacomo brothers, who were developing their soon-to-be 700-acre vineyard in Los Carneros. Phelps invested in the vineyard and as a result soon met Bud Mueller, another investor, who was also putting together a partnership to build a winery in Napa Valley to be known as Souverain of Napa and later on as Rutherford Hill Winery. By the time Phelps finished building that facility and also the sister winery, now known as Chateau Souverain in Sonoma County, he owned land in Napa Valley and had decided to build his own winery.

Located in a small indentation known as Spring Valley in the hills east of the Silverado Trail, the Phelps property covered 670 acres. Over the next few years he developed 175 acres to a variety of grapes adjacent to the winery. Walter Schug, originally from Germany, became the winemaker, and largely because of his presence and preferences the winery was typecast as a white wine specialist. Though it produced some of California's most successful Rieslings in all sweetness categories, as well as successful Gewurztraminers and Sauvignon Blancs, the winery always devoted considerable attention to red wines, and developed what had grown to be a powerful stable of four Cabernet-type bottlings. In 74, Phelps made a Bordeaux blend, marketed under the proprietary name "Insignia," which has become a genuine collector's item. In 75 the winery produced a limited-volume Cabernet from the Eisele Vineyard in the hills east of Calistoga. In 77, the Backus Vineyard Cabernet, a second vineyard designate, was first produced. Made from a small vineyard just off the Silverado Trail, the Backus bottling has received as many plaudits as any Cabernet made. Though some earlier vintages (77, 79) of Phelps regular Napa Valley Cabernet Sauvignon aged well, the style was variable until 83, when the winery issued the first of a string of lovely, fruit-highlighted Cabernets. Current winemaker Craig Williams replaced Schug after 82. The various Cabernet bottlings represent over 20,000 cases a year.

Among other achievements, Phelps was the first in California to produce a bona fide Syrah—in 78—and also the first to experiment with Scheurebe, a cross variety from Germany. "Vin du Mistral" designates a group of Rhone types now bottled, ranging from Viognier to a Rosé made from Mourvedre and Grenache, Mistral Rouge (blend of Syrah, Grenache, and Mourvedre), and Syrah. The winery's holdings have been augmented to include 50 acres south of Yountville planted predominantly to Chardonnay, 45 acres in Stags Leap planted to Cabernet Sauvignon, and 35 acres in Rutherford consisting of Cabernet Sauvignon, Merlot, and Cabernet Franc. Phelps also purchases Chardonnay from the Carneros region, and has bottled both a Napa Valley and a Carneros Chardonnay.

Since 75 Phelps has made Zinfandel from many regions and in a range of styles. By the mid-80s, the winery settled on the Alexander Valley as its regular source for a ripe, concentrated style of Zinfandel. In 86 Phelps added Merlot to its roster. In the winery's 80,000-case annual output, Cabernet, Chardonnay, and Sauvignon Blanc account for 75% of the total. Both Gewurztraminer and Riesling (early harvest, late harvest, and select late harvest), are regularly in the lineup. Neyers Winery and Innisfree Wines are other labels produced on the Phelps property.

Cabernet Sauvignon

(Napa Valley) 73   74   75**   76*   77**   78   79   80   81*   82   83**   84*   85**   86

(Backus Vineyard) 81**   83**   84***   85**   86**   87*

(Eisele Vineyard)   **77***   **78****   **79***   **81***   **82**   **84****   **85**   **86**

All relatively full-bodied wines, the Napa Valley bottling stresses fruit more than weight and tannin, while the Eisele is loaded with ripe cherry, chocolate, and hints of dried brush to go with its imposing tannins. The Backus, now surpassing the Eisele in quality, melds ripeness and tannin with black-cherry, currant, mint, and herb characteristics

Chardonnay

(Napa Valley)   **84***   **85***   **86***   **87**   **88***   **89**

Medium-depth wines with appley and slightly citrusy fruit, filled out by moderate oakiness

Insignia

74**   **75***   **76****   **77***   **78****   **79****   **80*****   **81***   **82***   **83***
84***   **85*****   **86**

Easily the most refined of Phelps's upscale reds, this blend of Cabernet Sauvignon (usually 50–60%), Merlot, and Cabernet Franc typically offers soaring fruit, redolent of cherries and currants, with hints of strawberry, mint, chocolate, and herbs often evident as well. While not as massively tannic as the winery's Eisele or Backus bottlings, this one seems to age equally well on the basis of its livelier fruit and impeccable balance

---

R. H. PHILLIPS VINEYARD   *Yolo 1983*   Phillips is an offshoot of a large agricultural venture owned by the Giguiere family. The vineyard project is near Esparto, in the eastern part of Yolo County about 30 miles from Davis. In the late 70s and early 80s this well-known farming family experimented with a few hundred acres of vineyards in an area they referred to as the Dunnigan Hills. With no history of grape growing in this remote area, and as the single pioneers, they needed to create a demand for their grapes. As a result, they made wines in 83 on what they considered would be a one-time-only basis. The varieties they were pushing were mostly whites, led by Chenin Blanc, Colombard, Semillon, and Sauvignon Blanc. The only significant red was Zinfandel. Priced on the low end, the wines sold so well that the owners were encouraged to plunge into winemaking. They took on a winemaker (since departed) as a partner, built a facility, and grew rapidly.

Thanks to low prices and some creative marketing, Phillips has expanded to close to 200,000-case production level, with its sights on 300,000. The vineyard holdings have been expanded to 500 acres, led by Chardonnay (140), Sauvignon Blanc (115), Chenin Blanc (60), and Syrah (50). One of its most successful wines is a blush made from Chenin Blanc and Zinfandel. Bottled as Chateau St. Nicholas and labeled the "White Christmas Cuvée," its sales top 50,000 cases. The same cuvée is used for the summertime release, renamed "Poolside Blush." Three wines—White Zinfandel, Sauvignon Blanc, and Cuvée Rouge—are grouped as the "Night Harvest" line, which as a whole represents the second biggest volume item. Varietals under the R. H. Phillips label are led by Sauvignon Blanc (30,000 cases) and Chardonnay (23,000). Chenin Blanc, Fumé Blanc, and Colombard have all disappeared from the varietal roster. With 88% of its production in white wines, the winery joined the Rhone Valley varietal brigade and is making both Syrah and Mourvedre, as well as Rhone-style blends. The owners' sentimental favorite is Semillon, holding steady at 4,000 cases a year. In order to demonstrate an ability to produce serious, ageworthy wines, Phillips has created a limited line of Special Reserve wines, with emphasis on barrel-fermented Chardonnay and a Reserve Syrah. So far the quality has been spotty, with Chardonnay occasionally earning ***** ratings.

Chardonnay

84*   **85**   **86***   **88**   **89**

Straightforwardly fruity, with supporting oak, medium body, and early drinkability, and at an attractive price

PICONI WINERY   *Riverside 1981*   After setting up his medical practice in Fallbrook, just north of San Diego, Dr. John Piconi began pursuing his second interest, winemaking. In 78 he and Vincent Cilurzo formed the Cilurzo-Piconi Winery, which operated under that name for two years. After they parted company, he purchased property just to the east of Temecula and began planting a 6-acre vineyard. In 80 Piconi purchased grapes to produce a line of varietals under this brand featuring his favorite, Petite Sirah. The winery, completed in 82, also offers Chardonnay, Fumé Blanc, Chenin Blanc, and Cabernet Sauvignon. The production goal is 6,000 cases a year maximum.

PIGEON CREEK   *Amador 1983*   In the town of Plymouth one finds the largest single vineyard in the county, called Clockspring Cellars. Of the total 350 acres planted to vines, 270 acres contain Zinfandel, with 60 planted to Sauvignon Blanc and the remainder to Muscat and port-type varieties. Most of the crop is sold. The owners have ventured slowly into wine production, but decided to bottle their wines under the Pigeon Creek brand. Three wines are regularly offered—White Zinfandel, Zinfandel, and Sauvignon Blanc. Production now stands at 3,000 cases a year, with 5,000 set as the annual maximum.

PINA CELLARS   *Napa 1979*   The Pinas—a well-respected Napa Valley family with years of experience as grape growers—decided to make wines from their own small vineyard in the Rutherford region. Most of the wines are sold locally. The original 5-acre vineyard has been expanded to approximately 16 acres of Chardonnay and 4 acres of Cabernet Sauvignon. When the vines reach full maturity, Pina Cellars will level off at 8,500 cases a year, with Chardonnay accounting for 80% of the total.

PINE RIDGE WINERY   *Napa 1978*   A limited partnership headed by Gary Andrus, Pine Ridge Winery is located on the Silverado Trail in the Stags Leap District. In 78 Andrus purchased a 50-acre site which was partly planted to Chardonnay. After adding Merlot, Cabernet Sauvignon, and more Chardonnay acreage, he built a small winery that by 80 was producing 12,000 cases a year. Over the next decade Pine Ridge expanded, and the winery now owns about 140 acres scattered through several Napa Valley appellations. About one-third of the Pine Ridge output consists of Cabernet Sauvignon, of which there have been as many as five bottlings in a given year. The major bottling is the "Rutherford Cuvée," which is accompanied by the Stags Leap Vineyard bottling, Diamond Mountain, and by an Andrus Reserve. A Cabernet labeled "Cuvée Duet" was introduced in 85 but only performed once.

The most expensive wine is the Reserve, made in part from the Cabernet acreage adjacent to the Andrus home in Rutherford. Two Chardonnays are annually bottled—"Knollside Cuvée," earlier called "Oak Knoll Cuvée" (about 10,000 cases) and Stags Leap Vineyard (2,000 cases). The Merlot, called "Selected Cuvée," is blended with small amounts of related Bordeaux varieties. Chenin Blanc remains an important item in the roster; produced in a slightly sweet, fruity style that rises to ❋, it has been a runaway sales success in some vintages, making it a welcome cash-flow wine. By 90 the winery's annual production was close to the 40,000-case capacity.

Cabernet Sauvignon

(Andrus Reserve)   **80**❋   **83**❋   **84**❋   **85**❋❋   86❋

(Stags Leap Vineyard)   **81**   **82**❋   **83**❋❋   **84**❋❋   **85**❋❋   **86**

(Rutherford Cuvée)   **78**❋   **79**   **80**   **81**❋❋   **82**❋   **83**   **84**❋   **85**❋❋   **86**

(Diamond Mountain)   **86**   87

Lavish oak accompanies all of these wines and, in the Andrus Reserve, which is the tightest-structured of the bunch, can sometimes seem the prime focus in lesser vintages; the "Duet" was bottled as the 85 Reserve, and it captured the deepest fruit found under that label to date; Stags Leap Vineyard wines are rich and supple in the style of wines that typify the area; the Rutherford bottling follows the geographic pattern as well in its delivery of rich, curranty flavors supported by moderate tannins; the Diamond Mountain bottling in its initial appearance displayed the sinewy, reserved, somewhat spicy character often associated with hillside grapes

Chardonnay

(Knollside Cuvée) 84 * 85 86 * 87 * * 88 89

(Stags Leap Vineyard) 84 * * 85 * 86 87 * 88

In years when the grapes ripen enough to give the wine some flesh, the Knollside Cuvée combines deep, firm fruit with toasty oak in a well-knit package; the Stags Leap Vineyard offering is generally more lush and rich, and tends toward riper fruit character than the Knollside Cuvée

Merlot

(Selected Cuvée) **80** * 81 * 82 * 83 * **84** **85** * 86 87 * * 88

Ripe cherries, hints of brush and herbs, and rich oak are blended in this medium- to full-bodied series of wines

PINNACLES VINEYARD *Monterey 1988* As part of the Franciscan Vineyard family (Estancia, Mount Veeder Winery), this label specializes in Monterey-grown Pinot Noir and Chardonnay. Production methods lean to a minimalist approach, and the Pinot Noir is neither fined nor filtered. From 20 mature acres in the eastern foothills of Monterey, the winery is currently making 1,000 cases of Pinot Noir, and plans to offer a few hundred cases of Chardonnay from Monterey. Its ultimate production goal, to be sought through vineyard expansion, is 7,000 cases.

PIPER SONOMA CELLARS *Sonoma 1980* When it began in 80, Piper Sonoma represented a 50–50 venture between Piper Heidsieck and Renfield Imports, but since 88 it has been solely owned by Piper Heidsieck. The company has settled on four styles of *méthode champenoise* wines—Brut, Blanc de Noirs, Brut Reserve, and a Tête de Cuvée. All four are vintage-dated and from the Sonoma County appellation. The Brut (75% Pinot Noir, 25% Chardonnay and Pinot Blanc) has improved since 85, and offers refined fruit, subtle yeastiness, and lively, austere character. One of our favorites is the Blanc de Noirs (100% Pinot Noir), noted for its restraint and balanced impression. The Reserve Brut is offered on occasion and is aged for four years *en tirage* and two years on the cork prior to release. The winery's most expensive product is its "Tête de Cuvée" (50% Pinot Noir, 50% Chardonnay), which is disgorged after spending seven years or more *en tirage.* The annual output is approaching 150,000 cases. The winery owns 40 acres in Sonoma County, and buys most of its tonnage from growers under long-term contract.

PLAM VINEYARDS & WINERY *Napa 1984* Ken Plam, an engineer in the Bay Area, frequently worked on projects in the Napa Valley. In the early 80s he purchased an old winery (Hopper Creek Vineyards) in Yountville in southern Napa Valley and began renovating it and expanding the vineyards. Plam's 26-acre vineyard is planted to three varieties—Cabernet Sauvignon, Chardonnay, and Merlot. As the winery was building toward its 10,000-case-a-year objective, those three were its leading varietals, with Sauvignon Blanc accounting for 10% of the total. Over its first few years the winery experienced erratic quality with Cabernet Sauvignon, but its Chardonnays showed much better.

PORTER CREEK VINEYARDS *Sonoma 1982* Owner and winemaker George Davis began developing a 21-acre vineyard in the early 80s. His first vintage was 87, and since then Davis has been specializing in Pinot Noir and Chardonnay. From the inaugural vintage of 2,000 cases, he plans to grow slowly to a maximum of 8,000 cases.

BERNARD PRADEL CELLARS *Napa 1983* French-born Pradel was a successful chef in Oregon before settling in the Napa Valley. Though his family is connected with the wine trade in Chablis, he was making Chardonnay over the first few California vintages only while awaiting the maturity of his own vineyard, planted exclusively to Cabernet Sauvignon and Merlot. He has 10 acres and leases another 5, giving Pradel 12 acres of Cabernet Sauvignon and 3 of Merlot to work with. By the end of the 80s, Pradel was specializing in Cabernet Sauvignon, with production at 2,600 cases. With vineyard maturity he intends to see production grow to 4,000 cases a year.

Cabernet Sauvignon

84* 85 86* 87

Somewhat inconsistent from year to year, these wines seem to have exaggerated the differences caused by vintage variation, with the result that they have ranged from underfilled to more ripe than necessary; to their credit, they uniformly contain focused varietal fruit and attractively rich oak

PRAGER WINERY & PORT WORKS *Napa 1979* Tucked behind the Sutter Home Winery visitors center just south of St. Helena, the Prager Winery specializes in port. Jim Prager left a long career in the insurance business to settle in Napa. All of the ports, often labeled with proprietary names, are 100% varietal in composition. The three varietals he works with regularly are Cabernet Sauvignon, Petite Sirah, and Pinot Noir. Most grapes are purchased, but Prager has under 1 acre of Cabernet Sauvignon in his estate vineyard. His first estate-bottled Port was a blend of 82/83. As a rule, the wines are aged in small oak for close to four years, and most are unfined and unfiltered. The minimal handling approach sometimes allows a degree of volatile acidity to develop that some find distracting. Maximum production is set at 4,000 cases a year.

PRESTON VINEYARDS *Sonoma 1975* In the northern end of the Dry Creek Valley, the Prestons developed 120 acres in the early 70s. With the intention of selling most of their crop, they planted 13 varieties. Their first vintage consisted of 1,200 cases of Zinfandel. Having steadily expanded production since then to the current 30,000-case-a-year level, the winery continues to offer a variety of wines, almost all from the estate vineyard. In 84 Lou Preston, trying to tame the aggressiveness of his Sauvignon Blanc, blended it with Semillon and Chenin Blanc. Labeled "Cuvée de Fumé," this lively, medium-bodied wine captures well-focused fruit and is capable of * * performance. It has become the best-seller at 8,000 cases and Preston's only non-estate-bottled wine. Other major wines offered by Preston are Cabernet Sauvignon (4,000 cases), Zinfandel (3,500), and a Reserve Sauvignon Blanc (2,500). Rounding out the line are a Chenin Blanc in a dry style, Barbera, a fruity Gamay Beaujolais, and a 50-50 blend, (Petite) Sirah-Syrah.

Encouraged by the reception of that wine, Preston has expanded the acreage of Syrah and added the other red Rhone varieties. When he feels the urge, he will blend a small percentage of Carignane, Barbera, or Petite Sirah, or even all three, into his Zinfandel, which thereby end up being unusually full-bodied. Several producers buy grapes from Preston. One of the most in demand, after Zinfandel, is Muscat Blanc, which once went to Paulsen Vineyards. What is not sold is usually made into a refreshing low-alcohol Muscat Canelli.

Cabernet Sauvignon

83* 84 85 86 87

Ripe black-cherry fruit has often been undermined by hints of earthiness in this medium-full-bodied, moderately tannic wine

Zinfandel

82 83** 84 85 86* 87* 88*

Centered on berryish, spicy fruit, and quietly enriched by sweet oak, the wine typically carries light-medium tannins and is capable of several years aging, especially in its best vintages

QUADY WINERY *Madera 1977* As head winemaker for a large, now defunct Lodi winery, Andy Quady was encouraged to try his hand at port-making in 75. The request came from Sacramento wine merchant Darrell Corti, who was convinced that Amador County Zinfandel would make quality port. Quady made 600 cases that year, and has been associated with dessert wines ever since. As production grew gradually, Quady expanded the original winemaking facility behind his home. In 81 he decided to devote full time to his own winery. As he worked with port, both vintage and blended, Quady became familiar with many growers in the Central Valley. In 80 he found a few remaining acres of an otherwise abandoned variety, Orange Muscat, which he made into a fortified wine. Since the variety was unknown to consumers, Quady sold the wine as "Essensia," a proprietary name, and presented it in a striking oversized label. Fortified at low levels (14–16% alcohol), Essencia was an immediate sales success and quickly became Quady's flagship wine. In 83 he added a Black Muscat fortified wine which he named "Elysium." It is his second best-selling wine at 4,000 cases a year. "Electra," a low-alcohol Orange Muscat, was added in the 90s.

Amador County continues to supply Zinfandel for his two types of port. Quady uses "Port of the Vintage" for batches in need of only nominal cellaring, and Vintage Port for those with long-aging potential. In 82, a third port was introduced, first identified as "Frank's Vineyard" and now bottled as "Starboard." This Vintage Port is made from a trial planting in Amador of several traditional port varieties—Tinta Cao, Tinta Amerela, Valdepeñas, and Bastardo. Total port production is steady at 3,000 cases a year.

QUAFF (Z MOORE WINES) The first Gewurztraminer produced by Z Moore was a sweet, 2%-residual-sugar wine in 85. The lighthearted "Quaff" name was an attention-getter, and the general quality of the wine made it an appealing, picnic-style Gewurztraminer. Each year about 1,000 cases of this pleasant wine from Sonoma County are produced.

QUAIL RIDGE CELLARS & VINEYARD *Napa 1978* In the mid-70s founders Elaine Wellesley and her late husband, Jesse Corallo, developed 10 acres of Chardonnay in the Mount Veeder district of the Mayacamas Mountains. The wines were made in an historic aging cellar located on Atlas Peak Road. For several vintages the winery produced limited amounts of barrel-fermented Napa Chardonnay, a fruity-styled Sonoma Chardonnay, and a dry barrel-fermented French Colombard. With expansion of the vineyard to 20 acres of Chardonnay in 83, the winery increased its Chardonnay production, dropped French Colombard, and added Cabernet Sauvignon. Merlot and Sauvignon Blanc have since been made.

By 88 Quail Ridge needed repairs and improvements, and the marketing division of the Christian Brothers, wanting a limited-volume winery with a hand-crafted image for its portfolio, purchased it. After upgrading the winery, the owners secured 20 additional Chardonnay acres in the Yountville area. Its annual production has now reached the desired 30,000-case level, with Chardonnay leading the way at 17,000 cases. Cabernet and Sauvignon Blanc are each at 5,000 cases a year. Though still barrel-fermented and oak-influenced, recent Chardonnays have been less showy than earlier versions. Merlot, blended with 20% Cabernet as a rule, is an up-and-coming varietal that in its first vintage achieved ✳ ✳ ✳ results.

Cabernet Sauvignon

82 83✳ 84✳ 85✳ 86

Even when fleshed out with Merlot, the wine remains on the firm, hard side, with curranty and cherryish fruit set against oak and tannin; fairly good aging potential in best years

Chardonnay

84*   85   87   88

Typically firm in construction, with oak a major player within the citrus and apple flavors

QUIVIRA VINEYARDS   *Sonoma 1981*   Fitting the definition of an estate winery quite literally, Quivira began in 81 with the purchase of an old vineyard site that was expanded into a 75-acre vineyard on the western side of the Dry Creek Valley. An ultra-modern, functional winery was ready for the 87 harvest. Since then, Quivira has moved steadily toward its annual 25,000-case goal, and is on course to produce wines entirely from its own vineyard by the mid-90s. The winery makes three varietals and a blended red. Sauvignon Blanc, Zinfandel, and Cabernet Sauvignon are the major varietal offerings, but the vineyard also contains sufficient amounts of Semillon, Petite Sirah, Merlot, and Cabernet Franc. The first proprietary blend marketed is the "Dry Creek Cuvée," made from Zinfandel, Grenache, and Petite Sirah. The winery has developed 6 acres to red Rhone varieties with the intention of offering a Rhone blend in the future. Winemaker Doug Nalle, who departed after the 89 vintage, got the winery off to a good start with its Zinfandels and its Sauvignon Blanc. The Sauvignon Blanc has earned ✳ for its melon-figgy aroma, forthright oakiness, and well-stuffed flavor impression. The winery's first vintages of Cabernet showed excellent promise.

Zinfandel

83***   84***   85*   86*   87**   88***

Attractive, well-proportioned wines, carrying bright, ripe-berryish fruit, are enriched by moderate oak; somewhat rough tannins suggest a few years of cellaring, but are not overbearing

QUPÉ   *Santa Barbara 1982*   Owner Bob Lindquist is part of an innovative trio (which includes the two owners of Au Bon Climat), all of whom once worked together at Zaca Mesa. Each went off to explore different wine types and appellations and ended up creating exciting wines that brought badly needed excitement to Santa Barbara. By the end of the 80s, they all finished up sharing one facility built by the owners of Bien Nacido Vineyard. Initially with Qupé (an American Indian name for a poppy), Lindquist moved in the direction of Rhone Valley wine types. Qupé was among the pioneers of Syrah in California through several vintages made from grapes grown by Estrella River vineyards. It now makes Syrah from the Bien Nacido Vineyard, a source shared with Bonny Doon Vineyards. In addition, Qupé bottles small batches of Syrah from two other appellations—Los Olivos (blended with Mourvedre) and Central Coast. Overall, the winery has regularly earned ✳ for its Syrahs.

By 90, Qupé was making 2,000 cases of Syrah, and was among the first to bottle Mourvedre, Marsanne, and Viognier. Lindquist has a 1-acre experimental vineyard containing most of the Rhone varieties. Purchasing grapes from the Sierra Madre Vineyard in the Santa Maria Valley, Qupé has produced a series of Chardonnays, including on occasion a full-blown Reserve. As the winery grows gradually to the 10,000-case-a-year target, the amount of Chardonnay will level off at 3,000 cases. Qupé's companion label is Vita Nova (see entry).

Chardonnay

84*   85*   86   87*   88**   89*

Toasty, somewhat buttery notes overlie broad, appley fruit in this series of consistently rich wines

RABBIT RIDGE VINEYARDS   *Sonoma 1985*   Erich Russell and his wife, Catherine, began developing a 35-acre vineyard adjacent to their Russian River Valley home in the early 80s. Erich is a well-known winemaker who became the head enologist for Belvedere in 88. He made small quantities of Rabbit Ridge varietals for a few years, but by 89, from his mature vineyard and from purchased grapes, his winery was offering a full line of wines. From 17 acres planted, Russell bottles a Rabbit Ridge Ranch Chardonnay; a Sonoma County bottling is made in larger quantities. Zinfandel and Cabernet Sauvignon are the next in importance, followed by Merlot and Cabernet Franc. Russell markets the Merlot under the "Clairvaux" brand, and he has developed "Meadow Glen" as a second label for Sauvignon Blanc and wines that were not used for the Rabbit Ridge line. The two Rabbit Ridge Chardonnays offered represent two-thirds of the winery's total output and have become the quality leaders in the winery's initial vintages. In 90, the winery made 9,000 cases. The production goal for all brands made in this facility is 15,000 cases.

Chardonnay

(Sonoma County)   85   86*   87   88**   89*

(Rabbit Ridge Vineyards)   86   87*   88*

Both wines are balanced, fairly generous, and full of ripe, bright fruit, seasoned with rich, somewhat toasty oak in a straightforward style

---

RADANOVICH WINERY   *Mariposa 1986*   This is a family-owned venture that began with the planting of 7 acres in the early 80s. The varieties planted are Zinfandel and Sauvignon Blanc. With another 15-acre vineyard controlled on a long-term lease, Radanovich is gradually increasing production from the initial annual 2,000-case output. Zinfandel, White and Red, has represented 50% of its production, and Sauvignon Blanc is the second most important wine offered. Production could grow to 10,000 cases a year.

A. RAFANELLI WINERY   *Sonoma 1974*   As grape growers, the Rafanelli family have always been held in high esteem by their peers. After selling grapes from their own vineyard and managing vineyards owned by others, the family eased into winemaking in 74. In the early vintages, Cabernet Sauvignon, Zinfandel, and Gamay Beaujolais were offered. By the late 70s the winery was beginning to make a name for itself and helped focus attention on the Dry Creek Valley appellation through a series of magnificent Zinfandels and good, solid Cabernet Sauvignons. Today, Rafanelli has 50 acres, with 22 acres devoted to Zinfandel, 10 acres to Cabernet Sauvignon, and the rest to a mix of varieties. Located midway between Healdsburg and the Warm Springs Dam, the Zinfandel plantings are situated in the hills above the west side of the valley floor. The location is slightly warm, and the nonirrigated hillside vines grow under stress conditions that intensify flavors.

Dave Rafanelli, who now runs the winery, believes, as did his father, Americo, in the special flavors obtained from old, old vines. The Zinfandels made by the winery are characterized by deep, well-defined fruit and berry-like flavors with great substance. Blended with Merlot in some vintages, Rafanelli Cabernet is also intense, sturdy, and imposing. The annual production is at 6,000 cases, with 4,500 of Zinfandel and 1,500 of Cabernet Sauvignon. Both are bottled unfiltered and tend to throw a deposit in the bottle.

Zinfandel

78*   79*   80*   81*   82*   83*   84   85*   86***   88***

Consistently well made, ripe, spicy, fruity, deep, and fairly full in body, this is prototypical Dry Creek Valley Zinfandel

---

RANCHO SISQUOC WINERY   *Santa Barbara 1977*   The Flood Ranch in the Santa Maria Valley covers 38,000 acres and grows a variety of crops. Rancho Sisquoc is the name for the wine and vineyard sides of this diversified agricultural enterprise. With the oldest parcels established in 68, Rancho Sisquoc is one of the oldest vineyards in the county. Over the first decade it has sold grapes to almost every winery in Santa Barbara, as well as to many outside the region. Its vineyards have been expanded to 211 acres, and the leading varieties planted are Cabernet Sauvignon, Chardonnay, Sylvaner, Merlot, Johannisberg Riesling, and Sauvignon Blanc. Of the 3,000 cases produced by the winery each year, the primary wines are Cabernet Sauvignon, Chardonnay (barrel-fermented), and Riesling, with small quantities of Merlot, Sylvaner, and Sauvignon Blanc. The whites enjoy a much better quality record than the reds. The Sylvaner is often zesty and fruity, and on a par with most of the better Chenin Blancs. The output remains steady at 6,000 cases.

KENT RASMUSSEN WINERY *Napa 1986* Kent Rasmussen acquired 10 acres in Los Carneros and planted Pinot Noir, financing the construction of a winery by a system of patronage in which each member-patron would receive wine at cost and/or have the right to custom-make wine at the facility. The scheme worked long enough to get the winery under way, and with the release of the inaugural Pinot Noir and Chardonnay Rasmussen earned enough critical acclaim to keep afloat. His wines are now distributed through traditional channels, except for what is offered to the original patrons. Chardonnay (2,000 cases) and Pinot Noir (1,000 cases) from the Carneros are his primary wines. Small (100–200) case lots of Sauvignon Blanc and a Cabernet-Merlot blend are also made. Entirely run by Rasmussen and his wife, the working winery has no stainless-steel tanks. All white wines are fermented and aged in barrels; the reds, in small open-top vats. A self-proclaimed tinkerer, Rasmussen makes small batches of odd wines every year and bottles most of them under Ramsey, his second label.

Chardonnay

86** 87 88*

Toasty, sometimes buttery, often carrying a citrusy undertone, and usually tight in fruit and structure, the wine is capable of aging for several years after release

RAVENSWOOD *Sonoma 1976* Co-owner and winemaker Joel Peterson was raised by wine-collecting parents, and his father helped form the Vintner's Club (an influential wine-tasting club) in San Francisco. Peterson served as an apprentice with Zinfandel-master Joseph Swan in the early 70s, and in 76 made 500 cases of Zinfandel in a rented corner of Swan's winery. In 81 he formed a partnership and moved into a facility just south of the town of Sonoma. Over the first few vintages Ravenswood made Zinfandel from appellations in Sonoma, Napa, and El Dorado County. The early style of winemaking was a no-holds-barred approach that occasionally went too far. Today's style has been tempered somewhat, though it is still muscular and brawny.

Most of the wine made is Zinfandel, which in any given vintage may be represented by five or six separate bottlings. The volume-leading "Vintner's Blend" Zinfandel (10,000 cases) also tends to be the most approachable. The second regularly offered version is the Sonoma County Zinfandel (2,500 cases), which is made from the Dry Creek Valley. The single-vineyard Zinfandels are regularly from Old Hill Ranch in Sonoma and from the Dickerson Vineyard in Napa Valley. Ravenswood also makes Cabernet Sauvignon (blended with Merlot) from Sonoma County and a blended Cabernet-based wine called "Pickberry," named after a hillside vineyard in the Sonoma Mountain area. Both are often exciting and, like the Zinfandels, are aged in French oak barrels. A Sonoma County Merlot combining grapes from Knight's Valley and Sonoma Valley is an up-and-coming varietal. The only white wine attempted is a heavy-handed style of Chardonnay. The winery owns no vineyards. Its annual production has hit the facility's 15,000-case capacity.

Cabernet Sauvignon

(Sonoma County) 82* 84* 85* 86* 87* 88*

Sometimes reminding us of Zinfandel in its ripeness and near-berryish fruit, the wine is bold, full, and tannic in structure

Zinfandel

(Dickerson) 83*   84**   85*   86*   87**   88*

(Old Hill) 84**   85***   87*

Ripe, aromatic, enormously fruity in most years, highly oaked, tannic, bold, and absolutely stamped by the winemaker's hand—and very much in the style of his mentor

---

RAYMOND VINEYARD *Napa Valley 1974* The Raymond family has been involved in Napa Valley winemaking since Prohibition. Roy Raymond, Sr., married a member of the Beringer family and worked at Beringer Vineyards for over three decades before forming this winery with his two sons, Roy Jr. and Walt Raymond. Together, they began developing their 80-acre vineyard in 71, and made their first wines three years later. Today, Roy Jr. is the vineyardist and Walt the winemaker. After planting a range of varieties and making a wide assortment of wines in the 70s, they decided to concentrate on three varieties—Chardonnay (40 acres), Cabernet Sauvignon (35 acres), and Merlot (5 acres). Chenin Blanc was dropped from the line after 84, and Johannisberg Riesling a year later.

The roster now consists of three bottlings of Chardonnay (Napa Valley, California, and estate-bottled Reserve), two Cabernet Sauvignons (Napa Valley and estate-bottled Reserve), and Napa Valley Sauvignon Blanc. All Chardonnays are aged in French oak, with the popular-style California given three to four months in barrel, while the Napa Valley and the Reserve are barrel-aged six and nine months respectively. Raymond's Cabernets of the 80s have followed the statewide trend by becoming somewhat softer and less tannic than their brethren of the 70s. The Private Reserve Cabernet is 100% Cabernet, and the Napa Valley Cabernet is usually blended with 10% to 12% Merlot. Over recent vintages, Raymond's Sauvignon Blancs are generally on the fruity, modestly varietal side. All told, Raymond produces 110,000 cases, half of that Chardonnay, 40% Cabernet Sauvignon, and 10% Sauvignon Blanc. Raymond introduced a second label, La Belle (see entry) in the mid-80s for a line of modestly priced varietals. In early 89, the Raymonds sold the majority interest in their winery and vineyards to Kirin Brewing, Inc., of Japan. The Raymonds retain a minority interest and are the company's managing partners.

Cabernet Sauvignon

(Napa Valley) 78*   79   80   82*   83   84*   85*   86*   87

Ripe cherry character, with moderate oak, light-medium tannins; usually good in better vintages and somewhat light in lesser years

Cabernet Sauvignon

(Private Reserve) 81**   82**   83*   84**   85**   86*

Ripe and rich in virtually every vintage, these highly oaked, currant- and cherry-flavored, full-bodied wines earn plaudits for depth, rugged handsomeness, and seeming long-term ageability

Chardonnay

(Napa Valley) 84**   85**   86*   87*   88*

(Reserve) 84*   85*   86*   87*   88

Consistently attractive wines, the Napa Valley is straightforwardly fruity, while the Reserve is strongly oriented to toasty oak and tends to be fuller-bodied

---

RENAISSANCE VINEYARD *Yuba 1978* With 365 acres of terraced vineyards on the western slopes of the Sierra Nevada Mountains, Renaissance claims to be the largest mountain vineyard in the world. Vineyards and winemaking are just one activity involved in this co-operative venture of arts and crafts lovers. A fine arts museum is adjacent to the winery, and all artifacts made on the premises are sold by the members. A few wines were made in 82, but it was years before Renaissance released substantial quantities. The wines made are Sauvignon Blanc, White Riesling, Cabernet Sauvignon, and Petite Sirah. Both white varietals are often made into late harvest versions. With Sauvignon accounting for 50% of the total, the winery's annual output climbed to 10,000 cases in 90, which included wines under Da Vinci, a second label. Long-term plans call for a maximum annual output of 50,000 cases.

REVERE WINERY　*Napa 1985*　This Chardonnay-only winery is owned by Ann and John Kirlin, who moved to Napa Valley in 79. Revere is a part-time project that relies on Chardonnay from an 11-acre vineyard and other grapes grown in the immediate vicinity. Both the winery and vineyard are located in the Coombsville area, a cool-climate zone about 3 miles northeast of the town of Napa. Revere produces a Napa Valley Chardonnay and a Reserve. Both are barrel-fermented and aged *sur lie*. Only 100 to 300 cases of Reserve are usually made. The winery currently produces 2,500 cases a year, and will grow to its capacity of 5,000 cases. The quality level has not risen above average to date.

Chardonnay

84　85　86

These heavy-handed efforts have been characterized by more oak than fruit

RICHARDSON VINEYARDS　*Sonoma 1980*　A limited partnership, Richardson is in the Sonoma sector of the Carneros District. Most of its wines originate in the Carneros, and the winery has developed somewhat of a following for its Pinot Noir. Other wines produced in this 2,000-case-capacity winery are Cabernet Sauvignon, Chardonnay, and Merlot. At times its Pinot Noirs (recent vintages have been from the Sangiacomo Vineyard) are a fantastic melange of flavors, with unusual depth and substance.

Pinot Noir

83　84*　85　86*　87**　88　89

Lots of ripe cherry and black-cherry fruit, with nuances of tar and orange rind, enriched by sweet, creamy oak in wines that are usually fairly full-bodied and youthfully tannic

RIDGE VINEYARDS　*Santa Clara 1962*　In 59 several members of the Stanford Research Institute bought an abandoned hilltop property as an ideal campground and retreat. When remnants of what was once the famous Monte Bello vineyard were discovered, partner Dave Bennion, who was reluctantly to serve later on as Ridge's first winemaker, convinced the others to preserve that vineyard. The first few harvests were sold, but by 62 Bennion was making 400 gallons of wine and the partners formed Ridge Vineyards. In 67 the partners committed themselves to winemaking by investing money in the property, hired Bennion as full-time winemaker, and began searching for grapes, especially Zinfandel, from old, dry-farmed, mountain vineyards.

Initially, making Zinfandels from Amador County, Paso Robles, Sonoma, and Mendocino, Ridge favored the heavy-duty approach. With the arrival of Paul Draper as winemaker in 69, Ridge continued to ferret out grapes— Zinfandels, Petite Sirah, and Cabernets—from various sources, but turned to more classical restraint in the winemaking. The adherence to proven traditional procedures such as natural yeast fermentations, small oak aging, and clarification by racking, helped set Ridge Zinfandels apart stylistically from the competition in the early 70s. Among the many vineyard-designated Zinfandels Ridge has offered, the most memorable are the "Geyserville" from the Trentadue Vineyard, first made in 66; the Lytton Springs in Sonoma County, introduced in 72; and the Howell Mountain Beatty Ranch, dating from 79. In retrospect, the success enjoyed by Ridge helped revive Zinfandel, and also may have spared numerous old vineyards likely to have been removed on the basis of simple economics.

Ridge is almost as well known for Cabernet Sauvignon. To some collectors, its limited Monte Bello Cabernet, first produced in 66, ranks among the best anywhere. In the 80s Ridge made a Cabernet Sauvignon from York Creek Vineyard located along Spring Mountain in the Napa Valley region. Starting in 83, Ridge began sorting out the softer, less distinctive lots from Monte Bello and the adjoining but slightly lower Jimsomare Vineyard to blend a Cabernet with the appellation of Santa Cruz Mountains. In the late 60s a few acres of Merlot were added to the Monte Bello and Jimsomare Vineyards. A varietal Merlot was not made until 85, when Ridge began working with grapes from Bradford Mountain in the Russian River Valley. Finally, Ridge has continued offering Petite Sirah from York Creek Vineyard to help sustain the otherwise neglected varietal. For close to two decades, Ridge has made small amounts of white wine. No more than a barrel or two of Chardonnay was normal until 84, but it is now expanding Chardonnay production, and makes one version from Napa Valley's Howell Mountain appellation. To prove it is not unaware of fads and trends, Ridge produced a White Zinfandel in the 80s, albeit in a dry, oak-aged style. Otsuka of Japan acquired Ridge in 86. Total output is holding steady at 40,000 cases.

Cabernet Sauvignon

(Monte Bello) 68** 70*** 71** 72* 73** 74** 75*
76*** 77 78* 80 82 83* 84*** 85*** 86 87 88*

Among the very best Cabernets produced in California, the wine usually is deep in concentrated, curranty fruit, and somehow suggests power and toughness while managing to avoid excesses of alcohol and tannin; the earliest vintages were not so refined but have outlived their rough exteriors and are now among the most desirable of older Cabernets

Cabernet Sauvignon

(York Creek) 80* 81 82 84 85* 86

Although Ridge has made exceptional Zinfandels and Petite Sirahs from this mountainside vineyard, it has had less success with York Creek Cabernet, which seems to display more structure than character

Zinfandel

(Geyserville) 78** 79** 80** 81* 82* 83 84*
85** 86** 87** 88*

Among the longest-lived and most outstanding Zinfandels, this one is loaded with quintessential varietal fruit of great depth, and while usually high in tannin and often approaching late harvest levels of alcohol, maintains its fruit as the foremost element in its large-scaled makeup

Zinfandel

(Lytton Springs) 84* 85*** 86* 87** 88*
(Howell Mountain) 82 83* 84** 85** 87 88**
(York Creek) 80** 81** 83* 84*** 85** 88*

As with most wines from Ridge, these vineyard-designated bottlings are long on flavor and full of aging potential; the Lytton Springs is deep and spicy, the other two more straightforwardly fruity and somewhat more tannic

RITCHIE CREEK VINEYARD *Napa 1974* In 64 owner Richard Minor, a dentist in Napa Valley, planted 4 acres to Cabernet Sauvignon and Merlot. Located on Spring Mountain, the low-yielding, extremely steep hillside vineyard did not provide a mature crop until 74. At that time, a small winery was built to produce 600 to 700 cases of Cabernet Sauvignon. Minor added 3 acres of Chardonnay in the early 80s, along with 1 acre of Viognier. His annual output has grown to around 1,200 cases, consisting of roughly 750 of Chardonnay, 350 Cabernet, and 150 Viognier. Ritchie Creek first offered Viognier from the 86 vintage and shares the pioneer's honor with La Jota Vineyard. On occasion, Richard Minor is used as a second label.

RIVERSIDE FARMS *(Foppiano Vineyards)* This second label covers a range of low-priced varietals along with a Dry Red and Dry White. All varietals are vintaged and from California. With annual production averaging 150,000 cases, the volume leaders are White Zinfandel and Chenin Blanc. Cabernet Sauvignon, Fumé Blanc, and Chardonnay are also bottled.

ROCHE WINERY *Sonoma 1988* In 77, anticipating retirement possibilities, John and Genevieve Roche acquired 2,500 acres of pastureland in the southwestern corner of the Sonoma Carneros region. At the time no vineyard was within 5 miles of the site. By the mid-80s, aware of the reputation of Carneros wine, they established a 25-acre vineyard consisting of Pinot Noir (10 acres) and Chardonnay (15 acres). A winery perched on a knoll overlooking the Sears Point Race Track to the south was operating for the 89 crush. The early annual production of 3,000 cases included a few hundred cases of a Blush Pinot Noir named "Tamarix." Roche Chardonnays are whole-cluster-pressed, barrel-fermented, and aged *sur lie*. The quality of the first few vintages bodes well for future Chardonnays. The first Estate Pinot Noir was made in 89. The owners would like to expand total production to 25,000 cases a year.

J. ROCHIOLI VINEYARDS *Sonoma 1979* The Rochioli family has been in the grape-growing business since the 30s. They now have 80 acres in the Russian River Valley, planted primarily to Pinot Noir, Sauvignon Blanc, Chardonnay, and Cabernet Sauvignon. In 82 they ventured into winemaking on a modest scale of 1,000 cases. In 85, they hired Gary Farrell (Gary Farrell Vineyards and Davis Bynum Winery) as consulting enologist, and he worked with them through the 86 vintage. Joe Rochioli is the vineyard manager, and his brother Tom now serves as winemaker. The winery's three mainstays are Pinot Noir, Chardonnay, and Sauvignon Blanc. Gewurztraminer is made, but primarily to be offered in the tasting room. The winery is best known for a refined, fragrant Pinot Noir, often made in a light style. It is developing a solid record for Sauvignon Blanc in a fruity, crisp, sometimes herbaceous style that is frequently of ✿ caliber. Production has reached the goal of 4,500 cases a year.

Chardonnay

86 ✿ 87 ✿ 88 ✿ 89 ✿

Green appley fruit and toasty oak are featured in these medium-full-bodied, crisp-edged wines that seem to benefit from a year or two in bottle

Pinot Noir

82 ✿ ✿ 83 84 ✿ 86 ✿ 87 ✿

Focused on bright, cherrylike fruit, and enriched by sweet oak, these attractive wines are moderately tannic and geared to enjoyment in their buoyant youth

ROEDERER ESTATE *Mendocino 1982* At the western edge of the Anderson Valley, the French firm of Louis Roederer found conditions that were felt to best approximate those of Champagne. It purchased over 500 acres, mostly within Philo where cool ocean breezes funnel into the valley. Beginning in the early 80s, Roederer of California developed vineyards on four separate parcels and eventually planted over 400 acres. The vineyards are a roughly 50–50 mix of Chardonnay and Pinot Noir. Though relatively large (40,000 square feet), the winemaking facility was designed to fit snugly into the landscape. Having evaluated numerous experimental cuvées, Roederer assembled a nonvintage cuvée, and after close to two years of aging *en tirage* its first Brut was offered in 88. Firm, crisp, and slightly austere, the Roederer Estate's first offering established a style that is unusual for California. Malolactic fermentation is prevented, and the dosage is low, even for a Brut. Under the direction of winemaker Michel Salgues, who had been a consultant to Roederer of France, California's Roederer Estate plans to grow steadily until leveling off at 90,000 cases. All of its production will originate in vineyards it owns, the same practice followed in Champagne by the parent company.

ROLLING HILLS VINEYARD *Ventura 1980* Located in Camarillo just to the north of Los Angeles, Rolling Hills takes its name from the site of its 5-acre vineyard in Temecula. The winery is owned by Ed Pagor, one of many former home winemakers in Southern California taught by John Daume. Renting space in an old warehouse, Pagor makes a few varietals, each in 200-case lots. He buys from several locations, but generally uses grapes from San Luis Obispo and Santa Barbara, as well as from his Temecula holdings. The line includes Chardonnay, Pinot Noir, Cabernet Sauvignon, Merlot, and Zinfandel. All told, Rolling Hills sets 1,000 cases a year as its limit. Quality has been uneven to date.

ROMBAUER VINEYARDS *Napa 1982* This winery, hidden behind a knoll at the northern end of the Silverado Trail, is owned and operated by Koerner Rombauer. Former commercial pilot and one-time investor in Conn Creek Winery, Rombauer built his winery in 80 and soon developed a thriving custom-winemaking business. Since opening, the winery has leased space to many labels and has also custom-made wines for many others. The best-known tenant renting from Rombauer is Dominus Estate. As it gradually expanded its own line, Rombauer has focused on Napa Valley Cabernet Sauvignon, Chardonnay (including 200 cases of a Reserve), Merlot, and a red Bordeaux blend, "Le Meilleur de Chai." All grapes are purchased under contract from Napa Valley. A family-owned 23-acre vineyard in Napa Valley grows Zinfandel, but the entire crop is sold.

Rombauer's Chardonnay is barrel-fermented and aged in small oak for 18 months. The winery's Cabernet Sauvignon is blended with Merlot and occasionally with Cabernet Franc. After a slightly shaky beginning with a few erratic Chardonnay vintages, Rombauer got over the jitters and improved its overall quality. In recent vintages, Rombauer's two red wines, which offer good value, have been outstanding enough to reach ✶✶ ratings. Rombauer is on course soon to join the upper echelon of Merlot and Cabernet Sauvignon producers. Annual output has grown from 3,000 cases in the mid-80s to about 12,000 cases today. Chardonnay and Cabernet Sauvignon account for close to 90% of the total.

Cabernet Sauvignon

81✶ 82✶ 83✶ 84✶ 85✶✶ 86

Blended with small amounts of Merlot and Cabernet Franc, this wine combines lavish oak and well-focused, fairly deep curranty fruit, sometimes seasoned with mildly herbal notes, in a tannin-laden, ageworthy setting

Chardonnay

(Napa Valley) 84 85✶ 86✶ 87 88

From time to time, this wine has suffered from an excess of acidity and more oak than its fruit could comfortably balance

ROSE FAMILY WINERY *Sonoma 1981* A family-owned, husband-and-wife-operated winery, the Rose Family made its wines in temporary facilities before settling into a small winery in the southwestern Russian River Valley. Pinot Noir and Chardonnay are the only wines produced, and the fruit is purchased, usually from the neighboring Cameron Vineyard. As production grows to the 3,000-case annual target, the winery has yet to perform consistently with either wine. Its Chardonnay is the better choice when wines are produced, but the Rose family has recently cut back on winemaking.

Chardonnay

(Cameron Vineyard) 84   85   86*   87

Vintage variations have seen the fruit ranging from pinched, nearly underripe, to pleasant and lean; the subtle oak is a constant

ROSENBLUM CELLARS   *Alameda 1978*   Beginning on an extremely small scale, Rosenblum Cellars eventually outgrew its original facility and moved into a larger one in 87. A full-time veterinarian in Alameda, Kent Rosenblum runs this winery with the help of his brother Roger, and friends who assist them during the crush period. Zinfandel, Petite Sirah, and Cabernet Sauvignon are the mainstays, and Rosenblum prefers making them from grapes grown in old, unirrigated hillside vineyards in the North Coast. Most red wines are vineyard-identified, and typically the winery bottles three or four Zinfandels per year. Often enough, Rosenblum's Zinfandels are intense, ripe and rich, with plenty of tannin and oak. The most successful Zinfandels reach * * levels when they display persistent berry fruit to see them through the cellaring warranted by their tannin levels. Ranking among the best in recent vintages, Rosenblum's Napa Valley Petite Sirahs offer an unusual level of deep, lively fruit for balance, and have risen to * * levels. Annual production currently stands at 6,500 cases, close to the winery's capacity.

Zinfandel

(Napa Valley)   81**   82*   83*   84*   85***   88

(Sonoma County)   83*   84***   85*   87**   88*

Made in limited quantities, these concentrated, intensely berryish wines are loaded with sweet oak and firmed by medium tannins

CARLO ROSSI VINEYARDS   *(E. & J. Gallo)*   Covering a line of generic wines in large bottles, Carlo Rossi was a rapidly growing brand in the 80s. Today, it still enjoys steady sales as it offers nonvintage blends of Central Valley wines. The best-selling table wine is Burgundy, followed by Vin Rosé, Pink Chablis, Rhine, and Paisano, described as a "Light Chianti." Sangria, a flavored wine, is also offered under this label. Charles "Carlo" Rossi is a cousin of Ernest and Julio Gallo. Under all Gallo-owned labels, sales of jug wines are in the 30-million-case-a-year range.

ROUDON-SMITH VINEYARDS   *Santa Cruz 1972*   In pursuit of a rural lifestyle away from Silicon Valley, two families became partners in this mountainside winery. After making their first vintages in the basement, Bob Roudon and Jim Smith, both electrical engineers, expanded their vision into a full-scale winery in 78. From the 5-acre estate vineyard and purchased varieties, they are edging close to their 10,000-case-a-year target. They focus on three wines from the Santa Cruz Mountain appellation: Chardonnay, the mainstay at 3,000 cases; Cabernet Sauvignon (700 cases); and Pinot Noir (300 cases). A Zinfandel from Sonoma Mountain and Petite Sirah from San Luis Obispo County are regularly offered. "Claret," their upscale generic red, is the best-seller and represents a third of the total output. The heavy-handed winemaking style, evident in the early vintages, has given way to some restraint. Overall, most of the wines are well made and true to type.

ROUND HILL VINEYARDS   *Napa 1977*   Beginning as a blender and bottler of bulk wines, sold primarily through a partner's retail chain, Round Hill evolved from a negociant label into a major producer by 87. Having long outgrown its original bottling facility north of St. Helena, Round Hill moved into a new (300,000-case-capacity) home just off the Silverado Trail in Rutherford in 87. As it grew, Round Hill made numerous roster changes. Today, among its four lines, one priced at the low end groups a line of generics and varietals under the "House" designation. Made mostly from purchased wine, the House line, all with the California appellation, is headed by White Zinfandel, and includes Chardonnay, Cabernet Sauvignon, and Zinfandel. Round Hill's mid-priced wines are from the Napa Valley appellation and consist of Cabernet Sauvignon, Chardonnay, Zinfandel, and Gewurztraminer. The Napa Valley line is made from grapes purchased from 40 growers throughout the valley and grapes grown by the winery's owners. In limited quantities, Round Hill makes its deluxe line exclusively from the 150 acres farmed by its owners. Labeled "Reserve," three wines are offered regularly—Cabernet Sauvignon, Chardonnay, and Merlot.

Introduced in 82, Round Hill's Reserve Cabernets, especially the 84 and 85, confirmed this winery's ability to hold its own against the competition in the prestige category. The fourth group of wines produced and bottled by the winery is labeled Rutherford Ranch (seen entry). About 60% of the winery's 300,000 cases fall into the House line, one that from time to time has produced Chardonnays and Cabernets earning praise for good value.

Cabernet Sauvignon

(Napa Valley)   81＊   82＊   83   85＊   86

(Reserve)   84＊＊   85＊   86

Both wines are medium-weighted, straightforwardly fruity, moderately tannic; the Reserve can be richer but has not always been better; both are good values when they succeed

Chardonnay

(Reserve)   84   85   86   87   88

The top-of-the-line Chardonnay from Round Hill, it has all too often been low on fruit and lacking in brightness

---

ROYCE VINEYARD   This label is owned by Jack Duarte, a wine specialist in Louisiana. He buys and blends ready made California wines and bottles them in rented space in Sonoma County. To date, Royce has offered Merlot and Chardonnay. In recent vintages Royce has been responsible for 3,000 cases of California Chardonnay.

CHANNING RUDD CELLARS   *Lake 1977*   A free-lance artist, Channing Rudd was once the art director for Paul Masson Vineyards, before branching out on his own. Beginning in 77 when living in Alameda County, Rudd started to make small quantities of wines, with emphasis on heavy, intense reds, and earned critical acclaim for both Zinfandel and Petite Sirah. Buying vineyard property, he ended up with 60 acres in the southern end of Lake County, where the elevation along the northern side of Mount St. Helena averages 1,500 feet. After Rudd and his family moved to the property in 82, and as the vineyard took shape, Rudd purchased grapes and made between 750 to 1,000 cases a year. Among the wines offered, his Napa Valley Cabernet Sauvignon from Bella Oaks Vineyards, a name usually seen in conjunction with Heitz Cellars, has been the most noteworthy. By 88 the estate vineyard was beginning to be used for Rudd's wines. From 6 acres planted to Merlot, Cabernet Sauvignon, Cabernet Franc, and Malbec, Rudd produces a Bordeaux-style blend. Chardonnay is made from the 2 acres on the estate.

RUSTRIDGE VINEYARD & WINERY   *1984*   In 72 Lu Meyer, a real estate agent from San Francisco, fell in love with a 450-acre ranch located in Chiles Valley. When a buyer backed out, she and her family bought the property, once home to a large thoroughbred horse ranch. The Meyer family's first attempt to develop vineyards was thwarted by the drought of 76. In 79 they harvested their first small crop. They continued to sell all or part of their crop, but experimented with winemaking in 82 and 84. In 85 Stan Meyer constructed a winery by renovating an old barn, and made 1,000 cases of Riesling that fall. The vineyard has been expanded to its present 54 acres, with Johannisberg Riesling (24 acres) predominating. Chardonnay, Zinfandel, and Cabernet Sauvignon are also grown. In its first vintages the winery mainly produced Riesling and promoted that one wine. Because of the weak demand for Riesling, the winery's annual output varied in the late 80s, from 3,000 cases to 6,500. After restructuring its vineyard, the winery began directing attention to Chardonnay and two reds, Cabernet Sauvignon and Zinfandel. As Rustridge grows to its 10,000-case goal, Chardonnay and Riesling will account for 60%, with the reds making up 40% of the total.

RUTHERFORD HILL WINERY *Napa 1976* Currently owned by a limited partnership whose members are also owners of Freemark Abbey, Rutherford Hill was previously owned by Pillsbury and was briefly operated as Souverain of Rutherford. With the compact Freemark Abbey winery unable to handle all of the partners' grapes, Rutherford Hill was snapped up as soon as it became available. Over the years, the winery's lineup has been considerably altered, and today emphasis falls on Merlot, Chardonnay, and Cabernet Sauvignon. Small amounts of Sauvignon Blanc and Gewurztraminer fill out the line. In its early vintages, Rutherford Hill gained some recognition for Merlot, and the rest of the line was generally acceptable. In the mid-80s the quality became inexplicably erratic, and a new winemaking team was brought in for the 87 crush. Over the course of time Rutherford Hill has used several different label designations, including a range of Reserve-type names, without any continuity. However, the winery has access to several fine vineyards, and the combined vineyard holdings of the partners come to 630 acres, all in Napa Valley. Included are 55 acres of Merlot on the Jaeger Ranch just north of Napa, one of the earliest Merlot vineyards in the valley.

In 85 the owners began constructing what turned out to be the biggest man-made aging caves in California, which now hold 6,500 barrels. Total annual production varied in the late 80s when the winery hit a few rough spots, but is now back to about 135,000 cases. After converting sizable acreage to Merlot in recent years, the winery plans to focus on Merlot and Chardonnay, which by the mid-90s will represent two-thirds of total production.

Chardonnay

(Jaeger) 85* 86* 87 88

Led by toasty oak, this medium-full-bodied, firmly structured wine is attractive in vintages that give it sufficient fruit to balance the oak and brisk acidity

Merlot

80 81 82* 83** 84** 85* 86 87

Always ripe and generally full-bodied, fleshy, and mouth-filling, this wine tends to be heavier than classic Merlots, but has plenty of richness from oak and deep fruit, and gains a needed firm edge from moderate tannin

RUTHERFORD RANCH (ROUND HILL VINEYARDS) This is the top-of-the-line label used by its owners for wines made from vineyards they own. The primary vineyard is located in the western hills of Napa Valley. In the early 80s Rutherford Ranch made several vintages of intense, dark, tannic Petite Sirahs and Zinfandels, but those wines were dropped from the line, which now features Chardonnay, Cabernet Sauvignon, and Merlot. Annual production usually turns out to be about 1,500 cases of each wine. With a sturdy constitution derived from their hillside origins, Rutherford Ranch's Cabernets are capable of * quality and often earn praise for good value. Merlot, when not made in a bombastic style, also reaches * quality levels in many vintages.

Cabernet Sauvignon

77** 78* 79* 80* 82 83* 84* 85* 86

Brawny, ripe, tannic efforts, this series of wines appeals to those who favor toughness over elegance

Merlot

84* 85* 86

Medium-intensity, fairly accessible fruit (especially in comparison to the Cabernet Sauvignon) is enriched by sweet oak and firmed slightly by moderate tannin

---

SADDLEBACK CELLARS   *Napa 1983*   Nils Venge has been making wines in the Napa Valley since 74 when he started with Villa Mount Eden. In the early 80s he developed a small vineyard near his home in the Oakville area. By 82, when he was hired by the newly formed Groth Vineyard, Venge began thinking about making wines under his own brand as a sideline. The following year he and his father-in-law built a small winery, and made a few hundred cases of wine. The vineyard has since been expanded and includes 8 acres of Cabernet Sauvignon, 5 of Chardonnay, and 2½ of Pinot Blanc. Venge is now making over 2,000 cases a year and has set 3,200 cases as a desirable goal. Over 50% of his annual output is Cabernet Sauvignon. Chardonnay and Pinot Blanc (the only such varietal made in Napa Valley) are the two other home-grown wines made. On occasion, Venge buys Sauvignon Blanc and markets it under his second label, Vine Haven.

ST. ANDREWS VINEYARDS   *Napa 1979*   Founded by Swiss-born Imre Vizkelety, St. Andrews is an 82-acre Chardonnay vineyard and winery located in southern Napa Valley, a mile north of Napa. Planted in 72 to several clones of Chardonnay, the vineyard's first four harvests were sold to sparkling wine producers. St. Andrews produced its first vintage in 80, and over the next four years averaged about 2,000 cases a year. In 83 Vizkelety decided to turn the management over to a winemaker, and the winery's production expanded to 13,000 cases a year of Chardonnay, and about 1,000 cases each of Cabernet Sauvignon and Sauvignon Blanc. The winery had earned a reputation for excellent value for both its estate-grown and Napa Valley Chardonnay. In 89, St. Andrews was sold to Joli Val, Ltd., a company headed by Bernard Portet, the president of Clos du Val. The new owner continues to make a partially barrel-fermented Chardonnay and a Cabernet Sauvignon from the Stags Leap appellation. Total production stands at 18,000 cases a year, the winery's full capacity.

ST. CLEMENT VINEYARDS   *Napa 1976*   San Francisco eye surgeon Bill Casey and family bought the site of the original Spring Mountain Vineyards in 76. A few hundred cases of 75 wine remained in the cellars, and represented the first to be sold as St. Clement. In 79 the facility was expanded as a second building was carved into the hills and connected to the original building. Beneath both buildings, a large underground storage facility and barrel-aging room were put into place without changing the appearance of the above-ground structures. The expansion enabled the winery to grow to 10,000 cases a year, with winemaker Dennis Johns in charge of the operation since 80. Johns, a self-taught winemaker, combined numerous small lots drawn from throughout the Napa Valley as he made Cabernet Sauvignon, Chardonnay, Sauvignon Blanc, and in the late 80s, Merlot. Most grapes were purchased, since the winery owned only the 3 acres visible from the house.

Within a few vintages the winery became well known for its Sauvignon Blancs. The style consistently combined deep, complex fruity character with firming acidity that provided a long life and often earned it ✷✷. An even clearer picture of consistency is St. Clement's Cabernet Sauvignons, which are ✷✷ caliber and beautifully proportioned. In late 87 Casey sold the winery to the Japanese brewers Sapporo, Inc. One of the changes made was the purchase of the well-established 22-acre Abbott's Vineyard in the Carneros, which is planted to Chardonnay. The new owners retained the services of Dennis Johns.

Cabernet Sauvignon

78✷   79✷   **80✷✷**   **81✷✷**   82✷   83✷   **84✷✷**   **85✷✷**

Classically constructed wines that are firm, tight when young, yet show plenty of curranty fruit underneath, and have a fair measure of rich oak; with a bit more stuffing, they would rate at the very top of the list

Chardonnay

84   85*   86   87*   88   89

Tight, somewhat appley fruit, with toasty oak background, but occasionally wanting greater depth

Merlot

85**   86**   87*

Ripe, deep, tannic, ageworthy wines, enriched with creamy oak, appear to possess good aging potential

---

ST. FRANCIS VINEYARDS   *Sonoma 1979*   Located in Kenwood directly across the wine road from Chateau St. Jean, St. Francis started out in 73 with the development of 100 acres. The first crush of 79 yielded 5,000 cases total, with the most promise shown by Gewurztraminer and Riesling. As production from its estate vineyard increased, St. Francis lacked a consistent focus until the 83 vintage, in which it produced ** quality Merlot. Now 20 acres are planted to Merlot, with the four oldest acres used for the winery's Reserve bottling. Both Merlots are 100% varietal, and they are aged in both American and French oak barrels (the Reserve aging six months longer).

The styles of Riesling and Gewurztraminer have evolved to the present slightly sweet level; each wine captures youthful fruitiness and at best is of * caliber. Since the beginning, Chardonnay has come from several appellations and been bottled under several designations. In the mid-80s, the winery removed its Pinot Noir and increased its acreage of Chardonnay. The estate Chardonnay along with a California Chardonnay combine for close to 20,000 cases, with Merlot amounting to 7,000 cases. Cabernet Sauvignon, a recent addition, can be exceptional, although only 500 cases are made a year. Since it began, St. Francis has served as a temporary home to several developing wineries, most notably Acacia and Van Der Kamp.

Cabernet Sauvignon

85**   86**

Ripe black-cherry fruit and lots of rich, vanillin oak are set in a moderately tannic frame

Chardonnay

(Estate)   84*   85   86   87*   88*

Toasty oak, appley, slightly blossomy fruit, crisp acidity

Merlot

(regular bottling)   80   81   82   83**   84**   85**   86**   87*
88

(Reserve)   83***   84**   85*   88

Both wines are ripe, intense, high in sweet, rich oak, and share a tendency to be a little soft in structure and round; appealing on the palate even when tannic

---

ST. MICHAEL WINERY   *Napa 1989*   André Bosc acquired a 175-acre estate in 60 in the Diamond Mountain area. Here, on the site of a winery that was operating in the 1860s, St. Michael was first scheduled to break ground in 89. About 100 acres on the estate will eventually be planted to vines. Bosc intends to produce Chardonnay, Pinot Noir, Cabernet Sauvignon, and Merlot, along with sparkling wines made by the *méthode champenoise*. However, after several attempts to launch the enterprise, both the winery and the vineyard remain mired in the planning stages, and, indeed, the future for St. Michael seems far from bright.

ST. SUPÉRY VINEYARDS   *Napa 1988*   This winery and adjoining old Victorian home are owned by Skalli Enterprises, a large wine company and distributor in southern France. In the early 80s, the Skallis, like many French vintners, wanted to invest in other regions, and ended up in California. In 82, they acquired a 1,500-acre cattle ranch in the Pope Valley, preparing it and gradually developing it into vineyards. In 86, when the 56-acre Rutherford estate and vineyard owned by fellow Frenchman Jean-Claude Boisset was put on the market, Skalli bought it and immediately began building a winemaking facility and office complex. In less than two years, a modern-looking 200,000-case-capacity winery was in place, along with a visitors center. The adjacent 50-acre vineyard was reworked and is now planted primarily to Cabernet Sauvignon.

By 90, the Pope Valley plantings, known as the Dollarhide Ranch, contained 400 acres of vines. The owners are expanding that to 650 acres, the major varieties planted being Sauvignon Blanc, Chardonnay, Cabernet Sauvignon, and Zinfandel. In 88, the winery began with a first crush of 20,000 cases. With expansion to 100,000 cases, the focus remains on Chardonnay, Sauvignon Blanc, and Cabernet Sauvignon. Wines not making the first team have been bottled under a second label, Atkinson House. Initial efforts have been clean, average quality, and fairly priced.

SAINTSBURY CELLARS *Napa 1981* Before starting Saintsbury, longtime friends Dave Graves and Dick Ward worked in the cellars of several wineries both in Napa Valley and Santa Barbara. In 81, they rented part of the Ehlers Lane stone winery north of St. Helena, bought Pinot Noir and Chardonnay from Sonoma, and made 3,000 cases total. They also raised enough money to build a winery in the Carneros where they intended to buy all grapes for their wines. Saintsbury caught people's attention with a style of Pinot Noir that burst with bright cherry varietal character, enriched by complementary oak. It suffered from no excesses, and was an unusual Pinot Noir in that nothing was out of proportion. In making Pinot Noir, Graves and Ward prefer a lengthy fermentation and employ both punching down and pumping over of the cap. In 83, Saintsbury's Pinot Noir was joined by a lighter version, called "Garnet," made from batches with less intensity and concentration. Their Carneros Chardonnay is barrel-fermented and undergoes malolactic fermentation. Starting in 86, a Reserve Chardonnay has been made from the most intense lots and fermented in new oak. Still without vineyards of its own at the end of the 80s, Saintsbury reached the 30,000-case-a-year level.

Chardonnay

(regular bottling) 84 * 85 * 86 * 87 * * 88 * 89 *

(Reserve) 86 87 * * **88 * * ***

Firm, solidly fruity wines combine brisk, appley fruit with toasty oak and quiet roasted-grain qualities

Pinot Noir

(Garnet) 83 84 85 86 87 * 88 * 89 *

(Carneros) 83 * **84 * *** 85 * **86 *** 87 * * 88 *

"Garnet" is the lighter, bouncier wine but, until recent vintages, seemed to lack adequate stuffing; the Carneros bottling is relatively fruity and bright in comparison to most of its competition and has a black-cherry and sweet oak personality

SALAMANDRE WINE CELLARS *Santa Cruz 1986* Owner-winemaker Wells Shoemaker is better known in the town of Aptos as Dr. Shoemaker, pediatrician. A believer in the minimal handling approach to winemaking, he specializes in Chardonnay and makes two versions, one from Arroyo Seco in Monterey and the other from Santa Cruz Mountains. In roughly 100-case quantities, he also makes on occasion Merlot, Sauvignon Blanc, Gewurztraminer, and Pinot Noir. Small-scale cuvées of *méthode champenoise* sparkling wines have been made. The annual output is 1,000 cases (75% Chardonnay). Shoemaker intends to continue on a small scale. In and around Aptos the long-toed salamander is plentiful and was adopted as the winery's symbol and logo.

SALMON CREEK VINEYARDS   A Chardonnay-only private label, Salmon Creek is owned by Daniel Baron, the enologist for Dominus Estate, and Peter McCoy of McCoy Vineyards. All grapes are purchased, and the origins have changed from year to year. The wines, made by Baron in rented space, are barrel-fermented in small oak and then given brief *sur lie* aging. The first vintages were far from successful. Production has been averaging 1,000 cases a year.

SAN PIETRO VARA   *Napa 1983*   Owned by two families, the Giordanos and Widmans, this small winery and surrounding vineyard is located a few miles northeast of Calistoga. The owners acquired the vineyard in 79, and cultivate it by certified organic farming principles. In 83 they decided to produce wines from their primary varieties—Charbono, Zinfandel, Merlot, and Cabernet Sauvignon. From the Rutherford region they purchase Gamay, which makes them producers of nothing but reds. The add-no-chemicals approach is applied to winemaking that also combines not too successfully with a long aging-in-oak regime. In addition to avoiding sulfur dioxide at all stages, the winemaking style calls for use of only the naturally occurring yeasts for fermentation. To date the Charbonos have been marketed five years after the vintage, and Zinfandels have appeared after being aged four years by the winery. By 90 San Pietro Vara was operating close to its 3,000-case-per-year capacity.

SAN SABA VINEYARD   *Monterey 1981*   From vineyards established in 75 in the foothills on the western edge of the Salinas Valley, San Saba makes Cabernet Sauvignon only. The 70-acre vineyard contains 62 acres of Cabernet and 8 of Merlot and Cabernet Franc. The vineyard is located approximately 2 miles north of the Smith & Hook Winery where the wines are custom-made and aged. Generally, the wines are aged for two years in French oak barrels, and a further year in bottle before being released. San Saba is owned by a physician who lives in Dallas, and the winery's first few vintages were available only in Texas. By 85 the annual production had grown to 5,000 cases and the winery began marketing outside Texas. To date, San Saba's Cabernets have suffered from an overly herbal, bell pepper character.

SANFORD & BENEDICT   *Santa Barbara 1972*   At the original winery he founded with Richard Sanford, Mike Benedict operated as the sole owner for many years. Covering 112 acres, the Benedict Vineyard grows Pinot Noir, Chardonnay, and lesser amounts of Riesling, Cabernet Sauvignon, and Merlot. In the 80s, Benedict left winemaking and put his efforts into the vineyard. He sold the crop to numerous wineries, and before long the Pinot Noir, the oldest in the county, was much in demand. Au Bon Climat, the Santa Barbara Winery, Gainey Vineyard, and several others regularly make Pinot Noir from Benedict Vineyard. In 90, Benedict sold the vineyard to Robert and Janice Atkins of London. They in turn signed on Richard Sanford as the vineyard manager, and all parties agreed that the Sanford Winery would use the grapes. The vineyard's name was changed to Talinda Oaks Ranch.

SANFORD WINERY   *Santa Barbara 1981*   In 80, by mutual consent, the co-owners of Sanford & Benedict Vineyards decided to dissolve the partnership. Mike Benedict continued operating the original winery as Sanford & Benedict and in 81 Richard Sanford established his own wine company. Sanford's initial vintages were made in leased space—the first two at Edna Valley Vineyards. Through his tasting room in Buellton and through his travels, Sanford developed a strong direct-mail clientele. Although several early vintages of Chardonnay originated in other parts of the Central Coast, all wines made today are from Santa Barbara County, primarily the Santa Ynez Valley.

On a 700-acre estate near Buellton, Sanford plans to build a winery. Meanwhile, his annual production, in leased space, is at its maximum of 30,000 cases a year, with Chardonnay (20,000 cases) and Sauvignon Blanc combining for 70% of the total. Both white wines are complex and full-bodied and, regardless of quality level, they often display a pronounced oak character. Typically,

Sanford ferments Chardonnay in new French oak, and encourages it to undergo malolactic fermentation. Even the Sauvignon Blanc is barrel-fermented (in American oak) and often undergoes malolactic fermentation.

Introduced in 82, a Vin Gris from Pinot Noir, barrel-fermented and made in a dry style, remains a regular item in the lineup. Over the years Sanford has earned a reputation for Pinot Noir, and produces about 4,000 cases a year. Fermented in open-top stainless-steel cooperage, Sanford's Pinot Noirs are made in a big, ripe style. Beginning in 90, Sanford has had access to grapes from the 112-acre Talinda Oaks Ranch, the former Benedict Vineyard, which he helped develop in 71.

Chardonnay

(regular bottling) 85 *** 86 * 87 * **88** * 89 **

(Barrel Select) 87 *** 88 *

Sanford wines, regardless of nomenclature, are high in oak and carry ripe, often broad and somewhat exotic fruit, with plenty of balancing acidity; the Barrel Select pushes the winery's outgoing style one step further

Pinot Noir

85 **86** * 87 **88** *

Lacking consistency, this often intense, sometimes too herbal, soft and ripe, tobaccoey wine succeeds in those years when its fruit and structure match up to its intensity level

---

SANTA BARBARA WINERY *Santa Barbara 1972* One of a handful of wineries located in downtown Santa Barbara, this is also one of the oldest in the county. It began in 62 by making an assortment of table and dessert wines for the local tourist trade. In 72, it took a more serious turn as its owners began developing what evolved into a 70-acre vineyard in the Santa Ynez Valley. Also under the winery's control is a neighboring 45-acre vineyard. The primary varieties planted include Chardonnay, Chenin Blanc, Sauvignon Blanc, and Riesling among the whites, and Cabernet, Zinfandel, and Pinot Noir among the reds. Among many wines offered, both its Riesling in a medium-sweet, full-fruity style (often ranked as a * wine) and its Chardonnay have stood out. The barrel-fermented Reserve Chardonnay consists of about 1,000 cases; production of the regular Chardonnay stands at 4,000 cases.

Among the more unusual wines offered, the winery's Chenin Blanc is barrel-fermented to total dryness. Usually blended with Semillon, the Sauvignon Blanc is average in quality, with some fruitiness and character. Also bottled is a Reserve Sauvignon Blanc that is 100% barrel-fermented. One of the more popular offerings is labeled "Beaujour," a Nouveau-style Zinfandel (50% made by carbonic maceration). On occasion, the Reserve Pinot Noir (300 cases) has been exceptional. In the 80s, the best-selling wine was the White Zinfandel (8,000 cases). Today, the winery is operating at its optimum production level of 30,000 cases.

Chardonnay

(regular bottling) 84 85 86 * 88 * 89 *

(Reserve) 85 86 * 87 ** 88 * 89 *

After a few years of average quality, the winery has begun to produce complex, rich, oaky Chardonnays whose vintage variations derive mostly from the fruit intensity exhibited

---

SANTA CRUZ MOUNTAIN VINEYARDS *Santa Cruz 1974* The search for an ideal site to plant Pinot Noir ended for Ken Burnap when he bought a long-defunct vineyard high in the Santa Cruz Mountain area. A former Los Angeles restaurateur (The Hobbit), Burnap was seeking a cool climate, relatively poor soils, and a southern exposure in which to develop his vineyard. Pinot Noir now covers 13 acres and Chardonnay 1 acre of his dry-farmed hillside site. Although Pinot Noir was the primary wine in the formative years, the winery currently makes Chardonnay, Merlot, and Cabernet Sauvignon in greater quantities. Only Merlot from the Central Coast appellation is purchased from outside the Santa Cruz Mountain area. The first several vintages of Pinot Noir generated excitement among wine collectors, but met with mixed critical reviews. Burnap insists on allowing his grapes to become very ripe before harvesting them, and he believes in using the native yeasts for fermentation. All wines undergo malolactic fermentation and are aged in French oak. The resulting wines have been somewhat erratic. After extended bottle aging, the winery's Pinot Noirs are released in their fourth year, the Cabernet Sauvignons in their fifth. For several years, the winery produced and labeled the only Durif made in California. The annual total output of this winery has reached the 4,000-case maximum.

SANTA MARGARITA VINEYARD & WINERY *Riverside 1985* Starting out as one of the few wineries in the Temecula region to specialize in red wines, Santa Margarita makes only Cabernet Sauvignon. Owner Barrett Bird has developed 3½ acres to Cabernet Sauvignon. By 90, he was making close to 750 cases, about half of his intended maximum annual output.

SANTA YNEZ WINERY *Santa Barbara 1976* Using a refurbished dairy barn, the original winery, known as Santa Ynez Valley Winery, began in 76 by specializing in white wines. Among its early successes, the winery made Sauvignon Blanc, and both the regular and Reserve offered enticing varietal character balanced by oak. In 88, the facility was purchased by Doug Scott, owner of Sterns Wharf Vintners, who contracts for grapes grown within Santa Barbara County to produce wines for both Sterns Wharf (see entry) and Santa Ynez Winery. The current Santa Ynez Winery lineup features Sauvignon Blanc, Semillon (usually barrel-fermented), Chardonnay, Pinot Blanc, and Riesling for the whites, and Cabernet Sauvignon, Zinfandel, and a Cabernet-Merlot blend among its reds. White Zinfandel was dropped after 89. Also, the winery makes port in limited volume. Production of Santa Ynez Winery is at the 18,000-case-per-year level, close to full capacity.

SANTINO WINES *Amador 1979* This winery is located in the middle of the Shenandoah Valley. Unlike many of its neighbors, Santino has always produced a range of wines to balance its interest in Zinfandel. Today, it offers three versions of full-bodied Zinfandel as well as several low-alcohol, picnic-style wines. After working as its winemaker for several years, Scott Harvey became a co-owner in 85. His 10-acre vineyard, the Grandpère Vineyards, was established in 1868, and the original vines remain in production. Santino offers a separate Grandpère bottling of Zinfandel to accompany an Amador County bottling and an occasional Fiddletown version. All Zinfandels are aged in French oak barrels and bottled-aged for two more years prior to release. All told, Zinfandel combines for about 5,000 cases.

The volume wine in Santino's 35,000-case annual output is a White Zinfandel named "White Harvest." Low in alcohol (under 11%) and finished with about 2% sweetness, this wine has seen its sales grow to over 10,000 cases a year. In 88 Santino entered the Rhone-blend division with "Satyricon," a blend of Grenache, Syrah, and Mourvedre. One year, Harvey produced a late harvest *Botrytis*-affected Zinfandel from frozen berries labeled "Frost Wine." Other wines made in small quantities include Barbera, late harvest Riesling, Orange Muscat, and Muscat Canelli.

Zinfandel

(Fiddletown)   80**   82   83*   84

(Shenandoah Valley)   83   84   85*   86*

(Grandpère)   84   86*   87*

Ripe, jammy, brawny wines, usually high in alcohol, deep in color but low on refinement

SARAH'S VINEYARD *Santa Clara 1978* One of the few small upscale wineries in the Hecker Pass region, Sarah's is located just west of Gilroy. Owned by Marilyn and John Otteman, the winery is directed by Marilyn, who is also the winemaker. Sarah is a name she dreamed up for the original vineyard, now covering 8½ acres and planted to Chardonnay and Pinot Noir. Chardonnays from both the estate vineyard and from Ventana Vineyards in Monterey represent the major wines offered. First made in 83, the estate Chardonnay has grown to 800 cases a year in quantity. Small amounts of Merlot and a proprietary red, "Cadenza" (made primarily from Grenache), fill out the line of this 2,500-case brand. Though offered in the 80s, Riesling has been dropped. After several generally successful, often noteworthy early vintages, Sarah's became surprisingly erratic. The near-stratospheric prices recently asked have greatly exceeded the quality offered.

Chardonnay

(Sarah's Vineyard) 86* 87 **88***

(Ventana Vineyard) **85*** 86 87 8̶8̶ 89

Initial vintages (early 80s) demonstrated richness and range, but more recent efforts have been overdone in oak while lacking the fruit to make them work—even in the face of sharply escalating prices

SATIETY VINEYARDS *Yolo 1983* Situated on the outskirts of Davis, the home of the University of California's large, diversified campus and its highly regarded winemaking and grape-growing school, Satiety is owned by the Chaykin family. They intended to develop a restaurant and visitors center in which a winery would play a part. By the mid-80s the winemaking side had taken over, and today Satiety produces close to 5,000 cases of table wine. From the family's own 29-acre vineyard and another 21 acres under contract, Satiety makes a White Table Wine and a Blush, which together represent about 95% of the annual output. Cabernet Sauvignon in a light, fruity style is the only red made.

V. SATTUI WINERY *Napa 1975* The "V." stands for Vittorio Sattui, great-grandfather of owner Daryl Sattui. With limited experience and financial support, Daryl started his own winery in 75, playing on the family name and winemaking history, even though the original winery was in San Francisco and went out of business in 20. He purchased a well-situated property in the heart of Napa Valley and immediately began courting the tourist trade. A small deli and tasting room along with inviting picnic grounds soon became a popular respite. With increased visitors, Sattui was able to develop a direct sales–marketing approach, and for many years his wines have been available only at the winery or through a mailing list.

In 85, with sales topping 20,000 cases, Sattui built a new winemaking facility and purchased 34 acres of vineyards. That vineyard is now planted to Cabernet Sauvignon, Sauvignon Blanc, and Zinfandel. Buying most of the grapes crushed, Sattui has enjoyed a long and successful arrangement with Preston Vineyard, located in Rutherford and responsible for a vineyard-designated Cabernet Sauvignon. Another dozen wines are produced by the winery. The best-seller, and often among the winery's quality leaders, is Johannisberg Riesling, made in both a Dry and Off-Dry style. In some vintages the Napa Valley Cabernet bottling has been preferred over its Preston Vineyard stablemate. In a typical year close to a quarter million people visit the winery— mostly for the picnic facilities. Annual sales have nudged up to the 30,000-case figure.

SAUCELITO CANYON VINEYARD *San Luis Obispo 1982* In 74 Bill Greenough bought a 100-acre ranch in the Arroyo Grande Valley that included the remains of a winery abandoned in the 40s. He soon discovered 3 acres of Zinfandel planted in the 1880s, and decided to revive both the winery and vineyard. The vineyard has been expanded to 15 acres, 14 of Zinfandel and 1 of Cabernet

Sauvignon. In 82 Greenough made his first wine. The annual production is holding steady at 1,500 cases—1,000 cases of Zinfandel and 500 of Cabernet Sauvignon. In general, the Zinfandels are ripe and heavy, and occasionally overdone.

SAUSAL WINERY   *Sonoma 1973*   In 56 the Demostene family acquired the Sausal Ranch in the heart of the Alexander Valley. Inheriting a parcel of red varieties planted in 25, the family eventually developed 100 acres of vineyards. For over a decade, the Demostene vineyard sold all of its grapes and gradually developed a strong reputation for Zinfandel. Grgich Hills has acquired much of its Zinfandel from this vineyard. It was also the source of the Alexander Valley Zinfandels once produced by Joseph Phelps Vineyards. In addition to Zinfandel, the vineyard contains Cabernet Sauvignon, Chardonnay, Colombard, and Pinot Noir. In 73, under the leadership of Dave Demostene, the family entered winemaking, first as bulk wine producers and by 74 as producers of bottled wine. Production has been led by its Zinfandel made in a full-bodied, but well-aged style. Special lots of longer-aged Zinfandel are bottled as a "Private Reserve." The Zinfandels, including a White version, account for 7,500 cases a year. The rest of the line consists of Cabernet Sauvignon (1,200 cases), Chardonnay, and a blend of Chardonnay and Colombard labeled "Sausal Blanc." All told, the winery is at its 12,000-case annual goal.

Cabernet Sauvignon
84*   85*   86**

Ripe, rich, full of black-cherry and berryish flavors, oaky, and fairly tannic in a style that makes up in exuberant, outgoing personality what it lacks in refinement

Chardonnay
86   87

Lots of oak and ripe grape character has sometimes been offset by old, tired characteristics; look for better results in future vintages

Zinfandel
81*   82*   83*   84**   86*   87*   88*

Briary, oaky, full-bodied, usually full of dense and ripe-berryish fruit; occasional hints of tar and raisins

SCHARFFENBERGER CELLARS   *Mendocino 1981*   John Scharffenberger was raised in Mendocino, and his family owns a highly regarded 75-acre vineyard in the Redwood Valley, growing mainly Zinfandel and Cabernet Sauvignon. After overseeing the family grape-growing business for a time, John decided to produce sparkling wine. Buying all grapes crushed, he slowly increased production to 25,000 cases by 85. Though the early cuvées were often acidic and a little green, Scharffenberger steadily improved the quality of his line, which now consists of a nonvintage Brut, vintaged Blanc de Blancs, nonvintage Rosé, and a Cremant. A tasting room was built in Philo, and the winery increased its production of table wine—Chardonnay and Sauvignon Blanc—under the Eaglepoint label.

In 89, Pommery, the French Champagne producer, acquired the majority interest in Scharffenberger Cellars, with John remaining as president and minority shareholder. Pomméroy also purchased 640 acres of bare land to be developed into a 180-acre vineyard and a winemaking site for future vintages. With Pommery's investment and direction, Scharffenberger Cellars will grow to an annual output of 60,000 cases.

SCHRAMSBERG VINEYARDS   *Napa 1966*   In 65 Jack and Jamie Davies purchased the defunct Schramsberg winery, an isolated mountainside estate founded in 1862, and Davies left a successful career in industrial management to specialize in *méthode champenoise* sparkling wines. After renovating the dilapidated winery and estate, he shored up the old aging caves and began developing vineyards, planting the first 5 acres on hillsides near the winery. From grapes purchased, Schramsberg's first offering was a 65 Blanc de Blancs. In 71 Schramsberg was the first in California to bottle a sparkling Blanc de Noirs, and in 72 made California's first Cremant sparkling wine, a style of sparkling wine deliberately low in effervescence.

As its production grew gradually to 25,000 cases a year by the end of the 70s, Schramsberg carved out a fine reputation for both quality and prestige. In the 80s Schramsberg expanded its own vineyard to the present 60 acres and moved toward an annual production goal of 50,000 cases. Today, it produces five types of sparkling wine. The Blanc de Blancs is primarily Chardonnay with some Pinot Blanc, while the Blanc de Noirs is typically made from Pinot Noir with upwards of 30% Chardonnay. In addition to those two mainstays, the winery offers Cuvée de Pinot Brut Rosé, a dry (under 1% sweetness) rosé made from Gamay and Pinot Noir. Its fourth bottling is Cremant, Demi-Sec, a medium-sweet, low-effervescence wine made from Flora and finished with 3% residual sugar. A Reserve bottling, aged at least five years with the yeasts, is offered in most vintages. The other four bottlings of Schramsberg sparklers age on the average for two to three years *en tirage.* A decade ago Schramsberg was arguably California's finest sparkling wine producer; though it is not quite at that level today, it is still among the best. Both its Blanc de Noirs and the Blanc de Blancs have been appealing in recent vintages.

SCHUG CELLARS *Sonoma 1980* Educated at Geisenheim in Germany, Walter Schug came to California and began his winemaking career in 61. For several years he worked for the Gallo winery, then headed winemaking for Joseph Phelps Vineyards from 73 until 83. By mutual agreement, Schug began developing his own brand in 80. Over the first several vintages, he worked out of a tunnel in Storybook Mountain Vineyards's winery, and later at his own facility in Yountville. Although he earned a good reputation at Joseph Phelps Vineyards for Gewurztraminer and Riesling in a range of styles, and occasionally for Cabernet Sauvignon, Schug prefers to specialize in Chardonnay and Pinot Noir. Until a vineyard was purchased and developed in 90, Schug's Chardonnays came from the Napa Valley–Carneros and were usually vineyard-designated. The Pinot Noirs were made from grapes grown in Los Carneros, along with a separate bottling from Heinemann Vineyard, a hillside vineyard in the Spring Mountain area.

With Chardonnay, Schug usually barrel-ferments but prevents the malolactic fermentation in order to make a wine he believes will live a long time. His style of Pinot Noir focuses on the minimal handling, no-filtering approach. In 90, Schug acquired 50 acres in the Sonoma side of Carneros and developed his own 42-acre vineyard. His winery, located next to the vineyard, is designed to produce 15,000 cases a year, a total Schug will achieve when his vineyard reaches full maturity. When that occurs, two-thirds of the total will be Chardonnay, the rest Pinot Noir. The quality has not risen above average levels in recent vintages.

SEA RIDGE WINERY *Sonoma 1980* Situated in the western Sonoma coastal town of Cazadero, Sea Ridge is an isolated winery in a cool region about 3 miles inland from the Pacific. Owner Dan Wickham planted 8 acres to Pinot Noir and 2 acres to Chardonnay, and has focused his winemaking efforts on Pinot Noir and Chardonnay, usually from the Sonoma Coast appellation. Always with a flair for the unusual, Sea Ridge has an erratic history with all of its wines, especially the Pinot Noir. In most vintages it makes small quantities of late harvest Zinfandel and medium-sweet Riesling. Annual production varied in the 80s, but averages close to 3,000 cases. About 40% of the total is barrel-fermented Chardonnay. The winery sells a good share direct from its tasting room, located in Bodega Bay along the coastal highway.

SEBASTIANI VINEYARDS *Sonoma 1889* The Sebastiani family history resembles that of a veritable wine dynasty. A small winery on the outskirts of the town of Sonoma was purchased in 04 by Samuele Sebastiani, the patriarch. Like many early winemakers in California, he was content, both before and after Prohibition, to sell wines to other producers, and often supplied wines to leading Napa Valley producers. In 44 his son August (Gus) Sebastiani took over the reins and the winery's bottled-wine business expanded under his guidance as he gradually developed a line of wines of all kinds under the Sebastiani Vineyard brand. By the early 60s Sebastiani was virtually out of the bulk wine business and was growing so fast with its generic wines that by the end of the 60s it was a major buyer of bulk wines. It began the 70s with a solid reputation, primarily for its red wines in a rustic, long-aged style. The winery was highly regarded for both Barbera and Zinfandel. In the 70s Sebastiani became known as a popular brand of jug wines, both generics such as its Mountain Chablis and Burgundy, and later as a producer of cheap, often thinly constituted varietals such as Cabernet Sauvignon and Chardonnay. The 70s ended with Sebastiani experiencing annual sales of over 4 million cases along with a sagging reputation.

In 80 Sam Sebastiani took over after his father's death. He tried to reverse direction by modernizing the winery, trimming the lengthy line, emphasizing varietals over generics, and crushing grapes only from Sonoma County and Sonoma Valley. The winery production was dramatically reduced, and many other changes occurred. However, the cost was considerable and dissension within the family surfaced. By 86, Sam was voted out, replaced by his younger brother, Don. Today, the winery offers several quality levels, and it is once again producing well over 4 million cases a year. However, it has gone through numerous changes in direction and its multiple lines have yet to be clearly delineated and consistently offered.

The top-of-the-line wines are collectively known as the "Estate Group." This consists of vineyard-designated Chardonnays and Cabernet Sauvignons, as well as a splashy-label Nouveau Beaujolais, low-priced varietals under the "Vendange" brand, and a line of imported wines. The Chardonnays, barrel-fermented to varying degrees and made in 2,000-case lots, originate in four vineyards: Wildwood Hill, Kinneybrook, Wilson Ranch, and Clark Ranch. The Cabernets are from the Bell Ranch and Cherryblock, which was once known as the Eagle Vineyard. The winery owns 310 acres in Sonoma County, but buys under contract from many of the biggest vineyards located in the county. To produce its line of "Country" wines and generics, it has refurbished an old facility in Woodbridge, near Lodi.

Sebastiani should be recognized for its accomplishments. It was among the first to produce a blush wine, its "Eye of the Swan," and it was likely the first to make a Nouveau-style red wine. Moreover, it has played a vital role in the evolution of Sonoma County as a rival to Napa Valley. Wine quality at Sebastiani has been inconsistent in the last decade owing to the many changes in production and direction. Some of the individual vineyard-designated bottlings can be quite good, and the regular Sonoma County Zinfandel and Merlot are frequently among the best values.

SEGHESIO WINERY *Sonoma 1983* Here is one of the last of many Sonoma County producers of bulk wine to make the switch to bottling wines under its own name. The Seghesio family bought vineyard land between Asti and Geyserville back in 1894, and by 02 they had finished building their winery. Before and after Prohibition, they supplied wines to Italian Swiss Colony and others. Business was brisk in the 40s, and in 49 they bought a winery in Healdsburg with 1.2-million-gallon-storage capacity. By the late 70s they began to modernize the facilities for the purpose of offering their own wines. Today, all wines made for their label originate in the family's 450 acres of vineyards, located in Sonoma and Mendocino counties.

In 83 Seghesio introduced a line of varietals led in volume by Zinfandel and Cabernet Sauvignon, and White Zinfandel, and including Chardonnay, Pinot Noir, and Sauvignon Blanc. Production, which began at 20,000 cases, grew to a target of 120,000 cases a year. Most of the wines have been rather modest in intensity and on the light side. However, their prices also tend to be relatively low, and we often find their Pinot Noir to represent good value.

THOMAS SELLARDS *Sonoma 1980* Near Sebastopol in southern Sonoma County, Sellards is producing wine out of an expanded shed close to his home. Purchasing most of the grapes crushed from the Alexander Valley, Sellards is currently producing 1,200 cases a year. To date, the line consists of Cabernet Sauvignon, Chardonnay, Zinfandel, and Sauvignon Blanc. The reds ferment in open-top tanks, and the whites follow the more conventional stainless-steel approach.

SEQUOIA GROVE VINEYARDS *Napa 1980* Jim Allen and his brother Steve are partners in this winery located between Oakville and Rutherford. The property, purchased in 79, was the site of a pre-Prohibition winery whose name is now long forgotten, and the estate contained a few acres of Chardonnay vines. The Allens increased the estate vineyard to its present total of 25 acres. Of the total, 20 acres grow Chardonnay, and the remaining 5 contain Cabernet Sauvignon and related blending varieties. The first estate Cabernet Sauvignon was made in 85. Sequoia Grove buys additional Cabernet to produce a second bottling, usually labeled Napa Valley. The Allens co-own 138 acres in the Carneros, planted primarily to Chardonnay and Pinot Noir. From this vineyard, they produce a Carneros–Napa Valley Chardonnay, and from the Rutherford vineyard they make a Napa Valley Chardonnay. Overall production stands at 20,000 cases, equally divided between Cabernet Sauvignon and Chardonnay. The winery's capacity is 25,000 cases a year. Quality has been quite high for Cabernet Sauvignon, generally good for Chardonnay.

Cabernet Sauvignon

(Napa) **84** * **85** *** **86** *

(Estate Bottled) **85** ** **86** *

Strong, curranty fruit is surrounded by sweet oak and, in some vintages, hints of herbs and tobacco, and wrapped in medium tannins

Chardonnay

(Carneros) 85   86   87 *   88

(Estate Bottled) 84 *   85 **   86   87 *   88 *

Tending a bit toward the pineappley side in both versions, the wines are typically fruity, moderately oaked, and high in brisk acidity

SHADOW CREEK CHAMPAGNE CELLARS (DOMAINE CHANDON) In the late 70s when Chateau St. Jean was experimenting with sparkling wine, it made numerous, often large, lots of wine. After settling on those that met its objectives, St. Jean offered the remaining trial cuvées for sale. An entrepreneur named George Vare purchased a considerable quantity for the purpose of marketing sparkling wines under his private label. Vare, former president of Geyser Peak Winery, selected Shadow Creek as his brand name. Priced just below the average retail for *méthode champenoise* wines, Shadow Creek developed a good track record. By the end of 81 it performed well enough to be purchased by Glenmore Distillers, owners of Corbett Canyon, who transferred all production to their Edna Valley facility. The appellation for the Brut, Blanc de Noirs, and Reserve Brut switched from Sonoma County to California.

Under Corbett Canyon's direction, Shadow Creek grew to about 30,000 cases a year. Glenmore by mid-87 was losing interest in its wine properties and did not expand production of Shadow Creek. In 88, Glenmore sold its California wine operations to the Wine Group, which in turn sold Shadow Creek shortly thereafter to Domaine Chandon of Napa. Through Shadow Creek, the owners of Chandon have been able to produce sparkling wine from non-Napa Valley sources. A 100-acre vineyard in Mendocino's Potter Valley was purchased to supply some of the fruit crushed for Shadow Creek. The line consists of a Brut, Blanc de Noirs, and limited amounts of Rosé.

SHAFER VINEYARDS *Napa 1979* In 72, John Schafer purchased a 210-acre estate in the eastern foothills of Napa Valley just beneath the Stags Leap palisades. The abandoned hillside vineyard had to be terraced before it was planted to 42 acres of Cabernet Sauvignon, Merlot, and Cabernet Franc, along with 8 acres of Chardonnay. In 82 the Shafers acquired and developed a 17-acre parcel in the Oak Knoll area near Trefethen Vineyards, and planted it all to Chardonnay. Starting out slowly as producers, Shafer made modest amounts of wine in 78 at another winery. While John's son Doug was finishing the enology program at U.C. Davis, the family was building its own winery. The 79 crush was split between two facilities, and by 80, with their own winery finished, the Shafers, with Doug as winemaker, were ready to focus on barrel-fermented Chardonnay and Cabernet Sauvignon. Zinfandel was made until 87, when it was dropped to make room in the lineup for Merlot, which has come to be an important part of the roster.

At present two Cabernets are bottled. One is Stags Leap in origin and is usually blended with Merlot; the other is "Hillside Select," a 100% Cabernet aged two years in barrel and two and a half years in bottle by the winery. This Hillside Select was first made in 83, and its production is level at 2,000 cases. Improving over each of its first few vintages, Shafer Merlot, blended with Cabernet Franc and Cabernet Sauvignon, has grown to just under 5,000 cases a year in quantity, and reached ✳ in quality. Both the Stags Leap Cabernet and the Chardonnay average 5,000 cases a year. When the winery's young Chardonnay acreage matures, the Shafers will be entirely self-sufficient for grapes. The winery's annual output will remain at 15,000 cases. Sustained quality improvements have placed Shafer among the top echelons of Napa Valley producers.

Cabernet Sauvignon

(Hillside Select) 83✳ 84✳✳ 85✳✳ 86✳✳

(Stags Leap) 78✳ 79✳ 80✳ 82 83✳ 84✳ 85✳ 86✳ 87✳✳

Both wines rely on ripe fruit and rich oak as their central themes; the Hillside Select is the bigger, brawnier of the two, and often has a more curranty cast to its fruit than the Stags Leap bottling, which tends more toward the ripe, black-cherry part of the varietal spectrum

Chardonnay

86✳ 87✳ 88✳ 89✳✳

Straightforwardly fruity, in a bright, crisp, appley manner, this one finds its fruit buoyed up by creamy, slightly toasty oak and lots of brisk acidity

Merlot

83✳ 84 85✳ 86✳ 87✳✳ 88✳✳

Rich, oaky, accessible, somewhat round fruit with moderate tannins giving a nice sense of supporting structure

---

CHARLES F. SHAW VINEYARD *Napa 1979* A graduate of West Point, banker Chuck Shaw in 72 purchased an established 35-acre vineyard just north of St. Helena growing Gamay grapes. Having studied the techniques for making French Beaujolais, Shaw was determined to replicate the wines in Napa Valley. He made two Gamay wines by carbonic maceration, one an early-bottled Nouveau and the other a wood-aged Gamay. Within a few vintages Shaw was producing close to 5,000 cases, and by 82 the market dictated the addition of white wines to his line. At first he offered a Gamay Blanc blush wine. In 83, with the assistance of consultant Ric Forman, he added Chardonnay and Fumé Blanc. He and Forman are partners in a 40-acre vineyard in St. Helena. The winery's annual output has grown to 20,000 cases.

Chardonnay

84✳✳ 85 86

Save for its success in the 84 vintage, Shaw has made a series of unexciting wines lacking the bright and bold fruit of its single success

SHENANDOAH VINEYARDS *Amador 1977* Home winemaker Leon Sobon decided in 77 to turn pro after becoming enthralled by Amador County Zinfandel. He purchased an old vineyard in the Shenandoah Valley and expanded it to 35 acres. From an initial output of 1,200 cases of Zinfandel, the winery grew to 60,000 cases by the end of the 80s, fueled by tremendous demand for its White Zinfandel. Sales of that wine topped 36,000 cases, and today hold steady at 30,000 cases a year. Regular robust Zinfandels (4,000 cases) have often been of ✿ quality. Since 84 only one bottling, labeled "Special Reserve" Zinfandel, has been offered. This Zinfandel combines grapes from the estate and neighboring vineyards. The winery's third most prominent varietal is a sweet-edged Sauvignon Blanc, made in a consistent forthright, fruity style. Sobon has always maintained an interest in fortified wines, first with port and more recently with fortified Orange Muscat and Black Muscat. The three speciality fortified wines have grown in output to 4,000 cases a year. Both the Orange and Black Muscat are very good in their respective categories. Though only 1,000 cases are made, Cabernet Sauvignon originates in the estate vineyard and has been a fixture since 77. In 89, Sobon bought the former D'Agostini Winery in Plymouth and renamed it the Sobon Estate.

Zinfandel

84✿ 85 86 87 88

Usually oriented to ripe fruit, with chocolatey and oaky overtones and fairly massive tannins; the milder 87 was an exception

SIERRA VISTA WINERY *El Dorado 1977* Electrical engineer and home winemaker John MacCready got the wine bug in 72 and purchased 70 acres of bare land next to his sister's home in El Dorado County. Over the next few years he developed a vineyard at the 2,900-foot level on rocky, granitic soils. The varieties favored in his now 37-acre holdings are Cabernet Sauvignon, Zinfandel, Sauvignon Blanc, and tiny amounts of Syrah and Chardonnay. Sierra Vista's Cabernet Sauvignon and Zinfandel are decidedly on the ripe, well-oaked side, but each has earned ✿ at least once with good value notations. Its estate-bottled Zinfandel and Herbert Vineyards bottlings have been among the best from El Dorado County. Though offering juicy fruit and appley character, Sierra Vista's Fumé Blanc is a bit simple and soft. Both the Syrah and barrel-fermented Chardonnay vary in quality and are available mainly at the winery. The addition of White Zinfandel and White Cabernet Sauvignon brought the winery's annual output in the mid-80s up to the optimum 8,000-case level.

SIGNORELLO VINEYARDS *Napa 1980* Ray Signorello, Sr., runs a successful natural resource (gold, silver) development company in Vancouver, Canada. In 77 he bought 100 acres near the Oak Knoll area in the eastern foothills of Napa Valley. The vineyard has been gradually developed and now covers all 100 acres. The major varieties established are Chardonnay (25 acres) Cabernet Sauvignon, Merlot and other Bordeaux reds (15 acres), and Sauvignon Blanc (5 acres). Signorello also has small plantings of Viognier, Nebbiolo, Sangiovese, and lesser Italian varieties. Over the first five vintages, the annual output averaged 2,000 cases each of Chardonnay and Sauvignon Blanc. Partially barrel-fermented, the top-of-the-line Chardonnay is identified as "Founder's Reserve." Also partially barrel-fermented and blended with Semillon, the winery's Sauvignon Blanc is aged in oak for about six months. When Signorello's vineyards are mature, the winery will focus on Cabernet Sauvignon, in addition to Chardonnay, Sauvignon Blanc, and Semillon. Pinot Noir continues to be made from purchased grapes. The overall quality has been consistently average. The winery anticipates increasing its production to 15,000 cases a year by the late 90s.

Chardonnay

85 86 87 88

Oak and ripe grape character, in need of deeper and richer fruit for balance

SILVER MOUNTAIN VINEYARD *Santa Cruz 1979* Ex-Air Force pilot Jerry O'Brien purchased 17 acres on a ridgetop high above Los Gatos. At the 2,000-foot-elevation level, he planted 7 acres to Chardonnay in 81. Chardonnay from Ventana Vineyards and Zinfandel from Sonoma County were purchased to make wines during his first several vintages. O'Brien is from the full-throttle school of winemaking. Chardonnays are 100% barrel-fermented, and every drop undergoes malolactic fermentation. In 85, the winery narrowly escaped a big fire, but was fully operational with a new bottling line in 86. It was not until 88 that O'Brien harvested a full crop of estate Chardonnay. Total production, including a few hundred cases of estate wine, had reached 2,000 cases by 89. In October 89, the winery was completely destroyed by earthquake damage and fire. Plans call for the construction of a new winery on the same site.

SILVER OAK CELLARS *Napa 1972* One-time member of the Christian Brothers Justin Meyer and his wife, Bonny, run this winery in partnership with Raymond Duncan. Meyer and Duncan first joined forces in the early 70s to buy the downtrodden Franciscan Vineyards. As they spruced that property up and improved its overall quality, they started Silver Oak as a sideline. In 79 they sold Franciscan to Eckes of Germany, and began focusing on Silver Oak, which until 79 was making only Cabernet Sauvignon from the Alexander Valley. Cabernet from the Napa Valley and another bottling from Bonny's Vineyard, adjacent to the winery in Oakville, were introduced in 79. After an uneven string of vintages, Silver Oak began to fulfill some of its promise in 78. Throughout the 80s, its Alexander Valley Cabernet has performed consistently well. Aged over two years in American oak, and close to two years in bottle, Silver Oak's Cabernets tend to be relatively mature when they reach the market. Total production has reached 25,000 cases. The Napa Valley Cabernet production is about 3,000 cases a year, Bonny's Vineyard around 1,000, and the Alexander Valley bottling has averaged 20,000 cases.

Cabernet Sauvignon

(Alexander Valley) 75* 76* 77* 78* 79** 80 81**
82** 83*** 84** 85*** 86*

(Napa Valley) 79 80 81* 82*** 83** 84** 85** 86***

(Bonny's Vineyard) 79** 82* 84* 85

The wines from the Napa and Alexander valleys have outperformed the pricier offering from Bonny's Vineyard, with the Alexander Valley the fruitiest of the three and the Napa often the richest, while the Bonny's has suffered from ripeness without fully adequate support

SILVERADO HILL CELLARS *Napa 1979* Located along the Silverado Trail a few miles to the north of the town of Napa, this winery has had several incarnations. Founded and operated for a brief period as Pannonia Winery, it failed to generate any interest and was sold to an investor, Louis K. Mihaly. For several years it was known as Louis K. Mihaly Vineyards, and its often strange wines were priced high and targeted exclusively for sale in restaurants and private clubs. That concept was less than totally successful. In 87 Mihaly sold his interest to Minami Kyushu Co. of Japan. The 34-acre vineyard is still planted primarily to Chardonnay and Sauvignon Blanc, with a smattering of Pinot Noir. In 89 the winery decided to make only Chardonnay, and phased out Pinot Noir and Sauvignon Blanc. Its annual production of Chardonnay is reported to be in the 10,000-case range. The winery's capacity is 25,000 cases.

SILVERADO VINEYARDS *Napa 1981* In 76 Lilian Disney (Mrs. Walter Disney) purchased vineyards in the Napa Valley. One, located in the Stags Leap District, was highly regarded for Cabernet Sauvignon and was previously owned by the

See family, owner of the See's candy company. The second vineyard and ranch, a Chardonnay vineyard situated in the Yountville area, was purchased by her daughter and son-in-law, Mr. and Mrs. Ronald Miller. After selling their grapes for several vintages, the Disney family decided to build a winery on a knoll overlooking the Silverado Trail, and the winemaking venture was launched. For a time the winery was unofficially known as "Retlaw," which is Walter spelled backwards. After that was dropped, the winery has never played up its association with the Disney family.

In 81 winemaker Jack Stuart, formerly of Durney Vineyards, assumed winemaking chores, and the winery has been a model of consistency and a success story ever since. Sauvignon Blanc and Chardonnay were the first wines offered, and helped establish the winery's style as one of immediate accessibility by combining bright, succulent fruit with moderate complexity. In a similar vein, Silverado's Cabernets usually offer lovely, intense young fruit against a backdrop of tannins and balancing acidity. The winery expanded production smoothly and was approaching 90,000 cases total in 90, with Chardonnay representing over half. When its vineyards (two of which were not planted until 89) reach full maturity, the winery plans to level off 150,000 cases. With vineyards at four locations including one in Los Carneros, Silverado Vineyards has 340 acres under vine. Chardonnay acreage stands at 110, Cabernet Sauvignon at 100, and Merlot has been expanded from the original 10 acres to 44. Both Cabernet Sauvignon and Merlot are 100% estate-bottled.

Cabernet Sauvignon

81* 82 83* 85* 86** 87* 89

Exuberantly fruity, moderately rich, well balanced, softly tannic for moderate aging potential, this one succeeds in a style more suited for near-term enjoyment rather than long-haul cellaring

Chardonnay

84* 85* 86** 87* 88*

Usually amiable in its round, near-juicy, inviting fruit and softly enriching oak

Merlot

83 84* 85 86** 87* 88*

The overriding winery style seems very well suited for Merlot, and results in wines that are fruity, moderately deep, accessible, and inviting

SIMI WINERY *Sonoma 1867* This historic winery in Healdsburg has gone through several ownership changes since being revived in the late 60s. Each owner enhanced the facility, and the current owner, Moët-Hennessy of France, which also owns Domaine Chandon in Napa and several major wine and Cognac properties in France, has added the finishing touches. Simi is run independently of Domaine Chandon, and since 81 has been under the guidance of Zelma Long, a well-known enologist who came to Simi from the Robert Mondavi Winery. She has strongly influenced the style of Chardonnay, Cabernet Sauvignon, and Sauvignon Blanc, and has brought each wine up to high-quality standards. As the annual output moves closer toward its 190,000-case goal, Simi is near to growing the majority of the grapes needed each year. Between 82 and 84, the winery developed 170 acres in the Alexander Valley, with Cabernet Sauvignon at 99 acres, followed by Chardonnay (29), Sauvignon Blanc (18), and Cabernet Franc (17). Another 120 acres will be developed over the next decade.

Simi's Chardonnay, representing 50% of its total production, is a blend of Sonoma and Mendocino grapes, and about 50% is barrel-fermented. The Cabernet Sauvignon from Sonoma County is 25% of total production. Among other wines offered, the Sauvignon Blanc is partially barrel-fermented and has in some vintages been a ** performer. A slightly sweet Chenin Blanc from Mendocino County usually earns * and is often one of the best of its type. On the roster since the mid-70s, a Rosé of Cabernet Sauvignon offers more character than most rosés, but sometimes is overly herbaceous. 1,000 cases each of a Reserve Cabernet Sauvignon and a Chardonnay, 100% barrel-fermented in new oak, are offered, representing the results from ongoing experiments conducted by winemaker Long, who is now the winery's president.

Cabernet Sauvignon

80   81   82   **84***   **85***   **86***

Somewhat ripe, but never heavy or bombastic, these wines are enjoyable for their well-focused fruit and their supple, moderately tannic structure

Chardonnay

84*   **85***   **86***   **87***   **88****   89

Bright, quietly floral fruit is teamed with creamy oak in well-balanced, medium-full-bodied wines

---

ROBERT SINSKEY VINEYARDS   *Napa 1988*   Eye surgeon Robert Sinskey was a partner in Acacia Winery before founding his own winery, located on the Silverado Trail just south of the Yountville Crossroad. The facility itself was first conceived as the wine center for Acacia's Cabernet and Merlot, wines Sinskey pushed to add to Acacia's roster. The winemaker for the only vintages of Acacia Cabernet and Merlot was Joe Cafaro, who became Sinskey's winemaker. In 83 Sinskey developed a 35-acre vineyard in Los Carneros, with 15 acres planted to Merlot, and 10 each to Chardonnay and Pinot Noir. 5 acres of Cabernet, Merlot, and Cabernet Franc are situated adjacent to the winery. Another vineyard site in Los Carneros has 72 acres under development. Once all of its vineyards reach full maturity, the winery will produce only estate-bottled wines.

Four wines are offered: Chardonnay, Pinot Noir, Carneros Claret, and Merlot. Partially barrel-fermented, the Chardonnay is aged in French oak for six to eight months. Pinot Noir fermentation occurs in small tanks specially designed to allow the cap to be punched down. With over 5,000 square feet of underground aging caves, the facility was from the start intended to be a highly frequented tourist stop. Chardonnay in a lively, crisp style was the early success story, with Pinot Noir evidencing some ups and downs in quality. The Meritage red is labeled "Carneros Claret," and this limited (1,500 cases) blend relies on Merlot for its appeal. The annual production has increased to 8,000 cases. The maximum output will be no more than 27,000 cases.

Chardonnay

86*   **87****   **88***

Brisk but bright appley fruit and toasty oak are supported by plenty of acidity

Pinot Noir

86**   87   **88****

Whether ripe and rich, as in 86, or pinched and lean, as with the 87, the wine comes focused on cherryish varietal fruit

---

SKY VINEYARDS   *Napa 1979*   On a ridgetop in the Mayacamas Range separating Napa from Sonoma counties, owner-winemaker Lore Olds farms 14 acres of Zinfandel. Planted in 73–74 at the 2,000-foot level, the vineyard is nonirrigated and extremely low-yielding. Total production of Zinfandel is 1,000 to 1,500 cases. Aging takes place in small French oak barrels. The quality ranges far and wide, but the Zinfandels in the better years have been powerful and reasonably balanced. Red House is a second label used occasionally for leftover batches of Zinfandel.

SMITH & HOOK WINERY   *Monterey 1980*   On beautiful terraced vineyards along the steep hills west of Soledad, Smith & Hook established 250 acres to red varieties in the mid-70s. Originally, the vineyard consisted of Cabernet Sauvignon (220) and Merlot (30), as the intention was to make only Bordeaux-style red wine. The winery itself is a renovated horse stable and carriage house. From the opening vintage of 79, the production of estate Cabernet Sauvignon has grown gradually and now surpasses 10,000 cases a year. Along the way Merlot was added to the line, and the winery developed 60 acres of Chardonnay. More recently, its Cabernet Franc acreage has been expanded to 10. While reserving the Smith & Hook label for its top-of-the-line red varietal wines, the winery bottles Chardonnay and less ageworthy batches of Cabernet Sauvignon and Merlot under a second label. At first, it selected Polo as the name of its second brand, but later changed to Goal and then to Deer Valley Vineyards. In the late 80s it adopted Lone Valley Vineyards for its 20,000-case-per-year second line. "Gabriel y Caroline" is a brand name once used for a late harvest Riesling. Now owned by N. L. A. Hahn, one of its founders, the winery has added a red Meritage wine named "The Baroness" as it moves on its way to a maximum production target of 50,000 cases.

Cabernet Sauvignon

81* 82 83* 85**

Always complex, the wine typically offers brushy, leathery, briary elements, tied to cherryish fruit, which shows vintage variations in depth and richness

SMITH VINEYARD & WINERY   *Nevada 1988*   Located in a scenic portion of Nevada County known as Grass Valley, Smith Vineyard is owned by longtime residents Sharon and Wayne Smith. In the mid-80s they began developing their 12-acre vineyard, which is farmed organically. The leading varieties are Chardonnay and Cabernet Sauvignon, with 1½ acres planted to Chenin Blanc. From the first small harvest of 88, the winery will expand production to the 2,000-case-a-year mark when its vineyard is fully mature.

SMITH-MADRONE VINEYARDS   *Napa 1977*   Brothers Stu and Charlie Smith bought 200 acres of forested land on Spring Mountain in 71. By the next year they had cleared the land at their hilly, 1,700-foot-elevation property, and planted 20 acres to Cabernet Sauvignon, Chardonnay, Riesling, and Pinot Noir. A graduate of U.C. Davis, Stu serves as vineyardist, and Charlie, a former schoolteacher, serves as winemaker. After focusing on Riesling for close to a decade, the Smiths decided in 85 to alter their vineyards and wine roster, and now emphasize Chardonnay, Cabernet Sauvignon, and Riesling. Pinot Noir was discontinued after 85. Their vineyard covers 41 acres and consists of 18 acres of Chardonnay, 18 of Cabernet, and 5 of Riesling. For blending with future vintages of Cabernet, a few acres of Cabernet Franc and Merlot were planted in 90. Total production averaged 6,000 cases a year in the late 80s, with 8,000 cases viewed as the absolute maximum. The winery's quality record has been spotty, although the 84 Cabernet Sauvignon ranked among the best in a highly competitive, strong vintage.

SMOTHERS BROTHERS WINES   *Sonoma 1977*   This brother wine act took a few years to get together. In 74 Dick Smothers bought an historic vineyard in the Santa Cruz Mountains named Vine Hill, which was located close to his home. Three years later he produced his first wine, 400 cases of late harvest Gewurztraminer, under the Smothers Winery name. That wine won awards, and the small winery was revived. By 85 it was operating at full capacity of 4,000 cases. Independently, in 71 Tom Smothers had moved to a 110-acre ranch in Glen Ellen, and developed a 35-acre vineyard named Remick Ridge. It was not until 86, when the brothers decided to team up as winemakers, that the brand name changed to Smothers Brothers. They came out with a line of varietals and highly successful blends, "Mom's Favorite White" and "Mom's Favorite Red," both made at another facility. Production was well over 25,000 cases by 87. Their search for a winery location in Sonoma County was slowed by the revival of their comedy act, and they finally ended up with a winery site and gift shop in Kenwood.

SOBON ESTATE *Amador 1856* In 89 the D'Agostini Winery in the Shenandoah Valley, the oldest in the county and the third oldest in the state, was bought by the Sobon family, owners of Shenandoah Vineyards. It was run-down and its vineyards were ancient and disease-ridden. Leon Sobon began renovating the old facility and replanting the 113-acre estate to 65 acres of Zinfandel, 11 of Sauvignon Blanc, and 7 acres of Cabernet Sauvignon. Close to 5 acres of Zinfandel remain from the old vineyard. The wines produced by the Sobon Estate are Zinfandel, Fumé Blanc, White Zinfandel, Muscat Canelli, and port. The initial offering was under 5,000 cases. When the vineyards are completely redeveloped and the vines mature, the winery aims to produce 20,000 cases a year.

SONOMA CREEK VINEYARDS *Sonoma 1987* John Larson and his father, Bob, were independent growers in the Carneros region for several years before starting their own winery. They own 40 acres planted to Chardonnay. A major portion of their crop is still sold, and the winery custom-crushes for various brands. Under its own label, Sonoma Creek is producing about 5,000 cases of estate-grown Chardonnay. Winemaker John Larson favors 100% barrel fermentation in new French oak for Chardonnay. He obtains Cabernet Sauvignon and Zinfandel from the Sonoma Valley, and produces about 1,000 cases of each. On a one-time basis he made 300 cases of 87 Howell Mountain Zinfandel, grown by Lamborn. The long-term capacity of Sonoma Creek is 20,000 cases.

SONOMA-CUTRER *Sonoma 1981* As a winemaking facility, Sonoma-Cutrer is "state of the art" and then some. Located in the cool western corner of the Russian River Valley, the winery was set up by winemaker Bill Bonetti for the exclusive production of Chardonnay. A few vintages of sparkling wine were once made on an experimental basis, but the notion was abandoned, and the winery now focuses all of its energies on its three Chardonnays. Two are vineyard-designated; one from the home Cutrer Vineyard, and the other from Les Pierres Vineyard in the Sonoma Valley. The third Chardonnay is made from several vineyards owned by the winery, and is bottled under the identity of Russian River Ranches. It is by far the volume leader at the 50,000-case level, as well as the least expensive. The other two, priced substantially higher, fall in the 10,000-case range.

All wines were well received during the early years and the winery has since continued to operate at a fairly high-quality level. In meticulous fashion, all Chardonnays are whole-cluster-pressed, barrel-fermented, and aged *sur lie*. However, the entire vinification process is a study in pampering, with hand-picked grapes transported in small, specially ventilated lug boxes to the winery, where the clusters are sent through a chilling tunnel (40°F.) before each is inspected and any defective grapes culled out. After fermentation and aging, the Russian River Ranches receives one year of bottle age, and the two others are given an additional six to ten months of bottle aging. The wines carry the Sonoma Coast appellation in addition to the individual vineyard names. Annual production reached 70,000 cases by 90.

Chardonnay

(Les Pierres) 84 *** 85 ** 86 * 87 * 89

(Cutrer) 84 ** 85 * 86 **87** * 88

(Russian River Ranches) 84 * 85 * 86 * 87 * 88 * 89 *

Emphasizing cleanliness and brisk acidity as their hallmarks, these Chardonnays combine a crisp, food-oriented style with varying amounts of oak and richness. The Les Pierres is the deepest in its best vintages, while the Cutrer can be the richest; the popularly priced Russian River Ranches tends to be the most immediately accessible of the trio

SOQUEL VINEYARDS *Santa Cruz 1979* Soquel was founded under the name of Grover Gulch Winery by home winemakers who tried to maintain two careers, finally giving up in 85. Two years later the small facility was acquired by a partnership headed by Peter and Paul Bargetto of the Bargetto Winery family, who renamed it Soquel Vineyards (though they might revive Grover Gulch in the future). Making wines exclusively from the Santa Cruz Mountains appellation, they obtain grapes from 14 acres under a lease arrangement. As they move toward the ultimate production goal of 2,000 cases, they are making only Cabernet Sauvignon, Chardonnay, and Pinot Noir. Soquel's initial releases (both the Cabernet Sauvignon and the Pinot Noir were highly rated) have been impressive.

SOTOYOME WINERY *Sonoma 1974* A little south of Healdsburg in the Russian River Valley lies this small winery and 10 acres of old vines. Named after a large land grant, Sotoyome made a range of wines at one time, including Chardonnay and Zinfandel. But it has developed a modest name for itself through a series of deep, dark Petite Sirahs, which after 85 were labeled Syrah. The winery was sold in 89 to the Mitchell family, which intends to continue making the Syrah and return production to the winery's 3,000-case capacity.

SPOTTSWOODE VINEYARD *Napa 1982* Moving to Napa Valley in 72 to "retire" and become grape growers, Mary and Jack Novak settled into an old (ca. 1882) Victorian house located on the western edge of St. Helena. The 46-acre estate was the site of a pre-Prohibition vineyard whose last known owner was the Spotts family. Beginning in 73, the vineyard site was planted to 22 acres of Cabernet Sauvignon and a few acres each of Merlot and Cabernet Franc. The next year they planted 8 acres to Sauvignon Blanc and about 2 acres of Semillon. After her husband's death in 77, Mary Novak sold the fruit to many wineries. The winery is run today by Mary and her daughter, Beth Novak. In 82 they hired winemaker Tony Soter, who has since produced extremely attractive vintages of Cabernet Sauvignon and Sauvignon Blanc. In most years the Cabernet is blended with 5% Cabernet Franc or Merlot. Partially barrel-fermented, Spottswoode's Sauvignon Blanc has been blended with as much as 25% Semillon. In better years the Sauvignon Blancs capture ample varietal character to accompany the usually rich-textured, ripe fruit, and oak-enriched style. The winery is producing 6,000 cases a year, with Cabernet Sauvignon tallying 4,000 cases and the remainder consisting of Sauvignon Blanc. During the 80s Spottswoode's Cabernets were consistently among the very best made in California.

Cabernet Sauvignon
82 ** 83 *** 84 *** 85 ** 86 *** 87 **

Deep, curranty fruit and rich oak are combined in a wine of substantial proportion, superb balance, and admirable aging potential

SPRING MOUNTAIN VINEYARDS *Napa 1968* In 62, Mike Robbins purchased a run-down Victorian home north of St. Helena with a large wine cellar, which he remodeled with the idea of using it for winemaking. Robbins started producing wines in 68, and within a few years was making Cabernet Sauvignon, Chardonnay, and Sauvignon Blanc. One of the most complex wines he ever made was one of his first—a Cabernet identified as Lot H 68–69, a blend of two vintages aged in oak barrels owned by Heitz Cellars. In the early 70s Spring Mountain's white wines were often leaders in their class. The winemaker (and later consultant) Chuck Ortman helped define an exciting style of oak-aged, moderately grassy, balanced Sauvignon Blanc and barrel-fermented Chardonnay.

In 76, with annual output over 20,000 cases, Robbins sold the property (which was renamed St. Clement) and bought another Victorian house on Spring Mountain Road. This second house was both bigger and more elaborate, with turrets and stained-glass windows throughout, and frequently served as the set for the TV series "Falcon Crest." In the 80s Spring Mountain Vineyards fell behind the competition, save for an occasional vintage of Cabernet Sauvignon. The winery became a tourist mecca, and Robbins began offering wines under the "Falcon Crest" label.

STAGS' LEAP VINTNERS   *Napa 1972*   This winery is part of an historic 240-acre estate and once prominent guesthouse known as Stags' Leap Manor. Built in 1890, the old mansion was badly damaged by fire and later only partially rebuilt. After being totally abandoned in the early 50s, the house and what remained of an old stone winery were bought and returned to life by Carl Doumani and family, who restored the winery and began replanting most of the old vineyard, keeping only a 5-acre patch of Petite Sirah planted in the early 1900s. That old parcel was eventually responsible for many intensely flavored, heavy-bodied red wines labeled "Petite Syrah" by the winery from 72 on. However, the winery became entangled in a long legal battle with its neighbor, Stag's Leap Wine Cellars, over trademark rights. Restoration and expansion plans fell behind schedule because of the legal issues.

It was not until 79 that Doumani crushed the fruit in his own winery. By then his 88-acre vineyard contained Cabernet Sauvignon (40 acres), Merlot (24 acres), Petite Sirah (16 acres), Cabernet Franc (4 acres), and Chardonnay (3 acres). For several years Cabernet Sauvignon and Merlot were marketed under the Pedregal brand. Once the legal dispute was resolved in 86, Doumani expanded production under his Stags' Leap label and grew quickly to the 12,000-case level. In its history, the winery made often superb Petite Sirah and some of the most full-bodied and full-flavored Chenin Blancs, purchasing the grapes from several growers. Doumani became partners with Steve Girard of Girard Winery in 87 and bought land in southern Oregon. He and Girard made wine in 87. The Napa Valley winery's annual production should reach 35,000 cases by the mid-90s.

Cabernet Sauvignon

81   **82**   **83**   84   **85**   86*

Heavyweight efforts are keyed on ripeness and boldness, and have often had the structures for long aging but not the necessary fruit to make the wait a sure thing

---

STAG'S LEAP WINE CELLARS   *Napa 1972*   Former University of Chicago professor of political science Warren Winiarski dabbled as a home winemaker before settling in the Napa Valley in the late 60s. He apprenticed with Lee Stewart of Souverain and worked two harvests at the Robert Mondavi Winery before buying land in 70 and developing vineyards and a winery in the Stags Leap District. The original vineyard consisted of 45 acres planted to Cabernet Sauvignon and Merlot. In 72, Stag's Leap produced 400 cases from its first crop, and though its 73 vintage was only slightly bigger, it became an overnight sensation by winning first place at a famous comparative tasting held in Paris in 76. With vineyard maturity, the winery's production increased, and by the end of the 70s Stag's Leap was offering a full line of varietals.

In 74 it produced its first Reserve-type Cabernet, labeled "Cask 23," made since then only in certain vintages. That same vintage saw the first bottling of Merlot, made on an irregular basis over the following decade. In 86 Stag's Leap acquired a well-known 75-acre Cabernet vineyard from Nathan Fay, and today bottles three Cabernets—"SLV" from the estate vineyards, "Cask 23" from a small parcel of that vineyard, and "Napa Valley," made from non-estate-grown grapes. The SLV has been further divided in some vintages into Lots 1 and 2, depending on the vintage. Total production of Cabernet Sauvignon approaches 25,000 cases a year.

Chardonnay (regular and Reserve), Sauvignon Blanc, and White Riesling from the Birkmyer Vineyard complete the line. Over the last few vintages, Stag's Leap's Cabernets became somewhat erratic in quality. At times the Reserve Chardonnay and the regular bottling have offered more excitement and interest. The winery's total production is 50,000 cases a year. A popularly priced line of wines is also offered under the Hawk Crest (see entry) label.

Cabernet Sauvignon

(SLV)   78 (Lots 1 & 2)*   79   **81***   82   83*   84*   85****   86
87

Capable of rich, round, cherry, and currant fruit, with added notes of loam and occasional hints of truffles and dried violets, the wine has been beset recently by offputting herbaceousness

Cabernet Sauvignon

(Cask 23) 74 *** 77 ** 78 ** 79 ** 83 * 84 * 85 86

The winery's most expensive Cabernet, claimed by some to be among the best in California, it has lost its standing in recent vintages. Its still intense and complex character is now often juxtaposed with offputting, intensely herbaceous, near-vegetal characteristics. Cask 23 is not offered in every year

Chardonnay

84 * 85 * 86 * 87 * 88 89

Green appley and quietly floral fruit, usually medium-intense and buttressed by toasty oak and brisk acidity, are the major themes in this generally attractive series of wines

Chardonnay

(Reserve) 85 * 86 *** 87 ** 88 *

Toasty oak and deep appley fruit combine in this brisk, well-balanced, amply stuffed wine; its typically tight structure seems to demand a few years of bottle aging

---

P. & M. STAIGER *Santa Cruz 1973* Paul Staiger and his wife, Marjorie, acquired a hillside site that was once home to a pre-1900 vineyard, and by 73 had built a small winery beneath their house in the Santa Cruz Mountains. Facing south, the hillside estate vineyard consists of 5 acres, half planted to Chardonnay and the other half to Cabernet Sauvignon and Merlot combined. In 79, they harvested their first estate-grown grapes. Now at full maturity, the vineyard yields about 250 cases of Chardonnay and the same of Cabernet Sauvignon. Pinot Noir made from a local vineyard has been occasionally offered. Working on a small scale, the Staigers follow traditional winemaking practices and rarely filter their wines. Most Cabernet Sauvignon vintages have been unfined as well.

STAR HILL WINERY *Napa 1988* Jake Goldenberg, a dentist, was an amateur winemaker before founding Star Hill. Located on a knoll in Napa, Star Hill is a small stone winery specializing in Pinot Noir and Chardonnay. The owner planted 4 acres of Chardonnay adjacent to the winery and buys grapes from growers in the Carneros and southern Napa regions. Early production of 1,000 cases consisted of 600 cases of Chardonnay and the remainder of Pinot Noir. The Chardonnay is 100% barrel-fermented in new French oak. Fermented by the native yeasts, Star Hill Pinot Noirs are unfined and unfiltered. The winery's production is projected to grow to a maximum of 3,000 cases a year. Star Hill's owners, Jake and Sally Goldenberg, also own a small vineyard and winery on the Mendocino coast named Pacific Star.

STELTZNER VINEYARDS *Napa 1977* A well-known grower, Dick Steltzner established his own vineyard in 66. Situated at the base of the Stags Leap cliffs, Steltzner's oldest vineyard contains 44 acres of Cabernet Sauvignon, and 5 acres each of Cabernet Franc and Merlot. Steltzner had previously carved out a reputation as a vineyard developer when he planted the vineyards of Diamond Creek, Spring Mountain, and several other producers. He also served as vineyard manager for several wineries. Starting in 77, he made his own wines in other facilities, and in 83 built a functional winery on his Stags Leap property. As a partner in a large vineyard located in the Oak Knoll area near Yountville, Steltzner draws from that source to make Sauvignon Blanc. Both as grower and wine producer, Steltzner has been associated with Cabernet Sauvignon.

The legendary 74 "Insignia" by Joseph Phelps Vineyard was made from

Steltzner's grapes. As a wine producer, he has at different times been his own winemaker, although Steltzner's ** achievements were made under the direction of consulting enologists. Nevertheless, in nearly every vintage made, the quality of the Cabernet fruit pushes the final product to some distinction. In 89, the winery made its first varietal Merlot, with the output expected to remain at 500 cases a year. In most vintages, Stelzner produces about 6,000 cases of Cabernet Sauvignon and just over 1,000 of Sauvignon Blanc. The facility has been expanded, with production moving toward a goal of 10,000 cases a year.

Cabernet Sauvignon

77 **   78 *   79 **   80 **   **81 **   82   **83 ***   **84 ***   85 *   **86 ***   87 *

Ripe fruit and lots of rich oak are braced by a decade's worth of coarse tannins; some wines will last up to 20 years

ROBERT STEMMLER   *Sonoma 1977*   Born and trained in winemaking in Germany, Robert Stemmler came to California and worked for several wineries, most notably Inglenook and Charles Krug. He became a consulting enologist in the 70s, and it was through his clients that he discovered available readymade wines and sources of grapes. With a partner, he started a winery to make a limited amount of wine through those contacts. However, by 82 he was crushing and fermenting wines, and before long he was making over 10,000 cases a year. Stemmler developed a reputation for rich, often heavy-duty Pinot Noir, in addition to a wide range of wines from Chardonnay to Sauvignon Blanc to Cabernet Sauvignon. In 88 Racke, USA, owner of Buena Vista, bought Stemmler and entered into an unusual arrangement whereby all Stemmler Pinot Noir, produced at the Buena Vista facility in the Carneros, is exclusively marketed by Racke. Other Stemmler wines are sold from his Dry Creek facility. With Pinot Noir production at 8,000 cases a year, Stemmler produces about 5,000 cases of other table wines.

Pinot Noir

84   85   86   8̶7̶

Ripe, exotic, not always clean, but usually rich and fully stuffed

STERLING VINEYARDS   *Napa 1967*   Just south of Calistoga on a bluff that disrupts the flat valley floor sits the white, monastic-looking Sterling Vineyards. In 64 four principals of Sterling International Paper Co. planted a 50-acre vineyard in Calistoga and joined forces to start this winery, with the goal of creating a striking facility that would draw thousands of visitors each year. An aerial tram was installed as the primary public approach to the knolltop facility, and a self-guided tour organized that deposited visitors in the tasting and sales room. A fee was charged for the tram ride, however, and in an era when many wineries offered free tours and tastings, Sterling's approach was not a hit. Nor were retailers thrilled by the news that all Sterling wines were to be sold exclusively from the winery. Sterling began making wines in temporary quarters in 69 under the direction of winemaker Ric Forman, who set out to make Bordeaux wines—Cabernet Sauvignon, Sauvignon Blanc (then labeled Blanc de Fumé), and Merlot (the second one made in California), with Chardonnay, Chenin Blanc, and Gewurztraminer filling out the line. The owners developed close to 400 acres of vineyards in and around the winery and in other generally warm sites, and in 73 completed a winery.

With the exception of a flawed 72 Cabernet Sauvignon, Sterling's quality was above average in most instances. Given the problems with tourists and retailers, however, the owners were forced to scramble to make ends meet. By the time Coca-Cola of Atlanta came along to purchase the whole package in 77, Sterling was making a wide array of wines. Under Coke, the facility was expanded and additional cask-aging areas built. Forman remained to work with a line trimmed down to Cabernet (regular and Reserve), Merlot, Sauvignon Blanc, and Chardonnay. Having ballooned to well over 100,000 cases a year, the winery's output was also reduced, to 65,000 cases. Coke expanded acreage and purchased the 110-acre Diamond Mountain Ranch, which contains Chardonnay, Cabernet, and a smattering of Merlot to bring the total acreage owned to 750. However, by 83 Coca-Cola had soured on the wine business in general and sold Sterling to Seagram. Since then, more acreage has been added, the well-known Winery Lake Vineyard in the Carneros being the most noteworthy. The winery now draws from its 1,180 total acres planted in 14 sites within Napa Valley.

The Winery Lake acquisition returned Pinot Noir to the lineup. Today, the majority of the production is the estate-bottled line of Sauvignon Blanc, Chardonnay, Cabernet Sauvignon, and Merlot. Vineyard-designated wines have grown to include bottlings of Chardonnay and Cabernet Sauvignon from Diamond Mountain Ranch, Pinot Noir and Chardonnay from Winery Lake Vineyards, and a Cabernet Sauvignon–Merlot blend from the Three Palms Vineyard. The top-of-the-line red is the "Sterling Reserve," a limited-volume (3,000-case average) Bordeaux-style blend.

Sterling's annual output approaches 200,000 cases, assisted by the popular non-estate-grown Cabernet Blanc, and the Sauvignon Blanc (blended with 20–25% Semillon), which is close to 33% of the total. Winemaking is in the hands of Bill Dyer, who began with Sterling in 77 and became head winemaker in 85.

Cabernet Sauvignon

78* 79* 80* 81 82* 83* 85* 86* 87*

A solid performer, this medium-depth wine has cherryish fruit underlaid by a bit of sweet oak, and has a fairly firm, never hard or heavy feel on the palate; the wines of the 70s were a little bigger

Cabernet Sauvignon

(Reserve) 73* 74** 75** 76 77* 78* 80** 82*
83*** 84** 85** 86** 87**

Ripe yet balanced, full-bodied and fairly intense without becoming ponderous, this rich, always highly oaked, curranty, sometimes minty Cabernet sets its deep, outgoing character against strong tannin; the wines of the 80s are somewhat more refined than their siblings of the previous decade

Chardonnay

(Napa Valley) 84* 85* 86* 87* 88*
(Diamond Mountain) 84 85** 86* 87
(Winery Lake) 86** 87 88*

Mostly above-average efforts from widely varying sources, yet sharing the same penchant for firm, crisp structure and for toasty, slightly creamy oak, these efforts have differed in the slightly broader, more direct fruit of the Napa Valley, in the near hardness of the Diamond Mountain, and in the slight pearlike and citrusy notes of the Winery Lake

Merlot

80* 81 82* 83 84* 85* 86* 87 88*

Light, sweet oak adds a note of prettiness to the cassis and cherry fruitiness of this moderately rough, fairly ageworthy, medium-intensity wine

STERNS WHARF VINTNERS *Santa Barbara 1982* In 79 Doug Scott purchased a popular tasting room and gift shop in Solvang named Copenhagen Cellars. Under the Sterns Wharf brand, he began producing limited amounts of wines to sell directly from the gift shop. He gradually expanded to seven varietals, all made from the Central Coast region. Through 40 acres on a lease arrangement and purchased grapes, the production of table wines approached 5,000 cases. The brand enjoyed a modest critical success with its Chardonnay and Riesling. In the same rented facility Scott began custom-making wines for the Warner West label. Warner, a large winery in Michigan, owns vineyard land in Santa Barbara County. In 88, Scott purchased the Santa Ynez Valley Winery (but not its vineyards) where he now makes the wines for Sterns Wharf and Santa Ynez. The roster for Sterns Wharf changes frequently, since almost all of the production is bought by tourists to the region. Currently, the lineup features Cabernet Sauvignon, Chardonnay, Muscat Canelli, and Riesling. On average, sales of Sterns Wharf wines are steady at 5,000 cases a year.

STEVENOT VINEYARDS *Calaveras 1974* The first winery since Prohibition to open and operate in Calaveras County, Stevenot grew out of an old cattle ranch bought by Bard Stevenot in 69. By 74 he had developed a 27-acre vineyard. His winery opened in 78 and produced 2,200 cases. Within two years it was producing about 10,000 cases as Stevenot bought grapes from vineyardists in El Dorado and Amador to supplement its own. The home vineyard was expanded to 18 acres of Chardonnay, and the first estate-bottled Calaveras Chardonnay was made in 83. Cabernet Sauvignon and Zinfandel are the next most significant varieties planted, both offered as varietals. In the 80s production jumped to 60,000 cases a year as Stevenot added White Zinfandel (accounting for 30,000 cases) and increased its production of Chenin Blanc, Fumé Blanc, and Muscat Canelli. It maintains a ratio of 80% white wines, 20% reds.

Chardonnay

84   85   86   87

Seemingly a little skimpy in its not-quite-varietal, melonlike fruit, and often on the thin side to boot

STONE CREEK BRAND This negociant label covers a line of varietal and generic wines from various appellations. Stone Creek was launched in 76 when the Bedford Wine Company, a San Francisco bottler and distributor, purchased an array of readymade wines from Souverain. At one time, at its peak level, close to 50,000 cases were bottled by Stone Creek, and at times a few noteworthy limited-volume wines made their way to the marketplace. However, the brand lost ground in the early 80s, and in 87 it was sold to the World Vintage Company, a division of the Simon Levi Company, Ltd. Stone Creek remains a negociant brand, and its owner buys grapes under contract as well as purchasing wines from both California and Northwestern producers. It offers a line of vintaged varietals from almost every appellation within California's North Coast, along with wines from the Columbia Valley. A few wines are identified as "American." At various times Stone Creek has had as many as four bottlings of Chardonnay on the market, under the appellations North Coast, Napa Valley, Alexander Valley, and American, as well as Cabernet Sauvignons from Mendocino and Napa Valley appellations. For the restaurant trade, it also markets nonvintage generics in 1.5- and 3.0-liter containers. Prices for all wines are generally on the low side. Quantity of all Stone Creek wines approaches 200,000 cases per year.

STONEGATE WINERY *Napa 1973* Jim Spaulding, a longtime home winemaker in Milwaukee, brought his family to California and purchased a mountainous vineyard in the Mayacamas Range in 69. Situated on the slopes of Diamond Mountain, the vineyard was planted to 35 acres and now contains Cabernet Sauvignon, Chardonnay, and Merlot. In 73, the Spauldings built a small winery in Calistoga, near Sterling Vineyards. A suitable area adjacent to the winery was planted to Sauvignon Blanc and Semillon. Over the first several vintages, as their vineyards were developing, the Spauldings made a wide range of table wines. One remarkable wine was the 75 Petite Sirah from the Maryroy Vineyard.

By 80 David Spaulding, Jim's son, had become the winemaker and today he handles the winery's day-to-day operation. As the winery has grown, it has relied more and more on its own grapes. For Chardonnay, Spaulding buys additional grapes from the Carneros to blend with his hillside crop. Production has reached the 17,000-case level, with Chardonnay at 9,000 cases, followed by Cabernet Sauvignon (4,500), Sauvignon Blanc (2,000), and Merlot (1,200). The

Cabernets, blended with 10% to 15% Merlot, are aged two years in oak and two years in the bottle prior to being marketed.

Stonegate's Merlot began as an afterthought when in some years there was Merlot remaining after the Cabernet blend was formulated. By the early 80s, however, Merlot was such a critical hit that the Spauldings added more acreage and contracted to purchase Merlot from a vineyard contiguous to theirs. Quality has varied from year to year at Stonegate and from variety to variety. Overall, although no consistent pattern has emerged, each wine in Stonegate's lineup has had its moments of success.

Cabernet Sauvignon

84* 85 86

Suggestions of black-cherry fruit are seasoned with oak in medium- to medium-full-bodied wines of average to above-average aging potential

Chardonnay

84* 85 86 87 88

Oaky but underfruited and somewhat weakly constituted wines are the rule of late

---

STONERIDGE *Amador 1975* A family-run winery small enough to handle on weekends, Stoneridge makes Zinfandel and Ruby Cabernet. These varieties are grown in the 6 acre vineyard located south of Sutter Creek. With the bottling of a White Zinfandel added in the mid-80s, annual production hit the winery's optimum level of 1,500 cases total.

J. STONESTREET WINERY *Sonoma 1989* Located in the Chalk Hill region of Sonoma County, this facility, originally known as Zellerbach Vineyard, was acquired by Jess Jackson in 89. Jackson, owner as well of Kendall-Jackson and Cambria, bought the winery and its 60-acre vineyard, but not the Zellerbach brand (see entry). Estate-grown Cabernet Sauvignon and Merlot are the main itmes in the Stonestreet line, though it includes Pinot Noir and Chardonnay. About 20,000 cases a year were offered in the initial vintages. The remodeled winery is capable of handling 40,000 cases a year.

STONY HILL VINEYARD *Napa 1953* To longtime observers of the California wine scene, Stony Hill merits a special place and special status. In 43 founders Eleanor and Fred McCrea bought an old ranch on a slope of Spring Mountain overlooking St. Helena. They began planting a vineyard consisting of Chardonnay, Riesling, Gewurztraminer, and Semillon. The early crops from their 35-acre vineyard were sold until by 51 a small stone winery was in place. Encouraged to make wines by Lee Stewart of the original Souverain, the McCreas started on a small scale, and even by 75 they were making little more than 1,000 cases total. However, by then Stony Hill was setting quality standards for Chardonnay, and its sales were primarily to those fortunate enough to be on the winery's mailing list.

Stony Hill eventually stopped selling grapes and its annual production expanded to a peak of 3,500 cases. Eleanor McCrea has operated the winery since her husband passed away in late 77. A continuity of style and quality has been maintained through winemaker Mike Chelini, at the helm since 72. Whether it was to do with the special Wente clone used in the vineyard or to the site's microclimate, Stony Hill's Chardonnays had the balance and structure needed for long, graceful aging in most vintages. Even the 76, a not overly successful vintage in general, was fit and attractive in the late 80s. By the mid-80s the winery's estate-grown Chardonnay output was decreased as the old vineyard, troubled by disease and age, was replanted in stages. During this time Stony Hill bought additional Chardonnay from Howell Mountain, which was once separately bottled under the SHV label and has since been blended with Stony Hill's home-grown crop. Generally, Stony Hill Chardonnays are reserved and lean in style, with appley and citrusy fruit played against a subtle oak background. Although they are long-aging, they have been bypassed in favor of newer producers who elevate oak and ripeness over restraint. Chelini has run the winery since Mrs. McCrea's death in 91.

STONY RIDGE WINERY *Alameda 1976* Back in 75 a partnership consisting of several winemakers purchased the historic property known as Ruby Hill Vineyard, founded in 1887. Operating as Stony Ridge, the new owners leased the old facility and surrounding vineyard property from the Southern Pacific Railroad. By 84 potential developers were lining up to build on the property, which was located in the middle of a rapidly growing area. Realizing that they could not stop progress, the winery owners closed down and sold off the inventory. At roughly the same time, the Scotto family were forced to close their own historic winery, Villa Armando in Pleasanton, and rather than give up winemaking, in 88 they bought the Stony Ridge name and revived it by making wines in leased space. In 90 the Scottos—Monica and her two brothers—built their own new facility in the Livermore Valley. As this chapter was unfolding, the new Stony Ridge was producing White Zinfandel, Sparkling Malvasia Bianca (similar in sweetness to Spumante), and low-priced Chardonnay and Cabernet Sauvignon. Output was close to 20,000 cases in 90. The new Livermore Valley facility has a capacity of 50,000 cases a year.

STORRS WINERY *Santa Cruz 1988* Owners Steve and Pamela Storrs, both enologists from U.C. Davis, started their own winery after working together for a few years at Felton Empire (now Hallcrest) Vineyards. All grapes are purchased, primarily from the Santa Cruz Mountains. Chardonnay from several small vineyards is the main wine produced, followed by White Riesling. As many as four bottlings of Chardonnay and two of Riesling have been made in recent years, each in 200- to 300-case quantities. Cabernet Sauvignon is also made from Santa Cruz Mountains, along with Petite Sirah from San Luis Obispo. Other red varietals have been made on a look-see basis. The annual production has reached 2,000 cases, with over half represented by the barrel-fermented Chardonnays.

STORY VINEYARDS *Amador 1973* With its original 23-acre vineyard among the oldest in the county, Story was a player in the Amador wine renaissance. It has 14 acres of Zinfandel, and 9 of Mission, both planted in the 30s. For years it made about 3,000 cases of Zinfandel and a blended wine based on the Mission grape. In the early 80s it developed a larger line to include generic wines and blush wines, and at one time was selling 25,000 cases a year. Today, the vineyard has expanded to 40 acres but the winery has returned to its original uncomplicated approach and is offering estate-grown Zinfandel, White Zinfandel, and a small amount of Chenin Blanc. Annual production is 7,500 cases.

STORYBOOK MOUNTAIN VINEYARD *Napa 1980* Former Stanford University history professor Jerry Seps decided to change careers in 76. Two years later, after apprenticing with several winemakers, he bought a 90-acre property north of Calistoga that was once the site of the Grimms Brothers Winery, dating to 1888, and named it Storybook Mountain. Building terraces on the moderately steep hillsides, Seps planted 36 acres to Zinfandel. The original aging caves were restored in time for the first crush in 80. Since the opening vintage Storybook has developed a reputation for long-lived, often high-quality Zinfandels that tend to be ripe, intense, and powerful. Through its first decade, the winery has offered three bottlings in most vintages—an estate, a Reserve estate, and Sonoma County (which has now been discontinued). Seps uses a combination of French and American oak for barrel aging. Production gradually increased and is approaching the maximum annual goal of 8,500 cases.

Zinfandel

(Napa)	81**	82*	83*	84*	85*	86***	87**	88*
(Napa Reserve)	81*	82**	83**	84**	86*			

Intense berryish fruit, lots of sweet oak, and strong tannins add up to some of the most flavorful, long-aging Zinfandels made

STRATFORD *Napa 1982* One of the first upscale négociant brands in California, Stratford is owned by a partnership headed by winemaker Paul Moser and marketing director Tony Cartlidge. The founders (a few have left the nest) originally focused on buying and blending Chardonnay that could retail for under $10 a bottle throughout the U.S. wine market. Buying Chardonnay from dozens of wineries in both the North and Central Coast regions, Stratford blended wines that often achieved ✷ rankings. The project was so successful that production expanded to include Sauvignon Blanc, Cabernet Sauvignon, and Merlot. Eventually, with production exceeding 75,000 cases a year, Stratford outgrew its original rented space, and the partners looked into the possibility of building a winery. A site was chosen in Napa Valley, and a facility was partially built before a major financial backer pulled out of the partnership. Since then Stratford, back in leased space, has reduced its annual production to 40,000 cases, including close to 18,000 cases of Chardonnay, with the remainder divided among Sauvignon Blanc, Cabernet Sauvignon, and Merlot. The two reds are usually made from Napa Valley grapes; the whites are bottled with the California appellation. The partners also own Canterbury (a line of lower-priced wines) and Cartlidge & Browne (see entry).

Chardonnay

(Napa Valley) 84✷ 85✷ 86 87 88

(Partner's Reserve) 86✷ 87✷ 88✷✷

The emergence of the medium-priced Partner's Reserve, a wine that started life successfully and has become the best under the Stratford label, coincides with the seeming loss of attractiveness in the regular bottling; the Reserve has round and fairly deep fruit with rich oak, while the other wine now seems to lack fruit intensity

STRAUS VINEYARDS *Napa 1986* After working in sales and marketing for several companies, including Sebastiani Vineyard, Phillip Toohey decided to make wine. He and his wife, Lisa, set out in 84 to make only Merlot. Their first vintages were made from blends of selected readymade wines from Napa and Sonoma appellations. Recent vintages are from Napa Valley. The style tends toward the full-bodied, with the occasional version having unchecked tannins. Most vintages have been blended with 10% to 15% Cabernet Sauvignon. Overall, given the general shortage of Merlot, the quality attained by Straus has been surprisingly acceptable, with an occasional vintage reaching ✷ quality. The brand was named after Phil Toohey's grandfather. After bottling close to 2,000 cases in each of its first several vintages, Straus is moving gradually toward a goal of 10,000 cases.

Merlot

86 87✷✷ 88 ✷

Tending toward ripeness and loaded with sweet oak in best vintage

STREBLOW VINEYARDS *Napa 1985* Longtime residents of the Napa Valley, the Streblow family own and operate the highly successful Basalt Rock Co. In the process of expanding that business, they acquired acreage throughout Northern California. In the early 70s the Streblows bought an old vineyard site on the slopes of Spring Mountain just west of St. Helena. In 79, after deciding to produce wine, the family (including all five sons) moved to the site. Once they had established terraces, they planted 11 acres to Cabernet Sauvignon and Cabernet Franc. On the valley floor south of St. Helena they own 3 acres once planted to Sauvignon Blanc and now to Merlot. A new winery was in place for the first crush in 85. Winemaker Bruce Streblow follows traditional vinification for Cabernet Sauvignon. Employing open-top fermenters, he punches the cap down by hand. Clarification is usually by racking and egg-white fining. The winery added a Napa Valley Chardonnay to the roster in 88. With vineyard maturity, the annual production will be about 2,000 cases of Cabernet Sauvignon and about the same of Chardonnay.

Cabernet Sauvignon

85   86*   87

Cherrylike fruit, tinged with herbs and cedar, comes wrapped in a moderately tannic, firm structure

---

RODNEY STRONG VINEYARDS   *Sonoma 1961*   Known until 84 as Sonoma Vineyards, this winery has gone through more changes than most. Originally, it was a tasting-room operation called Tiburon Vintners that expanded and moved to Sonoma County. It then became a wine-by-mail producer known as Windsor Vineyards, which was successful enough by 70 to give birth to a large winery, Sonoma Vineyards. Despite producing close to 500,000 cases in its peak years, the winery always seemed to be struggling. It was taken over in 84 by Renfield Importers, who changed its name to Rodney Strong Vineyards, but the name change did not provide greater stability. Renfield was acquired by Schenley Industries which, in turn, was acquired by Guinness. More recently, the winery has been in the hands of California-based Klein Foods.

Throughout the rapid changes in the 80s, which reduced its sales and annual output to under 200,000 cases, Rodney Strong, one of the founders of Tiburon Vintners, has hung on valiantly and once again runs the winery. Before the many ownership changes, the winery owned or controlled over 2,000 acres. Today, with holdings of 1,200 acres, it produces a line of Sonoma County table wines headed by several vineyard-designated varietals. Its most noteworthy is Cabernet Sauvignon from Alexander's Crown, first made in 74. It offers three Chardonnay bottlings, including two vineyard-designated versions, Chalk Hill and River West Vineyards. Pinot Noir originates in the River East Vineyard, and the winery's slightly sweet Riesling from the LeBaron Vineyard. One of its most unusual wines is an extremely brawny, powerful Zinfandel labeled "Old Vines." Overall, the Alexander's Crown Cabernet is its flagship wine and the trio of Chardonnays are its better values. The Windsor Vineyards mail-order brand remains alive, accounting for about a third of the facility's current 350,000-case output.

Cabernet Sauvignon

(Alexander's Crown)   81   82   84*   85*

Always ripe and dense, often with a tarry aspect, this wine frequently wants greater fruitiness to keep itself in balance

Chardonnay

(Sonoma County)   85   86   87   88   89

Citrusy fruit, somewhat lacking in depth, keeps the wine from higher ratings

---

STUERMER WINERY   *Lake 1977*   Owned by the Stuermer family, this winery was known as Lower Lake Winery until 87 when its name was changed. Lower Lake's reputation was not especially good, and in fact became notorious for a few overly vegetative vintages of Cabernet Sauvignon. The present approach calls for only one wine, a Reserve Cabernet Sauvignon, to be labeled Stuermer Vineyard. This wine represents 10% of the facility's 10,000-case annual output. The other wines made are Sauvignon Blanc, the mainstay, and a Lake County Cabernet Sauvignon, both of which are named Arcadia, the winery's second label. Under any and all names used so far, the wine quality has not been noteworthy.

SUGARLOAF RIDGE WINERY   *Sonoma 1985*   Sugarloaf Ridge refers to the northern part of the Mayacamas Range that separates Napa Valley from Sonoma Valley. High in the eastern hills at the 1,500-foot level, Sugarloaf Ridge Winery is located a short distance from Kistler Vineyards. Founded by Richard Putt-bach, an engineering consultant specializing in magnetic crystals and laser crystals, the winery is surrounded by 130 acres of bare land including about 45 acres suitable for vineyards. As of 90, Puttbach had yet to develop vineyards and bought Cabernet Sauvignon from a neighboring grower. Under the Sonoma Mountain appellation, he began making wine in 85, averaging 900 cases of Cabernet Sauvignon per year. All but the 85, which contained 15% Merlot, have been 100% varietal. In 89, on a one-time basis, he made 800 cases of Sonoma Valley Zinfandel. The winery's capacity is 2,000 cases a year, and the family plans to make only Cabernet Sauvignon.

SULLIVAN VINEYARDS *Napa 1972* Adjacent to Franciscan Vineyards in the area of Rutherford, Sullivan Vineyards began in 72 with the planting of 4 acres of Cabernet Sauvignon. The vineyard has since been expanded to include Mer-lot, along with small amounts of Chardonnay and Zinfandel. Jim Sullivan, who did the planting, is also the winemaker. During the first several vintages a range of wines were made in 200- to 500-case lots. Except for an occasional vintage of Cabernet Sauvignon calling attention to itself for over-enthusiastic astringency, most wines have not been noteworthy.

Cabernet Sauvignon

83* 84* 85 86

Merlot

83 84* 85 86

Both Cabernet Sauvignon and Merlot have often been loaded with excessive levels of volatile acidity

SUMMIT LAKE VINEYARDS *Napa 1986* In 71 Bob and Sue Brakesman purchased the site of a pre-Prohibition winery on Howell Mountain. With a degree in engineering, Bob began as a cellar worker for Freemark Abbey and later started designing and installing winery equipment. During the same period he was gradually clearing land and planting vineyards at the 2,200-foot level. A few acres of old Zinfandel were revived, and 10 new acres were planted to Zinfandel, Chardonnay, and Cabernet Sauvignon. In 86 their first wines appeared—82 Zinfandel and 84 Chardonnay—with 350 cases of each produced. The winery has also made Sauvignon Blanc. With vineyard maturity, it intends to peak at 2,000 cases a year. The Zinfandel is often worth a special search.

Zinfandel

82* 84** 85* 86* 88*

Tight, somewhat briary, berryish fruit; firm, moderately tannic structure for several years of aging potential

SUNNY ST. HELENA WINERY *Napa 1986* Built in 33 and used to make wines first by Charles Krug Winery and later by others, Sunny St. Helena is a winery building located just at the southern entrance to St. Helena. Though serving only as a storage facility in the 70s, it became a well-known reference point. In 86 it was purchased by five partners—three real estate developers (Bill Harlan, John Montgomery, and Peter Stocker), and Robin and John Lail. This same partnership owns Merryvale. Robin Lail, whose family owned In-glenook, serves as the manager of both Sunny St. Helena and Merryvale. The Sunny St. Helena line consists of Napa Valley varietals, generally made in a direct, straightforward style. The primary wines are Cabernet Sauvignon, Chardonnay, and Sauvignon Blanc; Zinfandel and Gewurztraminer are usually offered. Most wines are crushed and fermented by the winery, though on occasion readymade wine is purchased. Its early track record shows that most wines are easy to like, with Chardonnay offering the most depth and flavor interest. Production has been growing gradually. Currently, total annual output stands at 20,000 cases, with a potential capacity of 100,000 cases.

SUNRISE WINERY *Santa Clara 1976* The original Sunrise Winery was started by several partners who used an old facility north of Santa Cruz. A fire in 78 destroyed that property, and by 84 all but one of the founders had departed. Now owned by accountant Ron Stortz and his wife, Rolayne, who is the winemaker, Sunrise is situated on Monte Bello Road overlooking Cupertino. The owners have a long-term lease on the entire property, including 6 acres of old Zinfandel. A small line of table wines regularly includes Pinot Noir and Pinot Blanc from the San Ysidro Vineyard in Santa Clara County, along with Petite Sirah and Cabernet Sauvignon from the Santa Cruz Mountains. The owners hope the present output of 2,500 cases a year will grow to 5,000.

SUTTER HOME WINERY *Napa 1960* Sutter Home Winery has been in existence since 1874, but for many years it produced bulk wines. Owned by the Trinchero family since 47, the winery bottled an assortment of all types of wine until the late 60s. Distressed by soaring prices of Napa Valley grapes, Bob Trinchero eventually found what he wanted in Amador County. In 68 Sutter Home made an Amador County Zinfandel, starting the revival of interest in Amador County wine. By the mid-70s Sutter Home was enjoying enough success with its American oak–aged Amador County Zinfandels to have trimmed its line considerably. In 72, the Trincheros experimented with Zinfandel from Amador County in order to make a small batch of dry, wood-aged Blanc de Noirs. Labeled White Zinfandel, this wine was finished with sweetness for the first time in 75, but that bottling ushered in the blush wine era of the 80s.

In the mid-70s Sutter Home was focused on Amador Zinfandel, a sweet-finished Muscat of Alexandria, and White Zinfandel. Sales grew steadily and by 80 the winery was bottling 100,000 cases a year with well over half consisting of White Zinfandel. The demand for Sutter Home's White Zinfandel continued to grow in the 80s until, by the end of the decade, the winery was making 3 million cases of White Zinfandel a year. After greatly expanding the old winery south of St. Helena, the Trincheros developed a larger facility located on Zinfandel Lane in Napa Valley. Before 80 Sutter Home owned no vineyards, but it began acquiring land and now owns 3,000 acres. In Lake County, the winery has 300 acres planted mostly to Sauvignon Blanc and Chenin Blanc, while its 2,700 acres in the Sacramento Valley region are largely planted to Cabernet Sauvignon, Zinfandel, and Chardonnay.

Amador County is still represented: Sutter Home purchases all Zinfandel grown by the Deaver Ranch. Its Reserve Amador County Zinfandels, which occasionally earn ✩, continue its series of Amador County bottlings, and are the only wines currently offered with an appellation more specific than California. Cabernet Sauvignon is the second leading wine in terms of volume, with sales close to 240,000 cases. It is followed by Sauvignon Blanc and Chenin Blanc. Chardonnay was first offered from the 89 vintage. Sutter Home also owns Montevina Vineyards in Amador County.

JOSEPH SWAN VINEYARDS *Sonoma 1969* Joseph Swan, a soft-spoken, easy-to-like man, made Zinfandels of legendary proportions. In the 70s he and his winery developed something akin to a cult following. The Zinfandels from 68 to 77 and an occasional vintage of Pinot Noir created such excitement that they inspired many new winemakers, and became a galvanizing force for California wine during the 70s. Yet winemaking was Swan's second career. He retired early as an airline pilot, searched for a vineyard site, and in 67 finally selected a small patch in Forestville where he developed a 10-acre vineyard. Like many pioneers, Swan's preference was to make Burgundian wines—Pinot Noir and Chardonnay. As his vines were maturing, he experimented with Zinfandel grown in the Dry Creek Valley by Teldeschi Vineyard. He aged the Zinfandel in French oak and released it to friends and a mailing list in 72. By the time he released the 71, which was given ✩✩✩ in 74, Swan was well on his way to fame.

Typically, his legendary Zins of the 70s were full of ripe, deep fruit, creamy oak, and were indeed long-lived. A few of these early vintages were wonderful two decades later. After 77, Swan lost his favorite source of Zinfandel, so stopped making the varietal until he found an acceptable replacement in 82. However, the Zinfandel magic never fully returned and, in the 80s, it was Swan's Pinot Noir which set the pace. The average annual output rarely exceeded 1,500 cases. Most are regularly purchased by longtime friends on a mailing list. Joe Swan died in 89. The winemaking was turned over to his son-in-law, Rod Berglund, one of many young winemakers to apprentice under him.

Pinot Noir

78** 79* 80** 81* 82 83 84* 85* 86* 87

Varying by vintage according to the depth of fruit delivered by the grapes, these wines are all marked by black-cherry and herb flavors, firm structures, rich oak

Zinfandel

80** 81 82* 83 85* 86* 87

For their first 10 vintages, these were wines of heroic proportion—deep in fruit, high in rich oak, tightly focused on varietal character, solidly structured, long-aging; the wines of the 80s follow in style, but not in level of intensity or in finely focused varietal impressions

SWANSON WINERY *Napa 1989* Heir to Swanson Foods, Clarke Swanson purchased 80 acres in Oakville in 85. A few years later he bought the former Cassayre-Forni winery in Rutherford after a long search. As the old winery was being refurbished, Swanson acquired additional land adjacent to the Silverado Trail, and today Swanson Winery owns about 130 acres of vineyards. Chardonnay, Cabernet Sauvignon, and Merlot are the mainstays. The first offerings, an 87 Cabernet and 88 Chardonnay, added up to 5,000 cases. A Reserve Chardonnay debuted in the 88 vintage. Swanson also purchases grapes to produce Zinfandel from the Howell Mountain appellation. Long-term, Swanson Winery plans to grow to about 20,000 cases a year.

SYCAMORE CREEK VINEYARDS *Santa Clara 1976* In the quaint Uvas Valley west of Morgan Hill, Terry Parks and his wife purchased a defunct winery and renamed it after the Sycamore Creek that divides their land. When they bought the property in 75 it included 7 acres of Carignane and Zinfandel planted around 1900. The vineyard was expanded to 14 acres with the planting of 4 acres of Chardonnay and 3 of Cabernet Sauvignon. Acting as his own winemaker, Parks has averaged 4,500 cases a year, about one-third Chardonnay, and another third of various, slightly sweet whites. In late 89, the winery was sold to a Japanese sake producer, and the tasting room stayed in operation to sell the remaining wine inventory.

SYLVAN SPRINGS WINERY In early 88 Heublein introduced this new label for a line of low-priced varietals made and bottled in its Central Valley facility. Enhanced by the Vintner's Reserve designation, the wines offered are Chardonnay, Cabernet Sauvignon, Sauvignon Blanc, and White Zinfandel. The quality was no better or worse than Inglenook Navalle or most other wines bottled by Heublein in its Madera winery.

TAFT STREET WINERY *Sonoma 1982* What started as a part-time venture among Berkeley-based home winemaking friends and relatives evolved into a full-scale winery. The first vintage made in rented space consisted of 2,000 cases, and after muddling along, making some wines, buying and blending others for a small market, Taft Street settled down in 86. Though still in rented space, it now owns all of the latest equipment and cooperage, including small oak for barrel fermentations of its Chardonnays. After marketing a range of table wines, the winery now emphasizes Chardonnay from two appellations, Sonoma County and Russian River Valley. About 2,000 cases of the Russian River Chardonnay are produced, with the Sonoma County bottling amounting to 10,000 cases. Sauvignon Blanc from Napa Valley and Merlot from Sonoma County are regularly offered. A blended white, "White House White," is the only generic on the roster. The winery's annual production is at 25,000 cases.

TALBOTT VINEYARD *Monterey 1983* The Talbott family started their winery with the intention of producing only Chardonnay from the Carmel Valley, and midway up the valley developed a hillside vineyard that now covers 32 acres. Knowing that it would mature slowly, the family made their first vintages from grapes obtained from the Gonzales area of the Salinas Valley. After a good debut in 83, it was decided not to market the 84 Chardonnay. In 86, when Robb Talbott took over the winery operation after his father's death, he felt they were outgrowing the original facility. Pleased with the wines produced from the Salinas Valley, the Talbotts decided to build a larger winery there near Gonzales and to develop a 60-acre vineyard adjacent to it. Only Chardonnay is produced, but from two separate appellations today. The primary wine labeled Talbott originates in Monterey County; the second, grown exclusively in the family's Carmel Valley holdings, is labeled "Talbott Family Estates." Both Chardonnays display ripe fruit character and are barrel-fermented, and French oak-aged for at least 1 year. The Monterey Chardonnay is bottle-aged for one year; the Family Estate is given two years of bottle aging. The long-term production goal for both lines combined is 7,000 cases. In 88, the winery introduced another Chardonnay labeled Logan (see separate entry). Since 90 all production has taken place in the Gonzales facility.

Chardonnay

85   86*   87***   88**

Potentially among the tops in California, as it was in the 87 vintage, the wine can be rich, appley, buttery, deep, and mouth-filling at its best

TALLEY VINEYARDS *San Luis Obispo 1986* Settling in the Arroyo Grande region, the Talley family began by developing their own 65-acre vineyard. In 86, after expanding the holdings to 85 acres. Talley ventured into winemaking. Chardonnay at 60 acres is the primary variety planted, followed by Pinot Noir (10), Sauvignon Blanc (7), and Riesling (3). Early vintages were led by Chardonnay and White Zinfandel made from purchased grapes. When the estate vineyards are mature, Talley has set 15,000 cases as its maximum annual production. All estate-grown wines are identified as originating in the Arroyo Grande Valley, a subregion of San Luis Obispo County. Talley's initial vintages of Chardonnay and Pinot Noir have been well received.

IVÁN TAMÁS WINES   This is a negociant brand, owned and operated by Iván Tamás Fuezy and Steven Mirassou. In 84 Mirassou left his family winery to join Fuezy, a long time wine-marketing professional. In the first two vintages they offered varietals from both Central and North Coast appellations. For a few years after, most of their wines originated in Mendocino County. The line has remained constant, and features White Zinfandel, Chardonnay, Cabernet Sauvignon, and Sauvignon Blanc. As they grew to the 15,000-case-a-year level, White Zinfandel and Chardonnay combined represented 80% of their sales. In the late 80s, they decided to switch to the Livermore Valley as the primary source of wines. Trebbiano, a seldom-seen varietal, has been added to the lineup. Overall, the wines are priced on the low end and in some vintages have offered good value. With hoped-for steady growth, the annual output will level off at 40,000 cases.

TAYLOR CALIFORNIA CELLARS *Monterey 1978* Started from scratch in 77 by Coca-Cola of Atlanta's wine division, the Wine Spectrum, Taylor California Cellars brought together the name of the best-known New York State winery, Taylor, and the California identity in what was envisioned as a "can't-miss" brand of wine. With tremendous promotional efforts and generally agreeable wines, Taylor California Cellars quickly became part of the second largest wine empire in the U.S. In the tiny Monterey County town of Soledad, Coke built a large (30-million-gallon-capacity) winemaking facility, and was on a roll. In 80, it bottled over 10 million cases. The only problem was that Taylor California was still second behind Gallo, and it would take a long, tough, and possibly futile effort to try to unseat Gallo as the largest producer. In 83 Coke of Atlanta sold all of its wine properties—Taylor of California and New York, Sterling, and the Monterey Vineyard—to Seagram. Taylor California Cellars continued as one of the biggest wine producers, but its sales were not growing.

In 87, Seagram sold Taylor along with Paul Masson, a brand it owned since the 40s, to the corporation named Vintners International. Most of the major stockholders were former executives with Seagram and other wine and spirits companies, and Seagram retained 20% of the stock. Under this ownership, Taylor California Cellars was positioned as a generic wine brand, offering wines in all sizes from standard-bottled to bag-in-the-box to kegs. A modest line of varietals includes Cabernet Sauvignon, Chardonnay, and the volume item, White Zinfandel. In the 90s, it will be bottling low-calorie wines such as "Diet Chablis" and "Diet White Zinfandel." Annual production today, 90% of which is generic wine, is 5 million cases.

THE TERRACES   *Napa 1985*   This is a red wine–only brand owned by Wayne Hogue Vineyard of Rutherford. With 5 acres planted in 81 to Zinfandel and Cabernet Sauvignon, Hogue produced his first wine in 85. The terraced vineyard is located in the east Rutherford hills above the Silverado Trail. Originally Hogue intended to use the family name, but the Hogue Winery in Washington owned the trademark and thought otherwise. In general, Wayne Hogue favors fairly long aging, releasing his Zinfandel three years post-harvest, and his Cabernet Sauvignon four. All vintages through 89 were custom-made at Caymus Vineyards, with Hogue's small winery in place for 90. The annual production struggles to hit 1,000 cases, and is averaging 400 cases of Zinfandel, 500 of Cabernet. When it is in top form, the Zinfandel, aged in French and American oak, offers bright, ripe-berry fruit in a rich, creamy oak presentation.

THACKREY & CO.   *Marin 1982*   Owner of Thackrey & Robertson, an art store in San Francisco, Sean Thackrey is a weekend winemaker. Using space next to his home on the Marin Coast, he began dabbling with Pinot Noir before turning his attention to Rhone varietals and proprietary red blends. Favoring proprietary wine names, he first came to our attention with "Aquila," a Merlot–Cabernet Sauvignon blend. The Syrahs, 100% varietal, are marketed under the name of "Orion," and Thackrey prefers Syrah from the Rutherford Bench area. Initial vintages of Mourvedre came from the Cline Vineyard in Oakley and were given the name "Taurus." A house red blend following no specific formula each year is dubbed "Pleiades." Thackrey gained modest national recognition through his Syrahs, which became part of the Rhone variety revival in the late 80s. He intends to add a wine made from Viognier. His annual production reached 1,500 cases, with 5,000 set as the maximum.

THOMAS-HSI VINEYARD   *Napa 1988*   A small winery specializing in Chardonnay from the Mount Veeder area, Thomas-Hsi made its first wine in 87. Charles Thomas and his wife, Lili Hsi, have worked for many wineries within Napa Valley, and own a small vineyard near their Mount Veeder home. Thomas is part of the enological team at Robert Mondavi Winery, and Lili Hsi works for St. Supéry. The Thomas-Hsi Chardonnay is 100% barrel-fermented, and about half goes through malolactic fermentation. Aging in small oak barrels is *sur lie* for several months. After the first release of 200 cases, the owners hope to expand to 1,000 cases.

TIFFANY HILL   *San Luis Obispo 1986*   Ed Nivens, who owns Paragon Vineyards in the Edna Valley, also owns this brand. Most of the grapes grown by Paragon are crushed by Edna Valley Vineyards, which Nivens co-owns with Chalone, Inc. However, a few acres of Chardonnay grown on a knoll in Paragon Vineyards referred to as Tiffany Hills are set aside for this brand. In space rented in Santa Barbara, the Tiffany Hills Chardonnays are 100% barrel-fermented, and aged in oak for a year or more. Nivens gives this Chardonnay six months to a year of bottle aging before selling it. His annual output has been about 3,500 cases.

Chardonnay

86*   87*   88*

Lots of toasty oak enriches the aroma but somewhat obscures the medium-deep fruit

---

TIJSSELING VINEYARDS   *Mendocino 1981*   When the Tijsselings founded the adjacent Tyland Vineyards in 79, they intended to produce only table wines. However, two years later they decided to enter the sparkling wine market and converted the building next door into a separate facility. The Tijsselings had developed 300 acres of vineyards in Ukiah by then, and were using only a small portion for their sparkling wines. By 87 they had come to believe that the Tijsseling name was both acceptable to the public and conducive to family pride, so they consolidated most wines under Tijsseling Vineyards. A popular line of generic red and white wines bottled in 1.5-liter magnums has grown to 15,000 cases a year. The family's line of varietals averages close to 8,000 cases a year, and sparkling wines now account for 8,000 cases annually. Among Tijsseling's varietals, the mainstays are Chardonnay, Cabernet Sauvignon, Zinfandel, and Petite Sirah. Brut and Blanc de Blancs head the sparkling wine line. Annual production is steady at 35,000 cases

---

T.K.C. VINEYARDS   *Amador 1981*   A small winery located east of Plymouth, T.K.C. makes nothing but Zinfandel. Its owner, Harold Nuffer, has 9 acres of Zinfandel. The maximum annual production is slightly over 1,500 cases. While its vineyards were maturing, the winery made Zinfandel from the Bowman Vineyard, a neighbor in the Shenandoah Valley.

TOBIAS VINEYARDS   *San Luis Obispo 1980*   Perched on a mountaintop between Paso Robles and Templeton, Tobias specializes in Zinfandel and Petite Sirah from the local area, usually the Paso Robles appellation. Its Zinfandel is usually from the Dusi Ranch. Overall, the winemaking style favors ripe, sturdy, brawny wines. When they are not too volatile, they are acceptable for their style. With a maximum production goal of 5,000 cases a year, the winery has been holding steady at 1,000. Located on Peachy Canyon Road, the Tobias Winery has registered a second label, Peachy Canyon Winery.

PHILIP TOGNI VINEYARD   *Napa 1986*   Journeyman winemaker Philip Togni first came to California to work for Mayacamas Vineyards in 58. Over the ensuing years he made wines at Chalone, Chappellet, and Cuvaison. An extremely meticulous person, even by winemaker standards, Togni developed a reputation for single-mindedness and extreme attention to the smallest detail. After leaving Cuvaison in 81, he began developing his own 10-acre vineyard near his home on Spring Mountain. For several years he was a consultant to several wineries, most notably Chimney Rock. His own winery makes Cabernet Sauvignon and Sauvignon Blanc, both in an assertive style. A small amount of Black Muscat is also bottled. From a 300-case first harvest in 83, Togni has expanded production to the 1,200-case mark.

Cabernet Sauvignon

84   85   86   87   88

Inky, tannic, highly extracted wines, often lacking the fruit to bring themselves into balance and to justify the lengthy cellar aging demanded

---

TOPOLOS AT RUSSIAN RIVER   *Sonoma 1978*   South of Forestville, the Topolos family property consists of a winery and a restaurant. Both have gone through many changes in direction over the first decade. Mike Topolos directs the wine operation and owns a 26-acre vineyard in Sonoma, leasing another 37 acres close to the winery. The winery once offered a broad range of table wines—Red, White, and Blanc de Noirs. By 88 the annual production topped 10,000 cases. Unhappy with their lack of focus, the owners decided to trim the line, reduce production, and emphasize red wines only. The current mainstays are Zinfandel, Petite Sirah, and Alicante Bouschet. Limited bottlings of vineyard-designated Zinfandel and Petite Sirah from the Rossi Ranch represent the top of the line. Total production is 7,500 cases a year.

TOWNSEND & WALSH Until recently, this was a brand for sparkling wine only that was custom-made at Chateau St. Jean. Townsend & Walsh is owned by George Vare, one-time president of Geyser Peak, who went on to develop the highly successful Shadow Creek brand. After selling that brand of sparkling wine, he developed this one, and at one time was making close to 10,000 cases a year. Production ceased in 89.

TREFETHEN VINEYARDS *Napa 1973* The Trefethen family purchased an old ranch and vineyard named Eshcol Estate in 68. Soon to retire from Kaiser Industries, Gene Trefethen was looking for a rural home site, and with encouragement from his son John and daughter-in-law Janet, he began restoring the century-old wood frame winery and replanting the surrounding vineyard. Located in the cool-growing area between Napa and Yountville, the vineyard was gradually planted to Chardonnay, Pinot Noir, Riesling, and Cabernet Sauvignon. With good timing on their side, the Trefethens were awaiting their first harvests about the time Domaine Chandon was setting up a few miles to the north. Chandon, needing a grape supply while its vineyards were being developed, entered into an arrangement to buy grapes from Trefethen and crush some of the fruit there as well. Other producers purchased Trefethen grapes, including Schramsberg Vineyards in the 70s.

These arrangements allowed Trefethen to expand its vineyard to 600 acres and to move into winemaking at a leisurely pace, which it did with a small first vintage of Chardonnay in 73. Gradually more of the home grapes went into Trefethen wines, and today's lineup consists of Chardonnay, the mainstay, Cabernet Sauvignon, White Riesling, and two proprietary blends, "Eshcol White" and "Eshcol Red." Among its varietals, Chardonnay remains the volume leader, usually made in a medium-intense, crisp, balanced style. Its Riesling remains true to the original, holding to a floral, light-bodied, dry style. The production of Pinot Noir was gradually reduced in the 80s and may be phased out by the owners. Reserve-style Cabernet and Chardonnay appeared in the late 80s, and the popular Eshcol blends remain as important items in the winery's 80,000-case-a-year output.

Chardonnay

84* 85* 87 88

Crisp, bright, but narrow green appley fruit, with oak appearing only in the background

TRENTADUE WINERY *Sonoma 1969* Directly east of Chateau Souverain in Geyserville lie a well-manicured vineyard and a small building partially hidden by an oak grove. That property belongs to the Trentadue family, which farms 200 acres planted to a range of varieties, from Zinfandel, which is well suited to the region, to Chardonnay, which is not. For many years it has sold Zinfandel to Ridge Vineyards for separate bottling under the identity "Geyserville" Zinfandel. Still selling much of its crop to others, Trentadue eased into winemaking, and by 80 was making 12,000 cases. A new winemaker in 83, combined with the introduction of a White Zinfandel, increased production to 20,000 cases a year. The winery sells much of its wine out of its tasting room and gift shop. Hearty old-style red wines are still its stronghold.

MICHEL TRIBAUT *Alameda 1982* A partnership between Michel Tribaut and Bertram Devavry, both from the Champagne region, this winery specializes in *méthode champenoise* sparkling wine. Beginning as a low-overhead operation using a rented warehouse in Hayward, it enjoyed enough success over the first few years to expand its facility and production. Devavry sold his interest in 88. Three types of wines are available—Brut, Blanc de Noirs, and Rosé. All cuvées are from Monterey County grapes, and only Chardonnay and Pinot Noir are used. Adhering closely to the traditional approach followed in Champagne, the winemaker ages the wines in mature oak barrels prior to assembling the cuvée. Both Chardonnay and Pinot Noir undergo malolactic fermentation. By 90, annual production was halfway to the maximum goal of 50,000 cases. Pinot Noir is the only nonsparkling wine produced.

TUDAL WINERY *Napa 1979* Owner and self-taught winemaker Arnold Tudal is a farmer by experience, and proud of it. After growing produce in Alameda County for close to three decades, Tudal, once known as the "king of radishes" to his friends, was crowded out by urban growth in the late 60s and moved to the Napa Valley in 73. Having experienced little financial success growing walnuts on his 10-acre ranch not far from the Napa River between St. Helena and Calistoga, Tudal decided to start over and eventually planted all 10 acres to Cabernet Sauvignon. In 79, after reading a few enology textbooks and making a few barrels of wine in his basement, he made his first professional wine. By 80 he was making 100% Cabernet Sauvignon that was definitely above average. Through the 80s he continued using basic equipment, including an old basket press. The annual output varies from 1,500 to 3,000 cases because his dry-farmed vineyards are low-yielding in drought-plagued vintages. On average, Tudal makes 2,000 cases a year, usually of admirable quality.

Cabernet Sauvignon
80* 81* 82* 83* 84** 85** 86** 87*

Always deep, sometimes stressing ripeness more than finesse, and showing rich, sweet oak, this medium-long-aging wine wins plaudits for its direct, black-cherry fruit

TULOCAY WINERY *Napa 1975* Owner Bill Cadman was a stockbroker who decided to enjoy life fully and moved to the wine country. For many years he worked for Beringer and Charles Krug before joining Robert Mondavi Winery. When he is not leading tours through Mondavi's winery, he makes about 2,000 cases a year. All wines are from Napa Valley, and the roster usually consists of Chardonnay and Pinot Noir, the primary wines, and Cabernet Sauvignon and Zinfandel. Tulocay wines have been quite erratic, which is to say some have been of * quality and an equal number have been below par. A few Pinot Noirs have been above average more often than others; but, in general, most wines betray a heavy hand.

TWIN HILLS RANCH WINERY *San Luis Obispo 1980* Jim Lockshaw, owner of an aerospace company in Orange County, decided to purchase a 118-acre ranch outside of Paso Robles that contained several crops, including wine grapes. In 79 he began expanding the vineyard portion to its present 40-acre size. The primary varieties planted are Chardonnay, Sauvignon Blanc, Chenin Blanc, and Zinfandel. The biggest item is the Zinfandel, made into three styles—Blush, Rosé, and standard Red. From 4 acres planted to Palomino, Twin Hills is making about 1,000 cases of sherry by the *solera* process. Total annual output has hit the optimum 10,000-case mark.

TYLAND VINEYARDS *Mendocino 1979* Tyland is a brand name that was widely used from 79 to 87 by the Tijsseling family for a line of table wines. The winemaking facility in Ukiah is still identified as Tyland. In 81 an adjacent facility was created to produce only sparkling wine under the Tijsseling Vineyards name. In early 88, the Tijsseling family decided to put most of the wines made from their own vineyards under one brand, Tijsseling Vineyards. However, they still sell modest amounts of wines labeled "Tyland" in the Ukiah market and "Tyland Vineyards" in the export market.

M. G. VALLEJO WINERY *(Glen Ellen Winery)* In 86 the owners of Glen Ellen Winery (the Benziger family) trotted out this brand to see if it too would catch fire the way the primary brand did in 82. M. G. Vallejo was a general who directed all military affairs in the 1830s in what is now California. Among many accomplishments, he established the town of Sonoma, and once owned the land upon which Glen Ellen Winery stands. From the beginning the M. G. Vallejo brand donated part of its profits to restoration of the general's home and grounds, a State Historic Park near Sonoma Plaza. After cautiously entering the market with Chardonnay and Cabernet Sauvignon made from purchased wines and sold for below $5 a bottle, the Vallejo brand added White Zinfandel, Fumé Blanc, and Merlot a few years later. All have a California appellation. By the end of 90, sales were approaching 350,000 cases, with major marketing emphasis on the 1.5-liter magnum market.

VALLEY OF THE MOON WINERY *Sonoma 1943* On a peaceful cross street near the town of Glen Ellen, the Valley of the Moon Winery has quietly enjoyed a steady roadside business. It was a major supplier of jug wines to San Francisco restaurants up until the mid-70s. Since then, in order to catch up with the times, the winery has slowly worked to upgrade its varietals. With a 200-acre vineyard, the Parducci family (no relation to the family directing the Parducci Winery of Mendocino) has focused on its red varietals, notably Zinfandel and Cabernet Sauvignon, still made in a well-aged, sometimes over-aged, style. Production remains weighed heavily toward generic table wines, and the annual output is steady at 50,000 cases.

VAN DER KAMP CHAMPAGNE CELLARS *Sonoma 1981* In 81, using a corner of the St. Francis facility and buying grapes from St. Francis and others in the Sonoma Valley, jeweler Martin Van der Kamp produced 2,000 cases of sparkling wine. Production is now at the optimum 5,500-case level. Of the three sparklers offered, the Brut—which is aged four years on the yeast—is the mainstay at 3,000 cases. Next in importance at 2,000 cases is the Brut Rosé, labeled "Midnight Cuvée" and made 100% from Pinot Noir. The last wine is the "English Cuvée," aged for three years, which when produced amounts to 500 cases. Every so often Van der Kamp will set aside 100 cases of his Brut in magnums, and then after six years of aging offer them as a Brut Reserve. In 89 Van der Kamp moved his operation to Landmark Vineyards after its its new facility was built next to his home in the Sonoma Valley. He is developing 35 acres on the eastern slopes of Sonoma Mountain which in the mid-90s will supply most of his grape requirements.

VENTANA VINEYARDS *Monterey 1978* Named after a gigantic wilderness area in Monterey County, Ventana Vineyards has brought considerable recognition to Monterey as a grape source. In the early 70s owner Doug Meador developed what grew to be a 300-acre vineyard on the west side of the Salinas Valley in the Soledad-Greenfield area. A compulsive experimenter with grape varieties and growing techniques, Meador has paved the way for other growers in the county. Chardonnay covers 131 acres, and is easily the greatest success. Numerous producers have made vineyard-designated Ventana Chardonnays, and many are long-term buyers, among them Cronin, Fogarty, Sarah's Vineyard, and Boyer. Johannisberg Riesling at 38 acres is his second most in-demand grape, and Obester Winery, among others, has regularly made a pretty version. Chenin Blanc (38 acres) and Sauvignon Blanc (26 acres) are the other more prominent varieties grown.

As a wine producer, Ventana has offered a dazzling range of wine types in a variety of styles and under several label designations. The winery once produced as many as 30,000 cases a year, but in 85 hit a 5,000-case low. It is now holding steady at 20,000 cases per year. The Gold Stripe Chardonnay (14,000 cases) is followed by White Riesling (4,000) and Sauvignon Blanc (2,000). Under Magnus, a separate label, Meador produces a Cabernet/Merlot/Cabernet Franc blend that has not been impressive to date.

Chardonnay

(Gold Stripe)   85*   86*   88   89

Medium-intensity fruit, with toasty oak and dried-leaf flavor notes

---

VIANSA WINERY *Sonoma 1988* Within a year after being ousted from the family-run Sebastiani Vineyards, Sam Sebastiani was in business on his own. He rebounded quickly with three varietals under his own label, Sam J. Sebastiani. Though the wines were of decent enough quality, Sam had second thoughts about displaying the family name and having his wines confused with those of his former winery, so by the next vintage the brand name was changed to Viansa. The focus remains on three varietals, all blends of Napa and Sonoma County regions—Sauvignon Blanc, Chardonnay, and Cabernet Sauvignon. A new winery and visitors complex are located in the Sonoma-Carneros District, where a portion of the 85-acre estate is planted to Chardonnay. Production is at 14,000 cases, with Cabernet and Chardonnay combining for 80% of the total. Small amounts of Muscat Canelli and Barbera Blanc are available only at the winery. When the estate vineyards are fully developed and at full productivity, Viansa will produce a maximum of 30,000 cases per year.

Chardonnay

86*   87*   88

Direct fruit and background oakiness are found in the wine's successful vintages

---

VICHON WINERY *Napa 1980* For a winery that practically went belly up before its fifth harvest, Vichon has done well in making its mark on the wine industry. Founded and operated by an association of restaurateurs, Vichon was managed by three partners, winemaker George Vierra, Peter Brucher, and Doug Watson. Each gave two letters from his name to coin the brand name, Vichon. After making two vintages in rented space, the partners built a winery on the Oakville Grade, to the south of Robert Mondavi Winery. Vichon's main aim was to make and promote a style of white wines that were lively, balanced, and varietal. Winemaker Vierra fermented Chardonnay, Sauvignon Blanc, and Semillon in oak puncheons, and was among the first to age the wines *sur lie* for several months. A blend (approximately 50–50) of Semillon–Sauvignon Blanc was labeled Chevrier at first, and was an instant critical and sales success. Vichon's two Cabernets were generally ripe and fairly tannic, but Vierra was making headway by following the Bordeaux practice of extended maceration. However, the partnership was less successful than the winemaking and ill feelings were bringing down the house of Vichon by late 84.

In early 85 the winery was sold to the three children of Robert Mondavi—Tim, Marcie, and Michael. It is being run by Tim Mondavi, who managed to turn it around by the end of the 80s. Five wines are produced—Chevrignon (formerly Chevrier), Chardonnay, Cabernet Sauvignon, and Merlot. Vichon's Cabernet output consists of a Napa Valley version and one from the Stags Leap District labeled SLD. In the late 80s, it introduced its "Estate Red," a Meritage blend from its 4½ acres adjacent to the winery. All other wines are produced from purchased grapes, usually from the same growers contracted by Robert Mondavi Winery. Total production at Vichon is moving toward 50,000 cases a year.

Cabernet Sauvignon

(SLD)   85**   86*   87**

Rich, creamy oak is tied to ripe, curranty fruit in a supple, well-proportioned, moderately tannic wine, capable of aging nicely in the cellar

Chardonnay

85**   86**   87*   88*   89

Firmly structured, tightly balanced, and crisp, oaky, rich

Merlot

85* 86* 87* 88

*Ripe, supple, somewhat round wines, with lots of rich oak, hints of herbs,
and suggestions of cocoa; they are wrapped in a veneer of youthful tannins
needing half a decade of aging*

VILLA HELENA WINERY *Napa 1984* Located south of St. Helena, Villa Helena is
one of Napa's smallest wineries. Owner and winemaker Don McGrath started
this weekend winery shortly after retiring as a materials engineer in the early
80s. He specializes in Chardonnay, and also makes Sauvignon Blanc in small
quantities. In a typical vintage, about 500 cases of partially barrel-fermented
Chardonnay are produced. By the late 80s Villa Helena added an estate Chardonnay from the McGrath vineyard. The winery also grows less than an acre
of Viognier.

VILLA MT. EDEN *Napa 1974* Ann and James McWilliams revived a pre-Prohibition
winery in 70 and used the adjoining home as their part-time residence. As they
modernized and equipped the winery, the owners maintained the integrity
of the original structure, and today its design typifies the style of winery that
dotted the Napa landscape in the 1880s. Under the direction of winemaker-
manager Nils Venge, the vineyard was planted to 80 acres, with Cabernet
Sauvignon, Chardonnay, Gewurztraminer, and Pinot Noir predominating. By
80 Villa Mt. Eden was making 15,000 cases a year, 80% of which was Cabernet
Sauvignon and Chardonnay. After several roster changes, the winery dropped
Gewurztraminer and Pinot Noir, and increased its production of Chenin
Blanc.

Over its first decade, Villa Mt. Eden developed a modest reputation for its
100% varietal Cabernet Sauvignon. Save for the 74 Reserve, the Cabernets
were generally on the oaky, tannic, and slightly heavy-handed side of the
spectrum. In 82 Mike McGrath replaced Venge, who left to work for Groth
Vineyards. In 86 the McWilliamses sold the facility and the name to Stimson
Lane, the wine division of the U.S. Tobacco Co. (also owners of Chateau Ste.
Michelle and Conn Creek Winery), but they retained the surrounding vineyard, which now occupies 77 acres.

This vineyard remains the winery's most significant grape source and is
indeed responsible for the estate-bottled wines. Additional Cabernet Sauvignon and Merlot are purchased within Napa Valley. The revamped wine
roster now offers, in addition to Chardonnay and Cabernet Sauvignon, limited
amounts of Chenin Blanc, Zinfandel, and Pinot Noir. A Carneros bottling of
Chardonnay was added in the 88 vintage. With Chardonnay and Cabernet
Sauvignon each accounting for 8,000 cases a year, the winery's total production is level at 25,000 cases. The new owners are working to recapture Villa
Mt. Eden's early successful track record.

VILLA ZAPU *Napa 1988* After buying a 130-acre estate on Mount Veeder in 84,
Swedish-born financier Thomas Lundstrom hired an architect to build a winery and a villa. Though construction was delayed by the local planning com-
mission, Lundstrom persevered, and his villa and personal mansion, best
described as a science fiction fortress, is marked by a stark white tower with
large red banners blowing in the winds. Chardonnay and Cabernet Sauvignon
are the main wines produced by Villa Zapu. About 2,500 cases were made in
its first vintage in 86. The production emphasis falls on Chardonnay, which
represents about 80% of the total output. By 90, the winery was making 10,000
cases, midway to its ultimate goal. After a somewhat shaky beginning, the
winery has begun to show signs of success with both Chardonnay and Cabernet Sauvignon.

Chardonnay

85 86* 87 88* 89

Medium-intensity fruit, sometimes on the citrusy side, is filled out with noticeable oak

VINA VISTA WINERY *Sonoma 1971* A small winery in Geyserville, Vina Vista produces a modest line of varietals from the Alexander Valley appellation. Cabernet Sauvignon, Merlot, and Chardonnay are the primary wines. In recent vintages, Vina Vista's best efforts have been with a cherry-fruited, slightly herbal Merlot that attains ✿ status on occasion. The annual production is steady at 4,000 cases.

VITA NOVA *Santa Barbara 1986* The co-owners, Jim Clendenen of Au Bon Climat and Bob Lindquist of Qupé, originally joined forces to make a Bordeaux-style Cabernet Sauvignon blend. The components used in each vintage have varied since the release of their 86 bottling. Generally, the red has been a combination from Santa Barbara and other Central Coast regions emphasizing, in order of importance, Cabernet Franc, Merlot, and Cabernet Sauvignon. A Chardonnay from the Rancho Vinedo Vineyard is now also made. About 3,000 cases are produced annually under this label, with Chardonnay representing 60% of the total. Today, the label includes a barrel-fermented Sauvignon Blanc–Semillon blend from the Santa Ynez Valley. "Reservatum" is the proprietary name now used for the Bordeaux blend.

Chardonnay

87✿✿ 88✿✿ 89✿✿

Simply loaded with rich, toasty, and buttery components, presented in league with deep, broad, appley fruit and brisk balancing acidity

WEIBEL VINEYARDS *Mendocino 1945* One of the largest and oldest family-run wineries in California, Weibel is probably best known for its Green Hungarian. It began operations in Fremont, near San Jose, where it produced large quantities of sparkling wines. For many years, Weibel was remarkable for its private-label business; at one time it was bottling wines for close to 400 brands. In the 70s, Weibel gradually shifted its base of operation from the urban area of Fremont to Ukiah in Mendocino County. The family acquired vineyards, built a large winemaking facility, and in 73 opened a tasting room just north of Ukiah. As its output grew to 700,000 cases a year, Weibel began making most of its sparkling wines by the Charmat or transfer process. Among the many sparkling wine brands owned by Weibel are Stanford and Chateau Napoleon. In the early 80s, under the direction of Fred Weibel, Jr., the winery shifted its focus to varietal table wines. In 76, 90% of its production was sparkling; in 90, the percentage was down to 50%.

With 60 acres still under vine in Fremont, Weibel has fought a losing battle against housing developments, increasing its vineyard holdings to 1,300 acres of vineyards in Mendocino by the end of the 80s. A line of table wines that once stretched to 36 items has been trimmed to 20. The best-seller remains Green Hungarian, at 45,000 cases a year. As it produces more and more wines from Mendocino grapes, Weibel is increasing its output of Cabernet Sauvignon, Chardonnay, and Pinot Noir. To date, the line of varietal wines has enjoyed modest success at best. The Weibel line of sparkling wine is now made by the *méthode champenoise*.

WEINSTOCK CELLARS *Sonoma 1984* The Weinstock family, which founded and operated a large clothing emporium on the West Coast, acquired 92 acres in Sonoma County in 72. Under the direction of Rob Weinstock, who serves as winemaker, the family began producing limited amounts of Kosher wines from their vineyards in 84, using rented space. In 88, Weinstock decided to expand production to over 30,000 cases and reduce the number of wines offered. Today, he uses grapes from the original acreage in the northern end of the Dry Creek Valley to make White Zinfandel, Chardonnay, Sauvignon Blanc, and Gamay Beaujolais. On a limited-production basis he produces a Reserve Chardonnay and a Pinot Noir. The annual output has leveled off at just under 40,000 cases. In general, the wines are varietally correct and enjoyable in an early-maturing style.

WENTE BROS. *Alameda 1883* A veritable pioneer and family wine dynasty, Wente Bros. is now is the hands of the fourth generation. From a modest 50-acre vineyard developed in 1883 in the heart of the Livermore Valley, Wente Bros. made a range of wines that were highly regarded before Prohibition, especially its sweet white wines produced from Semillon and Sauvignon Blanc. Though still known today as a name synonymous with Grey Riesling, Wente has been a pioneer and quality leader in many areas. In 36 Wente released a varietal Chardonnay, the first in California to be varietally labeled. In 60, a decade before Chardonnay became popular, Wente was the leading proponent and grower with 70 acres planted to Chardonnay—about one-third of the state's total. In 33 Wente also offered the first California wine labeled Sauvignon Blanc. In the mid-60s the family, needing to develop new vineyards to meet the anticipated demand for its white wines, became one of the pioneers in Monterey County viticulture. Today, Wente has 650 acres of vineyards in northern Monterey County.

The winery was the first to market a late harvest Riesling made from *Botrytis cinerea* when it released its 69 Monterey County Johannisberg Riesling, "Spatlese." In 70, it added a sweet-finished Blanc de Blancs to accompany its ever popular Grey Riesling, Chenin Blanc, and Sauvignon Blanc. By the end of the 70s, popularity was forcing the winery to market some of its wine too early, and even its true-to-type Sauvignon Blanc and no-oak-aged Chardonnays were becoming erratic. Today, back on a steady course, Wente Bros. owns 1,200 acres in Livermore Valley, with 527 acres devoted to Chardonnay. Its Livermore Valley holdings emphasis Sauvignon Blanc and Chardonnay, along with a dozen other varieties. From the Arroyo Seco holdings in Monterey, Wente bottles Riesling, Gewurztraminer, and on occasion a Chardonnay.

In the 90s Wente consolidated its numerous wines into two categories, estate-grown varietals and estate Reserve, a line of limited-volume varietals. In the mid-80s it restored the neighboring historic Cresta Blanca Winery, and turned it and the surrounding land into a champagne-making facility and restaurant. Produced here now is a Brut from Monterey County–grown Chardonnay and Pinot Noir, along with a Blanc de Blancs, Blanc de Noirs, and Reserve Brut, all made by the *méthode champenoise*. Annual production at Wente Bros. is just in excess of 600,000 cases, almost all white and sparkling wine.

Chardonnay

(Arroyo Seco) 84* 85* 86 87 88 89

Medium-intensity wines, often exhibiting suggestions of tropical fruits and flowers as adjuncts to the straightforward fruit, are structured on the round and accessible side

WERMUTH WINERY *Napa 1982* What began as a hobby with home winemaker Ralph Wermuth developed into a small wine business. The Wermuth winery is located on the Silverado Trail, just south of Calistoga. A small tasting room was built to sell the winery's first and only wine at the time, a Dry Colombard. The winery has since developed its direct sales program, and now produces several varietals, led by Colombard, Gamay, Cabernet Sauvignon, and Sauvignon Blanc. By 90 it reached its production goal of 3,000 cases.

MARK WEST VINEYARDS *Sonoma 1976* A scenic pastoral property bordering the Mark West Creek, the Mark West Winery and Vineyards are owned by Joan and Bob Ellis. Located in the cool lower portion of the Russian River Valley, the vineyards were planted in 74 predominantly to early-ripening varieties—Gewurztraminer, Riesling, Chardonnay, and Pinot Noir. Now with 62 acres under vine, the winery makes about 22,000 cases a year. Chardonnay, produced in two styles, accounts for 10,000 cases per year of the total. The estate-grown fruit is bottled as a vineyard-designated version, Le Beau Vineyard. During the blush wine era, most of the estate Pinot Noir was converted into the then best-selling Pinot Noir-Blanc. A regular Pinot Noir was reinstated to the line in 87. One of the winery's specialties has been Gewurztraminer finished with under 1% sugar; in some vintages, that wine achieves ✻ status. In the early 80s the winery began producing Zinfandel from the Robert Rue Vineyard, and the quality has been up and down. In the 90s Mark West plans to grow to 40,000 cases a year.

Chardonnay

(Sonoma County)   85✻   86✻   87✻

(Le Beau Vineyard)   85✻   86✻   87   89✻

Both wines are well balanced and nicely fruity; greater oakiness and complexity is evident in the Le Beau, but the more obvious fruit in the Sonoma County bottling lifts it to very satisfactory ratings

Zinfandel

(Robert Rue Vineyard)   83✻✻   84✻   85✻   86   88

Can show deep, ripe-berryish fruit at its best, with plenty of aging potential

---

WESTWOOD WINERY   *El Dorado 1987*   Following a simple system, the winery is owned by two families that use two brands for two distinct lines of wines. The Westwood brand belongs to winemaker Bert Urch, who generally emphasizes wines from Burgundian varieties—Chardonnay, Pinot Noir, and Gamay. All grapes for Westwood wines are purchased from varying cooler-climate sources. Fermented in open-top containers with whole clusters added during fermentation, the Pinot Noirs have shown considerable promise. All Chardonnays are barrel-fermented. Production, which was minuscule over the first vintages, is now close to the 1,200-case-per-year goal. The related brand is Wolterbeek (see entry).

WHALER VINEYARD   *Mendocino 1981*   On a 35-acre ranch south of Ukiah, owners Russ and Ann Nyborg developed a 24-acre vineyard. Planted in 72, the vineyard consisted of Zinfandel which over the first several harvests was sold to other producers. In 81, the Nyborgs began making Zinfandel from their own vineyard. The style of the first few vintages was light and simple, emphasizing berry fruitiness. The 85 vintage showed more depth in a medium-bodied style. With the addition of a White Zinfandel made in part from purchased grapes, Whaler have reached the 5,000-case-a-year level. But the owners have since dropped White Zinfandel and are currently making only 2,000 cases of regular Zinfandel.

WILLIAM WHEELER WINERY   *Sonoma 1981*   The Wheelers, a husband-wife team, purchased 175 acres in the Dry Creek Valley in 70. Over the next few years they planted the steeper hillsides to Cabernet Sauvignon and Zinfandel for a total of 30 acres. This estate Cabernet vineyard came to be known as the Norse Vineyard. Venturing into winemaking in 79, the Wheelers built a barrel-aging and tasting-room complex in Healdsburg, and followed by building a crushing and fermenting facility adjacent to their vineyards. Though unusual, this setup has worked well, and the winery has steadily grown to its present 20,000-case production level. Chardonnay (8,000 cases) and Sauvignon Blanc (5,000) are from the Sonoma County appellation and are usually successful in a crisp style. The Sauvignon Blanc is strongly varietal, with a firm structure and light oak; it earns ✻ regularly, and ✻✻ on occasion.

Plans to make a medium-bodied Zinfandel were delayed for several years by the success of a White Zinfandel that was originally meant to have been made only while the vines were maturing. This turned out to be an exemplary version, which once earned ✻✻✻. Two Cabernet Sauvignons are made. The main one, from the Dry Creek Valley (4,500 cases), is available a year ahead of the "Norse" Reserve (700 cases), which is given four years aging by the winery. In the late 80s, experiments with a red Rhone blend were under way, with Petite Sirah and Mourvedre playing important roles. In 89 the French firm of Paribas Domaines, owner of many wine properties (Château La Lagune and Champagne Ayala) acquired the majority interest in the winery. The Wheelers remained in charge of operations.

Cabernet Sauvignon

79* 80* 82 83* 84* 85 86*

Cherryish fruit is offered in a narrow, slightly low-keyed manner

Chardonnay

84* 85* 86* 87 88

Somewhat lighter, fruity style, often with floral and appley tones, broadened by subtle oak

---

WHITE OAK VINEYARDS *Sonoma 1981* The White Oak facility was built by owner Bill Myers in 80, just a few blocks away from the Healdsburg town plaza. He owns 6 acres planted to Chardonnay and Cabernet in the Alexander Valley, and buys from growers throughout Sonoma County. Chardonnay (partially barrel-fermented) and Sauvignon Blanc account for 70% of the 10,000 cases produced annually. A dry Chenin Blanc (1,000 cases) aged in small oak is regularly offered, along with lesser amounts of Zinfandel. White Oak's Sauvignon Blancs are clean and usually show a pleasant mix of oak and blossomy-grassy fruit. A series of "Limited Reserve" Chardonnays (100% barrel-fermented) and Cabernet Sauvignons have been offered, with the majority of the grapes for each originating in Myers's own vineyard.

Chardonnay

84 85 86* 87* 88* 89

Direct, bright citrus and fresh appley fruit, with just enough background oak to add breadth to the crisp flavors

---

WHITE ROCK VINEYARDS *Napa 1987* In the southern foothills of the Stags Leap District, Claire and Henri Vandendriessche purchased vineyard land and a pre-Prohibition winery site in 77. In 79 they began developing 35 acres, planting Chardonnay and Cabernet Sauvignon, and including 5 acres of Cabernet Franc, Merlot, and Petit Verdot. Situated on steep terraces, the vines are planted closely together in European fashion, and the owners are proud of the fact that they use neither insecticides nor herbicides in vineyard cultivation. White Rock's first few harvests of red grapes were sold to wineries such as Quail Ridge, Ehlers Lane, and Merlion. In 86, to test the waters, they had their own Bordeaux blend of red wine made, which they labeled "Claret." That first bottling consisted of 600 cases, and the quality level encouraged the owners to go commercial. In 88 the Vandendriessches built an underground winery and aging caves, with the expectation of eventually producing 2,000 cases a year. Their Chardonnay, first made in 88, is entirely fermented in new French oak barrels, and all of its barrel aging is *sur lie*.

WHITEHALL LANE *Napa 1980* After vacationing in Napa Valley with their wives for several years, architect Art Finkelstein was ready to design a winery, while his brother, Alan Steen, a plastic surgeon, was prepared to take charge of a vineyard. In 79 they bought an old vineyard site on the main wine road south of St. Helena. The 26-acre vineyard had to be pulled and replanted, and the owners put in Chardonnay, Sauvignon Blanc, and Merlot. Forced to buy grapes until 85, Whitehall Lane experienced a few rough times, but also discovered some excellent fruit and developed definite notions on winemaking. Its Cabernet Sauvignon, blended with Merlot and Cabernet Franc, is a selection from as many as a dozen growers. Every now and then a Reserve Cabernet representing the most intense batch is bottled, but the quantity is usually only about 200 cases.

In 84, choosing Merlot from a grower in the Knight's Valley, the winery began building an impressive record for Merlot. The Chardonnay comes from the estate vineyard surrounding the winery; after being barrel-fermented, the wine ages in a combination of several types of oak. Somewhat erratic, White-hall Lane's Pinot Noir is usually made in a fruity style, and aged in American oak. A cold-fermented blush wine, Blanc de Pinot Noir, completes the line. Annual production was close to 11,000 cases in 90. In 88 the winery was sold to Hideaki Ando of Japan, with Art Finkelstein remaining as its general manager. The production goal is 20,000 cases a year.

Cabernet Sauvignon

(regular bottling) 81* 82* 83* 84** 85** 86** 87**
88

(Reserve) 84** 85** 86

Made in similar styles, these wines feature very ripe, open fruit, plenty of depth, lots of sweet oak, and carry abundant tannins that assure good aging capability

Merlot

82 83 84** 85** 86 87 88**

Like the Cabernet, this is a ripe, rich, tasty wine, with oak adding to its sweet, forward character; tannins are a bit lighter and the wine is a little softer, but it too can age

---

WILD HOG HILL WINERY *Sonoma 1988* As amateur winemakers, Michele Andrian and Joanne Wirth named their homemade wines after a small hill not far from downtown Healdsburg, where for many years they hiked and picked mushrooms. They decided to keep the Wild Hog Hill name once their winemaking venture went commercial in 88. All grapes are purchased, the majority from the Dry Creek Valley. The wine roster consists of Chardonnay, Pinot Noir, and, when nature permits, a late harvest Johannisberg Riesling. Initial yearly output was close to 1,500 cases. The maximum annual production target is 3,500 cases.

WILD HORSE WINERY *San Luis Obispo 1982* Owner-winemaker Ken Volk built a solid reputation surprisingly fast, but he earned it the old-fashioned way—by making outstanding wines. He first rose to prominence on the strength of small batches of vineyard-designated (Sierra Madre Vineyard, Bien Nacido) Pinot Noir from Santa Barbara County. He has added Chardonnay, Merlot, and Cabernet Sauvignon to the line, and has expanded the volume of Pinot Noir. Volk's winery is located in Templeton and his 33-acre vineyard is adjacent. The vineyard contains 20 acres of Chardonnay, 5 of Cabernet Sauvignon, and 8 combined of Merlot and Cabernet Franc. By 90 the winery was producing 25,000 cases, with Chardonnay as the leader, followed by Pinot Noir, Cabernet Sauvignon, and Merlot. The primary bottling of Pinot Noir is labeled Santa Barbara County. Long term, Volk, who started in 83 with one tank and an old barn, intends to level off production at 40,000 cases a year.

Chardonnay

86* 87** 88 89*

Full of ripe and luscious fruit to balance its imposing oaky, toasty seasonings

Pinot Noir

(Santa Barbara) 85 86** 87* 88*

Plenty of bright, cherryish, available fruit and moderate tannins combine for wines capable of improving for several years

---

WILDCAT WINES *Sonoma 1985* Part-time grower Charles Illgen cultivates Merlot in his small vineyard close to the historic Buena Vista Winery in Sonoma

Valley. He buys Chardonnay, Semillon, and Gamay Beaujolais to offer a 3,000-case line of wines, all made in rented space. To date, the Merlots have not been cleanly made, and the other wines have yet to impress.

J. WILE & SONS *(Bergfeld Winery)* Until it was bought in 90 by Bergfeld Winery, J. Wile & Sons was owned by Whitbread of England, which also owned Atlas Peak Winery. Under Whitbread's direction, the J. Wile line, which was introduced in 87, was aged and bottled in space rented from Bergfeld. With a list consisting of relatively low-priced Napa Valley varietals, Wile was enjoying annual sales of over 70,000 cases by 90. After Whitbread was bought by Allied-Lyons of England, it did not figure into their plans and was sold to Bergfeld. The primary wines in the line are Chardonnay, Sauvignon Blanc, and Cabernet Sauvignon. All are from Napa Valley.

WILLIAMS SELYEM WINERY *Sonoma 1981* Owned by Ed Selyem and Burt Williams, this brand started out making wine, primarily Zinfandel, under the name of Hacienda del Rio, a name never officially registered. However, when its use was challenged by Hacienda Winery, the name was quickly changed. The original winery was actually a converted garage behind a house on River Road in the southern corner of the Russian River Valley. In 83 the partners began to specialize in Pinot Noir purchased from several vineyards within Sonoma County. To date they have made small batches (300–600 cases) of Pinot Noir from the Howard Allen Vineyard and the Rochioli Vineyard, as well as from the Sonoma Coast and Sonoma County appellations. In 90, they moved the winemaking operation to a larger building owned by vineyardist Howard Allen. The winemaking style is quite traditional, with open-top fermenters used and warm fermentations that include stem retention. The wines are aged for an average of 18 months in heavily toasted barrels. Typically, this winery's Pinot Noirs have been full-blown without much restraint in evidence, and have varied in their degree of fruitiness and in their degree of success. Zinfandel from the Martinelli Vineyard in the Russian River Valley is also made. Total production is 2,000 cases, with 3,000 a year set as the maximum.

WINDEMERE WINES *Sonoma 1985* Cathy MacGregor worked in the enology department of several Sonoma County wineries before founding her own winery in 85. Only Chardonnay from the Edna Valley is made, and the production is limited to 1,000 cases a year. The grapes are grown at the MacGregor Vineyard, a well-known 90-acre vineyard in the Edna Valley owned by her parents. Windemere's wine is 100% barrel-fermented, and half undergoes malolactic fermentation. Early vintages were capable of earning ✣. Experimental batches of Napa Valley Cabernet Sauvignon have been made.

Chardonnay

85 ✣   86   87 ✣   88

Capable of offering bright, appley, and underplayed tropical fruit, backed by rich oak; medium intensity

WINTERBROOK VINEYARDS *Amador 1984* In the town of Ione, in what's known locally as the Jackson Valley, the Winterbrook winery sprang up quickly in 84. The founder began in 80 by developing what grew to be a 90-acre vineyard containing 35 acres of Chenin Blanc, 25 of Chardonnay, and 30 of other varieties. Neither was ideally suited to the region, and the intent to sell all of the crop was soon discouraged by a lack of demand. A barn was quickly converted into a 25,000-case-capacity winery, and before long the line was expanded to Sauvignon Blanc, Zinfandel, and White Zinfandel. After one ownership change, the winery and vineyard were acquired in 91 by Sacramento businessman, Fred Anderson and other partners. Annual output currently is 6,500 cases. To date the quality has been inconsistent.

WINTERS WINERY *Yolo 1980* Winters is a small farming community just a few miles south of Davis, better known for rice and almonds than for grapes.

Winters happens to be the home of David Storm, a sanitation engineer who has designed water and waste systems for dozens of large, well-known wineries. As a highly sought-after consultant, Storm became familiar enough with wine facilities to begin making wines at home as a hobby. When a large building in Winters became available in 76, Storm converted it into a modest (5,000-case-capacity) winery. He enjoys making red wines from old vines. Among the many produced, he regularly offers Zinfandel from Amador County and Petite Sirah from Yolo County. Most of the white wines have been Chardonnay and Sauvignon Blanc from Napa Valley.

WOLFSPIERRE VINEYARDS *Sonoma 1986* This is a rent-a-winery brand that covers vineyard-designated wines from four growers in Sonoma Valley. Started by winemaker Rod Berglund (formerly of La Crema) before he assumed the winemaking role at Joseph Swan Vineyards, Wolfspierre highlights each vineyard on its label. All of the vineyards contributing to Wolfspierre are situated within the Sonoma Mountain appellation. To date, the Steiner Vineyard Cabernet Sauvignon has been the only real noteworthy effort. Berlin Vineyard is the source of a Sauvignon Blanc, Farina Vineyard gives its identity to Pinot Noir, and Wolfspierre Vineyard grows and supplies Chardonnay to the cause. Production of each varietal ranges from 200 to 500 cases. Recent vintages have been produced at the Vinwood facility operated by the Gauer Estate in Geyserville.

WOLTERBEEK WINERY *El Dorado 1987* Owned by the Wolterbeek family, this label shares a winery with Westwood, and its wines are made by the same winemaker. Wolterbeek owns an 8-acre vineyard in the town of Shingle Springs planted primarily to Bordeaux varieties, led by Sauvignon Blanc. Combined production of a Bordeaux red and Sauvignon Blanc is expected to reach 1,000 cases a year when the Wolterbeek vineyard reaches full production.

CHRISTINE WOODS VINEYARDS *Mendocino 1982* Longtime growers in the Anderson Valley, the Vernon Rose family owns two vineyards, both located opposite the Roederer Estate in Navarro. The main vineyard is planted on the valley floor and is devoted to Chardonnay and Pinot Noir; most of the crop from this vineyard is sold. The other parcel is situated at higher elevations to the south and contains Cabernet Sauvignon and Gamay Beaujolais. Fewer than 2,000 cases a year were made during the first several years. The only offering creating some interest was a barrel-fermented Chardonnay. Christine Woods is the name of one of the early settlers in the Anderson Valley. The winery's total plantings amount to 20 acres.

YORK MOUNTAIN WINERY *San Luis Obispo 1882* The old stone winery was built in 1882 by the York family, which also planted the mountainside vineyard to the west of Templeton. In 70 the Goldman family purchased the property and set about refurbishing both winery and vineyard. 5 acres have been replanted to a mix of varieties—Pinot Noir, Cabernet Sauvignon, Zinfandel, and Chardonnay. The winery has an old and honorable association with Zinfandel, and it is the leading variety planted. Augmented by grapes purchased from the Central Coast, York Mountain currently offers Zinfandel, Pinot Noir, Merlot, and Cabernet Sauvignon, with Chardonnay as its only white. Sparkling wine production was under way by 90. Total output is at 6,000 cases a year, 75% of the owners' planned maximum.

Z MOORE WINES *Sonoma 1985* With a definite emphasis on Gewurztraminer, the family-owned Z Moore winery has performed remarkably well with that varietal. The winery is a renovated hop kiln located in the Russian River Valley, owned by Dan and Natalie Zuccarelli-Moore, who buy grapes from the Russian River Valley, Alexander Valley, and the Carneros District. Most of the Gewurztraminer comes from the neighboring Martinelli Vineyard. Two radically distinct styles of Gewurztraminer are made. The serious, totally dry version is barrel-fermented and then aged *sur lie* for a few months. It is full of spice and honeysuckle character, with enough complexity to consistently earn ✻. Gewurztraminer made in a medium-sweet style is bottled under Quaff (see entry). A Sonoma County Chardonnay is Z Moore's second most important wine. The winery ferments Chardonnay in oak puncheons and ages it *sur lie* for several months. On a modest scale, Z Moore produces Zinfandel and a proprietary red wine blend. Total annual production is at the optium 6,000-case level.

ZACA MESA WINERY *Santa Barbara 1976* Second only to Firestone Vineyards in terms of production in Santa Barbara, Zaca Mesa has had a rather tumultuous early history. It was founded by oil executive Louis Ream, and at one time the winery owned or controlled 340 acres of vineyards in the county. In the early 80s it was cranking out a range of wines for an annual production of close to 100,000 cases. By 86 Ream had sold his interests, and Zaca Mesa was reorganized into a corporation while the winery also underwent changes. Resurfacing with 235 acres in the Santa Ynez Valley, Zaca Mesa produced a range of usually sound table wines from the Santa Barbara appellation. Chardonnay, Johannisberg Riesling, and Sauvignon Blanc, Cabernet Sauvignon, Pinot Noir, Zinfandel, and Syrah were offered. For a few years it offered limited quantities of "American Reserve" Chardonnay, Cabernet Sauvignon, and Pinot Noir. Fewer than 1,000 cases of Syrah were available each vintage. In 90, the owners decided to focus almost exclusively on Chardonnay and Pinot Noir, offering a regular and Reserve bottling of each. Zaca Mesa's latest efforts with Chardonnay and Pinot Noir have been solidly ✻ in quality. The winery's annual production is 60,000 cases.

ZD WINES *Napa 1969* Originally located in Sonoma Valley, ZD was founded by Gino Zepponi and Norman de Leuze, aerospace engineers who worked in Sacramento. After outgrowing the first facility, they relocated in Napa Valley in 79, building a winery about midway along the Silverado Trail. To the west of the winery, they planted 3.2 acres to Cabernet. As their production expanded, de Leuze served as winemaker while Zepponi became active with Domaine Chandon, serving as plant engineer there until his death in 85. Now owned and operated by the de Leuze family, the winery continues to produce Chardonnay with a California appellation and Pinot Noir from Napa Valley or Los Carneros. The third most important wine, Cabernet Sauvignon, is usually labeled Napa Valley.

ZD's first estate-bottled Cabernet was made in 87. Entirely barrel-fermented, ZD's Chardonnays are a blend derived from Napa, Sonoma, and the Central Coast regions. ZD was one of the first Napa Valley wineries to buy Chardonnay from the Tepusquet Vineyard in Santa Barbara County. Aged in barrel for close to a year, ZD's Chardonnays are noted for a ripe, viscous texture and a rich, tropical fruit aroma. The winery developed such a strong reputation for Chardonnay that by the end of the 80s, over 18,000 cases were being produced per year. The winery's total output is 21,000 cases.

Cabernet Sauvignon

(Napa Valley) **83**✻ **84**✻ 85 **86** **87** **88**✻✻

Often showing more tannin than fruit, the wine is always long-aging

Chardonnay

84✻✻✻ 85✻✻ 86✻✻ 87✻✻ 88 89✻

Among the top Chardonnays in most years, the wine typically combines ripe and broad appley fruit with toasty oak and roasted-grain flavor complexities

Pinot Noir

82✻ 83✻ 84 85 86 87✻ 88✻✻

Cherryish fruit, moderate oak, light-medium tannins, and good depth in some years

ZELLERBACH VINEYARD *Sonoma 1978* In the Chalk Hill area of the Alexander Valley, Stephen Zellerbach completed a winery in 78 to process his first harvest. His 54-acre estate vineyard was planted in 72 to Cabernet Sauvignon and Merlot, and he produced Chardonnay from a vineyard under contract. It was business as usual for Zellerbach until 86 when with a production of 20,000 cases he found he was gaining neither inner peace nor financial bliss. He leased the winery along with his brand to William Baccala, who had just sold his own winery in Mendocino County to Robert Jepson. Baccala hired a winemaker and marketing team. Within a year, they were selling existing inventory at reduced prices and had built a strong following for Zellerbach Chardonnay. The next year they added a Sauvignon Blanc. In 88 entrepreneur Jess Jackson of Kendall-Jackson picked up the lease/option to buy from Baccala and bought the whole shebang—winery, 165-acre estate, and what was by then a 65-acre vineyard. The trademark name Zellerbach was retained by the Baccala family, which continues to use it as a negociant brand for Chardonnay, Sauvignon Blanc, and Cabernet Sauvignon.

The Northwest

ADAMS VINEYARD WINERY *Willamette Valley, Oregon 1985* Owners Peter and Carol Adams eased into winemaking by producing their first few vintages at Adelsheim Vineyard. By 75–76 they had developed a 13-acre vineyard next door to Adelsheim. However, the Adamses felt a need to operate a winery closer to Portland, where Peter was running a successful construction company, so in 85 they moved their winemaking operation from Newberg to northwest Portland. Carol Adams is the winemaker and runs the winery on a daily basis. The estate vineyard has been expanded to 19 acres, and contains 13 acres of Pinot Noir and 6 acres of Chardonnay. In winemaking, Adams favors 100% barrel fermentation for Chardonnay. For Pinot Noir fermentation, the winery ferments in 1,200-gallon tanks and adds about 20% whole clusters. The current lineup consists of Pinot Noir, Chardonnay, and Sauvignon Blanc. A limited-volume Reserve Pinot Noir is produced in some vintages. Adams makes one of only a few Oregon-grown Sauvignon Blancs, which is usually barrel-fermented and aged in small oak. In some vintages, its Reserve Pinot Noirs rise to * levels. Overall, production is holding steady at 3,500 cases.

ADELSHEIM VINEYARDS *Willamette Valley, Oregon 1978* In 72 Dave Adelsheim began developing a vineyard that now covers 18 acres. As his vineyard was maturing, he studied winemaking and learned the practical side by working in the cellars at Eyrie Vineyards. On a hill overlooking the vineyards, Adelsheim built a winery and crushed in it for the first time in 82. The winery's vineyard contains Pinot Noir, Chardonnay, and Riesling. Adelsheim also makes a Pinot Gris and on occasion a Sauvignon Blanc. From grapes grown by Sagemoor Farms in Washington State, the winery has produced Merlot and Semillon. Cold-fermented to dryness, and not oak-aged, Adelsheim Pinot Gris usually captures both fruit and some depth of flavor. Best known for its Pinot Noir, the winery makes a Reserve and Willamette Valley bottlings, each of which has earned good ratings. The winery's annual production has reached 7,500 cases, about halfway to its full capacity.

Pinot Noir

(regular bottling) 82   83   84*   85*   86*   87*

(Reserve) 87**

Straightforwardly fruity wines are, in the latest vintages, showing greater range of character; the Reserve goes one step further into a richness and suppleness that is somewhat rare in Oregon Pinot Noirs

AIRLIE WINERY *Willamette Valley, Oregon 1986* Located in the Salem area in the small town of Monmouth, Airlie is owned by Larry Preedy, who settled in Oregon originally to grow Christmas trees. In small stages he developed a 15-acre vineyard that now consists of Pinot Noir, Müller-Thurgau, and Gewurztraminer. The first vintages of Pinot Noir leaned toward the simple, fruity style. The winery also makes a popular blush wine from Pinot Noir labeled "Crimson." With maturity of the estate vineyard, the owner anticipates production will gradually grow to a maximum of 3,500 cases.

ALPINE VINEYARDS *Willamette Valley, Oregon 1980* Located in the southern Willamette Valley near Monroe, Alpine Vineyards is owned by Dr. Dan Jepsen, who also is its winemaker. Alpine makes wine only from its 20-acre estate vineyard, which is planted to Riesling, Cabernet Sauvignon, Pinot Noir, and Chardonnay. Situated on slopes high above the valley floor, the vineyard is one of the few in the Willamette Valley to enjoy some success with Cabernet Sauvignon. However, in cool vintages it produces a Rosé of Cabernet as well as a Pinot Noir-Blanc. It has been holding steady at the 4,000-case-a-year level.

AMITY VINEYARDS *Willamette Valley, Oregon 1976* In 74, owner Myron Redford purchased the 70-acre site in the town of Amity, just in the southern part of the Eola Hills. His vineyard now covers 15 acres supplying just under half of the grapes crushed. He has 7 acres of Pinot Noir and 3 acres of Chardonnay. Amity began by making 350 cases in 76; production has grown steadily to the present 7,500-case level. It is currently producing Pinot Noir, White Riesling, Gewurztraminer, and Chardonnay. The Pinot Noir is made in two styles—a Nouveau and a traditionally fermented version. The conventional Pinot Noirs are fermented in small vats, punched down by hand, and aged in French oak barrels. A portion of each vintage is made by carbonic maceration. In some vintages, Amity bottles a Reserve Pinot Noir.

In general, we have found the regular bottling of Pinot Noir to display more fruit and balance than the Reserve. One of the most noteworthy vintages for Amity Pinot Noir was 78. Amity has been making a Nouveau by carbonic maceration since 76, longer than any other U.S. winery. It is also working with the true Gamay Noir of Beaujolais, making its first batch of 200 cases in 88. In most years, Amity's Gewurztraminer is one of Oregon's best.

ARBOR CREST WINERY *Spokane, Washington 1982* Among Washington's first quality-minded producers, Arbor Crest was also among the first with an aggressive out-of-state marketing program. Located on a bluff 450 feet above the Spokane River, the current winery was built in 87. The adjacent historic mansion has been converted into a tasting room. Owned by the Mielke family, longtime growers and orchard owners, Arbor Crest has specialized in white wines from its first harvest, and today three fourths of its 30,000-case production consists of Sauvignon Blanc and Chardonnay. Cabernet Sauvignon and Merlot complete the lineup. The winery has enjoyed moderate success with an oak-aged Chardonnay and a full-bodied, tannic-style Cabernet Sauvignon. Arbor Crest owns 80 acres of vineyards in the Columbia River appellation, over 100 miles to the south. Annual production will level off at 40,000 cases.

ARGYLE *Willamette Valley, Oregon 1987* Australian winemaker Brian Croser teams up with local grower and investor Cal Knudsen in this joint venture. They operate the business as the Dundee Wine Company, but use Argyle as their wine label. A winemaking facility is located in the industrial section of Dundee, and all grapes crushed are purchased under long-term contract. Sparkling wine made by the *méthode champenoise* is the main thrust, and the line consists of Brut, the volume leader, along with a Rosé and a Blanc de Blanc. Two varietal wines—a barrel-fermented Chardonnay and a dry Riesling—are offered under the Argyle label. Croser is the winemaker and manager for Petaluma Wines in Australia, and produces sparkling wine under the

Croser label along with Petaluma table wines. He plans to take Argyle's sparkling wine to an annual production level of 25,000 cases. The output for Chardonnay and Riesling will remain at 3,000 cases each.

ARTERBERRY WINERY *Willamette Valley, Oregon 1979* With a degree in enology from U.C. Davis in hand, Fred Arterberry moved to Oregon intending to make only sparkling wine. While he was renovating and enlarging his winery in downtown McMinnville, he produced sparkling cider to help finance the project, and for several years his cider was coveted in the local market. It is generally agreed that in 79 Arterberry made the first traditional *méthode champenoise* Oregon wine. He remains an advocate of Oregon sparkling wine, but in 82 he began producing a line of table wines that has steadily increased in importance. Buying all grapes crushed, the winery currently offers a regular and "Winemaker Reserve" Pinot Noir, Chardonnay, and Riesling, along with sparkling wines. The overall quality of the well-balanced Pinot Noirs has been above average. The winery produces about 4,000 cases of wine a year.

AUTUMN WIND VINEYARD *Willamette Valley, Oregon 1987* Situated about 7 miles west of Newberg, Autumn Wind sits on a hilltop surrounded by tall oak trees. Escaping from Los Angeles, owner and winemaker Tom Kreutner purchased a 50-acre neglected cherry orchard in 82. About 10 acres have been planted to vines, with Pinot Noir predominating. Over the first few vintages Autumn Wind has made Pinot Noir, Müller-Thurgau, and Sauvignon Blanc. When the estate vineyard is fully mature, Autumn Wind will focus on Pinot Noir and Chardonnay. Optimum capacity is 4,000 cases a year.

BARNARD GRIFFIN WINERY *Kennewick, Washington 1983* Rob Griffin, winemaker for Hogue, and Deborah Barnard, his wife, operate this winemaking business. Using the original small facility in Prosser built by Hogue, they have been making wines entirely from purchased grapes. About 75% of their efforts are devoted to making Fumé Blanc and Chardonnay, with 400-case batches each of Merlot and Cabernet Sauvignon. Both Sauvignon Blanc and Chardonnay are barrel-fermented and aged *sur lie* in a no-holds-barred approach. Most wines are available only in Washington. Currently, annual production is under 4,000 cases. The owners intend to expand to 10,000 cases by the end of the 90s.

BETHEL HEIGHTS VINEYARD *Willamette Valley, Oregon 1984* Twin brothers Terry and Ted Casteel began developing a vineyard on property located in the Eola Hills region, northwest of Salem, in 77. They planted 51 acres on a south-facing slope on typically thin volcanic soils. Pinot Noir is the primary variety, with 23.5 acres planted, followed by Chardonnay at 14.5 acres. The Casteels sold their entire crop until 84, when they made their first wine. Ted is the vineyard manager and Terry is winemaker. As growers, they became quickly respected for the quality of their grapes by selling to producers within Oregon and a few in California, most notably Bonny Doon. Bethel Heights still sells grapes under contract. Today, the winery makes Chenin Blanc in a slightly sweet style, producing a more than pleasant wine in most vintages. It also makes Pinot Noir every year, as well as an occasional Reserve bottling. Winemaker Terry Casteel believes in using about 25% new French oak for Pinot Noir aging. Also, his Pinot Noirs are given minimal handling and are only lightly filtered, if at all. The winery's Chardonnays are 100% barrel-fermented, and aged entirely *sur lie*. An average of 3,500 cases of Chardonnay is made each year. The winery's total annual production is 7,500 cases.

Chardonnay

85* 86* 87 89

In most vintages, the wine is fruity, with citrus blossom notes and restrained oak adding extra interest

Pinot Noir
84 * *   86 *   87   88 *

Direct, slightly narrow, cherrylike fruit, occasionally displays the depth and suppleness needed to earn high ratings

---

BLACKWOOD CANYON VINTNERS   *Benton, Washington 1982*   At the eastern corner of the Yakima Valley, owner Mike Moore and his family planted grapes on the 100-acre ranch and eased into winemaking. In 85, just when the winery was beginning to make a name for itself, it was destroyed by a fire. After rebuilding, Moore resumed a range of wines in a highly individualistic mode. His whites (Chardonnay and Semillon) display considerable evidence of extended oak and *sur lie* aging. Blackwood Canyon has produced several unusual sweet dessert wines from *Botrytis*-affected grapes, including Semillon, Riesling, and a most unusual wine labeled "Penultimate Gewurztraminer. Ice Wine." Another sweet wine that is made in most vintages is labeled "Ultra Late Harvest" without any varietal identity given. By 90, the winery's total production had reached the optimum level of 15,000 cases.

BOOKWALTER WINERY   *Pasco, Washington 1984*   Owner/winemaker Jerry Bookwalter runs his small winery on a part-time basis; the rest of his time is given over to a vineyard management service. Formerly manager for Sagemoor Farms, the Northwest's largest vineyard, Bookwalter prefers to select grapes from growers for his own wines. He offers Chardonnay and Riesling regularly, and in most vintages he has bottled Cabernet Sauvignon, Chenin Blanc, and Muscat. Production has varied, but on average about 3,000 cases are made per year.

BRIDGEVIEW VINEYARDS   *Illinois Valley, Oregon 1986*   Situated in this southern Oregon valley, Bridgeview began in 80 with the development of a 75-acre vineyard. Reflecting their German heritage, owners Robert and Lelo Kerivan planted Gewurztraminer, Müller-Thurgau, and Pinot Gris, along with Chardonnay and Pinot Noir. The owners are proud of the fact that their vines are planted in the European tradition of close spacing, so they crowd in more vines per acre than the typical California vineyard and most Oregon vineyards. In 86 they built their large (45,000-case-capacity) winery. The winery's first crush of 5,000 cases in 86 has since doubled, and is expected to grow steadily through the 90s. The leading wines by volume are Riesling and Müller-Thurgau.

BROADLEY VINEYARDS   *Willamette Valley, Oregon 1986*   Leaving California in pursuit of the lifestyle of small winery owners, Claudia and Craig Broadley ended up in the southern Willamette Valley. Starting from scratch, they cleared the land along the eastern slopes above the small town of Monroe and planted 18 acres of Pinot Noir and Chardonnay, along with 2 acres of Pinot Gris. The Broadleys are producing a regular and "Reserve" Pinot Noir and Chardonnay. The first vintages of Reserve Pinot Noir showed considerable promise. When its vineyards are fully productive, the winery is expected to reach its capacity of 3,000 cases a year.

CAMERON WINERY   *Willamette Valley, Oregon 1984*   This winery is a three-way partnership of winemaker John Paul, vineyardist Bill Wayne, and builder Marc Douchez. They have taken it from a small operation in a rented warehouse to a modern facility located just above the town of Dundee. Winemaker John Paul gained experience in California with Konocti and Carneros Creek Winery. With 20 acres of vineyards to rely on, the winery focuses on Pinot Noir and Chardonnay, making a regular and "Reserve" version of each in most years. Most of the wines are of average quality, with few of real distinction to emerge in its short history. Its production is about 3,500 cases; capacity is 4,000 cases.

Chardonnay

(Reserve)   85 *   86   87

Generally tight wines, sporting crisp, appley fruit and toasty oak

Pinot Noir

84   85   86   87

Narrow, somewhat thin, cherrylike fruit is surrounded by oak

CANOE RIDGE VINEYARD   *Walla Walla, Washington 1990*   On 200 acres of land overlooking the Columbia River, Canoe Ridge first began to take shape with the development of 44 acres in the late 80s. The initial planting consisted of Cabernet Sauvignon and Merlot. In 90, Chalone, Inc., of California (owners of Acacia, Carmenet, Chalone, and other wine properties) acquired a 50% interest in Canoe Ridge. Shortly thereafter, 50 additional acres were planted to Merlot and Chardonnay, and a 25,000-case-capacity winery was under construction. With vineyards located adjacent to Chateau Ste. Michelle's River Ridge Vineyards, Canoe Ridge is slated to focus on Merlot and Chardonnay. The facility is scheduled for completion in 93.

CAROWAY VINEYARDS   *Kennewick, Washington 1984*   Vineyard owner Wayne Miller established 40 acres to several varieties in the early 80s. Located 5 miles from the Columbia River, the vineyard came into bearing in 83, a time when there was a grape surplus in Washington. As a result, the Millers made wines from their own grapes that year. Every year since, if and when some of the crop is not purchased, Miller produces Caroway wines. Riesling, Chardonnay, and Chenin Blanc are the major grapes planted.

CASCADE ESTATES   *Sunnyside, Washington 1988*   The owners of this ambitious winery include Toby Halbert, once associated with Chateau Ste. Michelle, and Robert Fay, vineyard manager for the 250-acre Sunnyside Vineyard. The first vintages (starting at 70,000 cases) were made at other wineries, but their own 100,000-case-capacity facility, in a former Sunnyside dairy plant, was completed in time for the 89 crush. Over its first vintages Cascade Estates produced Sauvignon Blanc, Semillon, Chardonnay, and Cabernet Sauvignon as its major varietal offerings.

CAVATAPI WINERY   *Kirkland, Washington 1984*   In Seattle, owner-winemaker Peter Dow is better known for his restaurant, Café Juanita, than for his wines. The restaurant in suburban Kirkland features northern Italian fare, and Dow wanted to offer his own house wine to go with it. After a long battle with local officials, he got the go-ahead. Cavatapi (the name means "corkscrew" in Italian) makes Sauvignon Blanc, Cabernet Sauvignon, and Nebbiolo. From a small planting in the Red Willow Vineyard, Dow produced Washington's first Nebbiolo in 87. Total production remains under 1,000 cases.

CHAMPS DE BRIONNE   *Quincy, Washington 1980*   In a remote, scenic site overlooking the Columbia River, Carol and Vince Bryan believed they had located the ideal soil for growing sensitive vinifera varieties, especially Pinot Noir. On a 700-acre parcel, they planted 100 acres to Pinot Noir, Chardonnay, Semillon, and Riesling. For years, this was the only winery in Washington trying to make Burgundian-style Pinot Noir, and it is one of the last wineries still trying to specialize in that varietal. Under a succession of winemakers from California and Switzerland, the winery has yet to win many accolades. Its large facility is partly given over to custom-crushing for other producers.

CHATEAU BENOIT   *Willamette Valley, Oregon 1979*   Situated on a hilltop, Chateau Benoit affords visitors a wonderful view of Oregon farmlands and the Willamette Valley. Back in 72 the Benoit family built their first winery in the south, due west of Eugene. But when owner and then-winemaker Fred Benoit decided to devote all his time to winemaking, he also decided to move closer to the winemaking center near McMinnville. While still farming 10 acres of Pinot Noir in the south, the Benoits have planted 22 acres to vines on their 65-acre estate. After several vintages, they hired a winemaker in 86. For a few years the winery was known for its balanced, fruity Müller-Thurgau and Riesling. However, in the mid-80s it began focusing more on Pinot Noir and Chardonnay. The quality of those two wines has been erratic. The winery is now at the 7,000-case-a-year production mark, about halfway to its goal.

CHATEAU STE. MICHELLE, *Woodinville, Washington 1934* This winery, which was originally located in the industrial sector of Seattle, produced fruit and berry wines for many years. In 67, it made a few thousand cases of vinifera varietals from an experimental vineyard in the Yakima Valley. Then in 74, the U.S. Tobacco Company purchased Chateau Ste. Michelle and invested several million dollars in vineyard development and in winemaking facilities. A new winery/visitors center was built in 76 in the woodsy area of Woodinville, just outside Seattle. In the 70s, the winery developed a reputation for varietally correct Riesling, Gewurztraminer, Semillon, and Grenache. Its early efforts with red wines, especially Pinot Noir, led to disapointment. Most of its wines were made in an old facility located in the Yakima Valley town of Grandview; but as production grew in the 80s, the owners constructed a third facility, known as River Ridge, along the Columbia River and closer to the company's 3,000 acres of vineyards.

From these three facilities, Ste. Michelle enjoyed solid growth throughout the 80s, and as the wine market evolved into different segments, Ste. Michelle created new brands to keep pace. Out of the River Ridge facility, the winery introduced the Columbia Crest label, originally for low-end-priced white wines, but now a complete line (see entry). Under the Ste. Michelle label, the focus falls on a line of varietals led by Riesling, Chardonnay, Blush Riesling, Cabernet Sauvignon, and Merlot. In the late 80s Ste. Michelle released a series of vineyard-designated Chardonnays, Merlots, and Cabernet Sauvignons. Its sparkling wines, for years the object of considerable research, are now labeled "Domaine Ste. Michelle." Made by the *méthode champenoise,* this line has grown to 7,500 cases. Overall, Ste. Michelle table wine production (excluding Columbia Crest) is moving toward 750,000 cases a year.

Cabernet Sauvignon

83* 85 86* 87

Medium-intensity fruit suggesting currants and cherries is quietly supported by sweet oak and firmed by moderate tannins; the wines seem to age well for several years

Cabernet Sauvignon

(Cold Creek Vineyard) 78* 80* 85*

(River Ridge Vineyard) 85

In their initial appearance, the wines from the Cold Creek Vineyard and the River Ridge Vineyard both showed bold tannins but only medium fruit; each will age longer than the winery's regular bottling, and future vintages may carry greater depth and earn higher ratings. But for now, these wines have not exceeded the regular bottling in quality

Chardonnay

84 86 87 88

Mild fruit, slightly citrusy in cast, is filled out partially by oak in these brisk, firm, sometimes too lean wines

Merlot

(regular bottling) 81 82 84 86*

(River Ridge Vineyard) 83* 85*

> *If inconsistent with its regular bottling, a medium-bodied wine with cherryish and herbal flavors, the winery has produced a fairly deep, somewhat brusque, potentially superb wine from its River Ridge Vineyard*

CHINOOK WINES *Prosser, Washington 1983* Owners Kay Simon and Clay Mackey both worked for Chateau Ste. Michelle before starting Chinook. Simon was a winemaker, and Mackey was in charge of vineyard operations. Both left to start independent consulting businesses, but a short time later they married and decided to run their own winery. All grapes are purchased for the winery's line of Chardonnay, Sauvignon Blanc (blended with Semillon), Merlot, and occasionally a sparkling Riesling. Production has been steady at 2,000 cases per year. The goal is about 6,000 cases.

COLUMBIA CREST *Paterson, Washington 1984* This brand developed almost by chance. In the early 80s Chateau Ste. Michelle bought a huge processing plant and surrounding corn fields and turned them into a winemaking facility and vineyards covering about 2,000 acres. In 84, with a grape surplus on its hands, the owners used this winery at River Ridge to process the excess grapes and divert them toward a stopgap generic wine program. Under the name of Columbia Crest, they bottled a blended-white Table Wine and a Blush. Experiencing strong demand, Columbia Crest was converted into its own brand by 87, offering a line of six low-priced varietals. The mainstays are Chardonnay and Sauvignon Blanc among whites, and Merlot and Cabernet Sauvignon for reds. A Semillon-Chardonnay blend is among its best sellers.

With strong advertising support and good value in the bottle, Columbia Crest grew to sales of over 400,000 cases by 90. The $26 million winery has become the showcase of the area and is in effect run today as a separate but equal sister brand of Chateau Ste. Michelle. Recent additions to the Columbia Crest line include Reserve-type Chardonnay and Merlot under the "Barrel Select" name; a line of magnums is on the market identified as Columbia Crest "Allison Combs." Annual production is around 600,000 cases today.

COLUMBIA WINERY *Bellevue, Washington 1962* This brand evolved over time from a winery known as Associated Vintners. Started in 62 as an association of amateur vintners, many of them working for the University of Washington, Associated Vintners acquired acreage in the Yakima Valley. Its commercial wines made in 67 were of high enough quality to gain the attention of winemakers in Washington and elsewhere. The first well-publicized Washington vinifera wine was this winery's Gewurztraminer. After moving to a larger facility in 76, the partners increased production to close to 10,000 cases a year. They moved to yet larger premises in 81. By 84 the winery was suffering financially and sold its vineyards. At that time David Lake, winemaker since 79, was put in charge of the entire operation, and the brand name was changed to Columbia Winery.

Production increased from 12,000 cases to 45,000 cases by the late 80s. Most wines were custom-made at the large Coventry Vale facility in Prosser. In 88, with production at the 100,000-case mark, Lake moved the winemaking operation to Woodinville. Though presently offering a large line of varietals, Columbia is focusing attention on Chardonnay, Semillon, Cabernet Sauvignon, and Merlot. Two vineyard-designated Cabernets—Red Willow Vineyard and Otis Vineyard—have been especially noteworthy. Two Merlots are offered, including one from Red Willow Vineyard. Experimental batches of Pinot Noir and Syrah have been made, and Lake may add both varietals to Columbia's line by the mid-90s. Production is steady at 110,000 cases a year.

COOPER MOUNTAIN VINEYARDS *Willamette Valley, Oregon 1987* About 15 miles southwest of Portland, Cooper Mountain is an extinct volcano that overlooks the Tualatin Valley. In 78 vineyardist Bob Gross purchased a 125-acre estate on the mountainside and began developing a vineyard. He now has 75 acres planted to Pinot Noir, Chardonnay, and Pinot Gris. Most of the crop from his vineyard is sold to others. However, in 87 Gross hired a winemaking consultant and has since been producing 2,000 cases of estate-grown Pinot Noir and Chardonnay. The early vintages of Pinot Noir were a little uneven in quality.

COVENTRY VALE WINERY   *Grandview, Washington 1983*   From its inception until 86, this 1-million-gallon winemaking facility was a custom-crush outfit. Several rapidly expanding wineries in the 80s, especially Columbia Winery, used to handle the bulk of their crush. In 86 owners David Wyckoff and Donald Toci decided to bottle some of their own wine. The first bottling was something less than 1,000 cases of an estate-grown Cabernet Sauvignon. A modest line of *méthode champenoise* sparkling wines also is available under the Coventry Vale label. With over 600 acres of vineyards established, the owners may move into the bottled-wine business in a significant way by the mid-90s.

COVEY RUN VINTNERS   *Zillah, Washington 1980*   Known as Quail Run until 86, Covey Run changed its name in order to avoid legal battles with Quail Ridge, a California winery. In the process of changing names, the winery may have lost some patronage. The winery is a limited partnership, and several of the partners own vineyards in the Yakima Valley and sell the grapes to them. The vineyards are planted to Riesling (70 acres), Chardonnay (30 acres), Cabernet Sauvignon (30 acres), Merlot (20 acres), and Chenin Blanc (25 acres). Producing 65,000 to 70,000 cases a year, Covey Run purchases Sauvignon Blanc as well as additional tonnage of Merlot and Chardonnay. Offering one of the largest lines of table wines in the state, Covey Run devotes 50% of its attention to Riesling and Chardonnay; the other half is given over to Chenin Blanc, Fumé Blanc, Merlot, and several others. Among them are three seldom-seen wines: Aligote, Morio Muscat, and Lemberger. A red grape developed in Germany, Lemberger has been made in a variety of styles by Covey Run. More recently, the winery has been favoring a light-bodied, Beaujolais-style wine labeled "Lemberger Nouveau." In addition to Fumé Blanc, the winery offers "La Caille de Fumé," a proprietary blend of Semillon and Sauvignon Blanc. Covey Run also produces a limited line of *méthode champenoise* sparkling wines.

Chardonnay

84✱ 8̶5̶ 87

Inconsistent to date, these wines are simple, straightforward, fruity, low in oak, and sometimes a little on the earthy side

DOMAINE DROUHIN   *Willamette Valley, Oregon 1988*   In 87, Maison Joseph Drouhin, the highly respected wine firm in France's Burgundy, purchased 100 acres in the Red Hills of Dundee for the purpose of producing Oregon Pinot Noir. Today, the Drouhins own 180 acres in the area where they have built a 15,000-case-capacity facility. The eight-floor-high winery is designed to allow all wine to be moved by gravity only. Over its first three vintages, Domaine Drouhin made about 2,000 cases a year, all from purchased grapes. As of 91, its wines are made entirely from grapes from the Drouhin vineyards adjacent to the winery. The initial vintages displayed plenty of promise.

ELK COVE VINEYARDS   *Willamette Valley, Oregon 1977*   After outgrowing their original winery, a converted barn, Joe and Pat Campbell moved into a new winery in 81 which enjoys a spectacular setting on a ridgetop separating Yamhill from Washington County. The initial 22-acre vineyard has been expanded to 45 acres. The Campbells grow Pinot Noir, Chardonnay, Riesling, and lesser amounts of Gewurztraminer and Pinot Gris. Theirs was among the first vineyards on the West Coast to adopt the French system of close vine spacing. Among the wines offered, Elk Cove routinely produces Cabernet Sauvignon and a late harvest Riesling. In most years, Elk Cove bottles one or two vineyard-designated Pinot Noirs in addition to its own estate-bottled and Reserve Pinot Noir. The winery's style of Pinot Noir captures enough depth to place some wines in the ✱ category.

Usually Elk Cove ferments Pinot Noir in 200-gallon bins for maximum extraction and to allow for frequent punching down of the cap. Its barrel-fermented, *sur lie*–aged Chardonnays have not appealed as much, lacking real focus in some vintages. However, Elk Cove's Rieslings are among the best made in Oregon, and the winery's Pinot Gris are also noteworthy. All told, Elk Cove has earned its stripes for good winemaking, and it is one of the more reliable names in the Northwest. It is making about 7,000 cases a year. With vineyard maturity, the winery could be at its full capacity of 20,000 cases a year within a decade.

Pinot Noir

(Dundee Hills) 86 **87** * **88** * *

(Estate) **86** * 87 **88**

(Wind Hill) 86 **88** *

With few exceptions, most of these are straightforwardly fruity, moderately rich in sweet oak, and light in tannin, with but few years of aging potential; occasionally an earthy, almost cedary, tobacco streak will appear

---

EOLA HILLS WINE CELLARS   *Willamette Valley, Oregon 1986*   Eola Hills Wine Cellars is owned by Tom Huggins, a well-known vineyardist who worked with Elk Cove for several years. Huggins built his own winery in 86, and is focusing on estate-grown wines. The vineyard, located in the emerging Eola Hills region, now has 66 acres under vine. The primary varieties planted are Chardonnay, Pinot Noir, Sauvignon Blanc, Chenin Blanc, and Cabernet Sauvignon. Winemaker Ken Wright, formerly with Ventana Vineyards and Talbott in Monterey County, arrived in 86 and made the Eola Hills wines for three vintages before giving way to another winemaker. The early vintages of Eola Hills Pinot Noirs have been acceptable in quality, and its Cabernet Sauvignons showed some promise, especially when compared to other Oregon Cabernets. A barrel-fermented Chardonnay is the primary white wine offered. With vineyard maturity, this winery will peak at 10,000 cases a year.

EYRIE VINEYARD   *Willamette Valley, Oregon 1970*   The indisputable champion for Pinot Noir in Oregon, owner-winemaker David Lett arrived in 66 and selected the Red Hills of Dundee as the site for his vineyard. Lett, a graduate of U.C. Davis, was the first to plant vinifera grapes in the northern Willamette Valley, and ended up with 26 acres planted to Pinot Noir and Chardonnay. In the late 70s a few acres of Riesling were replaced by Pinot Gris. Today, Eyrie has close to 50 acres. Unlike most Oregon winemakers, Lett never supported the Riesling variety. However, beginning in the early 80s he began campaigning in favor of Pinot Gris as Oregon's second best white wine after Chardonnay. In the town of McMinnville, Lett converted a turkey-processing plant into an efficient winery, with a production capacity of 15,000 cases.

Eyrie's lineup today consists of Pinot Noir, occasionally a Reserve Pinot Noir, Chardonnay, Pinot Gris, and Muscat Ottonel, made in a dry style. Pinot Gris has emerged as the volume leader. Pinot Noir remains the flagship, though. In its history, Eyrie has produced some of Oregon's finest Pinot Noirs. Eyrie's Chardonnays are generally well made and typical of the respective vintages. On occasion, they have enough depth to merit *. Despite the attention devoted to Pinot Gris, Eyrie has been surprisingly erratic with this wine, managing only to confirm its potential.

Pinot Noir

83 * 84 **86** 87 **88** *

Exhibiting more range than depth, this set of fruity, sometimes thin wines can capture elusive hints of spices and herbs to go along with medium body and oaky richness in better vintages

FACELLI WINERY   *Redmond, Washington 1984*   Louis Facelli, the owner and wine-maker, started making wines under this label in Idaho. It was there that he made a noteworthy vintage of Chardonnay from Washington grapes and first developed a modest following. However, in an attempt to raise capital, he sold controlling interest in that business venture and was ultimately edged out. He moved to the present location, taking his name with him, and started over. In 88 Facelli was back in business with a line of Washington varietals. The main-stays in this 2,500-case-capacity winery are Chardonnay, Semillon, Riesling, and Merlot.

E. B. FOOTE WINERY   *Seattle, Washington 1978*   Gene Foote, an engineer with Boeing Aerospace, was a home winemaker for years before turning pro. In a modest winery in Seattle's Southpark area, home to truck farmers, he special-izes in Chardonnay and Gewurztraminer from the Yakima Valley. His annual production is averaging 2,500 cases.

FORGERON VINEYARD   *Willamette Valley, Oregon 1977*   In 71–72 Lee Smith began developing his 17-acre vineyard in a then-untried wine region west of Eugene in the southern Willamette Valley. Acting from instinct, Smith planted the typical varieties for Oregon, Pinot Noir, Chardonnay, Riesling, and Pinot Gris, but added a few acres of Cabernet Sauvignon. The Smiths celebrated their first crush in 77. As time went by, their production came to focus more and more on Pinot Noir, Riesling, and Pinot Gris, although the interest in Cabernet Sauvignon has not diminished. As the winery's annual output moves closer to its 10,000-case goal, Forgeron continues making popular, tasting-room-type wines, such as a slightly sweet Pinot Gris, a Chenin Blanc, a White Pinot Noir, and a Rosé of Pinot Noir.

FRENCH CREEK CELLARS   *Woodinville, Washington 1983*   An offshoot of a home winemaking/wine-tasting club, French Creek is a limited partnership that has been shuffled a few times since originally formed. Its first vintages were made in Redmond, but the winemaking center was moved to Woodinville in 87, where it is much more accessible to visitors. The winemaking style emphasizes strength over finesse, as epitomized by its high-alcohol Chardonnays and tough rustic Cabernets and Merlots. Lemberger (both a red and a "white"), Chenin Blanc, Sauvignon Blanc, and an assortment of exotic late harvest whites have been produced. Reserve-style Cabernet Sauvignon and Merlot have been the most noteworthy offerings to date. Annual production is mov-ing toward the targeted 6,000-case goal.

GIRARDET WINE CELLARS   *Umpqua Valley, Oregon 1983*   In 72 Bonnie and Phi-lippe Girardet, with limited experience in grape growing, deciding to quit the academic profession and move to Oregon to start a vineyard. They bought 55 acres in the foothills west of Roseburg, and planted 18 acres to Pinot Noir, Chardonnay, Riesling, Sauvignon Blanc, and a range of hybrids on an experi-mental basis. Girardet's first crush was in 83, but it was not until 86 that the winery began making Pinot Noir and Chardonnay in significant quantities. In addition, it now offers blended red and white table wines from the hybrids and vinifera, labeled "Vin Blanc" and "Vin Rouge." These blends represent over one-third of the winery's annual output, which is close to the maximum level of 9,000 cases.

GLEN CREEK WINERY   *Willamette Valley, Oregon 1982*   Situated in the southern tip of the Eola Hills region west of Salem, Glen Creek is owned by Thomas Dumm, a one-time wine merchant in Southern California. He focuses on white varietals, primarily Chardonnay, Riesling, Sauvignon Blanc, and Ge-wurztraminer. The only Pinot Noir made has been in an early-bottled, Nou-veau style. On an experimental basis, Dumm has planted Cabernet Franc in his vineyard. For all varieties, the total planted area has reached 20 acres, and the winery's production capability is 5,000 cases. Through the 80s it has yet to make wines that have been consistently above the ordinary.

GORDON BROTHERS CELLARS *Pasco, Washington 1983* Potato farmers for many years, Bill and Jeff Gordon decided to try their hand with wine grapes. On family property located 10 miles northeast of Pasco above the Snake River, they began vineyard development in 80 and now have over 80 acres of vineyards. Their primary varieties are Chardonnay, Sauvignon Blanc, Cabernet Sauvignon, and Merlot. Selling most of their crop to other wineries, they make close to 3,000 cases under their own name.

HENRY ESTATE WINERY *Umpqua Valley, Oregon 1978* After working for several years in the aerospace industry in California, Scott Henry returned to Oregon to begin running the family ranch and to explore the possibility of developing a vineyard. Started in 72, the now 31-acre vineyard beside the Umpqua River contains Pinot Noir, Chardonnay, and Gewurztraminer. Henry also produces Müller-Thurgau and Riesling, the latter occasionally in an award-winning *Botrytis*-affected dessert-wine style. The winery is expanding steadily, and its annual output, led by Pinot Noir and Chardonnay, has increased from 4,000 cases in 85 to 14,000 cases in the 90s.

HIDDEN SPRINGS WINERY *Willamette Valley, Oregon 1980* Situated northwest of Salem along the upper slopes of the Eola Hills area, Hidden Springs is a joint venture between two families, the Byards and Alexandersons. From vineyards developed in 72, they are focusing on Riesling, Chardonnay, Gewurztraminer, and Pinot Noir. To fill out the line the owners also make a Pinot Noir Blanc and a blend, "Pacific Sunset." Some vintages of Pinot Noir have often displayed well-focused fruit, but the winemaking performance has otherwise been erratic.

HILLCREST VINEYARD *Umpqua Valley, Oregon 1963* As indicated by the founding date, Hillcrest was the true pioneer in the state, especially with vinifera wines. After graduating from U.C. Davis, Dick Sommer went north in search of a vineyard site and settled on a farm about 10 miles west of Roseburg. This was the first post-Prohibition vinifera vineyard to be established in Oregon, and today it covers 35 acres. Sommer has always devoted most of his attention to viticulture, leaving the winemaking to others for most of the winery's history. Hillcrest's specialty is Riesling, usually in a dry style, but a late harvest version is produced whenever possible. It is one of Sommer's beliefs that Riesling improves with bottle aging, and to prove his point he releases his Riesling a year or more after the vintage. In 78 Hillcrest produced a rare Ice Wine from Riesling. Chardonnay, Pinot Noir, and Cabernet Sauvignon are the other key wines offered. Hillcrest is one of the few Oregon wineries to grow and produce Zinfandel. The winery's annual production reached the peak level of 8,000 cases by 80.

HINMAN VINEYARDS *Willamette Valley, Oregon 1979* Located about 10 miles southwest of Eugene, Hinman emerged in the 80s as the renegade Oregon winery. Its production, with a strong emphasis on Washington State grapes, approached 40,000 cases a year, and in the late 80s the facility was custom-crushing for several brands, including California's Fetzer Vineyards. Hinman also made a point in its marketing to offer wines priced below the norm for Oregon. Most of its grapes come from the large Bordman Farms in Washington; the winery itself is surrounded by 27 acres of vineyards. The low-priced blends named "Tior" are from the Columbia Valley appellation. The primary varietals offered today are Pinot Noir, Chardonnay, Riesling, Gewurztraminer, and a White Pinot Noir. A line of Charmat sparkling wine is also made.

HINZERLING VINEYARDS *Prosser, Washington 1976* Mike Wallace, owner and winemaker, was one of the pioneer grape growers in the Yakima Valley. His first vineyard was planted in 72, and when it was reaching maturity, he built a winery in the valley, the first to be established there. The 30-acre vineyard contained Cabernet Sauvignon, Chardonnay, Gewurztraminer, and Riesling. Over the winery's first decade, Wallace produced several acceptable Cabernets, and a host of late harvest, *Botrytis*-affected Gewurztraminers (labeled "Die Sonne") and Rieslings. In 87 Wallace sold the winery to pursue other interests, then bought it back in 89. Today it is making about 3,500 cases a year.

HOGUE CELLARS *Prosser, Washington 1982* The Hogue family own a 1,500-acre ranch and farm, and for many years were the most important hop growers in the state. Gradually, they became diversified farmers, adding potatoes, mint, asparagus, Concord grapes, and row crops, and moved into cattle farming. In 74–75, they established a small vinifera vineyard, and by 82, when the vines were producing, they began making wines. Hogue's first vintages of Riesling and Chenin Blanc emphasized fruitiness in a refreshing, slightly sweet style. Both became quite popular, and Hogue began to augment its vineyard holdings. In 84, Rob Griffin came to Hogue from Preston Vineyards and served as winemaker, guiding the winery through the next growth phase.

Today, Hogue's vineyard covers 220 acres, with Chardonnay (60 acres) and Riesling (50 acres) as the leaders, followed by Sauvignon Blanc, Chenin Blanc, Cabernet, and Merlot, each in the 20–25-acre range. In 85, the winery produced 45,000 cases; in 89, it made 175,000, with plans to grow to 200,000 by the mid-90s. It grows about 40% of the grapes now crushed. At times, Hogue has produced a caliber zesty Fumé Blanc, and a Semillon of some interest. These two are its most consistent successes. Its red wines are led by a solid-quality Cabernet Sauvignon, and some of the most attractive Merlot from the Northwest. In better vintages, its Reserve Cabernet Sauvignons and Merlots are especially rich and ageworthy.

Cabernet Sauvignon

(Reserve) 83 * * * 84 * 85 86 * 87

Blended with up to 25% Merlot, this wine is rich, ripe, curranty, a bit on the astringent side, usually with lots of oak

Chardonnay

(regular bottling) 85 86 88

(Reserve) 86 * * 87 * 88

Less ambitious in approach (or price) than Hogue's reds, these wines offer medium fruit, somewhat brisk acidity, and in the Reserve especially, a background of oak

Merlot

(regular bottling) 85 * * 86 * 87 * 88 * 89 *

(Reserve) 84 * * 86 * 87 *

Oak is an overriding theme in these ripe, round, cherrylike wines of supple texture and moderate tannins

HONEYWOOD WINERY *Salem, Oregon 1934* The state's oldest wine producer, Honeywood offered only fruit and berry wines for many years. In the late 70s it began developing a line of vinifera varietals. Today it produces the typical range—Chardonnay, Pinot Noir, Riesling, and Gewurztraminer. In the 80s, as sales continued to increase, Honeywood began making what it calls "Twin Harvest" wines that combine vinifera wine with fruit juice. With two tasting rooms, a gift shop, and a full lineup, Honeywood is one of Oregon's biggest producers, making more than 70,000 cases of assorted products.

HOOD RIVER VINEYARD *Hood River, Oregon 1981* East of Portland in an area where few vines grow, owner and home winemaker Cliff Blanchette started his own winery. After making fruit wines for a few years, in 74 he began planting a vineyard at the intersection of the Columbia River and the Cascades. From this 12-acre vineyard in an area known as the Hood River, he produces Chardonnay, Pinot Noir, Cabernet Sauvignon, Riesling, and Gewurztraminer. The winery also makes wines from locally grown pears and raspberries. The grape wine line has grown to about 3,000 cases a year.

HOODSPORT WINERY *Hoodsport, Washington 1980* One of the few wineries on the western Olympic Peninsula, Hoodsport is best known for a line of fruit wines, but in the mid-80s it branched out with a line of vinifera. Although most of the winery's 15,000-case output continues to consist of fruit and berry wines, it started upgrading its grape wine production in 87. Chardonnay, Riesling, Gewurztraminer, and Merlot have become regular items.

HORIZON'S EDGE WINERY *Zillah, Washington 1985* Aptly named, Horizon's Edge is perched on a ridgetop overlooking the Yakima Valley. Founded by Tom Campbell, one-time winemaker for Jekel Vineyards and Chateau Ste. Michelle, Horizon's Edge has a 20-acre vineyard planted half to Chardonnay, with the remaining acreage planted to Muscat and Pinot Noir. Favoring ripe grapes and barrel fermentation for Chardonnay, Campbell has enjoyed some success with the early vintages. Cabernet Sauvignon and Muscat are also part of this 3,000-case winery's line.

HUNTER HILL VINEYARDS *Othello, Washington 1984* In the northern sector of the Columbia Valley appellation, Hunter Hill is part of a 200-acre farm owned by airline pilot Arthur Byron. In 81 he began developing 28 acres of Riesling, Gewurztraminer, and Merlot. The first few vintages were produced in leased space by a succession of consultants. A winery is planned for the 90s. Annual production has averaged 2,000 cases.

HYATT VINEYARDS *Zillah, Washington 1987* With their vineyard located in the foothills of the Rattlesnake Mountains north of Zillah, the Hyatts have been grape-growers for many years. However, they were basically growing Concord until coverting 73 acres to vinifera in the early 80s. Chardonnay, Chenin Blanc, Sauvignon Blanc, Riesling, and Merlot are the primary varieties planted. The first crush in 87 doubled in 88 to 5,000 cases. The Hyatts built a winery with a capacity of 12,000 cases, and with vineyard maturity they intend to be at full capacity by the mid-90s. The first vintages of Chardonnay and Merlot displayed sound varietal character and were attractive.

INDIAN CREEK WINERY *Kuna, Idaho 1987* Owner William Stowe is a native of Idaho who returned after retiring from the Air Force. In 82 he began developing 15 acres of vineyards, and a few years later converted a mule barn into a small winery. With a production capacity of 4,000 cases a year, Stowe is producing White Riesling, Pinot Noir, Chardonnay, and Chenin Blanc. The Riesling, labeled "Almost bone dry," is the best-selling wine.

KIONA VINEYARDS *Benton City, Washington 1980* On the eastern side of the Yakima Valley in a subregion known locally as Red Mountain, the owners of Kiona planted 30 acres in 75. On otherwise barren land growing little save sagebrush, they drilled their own well, a rarity in the area, and began planting Chardonnay, Chenin Blanc, Riesling, Cabernet Sauvignon, Merlot, and Lemberger. A partnership of two families—Pat and Jim Holms, and Ann and John Williams—Kiona has continued to sell grapes as it eased into winemaking. After moving into a new facility in 83, annual production increased to 12,000 cases. At various times, Kiona has been successful with barrel-fermented Chardonnay, the slightly sweet Riesling, and Chenin Blanc. The owners prefer making Lemberger in a ripe, oak-aged style. One of the most popular wines in local markets is Kiona's Merlot Rosé.

KNUDSEN-ERATH WINERY *Willamette Valley, Oregon 1968* One of the oldest producers and, until recently, one of the largest, Knudsen-Erath is located high in the Red Hills area of Dundee. In 68, on the advice of Dick Sommer of

Hillcrest Vineyards, Dick Erath came to Dundee from California to develop a vineyard. The spot he picked in the Red Hills area ranks among the more picturesque vineyards today. In 72, he became partners with Cal Knudsen, who also owned a vineyard, and their first crush, made in a basement, yielded 400 cases. Currently Erath is once again the sole owner, and Knudsen is a partner in Argyle. The winery owns a total of 45 acres outright, and contracts with local growers for more grapes in order to bottle the most Pinot Noir made by any one winery in Oregon. Its Reserve-type Pinot Noir is named "Vintage Select" and is from the Yamhill County appellation. Erath believes in fermenting Pinot Noir in small, closed, stainless-steel tanks, but at high (90–95°F.) temperatures. The malolactic fermentation is encouraged to occur simultaneously with the alcoholic fermentation. Erath also insists on an extended maceration period after fermentation.

Chardonnay, 100% barrel-fermented with extended *sur lie* aging, and Riesling (as a rule made slightly sweet), are the other major varietals offered. Occasionally when the Riesling develops *Botrytis*, Erath offers a "Vintage Select" dessert-style Riesling. Made in modest quantities, Gewurztraminer and Cabernet Sauvignon fill out the varietal lineup. A small-volume line of *méthode champenoise* wines is only available locally. The winery's total production now stands at 40,000 cases a year, with Pinot Noir accounting for about 40% in a typical vintage.

Pinot Noir

(Vintage Select) 82 83 * 85 86 *

Bright, cherryish fruit and lots of sweet oak are highlighted in the better vintages of this well-balanced, medium-bodied wine

---

LANGE WINERY   *Willamette Valley, Oregon 1987*   Don Lange was teaching school in Santa Barbara when he first became interested in wine. In his spare time, he began working for Ballard Canyon and the Santa Barbara Winery, and became intrigued by Pinot Noir. He and his wife first visited Oregon in March 87, returned to buy 27 acres in the Dundee area in May, and moved in by June. In September, the Lange Winery made its first commercial wine. The roster focuses on Chardonnay, Pinot Noir, and Pinot Gris. Lange's estate vineyard consists of 6 acres of Pinot Noir and 2 acres of Pinot Gris. Traditional winemaking practices are followed, even for the Pinot Gris, which is barrel-fermented and aged *sur lie*. Production is expected to grow gradually to an annual level of 2,000 cases.

LANGGUTH WINERY   *Mattawa, Washington 1982*   This winery was founded by a successful German wine company, F. W. Langguth, and the capital came from a group of prominent local investors. They agreed to develop 275 acres of vineyards on the Wahluke Slope in the Columbia Valley and to spend over $5 million to build a state-of-the-art winery. Within a few years Langguth pulled out of the venture and the winery was taken over by the local investors, who formed a company named Snoqualmie Hills. Wines were made under the Snoqualmie label for a year or two before a second round of dissension and legal debates began. As the debates continued, the facility was turning out wines under three brands—Langguth, Snoqualmie, and Saddle Mountain Winery, a label originally intended for low-priced items. By 88 the production of bottled wine had been reduced to 10,000 cases, but the facility was making wines for other wineries, including Fetzer of California.

LATAH CREEK WINE CELLARS   *Spokane, Washington 1982*   Owner Mike Conray gained experience by working four years at Hogue Cellars before establishing his own winery in Spokane. In the first few vintages, Latah Creek developed a following in the Northwest for Riesling and Chenin Blanc. However, Merlot is the wine Conray set out to focus on. Owning no vineyards, he has bought Merlot from Hogue as well as other growers. Chardonnay, Cabernet Sauvignon, and Semillon are other wines in his lineup. Latah Creek's annual production has grown to 14,000 cases, close to full capacity.

LAUREL RIDGE WINERY *Tualatin Valley, Oregon 1986* On one of the oldest vineyard sites in Oregon, Laurel Ridge is the latest and probably the last winery to operate there. Located on a knoll just west of Forest Grove, the winery has been involved in several ownership changes. One of the first to commence here in the modern era was the Charles Coury Winery, making wines that ranged from acceptable to below average. After Coury left the business, the same facility was soon making wines under the name of Reuter's Hill Vineyard. When it too went out of business, three couples in the Portland area formed a partnership and rescued the facility in 86, giving it a fresh start under the Laurel Ridge name. The 24-acre vineyard adjacent to the winery has been brought back to life, and the owners also have another 50 acres under vine in Yamhill County. The primary varieties planted are Pinot Noir, Gewurztraminer, Semillon, Sylvaner, and Riesling. White varietal wines and blends top the list of table wines, and *méthode champenoise* sparkling wines, headed by a Brut, represent about 30% of the total output. The winery's maximum capacity is 10,000 cases.

L'ÉCOLE NO. 41 *Lowden, Washington 1983* In a building that once housed classrooms for School District 41, Jean and Baker Ferguson occupy one floor as their home, using the two others for a winery and tasting room. Located 12 miles west of Walla Walla, it is the only building of any size in the area. Merlot and Semillon are the major wines offered. The Semillon is unusually full-bodied for the type. Total production is at the maximum of 2,500 cases per year.

LEONETTI CELLAR *Walla Walla, Washington 1977* A red-wine-only winery, Leonetti specializes in Merlot and Cabernet Sauvignon, offering regular and Reserve bottlings in most years. Owner-winemaker Gary Figgins started out in a makeshift building behind his home and by the early 80s was producing 500 cases a year. However, several early vintages gained awards and distinctions, and along the way Leonetti became something of a cult winery. A new winery on the property has allowed production to expand to 2,000 cases. Generally, we find Leonetti's style of winemaking to be in need of some restraint. However, the Merlot and Cabernet have earned high ratings at times.

MCCREA CELLARS *Lake Stevens, Washington 1988* A family-owned winery, McCrea is focusing on Chardonnay, with Cabernet Sauvignon and a proprietary red filling out the line. Doug McCrea came to winemaking from a musical career, and his winemaking remains a part-time venture. The winery's production is under 1,000 cases a year. To date, McCrea's barrel-fermented Chardonnays reveal competent winemaking.

MCKINLAY VINEYARDS *Portland, Oregon 1987* One of only two wineries within the metropolitan area, McKinlay made its first wines in 87. Its owners, the Kinne family, are making only Pinot Noir and Chardonnay in their small winery. The maximum combined output is about 800 cases.

MERCER RANCH VINEYARDS *Prosser, Washington 1985* In the early 70s Don and Linda Mercer established a 130-acre vineyard just beyond the boundary of the Yakima Valley. For several years they were one of the largest and most respected independent growers. The vineyard was developed on a large (30,000-acre) sheep ranch that has been in the Mercer family since the 1800s. The Mercers grow a variety of wine grapes, most of which are sold. As small-scale winemakers, they believe in red wines and produce only Cabernet Sauvignon and Lemberger. There are no plans to expand production beyond the current 2,000-case-per-year level.

MONT ELISE VINEYARDS *Bingen, Washington 1975* After experimenting with almost every available grape variety, owner Charles Henderson selected Gewurztraminer, Pinot Noir, and Gamay as the most suitable for the Bingen area. He developed 50 acres in a subregion known as the Columbia River Gorge, and built a winery to the east of Bingen. At one time Henderson had several partners, and his winery was known as Bingen Wine Cellars. In 78 he bought out the partners, and the winery's name was changed to Mont Elise, after his daughter Elise. The winery specializes in Gewurztraminer, Gamay, and sparkling wine made from Pinot Noir. It has a production capacity of 7,500 cases.

MONTINORE VINEYARDS *Tualatin Valley, Oregon 1987* On a 600-acre estate, the Graham family began developing vineyards in 82. Located just south of Forest Grove, the vineyards covered 450 acres by the late 80s, and the winery—which resembles a grand old manor house—stood out in the middle of them. The major varieties planted are Pinot Noir (150 acres), Chardonnay (108 acres), White Riesling (45 acres), and Pinot Gris (35 acres). From its beginning, this winery wanted to become Oregon's biggest and most ambitious. It is geared to making a line of varietal wines and for sparkling wines that will be aged in specially built caves. In 87 it began by making limited amounts of varietals, and by 90 it was making close to 50,000 cases. The lineup of varietals is led by Pinot Noir and Chardonnay, and includes Riesling, Pinot Gris, and Gewurztraminer. The winemaking facility was built to handle a maximum of 150,000 cases.

MOUNT BAKER VINEYARDS *Everson, Washington 1982* One of the first wineries trying to grow grapes successfully in western Washington, Mount Baker is in the northwest corner of the state about 11 miles east of Bellingham. It has two vineyards totaling 25 acres, with the older planting started in 77. It grows conventional cool-climate varieties, such as Gewurztraminer, Müller-Thurgau, and Chardonnay, but plantings also contain some obscure grapes, such as Madeline Angevine (from the Loire Valley) and Okanogan Riesling (a Canadian variety). Enjoying some success with whites in a slightly sweet style, the winery began to show improvements with oak-aged Chardonnays in the late 80s. Production overall has averaged between 10,000 and 12,000 cases per year.

OAK KNOLL WINERY *Tualatin Valley, Oregon 1970* West of Portland in the northern Tualatin Valley, Oak Knoll has a history which mirrors that of the Oregon wine industry. Founded in 70 by the Vuylsteke family, who converted their hobby, homemade fruit and berry wine, into a part-time business, it was within a few years turning out some of the best fruit and berry wines made anywhere. Beginning in 75, the winery started making vinifera wines and gradually over the years shifted its emphasis more and more to varietals. Now producing about 32,000 cases of vinifera wines, over 80% of its output, Oak Knoll buys all grapes from several Oregon growing regions. Heading its list are Pinot Noir, Chardonnay, Riesling, Cabernet Sauvignon, Gewurztraminer, and generic blends, and it still makes a highly enjoyable Loganberry and Raspberry wine. On occasion, Oak Knoll's Pinot Noirs rise above the crowd.

PANTHER CREEK CELLARS *Willamette Valley, Oregon 1986* After making wines in California from 79 to 85, winemaker Ken Wright moved to Oregon in 86 primarily because he wanted to work with Pinot Noir. In order to start his own winery, he moonlighted to raise money and finally found a site in an industrial part of McMinnville. At Panther Creek, he makes about 3,000 cases of Pinot Noir. Buying grapes from the Eola Hills area, he believes in a long fermentation and maceration period of over three weeks for Pinot Noir. The first vintages were among the most intense and tannic produced in Oregon. The winery also produces a Mélon varietal. With greater financial stability and familiarity with the region, Wright could possibly take Panther Creek to the top spot in Oregon Pinot Noir. The maximum production target is 7,500 cases a year.

Pinot Noir

86* 87** 88*

All lovely efforts, the wines are fairly deep in character and exhibit ripe cherry and black-cherry fruitiness, filled out by generously laid-on, rich oak

PELLIER CELLARS *Willamette Valley, Oregon 1985* Owned by Mitchell Mirassou, who is related to the Mirassou wine family of California, Pellier began its existence as a nursery. In the early 80s when Oregon wines were gaining recognition and the grape supply was short, Mirassou decided to move into the vineyard business. Today, 45 acres are planted in the Eola Hills region, just a short distance from Bethel Heights Vineyards. Mirassou turned professional winemaker in 85 and his winery offers an array of table wines. Riesling is the volume leader, joined by Pinot Noir, Chardonnay, Gewurztraminer, and Cabernet Sauvignon. The quality has been on the erratic side, but the vineyard location is well suited to Pinot Noir and Chardonnay. The winery's capacity is 14,000 cases a year.

PINTLER WINERY *Nampa, Idaho 1988* Longtime agriculturists in the Snake River area, the Pintler family started growing grapes in 83. In 87 the buyer for their first full crop backed out at the last minute, so the Pintlers custom-crushed it themselves at another facility. After making their first vintage under the Desert Sun name, they built a winery and changed their brand to the present name in 88. Pintler now has 12 acres under vine. The wine roster consists of Riesling, Semillon, Chardonnay, and Pinot Noir. Currently, annual production is close to the winery's 4,500-case capacity.

PONTIN DEL ROZA *Prosser, Washington 1984* With both vineyard and winery situated beside the Roza Canal, the Pontin family have been farming in the Yakima Valley since the early 50s. They began developing their 15-acre vineyard in 79, and planted Riesling, Chenin Blanc, and Chardonnay. Using the Coventry Vale facility, they started making wines in 84. To date, Riesling in a slightly sweet style has been the most consistent wine.

PONZI VINEYARDS *Willamette Valley, Oregon 1974* One of the pillars of Oregon winemaking, Ponzi is jointly managed by Dick and Nancy Ponzi. The winery is located in Beaverton, about 15 miles southwest of Portland, tucked away in the middle of rolling farmlands. From its initial 10 acres planted in 70, Ponzi now has 12 acres near the winery and contracts with two local growers within a close radius. The majority of the purchased fruit comes from Five Mountain Vineyard in Washington County. On the estate Ponzi grows Pinot Noir (two distinct clones), Chardonnay, Pinot Gris, and Riesling. The winery was among the first in Oregon to make a Pinot Gris, and Ponzi was among the first to produce a "white" Pinot Noir; it is now proud of being among the first to quit making it.

Producing a truly dry Riesling since 75, Ponzi manages to be successful with this wine the majority of the time. Chardonnays are 100% barrel-fermented in a combination of Allier and Limousin oak, and the quality level is usually average. Ponzi's Pinot Noirs often display a minty, earthy, and tobacco leaf combination that is unusual, but not always easy to appreciate. In making Pinot Noir, Ponzi ferments in 300-gallon open vats and at mid-80F° temperatures. Aging takes place in French oak with about 30% new barrels each year; the Reserve Pinot Noir is aged longer in barrel. The winery's total production is 8,000 cases a year. The Ponzis also own Bridgeport Brewing Co., a small brewery.

PORTTEUS VINEYARDS *Zillah, Washington 1987* The Portteus family purchased property in the Yakima Valley and developed a 50-acre vineyard. Cabernet Sauvignon and Chardonnay dominate the planting, with a few acres devoted to Semillon. Barrel-fermented Chardonnays have not been as impressive as the early Cabernet Sauvignon vintages. Long-term, the winery will expand to about 10,000 cases.

PRESTON WINE CELLARS *Pasco, Washington 1976* By 80 this family-owned winery was earning critical praise and winning many awards on the strength of its Fumé Blancs and Chardonnays. Then the winery seemingly lost its winning ways and faded into the background. Since 84 it has had a succession of winemakers. The quality became inconsistent in the late 80s, and even the Fumé Blancs have not been as successful as in the early vintages. The winery owns 180 acres of vineyards in the southern part of the Columbia River Valley. Annual output has averaged 60,000 cases.

Chardonnay

85   86   87 *   88   89

Although capable of good results, in too many vintages the wine lacks focus and the fruit is meager

QUARRY LAKE VINTNERS   *Pasco, Washington 1985*   From a large (3,000-acre) farming partnership between two local potato growers, the Balcom & Moe Corporation was formed. In the early 70s the principals began developing a 106-acre vineyard, making it the second largest at the time. For a decade the crop was sold to many wineries. The vineyard contains 36 acres of Chardonnay, 17 of Chenin Blanc, 15 of Sauvignon Blanc, and 10 acres each of Merlot, Pinot Noir, and Cabernet Sauvignon. In 85, using rented space, the owners made close to 18,000 cases, and through the 80s production has gradually grown to 30,000 cases. It is expected to increase to 40,000 when a new facility is built in the Pasco area. Chardonnay, Sauvignon Blanc, and Chenin Blanc are the three volume leaders. The lineup also includes Merlot, Cabernet Sauvignon, and Pinot Noir.

QUILCEDA CREEK VINTNERS   *Snohomish, Washington 1979*   Cabernet Sauvignon is the only wine made by this small winery located just 25 miles north of Seattle. Owner-winemaker Alex Golitzin graduated from U.C. Berkeley with a degree in chemistry and moved to the Northwest, where he has been working for a paper company. Making wines in his spare time, Golitzin buys Cabernet from the Yakima Valley, Kiona Vineyards being a frequent supplier. He was encouraged to pursue winemaking commercially by his uncle, the famous winemaker André Tchelistcheff. In each of the first two vintages he made 200 cases of Cabernet. Today, he keeps production under 1,000 cases. The wines are aged for two years in French and American oak barrels, most of which are new each year.

REX HILL VINEYARDS   *Willamette Valley, Oregon 1983*   Situated on a hilltop overlooking the town of Newberg, Rex Hill is by Oregon standards a fairly ornate winery. Although its large tasting room has a few more gold fixtures than might be necessary, it occupies a building that was formerly a fruit and nut drying shed. Founded in 83 by Paul Hart, who now is chairman of the corporation, Rex Hill has a knack for gaining attention. It was the first Oregon winery to price its wines over $15 a bottle, and it changes prices each year based on the perceived quality. The winery occupies a 22-acre site, with 11 acres planted to Pinot Noir and 4 acres to Chardonnay. All wines were produced from purchased fruit through 88.

Crushing grapes from as many as 12 suppliers within the Willamette Valley, Rex Hill developed a reputation for vineyard-designated Pinot Noirs; about 60% of its total production is Pinot Noir. Its white wines consist of Chardonnay, Pinot Gris, Riesling, and Symphony. However, Pinot Noir is the mainstay, and in some vintages Rex Hill has bottled five vineyard-designated and two blended Pinot Noirs. Many of its Pinot Noirs have been firmly structured, medium-bodied wines, often earning * ratings.

ROGUE RIVER VINEYARDS   *Illinois Valley, Oregon 1984*   Situated in southwestern Oregon, Rogue River Vineyards is owned by four families who pooled their resources and talents in 81 and began working on weekends to build the winery over the next three years. From its 5-acre vineyard and purchased fruit, it produces a line of popular-styled table wines such as slightly sweet blush wines and Nouveaux reds. Its two conventionally made wines are Chardonnay and Cabernet Sauvignon. Most of the winery's efforts are focused on the wine types that sell in its tasting room in Portland as well as at the winery. Rogue River is currently operating at its full capacity of 8,000 cases a year.

ROSE CREEK VINEYARDS *Hagerman, Idaho 1984* Having at one time been involved in potato and wheat growing, Jamie Martin became interested in vineyards in 80. With both winery and vineyards located southeast of Boise and just a few miles east of the Snake River, the Martin family has the only winery in the area and sold most of its first few vintages directly to visitors. Riesling and Chardonnay are the two primary varieties planted in the 30-acre vineyard. As production grew to the 4,000-case per year level, Rose Creek has settled on Riesling, Cabernet Sauvignon, and Chardonnay from Idaho and Pinot Noir from Oregon-grown grapes. A popular Blush, "Rose Creek Mist," has been the best-seller in the tasting room.

STE. CHAPELLE VINEYARDS *Caldwell, Idaho 1976* The winery to first put Idaho on the wine map, Ste. Chapelle is the second largest in the Northwest today, following only Chateau Ste. Michelle. Founded in 76, Ste. Chapelle was originally located in Emmett, where its founder, Bill Broich, built a small winery. Grapes were purchased primarily from the Symms Ranch, a large 200-acre vineyard located in the warmest viticultural region of Idaho, known as Sunny Slope. In 76 the Symms family became a partner in the business, and by 79 the Symms were controlling owners and immediately built a large (175,000-case-capacity) winery in Sunny Slope. Broich stayed as winemaker until 85.

From the winery's 180-acre vineyard, Ste. Chapelle produces Riesling, Chardonnay, Gewurztraminer, and several sparkling wines, the majority of which are made by the Charmat process. It also produces Cabernet Sauvignon and Merlot grown in Washington, along with Chenin Blanc, sometimes from Idaho, sometimes from Washington. But Riesling is the primary wine produced, and in copious years such as 76 the amount bottled exceeds 40,000 cases. In most vintages Ste. Chapelle's Rieslings retain about 2.5% residual sugar. An experiment with a drier version (1% sugar) in 87 resulted in the regular production of a Dry Johannisberg Riesling. Two Chardonnays are in the line; one is an inexpensive, no-oak Canyon Chardonnay; the second is oak-aged and labeled as Idaho Chardonnay. Although the winery is experimenting with *méthode champenoise* sparkling wine, it turns out close to 30,000 cases a year of Charmat-produced Riesling, Chardonnay, and Blanc de Noirs sparklers. Annual production has edged up to 150,000 cases.

SALISHAN VINEYARDS *La Center, Washington 1976* In southwestern Washington about 30 miles north of Portland, Linc and Joan Wolverton planted 11 acres to wine grapes. Beginning the vineyard in 71 when they were both amateur winemakers, they moved the family close to the vineyard and started this commercial venture in 76, though until 82 they actually made wine at other wineries. In their own 4,000-case-capacity winery, they are emphasizing Pinot Noir and Chardonnay (partially barrel-fermented), along with Riesling and Chenin Blanc.

SERENDIPITY CELLARS *Monmouth, Oregon 1981* After an apprenticeship at Amity Vineyards, owner Glen Longshore began developing a vineyard and winery in the Eola Hills region. The 3-acre vineyard is adjacent to his home and contains two varieties atypical for the region, Maréchal Foch and Chenin Blanc. Regularly produced in quantities of 200 cases each are Pinot Noir, Chardonnay, Müller-Thurgau, and Cabernet Sauvignon. In light or cool seasons, the red varieties are made into blush wines. All told, the annual output is holding steady at 2,000 cases.

SHAFER VINEYARD CELLARS *Willamette Valley, Oregon 1981* After developing a 20-acre vineyard in 73, owner Harvey Shafer sold his crop until his own winery was constructed in time for the 81 crush. Located in the Tualatin Valley area, unlike most of its neighbors the winery both outside and inside resembles a small modern California facility. The estate vineyard provides most of the

Pinot Noir, Chardonnay, and Riesling grapes needed to produce the three primary varietals. Lesser amounts of Sauvignon Blanc are also grown and made as a varietal that in some warm years has the depth to soften its pungent nature. Barrel fermentations have been the norm for Shafer's Chardonnays, while for Pinot Noir the winery uses small-scale bins to facilitate punching down of the cap by hand. By the late 80s Shafer yielded to popular tastes and began making its Riesling in a slightly sweet style. With Chardonnay and Pinot Noir leading the way, the winery's annual production is at the maximum 8,000-case level.

SILVER FALLS WINERY *Willamette Valley, Oregon 1983* A corporation formed by four friends, Silver Falls is located midway between Salem and Silver Falls State Park. Two of the principals own 28 acres of vineyards which supply most of the grapes crushed. Over the first several vintages, the winery has offered Pinot Noir, Chardonnay, Pinot Gris, and Riesling. After a slow start in which its first two vintages were never bottled, the winery got organized in 87 and is now making about 4,000 cases a year. Capacity is 12,000 cases, a figure the owners hope to reach by the end of the 90s.

SILVER LAKE WINERY *Bothel, Washington 1988* Located about 20 miles north of Seattle, Silver Lake brings together several Washington wine veterans. Winemaker Brian Carter, the best known, joined the winery in 89. However, to establish the brand, he selected and bottled a line of wines made elsewhere. The first white wines labeled Silver Lake were from 88; a Cabernet Sauvignon in the first offering was from 86. Beginning in 89, all Silver Lake wines have been crushed and fermented at the winery. Its emphasis today is on Chardonnay (barrel-fermented), Riesling, Sauvignon Blanc, Cabernet Sauvignon, and Merlot. Its initial bottling of the 89 vintage totaled 5,000 cases. Production is scheduled to grow to 16,000 cases by the mid-90s.

SISKIYOU VINEYARDS *Illinois Valley, Oregon 1978* One of the pioneer wineries in southern Oregon, Siskiyou began developing its 12-acre vineyard in 74. Located at 1,800 feet above sea level, the vineyard site is hospitable to late-ripening varieties, and the two primary grapes planted are Cabernet Sauvignon and Semillon. The winery has been operated by Suzi David since 83, and produces Cabernet Sauvignon, Pinot Noir, Semillon, Müller-Thurgau, and Chardonnay. Annual production tops 7,000 cases.

SNOQUALMIE WINERY *Snoqualmie, Washington 1983* What began as an exciting, dynamic new wine venture ran into many problems in the first few years. This winery was started by well-known winemaker Joel Klein along with several investors. The business went well enough until 87, when Klein and his partners became involved in the Langguth Winery. Before the year was done, Klein was out of both wineries. Snoqualmie has bounced back under a new winemaking team and now makes close to 40,000 cases a year. The line of varietals includes Chenin Blanc, Chardonnay (regular and Reserve), Fumé Blanc, Gewurztraminer, Semillon, Cabernet Sauvignon, and Merlot. The winery was acquired by Stimson Lane (owner of Chateau Ste. Michelle and other properties) in 91.

SOKOL BLOSSER WINERY *Willamette Valley, Oregon 1977* In 71 Bill Blosser and Susan Sokol purchased 125 acres of bare land in Dundee, close to a vineyard owned by Eyrie Vineyard. By 74 they were selling the first crop from their 45-acre vineyard and raising capital to build a winery. Both the winery and tasting room were completed by 77, and the 30,000-case-capacity winery was one of the biggest in Oregon for a decade. In 78 it made what is believed to be the first varietal Müller-Thurgau in the U.S. Over the next few years the owners gradually increased production and were operating at peak capacity by 85.

The home vineyard contains Riesling, Pinot Noir, Chardonnay, and Gewurztraminer. In addition to a Sokol Blosser bottling, Pinot Noir is made from the Hyland Vineyards and the Durant Vineyards, whose owners became shareholders in the winery in 87. These two grape-growing partners combine to bring the total acreage controlled by the winery to 135. A fourth Pinot Noir offered is a blend of the estate vineyard and the Durant Vineyard labeled Redland. A fifth Pinot Noir bottling, and the lightest in style, is identified as Yamhill County. Sokol Blosser produced some of the finest Pinot Noirs in 83, but has not been able to equal that performance over the ensuing vintages. Both its Chardonnays and Pinot Noirs tend to be medium- to medium-full-bodied wines, with moderate oak, and they rise to ✹ rankings on occasion.

STATON HILLS VINEYARD & WINERY *Wapato, Washington 1984* An attorney by training, David Staton moved to San Francisco to head a new company and promptly got bitten by the wine bug. Unhappy with California's real estate prices, he purchased an apple orchard in the Yakima Valley, just a few miles outside of Yakima. After several experiments, he planted 16 acres to wine varieties and began making wine in 84. Today, Staton's 50,000-case-capacity winery, modeled after a country-style château, is one of the few genuine tourist attractions in the area. A smaller facility in Seattle ages the winery's sparkling wines, and operates a busy tasting and sales room. The winery makes a line of varietals, including Chardonnay (barrel-fermented), Sauvignon Blanc, Semillon, Riesling, Cabernet Sauvignon, Merlot, and Pinot Noir. Its sparkling wines, made by the *méthode champenoise,* consist of a Brut and a Blanc de Noirs. Staton Hills became famous (or notorious) for being the first in Washington to make a "Pink Riesling," a blush wine made by adding a splash of red wine to the over-produced Riesling. Finished with 4.5% residual sugar, this wine, Washington's answer to White Zinfandel, has been copied by several Northwest producers. Riding the crest of its Pink Riesling, Staton Hills was considering expanding its overall production to 100,000 cases in the mid-90s.

STEWART VINEYARDS *Sunnyside, Washington 1983* Dr. George Stewart established his medical practice in Sunnyside in the early 60s. He purchased an old estate where grapes once grew, and his interest in grape growing commenced. In the late 60s he purchased 160 acres along the Wahluke Slope, and started planting what turned out to be 70 acres of vinifera. A winery was constructed, and has since been expanded to its current 14,000-case capacity. Though producing a large line of wines for its size, Stewart has been able to handle them all with moderate success. Chardonnay Reserve, Gewurztraminer, and Riesling (ranging from dry to late harvest) are highlights. Cabernet Sauvignon, Muscat Canelli, Sauvignon Blanc, Merlot, and a Blush wine have also been produced.

TAGARIS WINERY *Snoqualmie, Washington 1987* Making their first vintages in rented space, vineyardist Mike Taggares and winemaker Peter Bos plan to locate in the town of Snoqualmie. Taggares (who altered the spelling of his name for the brand) owns 120 acres of vines in the Columbia Valley. The major varieties established are Riesling, Chardonnay, Sauvignon Blanc, Cabernet Sauvignon, and Pinot Noir.

PAUL THOMAS WINERY *Bellevue, Washington 1979* Paul Thomas first became known in the Northwest for his Crimson Rhubarb wine and fruit wines. In 79, Thomas set up a modest winery in an industrial sector of Bellevue, just outside Seattle. For a few years he specialized in fruit wines and raspberry wine before branching out to offer a line of vinifera wines. Buying all grapes, Thomas offers Chenin Blanc, Chardonnay, Riesling, Cabernet Sauvignon, and Merlot. As the winery grew to 25,000 cases a year, Chardonnay became his biggest item and his most praised wine, yet the second most popular wine remains Crimson Rhubarb, a wine that looks like a blush wine. A Reserve Chardonnay, entirely barrel-fermented, was added in 87. Accentuating forthright fruitiness in his wines, Thomas has been consistent with his light-style Chenin Blanc and Riesling. Cabernet Sauvignon and Merlot have both been award winners in local judgings.

TUALATIN VINEYARDS *Willamette Valley, Oregon 1973* Near the town of Forest Grove some 30 miles west of Portland, owners Bill Fuller and Bill Malkmus founded their winery in the middle of the Tualatin Valley. Fuller is a wine-maker from California who worked for the Louis Martini Winery for nine years before moving north to join Malkmus, the marketing director, who is a graduate of Harvard Business School. After a long search for a site, they bought land and planted 85 acres to several cool-climate varieties with Riesling, Char-donnay, and Pinot Noir predominating. Also grown are Gewurztraminer and Müller-Thurgau. Best known for its Pinot Noir Reserve from 85, Tualatin has also earned ✿ for its Chardonnay in several vintages. As the winery reached the 25,000-case annual goal, Riesling and a generic white wine were its biggest sellers.

TUCKER CELLARS *Sunnyside, Washington 1981* One of the longtime growers in the Yakima Valley, the Tucker family have grown almost everything on their 500-acre farm. In the early 80s when the market for sugar beets turned sour, the family looked around for another crop. Under the supervision of Dean Tucker, they planted 22 acres of vinifera varieties. Today, the vineyard covers 60 acres. Randy Tucker, Dean's son, manages the vineyard and winery opera-tion. Cabernet Sauvignon, Chardonnay, Riesling, Gewurztraminer, and Mus-cat Canelli top the list of varietals produced. About 8,000 cases are made annually.

TYEE WINE CELLARS *Corvallis, Oregon 1985* This small winery is a partnership led by Barney Watson, the head of Oregon State University's Enology Depart-ment. So far 6 acres have been developed to several varieties, including Pinot Noir, Chardonnay, Pinot Gris, and Gewurztraminer. The winery has a capac-ity of 2,000 cases a year.

UMPQUA RIVER VINEYARDS *Umpqua Valley, Oregon 1988* Within the Roseburg area, the DeNino family have developed a 20-acre vineyard. The plantings were oriented toward warm-weather varieties such as Cabernet Sauvignon and Sauvignon Blanc. By 88 the winery was making about 1,000 cases of table wine, with Cabernet Sauvignon the volume leader.

VALLEY VIEW VINEYARDS *Applegate Valley, Oregon 1978* The southernmost win-ery in all of Oregon, Valley View's 26-acre vineyard is at the 1,500-foot level of the Applegate Valley, a region that is the sunniest and warmest in the state. Developed in 72, the vineyard contains Cabernet Sauvignon, Merlot, and Chardonnay. From purchased grapes the winery produces Pinot Noir and Gewurztraminer. In terms of emphasis, this winery is trying to make a name for itself for Merlot and Cabernet Sauvignon. To date it has not developed a consistent quality record. Total production is closing in on the target of 20,000 cases.

VERITAS VINEYARD *Willamette Valley, Oregon 1983* On a knoll north of Newberg, Dr. John Howieson established a 20-acre vineyard and a small winery. The vineyard is planted to Chardonnay, Pinot Noir, and Riesling. As his vineyard was maturing, Howieson produced wines from locally grown grapes and earned some recognition for his Chardonnays. By the late 80s he decided to increase the production of Chardonnay and limit the Pinot Noir to local distri-bution. The total production is expanding to the 4,000-case optimum level.

WATERBROOK WINERY *Lowden, Washington 1984* This family-owned winery is located in the Walla Walla region. Buying grapes from the Columbia Valley and elsewhere, Waterbrook concentrates on Sauvignon Blanc and Chardon-nay for whites, and Cabernet Sauvignon and Merlot for reds. Owners Janet and Eric Rindal are among a small group of local vintners who have never made a Washington Riesling. As their production moves toward its 10,000-case goal, Waterbrook has gained recognition for its Chardonnays.

WESTON WINERY *Caldwell, Idaho 1982* One-time filmmaker and river guide Cheyne Weston decided to settle down and become a winery owner. To learn the trade, he apprenticed at Chateau Ste. Chapelle. He also developed 20 acres of vineyards in the Sunny Slope area above the Snake River. Riesling and Chardonnay are the major grapes planted, but Weston grows Gewurztraminer and Pinot Noir as well. He experimented with Zinfandel for several years, and continues to buy Cabernet Sauvignon from Washington State. With a capacity of 4,000 cases a year, Weston Winery devotes about 50% of its production to Riesling, with a barrel-fermented Chardonnay in second place. In recent years the winery has been producing a few hundred cases of sparkling wine by the *méthode champenoise.*

WITNESS TREE VINEYARD *Willamette Valley, Oregon 1987* In the Eola Hills area 9 miles northwest of Salem, owner Doug Gentzkow developed 35 acres of vineyards in 80. After making wines as a hobby for a few years as well as selling grapes, he built a winery and hired a consulting enologist, Rick Nunes from Knudsen Erath Vineyards, to help out. Witness Tree is specializing in Pinot Noir and Chardonnay, and plans to grow to an annual output of 4,000 cases.

WOODWARD CANYON WINERY *Lowden, Washington 1981* Rick Small, owner-winemaker of this winery, had been involved in his family's agricultural endeavors (wheat, cattle raising) for years before planting a vineyard in the late 70s. Small is a strong promoter of the Walla Walla Valley appellation, but in his first decade of winemaking he made wines from several sources. Using a renovated machine-shop building as his winery, Small emphasizes two varietal wines: Chardonnay barrel-fermented in new oak, and Cabernet Sauvignon. In recent years he has added two proprietary wines, Charbonneau Red (Cabernet Sauvignon, Merlot) and Charbonneau White (Semillon, Sauvignon Blanc). The winery is operating at its peak capacity of 5,000 cases per year.

WORDEN WASHINGTON WINERY *Spokane, Washington 1980* Opening the first winery in Spokane in the modern era, owner Jack Worden started using a shed as his winery and an old log cabin as his tasting room. Making wines primarily from Columbia River Valley grapes, he has emphasized the popular, slightly sweet style of Riesling, along with Chenin Blanc, Rosé of Gamay Beaujolais, and Gewurztraminer. In the 80s, with annual production close to 20,000 cases, Worden offered a blush labeled Nouveau Blush. In the late 80s he began working with a Cabernet Sauvignon–Merlot blend, a dry-style Fumé Blanc, and oak-aged Chardonnay. Close to 50% of the winery's output is Riesling.

YAKIMA RIVER WINERY *Prosser, Washington 1979* Among the first five wineries in the region, Yakima River Winery was founded by John and Louise Rauner, both involved in home winemaking prior to moving from New York. Over its history, the winery has purchased grapes from many sources, the Ciel du Cheval Vineyard being its favorite. Though better known for its late harvest–style white wines, Yakima River Winery produces much more red wine than white. Cabernet Sauvignon and Merlot are the major reds, with small amounts of Pinot Noir also produced. Among the sweet, dessert wines, an 88 Riesling Ice Wine remains its greatest accomplishment. The winery's production has been averaging 10,000 cases a year.

YAMHILL VALLEY VINEYARDS *Willamette Valley, Oregon 1985* Dennis Burger and his longtime friend Dave Hinrichs are partners in this winery. They located a 200-acre site that contained a few acres under vine in the foothills 5 miles west of McMinnville, which they bought in 82. They have since expanded the vineyard to its present total of 100 acres. Pinot Noir, Chardonnay, and Pinot Gris are the primary varieties established. In 83 and 84 they purchased grapes and produced wines, but their own winery was not completed until 85. The flagship wine is Pinot Noir, fermented in stainless-steel tanks, an unusual practice in Oregon. A barrel-fermented Chardonnay is joined by Riesling, Gewurztraminer, and Pinot Gris. Also produced is an intriguing beverage labeled "Elderblossom." First produced in 85, it is a Riesling wine with a dollop of elderblossom extract added. The winery is growing toward a target production goal of 10,000 cases.

ZILLAH OAKES VINTNERS   *Zillah, Washington 1987*   The grape-growing partners behind Covey Run responded to the surplus of grapes in 87 by building a second facility and launching this brand. With a capacity of 8,000 cases, its initial efforts went into table wines headed by Riesling, Muscat, Chardonnay, and the proprietary pink blend made from Cabernet Sauvignon, "Zillah Blushed."

The Producers Rated

With few exceptions, every winery that regularly offers one of the major varietals or *méthode champenoise* sparkling wine is rated in the following tables according to the winery's past performance with that wine (see WINERIES AND WINES for individual vintage reviews). The producers are categorized in lists as follows:

OUTSTANDING PERFORMERS	These wines often earn ✿✿✿ and rarely are rated lower than ✿✿
ADMIRABLE PERFORMERS	These wines often earn ✿✿ and rarely are rated lower than ✿
ABOVE-AVERAGE PERFORMERS	These wines earn ✿ more often than not
AVERAGE PERFORMERS	These wines fail to earn at least ✿ ratings in a majority of vintages
BELOW-AVERAGE PERFORMERS	These wines rarely if ever earn ✿ and have been substantially below average in some vintages

These lists also include other important information. Special attention is called to wines that tend to be more capable of improvement with age than their peers and to wines that are more (or less) consistent in quality than similarly rated wines. Some ratings are marked † ("preliminary") because the wines have not been offered long enough to warrant a firm rating. Wines considered to be especially good value for price within their quality range are also indicated.

.   .   .

Symbols used in this section:

⚥   These wines are good values within their quality
range

➠   These wines tend to be more ageworthy than
other wines in their quality range

ACACIA   Wines printed in boldface tend to be more
consistent than others in their quality range and
occasionally have earned higher ratings

~   These wines tend to be less consistent than others
in their quality range and occasionally have
earned lower ratings

†   These wines are assigned preliminary ratings
pending future vintage results

Ratings of Chardonnay Producers

The best of California's white varietals, Chardonnay is made by more
wineries than any other. Vintage variations influence its success almost as
much as winery intention and vineyard location; overall, Chardonnay rates
as a moderately consistent performer. Chardonnays are usually enjoyable
when released, but many of the top bottlings seem to hold for up to a
decade and even improve somewhat with age.

Outstanding Performers
CRONIN Ventana Vineyards ➠
CRONIN Napa Valley ➠
CRONIN Sonoma / Alexander ➠
KISTLER Kistler Vineyard ➠
PETER MICHAEL †
ROBERT MONDAVI Reserve ~
MOUNT EDEN Santa Cruz ➠

Admirable Performers
ACACIA Carneros ~
ALDERBROOK Reserve †
BABCOCK Reserve †
CHALONE ➠ ~
CHAMISAL † ~
CHATEAU MONTELENA
Napa Valley ➠
CHATEAU MONTELENA
Alexander Valley

CRONIN Santa Cruz †
CUVAISON ➠
DE LOACH ➠
DE LOACH "OFS" ➠
EDNA VALLEY ⚥
FERRARI-CARANO Reserve †
FLORA SPRINGS Barrel Fermented
GIRARD Reserve †
GRGICH HILLS ➠
HANNA ~
HANZELL ~
WILLIAM HILL Gold Reserve ~
KALIN ~
KISTLER Durell ➠
KISTLER Dutton ➠
KISTLER McCrea †
LA CREMA Reserve
MATANZAS CREEK

PETER MCCOY

MORGAN Reserve

SAINTSBURY Reserve

SANFORD Barrel Select †

STAG'S LEAP WINE CELLARS Reserve †

TALBOTT

VITA NOVA †

WHITE ROCK †

ZD ~

Above-average Performers

ACACIA Marina Vineyard ~

ALDERBROOK

S. ANDERSON

ARGYLE †

ARROWOOD

AU BON CLIMAT

BALLARD CANYON † ~

BEAULIEU Carneros

BERINGER Private Reserve ~

BERINGER Napa Valley

BLACK MOUNTAIN Gravel Bar †

BONNY DOON La Reina

BOUCHAINE Carneros

BOYER Ventana

BUENA VISTA Private Reserve

BURGESS Triere ➡ ~

BYRON Reserve

CAMBRIA

J. CAREY ~

CHATEAU ST. JEAN Robert Young ➡

CHATEAU ST. JEAN
  Sonoma County ~ ⍨

CHATEAU WOLTNER ~

CLOS DU BOIS Calcaire

CLOS DU BOIS Flintwood

CONGRESS SPRINGS Reserve †

CONGRESS SPRINGS
  Santa Clara County ~

CORBETT CANYON Reserve ~

CRESTON MANOR

DEHLINGER ➡

DRY CREEK Sonoma

DRY CREEK Reserve †

FAR NIENTE ~

FARELLA-PARK †

GARY FARRELL

FERRARI-CARANO

FETZER Barrel Select ⍨

FIELD STONE †

FISHER Coach Insignia

FLORA SPRINGS Napa Valley

THOMAS FOGARTY
  Paragon Vineyard ~

THOMAS FOGARTY
  Ventana Vineyard ~

FOLIE À DEUX

FORMAN ➡

FRANCISCAN ~

FREEMARK ABBEY ~

GAINEY Limited Selection

GAINEY Santa Barbara ~

GARRIC-LANGBEHN

GIRARD ~

GROTH

GUNDLACH-BUNDSCHU ~

HACIENDA ~

HANDLEY

HOGUE Reserve

HUSCH

INGLENOOK Reserve

IRON HORSE ~

JEKEL ~

JEPSON

JORDAN

JORY San Ysidro ~

KARLY

KEENAN Napa Valley

KEENAN Ann's †

**KENDALL-JACKSON
  Proprietor's Reserve**

KENDALL-JACKSON Vintner's Reserve

KENWOOD Beltane ~

KENWOOD Sonoma Valley

KONOCTI ~ ⍨

LAMBERT BRIDGE

J. LOHR Riverstone

LONG ➡

MACROSTIE

MAYACAMAS ~

MAZZOCCO River Lane

MERIDIAN

MERRY Reserve

MERRYVALE ~

ROBERT MONDAVI Napa Valley

MONTEREY VINEYARD
  Limited Release †

MONTICELLO Corley Reserve ~

MONTICELLO Jefferson ~

MORGAN

MOUNT EDEN MacGregor

NAVARRO

NEWLAN

NEWTON

GUSTAVE NIEBAUM ~

OAK KNOLL †

OPTIMA †

PATZ & HALL †

ROBERT PECOTA Canepa ~

PEDRONCELLI ~ ⩎

ROBERT PEPI

JOSEPH PHELPS Napa Valley

JOSEPH PHELPS
  Sangiacomo ~

PINE RIDGE Knollside

PINE RIDGE Stags Leap

PLAM

QUPÉ Sierra Madre

QUPÉ Sierra Madre Reserve †

RABBIT RIDGE

RASMUSSEN

RAYMOND Napa Valley

RAYMOND Reserve

RIDGE

ROCHIOLI

ST. CLEMENT Napa ~

ST. CLEMENT Abbott's †

ST. FRANCIS Barrel Select

SAINTSBURY ▬

SANFORD

SANTA BARBARA Reserve

SEQUOIA GROVE Estate

SHAFER Napa Valley

SILVERADO VINEYARDS

SIMI

SINSKEY

SONOMA CUTRER Cutrer

SONOMA CUTRER Les Pierres

SONOMA CUTRER
  Russian River Ranches ⩎

STAG'S LEAP WINE CELLARS
  Napa Valley

STAR HILL †

STERLING Diamond Mountain ▬

STERLING Napa Valley ▬

STERLING Winery Lake ▬

STRATFORD Partner's Reserve

THOMAS-HSI †

TIFFANY HILL

TREFETHEN ~

TUALATIN Reserve †

VIANSA ~

VICHON

MARK WEST Reserve LeBeau †

WM WHEELER ~

WHITE OAK Sonoma ~

WHITE OAK Myers † ~

WILD HORSE

WINDEMERE ~

Average Performers

ADAMS

ADELSHEIM

ADLER FELS ~

ALEXANDER VALLEY

ALTAMURA

AMITY

DAVID ARTHUR

BABCOCK ~

BALDINELLI †

BALVERNE

BARGETTO

BARROW GREEN

BEAULIEU Beaufort

BELVEDERE

BENZIGER

BLACK MOUNTAIN Douglas Hill

BOEGER

BONNY DOON Santa Cruz †

BRUCE

BUENA VISTA

BYINGTON †

BYNUM

BYRON

CAIN Carneros

CAIN Napa Valley

CAKEBREAD

CALERA Central Coast

CALLAWAY Calla-Lees

CAMERON

CANTERBURY

CARNEROS CREEK

CARTLIDGE & BROWN

CHAPPELLET

CHÂTEAU JULIEN

CHATEAU POTELLE

CHATEAU STE. MICHELLE

CHATEAU SOUVERAIN

CHESTNUT HILL

CHIMNEY ROCK

CHRISTIAN BROTHERS

CHRISTOPHE ⚄

CLARK RANCH (by Sebastiani) †

CLOS DU BOIS Alexander Valley

CLOS DU VAL

CLOS PEGASE

CLOS ROBERT

B. R. COHN

COLUMBIA CREST

CONCANNON

COSENTINO The Sculptor

COSTELLO

CRIGHTON HALL ～

DE MOOR

DEVLIN

DION †

DOMAINE BRETON †

DOMAINE LAURIER

DOMAINE NAPA

DOMAINE ST. GEORGE

EBERLE

ELK COVE

ESTANCIA ⚄

ESTRELLA RIVER

EYRIE

FALLEN LEAF †

FELTON-EMPIRE

FETZER SUNDIAL ⚄

FIRESTONE

FISHER Napa/Sonoma

FLAX

FOPPIANO

FOREST HILL Private Reserve

FRITZ

FROG'S LEAP

GAN EDEN

GAVILAN Chalone †

GEYSER PEAK

GOOSECROSS

GRAND CRU Premium Selection †

GREEN & RED ～

GREENWOOD RIDGE †

GUENOC

HAGAFEN

HALLCREST

HAWK CREST

HAVENS †

HAYWOOD

HESS COLLECTION

HIDDEN CELLARS

WILLIAM HILL Silver

HOGUE Washington

HUNTER ASHBY

IMAGERY †

INGLENOOK Napa Valley

INNISFREE

KNUDSEN-ERATH

KRUG

LA BELLE

LA CREMA

LAKESPRING ～

LANDMARK

LEEWARD ～

LIBERTY SCHOOL ⚄

LOGAN ～

LOLONIS †

MARION ～ ⚄

MARKHAM

MARTIN BROTHERS

LOUIS MARTINI

PAUL MASSON

MAZZOCCO Sonoma County

MCDOWELL VALLEY

MEEKER

MERLION

MERRY Sonoma County

MILANO
MILL CREEK ∼
MIRASSOU
ROBERT MONDAVI Woodbridge
MONTEREY VINEYARD Classic ∉
J. W. MORRIS
MOUNT VEEDER
MOUNTAIN VIEW
MURPHY-GOODE
NAPA RIDGE
NEVADA CITY
NEYERS
NOBLE HILL †
OBESTER
OLIVET LANE †
OLSON
PARDUCCI
PARAISO SPRINGS †
PARSONS CREEK
MARIO PERELLI-MINETTI
R. H. PHILLIPS ∼
PONZI
PRESTON (Washington)
QUAIL RIDGE
RAYMOND California
RITCHIE CREEK
RIVER OAKS
ROMBAUER
ROSE FAMILY Cameron
ROSENBLOOM
ROUND HILL House ∉
ROUND HILL Napa Valley
ROUND HILL Van Asperen
RUTHERFORD RANCH
ST. ANDREWS Estate
ST. ANDREWS Napa
ST. FRANCIS California
ST. SUPERY †
STE. CHAPPELLE Canyon
STE. CHAPPELLE Idaho
SALAMANDRE †
SANTA BARBARA Santa Ynez Valley
SARAH'S Estate
SARAH'S Ventana ∼
V. SATTUI
SEBASTIANI

SEGHESIO
SEQUOIA GROVE Carneros
CHARLES SHAW
SHV (by Stony Hill)
SIGNORELLO
SOQUEL †
P. & M. STAIGER
STEVENOT
STONE CREEK
STONEGATE
STORRS † ∼
STRATFORD
RODNEY STRONG Chalk Hill
RODNEY STRONG Sonoma County
JOSEPH SWAN
SWANSON †
TAFT STREET
IVÁN TAMÁS
TIJSSELING
TUALATIN
TULOCAY
VALLEY VIEW
VANINO †
VENTANA Gold Stripe ∼
VERITAS
VILLA HELENA Hughes
VILLA HELENA McGrath
VILLA MT. EDEN Carneros ∼
VILLA MT. EDEN Napa
VILLA ZAPU
WATERBROOK
WEIBEL ∼
WEINSTOCK
WENTE Arroyo Seco
MARK WEST LeBeau
WHITEHALL LANE Napa Valley
WHITEHALL LANE Le Petit ∼
WOLFSPIERRE
WOODWARD CANYON
ZACA MESA
ZELLERBACH ∉

Below-average Performers
AHLGREN
BANDIERA
BRANDER

CAPORALE	RICHARDSON
CECCHETTI-SEBASTIANI	SANTA CRUZ MOUNTAIN
DUNNEWOOD	SAUSAL
MICHTOM	VENDANGE
RAVENSWOOD Sangiacomo	WESTWOOD
REVERE	WINTERBROOK

Ratings of Sauvignon Blanc Producers

This direct, perky white wine has not proven to be as consistent in year-to-year performance as Chardonnay or as the important red varietals. While some of the best wines can age well for a half decade or more, most Sauvignon Blancs seem not to benefit from extended cellaring.

Outstanding Performers
BABCOCK Eleven Oaks †
DUCKHORN
GRGICH HILLS
HAYWOOD ~
KENWOOD
MATANZAS CREEK

Admirable Performers
BYRON ~
CARMENET
CHATEAU ST. JEAN La Petite Etoile ~
DRY CREEK
FLORA SPRINGS
GRAND CRU Premium Selection ~
HANNA
HOGUE
HUSCH
MORGAN
MCDOWELL VALLEY ~
ROBERT MONDAVI Reserve ~
QUIVIRA
ST. CLEMENT
SIMI

Above-average Performers
ADLER FELS
ALDERBROOK
BEAULIEU
BYNUM

CAKEBREAD
J. CAREY
CAYMUS
CHATEAU POTELLE †
CHRISTOPHE † ⌀
CLOS DU BOIS
DE LOACH
DE LORIMIER
FERRARI-CARANO
FRITZ
GREENWOOD RIDGE †
GUENOC
HANDLEY
HIDDEN CELLARS
HONIG
IRON HORSE
KARLY ~
KENDALL-JACKSON ~
LAKESPRING ~
LONG
LYETH
MAYACAMAS † ~
ROBERT MONDAVI Napa Valley
MURPHY-GOODE
PEDRONCELLI ⌀
PLAM †
PRESTON Estate Reserve
PRESTON (WA) †
ROCHIOLI
SILVERADO

SPOTTSWOODE

STERLING

TAFT STREET Napa †

Average Performers

AMADOR FOOTHILL

AMIZETTA

ARCADIA

BABCOCK

BERINGER Knights Valley

BERINGER Napa Valley

BOEGER

BUENA VISTA Lake County

CAIN

CALLAWAY

CHATEAU ST. JEAN Sonoma County

CHATEAU SOUVERAIN

CHIMNEY ROCK

CLOS PEGASE †

CONCANNON

CONN CREEK

CRESTON MANOR

DOMAINE NAPA †

DOMAINE ST. GEORGE †

ESTANCIA ⚡

FARELLA-PARK ~

FETZER Valley Oaks ⚡

FIRESTONE

FOGARTY †

FROG'S LEAP

GEYSER PEAK

GROTH

HACIENDA

JEPSON

KONOCTI ⚡

MARKHAM

MERLION Sauvrier †

ROBERT MONDAVI Woodbridge ⚡

MONTEREY VINEYARD

MONTEVINA

J. W. MORRIS

OBESTER ~

PARDUCCI

ROBERT PECOTA

ROBERT PEPI

JOSEPH PHELPS

R. H. PHILLIPS

PRESTON Cuvée Fumé

QUAIL RIDGE

ROUND HILL

RUTHERFORD RANCH

ST. ANDREWS

SANTA BARBARA

SATTUI

SEBASTIANI

SHENANDOAH

SIERRA VISTA ~

SIGNORELLO

STAG'S LEAP WINE CELLARS ~

STONEGATE

STRATFORD

SUTTER HOME

VICHON Chevrignon

WENTE

WHITE OAK

Below-average Performers

CECCHETTI-SEBASTIANI

CHÂTEAU JULIEN †

DUNNEWOOD †

GLEN ELLEN Proprietor's Reserve

HAWK CREST

Ratings of Cabernet Sauvignon Producers

The best of California's red wines, Cabernet Sauvignon tends to follow vintage trends more closely than most other varietals. The top performers almost always produce very fine wines in the best vintages and sometimes in lesser years as well. The top ones are usually expensive and can be expected to age well for one to two decades.

Outstanding Performers

BEAULIEU Private Reserve (to 1970) ➡

BURGESS Vintage Selection ➡

CAYMUS Special Selection ➡

DIAMOND CREEK
  Red Rock Terrace ~ ➡

DUCKHORN ➡

DUNN Howell Mountain ➡

DUNN Napa Valley ➡

GROTH Reserve †➡

HEITZ Martha's Vineyard (to 1980) ➡

ROBERT MONDAVI Reserve ➡

MOUNT VEEDER (73–75 only) ➡

OPUS ONE ➡

JOSEPH PHELPS Insignia ~

RIDGE Montebello ➡ ~

SPOTTSWOODE ➡

STAG'S LEAP WINE CELLARS
  Cask 23 (1970s)

Admirable Performers

ARROWOOD †➡

BEAULIEU Private Reserve (71–79)

BERINGER Private Reserve ➡

BUEHLER ~

CAFARO †➡

CAIN Five †➡

CAKEBREAD Reserve †➡

CARMENET ➡

CAYMUS ➡

CHATEAU MONTELENA ➡ ~

CLOS DU BOIS Briarcrest ~

CLOS DU BOIS Marlstone

B. R. COHN †➡

CONN CREEK Private Reserve

CUVAISON ~

DIAMOND CREEK Gravelly Meadow ➡

DIAMOND CREEK Volcanic Hill ~ ➡

FISHER Coach Insignia

FORMAN ➡

FROG'S LEAP ~

GIRARD Reserve †➡

GRACE FAMILY ~ ➡

GRGICH HILLS ➡

HEITZ Martha's Vineyard (81 on) ~

WILLIAM HILL (Gold) Reserve

INGLENOOK Niebaum Cask Reserve †

INGLENOOK Reunion †

KEENAN

KENWOOD Artist Series ➡

KENWOOD Jack London

KISTLER Kistler Estate †➡

LAUREL GLEN

LIVINGSTON ~

MARKHAM ➡

MAYACAMAS
  (late 60s and early 70s) ➡

MOUNT EDEN ➡ ~

JOSEPH PHELPS Backus ➡

PINE RIDGE Stags Leap Vineyard

RAYMOND Private Reserve

ST. CLEMENT

ST. FRANCIS †

SHAFER Hillside †

SILVER OAKS Alexander Valley

SILVER OAKS Napa Valley

STAG'S LEAP WINE CELLARS
  Stag's Leap Vineyard (70s)

STERLING Reserve ➡

TUDAL ⚉ ➡

VICHON "sld" ➡

VILLA MT. EDEN (mid-70s) ➡

WHITEHALL LANE Napa Valley

WHITEHALL LANE Reserve †➡

Above-average Performers

ANTARES (by Hacienda) † ➤

BAY CELLARS †

BEAULIEU Private Reserve (1980s) ~

BELLEROSE ~ ➤

BENZIGER

BOEGER ~

BUENA VISTA Private Reserve ~

CAIN Napa Valley

CAKEBREAD Napa Valley ➤

CARNEROS CREEK ~

CHAPPELLET ~

CHATEAU POTELLE

CHATEAU ST. JEAN

CHIMNEY ROCK † ~

CLOS DU BOIS
   Alexander Valley

CLOS DU VAL

CLOS PEGASE †

CONN CREEK Barrel Select ~

CORISON †

COSENTINO Poet

COSENTINO Reserve

CRONIN Robinson

CUTLER Batto †

DE LOACH

DE MOOR

DEHLINGER

DOMAINE LAURIER

DOMAINE MICHEL †

DOMINUS † ~ ➤

ESTANCIA Meritage † ⚶

ETUDE † ~ ➤

FAR NIENTE ~

FETZER Barrel Select

FETZER Special Reserve

FLORA SPRINGS Napa Valley

FLORA SPRINGS Trilogy

FOLIE À DEUX † ~

FOX MOUNTAIN ~

FRANCISCAN Meritage †

FREEMARK ABBEY Bosche

FREEMARK ABBEY Sycamore †

FREY ~

FRITZ †

GEYSER PEAK Reserve Alexandre †

GIRARD Napa Valley ➤

GRAND CRU Collectors

GROTH Napa Valley

HAGAFEN

HANNA † ~

HANZELL ➤ ~

HAYWOOD

HEITZ Bella Oaks ~

HESS COLLECTION Napa Valley † ~

HESS COLLECTION Reserve † ~

HOGUE Reserve ~

HOP KILN

INGLENOOK Cask Reserve

JOHNSON-TURNBULL ~

JORDAN

KENDALL-JACKSON Cardinale †

KENDALL-JACKSON
   Proprietor's Reserve †

KATHRYN KENNEDY ~

KENWOOD Sonoma Valley

KONOCTI ⚶

LA JOTA ➤

LA VIEILLE MONTAGNE † ~

LAKESPRING

LONG ➤

LYETH

LYTTON SPRINGS †

LOUIS MARTINI Monte Rosso

MAZZOCCO †

MEEKER †

MERLION † ~

MERRYVALE † ~

ROBERT MONDAVI Napa Valley

MONT ST. JOHN ➤

MONTEREY PENINSULA
   Doctor's Reserve ➤

MONTEREY VINEYARD
   Limited Release

MONTICELLO Corley Reserve

MONTICELLO Jefferson Cuvée ~

MORGAN †

NEVADA CITY †

NEWTON

NEYERS ~

GUSTAVE NIEBAUM †

NIEBAUM-COPPOLA ➤

OPTIMA ⬛

PAHLMEYER Caldwell † ⬛

PALISADES †

ROBERT PECOTA Kara's

PEJU PROVINCE † ⬛

ROBERT PEPI Vine Hill ~

JOSEPH PHELPS Eisele ⬛ ~

JOSEPH PHELPS Napa Valley

PINE RIDGE Andrus Reserve ⬛

PINE RIDGE Rutherford

BERNARD PRADEL ~

QUAIL RIDGE ~

QUIVIRA † †

RAVENSWOOD Sonoma County

RAYMOND Napa Valley

ROMBAUER
Le Meilleur du Chai † ⬛ ~

ROMBAUER Napa Valley

ROSENBLUM ~

ROUND HILL Reserve

CHANNING RUDD ~

RUTHERFORD HILL

RUTHERFORD RANCH ⬛

SADDLEBACK †

SAUSAL †

SEQUOIA GROVE Estate Bottled

SEQUOIA GROVE Napa Valley

SHAFER Stags Leap District

SIERRA VISTA ~

SILVERADO VINEYARDS

SILVER OAKS Bonny's Vineyard

SIMI

SMITH & HOOK ~

SMITH-MADRONE ~

SOQUEL ~

**STAG'S LEAP WINE CELLARS
Napa Valley** (70s)

STAG'S LEAP WINE CELLARS
Stag's Leap Vineyard/
SLV (80s) ~

STELTZNER

STERLING Diamond Mountain † ⬛

STERLING Napa Valley

STERLING Three Palms †

STONEGATE

RODNEY STRONG
Alexander's Crown ~

TERRA ROSA †

TERRACES † ⬛

VILLA MT. EDEN
(late 70s to present) ~

VILLA ZAPU †

WM WHEELER Dry Creek Valley

WM WHEELER Private Reserve

WHITE ROCK Claret †

WOODWARD CANYON †

ZD ⬛ ~

Average Performers

ALEXANDER VALLEY

AMIZETTA †

VINCENT ARROYO ⬛

AUDUBON

BEAULIEU Rutherford

BERINGER Knights Valley

BUENA VISTA

DAVIS BYNUM

J. CAREY

CHATEAU STE. MICHELLE

CHRISTOPHE

CINNABAR †

COLUMBIA CREST

CONCANNON

COSENTINO North Coast

CRESTON MANOR

DEER VALLEY

DOMAINE ST. GEORGE

DRY CREEK

EBERLE

ESTANCIA ⩎

FIELD STONE Alexander Valley ~

FIELD STONE Hoot Owl ~

FIRESTONE

FOPPIANO

FRANCISCAN Oakville

FREEMARK ABBEY

GAN EDEN ~

GEYSER PEAK

GUENOC

GUNDLACH-BUNDSCHU

HACIENDA ~

HALLCREST †

HAWK CREST

HEITZ Napa Valley ~

WILLIAM HILL Silver Label ~

HUSCH

INGLENOOK Napa Valley

INNISFREE

IRON HORSE

JEKEL

KENDALL-JACKSON
  Vintner's Reserve †

CHARLES KRUG Vintage Selection

LAMBERT BRIDGE

LEEWARD †

J. LOHR

MARIETTA

MARION

LOUIS MARTINI North Coast

MAYACAMAS (mid-70s to present)

MCDOWELL VALLEY

MILANO †

MONTEREY VINEYARD Classic

MONTEVINA

MOUNT VEEDER (1975 to present)

MURPHY-GOODE †

NEWLAN

OAKFORD †

PARDUCCI

PARSONS CREEK

PAULSEN

PEDRONCELLI ⚓

R. H. PHILLIPS †

PRESTON (CA)

PRESTON (WA)

RABBIT RIDGE †

RANCHO SISQUOC †

KENT RASMUSSEN †

RAVENSWOOD Pickberry †

RIDGE York Creek ➡ ~

RITCHIE CREEK

ROUND HILL Napa Valley

ST. ANDREWS ~

ST. SUPÉRY †

SANTA BARBARA

SANTA CRUZ MOUNTAIN

V. SATTUI Napa Valley ~

V. SATTUI Preston Vineyard †

SEGHESIO †

SHENANDOAH

SPRING MOUNTAIN

STAG'S LEAP WINE CELLARS
  Napa Valley (80s)

STAG'S LEAP WINE CELLARS
  Cask 23 (80s)

STAGS' LEAP WINERY

STEVENOT

STONE CREEK

STRATFORD

STREBLOW † ~

STUERMER

SUGARLOAF RIDGE

SUNNY ST. HELENA

SUTTER HOME

TAFT STREET

IVÁN TAMÁS

PHILIP TOGNI ➡

TREFETHEN

TULOCAY

VIANSA

VINA VISTA

VITA NOVA †

WHITE OAK Myers

WILD HORSE

J. WILE

ZACA MESA

Below-average Performers

DAVID BRUCE ~

COTURRI

GAINEY

GLEN ELLEN Proprietor's Reserve

CHARLES KRUG Napa Valley

MILL CREEK

MIRASSOU

NAPA RIDGE

PLAM †

ROLLING HILLS

SAN SABA †

SEBASTIANI

SULLIVAN

Ratings of Merlot Producers

Less sturdy than Cabernet Sauvignon but often of equal attractiveness, Merlot seems to perform better in vintages that are a bit too cool for Cabernet. The best wines are moderately expensive and often improve in bottle for 8 to 12 years.

Outstanding Performers

CAFARO †
DUCKHORN Three Palms

Admirable Performers

BERINGER Bancroft † ▭
CHATEAU CHEVRE
CLOS PEGASE †
CUVAISON
DUCKHORN Napa
INGLENOOK Reserve †
KEENAN ~
MARKHAM ¢
MATANZAS CREEK ~
MONTEREY PENINSULA
   Doctor's Reserve
ST. CLEMENT ~
ST. FRANCIS ~
ST. FRANCIS Reserve ~
SHAFER
WHITEHALL LANE

Above-average Performers

BELLEROSE ~ ▭
BENZIGER †
J. CAREY
CHATEAU STE. MICHELLE
   River Ridge ▭
CHATEAU SOUVERAIN
CLOS DU BOIS ~
CLOS DU VAL ~ ▭
CONN CREEK
COSENTINO
DEHLINGER
DRY CREEK
DUCKHORN Vine Hill
FLORA SPRINGS
FRANCISCAN

GEORIS † ▭
GUNDLACH-BUNDSCHU Rhinefarm
HOGUE Washington
JAEGER Inglewood
KENDALL-JACKSON †
LEONETTI †
MURPHY-GOODE †
NEWTON
PINE RIDGE Select Cuvée
QUAIL RIDGE † ~
RAVENSWOOD
ROMBAUER
ROUND HILL ~
RUTHERFORD HILL ~
RUTHERFORD RANCH
SARAH'S
SEBASTIANI ~ ¢
SILVERADO
SINSKEY †
STAG'S LEAP WINE CELLARS
STERLING
STONEGATE Spaulding
STRATFORD
STRAUS
VICHON
WILD HORSE

Average Performers

ALEXANDER VALLEY
ARBOR CREST
BOEGER
BOGLE
BRAREN-PAULI
BUENA VISTA
CHAPPELLET
CHATEAU JULIEN
CHATEAU STE. MICHELLE
CHESTNUT HILL

COLUMBIA	NAPA CREEK
DEVLIN	PARDUCCI
FERRARI-CARANO	RICHARDSON
FIRESTONE	RIDGE Bradford Mountain
GAINEY †	STAGS' LEAP VINTNERS
GEYSER PEAK	
HAVENS † ~	**Below-average Performers**
KONOCTI ⚋	GLEN ELLEN Proprietor's Reserve
LAKESPRING	CHARLES KRUG
LAMBERT BRIDGE ~	MOUNT MADONNA
LOUIS MARTINI Los Vinedos	STE. CHAPELLE
LOUIS MARTINI North Coast	SULLIVAN
MILL CREEK ~	WILDCAT

Ratings of Pinot Noir Producers

California's great enigma, Pinot Noir performs best in cool, long growing seasons. Only a handful of wineries have proven consistently successful with this variety (or even consistent at any level of achievement); as a result, generalized ratings of this sort are less reliable predictors of future success than ratings for grapes like Cabernet Sauvignon and Chardonnay. Oregon Pinot Noirs, still in their infancy as an industry, have been suggesting a promise of better things to come. Most good Pinots can age for up to a decade, with a few reaching well into their second decade.

Outstanding Performers
CALERA Selleck ▬
CALERA Jensen ▬
DEHLINGER

Admirable Performers
ACACIA St. Clair
ACACIA Madonna ~
CARNEROS CREEK
CARNEROS CREEK
  Signature Reserve † ▬
CAYMUS Special Selection
ETUDE
GARY FARRELL Allen ~
GAINEY †
ROBERT MONDAVI Reserve
MOUNT EDEN ▬ ~
PANTHER CREEK † ~
SAINTSBURY
SINSKEY † ~

Above-average Performers
ACACIA Carneros ~
ADELSHEIM
AMITY ~
BAY ~
BEAULIEU Los Carneros Reserve
BETHEL HEIGHTS ~
BETHEL HEIGHTS Reserve † ~
BOUCHAINE Carneros ~
BOUCHAINE Reserve † ~
BYRON ~
CALERA Central Coast ~
CHALONE ▬
CLOS DU BOIS ~
CLOS DU VAL
ELK COVE Dundee Hills
GARY FARRELL Russian River
HACIENDA Reserve
HANZELL ▬
HUSCH

KISTLER DUTTON

KNUDSEN-ERATH Vintage Selection

MERLION Hyde †

ROBERT MONDAVI

NEWLAN

REX HILL † ~

RICHARDSON Sangiacomo ~

SAINTSBURY Garnet ⚭

SANFORD ~

SOKOL-BLOSSER Redland †

JOSEPH SWAN

TULOCAY Haynes ~

WHITEHALL LANE ~

WILD HORSE

WILLIAMS & SELYEM ~

ZACA MESA Reserve

ZD ~

Average Performers

ADAMS

ALEXANDER VALLEY

AU BON CLIMAT Benedict † ~

BARGETTO

BEAULIEU Napa Valley Beaumont

DAVID BRUCE

BUENA VISTA Private Reserve

DAVIS BYNUM Limited Reserve

CALLAHAN RIDGE †

CAMERON

CARNEROS CREEK
   Fleur de Carneros †

CHATEAU STE. MICHELLE

CONGRESS SPRINGS

CORBETT CANYON

CRESTON MANOR Petite

CRONIN

DE LOACH

EDNA VALLEY

ELK COVE Estate

EYRIE

FOGARTY Carneros

GIRARD †

GUNDLACH-BUNDSCHU Rhinefarm

INGLENOOK

IRON HORSE

JORY

KNUDSEN-ERATH

CHARLES KRUG

LA CREMA

LANGE †

LAZY CREEK

LOUIS MARTINI

MONTEREY VINEYARD

MONTICELLO

MORGAN

MOUNTAIN VIEW

NEVADA CITY

OAK KNOLL Vintage Select †

PARDUCCI

PEDRONCELLI

PONZI ~

RASMUSSEN

ROBERT STEMMLER ~

STERLING Winery Lake †

RODNEY STRONG River East

TREFETHEN

TUALATIN

VERITAS †

Below-average Performers

AU BON CLIMAT Rancho Vinedos †

SANTA CRUZ MOUNTAIN Jarvis

Ratings of Zinfandel Producers

Relying primarily on their berryish, zesty fruit for appeal, almost all Zinfandels possess early-drinking charms. However, the sturdiest, most highly oaked Zinfandels have the ability to improve for a decade or more. Vintage-to-vintage performance has been less predictable for Zinfandel than for Cabernet Sauvignon or Merlot, with the result that many well-regarded wines listed below are rated as having less-than-average consistency.

Outstanding Performers

RAFANELLI
RAVENSWOOD Dickerson ➖
RAVENSWOOD Old Hill
STORYBOOK MOUNTAIN Napa ➖
JOSEPH SWAN (1970s)

Admirable Performers

BURGESS ➖
CLOS DU VAL ~ ➖
EDMUNDS ST. JOHN †
FRANCISCAN †
HAYWOOD ~
KENWOOD
LAMBORN FAMILY ~
LYTTON SPRINGS ➖ ~
MAZZOCCO †
NALLE
QUIVIRA
RIDGE Geyserville ➖
RIDGE Lytton Springs ➖
ROSENBLOOM ~
STORYBOOK MOUNTAIN
   Reserve ➖
TERRACES † ~

Above-average Performers

AMADOR FOOTHILL Special Selection
BERINGER
BRANDBORG †
BUEHLER ~
CAYMUS
CHATEAU MONTELENA
CUVAISON ~
DE LOACH ~
DE MOOR ~

ELYSE †
FETZER Ricetti Reserve
FRITZ ~
FROG'S LEAP ~
GRANITE SPRINGS
GRGICH HILLS ~ ➖
GUENOC ~
GUNDLACH-BUNDSCHU Sonoma Valley
HIDDEN CELLARS Pacini ~
HOP KILN Primativo † ➖
HOP KILN Russian River
KENDALL-JACKSON ~ ➖
LA JOTA ➖
MARIETTA
MEEKER ➖
PRESTON
RUTHERFORD RANCH
SANTINO Grandpère †
SAUSAL
SEBASTIANI ⚕
SIERRA VISTA ~
SKY
SUMMIT LAKE ➖
SUTTER HOME Reserve
JOSEPH SWAN (1980s)
VILLA MT. EDEN
MARK WEST La Rue ~

Average Performers

ALEXANDER VALLEY ~
AMADOR FOOTHILL
   Eschen † ➖
BALDINELLI ➖
BOEGER
BOGLE
CHATEAU SOUVERAIN

CONGRESS SPRINGS

CONN CREEK

D'ANNEO

DRY CREEK

FETZER North Coast

FREY

GREEN & RED

GREENWOOD RIDGE

GUNDLACH-BUNDSCHU Rhinefarm ~

KARLY

LOUIS MARTINI ⚛

MCDOWELL VALLEY

OLSON

PARDUCCI

PEDRONCELLI

JOSEPH PHELPS ➡

RAVENSWOOD Vintners Blend ⚛

SANTA BARBARA

SANTINO Fiddletown

SANTINO Shenandoah Valley

V. SATTUI

SEGHESIO

SHENANDOAH

STEVENOT

SUTTER HOME

WHALER

RIDGE Dusi

Below-average Performers

DUXOUP

Ratings of Sparkling Wine Producers

These are likely the most changeable of all the ratings provided. Most of the producers are relatively new and have rising production levels. Their grape sources expand and/or change from year to year, and many offer nonvintage wines only. We have chosen to list only those producers who employ the classic *méthode champenoise* because the other techniques for producing sparkling wine—while capable of yielding perfectly clean, drinkable wines—rarely, if ever, produce wines even of ✳ quality. Among the wines in the list, none is described as being "long-aging," since almost all of the character of sparkling wine is attained during the winemaking and *en tirage* processes in the winery.

Outstanding Performers

CHANDON
  Blanc de Noirs (in Magnum)

CHANDON Reserve (in Magnum)

MUMM NAPA VALLEY Reserve †

Admirable Performers

S. ANDERSON Blanc de Noirs

CHANDON Blanc de Noirs

CHANDON Brut (in Magnum)

CHANDON Reserve

DOMAINE CARNEROS Brut †

IRON HORSE Brut ~

MUMM NAPA VALLEY Brut Prestige

MUMM NAPA VALLEY Winery Lake †

ROEDERER ESTATE Brut

Above-average Performers

S. ANDERSON Brut

CHANDON Brut

CHATEAU ST. JEAN Blanc de Blancs ~

CHATEAU ST. JEAN Brut

CULBERTSON Brut

DOMAINE STE. MICHELLE
  Brut (vintage) †

GLORIA FERRER Brut

GLORIA FERRER Royal Cuvée †

HANDLEY Brut Rosé

IRON HORSE Blanc de Blancs

IRON HORSE Rosé

IRON HORSE Wedding Cuvée

KORBEL Brut Rosé ~

MAISON DEUTZ Brut

PARSONS CREEK Tête de Cuvée † ⚲

SCHARFFENBERGER Brut

SCHARFFENBERGER Brut Rosé

SCHRAMSBERG Blanc de Blancs

SCHRAMSBERG Blanc de Noirs

SCHRAMSBERG Reserve

SHADOW CREEK Brut

TRIBAUT Brut

TRIBAUT Brut Rosé

VAN DER KAMP Midnight Cuvée ~

Average Performers

ADLER FELS Mélange à Deux

BEAULIEU Champagne de Chardonnay

BEAULIEU Brut

CHANDON Club Cuvée

CULBERTSON Blanc de Noirs

CULBERTSON Brut Rosé

CULBERTSON Natural

RICHARD CUNEO
   Cuvée de Chardonnay

DOMAINE STE. MICHELLE
   Blanc de Blancs †

DOMAINE STE. MICHELLE
   Brut (nonvintage) †

HANDLEY Brut

KORBEL Blanc de Blancs

KORBEL Blanc de Noirs

KORBEL Brut

KORBEL Natural

HANNS KORNELL Blanc de Noirs

HANNS KORNELL Brut

MIRASSOU Au Natural

MIRASSOU Blanc de Noirs

MIRASSOU Brut

SCHARFFENBERGER Blanc de Blancs

TIJESSELING Blanc de Blancs

TIJSSELING Brut

WENTE Brut

Wine Language

ACETIC All wines contain acetic acid—vinegar. Usually the amount is quite small, being less than 0.06% and ranging as low as 0.03%. When table wines reach 0.07% or above, tasters begin to notice a sweet, slightly sour and vinegary smell and taste in the wine. Such wines are acetic and are also said to have ascescence. At low levels, ascescence often enhances the attractiveness of a well-made wine. At higher levels (over 0.10%), the acetic qualities can become the dominant character of the wine and are considered a major fault. A related substance, ethyl acetate, contributes the smell associated with the presence of acetic acid.

ACIDIC Describes wines whose total acid is so high that they taste tart or sour and have a sharp feel in the mouth.

ACIDITY Labels mentioning acidity express it in terms of total acid, a measure of the several most common acids. These are tartaric, malic, lactic, and citric. The acidity of balanced dry table wine falls in the range between 0.6% and 0.75% of the wine's volume. However, for sweet wines, 0.70% total acidity or less is considered low because the wine usually tastes flat or unbalanced. For balance, generally, the sweeter the wine, the higher the acidity should be. It is legal in California to correct deficient acidity by adding malic, tartaric, or citric acid to achieve a balanced wine.

AFTERTASTE The taste left in the mouth after the wine is swallowed. Both the character and the length of the aftertaste are considered. Finish is a related term.

ALCOHOL BY VOLUME Wineries are required by law to state the alcohol level on their labels—usually expressed as a numerical percentage of the volume. For table wines the law allows a 1.5% variation in either direction from the stated percentage as long as the alcohol does not exceed 14%. An alternative taken by a few producers is to describe the wine as a table wine or light wine, omitting the percentage notation. By definition, sherry ranges from 17% to 20% alcohol by volume; other dessert wines fall into the 18–21% range.

ANGULAR The combination of hard, often tart-edged flavors and tactile impressions given by many young dry wines. Angular wines are the opposite of round, soft, or supple.

APERITIF A legal classification for wines having not less than 15% alcohol by volume; vermouth is the best example. However, current fashion also uses the term generically to describe any wine likely to be enjoyed before a meal, regardless of alcohol level.

APPLEY   This term often carries additional modifiers. "Ripe apples" suggests a full, fruity, open smell characteristic of some Chardonnays. "Fresh apple" aromas are occasionally associated with Rieslings, whereas "green apple" aromas come from wines made from barely ripe or underripe grapes. And, should you encounter a wine with the aroma of "stale apples," you are probably smelling a flawed wine exhibiting the first stages of oxidation.

AROMA   Traditionally defined as the smell that wine acquires from the grapes and from fermentation, now it more commonly means the wine's smell, including changes that occurred in the bottle. One assesses the intensity of aroma and also describes its character with virtually any adjective that fits, ranging, for example, from appley to raisiny and from fresh to tired. Bouquet has a similar meaning in common usage.

ASCESCENCE   The sweet and sour, sometimes vinegary smell and taste that, along with a sharp feeling in the mouth, mark the presence of acetic acid and ethyl acetate.

ASTRINGENT   Many red wines and a few whites have a rough, harsh, puckery feel in the mouth, usually from tannin. When the harshness stands out, the wine is astringent. Tannic astringency is reduced with age, but sometimes a wine will fail to outlive the tannin.

AUSTERE   Said of wines that are low in fruit and firm, sometimes hard, in texture. Sparkling wine is often meant to be austere, in the sense that "fruit" is intentionally kept in the background so that the wine can show the richness it acquires in its aging process.

BALANCE   A wine has balance when its elements are harmonious—no one part dominates. Acid balances against sweetness; fruit balances against oak and tannin; alcohol balances against acid and flavor. Wine not in balance may be acidic, cloying, flat, or harsh, among other things.

BARREL-FERMENTED   Some wines are fermented in small casks (usually 55-gallon oak barrels) rather than in large tanks. Advocates believe that barrel fermentation contributes better harmony between the oak and the wine and increases body. Its liabilities are that more labor is required and greater risks involved. It is being used increasingly with California Chardonnay and for a few of the dry Sauvignon Blancs, Pinot Blancs, and Chenin Blancs.

BERRYLIKE   The expected aroma and taste of Zinfandel. "Berrylike" is equated with the ripe, sweet, fruity qualities of blackberries, raspberries, cranberries, and cherries. Other red grapes may also produce wines with berrylike character.

BIG   A wine, either red or white, possessing rich, full flavors and fairly full body. Big red wines are usually tannic. Big whites often are high in alcohol and glycerine.

BITTER   One of the four basic tastes (along with sour, salty, and sweet). Some grapes—notably Gewurztraminer and Muscat—often have noticeable bitterness in their flavors. Another major source of bitterness is tannin. If the bitter quality dominates the wine's flavor or aftertaste, it is considered a fault. In sweet wines a trace of bitterness may complement the flavors and make the wine more enjoyable.

BODY   The tactile impression of weight or fullness on the palate usually experienced from a combination of glycerine, alcohol, and sugar.

BOTRYTIS CINEREA   A mold or fungus that attacks grapes under certain climatic conditions, *Botrytis* requires high humidity and/or some moisture. When it commences just before the grapes reach maturity, it causes them to shrivel, concentrating both sugar and acid. It is beneficial and highly desirable for some white varieties, especially Johannisberg Riesling. The resulting wines are uniquely aromatic and flavored, sweet and luscious, if the *Botrytis* is widespread. Lacking official definition, wines said to have *Botrytis* vary both in flavor intensity and in sweetness.

BOTTLE-FERMENTED   Generally indicates the champagne was not produced by the bulk process. It could apply to either the *méthode champenoise* or the transfer process. However, since producers following the former method usually say so on their labels, champagne bearing this description is more likely made by the transfer method.

BOTTLED BY   When it appears by itself without the "produced" or "made," the indication is that the named winery played a very minor role in the wine's production. The wine could have been purchased readymade and simply bottled; or it could have been made under contract by another winery only to be transferred, aged, and then bottled by the designated producer.

BOUQUET   Technically, that part of a wine's smell that develops after it is put in the bottle. Since most of the smell develops before bottling and bouquet comes mostly with years of cellar aging, the term aroma is almost always more appropriate when discussing a wine's smell.

BRAWNY   Term used for wines that are full of muscle and low on elegance. The term is used mainly for younger reds with high tannin and alcohol levels—thus referring both to body and to texture. Petite Sirahs with Napa, Sonoma, and Mendocino appellations are more likely than not to be brawny. Most reds from Amador are brawny.

BREED   Used for the loveliest, most harmonious, and refined wines, those whose charms reach classical expectations of varietal character, balance, and structure. The term is usually reserved for wines from the best varieties and is rarely associated with common grapes like French Colombard or Ruby Cabernet.

BRIARY   Like the thicket of thorns from which the wine term is derived, a briary wine gives a prickly, aggressive tactile impression on the palate not unlike flecks of black pepper. The term is most often applied to young, dry red wines with noticeable tannin and alcohol.

BRIGHT   Wines with fresh, zesty, fruity qualities are said to be bright, or to have brightness. It is a characteristic expected in most younger wines, especially whites and rosés, and can be a pleasant surprise in older bottlings. The bright aspects of a wine are part of its overall balance, and of the interplay between acidity, body, oakiness, alcohol, and sweetness in determining how the wine smells and tastes.

BRILLIANT   Term describing the appearance of very clear wines: absolutely no visible suspended or particulate matter in evidence. Brilliant wines are often the product of heavy filtration, a process that may remove the flavor along with the solids. See also Unfiltered, Cloudy, and Hazy.

BRIX   Name of a system used by American winemakers to measure the sugar content of grapes, must, and wine. On labels Brix normally refers to the degree of ripeness (meaning the sugar level at harvest) and occasionally is used to indicate the sugar in the finished wine. For most table wines the usual range at the harvest is 20° to 25° Brix. By multiplying the stated Brix at harvest by .55, one obtains the approximate alcohol by volume possible if the wine were fermented to dryness.

BROWNING   The normal tints of young table wines contain no brown. Browning is a sure sign that wine is beginning to age. Wines with good depth and character can be quite enjoyable even though a good deal of browning shows. For lesser wines the onset of browning usually signals the downside of the hill.

BRUT   An exclusive champagne modifier widely used to designate a relatively dry-finished wine, often the driest champagne made by the producer. In the absence of a legal definition, however, Brut does not guarantee that the champagne will be dry. Wineries in the U.S. use the term as they see fit.

BULK PROCESS   A speedy, large-volume, and inexpensive method of making champagnes. The secondary fermentation that provides the bubbles takes place in a large, closed container, as opposed to a bottle. Wineries have the option of putting either "bulk process" or "Charmat" (a synonymous term) on their labels.

CANDYLIKE   Modern technology enables winemakers to capture the perfumed fresh fruit aromas and flavors of the grape. This candylike fruitiness can be attractive in wines intended for early consumption, such as *Nouveau*-style wines and slightly sweet whites and rosés. It is out of place in longer-aging reds and in the better white varieties.

CARBONIC MACERATION   A technical procedure in which grapes are placed whole into a fermenter. Their weight breaks the skins, beginning an intracellular fermentation. The resulting wines (usually red) are intensely fruity, light-bodied, and meant for early consumption. Some wines labeled "Nouveau" are made this way. Occasionally a winery may blend some carbonic maceration wine with conventionally fermented wine for added fruitiness and freshness.

CASK #   Sometimes attached to very special wines; sometimes used as a gimmick. It is meant to imply that the wine spent its entire cellar life in one cask and that it was produced in small amounts. Neither condition need be met for the term to be used.

CELLARED BY   Technically means the wine was not produced at the winery where it was bottled. Usually indicates that the wine was purchased from someone else and aged or cellar-treated by the bottling winery, but there is no minimum time requirement for aging. This lack of precision makes "cellared by" highly suspect, even though it occasionally appears on wines that received long aging and personal attention from the bottling winery.

CHARMAT   Same as the bulk process of champagne making. The second fermentation occurs in large tanks, not individual bottles. It is a large-volume method involving fewer hand procedures. Since the champagne can be made quickly and the costs are lower, it is the usual method for all inexpensive champagnes. Many wineries prefer this label term since it sounds better than "bulk process."

CHEWY   Rich, heavy, tannic wines are said to be chewy because, figuratively, one could not swallow them without chewing first.

CITRUSY   Term describing a wine with aroma and flavor constituents reminiscent of citrus fruits. Such wines need not be high in acid, since citrusy refers to taste sensations that go beyond the basic qualities of sour, sweet, salty, and bitter. Many white wines from colder climates, especially Monterey County, have a citrusy quality that recalls grapefruit.

CLASSIC   A meaningless term when used on wine labels (e.g., Classic Chardonnay), its appearance there derives from its use by wine tasters to describe a wine that conforms to expected norms of character for a certain type or style. In that latter context, "breed" is a similar term.

CLONE   A group of vines originating from a single, individual plant whose descendants have been propagated asexually, usually by means of cuttings or grafts. A clone is selected for its special viticultural and wine merits (productivity, adaptability to particular growing conditions, and wine quality). Clonal selection studies have improved California Chardonnay and could lead to improved Pinot Noir.

CLOSED-IN   Term for wines that are presently low in intensity, but high in concentrated, correct character, and that are expected to develop greater intensity with age.

CLOUDY   An obvious lack of clarity in wines is undesirable. With the exception of old wines not decanted properly, cloudy wines are usually the result of winemaking error. They are caused by a variety of unwanted occurrences, such as protein instability, yeast spoilage, and refermentation in the bottle. Cloudy wines usually taste unpleasant.

CLOYING   When the sweetness annoys by dominating flavors and aftertaste, a wine is said to be cloying. Such excessively sugary wines lack the balance provided by acid, alcohol, bitterness, or intense flavor.

COLD STABILIZATION   A clarification technique involving lowering the temperature to 32° F. for one to three weeks. The cold encourages the tartrates and other insoluble solids to precipitate, rendering the wine clear. The tartrates cast by the wine are actually tasteless and harmless and are removed for appearance only.

COMPLEX   A wine of beauty and balance harmoniously combining many aroma and flavor elements is considered complex. This is the elusive quality that separates a great wine from a very good one.

COOPERAGE   Those who build wooden barrels are called coopers. In present usage cooperage refers to any container for holding or aging wine. Collectively, it covers containers of all sizes and of all materials, from oak to stainless steel.

CORKED   Some corks are flawed by the presence of a chemical in their makeup which makes the wine in the bottle taste and smell musty and dank. For reasons not well understood by the wine industry or the cork producers, this phenomenon is increasing; according to some studies, corked wines (that is, wines destroyed in attractiveness by diseased corks) are appearing in as many as 1 bottle in 30. Unfortunately, there is no way to test every cork before it goes into the bottle, so wineries and producers can only sample each batch of corks in the hope of detecting an unusually high percentage of bad ones.

CREAM   Loosely used term for a style of sherry that is very sweet and is intended for enjoyment with desserts.

CRISP   A tactile sensation somewhat akin to hardness but less imposing, crispness is generally the result of a high level of acidity relative to other balancing aspects. Dry and slightly sweet white and rosé wines are often crisp, and when they are bright as well, are likely to be attractive.

CROSS   A grape created by mating 2 members of the same vine species. For example, the mating of two *Vitis vinifera* grapes, Cabernet Sauvignon and Carignane, produced Ruby Cabernet. Other notable crosses are Emerald Riesling, Flora, and Carnelian.

CRUSH   Popularly used in the U.S. for the harvest season or the vintage. It also refers more specifically to the breaking (or crushing) of grape skins, which begins the winemaking process.

CUVÉE   Commonly used in the U.S. to identify a specific batch or lot of wine (as in Cuvée 8). In general, it refers to a blend of wines. Seen on both champagnes and table wines as a substitute for a vintage date.

DECANTING   Procedure by which wine is poured slowly and carefully from the bottle into another container before serving. The purpose is to leave the sediment behind. Many old red wines and a few young ones made with a minimum of clarification tend to throw a deposit or sediment in the bottle.

DELICATE   Any wine of light to medium-light body and of lower-intensity flavors can be described as delicate. The term is usually, but not always, applied to attractive wines.

DEMI-SEC   For reasons now forgotten, the language of champagne relating to sweetness is misleading when interpreted literally. Although this word means half-dry, *demi-sec* champagnes are usually slightly sweet to medium sweet. The term is occasionally applied also to still wines.

DEPTH   A wine with flavors of good intensity that seem to fill the mouth from front to back is said to have depth. It is a characteristic that one should expect of most premium wines, save for youthful, lighter-bodied whites. See also LINGERING.

DESSERT WINE   A term with two meanings. The first is a legal classification of wines whose alcohol content is at least 17%, but not higher than 24% by volume, and whose higher alcohol was obtained by adding either brandy or neutral spirits. Such wines are also known legally as fortified wines. The second use is general, covering sweet and very sweet wines of any alcohol level that are customarily enjoyed with dessert or by themselves after a meal.

DIRTY   This term covers a multitude of vinous sins. All of the foul, rank smells that can show up in wine—from the musty cachet of unclean barrels to the cabbage and garlic odors of undesirable fermentation by-products—render a wine dirty.

DOSAGE   In bottle-fermented champagne, the yeast sediment collected is eventually removed. Along with it a little wine is lost. To replace the wine and to adjust the sweetness level of the final product, winemakers add a dosage, usually a mixture of sweet syrup and wine.

DRY   A wine with no perceptible taste of sugar in its makeup is dry. Wines fermented to dryness have 0.2% residual sugar or less. Most wine tasters begin to perceive the presence of sugar at levels of 0.5% to 0.7%. For our purposes, we use "dry" for any wine with residual sugar up to 0.5%. The term is used more loosely on wine labels.

DUMB   A young wine with undeveloped aromas and flavors is often called dumb because it seems unable to speak. Closed-in is a similar term. Both words are reserved for wines expected to improve.

EARTHY   Wine tasters use this term to cover characteristics that range from the pleasant, rich earthiness of loamy topsoil to the unpleasant, rotting-grass earthiness of the compost heap. Earth may be dirt, but an earthy wine is not necessarily dirty.

ELEGANT   Wines of grace, balance, and beauty are called elegant. The term is applied more often to white wines than to reds, although a few medium-bodied Cabernet Sauvignons of breed and complexity may also be called elegant.

EN TIRAGE   Sparkling wines are aged in the bottle during the secondary fermentation stage. This time spent *en tirage* (the French term means literally "in drawing" and refers to the fact that the wine has been drawn from the barrel) keeps the wine in contact with the dead yeast cells and adds a rich, toasty, sometimes creamy aspect. This is often regarded as a key component in the character of the best sparklers.

ESSENCE   Used for a time by wineries to describe a late harvest, sweet red wine. It appeared on several Zinfandels made from grapes picked at 35° Brix or higher.

ESTATE BOTTLED   Once used by producers for those wines made from vineyards that they owned and could see from the winery. Until recently, its definition had been stretched beyond recognition. New regulations have now tightened its definition and restricted its application.

ETHYL ACETATE   The sweet, vinegary smell that often accompanies acetic acid is ethyl acetate. It exists to some degree in all wines and can complement other elements in the aroma and taste, especially those of sweet, rich wines. In most wines, however, noticeable ethyl acetate is considered a flaw.

EXTRA DRY   In keeping with the French Champagne tradition, wines labeled extra dry are not. They usually possess residual sugar in the 2–6% range and bridge the gap between the drier *Brut*-styled wines and those still sweeter.

FAT   The combination of medium to full body and slightly low acid gives wine a fat impression on the palate. The wine feels and tastes a bit more obvious and often lacks a touch of elegance. In fuller-flavored wines the fat quality is highly prized by some tasters. A fat, oily Riesling would be less so, unless made in a late harvest style.

FERMENTATION   A complex chemical reaction by which yeasts through their enzymes transform the grapes' sugar into equal parts of alcohol and carbon dioxide. The process generates heat, so most winemakers control the temperature nowadays by circulating cooling agents within the jackets of their stainless-steel fermentation tanks.

FIELD BLEND   This was once a widespread practice in California. Vineyards were planted to several different varieties, and the grapes were harvested together to produce a single wine. Thus, the wine was blended in the field. A few such vineyards, mainly of red varieties, remain in California.

FIELD CRUSHING   Generally used in concert with mechanical harvesters. The grapes are picked and immediately crushed in the vineyards or field; the fresh juice (called "must") being ultimately transferred to the winery for fermentation. The advantages are that the juice avoids oxidation and, since a blanket of carbon dioxide surrounds it, the juice will not ferment too early. Still experimental and somewhat controversial with regard to wine character.

FILTERING   A mechanical process of removing yeast cells and other particles from wine after fermentation. Sometimes used before fermentation to clarify press juice. Most wines (except those labeled unfiltered) are filtered for both clarity and stability.

FINING   Technique of clarifying wine by introducing various agents. The most common fining agents are bentonite (powdered clay) and gelatin; the most traditional is egg whites. Such agents precipitate to the bottom of the tank or barrel, carrying suspended particles with them.

FINISH   The tactile and flavor impressions left in the mouth when wine is swallowed. The tactile sensations of the finish may be hot, harsh, tannic, smooth, or soft, and lingering, short, or nonexistent.

FLAT   Term for wine suffering a lack of balance or lack of flavor. Flatness means the absence of vigor and liveliness and is caused by very low acidity. Flat flavors are insipid or old.

FLOR   A specific yeast that imbues *flor* or Fino sherries from Spain with their unique aroma and flavor. This *flor* yeast *(Saccharomyces fermentati)* does not occur naturally in the U.S. or in other wine regions outside Spain. However, several Canadian and California researchers have developed a *flor* yeast culture that can be introduced to the would-be sherry and imparts a similar character. The technique is called the submerged flor or cultured flor process.

FLORAL (also FLOWERY)   Literally, having the characteristic aromas of flowers. Floral is employed without modifier to describe pleasant, often delicate aromas found in white wines. In particular, Johannisberg Riesling often displays such attributes, as do Chenin Blanc, Muscat, and Gewurztraminer to a lesser degree. Very few red wines are floral.

FORTIFIED   A wine whose alcohol content has been increased by the addition of brandy or neutral spirits is said to be fortified. In the U.S. sherries are fortified to a minimum of 17% alcohol by volume; other fortified wines have an 18% alcohol minimum. Dessert wine is a synonymous term when used to describe a wine that has been fortified.

FOXY   Poorly chosen word traditionally used to describe the unique musky and grapey characters of many native American labrusca varieties and many French-American hybrids.

FREE-RUN JUICE   The juice that flows freely after the grape skins are crushed and before the stems and pulp are pressed for the remaining yield. About 60–70% of the total juice yield is free-run; it is generally smoother, less bitter, and less tannic than press wine. A few special bottling wines are fermented entirely from free run. However, most winemakers choose to blend the two in some proportion.

FRESH   Having the lively, youthful, uncomplicated qualities sought in lighter reds, rosés, and most whites. Such wines are usually fruity and clean and have ample acidity.

FRUITY   Having the distinctive aroma and taste of fruit, a quality found mostly in young wines. A fruity wine usually has intensity, freshness, and distinctive character; for example, it is berrylike, appley, or herbaceous. Young wines lacking fruitiness, especially whites, are often sweetened to fill the holes in their flavor profiles.

GASSY   Said of table wines containing carbonation (gas) usually from unwanted fermentation in the bottle. The term "spritzy" also describes carbonation in wine, but does not carry the negative connotation of gassy.

GENERIC WINE   Any wine whose name is part of a general category or type, as opposed both to varietal wines (which are derived from a grape variety such as Cabernet Sauvignon) and to specially coined proprietary names (Caymus' Conundrum, Phelps's Insignia). The best-known generic designations are those with European place names (Burgundy, Chablis, Chianti, Champagne, and Rhine) as well as the type categories (Blanc de Blancs, Blanc de Noirs, Claret, Rosé, Sherry, and Table Wine).

GLYCERINE This by-product of fermentation is found to some extent in all wines. It is most noticeable in higher-alcohol and late harvest wines, in which high levels of glycerine give the wine a slippery, smooth tactile impression and contribute fullness to the wine's body. Glycerine has a sweet taste on the tip of the tongue.

GRAPEFRUITY Cold-climate white wines often exhibit a distinct grapefruity character. Such wines also may contain floral qualities that blend nicely with the more citrusy grapefruit notes. The young white wines of Monterey County frequently possess this intriguing, fresh quality.

GRAPEY Simple flavors and aromas more like fresh table grapes than fine wine are called grapey. Many of the native American varieties and French-American hybrids produce grapey wines.

GRASSY A light fresh grassiness can enhance some wines (especially Sauvignon Blanc). However, the more grassy a wine is, the more likely it is to be unappealing. In the extreme, grassiness can take over a wine and render it unattractive.

GREEN Wines made from unripe fruit have a green taste. The flavors are usually monochromatic, somewhat sour and angular, and often grassy. The color green (light tints in a straw/pale yellow color) is not unusual in many young white wines, especially Johannisberg Riesling, and does not necessarily signal a green wine.

GROWN, PRODUCED, AND BOTTLED BY Used by a few producers to declare explicitly that they performed all functions, from growing the grapes to bottling the wine. Much more precise and reliable than "estate bottled."

HARD Tactile firmness taken one step further by high acidity or tannin yields a hard wine. The quality is appropriate in young red wines suitable for aging and can also enhance dry white wines that are served with shellfish.

HARSH Highly astringent wines, often relatively high in alcohol, may give this nasty, rough tactile sensation. With age, some of the nastiness goes away, but the relevant question is whether the wine is worth the wait. "Rough" and "hard" are related terms.

HAZY Term for wines with moderate amounts of visible particulate matter. If you see a slight haze in wine, especially if it carries the words "unfined" or "unfiltered," there is probably no cause for alarm. But if the wine is so hazy that the suspended matter causes it to lose clarity, it may be flawed.

HEARTY Generally used to describe the full, warm qualities found in red wines with high alcohol, especially those made in straightforward styles such as the heavier red jugs, some Zinfandels, and Petite Sirahs.

HERBACEOUS Literally, having the taste and smells of herbs (undefined as to species). Herbaceousness is often said to be a varietal character of Cabernet Sauvignon and, to a lesser extent, of Merlot and Sauvignon Blanc.

HOT Wines high in alcohol that tend to burn or prickle the palate and nose are called hot. This character is accepted in dessert offerings like port, sherry, and late harvest Zinfandel. It is noticeable but less appreciated in Cabernet Sauvignon and Chardonnay and actually undesirable in light, fruity wines like Johannisberg Riesling.

HYBRIDS Varieties developed by geneticists through crossing (and often recrossing) grapes from two or more different species. Full-scale efforts began in the search for resistance to the *Phylloxera* disease. Grapes resulting from the cross-pollination experiments of vinifera with a native American variety became known as French hybrids or as French-American hybrids. Those hybrids presently cultivated in the U.S. were chosen for their ability to survive cold winters and to yield balanced wines in short growing seasons. Among the best known hybrids are Baco Noir, De Chaunac, Foch, Seyval Blanc, and Vidal Blanc.

JAMMY, JAMLIKE The combination of ripe, concentrated fruitiness and the natural grapey or berrylike character of certain red varieties yields wines that have jamlike aromas and flavors. Zinfandel from Amador County is frequently jammy.

JUG WINES Inexpensive wines generally sold in large containers. The term originates in the tradition of consumers' bringing their own containers, jug bottles, to wineries for their purchases. Most wines so described are generics, but a few varietals also appear in jug containers. "Jug-wine quality" describes wines low in character and palatable at best.

LABRUSCA Shorthand for the native American grape species, *Vitis labrusca*, whose wines have a heavy, grapey character of the sort typified by Concord grape juice.

LATE HARVEST On labels, a signal that the wine was made from grapes picked at a higher Brix than normal. The term describes the condition of the fruit, not the calendar date. It is possible, though not requisite, that the high sugar levels were achieved through the influence of *Botrytis cinerea*. The general implication for late harvest white wines is that the wine is finished sweet to some degree; for red wines it means they may be either high in alcohol or finished sweet. Most late harvest wines are enjoyed after the main course as unfortified dessert wines.

LEAFY Some wines, including attractive wines, exhibit a slightly herbaceous, vegetative quality analogous to the smell of leaves. When a wine is leafy, it is not necessarily flawed and may actually be more interesting if the leafy quality adds a note of complexity.

LEES The sediment falling to the bottom of a wine container. When mentioned on labels, it usually refers to the sediment precipitated during fermentation, most of which consists of dead yeast cells. Most wines are removed from the lees as soon as possible, since they are thought to contribute inappropriate, and sometimes unappealing, odors and flavors. However, some Chardonnays are left in contact with the lees for several months (see *sur lie*) and sparkling wines gain much of their character by being kept in contact with the lees aging *en tirage* (see entry).

LEMONY White wine with fairly high acid often takes on a lemony quality. Such wines are not necessarily tart or sour; the acid may be balanced by intense flavors or sweetness.

LIGHT WINE Through the confluence of high technology and Madison Avenue marketing techniques, Light Wine was spawned in 1981. By legal definition, a Light Wine should contain fewer calories per comparable serving than a regular glass of table wine. In order to make a claim of "fewer calories" on the label, the producer must authenticate and document that statement. Wines can be made Light by decreasing either one or both sources of calories—alcohol and sugar. Most commonly, the calories are reduced by picking the grapes very early, before full maturity, or by removing the alcohol in a finished wine through a vacuum distillation process. Used as a tasting term, "light" indicates that the wine's viscosity is hard to distinguish from that of water.

LIMITED BOTTLING In the absence of legal definition, this high-sounding phrase is used on bottlings that run the gamut from small lots of special wine to every drop of the designated wine that the producer has to offer.

LINGERING Both flavor and tactile impressions may remain in the mouth after the wine is swallowed. When the aftertaste or finish remains in the mouth for more than a few seconds, it is said to be lingering. One would hope that the character is also clean, balanced, and attractive.

LIVELY Wines that are fruity and fresh in character, usually with ample acidity, are called lively because of their vigor. Such wines may occasionally be spritzy and usually are relatively low in sweetness and alcohol. The term is applied more often to white wines, but sometimes to reds.

LOT # Used in several different ways. The most legitimate is to differentiate wines of the same type from the same vintage that were bottled at different times. It also can suggest that the wine is a blend of two or more different vintages or different growing regions. A very few use it to indicate that the same wine was aged in different kinds of barrels. However, the term has no legal definition and therefore means as little or as much as the winery wishes it to mean.

LUSH Wines with the soft, viscous tactile impression created by high levels of residual sugar (usually in the sweet and very sweet ranges) are called lush.

MADE AND BOTTLED BY Though sounding the same as "produced and bottled by," this term has an entirely different meaning. The only requirement is that the named producer fermented a minimum of 10% of the wine in the bottle. That is hardly an intimate personal involvement with the wine.

MADERIZED This term originates in the brownish color and slightly sweet, slightly appley, sometimes nutty character found in the wines of Madeira. However, it is not intended as a compliment when used in conjunction with table wines. Maderized wines have been exposed to air and have lost their freshness. Sherrified is a similar term, but oxidized is the most common synonym.

MALOLACTIC FERMENTATION A secondary fermentation occurring in some wines, this natural process converts malic acid into softer lactic acid and carbon dioxide, thus reducing the wine's total acidity. It is also accompanied by fairly unpleasant odors that blow off as the gas escapes into the air. If it is not complete before bottling, the gas and undesirable odors remain trapped in the wine, usually spoiling its appeal. Malolactic fermentation is said to add complexity as well as softness to red wines, but, with the exception of high-acid Chardonnay, is considered undesirable in whites.

MATCHSTICK An unpleasant smell coming from high levels of sulfur dioxide (a widely used chemical preservative); similar to the smell of burnt matches. A cardboard or chemically grassy note often comes across as well. Fairly common in newly bottled white wines, it should dissipate with airing.

MEDIUM SWEET We use medium sweet to describe wines with residual sugar levels in the range of 1.5–2.9%. Such wines are perceptibly sweet to the taste, yet are not so sweet as to be limited to use with dessert. However, wines labeled medium sweet may be much sweeter than our range, because there is no industry agreement on how the term should be applied. See also Sweet.

MERITAGE California wineries have adopted this made-up term ("merit" plus "heritage") as the name under which to bottle wines that are blends which mimic the proportions of some wines produced in France's Bordeaux region. For red wines, the grapes allowed are Cabernet Sauvignon, Merlot, Cabernet Franc, Petite Verdot, and Malbec. For whites, it is Sauvignon Blanc and Semillon. The need for a special term has been brought about by government labeling regulations, which (for consumer protection) require wines with varietal names to contain at least 75% of the named variety. Heretofore, when California wineries bottled blends of wines in proportions that did not fit the 75% requirement, they were forced to use a generic name for the wine (Red Table Wine, Claret, etc.) or to make up their own proprietary name (such as Phelps's "Insignia" and Flora Spring's "Trilogy"). Now, many wineries making Bordeaux-style blends, red and white, will label their wines Meritage, often in conjunction with their own proprietary names.

MÉTHODE CHAMPENOISE   The most labor-intensive and costly way to make champagne. Once the wine is placed in the bottle to begin its second fermentation, it never leaves that bottle until it is poured into a glass for drinking. When expertly done, the champagne achieves a persistent effervescence of extremely tiny bubbles. It is the only permitted method for all French Champagnes. On U.S. labels, producers normally state that their wine was made by the *méthode champenoise* and often add "fermented in this bottle." However, if the label reads "fermented in the bottle" or "bottle fermented," chances are that the wine was made by the transfer process.

MOUNTAIN   Labels carrying this term are often attached to wines of lowly jug-wine quality. Most come from grapes grown in the flattest and hottest areas of California, where the mountains are seen only on clear days.

MOUTH-FILLING   Wines with intense round flavors, often in combination with glycerine or slightly low acidity, are said to be mouth-filling. They seem to have character and tactile presence everywhere in the mouth.

MUSCATTY   The character of muscat grapes shows up from time to time in the wines of other varieties—most notably Flora and Gewurztraminer. (See Muscat Blanc in the GRAPES AND WINE TYPES chapter for a more complete description of muscatty character.)

MUST   The unfermented juice of grapes produced by crushing or pressing.

MUSTY   Term for a wine with dank, moldy, or mildewy smells, the result of being stored in improperly cleaned tanks and barrels, being made from moldy grapes, or victimized by a poor cork.

NATURAL   A champagne term indicating that the wine is either totally dry or the driest made by the producer. Variants occasionally seen are *naturel, natur,* and *au naturel.* The term lacks strict definition.

NOSE   The character of a wine ascertained through the olfactory senses is called its nose. This can also be called the aroma and includes the bouquet.

NOUVEAU   A style of light, fruity, youthful red wine often presented as harbinger of the new vintage. In the U.S. some are produced by carbonic maceration, and others are simply bottled as soon as possible. *Nuevo* and *premier* are synonyms. All indicate a wine that is best when young.

NUTTY   Table wines exposed to air will often take on a nutty smell similar to some sherries. The wine is usually oxidized and, thus, flawed.

OAKY   Having aroma or taste elements contributed by the oak barrels or casks in which the wine was aged. Both vanillin, which comes from the oak itself, and toasty or roasted qualities, derived from the char contributed by the open flame used to heat the staves during barrelmaking, are common characteristics of oaky wines.

OFF-DRY   On our scale of describing and measuring sweetness in wine, we equate off-dry with slightly sweet and mean that the residual sugar in the wine is barely perceptible (0.6–1.4% residual sugar). In wine labeling the term has no agreed-on definition and is used by wineries indiscriminately to indicate levels of sweetness from slight to overbearing. (See Sweet for a more complete discussion.)

OILY The fat, round, slightly slippery tactile impression on the palate created by the combination of high glycerine and slightly low acid. It is a characteristic found and enjoyed in many of the best Chardonnays and also in other big wines, as well as in sweet, late harvest wines.

OVERRIPE Grapes left on the vine beyond normal maturity develop a concentrated, often dried-out, sometimes raisiny character. Zinfandel can yield very attractive overripe-tasting wines; Chardonnay and Cabernet are generally not enhanced by overripe qualities.

OXIDIZED Wine exposed too long to air takes on a brownish color, loses its freshness, and often begins to smell and taste like sherry or old apples. Oxidized wines are also called maderized or sherrified.

PERFUMED Refers to the strong, usually sweet and floral aromas of some white wines, notably Johannisberg Riesling, Gewurztraminer, and Muscat.

PH A chemical measurement (hydrogen ions in solution) used by wineries—along with grape ripeness and acidity levels—as a possible determinant of grape and wine quality. pH generally affects a wine's color, taste, texture, and long-term stability. The desirable pH range for white table wines is 3.0 to 3.4, and for red table wines 3.3 to 3.6. However, in varieties that mature with a high degree of ripeness, the pH levels of the finished wines can be somewhat higher.

PHYLLOXERA A vine disease brought about by tiny aphids or root lice that attack *Vitis vinifera* roots. It was widespread in both Europe and California during the late 19th century. Eventually, growers discovered a solution, which entailed grafting vinifera onto native American root stocks that were naturally resistant to *Phylloxera*. Most vines today are grafted, except in the new vineyards of California's Central and South coasts and the Pacific Northwest.

POMACE The mass of grape skins, seeds, and stems left after a wine has been pressed.

PONDEROUS Wines that are full in body and low in acid or tannin are ponderous. They have weight on the palate, but nothing to give them balance and structure.

POWERFUL Wines high in alcohol (and tannin for reds), often with big flavors, are said to have power. Brawny is a similar concept. The term is applied most often to red wines, but may also be useful to describe big, dry white wines.

PRESS WINE Juice extracted under pressure after pressing for white wines and after fermenting for reds. It is the opposite of free-run juice. Press wine has more flavor and aroma, deeper color, and often more tannins—all resulting from longer contact with grape skins. Wineries usually handle it separately and later blend all or part back into the free run and bottle what is left under second labels, using generic or proprietary names; some may sell it off in bulk to other producers.

PRIVATE RESERVE This high-minded phrase may once have had meaning for special, long-aged wines. Lacking external regulation, it is now used inconsistently. It should apply to wines deemed worthy of special attention. Sometimes it does so, but not often enough to serve as a reliable guide.

PRODUCED AND BOTTLED BY   Indicates that the named winery crushed, fermented, and bottled at least 75% of the wine in the bottle. Quite different from the similar-sounding "made and bottled by."

PROPRIETOR'S RESERVE   A variant of "Private Reserve."

PRUNEY   Very overripe, dried-out grapes give a pruney, pungent quality that is undesirable in fine wines.

PUCKERY   Used to describe wines high in tannin, which tend to dry out the mouth and cause one's teeth and cheeks to feel as though they were stuck together.

RACKING   The most traditional way of clarifying a wine: transferring it from one container to another, leaving the precipitated matter behind. This labor-intensive practice has been augmented (and often replaced) by filtration, fining, and centrifugation.

RAISINY   Somewhat rich, almost caramel, concentrated, dried-grape taste. Some wines, such as late harvest Zinfandel and port, can be pleasant with a little raisiny character, but most other wines are not. Some wines made from Central Valley–grown grapes taste raisiny because the excessive heat of the area dries out the grapes even as they are ripening on the vine.

REFINED   Said of wines that are in balance, have distinct varietal character, and are not brawny or out of proportion. The term is almost always used in a highly favorable context with varieties that tend to be powerful if left unchecked.

REGIONS I–V   A classification of grape-growing regions according to the amount of heat to which the vines are exposed during the growing season. Its basis is the "degree day" system, using 50° F. as the base line. (There is almost no shoot growth below 50° F.) The mean temperature above 50° F. each day during the period of vine growth is multiplied by the number of days in the period, giving the total of degree days.

Using the degree-day system California is divided into five climatic categories. Region I is the coolest (fewer than 2,500 degree days) and is comparable to European areas where Johannisberg Riesling and Gewurztraminer thrive. Region II is warmer (2,501–3,000 degree days) and is comparable to Bordeaux. Region III (3,001–3,500) is comparable to the Rhone region in France and to Tuscany in Italy. Region IV (3,501–4,000) compares with the Midi of France, and Region V (4,000+) experiences conditions comparable to Mediterranean growing areas.

RESIDUAL SUGAR   A statement of the unfermented grape sugar in a finished wine expressed either as the percentage by volume or the percentage by weight. Thus, residual sugar either of 2.6% or of 2.6 gm/100 ml is exactly the same. Such information helps determine how the wine should be enjoyed and is most often found on sweet-finished white wines. For a detailed breakdown, see Sweet.

RICH   Wines with generous, full, pleasant flavors, usually sweet and round in nature, are described as rich. In dry wines, richness may be supplied by high alcohol and glycerine, by complex flavors, and by vanilla, oaky character. Decidedly sweet wines are also described as rich when the sweetness is backed up by fruity, often ripe flavors.

RIPE   The desirable elements within each grape's own special varietal character come out when the grapes reach optimum maturity in the vineyard. Ripe-tasting wine usually has round flavors, tends toward being rich, and is more sweetly fruity than other wines possessing the same levels of scientifically measurable sweetness.

ROTTEN EGG   The smell of hydrogen sulfide (H_2S) in wine, a flaw that ranges from mildly bothersome at low levels to vile at very high levels.

ROUGH   Used for the grainy, somewhat puckery, tactile sensation of young, tannic red wines. A related term, astringent, refers to more noticeable levels of harsh tannins.

ROUND   Used to describe both flavors and tactile sensations. In both contexts, round connotes completeness, the absence of angularity or any dominating characteristic. Round flavors are balanced and tend toward richness and ripeness. On the palate, round wines usually are slightly low in acid, often have glycerine or residual sugar to fill in the angles or cover any roughness, and are low in tannin.

SEC   Literally means "dry." However, tradition is that a champagne labeled *sec* falls in the sweet-to-very-sweet range.

SELECT   Implies that the wine has special qualities. Lacking legal definition and consistent application, it most often means nothing.

SELECT HARVEST   Absolutely inconsistent usage and, therefore, meaningless.

SELECTED LATE HARVEST   Seen on white wines, primarily Johannisberg Rieslings, but lacking consistent usage. A few producers use it to indicate that the grapes were riper and the wine finished sweeter than a late harvest style. However, the phrase has different meanings from winery to winery.

SHARP   The slightly biting tactile sensation of excess acidity, or high acetic acid, and the accompanying bite in the taste.

SHERRIFIED   When table wines are exposed to air over long periods, they become oxidized. One of the signs of oxidation is a nutty aroma and taste reminiscent of sherry. Maderized is a comparable term.

SIMPLE   Wines with very straightforward character—immediately accessible with no nuances or complex notes. Most of the world's wines are simple when compared to the highly praised château and estate bottlings, yet can be delightful if clean, fruity, and fairly well balanced.

SLIGHTLY SWEET   Most appropriately used to describe the levels of sweetness lying just above the threshold of perception (in the range of 0.6–1.4% sugar). Off-dry is a similar term. See Sweet.

SOFT   Describes wines low in acid or tannin (sometimes both) that are, therefore, not firm and hard on the palate. Also used for wines with reduced alcohol levels and less of the consequent hot impact of higher alcohol.

SOLERA   A blending system used for both sherries and ports. A *solera* consists of barrels stacked in tiers with the oldest wine on the bottom tier and the youngest on top. As wine is drawn from the oldest barrel for bottling, younger wine from each tier is moved forward a stage. The objective is to blend for uniformity and consistency. About 10 California wineries and several in New York and Michigan maintain *soleras*.

SOUR   When wine is so high in acid that it is out of balance, it tastes sour or very tart. As a tasting term, it is used for a wine high in acetic acid and volatile acidity.

SPICY   Denotes somewhat pungent, often attractive aromas and flavors suggestive of cloves, cinnamon, anise, caraway, and similar substances. The most typically spicy grape is Gewurztraminer; other varieties that may show lesser degrees of spiciness are Zinfandel and Chardonnay.

SPRITZY Wines with fairly modest degrees of pinpoint carbonation are described as spritzy. In slightly sweet and medium-sweet white wines, a little spritz can give a lively impression that enhances the wine's balance. Most dry wines are not enhanced by spritziness.

STALE Refers to wines that have lost their fresh, youthful qualities and have taken on dull, tired, sometimes stagnant qualities—often from being stored too long at the winery in large containers before bottling. Tanky is a related term.

STRUCTURE A wine's structure is determined by the interplay of those elements that create tactile impressions in the mouth: acid, tannin, glycerine, alcohol, body. It is a term that needs a modifier like firm, sturdy, or weak to be meaningful.

SUPPLE Used most often to describe the tactile impression of red wines possessing general amiability and underlying softness in spite of fairly firm structure, ample acid, and noticeable tannin. Young, hard wines are often allowed to age until they achieve more agreeable, supple qualities.

SUR LIE Wines aged *sur lie* are kept in contact with the dead yeast cells and other sedimentary matter that remain when the fermentation is completed. In the last decade, this practice has become fairly commonplace in the making of Chardonnay and is followed also on occasion for Sauvignon Blanc. The hope is that *sur lie* aging will add complex quality to the wine—often akin to a toasty, roasted-grain character.

SWEET One of the four basic tastes perceived by the tongue, as opposed to the hundreds of flavors that we actually experience with our olfactory senses. The presence of sugar (or occasionally of glycerine) is required to taste sweetness, according to the wine scientist.

A few wine writers, ourselves included, have attempted to define sweetness levels in terms that can be applied consistently. The gradations of sweetness appearing in *Connoisseurs' Guide to California Wine* and adopted in this book are:

Less than 0.5% residual sugar	Dry
0.6–1.4% residual sugar	Slightly Sweet
1.5–2.9% residual sugar	Medium Sweet
3.0–5.9% residual sugar	Sweet
More than 5.9% residual sugar	Very Sweet

The scents of intense fruitiness, of ripe or overripe grapes, and of vanilla oakiness often seem to be sweet, especially when found in conjunction with each other. For that reason, when we use sweet to describe a wine's aroma, we add other descriptive terms to indicate the probable source of the sweet scents. The sweet taste of wine may be similarly modified when describing a nonsugary sweetness. Varying levels of acid, alcohol, and tannin and the inherent bitterness of some grape varieties balance against sugar and affect the level of sweetness that is perceived in wine.

TANKY Used for the tired, somewhat dank qualities that show up in wines aged too long in large tanks.

TANNIN The puckery substance in red wines and a few whites is tannin. It is derived primarily from grape skins, grape seeds and stems, and the barrels in which wine is aged. Brawny, young red wines usually have substantial tannin that requires years of cellar aging to soften. Tannin serves as a natural preservative that helps the wine develop, but must be kept in balance with depth and potential. Excessively tannic wines can remain tannic long after the flavors have peaked. Tannin can dry out the aftertaste and can taste bitter if not kept in balance. Astringent is a related term.

TART   The sharp taste of acidity in wine is described as tart or sour.

THIN   Wines lacking body and depth are known as thin. Such wines tend to feel and taste watery. The French describe such wines as meager—a very apt word.

TIGHT   Young wines with angular flavors and a hard tactile impression in the mouth are called tight. "Closed-in" and "dumb" are related terms.

TOASTY   Toasty smells and flavors in wines are derived from the oak barrels in which the wines are aged, and from contact with dead yeast cells and other sedimentary matter following the completion of fermentation. This character is thought by some to be particularly attractive in Chardonnay and sparkling wine, and may also be observed in other varieties when the winemaker is seeking an extra measure of character and complexity.

TOPPING   Winery practice of adding wine to barrels and tanks to replace what was lost by evaporation. It minimizes contact with air and, thus, oxidation.

TRANSFER PROCESS   A modern method of making bottle-fermented champagne. At the end of its second fermentation, the wine is poured out of the bottle into pressurized tanks where it is filtered to remove the sediment prior to being rebottled. Such champagnes may be labeled "bottle fermented" or "transfer process," often accompanied by "fermented in the bottle."

UNDERRIPE   When grapes fail to reach maturity on the vine, their wines usually lack round flavors and tactile impressions. Typically, their varietal character remains undeveloped, they possess high acidity, and they display green flavors.

UNFILTERED   Indicates that the wine achieved its state of clarification and stabilization without being filtered. However, this does not mean that other cellar treatments, such as fining, centrifugation, and cold stabilization, were necessarily also avoided.

UNFINED   Seen on many Cabernets and Zinfandels to suggest the wine received minimal treatment. It means the wine was not fined, though it could well have been filtered or clarified by other methods.

VARIETAL   A wine named after the predominant grape variety in its composition. Regulations enacted in the mid-80s require a wine to have a minimum of 75% of the given grape in its makeup to qualify as a varietal. Until the 80s, varietal wines needed only to contain at least 51% of the named variety.

VARIETAL CHARACTER   The unique combination of smells, tastes, and tactile impressions typically offered by a grape when ripened to maturity. The most highly prized wine grapes have distinctive and attractive varietal character. Lesser grapes have less distinct varietal character. And some grapes, including such familiar names as Green Hungarian and Grey Riesling, have virtually no uniquely identifiable character. In Zinfandel the berrylike taste is the typical varietal character; in Cabernet it is black currants; and in Chardonnay it is a round, oily texture and generous, round, fruity flavors. Breed is a related concept.

VEGETAL   The smell and taste of some wines contain elements reminiscent of plants and vegetables. In Cabernet Sauvignon a small amount of this vegetal quality is said to be part of varietal character. However, when the vegetal element takes over the wine or when it shows up in wines in which it does not belong, those wines are considered to be flawed. Wine scientists have been able to identify the chemical constituent that makes wines smell like asparagus and bell peppers, but are not sure why it occurs more often in Central Coast vineyards than in others.

VERY SWEET   In our system of differentiation, wines that possess 6.0% or more residual sugar are described as very sweet. Their obvious, inescapable sweetness leads generally to enjoyment with dessert or by themselves after the meal. Some of California's most exciting (and expensive) wines fall into this category, including late harvest Rieslings and Gewurztraminers.

VINOUS   Literally meaning "winelike," vinous is usually applied to dull wines lacking enough character to be described in more vivid terms. Vinous and its noun, vinosity, are used with relatively clean wines.

VINTAGE DATE   To give a wine a vintage date, the winery must have made at least 95% of the wine from grapes harvested in the stated calendar year. Such dates provide useful information about a wine's freshness or its aging requirements. However, a vintage-dated wine is not necessarily a "vintage" wine, even though most high-quality wines carry vintage dates.

VINTED BY   A pleasant-sounding but meaningless phrase that may be used on wine labels even when the named winery had no more involvement with the wine than purchasing it in bulk from another winery and bottling it upon arrival.

VITICULTURAL AREA   This is now a legal entity, representing an effort by the federal government to upgrade the use of place names and grape-growing regions on wine labels when the area is smaller than a state and does not conform to county boundaries. Interested parties must petition the government and make a case for the uniqueness of the particular region on the basis of climate, soil, elevation, history, and definable boundaries. Beginning in 1983, only those areas approved and established may be used on labels and in advertising. The federal requirement is that 85% of the wine in question is made from grapes grown within that specified Viticultural Area. If the wine is a varietal bottling, a minimum of 75% of that wine must be made from the designated grape variety.

VITIS LABRUSCA   A species of wild grapevine believed to be native to North America. Few of the grapes used to make wine are pure labrusca because most have been accidentally cross-pollinated with other species, including vinifera. All labrusca-type wines share, to varying degrees, a characteristic aroma and flavor traditionally and inexplicably described as foxy. This is another way of saying that they smell like Concord grape juice and have a strong grapey personality. The best-known wine varieties are Concord, Catawba, Delaware, and Niagara.

VITIS VINIFERA   The species of grapevine responsible for the world's best wines. It probably originated in the Mediterranean basin and subsequently was cultivated throughout Europe. Today, the species is often referred to as the Old World or European vine. The vinifera (wine-bearer) family may have close to 5,000 members, but fewer than 100 are considered important as wine grapes. As a family, vinifera vines require sufficient heat to bring the grapes to ripeness and are not at all hardy to freezing winter spells. They are also vulnerable to numerous parasites and to many fungus diseases. Vinifera vines also interbreed easily and do not breed true when propagated from seeds.

Freezing winter temperatures have stymied their cultivation in many parts of the U.S.; high summer humidity encouraging various molds has eliminated their cultivation in many Southern states as well. With its mild, rainy winter and long, dry, warm summer, California offers a climate generally favorable to vinifera vines. Parts of Washington, Oregon, Michigan, and New York, and several Mid-Atlantic states have also been successful in cultivating the European vine.

VOLATILE   Denotes aromas that come out of the glass aggressively, almost fiercely. They are usually caused by high levels of volatile acidity and alcohol or by chemical faults.

VOLATILE ACID   The smell of ethyl acetate and the palate sharpness of acetic acid (they almost always occur simultaneously) are often referenced collectively as volatile acid or volatile acidity. Occasionally wine labels will tell the level of volatile acidity (VA) in the wine. In general, the lower the better. The threshold at which most tasters notice VA in wine is just under 0.1%—more than most wines contain. The legal limit of volatile acidity is just over 0.1%.

WARM   Some red wines—Cabernet, Merlot, Petite Sirah, and Zinfandel—possess both flavor intensity and balance to offset their high alcohol. Such wines are described as warm. This is a positive attribute, unlike the term hot, which refers to excessive alcohol.

WEIGHTY   Term for wines with a heavy, full-bodied sense of presence on the palate.

WOODY   The smell or taste of the wooden containers in which wines are aged—usually strongest for wines aged in new barrels. The aromas and flavors of some wines are substantially benefited by the extra dimension garnered from the wood. However, wines that stay too long in the barrel become excessively woody and lose their interest. Oaky is a closely related term.

YEASTY   Occasionally a very young wine will be so fresh from the fermenter when released to market that its character is affected by the taste of the fermentation yeast, reminiscent of freshly baked bread. In sparkling wines, the term refers to the toasty, vaguely soylike character imparted to the wine by the dead (autolyzed) yeast during its secondary fermentation and bottle-aging (en tirage) phase.

A NOTE ABOUT THE AUTHORS

Norman S. Roby is a columnist for *The Wine Spectator* and a well-known wine writer. Charles E. Olken is co-publisher of *Connoisseurs' Guide to California Wine,* the foremost newsletter covering the California wine scene. Both men live in California.

A NOTE ON THE TYPE

This book was set in Gael, a version of Caledonia, a type face designed by W(illiam) A(ddison) Dwiggins (1880–1956) for the Mergenthaler Linotype Company in 1939. Dwiggins chose to call this type face Caledonia, the Roman name for Scotland, because it was inspired by the Scottish types cast about 1833 by Alexander Wilson & Son, Glasgow type founders. However, there is a calligraphic quality about Caledonia that is totally lacking in the Wilson types.

Dwiggins referred to an even earlier type face for this "liveliness of action"—one cut around 1790 by William Martin for the printer William Bulmer. Caledonia has more weight than the Martin letters, and the bottom finishing strokes (serifs) of the letters are cut straight across, without brackets, to make sharp angles with the upright stems, thus giving a modern-face appearance.

W. A. Dwiggins began an association with the Merganthaler Linotype Company in 1929 and over the next twenty-seven years designed a number of book types, the most interesting of which are Metro, Electra, Caledonia, Eldorado, and Falcon.

Composed by ComCom, a division of The Haddon Craftsmen, Inc., Scranton, Pennsylvania.

Printed and bound by Kingsport Press, Kingsport, Tennessee.